The Science of Consciousness

Consciousness concerns awareness and how we experience the world. How does awareness, a feature of the mental world, arise from the physical brain? Is a dog conscious, or a jellyfish, and what explains what is conscious and what is not? How is consciousness related to psychological processes such as perception and cognition? *The Science of Consciousness* covers the psychology, philosophy, and neuroscience of consciousness. Written for introductory courses in psychology and philosophy, this text examines consciousness with a special emphasis on current neuroscience research, as well as comparisons of normal and damaged brains. The full range of normal and altered states of consciousness, including sleep and dreams, hypnotic and meditative states, anaesthesia, drug-induced states, and parapsychological phenomena and their importance for the science of consciousness, is covered, as well as the 'higher' states and how we can attain them. Throughout, the text attempts to relate consciousness to the brain.

Trevor A. Harley is Emeritus Professor of Psychology at the University of Dundee and a Fellow of the British Psychological Society. He is the author of *The Psychology of Language*, 4th edition (2013), *Talking the Talk*, 2nd edition (2017), and *The Psychology of Weather* (2018). He is very widely published across psychology, including papers on consciousness and dreams, and has kept a detailed dream diary for several years. He is always wondering what his poodle Beau is thinking about.

The Science of Consciousness

Waking, Sleeping and Dreaming

TREVOR A. HARLEY
University of Dundee

CAMBRIDGE
UNIVERSITY PRESS

CAMBRIDGE
UNIVERSITY PRESS

University Printing House, Cambridge CB2 8BS, United Kingdom

One Liberty Plaza, 20th Floor, New York, NY 10006, USA

477 Williamstown Road, Port Melbourne, VIC 3207, Australia

314–321, 3rd Floor, Plot 3, Splendor Forum, Jasola District Centre, New Delhi – 110025, India

79 Anson Road, #06-04/06, Singapore 079906

Cambridge University Press is part of the University of Cambridge.

It furthers the University's mission by disseminating knowledge in the pursuit of education, learning, and research at the highest international levels of excellence.

www.cambridge.org
Information on this title: www.cambridge.org/9781107125285
DOI: 10.1017/9781316408889

© Trevor A. Harley 2021

This publication is in copyright. Subject to statutory exception and to the provisions of relevant collective licensing agreements, no reproduction of any part may take place without the written permission of Cambridge University Press.

First published 2021

A catalogue record for this publication is available from the British Library.

Library of Congress Cataloging-in-Publication Data
Names: Harley, Trevor A., author.
Title: The science of consciousness : waking, sleeping and dreaming / Trevor A. Harley, University of Dundee.
Description: New York, NY : Cambridge University Press, 2021. | Includes bibliographical references and index.
Identifiers: LCCN 2020029739 (print) | LCCN 2020029740 (ebook) | ISBN 9781107125285 (hardback) | ISBN 9781316408889 (ebook)
Subjects: LCSH: Consciousness. | Consciousness–Physiological aspects. | Cognitive neuroscience.
Classification: LCC QP411 .H366 2020 (print) | LCC QP411 (ebook) | DDC 612.8/233–dc23

LC record available at https://lccn.loc.gov/2020029739

LC ebook record available at https://lccn.loc.gov/2020029740

ISBN 978-1-107-12528-5 Hardback
ISBN 978-1-107-56330-8 Paperback

Additional resources for this publication at www.cambridge.org/harley

Cambridge University Press has no responsibility for the persistence or accuracy of URLs for external or third-party internet websites referred to in this publication and does not guarantee that any content on such websites is, or will remain, accurate or appropriate.

To Allan Hobson, who started it, and to Ruth, who finished it.

CONTENTS

List of Figures	page xiii
Preface	xix
Acknowledgements	xxvi
List of Abbreviations	xxvii

PART I THE NATURE OF CONSCIOUSNESS

1 The Problem of Consciousness	**3**
Why Study Consciousness?	3
Consciousness and Psychology	3
Consciousness and Neuroscience	4
Consciousness and Philosophy	4
Box 1.1 The Homunculus Inside Us	5
Consciousness and Spirituality	5
How We Study Consciousness	6
Scientific Experimentation	7
Box 1.2 The Role of Falsification in Science	7
Box 1.3 The History of Neuroscience	8
Philosophical Thought Experiments	10
Artificial Intelligence	11
Defining Consciousness	11
Definitions of Consciousness	12
Awareness	12
The Problem of Other Minds	13
The Hard and Easy Problems of Consciousness	15
Intentionality: Are We Always Conscious of Something?	15
Types of Consciousness	16
Phenomenal and Access Consciousness	16
Other Types of Consciousness	17
Degrees of Consciousness	18
The History of Consciousness Research	20
The Problems of Consciousness	21
Chapter Summary	23
Review Questions	24
Recommended Resources	24
2 The Mind–Body Problem	**26**
Box 2.1 Philosophy: Terms and Disciplines	26
Thought Experiments	27
The Mind and the Brain	28
The Mind–Brain Problem	28
The Mereological Fallacy	29
Qualia	29
Dualism and Monism	29
René Descartes and Substance Dualism	30
Other Types of Dualism	31
Monism	32
Box 2.2 The History of Physics	33
The Knowledge Argument	34
The 'Mary' Colour Thought Experiment	34
For and Against Physicalism	35
The Inverted Colour Spectrum	36
The Problem of Pain	38
The Physical Aspect of Pain	39
The Mental Aspect of Pain	39
Pain in Babies	40
P-zombies	41
Box 2.3 Zombies	41
Is Consciousness Essential?	42
Being Conceivable	42
Materialism	43
Reductive Materialism	43
Eliminative Materialism	44
Functionalism	45
Silicon Neurons and Silicon Brains	45
Box 2.4 Neurons	46
The 'China Brain' Thought Experiment	47
Box 2.5 What is Computation?	48
Arguments Against Functionalism	49
Mysterianism	51
Chapter Summary	53
Review Questions	54
Recommended Resources	55
3 Do We Have Free Will?	**57**
People and Objects	57
Determinism and Free Will	58

Human Behaviour	59		Constructing an Artificial Brain	99
The Implications of Quantum Mechanics	60		Neuroprosthesis	101
Dualism and Free Will	60	The Future of AI		102
Box 3.1 What Is an Illusion?	61		The Technological Singularity	102
The Homunculus in the Cartesian Theatre	62		Box 4.3 Transhumanism	103
The Benefits of Believing in Free Will	62		Is AI a Threat?	104
Compatibilism	64	Chapter Summary		105
Environmental Effects on Behaviour	64	Review Questions		106
Box 3.2 *Toxoplasma*	65	Recommended Resources		106
Crime and Punishment	66			
Moral Responsibility	67	**5 Animal Consciousness**		**108**
Box 3.3 The Purpose of Punishment	67	Which Non-human Animals might be Conscious?		108
The Role of Psychology in Understanding Crime	68	The Mind of an Animal		109
Deciding to Act	69		Animal Intelligence	110
Libet's Experiments on 'Voluntary' Movement	70		Box 5.1 Learning Without Neurons	113
Box 3.4 Measuring Brain Activity with EEG	71		The Mirror Test of Self-recognition	114
Criticisms of Libet's Experiments	72		Animals and Pain	116
Involuntary Action	73		Box 5.2 Do Plants Feel Pain?	117
Alien Hand Syndrome	73	Theory of Mind		117
Skill and Habit	74		The Importance of Social Interaction	119
Psychological Compulsions	76	The Evolution of Consciousness		120
Chapter Summary	76		Protoconsciousness	121
Review Questions	77		The Importance of Language	121
Recommended Resources	78		Recursion	122
			The Bicameral Mind	123
4 Machine Consciousness	**79**	Panpsychism		124
Artificial Life	79	Chapter Summary		126
Artificial Intelligence	81	Review Questions		127
The Timeline of Progress in AI	82	Recommended Resources		127
Chess-playing Computers	84			
Box 4.1 Computer Beats Human	86	**PART II THE WORKINGS OF CONSCIOUSNESS**		
The Turing Test	86			
Early AI Models of Psychology	88	**6 Looking at Our Own Minds**		**131**
How Smart Are Computers Now?	89	The Contents of Consciousness		131
The Computational Correlates of Consciousness	91		The Stream of Consciousness	132
LIDA	92		The Process of Introspection	133
Could a Disembodied AI Ever Be Conscious?	93		Phenomenology	135
Robotics	94		Experience Sampling	136
Box 4.2 Aliens	96		The Limits of Introspection	137
Swarm Intelligence	96	Your Beliefs		138
Evolutionary Robotics	97		The Reliability of Beliefs	139
Robots and Consciousness	98		Box 6.1 Solipsism, Anti-realism, and Deceiving Devils	140
Building a Brain	98		Delusions	141

CONTENTS

Box 6.2 Schizophrenia	141	**8 Cognition and Consciousness**	**185**
Mass Hysteria	143	Consciousness Is About Limitations	185
Confabulation	144	Language and Consciousness	186
Box 6.3 The Tanganyika Laughter Epidemic		Language and Culture	186
of 1962	144	Thinking	188
Denial	145	Inner Speech	189
Box 6.4 Dementia and Alzheimer's Disease	146	Mental Imagery	191
Is Anything Unavailable to Consciousness?	147	Attention	192
Freud and the Unconscious	147	Visual Attention	194
Box 6.5 Satanic Child Abuse	149	The Default Mode Network	194
Jung and the 'Collective Unconscious'	151	Box 8.1 The Default Mode Network	196
Subliminal Processing	152	Global Workspace Theory	197
Chapter Summary	153	The Neuronal Workspace Theory	198
Review Questions	154	Box 8.2 The Neuroscience of the Neuronal	
Recommended Resources	155	Workspace Model	200
		The Multiple Drafts Model	201
7 Self and Identity	**156**	Modelling the World	202
The Self	156	Mental Models	202
The 'Self Model'	157	Mental Time Travel	203
Ego and Bundle Theories	159	Metacognition	205
Box 7.1 Face Transplants	161	Representational Theories	206
The Knower and the Known	161	Recursion (Again)	207
Damasio's Three Levels of Self	161	Box 8.3 What Is a Complex System?	209
Types of Self and the Executive Self	163	Emergence	209
The Continuity of Existence	165	Representation and Consciousness	210
Amnesia and the Loss of Memories	166	Free Energy	211
Box 7.2 *Herpes simplex* Encephalitis	167	Quantum Consciousness	212
The Neuroscience of the Self	169	Box 8.4 Quantum Mechanics	213
Disorders of the Physical Self	170	Chapter Summary	215
Split-brain Studies	171	Review Questions	216
Dissociative States	173	Recommended Resources	217
Box 7.3 Derealisation: A Case Study	175		
Dissociative Identity Disorders	175	**9 Perception and Consciousness**	**218**
The Boundaries of the Self	176	Empiricism	219
Phantom Bodies	176	Are You Dreaming Now?	220
Phantom Limbs and Phantom Pain	177	Box 9.1 The Brain in a Vat	220
The Rubber Hand Illusion	178	Normal Visual Perception	220
Awareness of Motor Control	179	Filling in	221
Is the Self Restricted to the Body?	180	Bistable Figures	221
Is the Self Just Another Illusion?	181	Binocular Rivalry	222
Chapter Summary	182	Change Blindness and Inattentional	
Review Questions	183	Blindness	224
Recommended Resources	184	Visual Illusions	225

No-report Paradigm	227
Disorders of Visuo-spatial Perception	227
Blindsight	227
Spatial Neglect	229
Synaesthesia	230
Proprioception	231
The Binding Problem	231
Box 9.2 Gamma Waves	232
Microconsciousness	234
Visual Awareness	234
Box 9.3 The Jennifer Aniston Neuron	235
The Grand Illusion	235
Chapter Summary	236
Review Questions	237
Recommended Resources	237

10 Consciousness and the Brain — 239

Box 10.1 Studying the Living Brain	240
The Neural Correlates of Consciousness	241
The 'Astonishing Hypothesis'	241
Mind Reading: Finding Internal Content from the Outside	242
The Electrophysiology of Consciousness	242
Box 10.2 Brain Waves	243
The Evolution of the Brain	244
The Development of Consciousness	245
Incomplete Brains	246
General Anaesthesia	247
Box 10.3 The History of Anaesthetics	248
How Do General Anaesthetics Work?	249
Post-operative Recall	250
The Thalamus and Thalamo-cortical Systems	251
Are NCC Frontal or Posterior?	252
Re-entry and the Dynamic Core Hypothesis	252
The Claustrum	253
The Role of Anterior Cingulate	255
Integrated Information Theory	256
Radical Plasticity	256
What Is Death?	257
Death as Loss of Higher Functions	259
Disorders of Consciousness	259
Coma and Coma-like States	260
Definitions of Death	261
Locked-in Syndrome	261
Can We Escape Death?	262
Chapter Summary	263
Review Questions	264
Recommended Resources	265

PART III OTHER STATES OF CONSCIOUSNESS

11 Altered States of Consciousness — 269

What Is an ASC?	269
Box 11.1 Psychonauts	270
Types of ASC	272
Sensory Deprivation	272
The Ganzfeld	273
Out-of-body Experiences	274
Box 11.2 Laboratory-induced OBEs	275
Explaining OBEs	275
Migraine and Epilepsy	277
Near-death Experiences	279
Box 11.3 How NDEs Reduce Fear of Death	280
Biological Explanations of NDEs	281
Encephalitis Lethargica	282
Other Types of ASC	283
Chapter Summary	284
Review Questions	284
Recommended Resources	284

12 Sleep — 286

What Is Sleep?	286
Do All Animals Sleep?	287
The Biology of Sleep	288
Circadian Rhythms	288
The Electrophysiology of Sleep	290
The Neurology of Sleep	291
The Neuropharmacology of Sleep	293
Box 12.1 Neurotransmitters	293
The AIM Model of Sleep and Dreaming	295
Sleep Disorders	296
Getting to Sleep and Staying Awake	296
Problems During Sleep	298
Box 12.2 Talking in Your Sleep	298
Box 12.3 Murder in Your Sleep	299
Sleep Deprivation	300

CONTENTS

Box 12.4 Sleep Deprivation for Depression	301
Why Do We Sleep?	301
Evolutionary Functions of Sleep	301
Sleep and Learning	302
Chapter Summary	303
Review Questions	304
Recommended Resources	304

13 Dreams   305

Are Dreams Real?	305
Box 13.1 Zhuangzi's (Chuang-Tzu's) Butterfly Dream	306
What Is a Dream?	307
How Well Do We Remember Our Dreams?	308
Lucid Dreams	310
Dream Content	312
Box 13.2 Dream Content	313
Nightmares	313
Box 13.3 Sleep Paralysis	314
Recurring Dreams	315
Why Do We Dream?	316
Dreaming and Creativity	317
Are Dreams a Way of Dealing with Threat?	318
Psychoanalysis and Dreams	319
Post-analytic Dream Theories	320
Dreams and Learning	321
Chapter Summary	321
Review Questions	322
Recommended Resources	322

14 Hypnosis   323

The History of Hypnosis	323
Box 14.1 Freud, Charcot, Hysteria, and Hypnosis	324
The Process of Hypnosis	325
Hypnotic Induction	326
The Hypnotic Trance	327
Individual Differences in Hypnotisability	327
Box 14.2 Categories of Question in the Tellegen Absorption Scale	328
Can We Learn Suggestibility?	329
What Makes a Good Hypnotist?	329
Box 14.3 Snake Charmers and Horse Whisperers	329

Is There a Special Hypnotic State?	330
Dissociation	330
Non-state Theories of Hypnosis	331
Effects of Hypnosis	332
Hypnotic Suggestions	332
Hypnosis and Memory	333
Box 14.4 Is Hypnosis Dangerous?	334
Hypnotic Anaesthesia	335
The Neuroscience of Hypnosis	336
Self-hypnosis	337
What Hypnosis Tells Us About Cognition	338
Chapter Summary	338
Review Questions	339
Recommended Resources	339

15 Drugs and Consciousness   341

A Classification of Psychoactive Drugs	342
Cannabis	343
Box 15.1 Medicinal Use of Cannabis	344
Amphetamine and Other Stimulants	345
Amphetamine	345
Box 15.2 Amphetamine Psychosis	346
Cocaine	347
Opiates and Opioids	348
Morphine	348
Heroin	349
Hallucinogenic Drugs	350
Deliriant Drugs	350
Dissociative Drugs	351
Psychedelic Drugs	352
Peyote	352
Psilocybin	353
DMT	353
LSD	355
Box 15.3 Urban Myths and LSD Use	356
The History of LSD Use	357
Box 15.4 The Summer of Love	358
Box 15.5 The Good Friday Marsh Chapel Experiment	359
The Neuroscience of Hallucinogens	359
The Social Context of Drug Use	361
The Dangers of Cannabis	361
Cultural Diversity in Drug Use	362

Therapeutic Use of Hallucinogens	362
Chapter Summary	363
Review Questions	364
Recommended Resources	364

16 Meditation and Transcendental Experiences — 366

Meditation	366
The Physiological Effects of Meditation	367
Box 16.1 Raising Body Temperature Through Meditation	367
The Neuroscience of Meditation	368
Mindfulness	370
Transcendental Consciousness	371
Box 16.2 The Life of Colin Wilson	372
Consciousness Raising	373
Religious Experiences	374
Box 16.3 The Nine Characteristics of Mystical States	374
Temporal Lobe Activity and Religion	376
Entheogens	378
Buddhism	378
Zen	380
Chapter Summary	381
Review Questions	382
Recommended Resources	382

17 Parapsychology — 384

ESP and Psi	385
Spontaneous Phenomena	386
Box 17.1 The Versailles Time Travel Incident	387
Box 17.2 Sonic Noise and Sonic Weapons	388
How Spontaneous Phenomena Change with Time	389
Experimental Findings in Parapsychology	389
Box 17.3 Psychic Superstars	390
Issues in Experimental Design	391
Psi and Altered States of Consciousness	391
Box 17.4 Hoax Mediums	392
Psi in the Ganzfeld	393
Remote Viewing	393
Bem's Experiments	394
Trait and State Studies	395
Experimenter Effects in Parapsychological Research	395
Psychokinesis	395
Box 17.5 Poltergeist	396
What Would Convince a Sceptic?	397
What Does Parapsychology Tell Us About Consciousness?	398
Survival	398
Box 17.6 Ghosts	399
Reincarnation	400
Chapter Summary	401
Review Questions	402
Recommended Resources	402

18 Bringing it all Together — 403

How Do We Define Consciousness?	403
The 'Hard Problem'	404
What Are the Neural Correlates of Consciousness?	404
What Are the Cognitive Correlates of Consciousness?	405
The Timing of Events	405
The Problem of Free Will	406
What Is the Self?	406
Why Are Some Things Unconscious?	407
Why Are We Conscious?	407
Solving the Binding Problem	408
What Are Altered States of Consciousness?	408
Consciousness Around the World	409
Can There Be a Science of Consciousness?	410
How This Book Will Help Your Life	411
Chapter Summary	412
Recommended Resources	412

Glossary of General Terms	415
Glossary of Basic Neuroanatomy Location Terms	422
Glossary of the Most Common Neurotransmitters	422
Glossary of the Most Important Neuroanatomical Structures	422
References	426
Index	464

FIGURES

1.1	Diffusion tensor image of the living brain.	page 4
1.2	Democritus (c. 460–c. 370 BCE).	4
1.3	Buddhist nuns practising kung fu.	6
1.4	Sir Karl Popper (1902–1994).	8
1.5	Accuracy or resolution of various neuroscience investigatory techniques.	9
1.6	Growing brain cells.	11
1.7	A bat using sonar.	13
1.8	Helen Keller with her teacher Anne Sullivan, in 1888.	14
1.9	Meet my miniature poodle, Beau.	14
1.10	Hofstadter's 'consciousness cone'.	19
1.11	B.F. Skinner (1904–1990) with the Skinner Box.	21
2.1	A red rose.	29
2.2	René Descartes (1596–1650).	30
2.3	The location of the pineal gland.	31
2.4	A monochrome rose.	34
2.5	A rainbow.	36
2.6	Colour spaces included in a version of a colour circle.	38
2.7	Chocolate.	39
2.8	Voodoo in Port au Prince, Haiti.	42
2.9	Humanoid robot dental therapy simulator 'Simroid'.	44
2.10	Neurons.	47
2.11	The roundworm *Caenorhabditis elegans*.	51
2.12	Publicity material from the 1957 Japanese science-fiction movie *The Mysterians*.	52
3.1	A clockwork solar system.	59
3.2	British stage magician Jasper Maskelyne (1902–1973), at Whitehall Theatre, London, 1948.	61
3.3	The brain's reward circuitry.	63
3.4	*Toxoplasma gondii*.	66
3.5	Wormwood Scrubs prison in the UK.	67
3.6	Readiness potential.	70
3.7	An EEG cap.	71
3.8	The premotor cortex and surrounding areas.	74
3.9	Brain circuitry involved in obsessive-compulsive disorder	76
4.1	A flock of starlings (*Sturnus vulgaris*).	80
4.2	The boids simulation.	81
4.3	Four-colour map of the United States.	83
4.4	Computer-generated algorithmic art, Composition #72 by Patrick Gunderson.	83

LIST OF FIGURES

4.5	Deep Blue v. Kasparov (1996 match, Game 1).	84
4.6	Alan Turing (1912–1954).	87
4.7	BLOCKSWORLD, the microworld of Winograd (1972).	89
4.8	A plot showing the acceleration of the rate of development of important cultural and technological events.	90
4.9	Elektro the smoking robot.	94
4.10	CRONOS the robot.	95
4.11	The uncanny valley.	96
4.12	Aliens with tentacles.	97
4.13	The Golem Project; this robot form is called Arrow.	98
4.14	A cochlear implant.	101
5.1	Beau the poodle.	109
5.2	A puffin with fish.	109
5.3	Alex the talking parrot and Irene Pepperberg.	111
5.4	Classical and modern views of a typical bird brain.	112
5.5	A common raven (*Corvus corax*) performing cognitive experiments.	112
5.6	'The blob'.	113
5.7	A slime mould.	114
5.8	The mirror test of self-recognition.	114
5.9	A forest fire: firefighters work to put out a forest fire on Signal Hill, Cape Town.	117
5.10	A group of chimpanzees at Ngamba Island Chimpanzee Sanctuary, Lake Victoria, Uganda.	119
5.11	Dr Louis Herman researches dolphin sensory abilities.	122
5.12	The first controlled, powered and sustained human flight, 17 December 1903, by the Wright brothers.	125
6.1	William James (1840–1910).	133
6.2	Types of introspection.	134
6.3	A landscape of rainbow and tree.	136
6.4	A Kanizsa triangle.	139
6.5	Beatles hysteria.	144
6.6	The occipital lobe of the brain.	145
6.7	Freud's iceberg model of the mind.	148
6.8	A Rorschach test item.	148
6.9	Jungian archetypes revealed in the major arcana of the Tarot.	151
6.10	Subliminal advertising in the 1957 movie *Picnic*.	152
7.1	David Hume (1711–1776).	159
7.2	Location of the thalamus.	163
7.3	Reconstruction of the wound to Phineas Gage.	164
7.4	The hippocampus, and the seahorse from which it gets its name, and its location in the brain.	167
7.5	The *Herpes simplex* virus.	168
7.6	Example of lesions to brain following a *Herpes simplex* encephalitis infection.	168

LIST OF FIGURES

7.7	The insular cortex.	170
7.8	The brainstem.	170
7.9	The corpus callosum.	171
7.10	Split-brain testing setup	172
7.11	The mirror box setup.	178
7.12	The rubber hand setup.	178
7.13	The Petkova and Ehrsson person-swapping setup.	179
8.1	Members of the Dani people of Papua, New Guinea.	187
8.2	The Muller–Lyer illusion.	188
8.3	Broca's area.	190
8.4	The default mode network.	197
8.5	The phi illusion.	201
8.6	The brain and metacognition.	205
8.7	The Droste cocoa tin, 1904 design, illustrating recursion.	208
8.8	Microtubules at the edge of a cell.	212
8.9	A wave.	214
8.10	A quantum computer: the IBM Q System One.	214
9.1	The Necker cube.	221
9.2	A bistable figure: which way up are the stairs?	222
9.3	The young girl–old lady figure.	222
9.4	'The Slave Market with the Disappearing Bust of Voltaire', by Salvador Dali (1940).	223
9.5	A concealed figure.	223
9.6	Stimulus used in change blindness experiment.	225
9.7	Stimulus used in inattentional blindness experiment.	226
9.8	Selection of visual illusions.	226
9.9	The dorsal and ventral visual streams in the brain.	228
9.10	How the world appears to people with spatial neglect.	229
9.11	The copying task and spatial neglect.	229
9.12	Representation of colour–letter synaesthesia.	231
10.1	Examples of EEG output.	243
10.2	The evolving brain (not to scale).	244
10.3	An infant being tested with EEG.	246
10.4	Hydrocephaly scan.	247
10.5	The location of the claustrum.	254
10.6	The location of the anterior cingulate.	255
10.7	Death is not always instantaneous.	257
10.8	Awareness plotted against arousal.	258
11.1	Normal waking state and some other states as revealed by EEG.	270
11.2	Timothy Leary (1920–1996).	271

11.3	A quiet place: inside an anechoic chamber.	272
11.4	A salt water sensory deprivation tank.	273
11.5	Lesions affecting the sense of self in space leading to OBEs.	276
11.6	Migraine aura.	278
11.7	EEG during an epilepsy seizure.	278
11.8	Encephalitis lethargica sufferer.	282
12.1	A typical sleep laboratory.	286
12.2	A manatee sleeping on the sea floor.	288
12.3	Melatonin production.	288
12.4	The location of the pineal gland.	289
12.5	Brain activation in sleep.	290
12.6	Brain transections: cerveau isolé and encéphale isolé.	292
12.7	EEG of a cat.	292
12.8	Brainstem structures.	293
12.9	Hobson's AIM model of consciousness.	295
12.10	Non-drug treatments of insomnia.	297
12.11	Randy Gardner.	300
13.1	Beau asleep.	306
13.2	Zhuangzi's butterfly dream.	307
13.3	Blood flow differences in high and low dream recallers.	309
13.4	Stimulation at 25–40 Hz of the frontal and temporal regions increases lucidity.	310
13.5	Frontal and parietal areas are more involved in lucid dreaming than in non-lucid dreaming.	311
13.6	'The Nightmare' (1802) by Henry Fuseli.	315
13.7	Activation of the default mode network in waking and REM states contrasted with slow-wave sleep as shown by fMRI.	317
13.8	The structure of benzene.	317
13.9	'The round dance of monkeys': six monkeys holding hands and paws.	318
13.10	Dream symbols.	319
14.1	Franz Mesmer (1734–1815).	324
14.2	Jean-Martin Charcot (1825–1893).	325
14.3	Group hypnosis.	326
14.4	Billy Graham (1918–2018).	329
14.5	A snake charmer.	330
14.6	A group of smokers trying hypnosis to kick the habit.	333
14.7	Betty Hill's star map.	334
14.8	A Caesarean operation carried out under hypnosis in the maternity ward of Saint-Gregoire hospital in Rennes, France.	335
14.9	Neural correlates of hypnotic induction.	337

LIST OF FIGURES

15.1	A cannabis plant.	344
15.2	Caffeine and adenosine.	345
15.3	Coca plant fields in Yungas, Bolivia.	347
15.4	Morphine opioids activating receptors.	349
15.5	The peyote cactus.	352
15.6	Magic mushrooms.	353
15.7	Plant source of ayahuasca from the Amazonian basin in Peru.	354
15.8	Ayahuasca ceremony in Yarinacocha, in the Peruvian Amazon, 2018.	354
15.9	LSD tabs.	355
15.10	Representation of fractals in a psychedelic LSD experience.	356
15.11	The Summer of Love, 1967.	358
15.12	Imaging the hallucinating brain.	360
15.13	Carlos Castaneda (1925–1998).	362
16.1	The brains of novice controls (left) and skilled meditators (right) while meditating.	368
16.2	Brain regions involved in mindfulness meditation.	369
16.3	Mindfulness training seems to affect many of the same brain regions as other types of meditation.	370
16.4	George Ivanovitch Gurdjieff (1877–1949).	372
16.5	Colin Wilson (1931–2013).	372
16.6	Women's liberation: an equal rights march.	374
16.7	Whirling dervishes perform the Sema Ritua.	375
16.8	Average additional brain activation of Carmelite nuns in mystical states.	376
16.9	The 'God helmet'.	377
16.10	A representation of the sacred Buddha, Wuxi city, Jiangsu province, China.	379
16.11	A group of westerners practising Zen Buddhism.	380
17.1	An 'unidentified flying object' (UFO).	385
17.2	Zener cards.	389
17.3	Uri Geller.	390
17.4	Sensory leakage.	391
17.5	Ectoplasm apparently appearing out of the head of the medium Marthe Beraud.	392
17.6	The ganzfeld.	393
17.7	Some targets in the ganzfeld.	393
17.8	Remote viewing.	394
17.9	Psychokinesis?	396
17.10	Poltergeist: pointing at the location of a rapping sound – or is it a portal to another dimension?	397
17.11	Victorian photograph of a ghost.	399
17.12	Reincarnation: the case of the Pollock twins.	400
18.1	Moon rocks.	403
18.2	Computer cables and power.	405

18.3	Guard on prison security tower.	406
18.4	Mountain (or eastern) gorillas, *Gorilla beringei*.	408
18.5	What changes in an altered state of consciousness?	409
18.6	Captain James Cook meeting indigenous people in the tropics, circa 1700.	409
18.7	Equations on a blackboard.	411

PREFACE

The late twentieth century saw the emergence of cognitive science as an interdisciplinary approach to studying the mind, a strategy that took what was needed from experimental psychology, computer science, philosophy, linguistics, anthropology, and comparative psychology, and, increasingly, neuroscience. As I have taught the study of consciousness over the past 30 years – first as part of an introductory cognition class, and then as an advanced option – I have seen the ways in which the evidence gleaned from neuroscience in particular has become essential to our understanding of consciousness. Indeed, all of psychology has become substantially intertwined with neuroscience. During this period, consciousness has moved from being a fringe topic to one taking centre stage, unifying different areas of psychology in the process.

Yet many students are surprised by the idea that there might be nothing more to us than our brain and bodies; and if psychology students are troubled by this notion, those without a psychology background are often shocked. This insight – that our brain is all there is, and therefore that neuroscience must play a major role in our discussion of consciousness – is the main reason for the creation of this text. As an instructor, I began to feel the need of a text that could succinctly address consciousness in light of the available scientific information by putting neuroscience front and centre in the discussion, while maintaining philosophical integrity. I want a text that can show that there is still a glorious mystery ever present in our lives, and that science can cast light on that mystery. *The Science of Consciousness* is that text.

Approach

Primarily an undergraduate text, *The Science of Consciousness* is appropriate for psychology and philosophy courses in consciousness and cognitive psychology. I hope, however, that it will reach a broader audience, and consequently have written with the educated lay person in mind. As a comprehensive introduction to the science of consciousness, the text is distinguished by the following characteristics.

A Multidisciplinary Approach. Because of the profound effect on the study of consciousness by discoveries in diverse academic fields, only an interdisciplinary approach can expose students to the broadest and most up-to-date understanding of consciousness. Consequently, the text examines every major subject in terms of the light that can be shed on it by a wide range of disciplines – from social sciences to biological sciences to computer science to philosophy.

Theoretical Framework. This book is a text, not a monograph, or a piece of original research, or a mission statement. I have endeavoured to be as neutral as possible while covering a range of material from many sources, some of which contradict each other.

Psychology is distinguished by a lack of consensus in the way that would not be evident in, say, an undergraduate physics text, where much more is known and certain about the discipline being studied. It is one of the challenges of a psychology or related course that the student has to learn to live with and evaluate the uncertainty.

Although bias has no place in a text, it might occasionally shine through. My views are closer to those of Chalmers than of Dennett. I think enormous progress has been made in understanding consciousness over the last few decades, mainly as a result of sophisticated psychology experiments and advances in neuroscience, while philosophy has sharpened the issues to be debated. There is a core of problems (the 'hard problem') where advances have been less rapid, and there may be some problems that are never solved. But progress isn't achieved by giving up, and nothing would be more depressing to a student than a defeatist text. This book is called *The Science of Consciousness* because I think science is humanity's greatest invention.

Little Prior Knowledge Assumed. An interdisciplinary approach brings the challenge that few readers have a background in all of the component disciplines. Not all readers of the text will have the same level of knowledge of these diverse fields, particularly when a major contributor to understanding consciousness is neurobiology, often a difficult subject for the nonspecialist under any circumstances. Students may be apprehensive, finding it difficult to remember all the names and acronyms used in the topic. Understanding the subject can seem more like a test of memory rather than a matter of understanding principles.

Consequently, I have tried to assume as little prior knowledge as possible. Explanations take into account the reality that readers are not students of neuroscience. In addition, rather than weigh down the text with background material that not all readers will need, I have put some information in boxes so that it does not interrupt the flow of the text. Also, I have focused on trying to make the text move seamlessly from subject to subject so that concepts build organically regardless of the discipline from which they emerge. The early part of the text contains a lot of philosophy and a few experiments; later, as we examine consciousness-related topics such as attention and sleep, the text focuses less on philosophy and a great deal more on experiments.

Strong Foundation in Neuroscience. Recent rapid advances in the study of the brain have transformed our ideas about consciousness. No serious consideration of consciousness can proceed without substantial input from neuroscience. Consequently, the discussion of discoveries in neuroscience is an essential aspect of the text. As neuroscience informs every aspect of the subject, the material is integrated throughout rather than shunted into one separate chapter. The glossary though provides a resource for students with less background in neuroscience.

Integration Throughout of 'Atypical' States of Consciousness. While other texts cover sleep and dream science very briefly, three full chapters are devoted to the recent discoveries in this field – discoveries that are especially important to psychology students interested in the latest psychotherapeutic interventions. Other chapters are devoted to 'atypical' states of consciousness; it is easy to gain the impression from the literature that consciousness is one simple state.

Inclusion of Cross-cultural Aspects of Consciousness. Most psychology experiments might be carried out on western young undergraduate students, but we must remember that they might not always be representative of the world's population of what is expected to soon be 8 billion. Different cultures have different views of consciousness; for example, contrast western and eastern approaches to consciousness and spirituality. Different religions place different emphases on altered states of consciousness and means of obtaining them (including prayer and drugs). Even differences between languages affect the way we think of the world.

Engaging Pedagogical Features. The text includes many pedagogical features. Students are encouraged to attempt activities, experiments, and thought experiments, labelled 'Try this', throughout the text; these exercises prompt them to examine different conceptual problems. No other subject lends itself so well to self-exploration as does consciousness. 'Try this' suggestions are clearly marked in the text.

To maintain the flow of the narrative, as well as to break up the text, boxes contain nonessential material that some students might find useful or interesting. In particular, I have provided background information about interdisciplinary approaches that many undergraduates might not know. I have illustrated the book as richly as possible, taking care to use illustrations that really add information or aid understanding, rather than being merely decorative or token. Each figure is captioned so as to aid skimming and remembering the associated material.

Each chapter contains recommendations for exploring further reading and other material. To make the supplemental reading as accessible as possible, I have focused on approachable secondary sources that will prepare the student for the primary sources of peer-reviewed journal articles and books.

Every chapter begins with a roadmap of what that chapter is about. At the end of each chapter is a clear bullet point summary telling the reader what they need to be able to take away from each chapter. The summaries can also act as another form of self-test for readers to be able to evaluate their understanding and knowledge of each topic. There are explicit self-test questions at the end of each chapter.

I think reading the text from Chapter 1 through to Chapter 18 is the best order, but have tried to make each chapter as independent as possible. There is a glossary to assist readers. Items in the glossary are in bold red on first mention (outside the introduction). There is a separate glossary of neuroanatomical location terms, with entries in the text in bold black italic, a glossary of common neurotransmitters with entries in non-bold red, and a glossary of neurotransmitter structures with entries in bold black. Other important technical terms whose scope is usually confined to one chapter are in italics. There is also a list of abbreviations and acronyms.

Online Resources

The field of consciousness research is fast changing and the reader will want a way of keeping up to date with what has happened since the book's publication. There is, of course, also far more material than can be presented in one book. In an attempt to deal with these issues, there is a website for this book at: www.trevorharley.com/consciousness.html.

Under *Consciousness* you will find corrections, additions, comments, news of recent work, informative reviews of other books on consciousness, and frequently asked questions.

One of the most difficult decisions for the writer is how many citations to include. If absolutely everything is referenced, the book will be enormous and the flow disrupted at least once a sentence. On the other hand, every statement must be obviously true or easily verifiable by the reader. If you think a particular assertion needs additional clarification or verification please email me. More generally, an enormous number of resources are available online. The number of blogs on consciousness alone is daunting, but the difficulty with blogs is that unlike journal articles they are not peer-reviewed. I have posted links to some of them on my website.

Some instructors will think this topic should be in and that topic should be out. If you think a particular topic should be covered, please contact me. If you think I should cite particular research, again please just email me. I hope that as time passes new research will overthrow old ideas and give us fresh understanding.

Organisation and Coverage

The early chapters focus on what consciousness is. After giving the matter some thought, I decided to put a chapter on machine and animal consciousness relatively early on. I think students new to the subject matter will find this discussion enhances their understanding of the nature of consciousness. In general, I have made each chapter as independent as possible, so the order of material can be determined by the instructor. I suggest though that the first three chapters be covered first.

The chapters are grouped into three parts.

Part I is on the nature of consciousness. We try to come to grips with what consciousness is.

Chapter 1 surveys the field of consciousness, explaining why it is such a difficult subject to study. The chapter summarises the whole book. The conclusion is that the 'problem' of consciousness is really several related problems.

Chapter 2 discusses the relationship between the mind and brain – a relationship that some have viewed as between hardware and software. This chapter is mainly a philosophical one. It is essential reading if you want to appreciate what the problems are, and how they might be solved. The focus is mainly on what has been called the 'hard problem' of consciousness: why does it feel like something to be me? This chapter summarises the main philosophical approaches to consciousness in the philosophy of mind.

Chapter 3 addresses the problem of free will. It asks who is making decisions about when to do something. It also examines the legal implications of this discussion; if we don't have free will, can we really be held responsible for our actions? Can we ever really be guilty of a crime? The chapter covers philosophical, psychological, and neuroscientific approaches to deciding to act.

Chapter 4 is the first of two about other types of consciousness. Could a computer or robot ever be conscious? How would we tell? Are there any ethical issues or fears associated with machine consciousness?

Chapter 5 talks about awareness in animals, asking this time how we might tell that an animal is self-aware. What are the ethical issues concerning possible consciousness in some animals? A related issue to animal consciousness concerns the evolution of consciousness. Why are some animals conscious (presumably) but not others, and why did consciousness evolve in humans? How is the development of consciousness related to the development of human consciousness and of social groups and organisation?

Part II is about the workings of consciousness. How does consciousness arise from the brain, and how is it related to cognitive and perceptual processing?

Chapter 6 examines introspection and what we can learn about consciousness. What do we think about? What are the contents of consciousness? We think we know all about our own consciousness because it is so immediate, but psychologists understand that appearances are deceptive. Our behaviour is prone to all sorts of bias and self-deception. Some illnesses and damages to the brain have interesting and revealing effects on our abilities to access information about ourselves. This chapter also examines Freud's conception of an actively repressed unconscious and his theory about the structure of the mind. The chapter concludes with an examination of subliminal processing and priming.

Chapter 7 is about the self and our views of our own identity. Do we have a stable identity that persists over time? Is there a core 'me'? The chapter focuses on the contrast between ego and bundle theories of the sense. The text examines various illusions that show how the self can be misled about what it is, which leads into a discussion of how brain damage can disrupt our identities. In particular, the chapter explores the extent to which we derive our sense of self from our memories and what happens when our autobiographical memories are extremely disrupted by brain damage. Again, we focus on the neuroscientific basis of our sense of self.

Chapter 8 focuses more on the cognitive psychology of consciousness. We are 'thinking' all the time we are awake, but what is thought? Many of us experience an inner voice commenting on our experience. Where does this inner voice come from, and how is it related to other language systems? We examine whether the form of our language affects the way in which we think and perceive the world. 'Attention' is an important topic in cognitive psychology and is clearly related to consciousness, but as the chapter shows, attention and consciousness are not the same thing. The text discusses the neuroscience of attention and particularly the idea that there is a 'default mode' network busy when we are doing nothing else – a system that generates daydreaming. The chapter presents several models of consciousness that emphasise cognition. Finally, we look at accounts of consciousness involving quantum mechanics.

Chapter 9 takes a look at the closely related topics of the relationships between visual perception, visual awareness, the brain, and consciousness. A great deal of research has been done on visual awareness. What have we learned from all this research?

Chapter 10 examines in detail the key question of how consciousness is related to the brain. At first sight we might need look no further than how anaesthetics function, but as we shall see, although the workings of anaesthetics are instructive, they provide no definitive answers. We can learn a great deal by examining how damage to the brain affects consciousness. We can also learn something with new techniques of imaging the brain, although some caution is needed in drawing conclusions from these results. Several models of consciousness and the brain are discussed in this chapter. It looks at death, the end of consciousness. Or is it? Is there any continuation of consciousness after death? And how should we define death in the first place? Is death a sudden or lingering process, and what affects the duration of any transition from consciousness to death? Is it possible to avoid death?

Part III is about states of consciousness other than normal waking consciousness – what are called 'altered states of consciousness', including sleep, dreams, hypnosis, and drug-induced states.

Chapter 11 introduces the notion of an altered state of consciousness, a state of consciousness that is in some way different from our normal waking consciousness. We consider what happens to make the state of consciousness seem altered: how do changes in the brain lead to changes in phenomenology? This chapter looks at a range of altered states with different origins, such as sensory deprivation and out-of-body experiences.

Chapter 12 looks at that most familiar altered state, sleep, in which consciousness is largely absent. The mechanisms that control the sleep–wake cycle are likely to reveal much about what maintains wakefulness and consciousness. We look at brain structures, the connectivity of the brain, and neurotransmitters. The chapter also examines the effects of sleep deprivation and sleep disorders. Finally, we ask why we sleep, and to what extent is sleep involved in learning?

Chapter 13 examines the related topic of dreams. Dreaming is the altered state of consciousness with which everyone is most familiar. What do people dream about, and why do we dream? The subject of dreams is naturally a time to revisit Freud, but there are many other accounts of dreaming, and they are not necessarily contradictory. We ask how the brain generates dream content, and we examine dream pathology – the nightmare. We also consider lucid dreaming, when people are aware that they are dreaming and can sometimes influence dream content.

Chapter 14 discusses hypnosis. There has been much debate among psychologists and psychotherapists about whether hypnosis is indeed an altered state of consciousness, and this chapter examines the debate and the evidence. How do we induce hypnosis, and why are some people more easily hypnotised than others? We look at how post-hypnotic suggestions work, and what the clinical applications of hypnosis are. And we also address the issue of whether people can be hypnotised to do things they don't want to do.

Chapter 15 reviews the effects of psychoactive drugs – drugs that influence our mental state. There are a huge number of such drugs with many different effects – some synthesised, some naturally occurring, some used as medical treatment, some for recreation, some legal, some illegal. This chapter focuses on those drugs that tell us the most about consciousness, particularly LSD. The key question is, how do changes to the brain (particularly the chemistry of the brain) lead to changes in perception and consciousness? We look at what the study of psychoactive drugs tells us about 'normal' consciousness. Also included is a brief discussion of the social context of these drugs, looking at how recreational drugs might have helped shape cultural changes.

Chapter 16 examines meditation. What is meditation, and does it work – and, if it does, how? An overwhelming amount of evidence suggests that regular meditation is beneficial in a large number of ways, and this chapter considers these. The chapter also examines the related idea of mystical and religious experiences. The chapter concludes by asking whether there is a state of consciousness that is in some way 'better' than our normal resting state, or at least a 'heightened' state of consciousness.

Chapter 17 reviews the existence of paranormal phenomena, and the methodological difficulties involved in testing for them. What is the evidence for extrasensory perception and related phenomena? And what if anything does the subject tell us about consciousness?

Finally, Chapter 18 revisits the questions posed at the end of the first chapter and summarises what we have learned.

ACKNOWLEDGEMENTS

I have many people to thank for this book. Several anonymous reviewers have improved the book immeasurably. The discussion of artificial intelligence has benefitted from years of argument with Richard Loosemore.

This book would not have happened in this form without the enthusiasm and encouragement of Allan Hobson. I am grateful for his generosity, hospitality, experience, knowledge and enthusiasm. I am conscious of the fact that he won't always approve of the approach I have taken, but nevertheless, Allan, this book is for you. Numerous other people helped. Matthew Bennett of Cambridge University Press (CUP) got the project rolling, and I am grateful to CUP for all their help and particularly their patience. I would like to thank Lisa Pinto for all her guidance and patience, and Linda Stern for all her detailed comments and hard work; I hope you think it has paid off. Jane Adams has been a superb editor. Particular thanks are due to Rachel Norridge for the extraordinary amount of time and help she has given me. I have had many conversations over many years with Richard Wilton about many of the topics in this book. We have recently written a book together (*Science and Psychology*), which has a chapter about consciousness and another about free will, and I am sure my current approach to the legal issues surrounding free will has been influenced by cowriting the latter chapter in particular. Frank John Snelling read chapters as an 'intelligent lay person', and his comments on what he found difficult or needing definition were illuminating.

Finally, here is a word of consolation. The study of consciousness is difficult; if you find it hard going at times, it isn't just you. It's right up there in conceptual difficulty with quantum mechanics and relativity. And more difficult than rocket science and brain surgery.

ABBREVIATIONS

ACC	Anterior cingulate cortex
AI	Artificial intelligence
AIM	Activation input modulation
APA	American Psychological Association
ASC	Altered state of consciousness
ASPD	Antisocial personality disorder
AVH	Auditory verbal hallucination
CBD	cannabidiol
CN	Caudate nucleus
CSF	Cerebrospinal fluid
CLIS	complete locked-in syndrome
DBS	Deep-brain stimulation
DCH	dynamic core hypothesis
DID	Dissociative identity disorder
DLPFC	Dorsolateral prefrontal cortex
DMN	Default mode network
DMT	N,N-dimethyltryptamine
DN	Default network
DSM	The American Psychiatric Association's Diagnostic and Statistical Manual of Mental Disorders
EEG	Electroencephalogram
ESM	Experience sampling method
ESP	Extrasensory perception
fMRI	Functional magnetic resonance imaging
fNIRS	functional near infrared spectroscopy
GWT	Global workspace theory
GESP	a general extrasensory perception
HPPD	hallucinogen persisting perception disorder
IIT	Integrated information theory
LIFG	left inferior frontal gyrus
LRE	life review experience
LIS	Locked-in syndrome
MAOI	Monoamine oxidase inhibitor
MEG	Magnetoencephalography
mPFC	Medial prefrontal cortex
MCS	Minimally conscious state
MRI	Magnetic resonance imaging
ms	Millisecond, 1/1000 th of a second
MSR	Mirror test of self-recognition

LIST OF ABBREVIATIONS

MVPA	multi-voxel pattern analysis
NCC	Neuronal correlates of consciousness
NDE	Near-death experience
NREM	Non-rapid eye movement sleep
OBE	Out-of-body experience
OCD	Obsessive-compulsive disorder
OFC	Orbito-frontal cortex
PCC	Posterior cingulate cortex
PCP	phencyclidine
PET	Positron emission tomography
PK	psychokinesis
PGO	Ponto-geniculo-occipital
POSTS	Positive occipital transients of sleep
PPC	posterior parietal cortex
PTSD	Post-traumatic stress disorder
PVS	Persistent vegetative state
REM	Rapid eye movement (sleep)
REST	Restricted environmental stimulation therapy
RP	Readiness potential
SCN	Suprachiasmatic nucleus
SSRI	Selective serotonin re-uptake inhibitor
SWS	slow-wave sleep
TUTs	task unrelated thoughts
TST	threat simulation theory of dreaming
THC	Tetrahydrocannabinol
TLE	Temporal lobe epilepsy
TMS	Transcranial magnetic stimulation

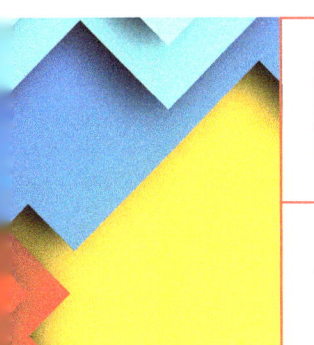

PART I

THE NATURE OF CONSCIOUSNESS

1 THE PROBLEM OF CONSCIOUSNESS

This chapter will introduce you to consciousness and its most important characteristics. We will look at definitions of consciousness, and examine what it means to say that consciousness is a private experience. We will look at the idea that it is like something to be you or me. The chapter mentions ideas and themes that will be covered in more detail in the rest of the book, and explains why the topic is an important one.

Research on consciousness is big on questions but shorter on answers. Nevertheless these questions are central to what it means to be human, or indeed at the heart of what it's like to be anything – what it's like to be conscious.

Think of yourself just now. What does it feel like to be you right at this moment? Think of a loved one. What do you think it is like to be them? Do they know exactly what they're feeling, and do you know just what they're feeling? We might have some idea, but the answer in both cases is no, and not only 'no', we can't see how we ever could know for sure. It's *my* consciousness and *your* consciousness.

Why Study Consciousness?

The study of consciousness is the study of what it means to be us. We perceive the world (or at least we think we do) through the lens of our consciousness. And how can we understand the universe if we don't understand how we experience it?

What is consciousness and how does it arise are two of the fundamental questions of science, along with others such as 'what is life?' and 'where did the universe come from?'.

The study of consciousness is at the limit of our understanding of natural science. For some researchers the gap between our understanding of consciousness and the laws of physics is so large that they think physics must either be incomplete, or that understanding consciousness is beyond physics.

Consciousness and Psychology

The study of consciousness is a unifying topic in psychology because consciousness links research on attention, executive processes, working memory, perception, decision making, and language. We think of consciousness as the result of all the processing that goes on in the mind. For example, when perceptual processing of an object is complete, it enters visual awareness. Is this view that consciousness is the last stage of processing correct?

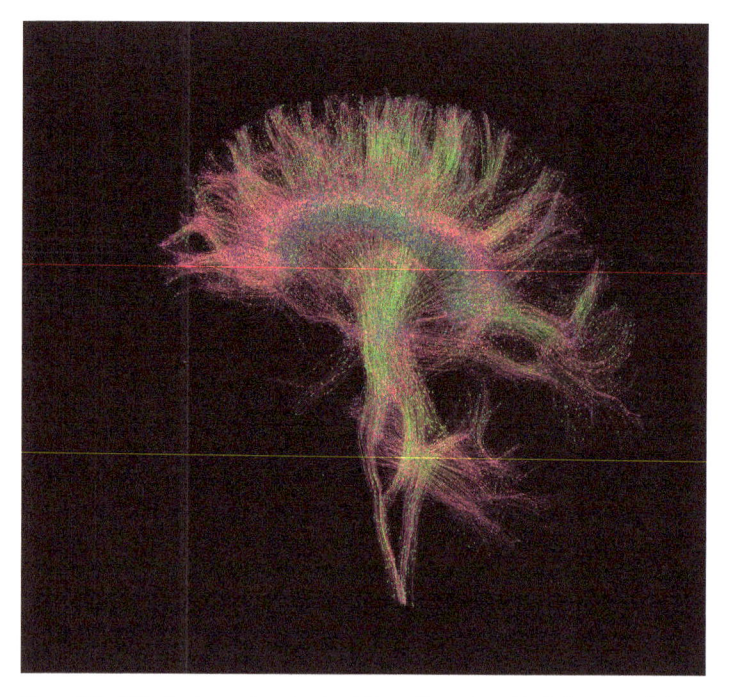

Figure 1.1 Diffusion tensor imaging is at the cutting edge of techniques available for imaging the living brain, and produces spectacular (and useful) images such as this one. Source: Callista Images/Cultura/Getty Images.

Figure 1.2 Democritus (c. 460–c. 370 BCE). Democritus was a Greek philosopher who argued that all things were made of 'atoms', with the motion of atoms determined by causal laws. There was no place for chance or choice in his scheme of things. Source: De Agostini Picture Library/Getty Images Plus.

Consciousness and Neuroscience

The search for the seat of consciousness in the brain has shown how parts of the brain are connected, and how information flow between these parts gives rise to consciousness. Neuroscience research on consciousness has advanced our understanding of how psychological processes are underpinned by brain systems, and how normal psychological processing depends on the delicate balance of many systems in the brain. It shows what can go wrong and what the results of dysfunction are. Some of the most exciting neuroscience research is currently being carried out on topics related to consciousness (see Figure 1.1).

Consciousness and Philosophy

Consciousness is one of the central problems in the philosophy of mind. How can matter give rise to awareness? How can my private experience be explained by the laws of physics?

Consciousness is also entwined with one of the fundamental concerns of philosophical thought, the problem of free will. It seems to me, as I sit here, aware and conscious writing this paragraph in a trendy coffee shop, that I am choosing not to pick up my mug of coffee and throw it on the floor. This choice is my free will in action. On the other hand, if all I am is determined by my genes and my past, and by the history of the universe up to now, that sense of free will is illusory. My future has already determined that I will remain seated here, sipping my coffee, polite, restrained, and demure. I have no choice – a conclusion very counter to my everyday beliefs. Philosophers have been aware of the problems with free will and choice since antiquity (see Figure 1.2), but there is still no widely accepted resolution.

The study of consciousness tells us who we are – or are not. Who is this 'I' that has a choice, or not? When 'you' are deciding to do something, who is the 'you'? Who is in control? We often think of ourselves as watching the world and observing our mental life, as though there is a person with us. We call this little person a **homunculus** (see Box 1.1), but the homunculus idea suffers from the problem of an *infinite regress*. A related idea is that we have permanent 'selfs' that experience things. I think of myself (myself is my self) as being the same person as I remember listening to a piece of music on my fifth birthday. Why do I think that? Does it make any sense to do so? I think of my self as having an identity that persists over time. Where does this notion of 'self' come from? As we shall see, many consciousness researchers argue that the self is an illusion. Research on consciousness will cast light on where our sense of ourselves and of our identities comes from.

Box 1.1 The Homunculus Inside Us

Homunculus means 'little person' in Latin. The idea is that there is a little person inside our heads who observes everything and decides how to act. The idea has its roots in the pre-scientific practice of alchemy. Some version of the homunculus idea is popular among non-psychologists (and some psychologists too): we don't really think there is a little person inside us, but we do have the impression that 'I' am looking out from inside my head at the world. The problem with the homunculus idea is that we have no idea how the homunculus works. Does the homunculus have another homunculus inside it, observing and controlling the bigger homunculus? If so, we have only displaced the problem, and quickly enter an infinite regress of an endless series of homunculi inside each other. The idea pops up in popular culture: the Numskulls was a comic strip in the D.C. Thomson comics the *Dandy* and the *Beano* that showed a team of tiny technicians who lived inside our heads working our senses and brains. But what ran the brain of the Numskulls? A team of even smaller Num-Numskulls?

The study of consciousness has implications for society. If we don't have free will, there are important consequences for how we view individual responsibility. If I had no alternative other than to rob a bank, why should I be punished for the crime?

Consciousness and Spirituality

Consciousness is the bridge between science and the humanities. Why do you find a particular piece of music moving, or a piece of art beautiful? Can you imagine a computer appreciating beauty or justice, and why not? Science does not tell us how to behave, while ethics in philosophy describes ways of living, and does suggest how we should behave. But what would such injunctions mean without consciousness?

Our consciousness is intimately involved with our *spirituality*, our deepest values and our sense of things beyond science. What do we find spiritual, and what creates these feelings of spirituality? You may meditate, or attend church, or practise a religion in some other way, and feel that some experiences are richer or on a higher plane than everyday experience (see Figure 1.3). Or you might have experienced some unusual state, such as feeling that your mind has left your body. Some people have taken drugs to 'expand' their consciousness; what, if anything, does this statement mean? What is the relationship between these different states of consciousness?

The study of consciousness also informs what happens when we are not conscious, including when we are asleep, when we are in a coma, and when we are dead. Is sleep merely the absence of consciousness? What happens when we are dying, and afterwards?

The study of consciousness informs our search for meaning in life. However, being conscious can be sometimes seen as a curse; as the Danish philosopher Søren Kierkegaard (1813–1855) put it in 1844:

> What does it mean to be a self-conscious animal? The idea is ludicrous, if it is not monstrous … It means to know that one is food for worms. This is the terror: to have emerged from nothing, to have a name, consciousness of self, deep inner feelings, an excruciating inner yearning for life and self-expression – and with all this yet to die. (Kierkegaard, 1980)

Without consciousness there would be no pain, but neither would there be pleasure, joy, beauty, or love. And it's one of the most fascinating topics in science, and a topic that bridges science and the arts. Those are pretty good reasons to study it.

Figure 1.3 The way in which religions are practised varies across the world. Here, Buddhist nuns practise kung fu at the Amitabha Drukpa Nunnery on the outskirts of Kathmandu. Source: AFP/Getty Images.

How We Study Consciousness

The scientific study of consciousness was once the sole domain of philosophers, but is now an interdisciplinary affair. For some time the study of consciousness was thought to be not quite respectable. I'm not sure whether the word 'consciousness' was used at all in my undergraduate degree in psychology at Cambridge (although that was a long time ago). Fortunately, that has changed, and consciousness is being studied by a coalition of psychologists, philosophers, neuroscientists, surgeons, computer scientists, and anthropologists. We call the research carried out by this joint enterprise of cognitive scientists *consciousness studies*.

One way of finding out about consciousness is simply to think about what you're experiencing. After all, you're conscious right now, so why not just consider what's going inside your mind? Surely that act more than anything else will tell us about consciousness? This process of observing ourselves and reporting on our experience is called **introspection**. Introspection has its uses, but it's not always that reliable. By definition, we can only introspect upon what we're conscious of at the time. Our knowledge of ourselves is limited, and we are often not aware of our limitations, as shown by the work of psychologists such as Daniel Kahneman (2012) on human reasoning. For example, when we make judgements about things such as spending money, we think we're making a reasoned judgement, but in fact we're influenced by all sorts of biases and prejudices of which we are mostly unaware. For example, we're usually strongly averse to taking risks. We might not actually be conscious of very much at any one time, but everything else of which we are not conscious might nevertheless be influencing us. So when we introspect and report on the contents of our consciousness, and think about why we're behaving in a certain way, our picture is at best incomplete, and occasionally quite wrong. We'll look in detail at the limits of introspection, and how difficult it is to know our own mind, in much more detail in Chapter 6.

So, to study consciousness, we must use a range of methods. Along with philosophical analysis, we carry out psychological experiments that measure some variable we think is associated with consciousness, and observe the effect of our experimental manipulations on that variable. We then make an inference from our results to construct a theoretical model of what is happening.

Scientific Experimentation

Psychology and neuroscience are experimental sciences (see Box 1.2 and Box 1.3), which means that typically we manipulate independent variables (such as the length of a word) and observe the effect of these manipulations on a dependent variable (such as how long it takes to name that word). Consciousness research is difficult because there is no way yet known of measuring consciousness, and so it is difficult or impossible to turn it into a dependent variable. There is no 'consciousnessoscope' that we can put on our heads and read out a number for how conscious we are, what we're really thinking, or what we're experiencing just now. This difficulty sometimes motivates pessimism about how far we can get with studying consciousness. But even if we cannot (yet) measure consciousness directly, we can measure variables that we assume are dependent on or related to consciousness, such as a verbal report of something, or a judgement about ourselves or the world.

Box 1.2 The Role of Falsification in Science

Science is a method of gaining knowledge about the world. We use the scientific method when we collect data about the world and construct theories to explain those data. Data is anything we can measure. Science is concerned with controlled observations, which involves making comparisons where as few things as possible are left to chance.

Theories then lead to novel predictions, which we can then test against more data. If the predictions are verified, then the theory is supported and gains in strength; if the predictions are wrong, then the theory has to be revised in some way. The eminent Austrian-British philosopher of science Sir Karl Popper (1902–1994) argued that science should proceed by *falsification*: instead of trying to prove our theories, we should be trying to disprove them (see Figure 1.4). It's only by finding that our predictions are wrong that science progresses and theories are overturned. We rejected Aristotelian physics because its predictions turned out to be wrong once experiments were carried out. We found that the velocity with

Box 1.2 (cont.)

Figure 1.4 Sir Karl Popper (1902–1994). Karl Popper was an Austrian-born philosopher who for many years was professor of logic and scientific method at Imperial College, London. Popper argued that science proceeded not by verification (proving things right, which is impossible), but by falsification – trying to disprove a theory. Source: ullstein bild/Getty Images.

which different objects travelled when dropped from the same height does not depend on the objects' weight, and that bodies in motion carry on in a straight line without decelerating if no other forces acted upon them. Newtonian mechanics gave a much better account of the world.

Although falsification is important, science doesn't always progress by rejecting falsified theories. There are two main reasons for this pattern. First, if a theory has done very well, people are understandably reluctant to reject it altogether and go back to scratch and design a whole new theory just because one prediction is falsified. Perhaps the whole theory isn't wrong, but just one of the assumptions we have made along the way? So when we drop a feather and a heavy ball from the top of a tower, and observe the feather floating down as the ball plummets, we don't reject Newtonian mechanics. Instead we think about factors such as air resistance, and realise that it's our assumption that the medium through which the objects are falling doesn't matter that is wrong, not the whole theory. Second, we have to make measurements to collect data. Perhaps our measurements or our observing devices are wrong. If I look at a section of a brain through a microscope, and see a perfectly circular black object in it, it's most unlikely that I'm observing a new brain structure that has amazingly been missed for centuries – and far more likely there's a mark on my microscope lens.

Box 1.3 The History of Neuroscience

Neuroscience is the scientific study of the nervous system, with cognitive neuroscience being the study of how the nervous system and associated biological processes underlie cognition.

For a long time, the only available means of studying how the brain is related to human behaviour was an autopsy performed on a person with brain damage; we observed the effects of damage while the person was living, and then later found out which parts of the brain had been damaged. In some cases, researchers could estimate which parts of the brain were affected by examining the location of the injury (such as the position of the blasting rod that perforated the brain of the American railway worker Phineas Gage in 1848; see Chapter 7 for more detail on his case). Neurosurgical operations told us exactly which parts of the brain had been damaged. For example, in *split-brain* patients, we knew that the only significant damage to the brain was to the body of nerve fibres called the **corpus callosum** that connects the two cerebral hemispheres, and then conducted experiments to see which aspects of behaviour changed as a consequence of this damage. We could also extrapolate from animal studies, although obviously some caution is necessary in linking

Box 1.3 (cont.)

animal studies to human models, particularly given animals do not use language, and the degree of self-awareness is limited and questionable.

More recently non-invasive techniques of brain imaging have enabled scientists to examine the structure of the brain and measure its electrical activity while working. The biggest revolution has come from a technique known as *functional magnetic resonance imaging* (fMRI), which allows us to observe what different parts of the brain are doing in real time, with reasonable spatial and temporal accuracy. The earliest scientific studies on humans were carried out in the early 1990s, but as the equipment has become cheaper and more accurate, and the skills necessary to carry out the research more widespread, the use of fMRI is widespread.

As with any technique, the use of imaging requires some caution. First, the brain is always doing more than carrying out the specific task under consideration, so methods are necessary to isolate the task of interest from the background noise. Second, these techniques do not measure neural activity directly, but do so through some intermediate measure, such as oxygen uptake (Lilienfeld et al., 2015). Third, at present there is something of a tradeoff between physical and temporal resolution (see Figure 1.5). Finally, we need to remember that knowing where and when something is happening might not tell us exactly what is happening. Nevertheless there is no doubt that psychology is a very different subject from 30 years ago, and our understanding of behaviour and the relationship between the brain and behaviour has advanced enormously.

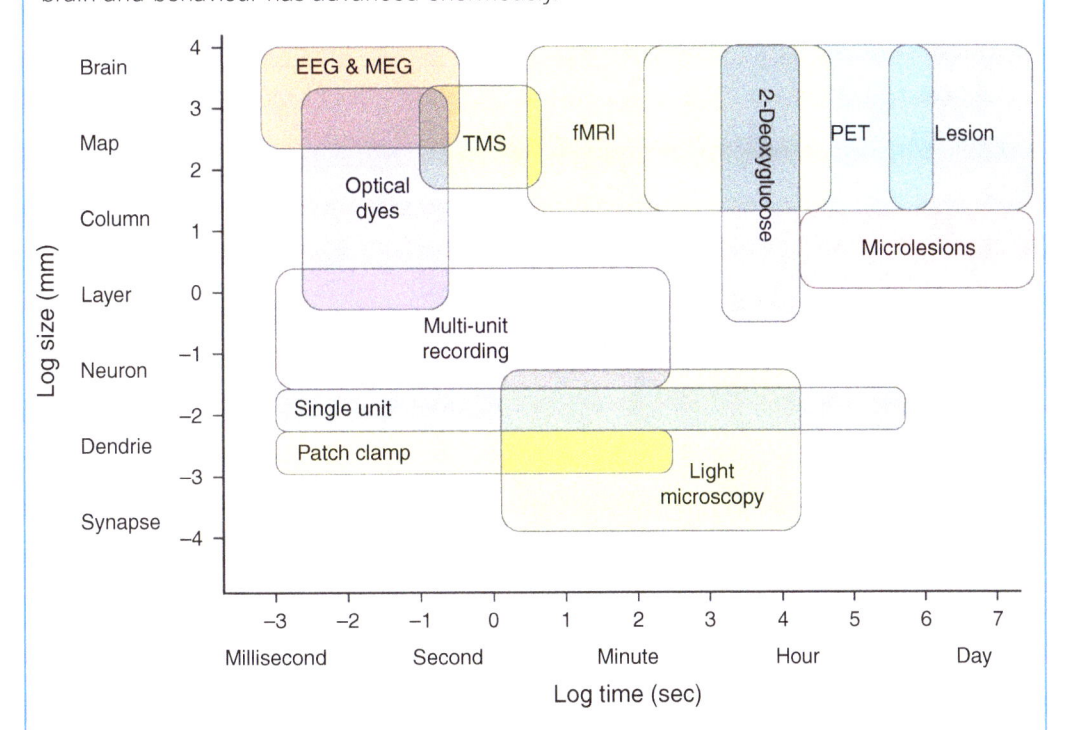

Figure 1.5 The spatial and temporal accuracy or resolution of various neuroscience investigatory techniques. The y-axis is size and x-axis time; the scales are logarithmic, meaning each tick on the axis is 10 times more than the preceding one. See text and glossary for the meaning of abbreviations.

Psychology and the study of consciousness has advanced rapidly with modern developments in techniques of brain imaging. Until not too long ago, the only way of looking at a brain was to wait until a person died and then carry out an autopsy, and even then a chain of inference was necessary to relate brain functions to psychological processes. Imaging enables us to look at the living brain, and modern functional imaging enables us to look at what the living brain is doing. Other techniques enable us to influence what the brain is doing, so for the first time we can see what is happening in the brain as we think and make decisions.

There are though a few caveats we should bear in mind. The first is that brain-imaging techniques are still restricted in what can be done: at the moment it takes a relatively long time to take measurements that are highly spatially accurate, so the *temporal resolution* of brain imaging is presently not that accurate. Other techniques that are more accurate in identifying when things are happening currently have relatively poor spatial resolution, and so at the moment there is a tradeoff between temporal and spatial accuracy (see Figure 1.5). The machines are still big and noisy, so it's going to be difficult (but not impossible) to test people when they're sleeping and dreaming, say. Of course, all these limitations will probably disappear, hopefully sooner rather than later. The second caveat is more important: we are not measuring consciousness directly, but what is going on in the brain, and as the only access to consciousness is through a person's verbal report, or some other indirect measure of what is happening, the best we can do is correlate our imaging data with aspects of consciousness. Furthermore we are not measuring brain activity directly, but some correlate of it, such as oxygen uptake. Nevertheless, the techniques are a huge advance in what has previously been available, and are in part responsible for the scientific study of consciousness being taken more seriously than it has previously been.

Another way of studying the relationship between the brain and consciousness is to examine the effects of brain damage, by injury, stroke, or surgery, upon consciousness. The effects of damage to the brain vary depending on exactly which parts of the brain are damaged, and by how much. We shall see that the study of brain damage reveals a great deal about the nature of consciousness. These neuropsychological studies are now often combined with imaging so that we know exactly which parts of the brain are damaged.

Philosophical Thought Experiments

Philosophy is the study of fundamental problems concerning the nature of knowledge, what exists, the nature of the mind, and the nature of values. In this book our primary concern is the sub-discipline known as the philosophy of mind. One of the most important weapons in the armoury of the philosophy of mind is the **thought experiment**, in which we consider some hypothesis or situation, and think through the consequences to what we think is a logical conclusion. Science is characterised by experiment, but thought experiments deal with scenarios that are impossible, or at least very difficult, to construct in reality, at least now. The idea is that the thought experiment reveals our prejudices, or shows how our prejudices lead us to surprising conclusions. A good thought experiment clarifies the problem and our assumptions. We will meet many in the next few chapters, including the China brain and Mary the clever neuroscientist.

Artificial Intelligence

Another way of investigating consciousness is to try to build it. Is it possible that a computer or robot could be conscious? Or is consciousness for some reason restricted to biological systems? Supposing we could build one, what would be the characteristics of a conscious machine – would we be able to say exactly what it was that we did to make the computer conscious, or would artificial consciousness be as baffling as human consciousness? Crucially, how would we tell if the computer was conscious or not? In the *Terminator* series of films (Cameron, 1984), the artificial intelligence (AI) SkyNet launches a nuclear attack on humans in an attempt to defend its self-awareness: if we do construct a sentient artificial intelligence, would we have anything to fear from it? Could we limit its powers so that it poses no threat?

As well as constructing an artificial intelligence, we could construct machines that move and interact physically with the world; such machines are better known as **robots**. Robots can be made to look more like humans, but appearances can be deceptive. How important is being able to interact with the world for the development of consciousness?

Although well beyond our current capability, we could aim to learn about psychology, neuroscience, and consciousness by trying to build a brain (see Figure 1.6). Attempts at doing so are already well underway, and to date we have attained large-scale models containing millions of nerve cells, or **neurons**. There are two ways of approaching the problem: simulating neurons, or building artificial neurons, with the first slower but currently easier. In a similar vein, we could augment, or 'upgrade', our brains with specialised components, ranging from very simple capabilities (fancy a GPS chip?) to much more wide ranging (such as more memory). What are the implications for consciousness of such changes?

Defining Consciousness

The British psychologist Stuart Sutherland once famously defined consciousness as: 'a fascinating but elusive phenomenon: it is impossible to specify what it is, what it does, or why it has evolved' (Sutherland, 1989).

Sutherland goes on to say that nothing worth reading has been written about it. I hope that, if nothing else, this book shows that this statement is no longer true. It is true, however, that consciousness is difficult to define. It's one of those things that you know when you see it.

Figure 1.6 Growing brain cells. A magnified view of mouse stem cells producing new neurons at a neuroscience lab at the Stanford Medical School. Building a biological brain depends on being able to grow nerve cells. Source: MediaNews Group/San Mateo County Times via Getty Images.

TRY THIS: Defining Consciousness

You probably think you know what consciousness is, so how would you define it? Then use a search engine to find some definitions of consciousness. How do they compare with your own?

Definitions of Consciousness

Consciousness is our experience of being us here now. It's what is lost when we are in a dreamless sleep and what returns next morning when we wake up (Tononi, 2004; Tononi & Edelman, 1998). Consciousness is permanently lost when we die, but as we shall see in Chapter 10, this statement also leaves plenty of room for discussion.

The American philosopher Thomas Nagel (1974) proposed that an organism is conscious if there is something it is like to be that organism. There is something it is like to be you reading this text at the moment; you will almost certainly think that there is something it is like to be a robin hopping around the garden hunting worms; but presumably you will think it is like nothing to be a laptop or lump of rock (see Gallagher & Zahavi, 2012).

We can further distinguish consciousness, which is equivalent to **awareness**, the experience of perceiving a sensation of some sort, from **self-consciousness**, which is awareness of our own awareness or consciousness.

Vimal (2009) reviewed the various meanings of the word consciousness used in the research literature, and identified 40 distinct meanings. He concludes that 'consciousness can be optimally defined as a mental aspect of an entity (system or process) that has dual-aspect: conscious experience and conscious function. In other words, a system or a process is conscious iff [an abbreviation of 'if and only if'] its mental aspect is conscious experience and conscious function' (p. 17). Note that we have the word 'conscious' in the definition of consciousness!

Awareness

The words 'aware' and 'awareness' crop up consistently in dictionary definitions of consciousness: being conscious involves being aware. When we ask people what they think consciousness is we might be told that it's what it's like to be awake, and it's what it's like to be aware of things. 'Awareness' then is clearly important in our conception of consciousness. Look up the meaning of 'awareness' and you get ... 'conscious'. Awareness is the state of feeling or perceiving sensations (Cohen & Dennett, 2011).

In addition to being aware, we can be self-aware, in that we can be aware of our being aware. While we think we are aware all the time we are awake, we are only self-aware when we turn our attention to our awareness. And while you may think many animals are aware, is it likely that few if any of them are self-aware? Perhaps self-awareness sets humans apart from other animals? That's an important question and one we'll discuss in Chapter 5.

Notice that we can only be conscious of our own experience. We cannot explain to another person what it is like to be us, and they can't explain to us what it is like to be them. They can't describe the pain they feel in a way that we can feel it. There is something essentially private about consciousness.

We can only be aware of our consciousness now. Of course our consciousness isn't completely trapped in the present because we have our memories, but when we remember something, it is the memory we're aware of, not the original event.

DEFINING CONSCIOUSNESS

> **TRY THIS:** Observe Your Mind
>
> Whatever you are doing, just observe your mind. What is happening? What are you aware of now? Were you thinking about something in particular? Were you thinking in words, or in pictures? Were you remembering something, or perceiving something? Now can you make yourself aware of something else? Try to hold on to the present moment for as long as possible; how soon is it before you would say things have changed and you're in a new moment? How would you characterise self-awareness, awareness of your awareness?

The Problem of Other Minds

There's something peculiar about our own experience: it's our own and nobody else's. Consciousness is very different to the world outside our heads, which is typically studied by science. There are several ways of describing this difference: we can say that consciousness is subjective, and everything else objective. We have the first-person perspective in our own mental life, whereas science uses the third-person perspective to describe the world. The outside world is public, but our experience is private.

This privacy of consciousness makes its study so difficult. What is it like to be you? Other minds are for ever closed to us. Our experiences are private, and we have no way of sharing them. The problem of other minds is that we have no way of knowing what anyone else is experiencing – I cannot access the contents of your consciousness, or you mine. We cannot truly share our pain. We can use words like 'pain' and 'red' and 'hot' and hope that you mean the same things with them as I do.

In 1974, Nagel wrote a famous paper called 'What is it like to be a bat?'. Bats navigate and find prey by sonar – a different kind of sense to the five human senses (see Figure 1.7). We can guess what it is like to be most other humans because we assume that we all have broadly similar types of experience, but we cannot begin to imagine what it must be like being a bat. A bat perceives the world primarily through a sense we do not possess, echolocation, a form of sonar. The bat emits a sound, mostly in a frequency range beyond the limits of human hearing, and detects the echo. The sense is accurate enough to enable the bats to hunt fast-moving insect prey. Presumably it is like something to be a bat, but we cannot conceive of

Figure 1.7 A bat using sonar. What is it like to be a bat? Source: Danita Delimont/Gallo Images/Getty Images Plus.

it. According to Nagel, we can never really grasp what it is *like to be a bat*; some aspects of 'bathood' are, as McGinn (1989) puts it, 'perceptually closed to us'. There's nothing special about bats – it's just that the differences between us and them are rather more extreme than between us and other mammals. At least that's the standard argument; perhaps we can have some idea what it is like to be a bat – after all, echolocation is a form of hearing, one that humans use to a much lesser extent – but we cannot completely appreciate what it is like to be a bat.

We are even limited in what we can conceive about human experience; I cannot imagine what it must be like to be blind from birth, and surely neither can a person who has never seen contemplate what sight must be like. Helen Keller was born in Alabama in 1880; at around 19 months old she contracted an illness, possibly scarlet fever or meningitis, that left her deaf and blind. When she was seven years old she started to learn to communicate through touch with her teacher, Anne Sullivan (see Figure 1.8). What would the experience of Helen Keller have been like before that moment of contact? Even after that in what ways would her experience be similar and dissimilar to ours? Keller's story is remarkable: she lived until the age of 88, and was the first deaf-blind person to obtain a degree in art.

Finally, meet my dog, Beau (see Figure 1.9). He's a miniature poodle, just over two years old. We'll consider his point of view a few times in the book. Beau is an interesting case: I know him extremely well. We are very close. I am sure he's conscious and I think at times he's self-conscious. He knows a few words of language (such as the name of all of his toys), but doesn't to my knowledge understand syntax, the details of word order. He perceives the world differently from me – his sense of smell is 300 times more sensitive than mine. I think I know something of what it is like to be Beau, although I am less sure what he thinks of me. Does he just think of me as a big dog? That part of him is closed to me.

Figure 1.8 Helen Keller with her teacher Anne Sullivan, in 1888. What was it like to be Helen Keller? Source: Bettmann/Getty Images.

Figure 1.9 Meet my miniature poodle, Beau. Does it make any sense to ask what does he think it is like to be Trevor?

The Hard and Easy Problems of Consciousness

The Australian philosopher David Chalmers called the central problem of consciousness, that of how phenomenal awareness arises in a physical world, the **hard problem**. Another way of putting it is by asking how do the objective processes studied by science, particularly the physical structure of the nervous system and brain, give rise to subjective experience? The hard problem is sometimes phrased in terms of the **explanatory gap**, which is the difference in our ability to explain physical properties of the universe with physical laws and our inability to explain mental properties. The hard problem is the problem we have in bridging this gap between mechanistic laws and feelings and experiences.

In contrast to the hard problem, the easy problems are everything else we want to know about consciousness. They're questions about psychological processes, such as what's the difference between being awake, asleep, or being in a coma, how do vision and the other senses work, how do we plan for the future and control our behaviour, what are the processes that control how we sleep and dream, what is attention, how do we access memories, how do we access and report our internal states, how do drugs affect us, how do we decide to act and move, how does brain damage alter cognitive processing, what can we report about our own mental processes, and many more. Note that these problems are only easy relative to the hard problem: in spite of a hundred years or more of experimental psychology, our understanding of many of them is patchy at best.

For philosophers such as Dennett (2014, 2018), once we have solved all the easy problems (which he thinks aren't that easy at all), the solutions to the 'hard problem' will either drop out or it will turn out not to be a problem at all. We just don't understand the field of research or the problems properly yet. He also argues that it is a mistake to separate consciousness from its functions, and it is this mistake that leads to there appearing to be a hard problem (Cohen & Dennett, 2011). A similar line is taken by Dehaene (2014), who also argues that the 'easy' problems are in fact the hard one, and our labelling of 'easy' and 'hard' changes as our knowledge of the field evolves. The philosopher Peter Hankins takes a different approach, also saying that the easy problems are actually hard ones, but that the hard problem is impossible to solve (Hankins, 2015).

If this book were about the hard problem alone, it could be a very short book. We have made enormous progress over recent years on the easy problems, but very little on the hard problem, other perhaps than understanding it better. As we shall see, some people argue that we can never, in principle, solve the hard problem. Others think we have as good as solved it, or at least know the way to solve it, while others deny even that there is a hard problem. Others just hope we will make progress one day.

Intentionality: Are We Always Conscious of Something?

'Conscious' is an ambiguous word – in everyday conversation we can use it in different ways. There's consciousness in the sense of awareness that we've just been looking at. You can be 'conscious of the time' – meaning that you are aware of the time and that the clock is ticking. We might also say something like 'I'm conscious that you need money.' In this sense of consciousness, we're conscious of something.

This point is an important one: consciousness when used this way is about or directed towards something. In fact, consciousness always seems to be directed towards something. We are always aware of something. We are conscious of our thoughts, or sensations coming in from the outside world, or of our body, and perhaps all of these at once. It seems impossible to be completely empty headed. Even if you try to think of nothing, that nothing becomes the something that consciousness is directed towards. The idea that consciousness is about something is called **intentionality**. Although the idea is an old one, it is most associated with the German philosopher Franz Brentano (1838–1917). Brentano was one of Sigmund Freud's PhD supervisors, and his ideas influenced early psychoanalysis and hence our later conception of the unconscious. Brentano (1874) said that intentionality is one of the major characteristics of thought and consciousness. Thoughts are always about something, and we can't just be aware; we are always aware of something, even if it is just being aware. Consciousness has content.

There are limits on what we can be conscious of. You can't be conscious of your digestion. Occasionally you might hear an embarrassing rumble, or be aware of indigestion, but these are side effects of digestion acting on the nervous system. But the processes of digestion themselves are completely opaque to us. Getting closer to home, when we accidentally stab ourselves with the rose thorn, we are conscious of the pain, but not of the nerve cells that carry that pain, no matter how hard we might try to think about them.

> **TRY THIS:** Being Conscious of Nothing
>
> Try to be conscious of nothing at all. Empty your mind. Do you think it is possible to be conscious without being conscious of anything? If you think it is, how do you know you're not thinking of anything?

Consciousness is also unable to access many psychological processes. When you hear someone say a sentence, you understand it (normally); but you can't make yourself aware of how you understood it. When you're a skilled driver or tennis player, the processes involved are automatic. Indeed, focusing on skilled performance can cause problems: if a skilled tennis player or golf player starts to focus consciously on their movements, performance can deteriorate quite dramatically.

Types of Consciousness

Psychologists and neuroscientists are justifiably proud of the progress they have made in understanding the brain and behaviour and the relationship between them over the last century or so, with the rate of progress accelerating over the last few decades. Many say that they've made huge progress in understanding consciousness as well. But this chapter has examined some of the fundamental problems of consciousness thrown up by researchers, and it should come as no surprise that several people have distinguished between different types or aspects of consciousness.

Phenomenal and Access Consciousness

The American philosopher Ned Block (1995) distinguished between **phenomenal consciousness** and **access consciousness**. Phenomenal consciousness is what we experience: it's what it's like to be us. It's the sensations of perception from the outside, and the experience of wanting, thinking, and feeling from the inside. It's what we've been talking about mostly in this chapter, and for many understanding phenomenal consciousness is the central 'hard problem' to be addressed. Access consciousness concerns language, thought, attention, the control of action, and reasoning. It concerns what we talk and think about and, importantly, it's what we can report – so it's our thoughts, feelings, and desires themselves (rather than our experience of them) and the representations that are manipulated in cognition. Block uses the abbreviations P-consciousness and A-consciousness. Most cognitive psychology experiments are on A-consciousness, while the *Try This* thought experiments in this chapter have mostly been about P-consciousness. A-consciousness is said to be definable within a computer program, but P-consciousness is not.

To what extent are P- and A-consciousness *dissociable* – that is, can we have one without the other? Normally, Block says, P-consciousness and A-consciousness interact, but in principle they could exist independently of each other. So Block believes that beings could exist that would have A-consciousness but not P-consciousness: for example, we might build a robot that does all the things we do but without phenomenal consciousness. On the other hand, many non-human animals may have P-consciousness but not A-consciousness; they have experiences but the experiences are not involved in cognitive processing, so they have experiences but not the sense of themselves experiencing anything. What this statement means in practice, and how we could tell for sure, are difficult to evaluate.

Block's division is controversial because P-consciousness is, by definition, non-computational – only A-consciousness can be manipulated symbolically. That is, it takes A-consciousness to solve a maths problem or write a sentence. Block (1995) stresses the importance of introspection, our ability to look into our own minds, and states that only events that are available to introspection can be manipulated symbolically. Furthermore, if we accept this type of distinction, we must also accept that sensations arise from non-computational mechanisms, an idea some researchers find unpalatable (see the Block, 1995, target article for many peer critiques of his ideas). Others take issue with the access–phenomenal distinction for how it accounts for partial awareness (Kouider et al., 2010; but see Block, 2005, for a differing view).

Another problem with this distinction is that many people feel P-consciousness is all we normally mean by consciousness; what Block calls access consciousness, while important for psychology, isn't really anything to do with consciousness. On the other hand, some researchers believe that everything can be explained by A-consciousness (Naccache, 2018).

Other Types of Consciousness

Other researchers make similar types of distinction as Block's between phenomenal and access consciousness. The Nobel Prize-winning American biologist Gerald Edelman distinguished primary consciousness, which is the awareness of the present arising from the binding together of information from different senses and the integration of the senses with recent memory, from secondary consciousness, which is awareness of our consciousness and the ability to access our thoughts, plans, and memory. Secondary consciousness enables us to manipulate our own thoughts and carry out abstract reasoning (Edelman, 2003).

What all these attempts at categorisation show is that we are aware that we need to make certain distinctions – between awareness and non-awareness, between awareness and self-awareness (awareness that we are aware), between feeling and emotion, and between living merely in the present, having a memory for the past, and a sense of the future. The lack of agreement in these divisions shows that we do not know how best to carve up the space of consciousness and awareness.

Many people are interested only in core consciousness and P-consciousness, and wonder why we need to be concerned with those peripheral psychological and neuroscience issues such as attention, memory, and vision. For these people (like Chalmers) we should tackle the hard problem head on, in as much as we can, because that's the only important question in consciousness research. On the other hand, for those like Dennett who believe that the hard problem will only be solved by attacking the easier ones, these 'peripheral' problems are the key to everything else.

Degrees of Consciousness

Consider whether you are conscious when you're dreaming. We can have vivid visual, auditory, and sometimes motor experiences. So, we're conscious, but in a way that's clearly different from 'normal' waking consciousness. We are though (usually) unable to reflect upon these experiences; they may be very bizarre, but they don't cause us to stop and think, 'hey, this is weird, this shouldn't be happening; am I dreaming?'. Our ability to influence our actions in our dreams is very limited. What about when we're asleep and not dreaming? Mostly, we say we're unconscious, but even then being unconscious isn't the same as not existing: if there's a loud noise in the room when you're sleeping, you'll most probably wake up.

What about a baby laughing away at some dangling toy? Infants don't yet have language; they don't yet have many memories; they can't move very far; their consciousness must be very different from ours, yet most people would say that they're conscious in some way.

What about a chimpanzee, or your companion animal, or a bird in your yard? They all seem to act as though they're conscious in some way. Most people think that other primates are conscious. Many animals clearly seem to show distress and signs of being in pain. If shown a series of photographs – a human, a picture of an early human, a chimpanzee, a dog, a bird, a fish, a shrimp, an ant, a bacterium, a tree, a rock – and asked which you think is conscious, what would you say? Answers can vary a great deal, but mostly draw the line of consciousness somewhere around fish and ant (Reggia et al., 2015). We have no way of knowing (at the moment) what the answer is, but clearly most people think that consciousness is not limited just to humans. And, as we shall see, people might be being tough on the fish (see Chapter 5).

Clearly the consciousness of babies and dogs is different from adult human consciousness, but does it make any sense to talk about *degrees* of consciousness? Am I more conscious than a dog or a baby? The noted polymath Douglas Hofstadter (2007) thinks so; in his book *I Am a Strange Loop* he presents a hierarchy of consciousness in which he talks about 'more' and 'less' consciousness. Are we more conscious when we're wide awake than

TYPES OF CONSCIOUSNESS

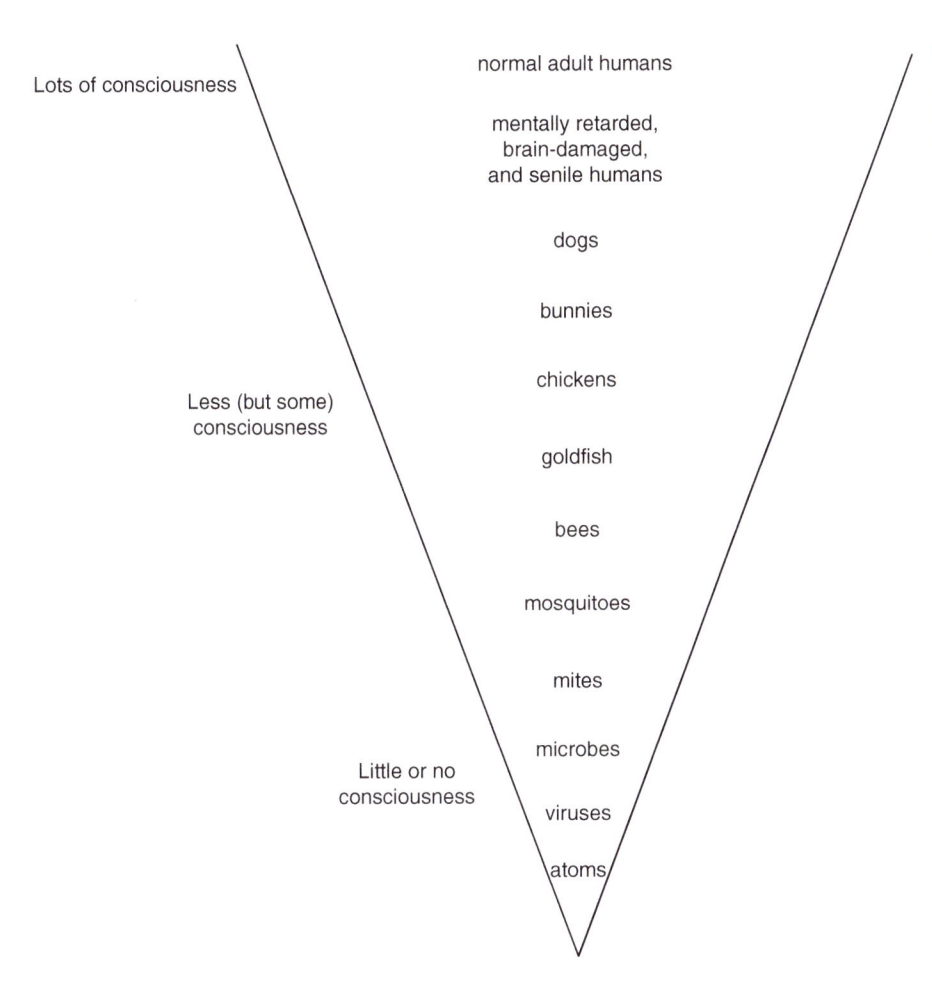

Figure 1.10 Hofstadter's 'consciousness cone'. (with his terminology) Most people think that consciousness is a graded phenomenon: some organisms have 'more' of it than others. Is this lay belief correct? Source: Hofstadter (2007).

Lots of consciousness — normal adult humans; mentally retarded, brain-damaged, and senile humans; dogs

Less (but some) consciousness — bunnies; chickens; goldfish; bees

Little or no consciousness — mosquitoes; mites; microbes; viruses; atoms

when we're dreaming? Hofstadter's proposed hierarchy of consciousness is illustrated by Figure 1.10. Note that there's guesswork involved: maybe some birds are more conscious than some dogs. Who knows? If we talk about 'more conscious', then we are presuming that consciousness has some kind of size dimension that can be measured, and it is most unclear what this dimension should be.

Research on anaesthesia, and on people in comas and with different types of brain damage, also suggests that it makes sense to talk about consciousness as a graded phenomenon (see Chapter 10 for more on this topic). And what about when you're waking up, particularly if you're confused as to when it is and where you are? We say, 'we're not quite awake yet', and that could be taken more literally than we might have intended.

Humans are not just aware of our surroundings, but are also self-aware in that we can be aware of our own awareness – we can reflect on our consciousness. This ability is mostly restricted to normal waking consciousness, because dreaming is usually characterised by a lack of self-awareness and an inability to stop and ask if we're awake or asleep. This apparently infinite regress of being aware of being aware of being aware is an example of what is called **recursion** – when something is defined or uses itself. Some researchers think that the ability to think recursively is limited to humans and is essential for the ability to learn human language (Corballis, 2014). If this idea is correct then it will be the case that only humans are capable of self-awareness.

Our consciousness can be changed from its normal waking state in various ways. Dreaming is an obvious example, but the most dramatic changes occur after taking mind-altering drugs. The effects of such drugs can be mild, depending on the drug and dose, or extremely dramatic, as with hallucinogenic drugs such as LSD. How do drugs alter the mind, and how do their chemical effects lead to changes in perception, cognition, and particularly our consciousness? How is the biology of drugs related to our phenomenology?

There are though many other ways in which consciousness can be altered. Meditation, mindfulness, and hypnosis are all techniques deliberately employed to change our normal waking state. What changes are involved, and how does the brain change in parallel? Profound mystical or religious experience also involves a change in consciousness. Sensory deprivation can be used both as a means to relax and as a method of torture.

Death is the final alteration of consciousness. Is that right – is death like a switch, which when pressed just leads to the permanent extinction of consciousness? How do we define death, and is it a sudden or gradual process? Some people who are close to death but then survive report near-death experiences, typically involving feeling peaceful, even joyful, and often travelling down a tunnel of light. What accounts for such unusual experiences? Are these people really going to heaven and coming back, as some of them think?

It's clear that our 'normal' waking state of consciousness is not the only type of consciousness. What accounts for the phenomenology of these states – what we feel and experience – and how are the changes in state related to changes in the nervous system?

The History of Consciousness Research

It is not surprising that consciousness has been of great interest to thinkers from the beginning of history given that we all experience the world, and that experience is the most prominent feature of our existence. The Greek philosophers speculated about it. Religions place human consciousness in the form of a non-material *soul* centre. In some religions the soul is immortal and persists after death in a number of ways, either existing independently from the body to await judgement (such as with Christianity) or being reincarnated in another body at some later stage (such as in Buddhism).

The scientific revolution began in the sixteenth and seventeenth centuries, originally with the work of astronomers such as Copernicus, Kepler, and Galileo. Most early science focused on the physical and then the biological sciences, with psychology and consciousness still topics in the realm of philosophy. The French philosopher René Descartes (1596–1650), for example, proposed that there were two fundamentally different types of substance, mind and matter, giving rise to an account of the mind–body problem called dualism (see Chapter 2).

In 1907, Duncan MacDougall, a physician from Haverhill, Massachusetts, hypothesised that souls have physical weight. He tried to measure the mass lost by a human when the soul left the body. He weighed six patients at the moment of death, comparing their weight just before and just after death. He concluded that the soul weighs 21 grams, a figure widely quoted in fantasy fiction and movies, a figure almost certainly generated by measuring error.

The science of psychology only really developed in the late nineteenth century with figures such as the philosopher Wilhelm Wundt (1832–1920) in Germany and the philosopher William James (1842–1910) in America (Schultz & Schultz, 2015). Early psychology focused, unsurprisingly, on what could be measured easily, such as perception and memory. The rise of behaviourists such as J.B. Watson and B.F. Skinner (see Figure 1.11) in the early part of the twentieth century in the United States saw consciousness research pushed to the margins as concepts that were considered vague, such as mind, were effectively abolished, to be replaced by observable behaviour.

Figure 1.11 The American behaviourist psychologist B.F. Skinner (1904–1990) with his invention, the Skinner Box. The Skinner Box was used for conditioning pigeons and rats. As the name implies, the behaviourists concentrated on animal behaviour, and there was no place for abstract constructs such as consciousness. Source: Joe Wrinn/The LIFE Images Collection/Getty Images.

Cognitive psychology became the dominant paradigm in psychology from the middle of the twentieth century with the work of the American linguist Noam Chomsky (b. 1928) and the development of the digital computer, which soon became a metaphor for how the mind works. Much of early cognitive psychology could be viewed as adopting essentially a dualist stance, with research on cognitive processes without much consideration of how the brain worked. There was very little research on consciousness at this time; it was considered a weird, almost taboo subject.

It was really only with the development of brain-imaging techniques at the end of the twentieth century that psychology became obsessed with the brain, and a new discipline, cognitive neuroscience, merging cognitive psychology and brain sciences, became the dominant paradigm. With the rise of brain imaging, consciousness came to the fore of psychology and is now one of the most exciting and researched topics. However, as we shall see, different researchers mean different things by consciousness.

The Problems of Consciousness

From the preceding discussion, it seems that the problem of consciousness is really several related problems. The following summary of 11 problems for consciousness researchers amplifies and extends our discussion above, introducing some key terms and ideas. The remainder of the book discusses our current state of knowledge about each of them.

1. The hard problem: Why does it feel like something to be me? Why do sensations appear to us as they are? What is this 'red sensation' we have when we see a red rose, and why can't we describe it to anyone else? Why do we have phenomenal experiences at all? When most people think about consciousness, they have the hard problem in mind.

2. The temporal problem: Why do I have the illusion of choosing to act when my brain has apparently made that decision for me some time ago? The brain activity associated with consciousness appears too late for consciousness to be involved in perceptual processing and motor action.
3. The free will problem: The free will problem How and why do I have the illusion of choice and control if all my actions are determined?
4. The why problem: We are only certain that humans are self-aware and conscious, although it is likely that some other animals are conscious to some degree. It is, however, likely that many animals get by perfectly well without self-awareness. So, why this additional complexity? Why are animals conscious but not beaches of sand or galaxies of stars even though they contain huge numbers of grains of sand and stars? Why is my laptop not conscious (I think)? Why is a horse more conscious than a fly (probably)?
5. The self problem: Who is this 'I' who thinks they have a choice? Who is experiencing my experiences?
6. The unconscious problem: Why are some things conscious, and others unconscious? What additional things does consciousness give us? Virtually all processing is unconscious, so why do a very few things become conscious – particularly if it is too late to affect anything?
7. The cognitive problem: Does something as complicated as an intact adult human have to be conscious? What is it about our cognitive machinery that gives rise to consciousness? Where does consciousness fit into cognitive processing?
8. The binding problem: How do different sensations get bound together so that we perceive one object with all the associated emotions? Why when I see a tiger do I see the orange and black stripes moving with each other and see the shape of the tiger distinct from the background? Why when I hear the tiger's roar does it seem to come from the tiger? And why does that object alone in the environment promote feelings of fear and awe? Binding is both within modality (so that we recognise one object with everything in the right place) and across modalities (the roar goes with the sight of the tiger).
9. The neural correlates problem: How does the brain give rise to consciousness? Are there particular brain structures we can identify that are active when we engage in certain sorts of processing? How does brain damage affect consciousness? Why does the cerebral cortex appear to give rise to consciousness, but not the cerebellum, even though it contains more neurons and is just as richly interconnected?
10. The altered state problem: What do we mean by a 'normal' state of consciousness? What causes an alteration in our state of consciousness? How do changes in neurotransmitters in the brain lead to changes in the phenomenology of consciousness? What is altered in an altered state of consciousness?
11. The science problem: Is it even going to be possible for science to provide a complete account of consciousness?

Broadly, problem (1) is a question about P-consciousness, and all the others about A-consciousness. In this chapter, we've examined what consciousness is, and hopefully you now also have some idea of why consciousness is more mysterious than it might first seem.

CHAPTER SUMMARY

There are many questions in this chapter, and if you're expecting definitive answers to all of them by the end of the book, you might be disappointed.

A final question: what should you take away from this book if you don't continue a career in this area? What will you remember five years later? You should remember that apparently simple questions are very complicated. You should remember the hard problem. And you should remember how the brain is related to behaviour and experience – and how it isn't.

Chapter Summary

- Consciousness is our sense of awareness and self-awareness.
- Consciousness is what it is like to feel like something.
- We study consciousness because it is the study of what it means to be us, and pushes the limits of our understanding of science.
- Consciousness is a unifying topic in psychology and philosophy.
- Consciousness is linked to the question of whether we possess free will.
- Consciousness involves the study of spirituality and higher states of consciousness.
- Consciousness can be altered through the use of drugs and psychological techniques, such as meditation.
- We can study consciousness by introspection, observing our own thoughts, but this method is limited and unreliable.
- We can study consciousness by carrying out experimental studies where we study the effects of manipulations on variables we think are associated with consciousness.
- We can study philosophical considerations in consciousness with thought experiments.
- We can attempt to construct robots and computer models of consciousness, and analyse the features necessary for a machine to perhaps acquire consciousness.
- There are many definitions of consciousness, but awareness and self-awareness are central concepts. It is difficult to provide a definition that does not involve some degree of circularity.
- Consciousness is private – no one else knows what we are thinking just now, and indeed we cannot describe to another person exactly what we are thinking.
- The 'hard problem', as posed by Chalmers, can be phrased in several different ways, but all can be reduced to trying to explain how subjective experience arises from the physical structure of the brain.
- We cannot really imagine what it is like to be another person or another type of animal.
- Consciousness is always about something.
- Different people appear to have different things in mind when they talk about consciousness, and sometimes even the same person uses the word differently at different times.

- Researchers have distinguished several types of consciousness, but they all reflect a distinction between core consciousness and psychological mechanisms that appear to rely on or make use of consciousness in some way, such as attention, memory, and perceptual processing.
- Core consciousness is the self-awareness that a person experiences in the moment.
- Block distinguished phenomenal consciousness, which concerns sensation and phenomenal experience, from access consciousness, which concerns self-report and the ability to manipulate ideas.
- Our state of consciousness changes when we sleep, or if we take certain types of 'mind-altering drugs', as well as in other ways.
- The degree of consciousness differs between organisms.
- We can identify 11 specific problems concerning consciousness: the hard problem, the temporal problem, the free will problem, the why problem, the self problem, the cognitive problem, the binding problem, the unconscious problem, the neural correlates problem, the altered state problem, and the science problem.

Review Questions

1. How would you define consciousness?
2. What is it that distinguishes consciousness from the rest of psychology so that we might wonder whether we could ever have a scientific account of it?
3. Evaluate the different methods used to study consciousness. Which is most likely to lead to significant progress over the next five years?
4. What are the hard and easy problems of consciousness, and how easy are the easy problems?
5. Does it make sense to talk about different organisms differing in the quality and quantity of their consciousness?
6. Is it possible to study consciousness scientifically if we are not sure what it is?
7. What do you hope to remember from this book in five years' time?
8. Imagine your university or institute has set up a department of consciousness studies. What would you write in a press release to the general public and local politicians? How would you justify them getting their money's worth?

Recommended Resources

General Introductions to Consciousness

Blackmore, S. (2017). *Consciousness: A Very Short Introduction* (2nd ed.). Oxford, UK: Oxford University Press.

Blackmore, S. (2005). *Conversations on Consciousness*. Oxford, UK: Oxford University Press.

Critchlow, H. (2018). *Consciousness*. London: Ladybird Books.

Parks, T. (2018). *Out of my Head: On the Trail of Consciousness*. London: Harvill Secker.

RECOMMENDED RESOURCES

Comprehensive Handbooks on Consciousness
Bayne, T., Cleeremans, A., and Wilken, P. (2009). *The Oxford Companion to Consciousness*. Oxford, UK: Oxford University Press.

Schneider, S., and Velman, M. (2017). *The Blackwell Companion to Consciousness*. Oxford, UK: Blackwell.

Zelazo, P.D., Moscovitch, M., and Thompson, E. (2007). *The Cambridge Handbook of Consciousness*. Cambridge, UK: Cambridge University Press.

Why Study Consciousness?
Keller, H. (2012 [1903]). *The Story of my Life*. Mineola, NY: Dover Press.

2 THE MIND–BODY PROBLEM

The mind–body problem is the philosophical problem of how the mind is related to the brain. How can subjective experience (consciousness) arise from a brain (a physical part of the body)? How does 1500g of pulsating pink goo give rise to our sensations, our feelings, our thoughts, and all our other mental activity? The philosophical consideration of the mind–body problem has a long and sophisticated history. The general area of philosophy concerned with the mind–body problem is called the *philosophy of mind*, although the philosophy of mind is concerned with more than just the mind–body problem (see Box 2.1).

Box 2.1 Philosophy: Terms and Disciplines

Philosophy is the study of ideas: it is the study of knowledge and where it comes from, of what exists and how we know that, of what is a good way to live, of what distinguishes good from evil, of what makes some things appear beautiful to us, and of logic, which is how we can deduce new knowledge from old. Like all disciplines it has several sub-disciplines, particularly for our purposes:

Epistemology is the study of knowledge. It asks, Where does knowledge come from? Do we acquire knowledge just from experience, or is some knowledge innate? What can we know for certain? Sceptics doubt that we can be certain of very much.

Ontology is concerned with the study of the nature of being and existence. What exists?

Metaphysics is an umbrella term combining epistemology and ontology for the study of fundamental questions about the basic cause and nature of things. 'Metaphysical' is sometimes used as a dismissive insult, but it shouldn't be – the questions of metaphysics are among the most fundamental humans can ask.

The *philosophy of mind* is about the issues raised in this chapter, and more besides: what is the mind, and how do we gain knowledge about ourselves and the world?

The *philosophy of science* is the branch of philosophy concerned with what scientists should do, and why. What is the nature of the scientific enterprise? What are its methods, its goals, and its foundations?

The ancient Greeks made no distinction between philosophy and natural science. It was only during the scientific revolution (starting with the astronomical work of Copernicus, Kepler, and Galileo in the early sixteenth century) that a distinction started to emerge between philosophy, religion, and science. Cambridge University didn't even start teaching a degree in natural science, including physics and chemistry, until 1851, although philosophy (and mathematics) were well established centuries before then.

This chapter considers two questions. First, what can we say about the nature of the relationship between consciousness and the brain – between mind and matter? We will look at the fundamental ideas of dualism and monism – how many types of 'stuff' are there? Is mind different from physical matter? And second, what is the nature of subjective experience? In terms of the problems of consciousness defined in Chapter 1, this chapter is mostly about problem number one: the hard problem. There are several other problems to solve, and perhaps their solution might illuminate the topics covered in this chapter.

We begin by introducing the philosophical tool known as a thought experiment. We then consider what for many is the most intuitive explanation of the main relation between mind and brain, that they are different kinds of stuff, and then discuss how most contemporary researchers prefer the alternative, that there is only one kind of stuff: matter. We then have to explain how sensations and private experience can be explained in a world comprised only of matter. We consider the knowledge argument, which is often cited as a key argument against physicalism, the idea that everything can be explained in terms of physical matter and the laws of physics. We consider the implications of another thought experiment, the inverted spectrum. We consider another problem for a purely material view of the world, the subjective experience of pain. We then examine another famous thought experiment, that of the philosophical zombie, a hypothetical being that looks like us and acts like us but has no conscious experience.

We then consider some formal models relating brain to mind, of which currently the most popular is functionalism. We then throw our hands up in despair when considering mysterianism, the possibility that we're just not biologically or cognitively equipped to understand our own consciousness.

It is worth noting that a textbook on physics or chemistry summarises knowledge and shows the way to carrying out further research. Such books are built on certainty. This chapter provides no assurances, just disagreement and argument. You might conclude that if, after centuries of thought, the leading philosophers who have spent their lives thinking about the subject can't agree on the basics, what hope is there? But do not despair; that is what makes the topic so fascinating.

Thought Experiments

We have noted that philosophers often conduct a particular kind of experiment: the thought experiment, where they ask 'what if' and carry out the experiment in their imagination. These experiments are not designed to provide definitive or proven answers. Rather, merely trying to answer these questions reveals our intuitions about the subject matter. It's important when we participate in a thought experiment to stop and think for a while about what our answer would be.

Thought experiments aren't confined to the philosophy of mind: the famous 'Schrödinger's cat' idea is a thought experiment in physics in which under one interpretation of quantum mechanics a cat might be simultaneously dead or alive. The American philosopher Daniel Dennett (2014) promotes a version of thought experiments he calls **intuition pumps**, which are simple thought experiments that focus our minds on the important aspects of a problem, simplifying our thinking by avoiding irrelevant detail. They may be structured to mislead our reasoning in a revealing way, and give a series of answers on the path to what he considers to be the correct answer. Their point is to illustrate or clarify our argument, not to reveal an answer, for, as we shall see many times, our intuitions are often wrong.

> **TRY THIS:** Swampman
>
> One of the most famous thought experiments discussed by Dennett was first formulated by the philosopher David Donaldson (1987). You go hiking in a swamp (don't ask why) and get struck and killed by lightning. At the same time, another lightning bolt hits a different part of the swamp and spontaneously rearranges a huge load of molecules so that, by coincidence, they take on exactly the same form as your body at the time of your little accident. Let's not worry too much about the physics and biology; this after all is a thought experiment. This being has been called 'Swampman'. As Swampman, looking just like you, wanders around the world, he will behave exactly like you. He will carry on reading the same book, and say hi to all your friends just as you would. Is Swampman (or Swampwoman) really just you? What is your intuition about this argument? What does it tell us about consciousness?

The Mind and the Brain

'Mind', like consciousness, is one of those words that we use all the time and that we think we know what it is, but can be difficult to define. The mind is everything about our mental life, both inside and outside of consciousness: the cognitive processes giving us perception, thinking, and memory.

The Mind–Brain Problem

The central issue is how the mind and the brain are related: how does the brain, a thing, permit us to have private mental experiences? Experiences are not things, so how do they arise from a thing? Or more precisely, things, because the brain has a complex structure and is made up out of 100 billion neurons. This problem, the **mind–body problem**, is the central one of this chapter. You can talk about the brain or parts of brains or neurons having size and being somewhere in space, but not fears, ideas, or wishes. A wish doesn't have physical size.

The problem is summarised in four simple propositions by Westphal (2016).

1. The body is a physical thing.
2. The mind is a nonphysical thing.
3. The mind and body interact.
4. Physical and nonphysical things cannot interact.

Each individual proposition seems correct, but put together they are clearly inconsistent! So at least one of them must be wrong, but which one?

DUALISM AND MONISM

The mind–body problem includes the problem of consciousness, but is more general, concerning the relation between all mental events and the physical.

The Mereological Fallacy

It is easy to fall into the trap of talking about the brain as though it's the same thing as the mind. It isn't, and making the mistake of doing so is called the **mereological fallacy**. Examples of the fallacy are to say the brain knows something, the brain thinks, the brain interprets, the brain makes decisions, and so on. What we mean in all these cases is that the mind knows something, and so on (Bennett & Hacker, 2003).

There is a type of metaphor called a metonym where one word is used for another very closely associated with it, such as calling the judiciary or the judges 'the bench', or calling business executives 'suits'. One might say that we could use 'brain' for 'mind' in this metaphorical sense. The trouble is speaking metaphorically can lead us into confusion; and after a while, we might come to think that it is the brain that is thinking and feeling, and that really there is no problem to solve. Science thrives on the exact usage of language, and sloppy usage is its enemy.

The mereological fallacy is very easy to fall into. Sometimes my brain doesn't know what it's thinking.

Qualia

Philosophers have given a name to the elements that make up a subjective experience: **qualia**. ('Qualia' is plural, with singular 'quale'.) Examples of qualia are our experience of the orange of a sunset, the red of a rose, the blue of the sky, the scent of a rose, the pain of accidentally jabbing a finger with a needle, the taste of a nice cup of coffee, the sound of a guitar, and the feel of your shoes around your feet. Open your eyes (and ears and mouth) and qualia are everywhere.

Qualia make up our experience – our experience of a rose is the sum of its qualia. But as we have observed before, our experience is *private*. You cannot describe the colour red to someone who has never experienced it before. And how do you know that you see red in the same way I do?

Another way of phrasing the hard problem is how can the nervous system generate qualia. What objective physical processes are responsible for the purely mental and completely subjective qualia?

Dualism and Monism

Mind and matter seem to be so fundamentally different that it's reasonable to wonder if they are completely different substances so that matter is part of the physical world but mind is not. This idea is called **dualism**, and has a long and respectable history. The

> **TRY THIS:** Describing Red
>
> Choose something with prominent qualia, such as a red rose (see Figure 2.1). How would you describe it to someone else? How would you describe colour to someone without sight?

Figure 2.1 A red rose. The redness and fragrance of the rose flower are examples of qualia, as is the pain you experience when you prick your finger on one of its thorns. Source: Rosemary Calvert/Stone/Getty Images.

> **TRY THIS: How Many Qualia?**
>
> Stop and consider your environment. How many qualia can you become aware of? Can you be aware of more than one at a time?

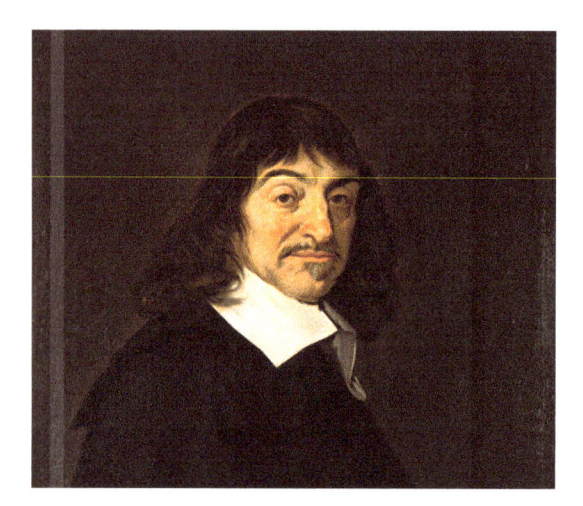

Figure 2.2 The French philosopher René Descartes (1596–1650). Descartes gave his name to Cartesian dualism and Cartesian coordinates in geometry. Source: Imagno/Hulton Fine Art Collection/Getty Images.

alternative is that there is only the physical world, an idea called **monism**, so mind must somehow arise from matter, or matter from mind, or are different aspects of something else.

René Descartes and Substance Dualism

Dualism has a long tradition, dating back to ancient Eastern philosophies, the ancient Greek philosopher Plato, and religious traditions. The idea was most clearly articulated by the French philosopher René Descartes in 1641 (see Figure 2.2). Descartes thought that the body, like all other matter, is made out of a material substance he called *res extensa* (it extends into the world), while the mind is made out of an immaterial substance he called *res cogitans*. *Res extensa* is the physical world we can reach out and touch; it is what's made out of quarks and atoms. *Res cogitans*, the mental stuff, is what we experience and what constitutes our consciousness. The type of dualism, in which mind and matter are different types of substance, is called **substance dualism** (often called **Cartesian dualism**).

Substance dualism is appealing to many non-scientists because it fits in well with what we experience: mind and matter do *seem* so very different. And for those who believe in the soul, there being mental stuff is a solution consistent with the idea of a permanent soul that can survive death. Some argue that substance dualism could also account for anomalistic phenomena such as extrasensory perception and telepathy, although the scientific evidence for these phenomena is controversial. Substance dualism does provide an answer of sorts to the hard problem: physical matter doesn't give rise to private experience at all because private experience takes place within the realm of mental matter.

There are two major problems with substance dualism. First, the mental material is outside the realm of physics: we have no idea what constitutes it, and it cannot be examined by physical or scientific methods. We are left with no way of making any further progress in the subject: mind must remain an eternal mystery. The second issue is even more problematic: how do mind and matter interact? Why is it that when you accidentally hurt yourself, such as stubbing your toe, the object hitting your toe gives rise to a sensation of pain in your awareness? How is it that, when your mental stuff decides to raise a finger, the finger then goes up?

Descartes recognised this problem and argued that the soul interacts with the brain and world through the **pineal gland**, a small gland positioned near the centre of the head (see

Figure 2.3). Descartes seems to have chosen the pineal gland for reasons that were known to be incorrect even at the time: that it was in the middle of the ventricles, the cavities in the grey matter of the brain (whereas it actually hangs from the underside of the brain) and that it is surrounded by arteries (whereas it was known from the time of the Greek philosopher and surgeon Galen, b. 129 CE, that it is surrounded by veins). Descartes thought that the movement of the pineal gland could cause movement in the ventricles, blood flow, and eventually muscles. We know this biology is totally implausible, and there remains no mechanism by which mental matter could interact with physical matter.

Other Types of Dualism

Attempts other than Descartes' to account for the interaction between mind and matter sound no less plausible. One idea, called *parallelism*, is that the physical and mental worlds have run in perfect unison from the start of time – like two enormous clocks, set up by God and kept in perfect synchrony. Another idea, called *occasionalism*, is that a rather busy God makes sure that every time something happens in the physical world, the corresponding thought or feeling happens in everyone's mental world.

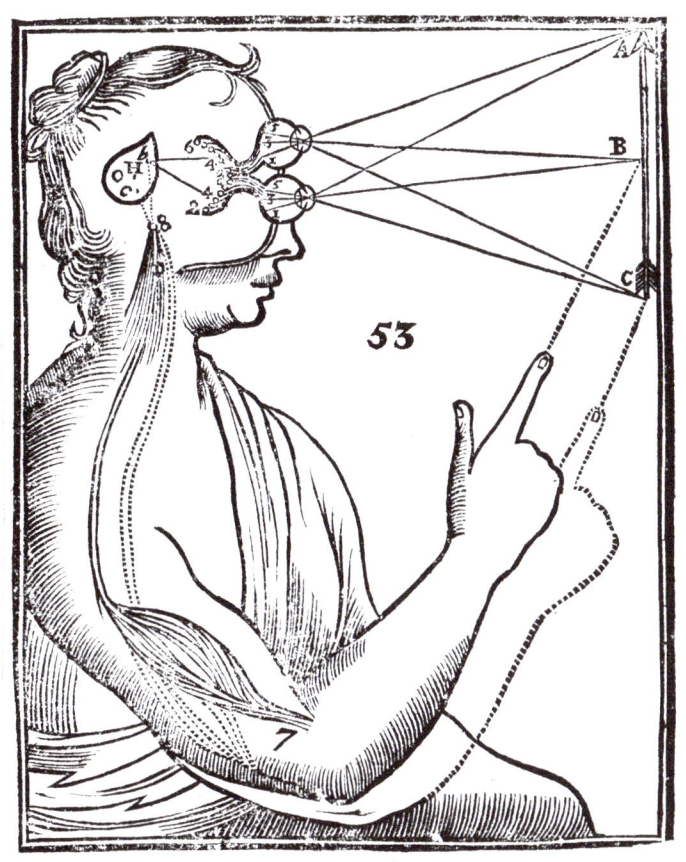

Figure 2.3 The location of the pineal gland, which Descartes believed was the location of the interaction between mind and matter. Descartes also wrote about perception and action. The figure also shows details of the eyes. Source: Print Collector/Hulton Archive/Getty Images.

For scientists seeking a simple, physical explanation without resort to divine intervention, the failure of substance dualism, in spite of any popular and intuitive appeal, to explain how the mind and material interact is a fatal flaw.

A few brave scientists have nevertheless attempted to produce a rigorous account of dualism. Perhaps the best known is the Nobel Prize-winning Australian physiologist and philosopher Sir John Eccles (1903–1997). Eccles was motivated by a strong Christian faith, and a belief that mind and matter must be different substances. He proposed that the **cortex** consists of fundamental units he called dendrons; each dendron is made up of a vertical cylindrical bundle of neurons, each cylinder being about 60 micrometres (60 millionths of a metre) in diameter. Groups of dendrons (about 40 million of them) link to a corresponding mental unit he called a *psychon* (Beck & Eccles, 1992; Eccles, 1994). Eccles proposed that psychons, through quantum mechanical-like processes, affect the release of neurotransmitters. The interactions are small and undetectable, so as not to violate physical conservation laws that say overall matter and energy are not lost or created in a system. But because these interactions are undetectable, they are forever destined to be outside the realms of science.

The problem with all substance dualism accounts is that our understanding of the physical laws of the universe, although not complete, is extremely good, and those laws do not seem to allow room for anything else. We already understand all the forces acting on protons, atoms, and molecules. The behaviour of neurons is also completely explicable in terms of the laws of physics. Saying that there is scope for some other influence on these elements other than the known physical laws would involve a revolution in physics for which there is no other basis.

Other kinds of dualism, in addition to substance dualism, have been proposed. The most popular is property dualism, which says that, although there is only one kind of substance in the world – physical substance – there are two kinds of properties: physical and mental properties. An example of property dualism is **emergentism**, the idea that, when matter is organised in certain complex ways, new kinds of property, such as mental properties can emerge. Emergentism is a popular recent idea, and we'll be looking at it again later. Property dualists say that, although there is only one kind of substance, mental phenomena cannot be reduced to physical phenomena. Examples are colour and heat: although a colour may be defined by the frequency of the light, the colour we perceive cannot be reduced to frequency; and although heat and warmth are defined by the kinetic molecular energy of the material, the heat we feel is something else.

Monism

The alternative to dualism is **monism** – the idea that there is only one sort of substance in the world. One monist theory, known as **idealism**, is that the world is fundamentally mental, an idea most associated with the Irish philosopher Bishop Berkeley (1685–1753). Berkeley argued that material objects exist only in the mind of the perceiver – and even if no person perceives these objects, God is still doing so. Although dismissed for some time as fanciful, variants of idealism have enjoyed something of a renaissance in recent times, such as *conscious realism*. In conscious realism, consciousness creates brain activity, and then creates properties and objects of the physical world (Hoffman, 2019).

Most scientists, psychologists, and philosophers now prefer a type of substance monism, where the only substance that exists is physical matter governed by the laws of physics, an approach known as **materialism**. (Materialism is also known as **physicalism**. Strictly speaking, materialism says that there is only physical matter, whereas physicalism says that there are only physical matter and the laws of physics. Many people now use the words interchangeably, and they are used interchangeably in this text.) Materialism/physicalism is appealing because we need to consider only one type of matter, so there is no issue about how anything interacts with anything else other than through the laws of physics, and all of consciousness research remains within the realms of natural science. Most contemporary consciousness researchers favour some form of materialism. We are left though with the hard problem of how private experience arises from physical matter.

Another view is that there is only one kind of substance, neither mind nor matter, and mind and matter are different ways of viewing or organising that substance. This view is called **neutral monism**, and variants of it have been held by some philosophers for centuries. Westphal (2016) argues that neutral monism is a complete solution to the mind–body problem. A variant of neutral monism is **anomalous monism** (Davidson, 1970), in which there is only physical matter, and mental events do not correspond to physical events in a strictly physical way. The main objection to versions of neutral monism is that it is difficult to characterise the nature of this neutral substance. Nevertheless, these ideas are currently enjoying something of a revival.

> **Box 2.2   The History of Physics**
>
> The *laws of physics* describe how matter and forces behave everywhere in the universe across all time. These laws constitute a fundamental limitation on our behaviour and on the universe. As Scotty says in *Star Trek*, 'I cannae change the laws of physics' (Daniels, 1966).
>
> Although the principles of physics themselves are unchanging across time, our understanding of them has changed considerably throughout history. We can describe three main phases.
>
> In the pre-scientific phase, as captured by the reasoning of the ancient Greeks, primarily Aristotle, the laws were based on observation and intuition. However, our intuitions are often wrong, and without testing of the hypotheses, incorrect assumptions are made and incorrect conclusions drawn. The Greeks thought, for example, that it was obvious that, if something is moving at a constant velocity, then force is being continuously applied to it, and when that force is no longer being applied, it will stop. If you roll a ball along the ground, it eventually comes to a halt. Similarly, they thought that, if you dropped a feather and a cannon ball from the top of a tower, the cannon ball, being heavier, would land first. The pre-scientific phase endured for thousands of years.
>
> The scientific phase began in the sixteenth century with the realisation by Copernicus, Kepler, and Galileo that the Earth was not the centre of the universe, but that the Earth moves around the Sun. Some earlier philosophers had postulated a heliocentric view of the world, but these scientists were the first to use observational data to construct a model of the solar system and to formulate the ideas mathematically and refute the prevalent geocentric view. The heliocentric model accounts for the observational data much better than the geocentric model.
>
> The task of explaining why these mathematical equations were as they were fell to Sir Isaac Newton (1642–1727). He postulated that objects act under forces according to his

> **Box 2.2 (cont.)**
>
> three famous laws: every object stays at rest or travels at constant velocity in a straight line unless a force acts upon it; force equals mass times acceleration; and for every action there is an equal and opposite reaction. Newtonian (or classical) mechanics provides a superb account of the behaviour of objects at rest and in motion. In everyday situations, the account of what happens is perfect, limited only by the accuracy of our measurements. Classical mechanics does such a good job of accounting for the world that it was said that there is nothing new to discover in physics now; physical science is now just a matter of making measurements to an increasing number of decimal places.
>
> Then, Einstein's miraculous papers in 1905 made it clear that, superb though classical mechanics is in everyday situations, it breaks down in explaining phenomena occurring at very high speeds and large distances, where relativity comes into play, and at very small, sub-atomic distances, where quantum mechanical effects come into play. Quantum mechanics says that energy is not continuous, but comes in very small packets, that there are limitations on how accurately we can measure things, and that some effects are best described probabilistically.
>
> The laws of physics are important because they appear to provide a complete account of how the universe works. But are they sufficient to explain consciousness?

The Knowledge Argument

Materialist monism has the virtue of simplicity, and doesn't suffer from any problem about different sorts of stuff interacting, but seems not to provide an answer to the hard problem: how can physical matter give rise to subjectivity, qualia, and private experience? The position that it does is called physicalism.

Perhaps we're overestimating the difficulty of the hard problem. We need to explore the problems more thoroughly, and a few thought experiments will clarify what is at stake.

The 'Mary' Colour Thought Experiment

The following thought experiment was devised by the philosopher Frank Jackson, and is called the **knowledge argument** (because Mary, the protagonist of the story, has complete knowledge of the world but limited experience of it). Let's imagine a woman we call Mary (Jackson, 1986). Mary has been brought up by an evil philosopher, let's call him Frank. Before opening her eyes at birth, Mary was given a special pair of contact lenses that turns the world monochrome, so that she only ever sees the world in black, white, and shades of grey. Figure 2.4 shows how Mary sees a red rose.

Figure 2.4 A monochrome rose. What Mary saw while growing up. Source: Rosemary Calvert/Stone/Getty Images.

THE KNOWLEDGE ARGUMENT

Mary devotes her life to studying everything to do with colour vision – the physics of colour, the biology of colour vision, the neuroscience of colour vision – and by the time she is 35 she knows everything there is to know about how humans see colour. It might well be that to understand colour vision properly she will have to end up learning everything there is to know about the world, but Mary is extremely clever and has a phenomenal memory, and plenty of time. Then on her 35th birthday she is given a red rose and her contact lenses are taken out. What will Mary say? Will she learn anything new about colour, or not? Will she say, 'Oh, that's just how I thought red would look' or will she say, 'Wow! So that's red!' What do you think she would say? Many people think that Mary's experience will be a total surprise to her, and she will say, 'Wow!' For these people, qualia, the private sensations of experiencing red and other colours, are not part of the physical world. All of Mary's complete understanding of the physical laws of the universe could not prepare her for the sensation of actually seeing the colour red. If that is our belief, we must reject physicalism and the idea that all knowledge can be derived from physical properties of the universe, as Jackson suggests. This thought experiment therefore leads to what is called the knowledge argument.

For and Against Physicalism

For many people, the idea that actually experiencing colour adds to our knowledge of colour sounds so immediately correct that they are surprised to learn that some leading researchers disagree with it. Perhaps the most extreme position in favour of physicalism is taken by Dennett (1991), who argues that Mary will not be at all surprised by the experience of the redness of the rose. He believes that the nature of sensation is indeed derivable from complete knowledge of the world. It is easy to say Mary would be surprised without really appreciating the enormousness of complete knowledge – something we can't really comprehend. Dennett's approach is certainly one way of answering the hard question – by saying there isn't really a hard question after all.

> **TRY THIS:** Mary the Monochrome Scientist
>
> With all thought experiments, it is important that you really do stop and think. There is no 'right' answer, just your intuition. What do you think Mary will think, and can you give reasons for your belief? Look at the image of the grey and red roses to focus your thoughts.

Another approach is to say that Mary does learn something new, but that this in itself does not reject physicalism. One way to argue this point is to say that Mary doesn't learn any new facts, but she learns about old facts in new ways. We can illustrate this idea with the following two sentences about a popular Marvel Comics character and his secret identity:

'Iron Man can zoom up into the atmosphere.'
'Tony Stark can zoom up into the atmosphere.'

Both are saying the same thing if you know that Tony Stark and Iron Man refer to the same entity. If you didn't know before that Iron Man is Tony Stark, when you do find that out, you're simply learning to look at the world in a different way. Needless to say, this argument is controversial, because you could argue that you are learning a new fact, that

Iron Man and Tony Stark are the same thing, so before your knowledge of the world was incomplete.

Paul Churchland (2004) proposed a much-discussed variant of this argument. Churchland makes use of the philosopher Bertrand Russell's (1910) distinction between knowledge by description and knowledge by acquaintance. If we read everything there is to know about giraffes, including an accurate verbal description of what one looks like, we have knowledge by description. But if we visit a zoo to see one, only then do we have knowledge by acquaintance. In all these cases, Churchland would say, we haven't exactly learned new knowledge, but it's clear that actually seeing a giraffe, or swimming in water, is different from just reading about these activities.

Finally, some people deny that it is possible to learn everything about the world by teaching alone; they feel that we may be able to acquire some physical knowledge only by experience. For them, the premise that Mary knows everything there is to know about the world is incorrect (Alter, 1998). So the contention that 'Mary knows everything' about colour is simply false because experience is part of knowledge and Mary has been deprived of that knowledge.

In spite of the attempts at rebuttal, for many people the knowledge argument is one of the strongest arguments against materialism.

We should note that sometimes people who were blind from birth (because of congenital cataracts) or deaf from birth acquire through treatment the ability to see or hear later in life. Their response to gaining the new sense is understandably extreme, ranging from joy to confusion. These experiences tell us nothing about Mary's plight, however, because no one would say these people had a complete physical account of what they were missing beforehand.

Figure 2.5 A rainbow. Richard of York gave battle in vain – but suppose you see the sensation of the colours reversed compared to me? Source: Danita Delimont/Gallo Images/Getty Images Plus.

The Inverted Colour Spectrum

The essence of the idea of **private knowledge** is that we can never really be certain what another person is experiencing. How do you know that when you see the colour red you experience the same thing as someone else who says they too are seeing something 'red'? Suppose instead that, when you have the sensation of seeing red, the other person has the same sensation as you have when you see 'green'? Or that, when I look at a rainbow, I see the colours in the same way as you do (see Figure 2.5)? This idea is called the **inverted spectrum**, and it dates back to the English philosopher John Locke (1632–1704). The idea is that the perception of colours could be systematically changed between people, and no one would be able to tell. As there is no way of describing the sensation of colours, we are left once again with the conclusion that qualia are real and ineffable (they cannot be expressed in words).

It doesn't seem plausible that we can tell how we perceive colours by looking at our brain states: what would we look for in the visual system that tells us how we're experiencing the sensation of a particular colour? There is nothing to look for in the brain because the brain is a physical system and our experience of colours a purely private experience. So we seem to be forced to accept again that, because we can conceive of colours being inverted and there is no physical way of telling if that has happened, there is something nonphysical going on and we must accept the existence of qualia. Knowledge of qualia is something over and above our knowledge of the physical world. One person who doesn't like the idea at all, and thinks the inverted spectrum argument is 'absurd' and 'ridiculously' incoherent, is the American cognitive scientist Douglas Hofstadter (Hofstadter, 2007). He gives examples of several other inversions and asks, 'Do they really make sense?' The most interesting is the inverted sonic spectrum; we have a simple continuum of high- to low-frequency sounds, where very low notes can shake the room, and very high notes, in Wagner's operas, for example, pierce us to the core. Is it really possible that I feel the high notes in the way that you feel the low notes, and vice versa? For Hofstadter the problem is in believing that we can have pure experiences that are detached from the brain and anything else in the world; he can't conceive of them. Philosophers pick on the electromagnetic spectrum and talk about inverted colours, because inverted sounds seem so grounded in the world. But it's just this question of whether sensations are attached to anything physical that's at stake.

You may think that we can say something about colours: red is a bit like orange, for example, and is closer to yellow than blue, while green seems to be closer to blue than orange. Red seems warm, while green seems cooler. In our example, the colour spectrum has been systematically inverted, however, so the references to other colours change too. One way of thinking about this inversion is to imagine that a rainbow is inverted, so that all the in-between colours shift too. Or we could swap opposite points on a colour wheel. And of course the feeling of warmth one person gets from red and orange, another person would get from green and blue, and vice versa.

We know a tremendous amount about the neuroscience of vision; is it really plausible that none of this knowledge is of any use in being able to tell us what we feel when we see red? Here, for a change, science does come to our help, at least a little. Colours can be described in terms of a colour space. There are different ways of covering the range of colours, but one easy way of doing so is to use hue (the underlying frequency, or the position on the rainbow, which is the main determinant of the colour), saturation (how pure the colour is, or how much it is mixed with white light), and lightness (how bright it is, or how far away it is from black). It's possible to specify any colour in a space with these three dimensions. Moreover, human colour vision is not equally sensitive to all colours. For example, it turns out that there are more perceptually distinguishable colours between red and blue than there are between green and yellow. So if we were to invert red and green we would be able to detect the inversion behaviourally by asking the person to make judgements about small differences in colours. And whereas dark blue is a shade of blue, a dark yellow is what we call brown. It's possible that there are enough asymmetries in colour space to make it impossible to find an inversion that is behaviourally undetectable (Clark, 1985; Hardin, 1993). A glance at the colour systems developed by commercial enterprises like Pantone and NCS Group gives an idea of the range of colours we're capable of seeing (see Figure 2.6).

Figure 2.6 Colour spaces included in a version of a colour circle. There are a number of ways of describing colour, but one way is a space contained by hue (frequency), saturation (how pure the colour is), and lightness (how bright it is). Source: Berezka_Klo/Getty Images Plus.

Could we take the argument further, and, if we were sufficiently knowledgeable, describe any colour uniquely to another person in terms of its position relative to its neighbours by reference to asymmetries? So perhaps spectrum inversion isn't a good argument for qualia after all. And if inversion doesn't work for colour, why should it work for any other spectrum of experience? For example, how do I know that what a lemon tastes like to me is what it tastes like to you? Perhaps we could eventually place its taste by reference to other tastes and their asymmetries relative to their neighbours. Maybe the inverted spectrum argument isn't a very good argument for the ineffable, private nature of qualia after all. On the other hand, there does still seem to be something left over about the redness of red and the greenness of green that isn't captured by their relation to other colours, as the knowledge argument shows.

The Problem of Pain

Think back to any painful experience. What did the pain feel like, and how would you describe the pain to others? Pain appears to share a quality with other qualia like colours: it is eventually private and ineffable – you can't explain it in words. In essence, you cannot really feel my pain – my pain is private.

The Physical Aspect of Pain

Pain has both a physical and a mental aspect in that we have the subjective experience of pain, which seems to correspond to particular activity in the nervous system. We know a great deal about the neuroscience of pain. Pain originating from an external stimulus is called nociceptive pain, and it occurs when a stimulus (heat, cold, sharpness, crushing force, or chemical) approaches harmful intensity. When the stimulus exceeds a certain threshold, nerve endings called **nociceptors** fire and the signal is passed to the spinal cord and then the brain. There are two main types of nociceptors: A-fibres, which are protected by a sheath of a fatty substance called **myelin**, transmit an electrical signal very quickly, and C-fibres, which are not protected by a myelin sheath, and as a consequence transmit a signal relatively slowly.

If you jab your finger or accidentally touch something hot, the first thing that happens is that you move your hand away very quickly. This quick motion occurs because of a reflex and because of the way the A-fibre nociceptors are connected to motor neurons at the spinal cord. The sensation of pain comes a bit later – maybe quite a bit later – and then persists. At the same time the C-fibres project (transmit information) to the spinal cord, where that information is then relayed to the brainstem and thalamus, before being processed by the rest of the brain. The slow conductive speed of the C-fibres explains the delay between a painful event and the feeling of pain, and why we often feel pain in two phases, a sudden sharp pain followed by a dull ache akin to burning. We can then describe our response to a painful stimulus in a biological causal chain (greatly simplified in this telling) that is very well understood. The trouble is that this chain doesn't appear to need the feeling of pain.

The processes involved in pain are much more complex than this overview suggests. The peripheral nervous system has 'gates' that can limit the transmission of pain signal (Melzack & Wall, 1965). It is also now well known that the body produces **opiate**-like chemicals known as *endorphins* that inhibit the transmission of pain signals and can even produce feelings of euphoria (see Figure 2.7). While important for understanding the physiology of pain, these further details are sideshows to the main issue of what pain is and why it hurts.

The Mental Aspect of Pain

Pain is a particularly interesting example of sensation because the sensation of pain is clearly associated with a very distinct physical state, so that all and only people with C-fibres firing will say they're in pain. Is pain anything more than C-fibres firing? Of course, because we do seem to have this additional sensation of pain. The issue then is the relationship of the feeling of pain to this very clearly defined physical state.

Now more questions arise. Could we have evolved with the aversive physical nature of pain but without the sensation of it hurting? Or could it even be that, if someone jabbed you with a pin, you would draw your hand away and say 'Ouch'

Figure 2.7 Cocoa in chocolate releases endorphins and produces mild euphoria. You'd need to eat a lot of dark chocolate to notice the effects though. Exercise is a more reliable way to generate euphoria. Endorphins are involved in pain control. Source: Irrin0215/Getty Images Plus.

but inside you would feel nothing? Suppose that you take a particularly effective painkiller and your physical state is otherwise the same, but you feel no pain. Would you still say you're in pain then? And given that we have a fairly detailed physiological account of pain, and can use brain imaging to see which parts of the brain become activated by painful stimuli, would we then want to go further and say that the feeling of pain is located in that specific area of the brain? Moreover, when we say, 'I feel a pain in my arm after you jabbed me,' do we really feel the pain there? Surely the pain arises after processing in the brain?

At this point, you might say, 'Look, this is all very well, and quite entertaining, but it's a bit theoretical and a bit silly really; I know what the world is like for me and, of course, it's surely the same for everyone else. If you jab me with a pin, I will feel pain in just the same way as you will if I jab you.' This argument is called the *argument by analogy to the existence of other minds*. There are two rejoinders to your scepticism. The first is that you may think you know what others feel, but you could never be certain. The second is that, as the Austrian philosopher Ludwig Wittgenstein (1889–1951) pointed out, why should there be anything special about you (Wittgenstein, 1953)? He called this kind of generalisation irresponsible: just because I am a certain way, why should I be so special that everyone else is like me, too?

In a rare condition called *congenital analgesia*, affected individuals are incapable of feeling pain. These individuals are very prone to injury and infection because they do not receive the warning signals that the rest of us get from pain. Furthermore, some drugs such as morphine cause people to report that they are still experiencing extreme pain, but also that it is not unpleasant – a state we call a **dissociation**. Hence, it seems that either we are wrong to think that people cannot be mistaken about being in pain (that is, wrong about what we call the infallibility of our sensations), or that pain need not necessarily be aversive (that is, wrong about the intrinsic awfulness). Dennett suggests that our concept of pain is so defective that it doesn't refer to anything real – which is, he argues, why we could never make a computer feel pain (Dennett, 1978b).

> **TRY THIS: Making a Robot Avoid Harm**
>
> You have built an extremely sophisticated human-like robot. Naturally you want it to stay safe and have some sophisticated means of self-preservation; who having spent years of their lives and millions of dollars wants their creation to sit up and then immediately walk straight into a fire. What would you need to do to ensure the robot avoids harm? Is knowledge of the world, that it should not walk off tall buildings or into fire, enough? But then what about surprising stimuli, such as hot pans and unexpected sharp objects? Is the ability to withdraw from the dangerous stimulus enough, or would you need to programme it to feel pain as well? And, if so, how could you do so?

Pain in Babies

Until recently there has been considerable controversy about whether or not babies feel pain. It might seems obvious to us now that they do, but until the mid-1980s it was, unbelievably, routine to operate on babies without giving them an anaesthetic or analgesic (de

Lima et al., 1996). To be fair, one of the issues was that anaesthetics are more dangerous for babies, so it was thought important not to give them when it was not considered necessary, and it was not considered necessary because it was believed that the nervous system of infants is not fully developed and not capable of feeling pain. Now safer anaesthetic protocols mean that infants can be anaesthetised with greater confidence about their safety. In addition, our understanding about the neurology of infants and foetuses is much more advanced.

Research now shows that older but not younger foetuses appear to feel pain. The brain systems supporting pain, particularly the cortex and relevant connections to it, are not fully developed before the 27th week (Lee et al., 2005). It does though seem extraordinary that anyone could look at a baby in distress screaming away and not believe that they were in pain.

P-zombies

Zombies are everywhere these days: they're all the rage in movies and shoot 'em up games, poor things. For our purposes, a zombie is a person who is behaviourally indistinguishable from us, but who does not have consciousness. A zombie does not experience sensations, such as those of seeing the colour red or of feeling pain, and while it is like something to be like me (and presumably you), the same isn't true of zombies. It isn't like anything to be a zombie. By 'behaviourally indistinguishable' we mean there is no behavioural test that would tell us whether the zombie is conscious or not. If we jabbed it with a needle, it would cry out in pain (and maybe take a swipe at us); it would claim that it thought it was seeing red just like anyone else; and if we asked it whether it was conscious, it would insist that of course it was, and possibly express badly hurt feelings that we could doubt such a thing. Nothing would expose its lack of consciousness. But inside, the zombie wouldn't actually feel any pain – it would just exhibit pain behaviour. As we're talking about zombies in a specific sense here, we can call them 'philosophical zombies', or '**p-zombies**' for short.

Box 2.3 Zombies

In movies, zombies are portrayed as mindless, flesh-eating, rotten undead walking slowly around with arms outstretched – they might move and pursue goals, of sorts, but they have no consciousness. In folklore, they are often placed in the Caribbean and associated with voodoo, mostly in Haiti as lifeless corpses animated by the magician to perform labour for the master (see Figure 2.8). One of the earliest studies of the zombie myth was the fieldwork of the American anthropologist Zora Neale Hurston in Haiti in the 1920s and '30s. Wade Davis's (1985) book *The Serpent and the Rainbow* controversially proposed that the myth arose from anecdotes of people being deliberately poisoned with datura, a hallucinogenic deliriant drug, and crucially *tetrodotoxin*, a potent **neurotoxin** extracted from the puffer fish. The puffer fish is considered a great delicacy in some parts of the world, particularly Japan, where it is served as fugu; it must be carefully prepared by specially trained chefs, and accidental deaths occasionally occur. Tetrodotoxin blocks the action of sodium ions in the nervous system so

> **Box 2.3** (cont.)
>
> muscles cannot contract and messages cannot be sent across the nervous system. The idea was that witch doctors could maintain people in a zombie-like state by giving people sub-lethal doses of 'zombie powder' containing tetrodotoxin; however, it is uncertain whether the effects described are physiologically possible. A less controversial explanation of the zombie myth is that zombies were simply exhausted workers in sugar plantations at night.
>
> Figure 2.8 Voodoo in Port au Prince, Haiti: the figure shows the graveyard from which it is reported that bodies are taken and turned into zombies. There are several theories about the origin of the zombie myth, but most likely they were just exhausted planation workers working at night. Source: Roger Hutchings/Corbis Historical/Getty Images.

Is Consciousness Essential?

Do you think a p-zombie is possible? Stop a moment to think about your answer.

If you think a p-zombie could in principle exist, then because p-zombies behave exactly like conscious entities, we have no way of distinguishing conscious from nonconscious things. Consciousness is therefore something else on top that doesn't do anything: it is a nonessential extra. David Chalmers (1996) is the most significant philosopher to have argued that p-zombies are possible; he uses the argument to conclude that physicalism must be false. Unfortunately, the conclusion also seems to follow that consciousness doesn't play any causal role in our physical states, a position called **epiphenomenalism**.

If you think a p-zombie cannot exist, then you are committed to the notion that consciousness serves some essential function: someone can't behave like a conscious person unless that someone is truly conscious. In that case you have to be prepared to answer questions such as, why is consciousness essential and what is its function? Several philosophers have argued that p-zombies cannot exist, including Owen Flanagan (1992) and Patricia Churchland (1996).

Being Conceivable

The possible existence of p-zombies is one of the most controversial thought experiments in the philosophy of mind. Neither of the positions just described – that consciousness is a nonessential extra or that it serves some function – is immediately appealing. Another way out of the problem of p-zombies is to say that it's meaningless to talk about them in the first place. It is helpful here to distinguish between something being conceivable and something being possible. Something is *conceivable* in that we can imagine it in the first place. Only if something is conceivable can we move on to considering whether it is actually possible. The idea that we can speak meaningfully about p-zombies depends on the idea that they are in fact conceivable. Some though argue that p-zombies are not in fact conceivable: they're inconceivable, if you like.

Dennett (1995) is the most notable proponent of the inconceivability argument; he argues that we are simply mistaken if we think we can conceive of a p-zombie. Dennett mounts several arguments against the conceivability of p-zombies, essentially saying that consciousness isn't a single thing that can be simply dispensed with, but a huge complex of mental states, behaviours, and dispositions, and people who think we can do without it underestimate the difficulty of the task of doing so. You cannot, for example, remove the hurt from pain and have a thing behave in the same way; it just isn't possible, says Dennett. So if p-zombies are not conceivable, it makes no sense to talk about them existing: the problem disappears. Needless to say, however, there is as little agreement on whether they are conceivable as on whether they are possible.

The arguments about the viability or not of p-zombies shows the essential difference between real and thought experiments: with real experiments, we just look at the data. With thought experiments, we can have different intuitions, and each of us thinks our intuition is right.

Materialism

Suppose we reject dualism. Somehow, we then have to make a monist materialist position work: the mind has to be explained in purely physical terms if it is completely dependent on the brain and nothing else. How then do we deal with qualia and private, subjective experience? That is, how do we solve the hard problem? The preceding thought experiments show how difficult it is going to be to accommodate subjective experience into a physicalist framework. Materialism is the idea that matter is all there is. There are two different approaches – **reductive materialism** and **eliminative materialism**.

Reductive Materialism

Reductive materialism or **reductionism** is the idea that we can explain one level of theorisation with lower-level theories. So we can explain the behaviour of atoms in terms of subatomic particles and quantum mechanics; we can explain chemistry in terms of physics; and we can explain biology in terms of chemistry and physics. We can eventually reduce behaviour to the operation of the brain, and the brain to biology and hence to physics. So reductive materialism says that all sensory experience can be explained in terms of, or reduced to, physical activity in the brain. At the moment this line of argument is very much 'in principle' for complex biological systems because the practicality of reducing phenomena at one level to a lower one is overwhelming.

Perhaps the simplest approach to physicalism is to deny that there is much of a problem at all, and assert that mental states are identical to brain states. That is, sensations and brain processes refer to the same thing. This approach is often called **mind–brain identity** theory. There are different versions of identity theory, but the most popular and most discussed is called *type identity theory*. According to type identity theory, mental events can be grouped into types, such as being in pain, and these types of mental events can be correlated with types of brain states, such as C-fibres firing. According to identity theory, the mental state of being in pain is identical to the physical state of C-fibres firing.

One of the most famous statements of type identity theory was put forward by the Australian philosopher J.J.C. Smart (1959). Smart was particularly impressed by the parsimony of identity theory. In science, the *parsimony* principle holds that the simplest explanation for a phenomenon is preferred. So if there is no very good reason to do so, why should we introduce anything else in addition to brain states to explain qualia? The strongest objection to identity theory is that the same mental state might be realised by different physical states. For example, the physiology of the pain system is very different in humans and birds (Putnam, 1988). If we one day encounter aliens, it is most unlikely that they will have evolved C-fibres like ours, yet they will almost certainly be capable of feeling pain. Who is to say that one day a silicon-based robot might not be capable of feeling pain (see Figure 2.9)? Pain does appear to be more than simply C-fibres firing.

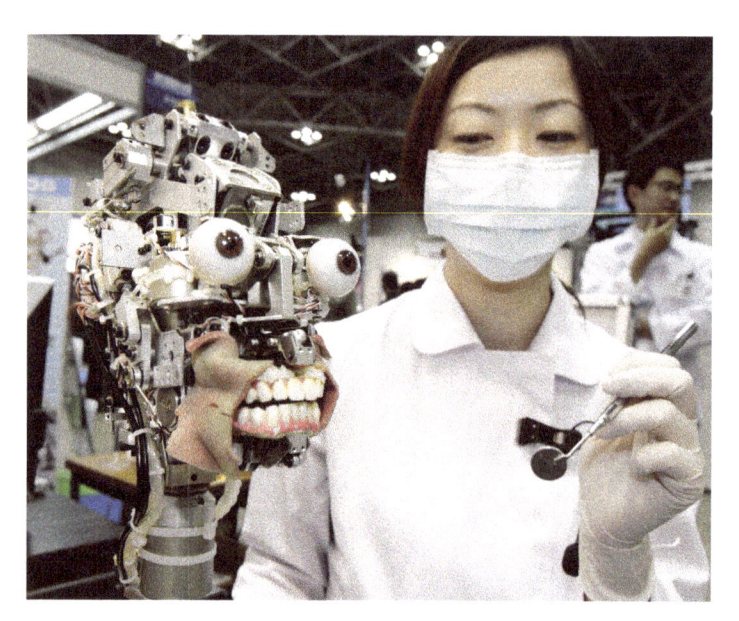

Figure 2.9 Japan's Nippon Dental University Hospital staff member Yuko Uchida shows the mechanism of a humanoid robot dental therapy simulator 'Simroid' for dentists and students at the International Robot Exhibition in Tokyo, 2007. It has sensors in its mouth and shouts 'Ouch' when the dentist gives the wrong treatment. The robot was developed by Japanese robot venture Kokoro and Nippon Dental University, and is now used for clinical training. Source: Yoshikazu Tsuno/Staff/AFP/Getty Images.

Eliminative Materialism

The second approach, pioneered by the philosophers Daniel Dennett (1988), Paul Churchland (1981, 1988), Patricia Churchland (1986), and Georges Rey (1997), is called eliminative materialism. It makes the bold claim that our everyday understanding of mental states is wrong. This approach is particularly well exemplified in Dennett's paper 'Quining qualia'. Now, no one could doubt that qualia exist; after all, the fact that I have a sensation of red when I look at something red is unquestionable – to me. It is giving qualia any special status in science that Dennett objects to; he instead argues that we should not reject materialism because it in some way fails to account for qualia (or 'reduce' them to lower-level phenomena). Instead, Dennett argues, materialism is perfectly consistent with the existence of qualia; there just isn't a problem. He gets rid of the problem of qualia by 'quining' them, coining the verb 'to quine', defined as 'to deny resolutely the existence or importance of something real or significant', in honour of the great American philosopher W.V.O. Quine

(1908–2000), who argued against the philosophical reality of another seemingly important distinction (the analytic–synthetic distinction, the details of which need not concern us).

Dennett makes this argument using an intuition pump. Here is an example: imagine two chaps who enjoy a particular cup of coffee. After a few years, they agree that the coffee isn't as good as it used to be. One says the flavour of the coffee has remained constant, but his response to that flavour has changed, so he no longer enjoys it; the other says that the flavour has changed, so he no longer enjoys it. One says the quale has remained the same but his response to it has changed; the other says the quale has changed. Can we distinguish the two views? They can't both be right, says Dennett, so which one of them is right? The problem is insoluble: one of the two people must be wrong about his own quale, but doesn't know so.

Dennett's approach has perhaps not surprisingly generated much debate, and many would take issue with some of the steps in his argument (see, for example, Flanagan, 1994). However, this approach does show that at least some people believe that qualia are not an obstacle to a completely materialist science. For Dennett, the philosophers Paul and Patricia Churchland, and others, the whole idea of qualia is so confusing and riddled with inconsistencies as to be unusable. Their position is that, since we know that our introspections are unreliable, this everyday 'folk' psychology has no place in modern science, better to do without it. The philosopher Galen Strawson (2018) calls these people 'deniers'.

Whether or not side-stepping the problem gets rid of it though is debatable, and not everyone is convinced. Although eliminative materialism appears counterintuitive to many, philosophers have found it difficult to reject eliminative materialism to everyone's satisfaction. Folk psychology clearly has many problems; the ideas we use in everyday life do not always stand up to scientific scrutiny.

Functionalism

Perhaps we're worrying too much about the detailed relationship between brain states and mental states: maybe there are many ways in which they can be related. After all, there are many ways of constructing a mouse trap: we have the classic spring that is sprung when a mouse tries to remove the piece of cheese, or boxes whose lids flip shut when the mouse goes in, or tubes that they can get into through the top but then can't get out of again. All that matters is what the mousetrap does: if it kills or captures the mouse, it's a mousetrap. Similarly, it could be that all human minds are similar: all that matters is what a particular mental state does, not what it looks like. And if that's true, the details of how mental states are realised physically are irrelevant. It's the function of mental states that matters. **Functionalism** is the idea that what makes a mental state what it is depends only on its function, and the role it plays in the system; it doesn't depend on its internal constitution or how it is realised physically.

Silicon Neurons and Silicon Brains

We are all perfectly happy with hip replacements and artificial valves being fitted to us, where our quality of life or even our lives are changed by artificial material. Some of us have qualms though about extending these changes to the brain. Let's start with a simple thought experiment. Imagine we could manufacture a little silicon neuron. It works in exactly the same way as a 'real' neuron does; you can swap it for an existing brain cell, and it does just the same thing, receiving inputs from neighbouring neurons, and firing and sending outputs to adjacent neurons just as the 'real' one would. Now, would you be troubled if we substituted the silicon neuron for one of your biological ones? I certainly wouldn't; it might even be more robust. After all, all that matters is the function of the neuron, the way it works, not the details of how it's made.

Perhaps you can see where this argument is going: why not substitute two silicon neurons for two biological neurons in your brain, each connected to all the other neurons it should be connected to? If we can work out the wiring and figure out exactly which neurons are connected to which, why not give us the transplant of a silicon hippocampus or silicon hypothalamus? Indeed, why not swap in an appropriately connected silicon brain? Most of us would be happy with one or two silicon neurons, but we baulk at larger structures, and few are happy with the idea of having a silicon brain swapped in. The point at which we start to say no varies.

With functionalism, the point is that it's only function that matters. If the silicon brain is behaving exactly like a biological brain, it doesn't matter what the brain is made of, as long as it is functioning in the same way. We have made enormous strides in the last few years in our understanding of how the brain is wired, thanks in part to the *Human Connectome Project* (Van Essen et al., 2013); in fact, we have known the complete neural wiring of one living animal, the roundworm *Caenorhabditis elegans*, for some time (White et al., 1986). So if we had a good model of the neuron, the dream of a silicon brain, if only for a worm, isn't as implausible as it might first seem.

> **TRY THIS:** How Much of your Brain Would you Give up?
>
> Consider the silicon brain and then answer these questions. Would you object to having one of your neurons replaced by a silicon one? Two? A thousand? Your hippocampus? The whole brain? Why does one neuron not matter to you but a million do? Would you still be you? Would you be conscious?

Box 2.4 Neurons

The neuron or nerve cell (and sometimes spelled neurone) is a special type of cell that is the basic unit of the nervous system, which comprises peripheral nerves, the spinal cord, and the brain. Like all cells, neurons have a body that is essentially a bag of chemicals, a nucleus containing genetic material, and a semi-porous membrane that you can think of as the bag itself. Unlike other cells, neurons also have two types of projection on their surface. **Axons** are long thin 'arms' that connect with other neurons. *Dendrites* are smaller flatter projections (see Figure 2.10). Axons transmit signals along the cell length while dendrites receive them from other cells. Signals are transmitted along axons as electrical waves called

Box 2.4 (cont.)

potentials, with ions (charged particles) of the elements sodium, potassium, and calcium being particularly important in the transmission of the signal.

Neurons do not touch other neurons directly but are separated by small gaps between the axon and dendrite called **synapses**. Synapses contain special chemicals called **neurotransmitters**, examples of which are serotonin, dopamine, glutamate, gamma-aminobutyric acid (GABA), and noradrenaline. Neurons communicate through neurotransmitters and electrical signals, although ultimately all communication results in a change in the electrical state of the cell.

Axons are protected and insulated by a fatty substance called *myelin*. Because myelin is an insulating material, a thick myelin sheath increases the speed at which an electrical impulse is propagated along the axon relative to a thinner myelin sheath. Disorders of myelin formation and distribution lead to widespread central nervous system disorders, the best known of which is multiple sclerosis.

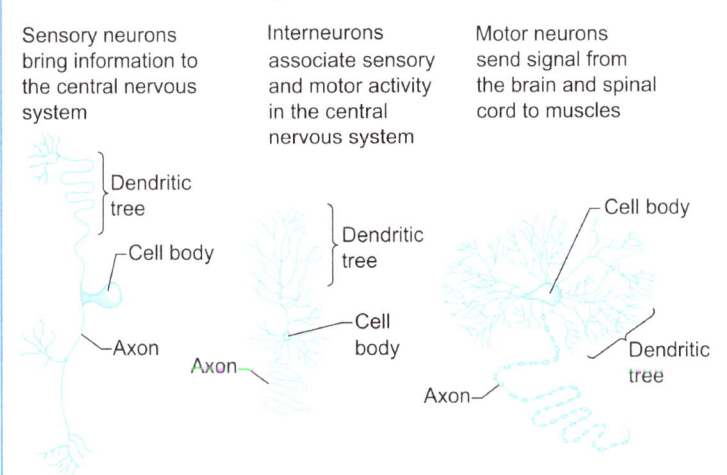

Figure 2.10 A neuron. A nerve cell – the brain has about 100 billion of them, and each neuron might be connected to a 1000 others. Does consciousness really arise from just a lot of these connected together?

The 'China Brain' Thought Experiment

At least it seems sensible to ask whether a silicon brain might be conscious, but a thought experiment called the Chinese nation, or China brain (Block, 1978), makes the question seem daft for many people – until they think about it. China is chosen because the population is so large – at least 1.4 billion. The typical human brain has about 100 billion neurons, so it's just a couple of orders of magnitude more. We let each person stand in for a neuron, and let them communicate with other people with cell phones (or radios in earlier version), just as neurons communicate with one another by firing. In the brain, every time a neuron 'fires', it sends an excitatory impulse to other neurons. In the same way, the person in the China brain corresponding to such a neuron would phone up all the people to which he or she is connected, and they would phone up their connections in turn, and so on. We could have people corresponding to neurons receiving input from sensory neurons, and have others corresponding to motor neurons if we wished, and we could even arrange a system to translate signals from the world to sensory neurons and from motor neurons to the world. In effect, China would constitute a brain.

Would the whole system – the China brain – be conscious? The property of consciousness doesn't reside in any individual neuron, but the brain as a whole, as a system; what's the difference between the human brain and an appropriately connected China brain?

Some philosophers, Dennett (1991), for example, conclude that the China brain is a form of mental state. Many others are less comfortable with that conclusion. In particular, Block (1978) noted that, although the whole system would receive an input, there would be nothing corresponding to qualia. This conclusion is however questionable: no individual neuron feels pain, but the mind, made out of many neurons, does. Why should a China brain be any different?

Following these examples, we can propose that mental states (such as beliefs, desires, being in pain, and so on) are constituted solely by their functional role – what they do and what they're connected to do. Mental states are related to other mental states, sensory inputs, and behavioural outputs only by virtue of the effects they have on each other (what is known as their causal role). This proposal is known as functionalism. (A word of warning: there are several types of functionalism in psychology and sociology.)

Because all that matters is the causal role, the physical form of what implements mental states does not matter, an idea known as multiple realisability. So a suitable silicon chip is as good as a neuron. A China brain is as good as a brain as long as it is connected up appropriately. The details of the implementation do not matter (an idea called *organisational invariance*), so there is nothing special about the 'wetware' of the brain.

In my experience, most students don't like the idea of a nation itself, such as China in this thought experiment, being conscious, but when pressed they find it difficult to explain why. We shouldn't think of the China brain working one neuron at a time; everyone is active simultaneously. If the worry is about speed, we could have people on speed dial or even have them send an immediate pulse to all the connected people. We can with a bit of imagination get rid of any systematic difference between the human and China brain. In that case, surely, like the functionalist, we must conclude that the Chinese nation as a whole would be conscious.

Box 2.5 What Is Computation?

In practice, **computation** is what a *computer* does. Given an input, the system follows a set of rules to produce an output. To give a very simple example,

$$2 + 3 = 5$$

Given two numbers as the input, the arithmetic operation of addition gives an output. The development of the theory of computation by the British mathematician Alan Turing (1912–1954) and others was essential for the development of the computer. A computational system is a formal system in that it is a well-described system based on mathematics. The rules a formal system follows are called the *syntax* of the system. Human language has a

> **Box 2.5** (cont.)
>
> complex system of syntactic rules for manipulating the words of a language; the conveyance of meaning in language is the domain of *semantics*.
>
> Cognitive psychology, which developed in the 1960s and '70s, took the computer as a metaphor for how behaviour arises, viewing psychological processes as *information processing* – that is, computation. The mind is given an input (for example, a pattern of light on a screen or on a retina, or a spoken word) and by a series of transformations (computations) produces an output (for example, the name of the object or access to the meaning of the spoken word). In this light, the task of cognitive psychology is to specify the nature of the intermediate transformations or computations, as well as the representational format of the inputs and outputs that the mind uses. Thinking is often said to be symbol manipulation – *symbols* stand for something, such as a representation of a dog standing for a dog. When we think we are manipulating these symbols.
>
> The extent to which this approach provides an adequate account of cognition and psychology has proved controversial. The essence of Searle's Chinese room argument (see the section *Arguments Against Functionalism* in this chapter) is that specifying the syntactic rules of computation alone is inadequate for understanding behaviour, and more consideration needs to be given to the semantics, and the way in which meaning in the mind is related to objects, attributes, and events in the world.

Arguments Against Functionalism

How does functionalism explain qualia? Some people think that there is something special about the biological substrate (although it is not at all clear what it might be that is special), and that a biochemical foundation is essential for qualia. The possibilities are: (1) that humans and other complex biological entities experience normal qualia (we will assume that our qualia are similar); (2) that some systems, no matter how complex, will not have qualia, an idea known as absent qualia; or (3) that a robot based on silicon chips might be conscious, but its consciousness would be very different from us (an idea known as different or sometimes inverted qualia). As two things that are functionally identical can yet have different mental states, functionalism cannot explain these individual differences in qualia.

As Chalmers (1995) says, there is currently something of a stand-off: proponents of the ideas that there is something special about biochemical systems and that a China brain's being conscious is preposterous just have a very different view of the world from those who think that all that matters is the way things are organised, and not how they are implemented. Both stick steadfastly to their positions thinking they must be right. And in the end, who can know for sure? Chalmers (1995), however, proposes an additional interesting thought experiment.

Consider your biochemical self and a silicon *isomorph* (that is, identical duplicate) of yourself in which all your neurons have been replaced by silicon chips that function in exactly the same way as your neurons and have exactly the same pattern of connectivity. Let's call this copy MyRobot. A functionalist would say that MyRobot would be conscious and have exactly the same experiences (and qualia) as you would in any situation. Some anti-functionalists would say that MyRobot has *absent qualia*. Now let's consider intermediate positions by revisiting a previous thought experiment. We'll take you and replace just one neuron (in the left prefrontal cortex, say) with one of these super-duper silicon chips. As we have observed, few people would say that this operation would make any difference to anything. Then we gradually replace more neurons.

At some point, the anti-functionalist is committed to the point of view that something changes. One possibility is that the qualia suddenly disappear, but if they do, at what point? When just one biological neuron is left? That doesn't sound right. Halfway? We don't know exactly when, but at some point with some configuration we have suddenly disappearing qualia. The other possibility is that the qualia gradually fade away the more we change, but does that idea even make sense? When you burn your finger, you feel a most unpleasant pain; will MyRobot just feel a slight ache? Will MyRobot see a faded pink when you look at our trusty red rose? As we replace more neurons, the qualia fade away altogether. Does it even make sense to talk of partial qualia? We can apply a similar thought experiment if we think that MyRobot has qualia, but they are different – inverted, say. As we change the neurons into chips, at what point do the qualia change? Do they suddenly flip over? Chalmers (1995) calls this idea *dancing qualia*.

Another substantial argument against functionalism is the *Chinese room* (Searle, 1980). Functionalism is linked to the computational theory of mind, the idea that mental processing is a matter of computation in the same way as a computer works through a program. Crucially, which computer you run the program on doesn't matter: 2 + 2 always equals 4 regardless of whether you're using a Mac or PC. Searle calls the idea that an appropriately programmed computer has mental states 'strong AI', and the Chinese room is one of the strongest arguments against strong AI. Imagine we have a woman sitting in a room; her knowledge of foreign languages is zero. In particular, she knows nothing whatsoever about Chinese. In her room though, she has a set of rules that enable her to produce an appropriate written Chinese output for any Chinese input. Someone slips a piece of paper under one door; she goes to her book of symbols and list of rules for manipulating those symbols, and by using just them, she creates an output in Chinese, which she then slips under another door. To the outside world, it is as though we have given the 'room' something in Chinese, and it has understood it and produced an answer in Chinese.

But would we say that the woman inside understands Chinese? Of course not. We have already said she doesn't understand a word. She has just 'blindly' been following a list of rules. Searle argues strong AI is the same: the computers just blindly follow rules, but have no understanding of what they are doing.

The argument provoked many critical responses, and responses to those responses, and as usual in consciousness research, there is no clear winner (see the original Searle article for many peer responses). Most of the original protagonists just moved on to new problems. The most common response is called the systems response; the woman might not understand Chinese, but the entire room, the whole system, does. When you hear a word in English, no single neuron can be said to understand English, but your whole brain clearly does. It's the system level that's important. Searle's response is that the system has to know

MYSTERIANISM

about the meaning of the symbols (the semantics): how the symbols refer to things, actions, and properties in the world. The set of rules in the Chinese room is just a formal syntactic system without semantics, meaning that the room manipulates the symbols without any idea of to what they correspond. To be conscious, he argues, you need meaning, and only biological systems have that. Although there are other responses to the Chinese room, the systems reply is the most popular (see the chapter on the Chinese room in Dennett, 2014, for a recent account).

> **TRY THIS:** What Is it Like to Be a Worm?
>
> The roundworm *Caenorhabditis elegans* is a free-living nematode that lives in the soil in temperate regions (see Figure 2.11). At the time of writing, it is the only organism to have had its complete **connectome** (neural wiring) mapped. We have also sequenced its DNA. It has around only 1000 neurons in its nervous system. How might you go about simulating a leech in a manner analogous to the China and human brains? Think of what a worm can do. Suppose you are in a class of a hundred people linked together by cell phones, passing messages around, simulating electrical impulses in the leech nervous system. Would any of you learn anything about what it is like to be a worm?

Mysterianism

Most people with at least a little scientific education are uncomfortable with substance dualism, so they usually conclude that they must be a kind of physicalist monist (that is, a materialist) – although they might not use those words! The trouble is that materialism is prone to all the sorts of problems that we've just looked at, particularly there doesn't seem much scope for the presence of feeling and experience something. Are there any other alternatives?

One possibility is that, unlike the rest of the scientific domain, consciousness is beyond human understanding. It might seem strange that something we all experience at first hand is ultimately incomprehensible, but it's not impossible. This type of approach is called the new mysterianism, or simply just **mysterianism**. The proponents of mysterianism are called the *mysterians*. The name comes directly from a 1960s American rock band (the band's full name was '? And the Mysterians'; yes, that's a question mark), which in turn took its name from a 1957 Japanese

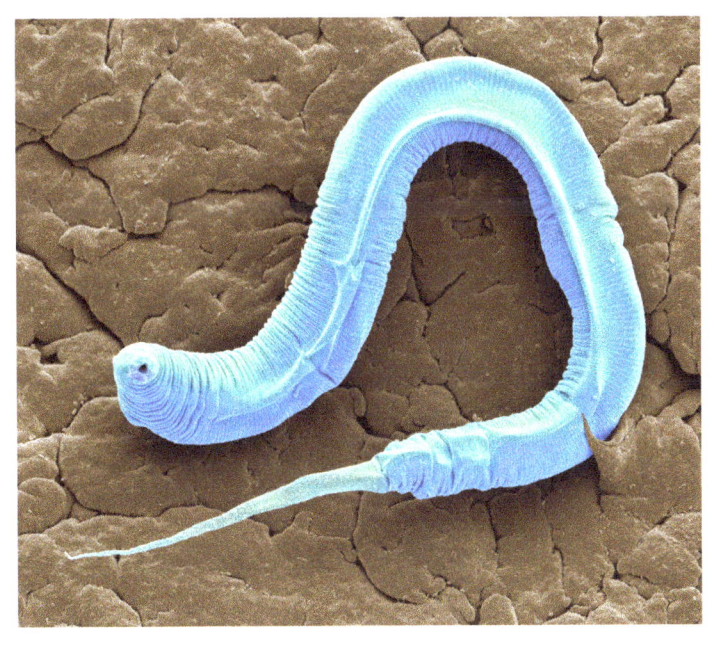

Figure 2.11 The roundworm *Caenorhabditis elegans*. We have sequenced its DNA and computed its connectome, but do we really know what it's like to be a roundworm? Is it like anything to be *Caenorhabditis elegans*? Source: Steve Gschmeissner/Science Photo Library/Getty Images.

Figure 2.12 Publicity material from the 1957 Japanese science-fiction movie *The Mysterians*, directed by Ishirō Honda (1957). The film is about an invasion by a race of aliens who are of course just after Earth women. Modern mysterians are much more reasonable, simply arguing that consciousness is too complicated for humans to understand. The Mysteries is the one on the right. Source: LMPC/LMPC/Getty Images.

science-fiction film, *The Mysterians* (Honda, 1957; see Figure 2.12). The original mysterians were dualists who thought that consciousness was a different type of substance that was therefore not subject to the laws of physics. Here is an analogy to help you understand new mysterianism. William James (1896) observed that dogs are 'in our life but not of it': all the time they are experiencing events that have meaning and purpose beyond their understanding. Imagine my poodle Beau looking at a book; of course, he could not be said to be reading it because it's not just that he can't read, but that he has no, and can never have any, comprehension of what reading is. The study of consciousness might be for us like reading is for Beau.

The most adamant proponent of new mysterianism is the British philosopher Colin McGinn. He argues that nature may not have equipped the human brain with the ability to solve the problems of consciousness; that is, nature has not provided us with the apparatus to understand ourselves (McGinn, 1989, 2000). When it is up against consciousness, science hits a brick wall, what McGinn calls *cognitive closure*. McGinn doesn't say that science simply can't explain consciousness at the moment, but that it necessarily never will: our minds are closed to it because the subject is beyond our limits of understanding. We're just not biologically capable of understanding our own minds.

Daniel Dennett again has been a trenchant critic of mysterianism (e.g. Dennett, 1991b). His objections are centred around the opinion that it is unduly pessimistic to conclude that consciousness is beyond our understanding. Indeed, the history of science is full of examples of problems that seemed intractable, or in fact even beyond our imaginings before their discovery, such as quantum mechanics. Dennett also argues that the form of the argument of new mysterianism is unscientific: people assert that we may never understand consciousness, but that assertion is not in itself any proof or guarantee that we won't.

Nevertheless the list of adherents to mysterianism is impressive. Leading researchers who have at least speculated that the explanatory gap between the generation of private experience and what we know of the physics and biology of the brain is so large that it may never be breached include Noam Chomsky, Steven Pinker, Martin Gardner, and Sam Harris.

Another possible resolution of the mind–body problem is that we have given up on dualism too soon. As we have seen, substance dualism isn't the only type of dualism, although it is the best known. Property dualism states that there is only one type of substance, but physical and mental properties are two different sorts of category, neither of which can be reduced to the other. Non-reductive materialism holds that, while mental properties can be mapped onto biological processes (pain in humans is associated with C-fibres firing), they cannot be reduced to them (that's not all there is). What though is the extra? While substance dualism is relatively straightforward to understand, many people find property dualism much more difficult to follow.

Chapter Summary

- The philosophy of mind studies the interaction of mind and brain.
- How the brain might give rise to private experience is known as the mind–body problem.
- Instead of traditional experiments, philosophy particularly makes use of thought experiments.
- Thought experiments help clarify problems and reveal our assumptions and beliefs about them.
- Qualia (single quale) is the name given to raw sensations, the basic components of experience, such as the redness of a rose.
- As formulated by Descartes, dualism says that mind and matter are different types of substance, and that mind does not obey the laws of physics.
- The main problem with dualism is in specifying how mind and matter interact.
- In contrast to dualism, monism says that there is only one kind of substance: matter, mind, or another 'neutral' substance.
- The problem facing physical monism lies in specifying how matter can give rise to private experience and qualia.
- Physicalism and materialism are terms now used interchangeably, and say that everything is ultimately physical.
- The knowledge argument asks us what we would need to know to be able to predict what a quale is like by considering Mary the neuroscientist.
- The knowledge argument is often taken as an argument against physicalism.
- Many are sceptical that Mary could know what a red rose was like before she experienced one.
- There are though several rebuttals of the knowledge argument.
- The most extreme rebuttal of the knowledge argument is Dennett's, which says that Mary would not be at all surprised by redness because it would be deducible from complete knowledge of the physical world.
- The idea of the 'inverted spectrum' asks whether it's possible for one person to sense red where another person senses green, seeing the same thing, yet experiencing different qualia.
- Pain is another example of a quale, and there has been much discussion over its function.
- Could we function just as well by withdrawing from some stimuli without those stimuli causing a feeling of pain?

- Could there be a hypothetical p-zombie (or philosophical zombie, or robot) that is behaviourally indistinguishable from a human that would also necessarily be conscious.
- If you think a p-zombie could exist, then we have no way of distinguishing conscious from nonconscious things, and consciousness is therefore something else on top that doesn't do anything: it is a nonessential extra. It is said to be epiphenomenal.
- A thing is conceivable if, in principle, we can grasp the concept, and the concept does not involve any logical contradictions.
- There has been considerable argument as to whether the philosophical zombie is conceivable.
- Materialism is the doctrine that all human experience arises from one sort of substance, and that substance is the matter studied in physics.
- Type physicalism, reductive materialism, and mind–brain identity theory are different names for the idea that a mental experience corresponds to a physical brain state, and nothing more.
- Eliminative materialism says that our everyday folk psychology beliefs about the world are misleading, very poorly defined, or even plain wrong, and hence we as scientists should not be too concerned about the subjective sensation of pain.
- Functionalism is the idea that mental states are defined by what they do rather than how they are made.
- According to functionalism, we could construct a mind from materials other than neurons – for example, silicon or even a human population – as long as the 'neurons' were connected in the right way.
- Many dispute that how a mind is constructed is irrelevant.
- A famous counter-argument is Searle's Chinese room thought experiment.
- According to the mysterians, consciousness is beyond our understanding because the mind is not equipped with the machinery to comprehend itself.

Review Questions

1. What is meant by 'substance' in the distinction between dualism and monism?
2. What are the advantages and disadvantages of property dualism?
3. Can you construct a thought experiment illustrating the knowledge argument for some sensation other than colour?
4. What distinguishes a p-zombie from a zombie as depicted in popular movies?
5. Is there something about the brain that is special for consciousness?
6. Most non-experts find the example of the China brain ridiculous. What are their objections, and how would you counter them? What objections remain?
7. What is Searle's Chinese room argument, and is it correct?
8. If mysterianism is correct, should we all just give up and go home, or are there aspects of consciousness research remaining that are worth doing?

Recommended Resources

General
Churchland, P.M. (2013). *Matter and Consciousness* (3rd ed.). Cambridge, MA: MIT Press.
Cohen, M. (2004). *Wittgenstein's Beetle and Other Classic Thought Experiments*. Oxford, UK: Wiley-Blackwell.
Dennett, D.C. (2013). *Intuition Pumps and Other Tools for Thinking*. Harmondsworth, UK: Penguin.
Kim, J. (2010). *Philosophy of Mind* (3rd ed.). Philadelphia, PA: Westview Press.
Searle, J.R. (1997). *The Mystery of Consciousness*. New York, NY: The New York Review of Books.
Searle, J.R. (2004). *Mind: A Brief Introduction*. New York: Oxford University Press.
The Stanford Encyclopaedia of Philosophy. 2020. Website. http://plato.stanford.edu.

Dualism and Monism
Uttal, W.R. (2013). *Dualism: The Original Sin of Cognitivism*. London: Routledge. An overview of dualism in religion, philosophy, and science.

The Knowledge Argument and Inverted Spectra
Nagasawa, Y. (2009). The knowledge argument. In T. Bayne, A. Cleeremans, and P. Wilken, *The Oxford Companion to Consciousness*. Oxford, UK: Oxford University Press, pp. 395–397.
Ludlow, P., Nagasawa, Y., & Stoljar, D. (eds.) (2004). *There's Something about Mary*. Cambridge, MA: MIT Press.

The Problem of Pain
Møller, A.R. (2018). *Pain: Its Anatomy, Physiology, and Treatment* (3rd ed.). Scotts Valley, CA: CreateSpace.

Philosophical Zombies
The Stanford Encyclopaedia of Philosophy. 2020. P-zombies. Website. http://plato.stanford.edu/entries/zombies/#3.

Materialism and Functionalism
The Stanford Encyclopaedia of Philosophy. 2020. Functionalism. Website. https://plato.stanford.edu/entries/functionalism.

History of Science and the Scientific Revolution
Chalmers, A.F. (2013). *What Is this Thing Called Science?* Milton Keynes, UK: Open University Press.
Koestler, A. (1959). *The Sleepwalkers*. London: Penguin.

Computation

Hofstadter, D. (1979). *Godel, Escher, Bach: An Eternal Golden Braid*. New York, NY: Basic Books.

Mysterianism

McGinn, C. (2000). *The Mysterious Flame: Conscious Minds in a Material World*. New York, NY: Basic Books.

3   DO WE HAVE FREE WILL?

You have a choice. How many times have you been told that? You could have worked harder at school or college, or had more fun: you decided, the choice was yours. Your life afterwards is a consequence of the decisions you made. How many times have you agonised over making a decision? Should I buy a new car, a new house, a new pair of shoes? You spend hours weighing up the pros and cons before you eventually make your choice (and sometimes instantly regret it).

This chapter examines whether we really do have a choice in everything, and indeed anything, we do. Are we more like balls than we think? We begin by examining the idea of determinism, that everything that happens must happen because of the way the laws of physics apply to the current state of the universe. We then consider how determinism affects our belief that we have free will, that at any time we are completely free to choose how to act. We then ask who is this 'I' that believes that they are acting and making a choice, and introduce the ideas of the homunculus and Cartesian theatre.

We examine the implications of the absence of free will – for example, should you be punished for committing a crime if you really had no choice? We then go on to examine the neuroscience of action – what is happening in the brain when we are making a decision or deciding to carry out some action? We conclude the chapter with an examination of cases of involuntary action, where our bodies appear to carry out some action without any apparent input from the 'I' that we think is in control.

People and Objects

You're currently reading this book, but if you want, you can now choose to put it down and go and do something else, or you can carry on reading. You feel that you are completely free to choose what to do at this moment.

Contrast our decisions and choices with the behaviour of a ball. Think of kicking or throwing a ball. We can choose whether to kick it or not, but does the ball have any choice in what to do when it's kicked? Of course not – the notion is nonsensical. The behaviour of the ball is completely *determined* by the laws of physics. When we kick the ball, the laws of physics kick in. At the level of objects, Newton's laws work perfectly, and if we could measure the starting conditions accurately enough (exactly where the ball is, when it is kicked, exactly where it is kicked, and with how much force in which direction), we could work out exactly how the ball would travel, for how long, how high, and precisely where it would land (and bounce, and eventually come to rest). The ball has no say in the matter. We would get the same answer every time we did the necessary computations, and we would always be right. Kick the ball again and we could predict the flight of the ball once again, with perfect accuracy. (For a brief comment on Sir Isaac Newton's place in the history of science, see Box 2.2 'The History of Physics' in Chapter 2.)

Determinism and Free Will

People and balls seem then to be very different types of things. We say the laws of physics determine the action of the ball, as indeed they determine the behaviour of all physical objects. The argument that all behaviour, mental and physical, is determined by physical laws is called **determinism**. As humans, on the other hand, we appear to be able to choose what we do. We say that we have free will – or at least we think we do. **Free will** is the ability to choose between alternative courses of action without being forced to choose one or another.

Let's move beyond an isolated ball to a more complicated system, for example, a pool, billiards, or snooker table. When you hit the cue ball with your cue, the ball moves off and hits the other balls, and they in turn move around, often hitting each other, until the force of friction causes them to come to rest. The level of control possible by professional billiards players can seem amazing; they can set up the balls for their next play and the play after that; they can make the cue ball swerve and recoil; they can pocket balls with ease. This system though, complicated as it seems, is clearly just a scaled-up version of kicking a ball; it's a completely determined system governed by the laws of physics. We don't need to restrict ourselves to stationary objects; if we know how an object such as a billiard ball is moving (its velocity; that is, its direction and speed), we can work out what will happen to it, even if it is hit by other objects.

Perhaps you can suspect the problems coming up. We can scale up even more. We can think of the Earth–Moon system, solar system, indeed universe, as nothing more than a much more complicated billiards table. At any one time, if we knew the exact state of the universe (the starting conditions), we could work out exactly what was going to happen next by just mechanistically applying the laws of physics. The idea that the next state of something is determined purely by its current state (which is in turn determined purely by the thing's history) is called determinism.

Of course, in practice, determining the exact path of something as relatively simple as a ball is extremely difficult because the accuracy of measurement and computer power necessary greatly exceed what we have available. Measuring and computing future states of the universe will remain impossible, in practice. But, *in principle*, given enough time and power, it could be done. It's this 'in principle' argument that's important. It means that all future states are determined by the current one, which is determined by history and the laws of physics. The universe runs as smoothly and as predictably as clockwork (see Figure 3.1). In 1814, the French philosopher and mathematician Pierre-Simon Laplace (1749–1827) worked on the theory of tides and planetary orbits, particularly using calculus to describe higher-level interactions in gravity between the planets (such as the effect of Saturn on the orbit of Jupiter around the Sun). Such thinking led him to propose that everything is

DETERMINISM AND FREE WILL

determined – with sufficient knowledge and time, a suitably clever person could compute everything about the later state of the universe from its current state. He postulated a super-intelligent demon; if that demon knew the position and velocities of all the particles in the universe at any one time, and all the forces acting on them, it could work out, in principle, all future states of the universe.

Human Behaviour

But what about us? Surely our thoughts and the actions arising from them can't be fully determined? There is a strong argument that they can. Our brains are made out of matter; if we are materialist monists (that is, we believe only physical matter exists), then we believe that our thoughts, and our consequent behaviours, arise from the action of matter. We are physical systems just like any other, somewhere in complexity between billiards tables and the whole universe. So, at any one time, our behaviour is also fully determined by our current state, which in turn is determined by our history (and our genes, of course, which are in turn only part of the universe).

Figure 3.1 A clockwork solar system. Everything is predictable from the beginning and runs like clockwork. Does the mind work in the same way? Source: Jamie Cooper/SSPL/Getty Images.

Think of it another way: how free are you really? Let's say your instructor asks you to do something embarrassing, for example, to go to a public place and shout 'Hello world!'. Some of you may do it; most of you probably won't. You think you have free choice. But according to many philosophers, you don't: whether or not you comply with this request depends, sure enough, on you, but you are the sum of your history. Your behaviour now is determined by what has happened to you before. That in turn depends on your genes and your history; you have no choice now in those. They've already happened. You are just as clockwork as the billiards table. You will behave in a certain way because of the current state of your neurons, the exact wiring in your brain. Given your exact current wiring, you can't act in any other way. There is only one possible future for you.

We can see how plausible this account is if we consider ourselves making a difficult decision. Imagine yourself at a juncture in your life, considering an important decision. I think back, for example, to being offered my first job as a university teacher. I remember thinking carefully about whether to accept it or not. I weighed the pros (money, a step on the career ladder) and the cons (it was a long way away from home; the fact that it was a teaching job meant that I would have less time available to do research). I'm sure you can think of similar big professional or personal decisions. In that situation I had a choice, a completely free choice (I decided to accept, and you will perhaps be pleased to know that things worked out very well).

But did I really have a choice? Was the outcome ever in doubt? Would I ever have said 'no'? I was worried about money, and that worry came from my background where we grew up with limited income. I was risk averse because in my family we never took risks. The outcome was never really in doubt. At any one time we are the products of our genes, environment, and history (and their interaction). Forces of genetics and history have shaped the wiring of our brains, and they will force the neurons to fire in a specific way. Sure, we spend time deliberating, but the electricity flows in an entirely predictable way.

> **TRY THIS:** Be Bold
>
> Do something (safe and legal!) that you would not normally do, because you would be embarrassed or inhibited. For example, resolve to go to a public place and shout 'Hello everyone!'. Even better if you can think of something that makes the world a better or happier place. I would be embarrassed to go up to someone and say, 'I like your shirt', for example. Can you do it? Do you chicken out at the last moment (as I invariably have when trying this exercise)? Then examine your feelings of choice as you act (or don't). Do you think your actions are free? Do they feel as though they are?

The Implications of Quantum Mechanics

At this stage (probably before) many people will raise an objection based on **quantum mechanics**. At the subatomic level, energy comes in very small packets (called *quanta*, plural), and the behaviour of particles is *probabilistic* – we can only say that a particle will do something not with certainty but with a certain probability. At this level the universe is non-deterministic and real chance does come into play, but quantum mechanics isn't much help when it comes to free will. First, non-determinism only applies at the quantum level, which is very, very small. When you roll a die or toss a coin at the macroscopic level, the outcome is not explained by quantum mechanics, but rather by the laws of classical physics – the laws that govern how billiard balls move.

Second, even if there are any quantum effects on the brain, they would just be another source of input to your current neural state; they would not in any way provide you with a choice. Suppose you want to choose between two alternatives by tossing a coin, and the coin is a quantum coin. The outcome of the coin toss would be completely random. You wouldn't in any way have chosen because your 'choice' would have been fully determined by the coin toss. So even taking quantum mechanics into account, the conclusion that the universe is non-deterministic to some degree doesn't give us free will. (Quantum mechanics does pose problems for Laplace's demon, however, because events at the quantum level are probabilistic, and therefore a demon could not have perfect knowledge of the universe; but this point is irrelevant to our purpose when we think we are deciding on an action.)

Dualism and Free Will

Others might conclude that the idea of having no free will is so unpleasant that they would rather give up materialism and go back to dualism. But we saw in Chapter 2 that dualism is highly problematic. In fact, it is not even clear why an immaterial soul will have free will. Will not your soul simply be the result of all its experiences up to the point it is seemingly making a choice? Will it not just act on the basis of its history, in the same way that our physical selves do?

Some people also respond, 'Well, if I don't have free will I might just as well …' and then say something like 'rob a bank', or 'go back to bed for the rest of my life'. Well, you might, but you still don't have a choice, I'm afraid. Any of those courses of action will already have been determined in advance. So, you might as well believe that you are going to choose to have a healthy productive life instead.

If you don't want to give up materialist monism, you seem forced to conclude that free will doesn't exist. You had no more choice in whether you saidm 'Hello, world!' than a thrown ball has in where it goes. Free will is an illusion.

Box 3.1 What Is an Illusion?

When an illusionist performs their magic, we know that things aren't as they seem (Figure 3.2). When the magician David Copperfield rises from a glass tank and then flies through the air, we know (or at least are very confident that we know) that he isn't really flying. When David Blaine or Derren Brown appear to read a person's mind and pick the right card, we know (or at least are very confident that we know) that they haven't really used telepathy. Something has happened, but it's an illusion.

When we look at a visual illusion, we don't deny that something is on the paper; things simply aren't what they seem.

To say something is an illusion is to say that something isn't as it first appears. It doesn't necessarily mean that something doesn't exist – after all, the illusionist David Copperfield does appear to fly through the air with the greatest of ease – but that appearances are misleading. To find out what is really going on, we have to dig deeper.

Figure 3.2 British stage magician Jasper Maskelyne (1902–1973) prepares to saw assistant Maisie Wright in half at the Whitehall Theatre in London, 1948. We know the assistant isn't really going to be cut in half – it's an illusion, but that doesn't mean that nothing is happening. Source: Hulton Archive/Getty Images.

The Homunculus in the Cartesian Theatre

Who is this 'I' in 'I can choose'? Who is the I who we think has free will? At first sight the answer seems obvious, but this question is one of the central questions in consciousness research. We think of ourselves as 'I', a 'self' that sits in our head and perceives the world and makes decisions. We often also produce a running commentary on the outside world and what we are thinking with an inner voice (inner speech), and we think of this voice as being produced by our inner self. It is as though there is a person within our person.

This view of the self as a separate inner person is called the homunculus theory of the self. We think of the perceived world – vision, sound, touch, smell, taste – as rather like a magnificent multisensory cinema surrounding us. But who is watching the screen? There is an inner person looking at what is going on and deciding to act on it. But then what happens in that inner person? What makes that inner person work? Another even smaller homunculus? We quickly enter an infinite regress, like Russian nesting dolls and discover that we haven't solved anything at all.

The idea that the mind assembles a multisensory representation that we then observe like watching a movie in *virtual reality* is usually called the myth of the **Cartesian theatre**. The philosopher Daniel Dennett has devoted much effort to trying to demolish the myth. Dennett (1991) uses the term 'Cartesian' in a negative way to remind us of Cartesian dualism: what else could the mysterious homunculus be other than an immaterial soul? And if we reject the soul, as most researchers do, then the theatre analogy cannot be correct.

The 'I' then doesn't watch a screen or produce inner speech; rather, the 'I' is the product of the activity of the whole brain. There isn't any real inner self that can weigh alternatives and make a choice between them. Instead, the brain produces an output in response to an input based upon its current state. The more we think about what could be making a choice, even if we had complete free will, the less it seems that we can comprehend what such an 'I' would be; a 'me' divorced from the rest of me, a free inner self. The whole idea of free will seems to be more and more confusing, and makes less and less sense.

The Benefits of Believing in Free Will

Some of our most cherished beliefs – that we know other people are just like us, and that we are free to choose to do what we want – are brought into question by consciousness research. Consciousness research teaches us that consciousness is caused by, rather than the cause of, brain events and that our belief that 'we' are causing our bodies to do things, our sense that we have conscious control over our bodies, might be little more than an illusion.

Consider the case of the guided rat, also called the *robo-rat* (Talwar et al., 2002). These rats had electrodes implanted in their **motor cortex** and in their ***medial** forebrain bundles*, a tract of fibres that passes through structures known as the forebrain and hypothalamus and which is an important part of the reward system of the brain (see Figure 3.3). These electrodes were connected through a small backpack to a transmitter.

Researchers sent the rats signals they felt as sensations in their whiskers and as pleasure. These combined signals were used to condition the rat to move in particular directions, jump, and climb walls. The rat doesn't know that it is under external control; due to how the electrodes work, from its point of view, if it could reflect upon the situation, it is acting of its own accord. It's moving due to its own free will, if you like. Many feel that we are to some extent like these rats, except the backpack is in our brain.

Why do we bother to maintain the illusion? Although I am aware of the problems with the concept, I carry on acting as though it is real, as, it seems, do all scientists and philosophers. Few of us give up and simply wait passively for events to unfold.

The American social psychologist Daniel Wegner (2002) argued that, although free will is an illusion, we deliberately construct the illusion for a purpose. We make up the feeling of conscious will, without being aware of doing so, to help us tell a story about our lives, to help us maintain and remember a narrative of events. Without this story, says Wegner, we would have no sense of responsibility and hence no sense of morality, and without our having a sense of right and wrong, it would be difficult for us to maintain the cohesion of a social group. Without believing that we control our future, we might not even bother ever to act.

Constructing a story about free will and responsibility means that we sometimes go too far: we attribute control when we have had no direct influence on events at all. Superstitious beliefs and magical thinking fall into this category. We dance during a drought, it rains, and we think we must have caused the rain. Hooray for us.

There is also much research showing that, if people are told there is no free will, or if they are reminded of it, their behaviour deteriorates, and they act less morally. People who have just read about how there is no free will are more likely to cheat on a mathematical problem-solving task (Vohs & Schooler, 2008), and emphasising the absence of free will also makes people more aggressive and less likely to help others (Baumeister et al., 2009). So a belief in free will appears to help us act more socially (although it should be pointed out that these effects have only been shown to act for a short time, and others have had difficulty in replicating some of these experiments).

It also seems very strange that everything is in fact decided unconsciously: we prepare our responses, we swing at the tennis ball, we even initiate an action at a particular time 'of our own free will' well before these events enter consciousness. The job is already done. What on Earth then is consciousness adding: we have already acted, so what is added by this new level of complexity?

Of course, ultimately whether you believe in free will or not, and how you respond to reading this chapter, isn't up to you; your behaviour is already determined.

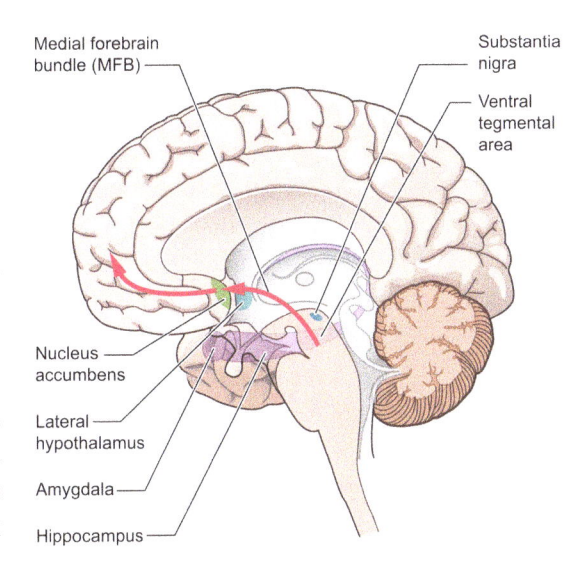

Figure 3.3 The brain's reward circuitry. All organisms need to be motivated to stay alive, ingest nutrients, and reproduce (examples of what we call *drives*), so it will come as no surprise that the brain systems involved in reward are complex.

Compatibilism

The arguments against free will seem convincing, but not quite all philosophers have given up on it. Some argue that determinism and free will can in some way coexist, or we can even give up on determinism.

The idea that determinism and free will are compatible is called **compatibilism**. (Philosophers who believe that free will and determinism are incompatible are called incompatibilists.) A compatibilist believes that, when people carry out an action, or make a choice – that is, when they use free will – they could have acted otherwise than they in fact do. Whereas in the classic determinist account there is only one possible future, in the free will account there are multiple futures, with people choosing among them.

This possibility is in line with most people's intuitions about how we and the world work, but the compatibilist then has to identify the flaw in the argument for determinism.

One possibility, which dates back to the work of the British philosopher Thomas Hobbes (1668 [1651]), is to say that we as individuals are the source of any decision. We believe that we have freedom of will, and that we could have done otherwise than what we have done. Thus we are still morally responsible for our actions. While this argument might be comforting for prison officers (as we shall see later in this chapter), it isn't really a solution because people are still merely mediating history when they act. Just because people believe they have free will doesn't make determinism wrong.

There are different versions of compatibilism with different emphases. For example, Dennett (1978a, 2004) argues that, although our actions are determined by the current state of our brains, we should consider the whole system, rather than just the illusory 'I' that we think is making a decision. Nevertheless, the objection remains that at any one time the state of our brain is completely determined by our history.

Incompatibilists deny that free will and determinism can coexist, but they can maintain free will by giving up on determinism. This position is called **libertarianism** (not to be confused with the political position that people should pay as little tax and be as free as possible, within certain constraints). There are several versions of libertarianism, some getting round the problems posed by determinism by accepting dualism, and others, such as that formulated by the philosophers Robert Kane (1998) and Robert Nozick (1981), which do not necessitate giving up materialism but still renounce determinism.

British philosopher Peter Strawson (1962) says that problems of free will and determinism have more to do with the way words are used than anything else; such problems are called *pseudo-problems*. Whatever the philosophical truth about free will, people will also think in terms of moral responsibility and right and wrong, and it's those things to which we should pay attention.

Environmental Effects on Behaviour

When you go into a supermarket, do you think you choose freely from among the goods on display? Do you think that expensive goods and merchandise that the shops want to move are at eye level just by chance? You think it's just coincidence that the pervasive smell of baking bread and rotisserie chicken, which is making you salivate and hungry, and urging you to buy more food right now, is accidental? Of course not: shops and advertisers know that our purchasing behaviour can easily be influenced (Lindstrom, 2011). Big decisions can be influenced by small things.

Our behaviour at any one time – the decisions we make – is the result of our genes, the sum of life experiences up to that point, and the environment. Some of those influences, such as those of major life events, will be large, but many will be small. We certainly are usually mostly unclear why we are acting in a particular way and could not describe the small environmental influences on our behaviour.

The idea of social priming is that subtle environmental cues can affect behaviour. In some of the early classic experiments, students primed by reading words associated with being rude tended subsequently to interrupt the experimenter more often and more quickly than students in the control condition. Similarly, students who read lists of words associated with being elderly (such as retired, old, and wrinkled) then walked more slowly after leaving the lab than control students (Bargh et al., 1996). This result is extraordinary, and there has been much controversy about it, particularly about whether the finding can be replicated (e.g. Doyen et al., 2012; but see Bargh, 2012). In general, however, enough studies in the area seem to support the general contention that our behaviour can at least sometimes be influenced by subtle features of the environment. For example, a recent study has shown that priming can affect whether gamblers bet or pass (Payne et al., 2016).

Box 3.2 *Toxoplasma*

Some very small things in the environment can affect our behaviour. *Toxoplasmosis* is a disease caused by the parasitic protozoan *Toxoplasma gondii* (see Figure 3.4), and is spread by contact with contaminated cat faeces. Often the disease causes no obvious symptoms, or at most mild flu-like symptoms on first being infected. One estimate is that in the United States almost one in four people are infected. Researchers have known for a while that mice and rats infected by *T. gondii* change their behaviour by behaving more riskily: they stay longer in the open and thereby make themselves more likely to be caught and eaten by cats (Berdoy et al., 2000).

Studies have shown that infection by *T. gondii* also affects human personality, particularly making men act more expediently and more likely to disobey rules (Flegr, 2007). The changes in personality were more profound the longer the person had been infected, suggesting that the infection changed behaviour, rather than that more expedient people were more likely to become infected. Infection also reduces psychomotor coordination; probably as a result of these factors, infected individuals are more likely to be involved in motor accidents, both as drivers and pedestrians. These effects, which signal a greater likelihood of taking risks, are similar to the effects the parasite has on rodents. The mechanisms involved are complicated, but include the increased release of the neurotransmitters dopamine in the brain in response to inflammation and increased levels of testosterone (Flegr, 2013). (*Dopamine* is a neurotransmitter particularly associated with the brain's reward system.) Infection has also been associated with increased suicide rates in women, with similar mechanisms being at work (Pedersen et al., 2012).

Box 3.2 (cont.)

So, in many senses, small things in our environment can affect our behaviour and the decisions we make – our choices – without our awareness. Do yourself a favour; always go shopping with a list. And always wash your hands after handling cats.

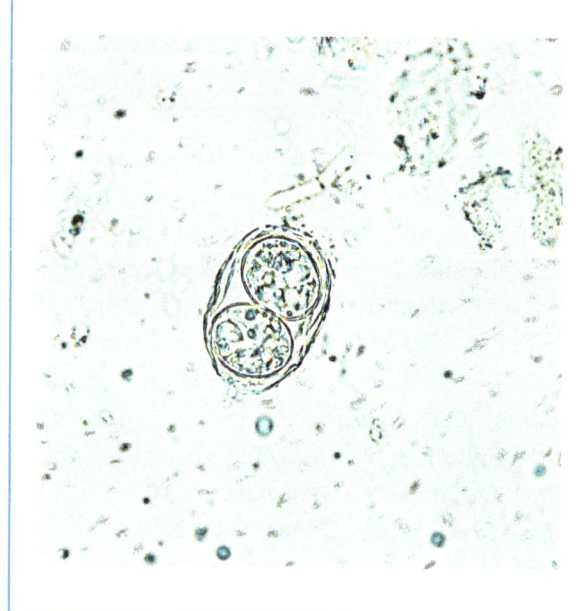

Figure 3.4 *Toxoplasma gondii*. Can this little creature really make us take more risks in crossing the road? Source: Todorean Gabriel/Getty Images Plus.

TRY THIS: Your Life's Turning Points

Look back at some major life decisions. Why did you choose the outcome that you did? Go back. What were the reasons for those reasons? Now consider a recent minor decision, such as why you ate the breakfast you did (or perhaps why you didn't have any breakfast at all). Why did you choose a cheese omelette this morning? Because you like eggs, and had them in stock, along with a piece of cheese that needed using up? Why did you have cheese and eggs hanging around? Why do you like eggs so much? And so on. You will probably realise that everything you do has many reasons for it, most of which you are clueless about.

Crime and Punishment

Questions about the existence of free will are of practical importance. Every legal system assumes that a person commits a crime through choice: the important idea in law is that a guilty person could have done otherwise. If someone decides to rob a bank, and then does so, that person should be found guilty. They had an alternative in which they could have decided not to perpetrate the robbery.

CRIME AND PUNISHMENT

There are of course many subtleties in law. Suppose I force you in some way to carry out the crime, then the legal system is likely to find you not guilty. Although you appeared to have a choice, the law would consider that the alternative to carrying out the robbery was so unpleasant that you should be exonerated of all blame (which should instead be placed on the head of the person who forced you to commit the crime).

The argument in this section is that the perpetration of any crime is analogous to the second case: although it might seem that the criminal had a choice, in practice they did not.

Moral Responsibility

But if a bank robber has no free will, then in what way can they be said to be responsible for their criminal actions? Why should they be sent to prison for a crime they couldn't do otherwise than commit? If they have no free will, then surely they are as innocent as if they had had a gun pointed to their head? Such worries are not limited to crime. Why castigate or punish a child for a naughty action if they could not have done otherwise?

As this issue of moral responsibility depends on the argument between free will and determinism, there is clearly going to be no straightforward resolution. The idea that we are not morally responsible for our actions, and at any time had no real choice, is not a palatable one. Hence it is little wonder philosophers have expended so much effort in trying to reconcile moral responsibility with determinism, or in trying to show that determinism is false (Wilton & Harley, 2018).

> **Box 3.3 The Purpose of Punishment**
>
> There are other ways in which consciousness research is related to the ideas of crime and punishment. You might argue, for example, that, although we agree that philosophy says that a criminal had no choice, the purpose of punishment is not really to punish the convicted criminal, but to deter others from committing similar crimes. Others argue that we need prisons to keep society safe; criminals can't commit any more crimes while they're safely locked up. The history of the argument about the purpose of punishment (whether it is truly to punish, to rehabilitate, to deter, to protect society, or all of these) is a long one (e.g. Hart, 1970). But we are just shifting the problem back a little: the effectiveness of punishment as a deterrence to others is also a meaningless question in a deterministic universe. It is already determined how the people who watch a public execution will act in the future. The existence of punishment as a deterrent is just yet another factor in conspiring to determine how an individual acts at any time (Figure 3.5).
>
> Figure 3.5 Wormwood Scrubs prison in the UK. What function do prisons serve if criminals had no choice in whether they committed a crime or not? Source: weerachonoat/Getty Images Plus.

The Role of Psychology in Understanding Crime

Even if we put aside fundamental concerns about free will, psychology and neuroscience pose other problems for our consideration of moral responsibility and how society should respond to crime and criminals. The law has long held that some individuals have diminished responsibility such that they cannot be held fully responsible for their crimes: not guilty by reason of insanity, or guilty but insane in the United States, insane in English law. Similar definitions apply across the world. A person who commits a crime when suffering from schizophrenia, for example, is usually treated differently from someone held not to be suffering from mental illness, because they are considered to be either not responsible for their actions, or have diminished responsibility. The outcome for serious crime is still usually some form of incarceration, but with an emphasis on treatment rather than punishment (often with the stipulation that the person cannot be considered for release until he or she is 'cured').

But who is mentally ill? A person with *antisocial personality disorder* (abbreviated to ASPD, and described in the American Psychiatric Association's Diagnostic and Statistical Manual of Mental Disorders or DSM), more commonly known as psychopathy, has very low or no empathy, does not show remorse, fails to conform to social norms, is capable of excessive deception, and may enjoy inflicting cruelty. Many serial killers have antisocial personality disorder. But given it is classified as a disorder, how should we respond to people with ASPD? Surely they are ill, as ill as someone diagnosed with schizophrenia, for example? Should we therefore treat them the same as people with schizophrenia and hold them not to be responsible for the crimes they commit? On the contrary: western law considers that they have a level of insight, which means that the law considers that they could have acted otherwise (whereas someone with schizophrenia could not).

But is this distinction between schizophrenia and psychopathy reasonable? Plenty of evidence now shows that the brains of people with ASPD are systematically different from people without. Most studies show that the **amygdala**, a small almond-shaped structure deep in each hemisphere, functions differently in people with ASPD, or that the connections to it are in some way different. For example, a study by Yang et al. (2011) found, using brain imaging, that the amygdala tends to be smaller and malformed in people with psychopathy than in a control sample. Fried (1997) suggests that the prefrontal cortex is hyper-aroused and inhibits the amygdala too much in individuals who learn to be violent. The amygdala is known to be highly involved in processing emotion, and particularly in identifying threat. There are several other differences between people with and without ASPD; for example, levels of the neurotransmitter serotonin are lower in psychopaths (Moore et al., 2002). Thus, the brains of individuals with ASPD are either different from most people's brains at birth or made different by early traumatic life events. In that case, surely a person with what is effectively brain damage should be dealt with sympathetically, and offered treatment, rather than be treated as a fully responsible adult and incarcerated, or even, in some countries, executed?

But all criminal behaviour has roots in the interaction between a person's environment and early upbringing. It is well known that early poverty, social deprivation, parental unemployment, and childhood trauma, neglect, and abuse are all likely to increase the probability that someone acquires a criminal record (see, for example, Milaniak & Widom, 2015; Minh et al., 2013). Should someone who turns to crime as a result of his or her upbringing be punished or treated? Let's think about what falls in the range of 'normal' personality types: we know that some people are more likely to take risks than others. Should they be punished for carrying out a crime on the spur of the moment just because of their personality, resulting from a peculiarity of the formation of their brain, or because they themselves were treated poorly when young? How unfair!

The field of applying neuroscience to the study of morality and ethics is called neuroethics, and to criminology in particular, *neurocriminology*. **Neuroethics** is a wide-ranging subject, covering everything from the philosophy and neuroscience of free will, to the use of smart drugs, to the application of treatment (and punishment). Is it right, for example, to treat someone with ASPD against their will?

Deciding to Act

Think about as simple a voluntary action as you can perform: choosing when to move your finger. Let's try a very simple experiment: assuming you're sitting at a desk or in a chair, hover your finger above a surface and, whenever you want, tap the surface with your finger. The subjective experience of this action is that there is a period while you're waiting to make a decision, then you decide, and then nerve impulses travel down from your brain to your finger, which then moves. Put at its simplest, we can say that action seems to comprise a decision to act followed by the action. And in making that decision about when to move your finger, you appear to be exercising your free will. You have a *sense of agency*.

Note that human actions can be described at several levels. You could say you're choosing to move your finger, but then we could ask, why are you choosing to lift your finger? Because you're reading this chapter and I've said it would be educational for you to try. You're reading this chapter because you want to find out about free will. Because you want to get a university qualification. Because you want to be in a better position to make a living. All of these explanations of why we are acting are simultaneously true of any action or any choice we make.

Let's put aside for now the question of free will and explore what is happening in the brain when we think we're making a decision. After all, even if we don't have free choice, the brain has to respond to the current situation in line with its history and environment, and this involves processing. What happens in that processing, and when?

> **TRY THIS: Choosing to Act**
>
> Sit with a solid surface in front of you. Place your hand on it and raise a finger suspended above the table. Whenever you like, decide to tap the table. Examine your processes and your muscles and hand position as you carry out this action. What is your experience of deciding to act? When did you choose? How long was it, do you think, before your finger moved?

Libet's Experiments on 'Voluntary' Movement

In a classic series of experiments, Benjamin Libet (1983) explored what was happening in the brain when it carried out such simple tasks as initiating a finger movement. Libet used apparatus discussed in Box 3.4. People watch a small dot move quickly around a numbered dial, rather like a clock face. Participants had to note the position of the dot when they were consciously aware of the decision to act. You decide when to move your finger while noting the position of the dot on the screen. Afterwards you report that position. At the same time we measure your readiness potential with EEG (explained below). Libet found that the readiness potential begins well before the person reports forming the conscious intention to move their finger, typically around 350 milliseconds before, although the exact figure depends on the setup.

The design is based upon the finding that, when we perform any movement, the brain shows a small electrical spike called the readiness potential, or RP, which is measured by an *EEG* (an electroencephalogram, a device that measures the brain's electrical activity; see Box 3.4 and move Figure 3.6 to here, so now reads see Box 3.4 and Figure 3.6). The RP is a complex wave pattern, but crucially with a clear spike in activity identifiable 0.5 s (500 ms) before the action occurs. So we know that at that specific time, 500 ms before an action, we have decided to act – to move our finger, say.

Figure 3.6 An ERP (event-related potential) - how the brain responds to a stimulus. A gradual increase followed by sudden fall in positive electrical activity in the brain associated with preparing a motor movement.

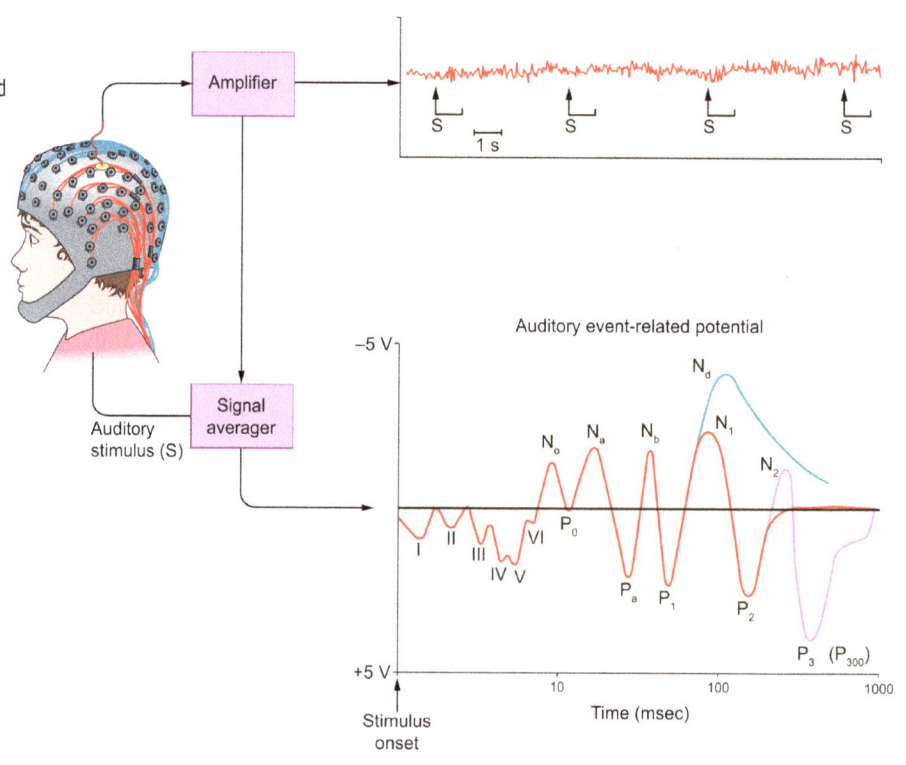

Libet found though that people reported awareness of the decision to act – the time at which they say they decided to flex their finger – only about 200 ms before action. So awareness of deciding to act comes 300 ms after the brain processing associated with deciding to act (some of the precise times reported vary by 50 ms or so, which doesn't affect these arguments in any way). Thus, the brain initiates voluntary movement before we experience the will to act.

Hence these results seem to show that our conscious decision to act is merely an illusion; our mind is made up unconsciously some time before we are conscious of making a decision.

Libet proposed a way in which his findings could still accommodate conscious will by proposing a two-stage model of volition. The brain carries out the processing that leads to the decision, leaving a brief window of time between the person becoming aware of the decision and the motor cortex irreversibly initiating motor action. Libet said that in this brief time window there was the possibility of a conscious veto, where we can decide to allow the movement or to veto it and prevent the motor cortex initiating action. The veto re-introduces the possibility of a free choice between possible alternatives (moving and not moving).

For some, this idea of a conscious veto seems a rather desperate move. First, it doesn't really save free will, just shifts responsibility to conscious will; and conscious will is fully determined, by all the previous arguments. Second, who or what makes the veto? We face the problem of the homunculus again, watching the Cartesian theatre of action. Doesn't the homunculus need time to make its little decision? Where does this time come from?

Box 3.4   Measuring Brain Activity with EEG

EEG stands for electroencephalogram. An electroencephalogram is a device that measures electrical activity in the brain by placing electrical sensors, usually in the form of small metallic discs, on specific, standard points over the scalp (see Figure 3.7). The discs are usually covered with a small amount of gel to improve the conductivity between the skin and the discs. There might be as few as 4 or as many as 256 sensors, although a few dozen is typical. The sensors pick up the brain's electrical activity as neurons fire. EEG is an important medical tool for diagnosing illnesses such as epilepsy in addition, as we shall see, to different states and depths of consciousness. The electroencephalography cap contains sensors called electrodes placed in standard positions that pick up the brain's electrical activity. It generates data in the form of information about the varying voltage for each position or channel. The temporal resolution of EEG – how finely the brain's activity can be resolved in time – is very good. But the spatial resolution – how accurately the activity can be resolved in space – is less so, as each electrode is picking up activity from quite a large area (and depth) of the brain, with the skull in between the sensor and the source of the signal. Nevertheless EEG has been used for several decades in an enormous range of psychological research.

Figure 3.7 An EEG cap. Source: Luca Sage/Stone/Getty Images.

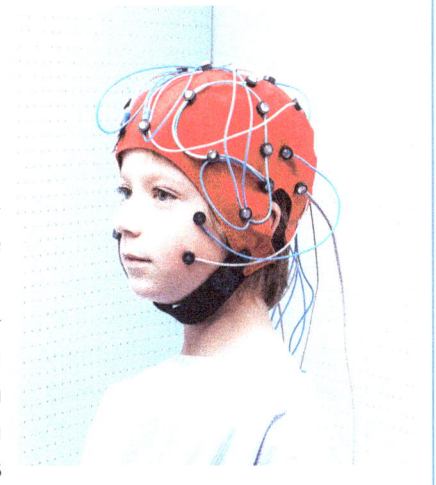

> **Box 3.4** (cont.)
>
> The readiness potential or RP (sometimes shown as BP, from the German *Bereitschaftspotential*) is a pattern of gradually increased positive electrical activity averaged across several specific electrodes (all electrical activity is either positive or negative), followed by a comparatively sudden fall into the negative zone, gradually recovering to neutral, over a second or so. The potential is found in sensors measuring activity in the motor cortex of the brain, and has long been conceptualised as associated with the planning and preparation of voluntary motor movement.

Criticisms of Libet's Experiments

Researchers have raised several problems with Libet's procedure. A number of criticisms can be made of the physical design of his device, which was forced on Libet by the lack of alternatives in apparatus at the time. Reporting a number on a clock face is a far from ideal method of reporting the timing of awareness, particularly given that we are dealing with relatively small times. A person has to do two things at once – both make the decision and note the position of the dot. People aren't very reliable when asked to carry out this sort of task (Danquah et al., 2008). Participants have to shift their attention from their intention to the clock, an act that takes time and introduces inaccuracy (Dennett & Kinsbourne, 1992).

Others argue that the RP may not be a very good measure of the neural preparedness to act (Guggisberg & Mottaz, 2013). For example, Trevena and Miller (2002, 2010) argued that the RP isn't associated with preparing movement in particular, because an equally large signal is shown when a person decides not to move. Instead, they say, the RP is associated with engaging attention with the planned movement. In a similar vein, others argue that the RP reflects background neuronal noise associated with gradually preparing to move rather than a specific and precise neural event corresponding to an explicit decision to move (Schurger et al., 2016). The philosopher Alfred Mele attempted the experiment himself, and he concluded that 'the awareness of the intention to move' is an ambiguous concept (Mele, 2010). Libet reports results averaged across trials, which shows that on average there is an RP before the urge to move, but doesn't show that it holds for every trial, which it should do if there is a direct link between the two (Haynes, 2011).

Although Libet's original technique may be problematic, more recent studies using more advanced technology have supported his general conclusion. Soon et al. (2008) used *fMRI* to examine the cortical activation of people as they chose to press a left or right button with an index finger. They found that much more of the brain was involved than simply the *supplementary motor area*, the region of the brain that controls motor movements, but regions of the **frontal** and **parietal** cortex were activated well in advance. Indeed, Soon et al. claimed that they could predict the outcome of the motor decision the participant had not yet reported having made – by up to 10 s in advance. This type of experiment is still prone to the accusation that the idea of becoming aware of an intention to move is ambiguous, but the time involved is so large as to outweigh any ambiguity. Note that we cannot conclude that we always need 10 s to decide to make a simple motor movement. These sorts of experiments suggest that with the right neuroscience equipment someone else might know what you are going to do before 'you' do – although as we have seen these are murky concepts. Nevertheless these ideas pose yet more difficulties for the concept of free will.

Finally these experiments all concern fairly simple decisions, such as when to lift a finger, and it is not clear how understanding how these relatively simple decisions are made generalises to more complex decisions, such as deciding what to have for dinner or whom to marry.

Regardless of the validity of these experiments, we are faced with the same questions about free will. Unless you are a dualist, consciousness doesn't just come from nowhere; it reflects brain activity. Why do we decide to act when we do? Because of processing in the brain. All these experiments show is that making a decision must take time.

Involuntary Action

We have all experienced situations where our limbs move slightly involuntarily; these movements are called **myoclonic jerks** and are occasionally experienced as we fall asleep. Another familiar type of myoclonic jerk is the hiccups, in which there is a contraction of the diaphragm followed by a relaxation. Myoclonic jerks are caused by involuntary muscle contractions, and are commonly and widely experienced. Usually they don't cause us any problems, although prolonged hiccups can be annoying, becoming distressing if they carry on too long. More severe myoclonic jerks are associated with a range of illnesses, ranging from poisoning, injury to the central nervous system, and neurological diseases such as multiple sclerosis, Alzheimer's disease, and Parkinson's disease.

Our limbs are usually under our voluntary control. I decide to lift my arm to grasp my computer mouse; notice how that 'I' is present again. Myoclonic jerks are movements of our body where the 'I' is not involved. They surprise us. And with hiccups, our body rebels against us; most of the time the 'I' cannot stop the body misbehaving. We may think we have free will, but we can't always control those parts of the body we usually think we can.

Alien Hand Syndrome

One of the most extreme examples of involuntary action is seen in *alien hand syndrome* (or *anarchic hand syndrome*) in which a part of the body (typically the left hand) appears to act of its own accord. The person might not know what the hand is doing until the movement is pointed out. In some cases, the left and right hands might act in opposition to each other. The syndrome is mostly observed in split-brain patients (discussed in detail in Chapter 7), in which the left and right hemispheres of the brain are disconnected by severing the tract of tissue that normally connects them. Brain imaging suggests that alien hand movements are initiated by activation of the **contralateral** (on the opposite side, so right motor cortex for left alien hand) motor cortex in isolation, while voluntary movements involve a much wider area of the brain, including the **premotor cortex** (see Figure 3.8), and parts of the left hemisphere (Aboitiz et al., 2003; Assal et al., 2007; Biran et al., 2006). The motor cortex and surrounding regions is the area of the surface of the brain responsible for controlling motor actions – making movements, although other regions of the brain are also involved. The premotor region sends commands to the motor cortex: while the motor region is concerned

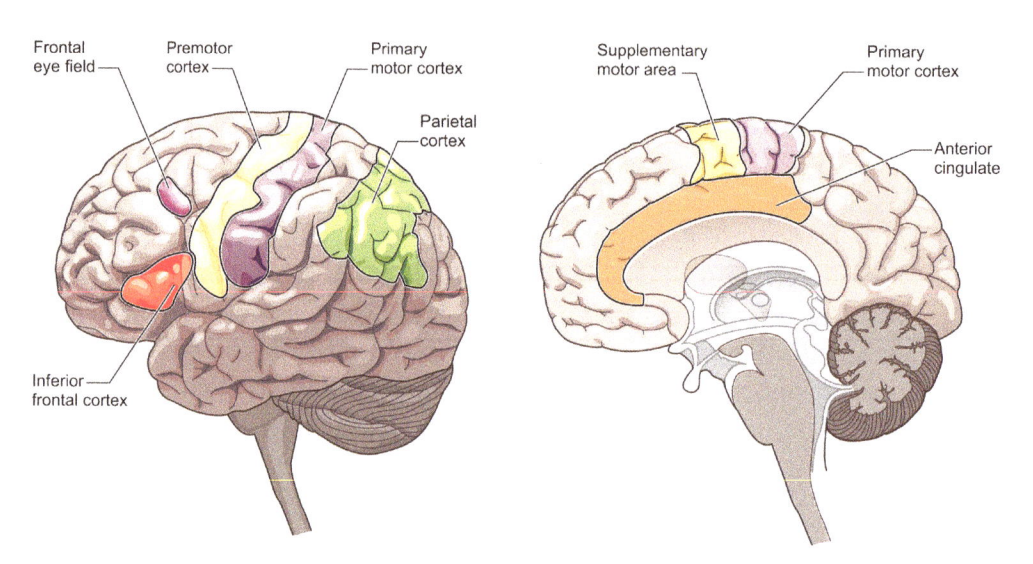

Figure 3.8 The premotor cortex and surrounding areas. This region of the brain is involved in preparing to act.

with executing the details of muscle movements, the *premotor* region is involved in planning action. This conclusion is the same as that of the previous section: the immediate control of movement involves the motor cortex, but deciding to move involves much more of the brain. If the motor cortex becomes in some way isolated, our movements start to feel strange and alien to us.

Alien hand syndrome is sometimes called *anarchic hand syndrome*, but Marchetti and Della Salla (1998) argue that these two conditions should be distinguished: alien hand is the sense that your hand is not your own, while anarchic hand is the sense that it is your hand but that you are not in control of it. They point out that different patients show this distinction, and that, while anarchic hand is associated with lesions to frontal areas of the *corpus callosum*, alien hand is associated with **posterior** lesions and maybe damage to the *parietal cortex*.

Skill and Habit

When you begin learning how to carry out some skilled task, such as driving a car, playing a musical instrument, or playing a sport, you need to give it your full attention. You have to think about – 'be conscious of' – every gear change, or turn of the wheel, or your arm position, or translating a note into sound, or whatever. However, as you become more skilled, your ability to carry out these tasks becomes increasingly automated. Eventually, you can carry out the skilled task without thinking about it at all; indeed, skilled game players and drivers find that forcing themselves to be conscious of the automated task may actually interfere with performance.

When you start learning to drive, you can't do two things at once; you can't talk and drive at the same time. But as you become skilled, you can chat happily away while driving quite safely. On the whole, though, doing two things at once is very difficult and leads to a substantial impairment on measures as performance, as studies using the dual-task paradigm have shown. The dual-task paradigm is simply an experiment in which a participant is asked to perform two tasks at the same time (e.g. Navon & Gopher, 1979).

Habit formation involves similar processes to become skilled at a task. More extreme than habits are behavioural addictions, such as gambling (Duhigg, 2013). Gambling and other addictive habits involve the activation of the reward circuitry of the brain; they share circuitry involved in initiating movement, including the **basal ganglia** and **brainstem**, among other areas. With both learning a skill and developing a habit, if we repeat something enough times, or perceive a large enough reward, the brain takes over, and conscious control over our actions is greatly reduced.

How do tasks such as driving or playing the piano become automatic? The answer is through sustained practice and repetition. The way in which tasks become automated has been well documented in the psychological research literature. Most researchers believe there are two modes of processing information, including executing motor acts (although it might be best to think of these modes as the ends of a continuum rather than a dichotomy). On the one hand, we have *attentional processing* (sometimes called controlled processing), which is slow and effortful, and takes up space in working memory, and which we can reflect upon with awareness. On the other, we have *automatic processing*, which is fast and effort free, which does not use space in working memory, and to which we do not have conscious access. Becoming skilled at a task means shifting from attentional to automatic processing (e.g. Schneider & Shiffrin, 1977).

Think about when you learned a new skill: you should be able to trace the shift in processing modes. When I learned to drive, having to do everything at once was overwhelming, and I particularly found having to check the mirror every time I wanted to do something to be extremely difficult. I just could not coordinate releasing the clutch with shifting the gear. For some time, I was so despondent that I almost gave up, until I reminded myself that many millions of people managed without difficulty. So I persevered, and the skill became automatic: I eventually no longer even had to think about what I was doing when changing gears. The skill became so automatic that I now occasionally find myself trying to change gears, even though I have been driving an automatic car for several years. You almost certainly have similar memories.

Although eventually we become automatic at carrying out some tasks, we must still be monitoring the environment. Though driving a car is a very complex (and dangerous) task, we can get to be so good at it that not only are we unaware that we're doing it, but we can forget the details of what we're doing. Perhaps you have had the experience of driving for some time, only to realise that your mind has been elsewhere and you can remember nothing of the drive, including how you got to your destination! Neither can you remember making any choices about the route, but nevertheless, you get where you wanted to be.

But this situation is not as dangerous as it sounds! If something untoward does happen on the drive, we can shift modes very quickly. If a child or animal suddenly appears in the road, or a car in front does something unexpected, we will respond extremely quickly. So, although our minds appear to be elsewhere, we are still monitoring the world and can respond appropriately. This ability is the same as what is called the *cocktail party effect*: you are at a noisy party paying rapt attention to the charming person talking to you, and in the distance you hear someone else mentioning your name. Suddenly, you pay attention to what is happening across the room. Having said that, there is a cost associated with paying too much attention to the non-automatic task: it is widely known that drivers are more likely to have accidents when using a cell phone, but simply talking or even just listening to music can raise the rate of accidents, particularly with novice drivers (Brodsky & Slor, 2013).

So, although there is a great deal of material outside of awareness, we are processing this material to some considerable depth. We will return to this topic in the chapter on cognition and consciousness.

Psychological Compulsions

It isn't just parts of the body that are sometimes outside our control. People with *obsessive-compulsive disorder* (*OCD*) are compelled to carry out actions 'against their will', such as repetitively washing their hands, or performing complex rituals. People with OCD fight against their obsessive thinking, but, however much they might want to stop acting or thinking about something, they find it extremely difficult to do so (Fornaro et al., 2009; Schwartz, 2017). OCD is a wide-ranging disorder, and, as with other such disorders, the causes are complex. Imaging studies show abnormal activation in several parts of the brain, including the **orbito-frontal cortex (OFC)**, the **anterior cingulate cortex**, and the **caudate nucleus (CN)**, in response to images associated with the obsessions. Tellingly, we will meet these structures again several times in our search for the seat of consciousness (see Figure 3.9). There is also a strong inherited component to the disorder (Fornaro et al., 2009). Obsessive thoughts take many forms, and may merge with compulsions: for example, a person might think about disease and becoming ill, and that compels the person to perform the act of repetitive hand washing. The key point though is that our mind can have thoughts against our will.

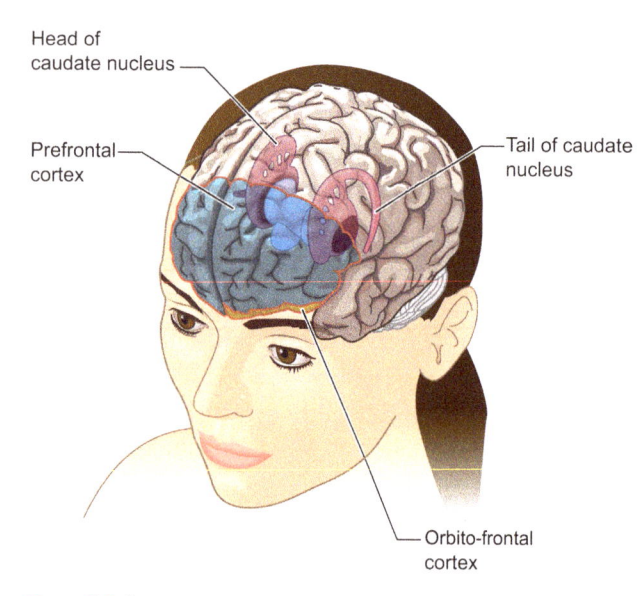

Figure 3.9 Brain circuitry involved in obsessive-compulsive disorder (OCD). People with OCD feel compelled to think or act against their will.

Chapter Summary

- Free will is the sense we have that we are choosing to act when we do.
- We think we can choose to lift a finger when we want; we can choose to study or go to work now if we want; we can choose to do nothing at all. We have free will.
- Most scientists believe we live in a deterministic universe, at least at the level of decision making and events influencing our behaviour, which means that every action is determined by prior events.
- Free will libertarians (not to be confused with political libertarians) keep free will and reject determinism, but theirs is a minority view.
- Compatibilism attempts to reconcile free will with a deterministic universe.

REVIEW QUESTIONS

- Quantum mechanics doesn't provide any escape from the illusion of free will because quantum effects only operate at a very small level; at the physical level every event is still determined.
- Most philosophers conclude that our sense of free will must be an illusion.
- Our behaviour is determined by our genes, our history, and our environment.
- There is a construct that appears to think that it has free will – the 'I'.
- This 'inner person' making a decision or observing the world is called the homunculus.
- The multisensory screen on which the world is portrayed and which the homunculus watches and acts upon is called the Cartesian theatre.
- Dennett and others reject the analogy of the Cartesian theatre because of problems with the homunculus and infinite regress.
- Small things in our environment, such as some parasites or social priming, can have big influences on our behaviour without our knowledge.
- Many feel that conscious control is an illusion but a necessary one because it helps us tell a story about our lives and is essential for developing a sense of responsibility and morality.
- If people do not have free will, perhaps they are not really responsible for their actions, and therefore perhaps criminals should not be punished.
- People with antisocial personality disorder show brain abnormalities resulting from the interaction of genes and environment; and it is arguable whether this disorder merits punishment.
- Deciding to act, even just deciding to make a small motor movement, takes time, and brain activity associated with making that decision is apparent before we are conscious of the decision.
- Alien hand syndrome is the feeling that a hand does not belong to the person and moves against the person's wishes; it results from brain damage disconnecting the motor cortex from other regions of the brain involved in control and planning.
- There are occasions when we move without conscious control, and also when we have thoughts that we do not want to have.
- When we are first learning a new skill, we find it very difficult to be conscious of anything other than the task at hand, but as we become more adept, the skill becomes automated.
- Automatisation involves repeated practice of the task, and involves many regions of the brain, including the deep-brain structures.
- When we are addicted to some stimulus or even when we have formed a habit, we may act without apparent control.
- People with obsessive-compulsive disorder can even be said to be acting against their will.

Review Questions

1. Why does quantum mechanics not provide any escape from determinism when considering free will?

2. Most people have the sense of there being an 'I' in our heads that observes the world and makes decisions about our next actions. What is wrong with this folk view?
3. How successful is compatibilism at dealing with the problems associated with free will?
4. If you don't have free will, why does everyone think they do?
5. Is it right to punish a psychopath?
6. We think that when we act we make a decision and execute that decision. What does neuroscience tell us about this description?
7. What are alien and anarchic hand syndromes, and why are they important in consciousness research?
8. Can you avoid answering this question?

Recommended Resources

Overall
Kane, R. (2011). *The Oxford Handbook of Free Will* (2nd ed.). Oxford, UK: Oxford University Press.

Free Will and Determinism
Baggini, J. (2015). *Freedom Regained: The Possibility of Free Will*. London: Granta.
Baron, P. (2016). *Free Will and Determinism* (2nd ed.). Scotts Valley, CA: CreateSpace.
Mele, A.R. (2014). *Free: Why Science Hasn't Disproved Free Will*. Oxford, UK: Oxford University Press.
Harris, S. (2012). *Free Will*. New York, NY: Free Press.
Dennett, D.C. (2004). *Freedom Evolves*. Harmondsworth, UK: Penguin.

Neuroethics
Fallon, J. (2013). *The Psychopath Inside*. New York, NY: Current Books.
Farah, M.J. (ed.) (2010). *Neuroethics: An Introduction with Readings*. Cambridge, MA: MIT Press.
Illes, J., and Sahakian, B.J. (2011). *The Oxford Handbook of Neuroethics*. Oxford, UK: Oxford University Press.

Deciding to Act
Libet, B. (2005). *Mind Time: The Temporal Factor in Consciousness*. Harvard, MA: Harvard University Press.
Sinnott-Armstrong, W., and Nadel, L. (2010). *Conscious Will and Responsibility: A Tribute to Benjamin Libet*. Cambridge, MA: Oxford University Press.
Wegner, D.M. (2003). *The Illusion of Conscious Will*. Cambridge, MA: MIT Press.

Involuntary Actions
Duhigg, C. (2013). *The Power of Habit: Why We Do What We Do, and How to Change*. New York: Random House.

4 MACHINE CONSCIOUSNESS

Are humans the only things that can be conscious? There is no obvious reason why it should be so; it is possible that there are conscious aliens elsewhere in the universe, perhaps worrying about just the same things as we are right now, wondering if they are the only conscious beings around. But any aliens are a long way away, so what about other things nearer to home? There are two candidates for other things that might be conscious: animals and computers (including robots).

The next two chapters examine whether consciousness is restricted to living things, and this chapter focuses on artificial beings – computers and robots. We begin by looking at computer simulations of key aspects of life, asking what it is about life that is so distinctive. Of course being alive isn't the same as being conscious, so we next look at artificial intelligence. Presumably some minimal level of intelligence is a prerequisite of consciousness. In particular, we look at the idea of general intelligence, as opposed to *domain-specific expert systems*, which can answer questions about narrow domains of knowledge, such as medicine or law. We then consider the importance of motion and interacting with the environment in our consideration of robotics. We conclude the chapter with an examination of attempts to construct brains and brain-like systems, and the effects on our consciousness of augmenting our biological selves.

It is difficult to answer questions such as 'is this robot conscious?' when we are unclear about what consciousness is; one advantage of examining consciousness in other domains, such as technology or animals, is that it helps us to focus on the nature of consciousness.

The idea of highly intelligent and indeed conscious computers is an important meme in science fiction, including the cinema. We can learn a great deal about what people think of consciousness by examining how it is reflected in art. The possibility of consciousness in computers and robots is often taken for granted, although the behaviour of these beings in the arts is frequently strange, and often threatening.

Artificial Life

What is life? Although like consciousness the boundaries are a little fuzzy (Is a virus alive? Is a prion, a misfolded protein, responsible for some neurological diseases such as 'mad cow disease', alive?), most researchers agree that something is alive if it is self-organising, self-perpetuating, and exhibits the capacity for growth and reproduction.

There have been several well-documented attempts to recreate aspects of living organisms, a fairly recent discipline known as *artificial life* (often abbreviated to *A-life*), named in 1986 by one of its most eminent practitioners, the American computer scientist Christopher Langton. The emphasis in modelling artificial life is on learning about the systems of life, at all levels, by building lifelike systems. There is often particular emphasis on evolution, or on how complex systems evolved from a small number of simple constraints. The field of A-life divides into software-based approaches and approaches using hardware (robots of some sort). None of the computer simulations developed so far comes close to doing anything that might be considered conscious, although, to be fair, it is not their primary aim. However, some of the ideas involved, such as evolution and complexity, might turn out to be important for understanding and possibly creating consciousness. The most important idea that comes from A-life research is that self-organisation is a relatively simple process that can emerge from a small number of low-level constraints.

The word *autopoiesis* is sometimes used to refer to a system capable of reproducing and maintaining itself, two characteristics of life. The term is often used as a synonym of self-organisation, with the cell being the most prominent example of an autopoietic system.

Figure 4.1 A flock of starlings (*Sturnus vulgaris*). A flock of starlings behaving in this way in flight is called a murmuration, and can produce complex and beautiful displays. Source: Fiona Elisabeth Exon/Moment/Getty Images.

One early topic was how animals such as birds and fish flock (or swarm) together. Animals form tight flocks primarily for safety: it is more difficult for a single predator to pick off an individual animal when many are grouped tightly together. There are many advantages of safety in numbers, including making it easier to find sources of food and spot predators, but we are concerned here with *flocking* in motion. Flocks serve many functions but in motion are primarily a means of a defence against predators (see Figure 4.1). When birds flock it is sometimes as though the group of birds has a collective intelligence; the flock appears to move as one thing. One of the earliest animal flocking simulations was the program boids (Reynolds, 1987), designed to model the flocking behaviour of birds (although the same principles might be applied to any creatures that flock or swarm). The program simulates birds as very simple creatures, or agents, each of which just applies three simple and uncontroversial rules (see Figure 4.2):

Separation – maintain enough distance from your neighbours to ensure that you don't fly into any of them.
Cohesion – move towards the centre of the flock.
Alignment – move towards the average direction of the flock.

If each 'boid' follows these rules, the behaviour of the simulated flock looks very like behaviour of a real flock of birds, and mimics how the flock seems to move as one. Note that no agent has been told about the behaviour of the flock at the larger scale; each agent just knows how to fly relative to its neighbours – the rules act locally. The complex behaviour, flocking, is said to emerge from the interaction of many simple entities following a few simple local rules.

Alvarez-Rodriguez et al. (2018) describe simulating life in a *quantum computer*. Quantum computers, still in a very early stage of development, use the principles of quantum mechanics to carry out computation at a much faster rate than is possible with transistor-based computers. They used an IBM QX4 to show how genetic evolution and replication could be implemented using *qubits* (the quantum computing analogue of bits), which 'organism' was represented by two qubits. Features of the genetic makeup are inherited through generations of these quantum individuals. Here the distinction between simulating life and implementing life is rather murky. If the simulation shows all these qualities, in what way is it not life? Although this research is at an early stage, it opens the way to showing the possible involvement of quantum mechanics in life.

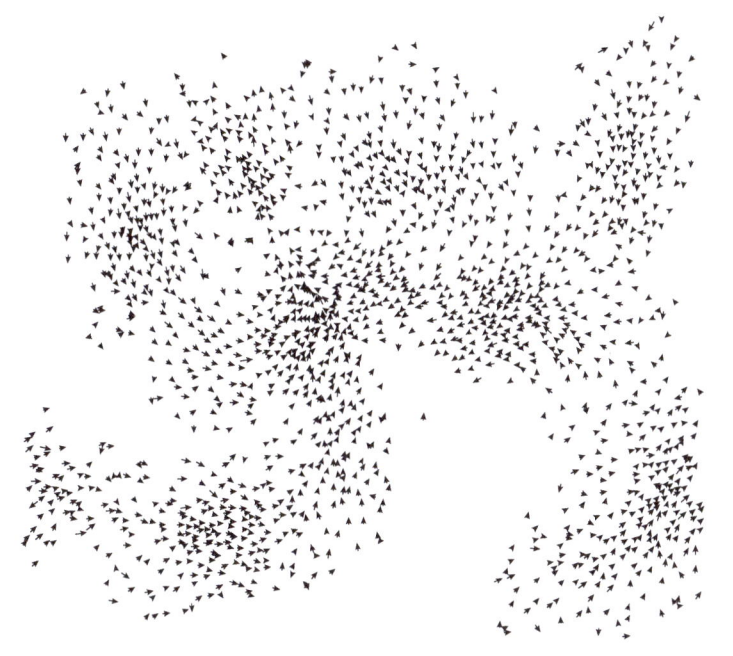

Figure 4.2 The boids simulation. Complex flocking behaviour emerges from three simple rules called separation, cohesion, and alignment.

Are these computer programs life or just simulations of life? They demonstrate some self-organisation but not self-perpetuation – but they illustrate some important principles, particularly the idea of *emergence*, an important idea we will look at in more detail in Chapter 8.

> **TRY THIS: Rules for Being a Bee**
>
> Honey bees are swarm insects, along with other examples, such as ants and locusts. Their lives are not limited to swarming, however, as they have to find food in the form of pollen, collect it in their pollen baskets, take it back to the hive, unload it, and tell other bees about the source of particularly rich nectar by the means of their well-known waggle dance. Although each bee can be considered a small, simple unit with limited individual intelligence, the hive as a whole exhibits complex behaviour. Write a small number of local rules that might determine the behaviour of an individual worker bee.

Artificial Intelligence

Could a computer ever be conscious? Sitting in front of my laptop, smart as it is, this proposition seems a ridiculous one. However, estimates by experts of when a computer will first exceed the intelligence of a human scatter around a surprisingly, alarmingly even, close date. Bostrom (2014) discussed surveys of computing experts about when computers were likely to achieve *human-level machine intelligence*, defined as 'one that can carry out most human professions at least as well as a typical human'. In 2014, the median estimate was 2040 (with the median being at least 50% of the experts thinking it will be achieved by that date). Around 10% think it will happen by 2022, and 90% by 2075.

One reason to be sceptical about these dates is that the history of **artificial intelligence (AI)** is littered with optimistic predictions and enthusiastic claims. Artificial intelligence is a self-explanatory term, coined by the computer scientist John McCarthy in 1956: it means getting computers to carry out tasks that require intelligence on the part of humans. Note that the computer does not have to do the task in the same way that humans do. Early AI research focused on *expert systems*, where a body of knowledge could be codified and interrogated to mimic or replace human experts, and problem solving, using conventional computer programming languages, particularly Lisp. Expert systems were domain-specific codifications of fields of knowledge, such as medicine or law, and comprised a database of knowledge and an inference engine for finding an appropriate answer to a question. An early example is the expert system MYCIN (Gorry et al., 1973), which answered questions about bacterial infections.

It is useful to distinguish between the pursuit of AI as technology (getting computers to do smart things regardless of how) and as science (using AI to understand human intelligence), without any presupposition that one is better than the other, and acknowledging that there is much crosstalk between the two approaches. Just because an expert system such as MYCIN doesn't answer a question about bacterial infection in the way a human does doesn't make it worthless; in fact, expert systems have many advantages, such as 'knowing' many more things, not being subject to bias when answering, and not forgetting critical information. It is also useful to distinguish between symbolic AI, which emphasises symbolic computation, where programs manipulate symbols representing something, from more general AI, which includes the study of neural networks and non-symbolic learning.

The Timeline of Progress in AI

In the early optimistic days of AI, Simon and Newell (1968) made five predictions (actually made in 1967) about computers that they expected to be fulfilled within 10 years.

1. A digital computer will be the world's chess champion (unless they are banned from competing).
2. A digital computer will discover and prove an important new mathematical theorem.
3. A digital computer will write music that will be accepted as having considerable aesthetic value.
4. Most theories in psychology will take the form of a computer program.

None of these came to pass within 10 years. How close were they?

1. A computer beat the world chess champion first in 1996; see the next section for details.
2. The first major mathematical theorem to be proved by computer was the four-colour theorem (the idea that you don't need more than four colours to complete a map without

any 'country' touching another with the same colour along a line (Appel & Haken, 1977; see Figure 4.3)). But this problem was long-standing, with the initial conjecture made by Francis Guthrie while trying to colour a map of the counties of England in 1852. Computers are now routinely used for checking mathematical proofs and constructing some (although these proofs are not without critics, one important objection being that many proofs are not verifiable by humans, and another being that they are not elegant in the sense of providing new insights). However, a computer-assisted proof is not the same as generating a novel interesting theorem, and there is no consensus that computers have come anywhere close to achieving this target.

Figure 4.3 Four-colour map of the United States. It was long believed that the maximum number of colours necessary to colour a map was four, but it needed computer assistance to prove it. Source: bergserg/DigitalVision Vectors/Getty Images.

3. Whether music or art is aesthetically valuable is a very subjective matter – some people love atonal music or expressionist art, others loathe them. Computers have generated music and art that pass for human-generated music art, but it is only recently that people have considered the artworks merit worthy (see Figure 4.4). Whether these creations have any artistic depth, or are truly comparable to art produced by humans, is debatable. But we can conclude, perhaps generously, that yes, computers can do these things, although it took more like 40 years than 10 to be any good at them, in the sense of many people finding them aesthetically pleasing. I'm listening to some computer-generated music right now, and I don't really like it. Somehow it doesn't sound very musical and it's somehow just not very good.

4. There were computer models of intelligent behaviour in the 1960s and '70s but it is doubtful whether they contributed much to our understanding of psychology. Examples include Winograd's (1972) BLOCKSWORLD program modelling language understanding; while technically impressive, most would say it didn't capture anything about psychological processes, and perhaps didn't really understand anything at all (see below for further detail). Many psychologists would probably say that it wasn't until the advent of connectionist modelling (most notably McClelland & Rumelhart, 1981) that computer programs began to express theories. Computational psychology has become highly influential, if not dominant, in cognitive psychology at least.

Figure 4.4 An example of computer-generated algorithmic art, Composition #72 by Patrick Gunderson. Aesthetics are subjective, but I think this one is rather good, comparable with the best of (human) expressionist art. What's your opinion? Source: Image supplied by artist.

> **TRY THIS: Art for Art's Sake?**
>
> Examples of computer-generated music and visual art are easily found on the web. Give them with similar examples of human-generated music and visual art to people who don't know which is which, and see if they can distinguish them. How would you characterise the differences, if you think there are any?

As a result of the failure of the AI to deliver quickly what had been promised or expected, funding for AI research dried up in the early 1970s and periodically again in the 1980s and '90s, times known as AI winters (contrasted with AI summers, when funding was easily available). In the UK, arguments within the AI community as to the best way forward led to a review of AI research that culminated with the 1973 Lighthill report, which all but ended government funding for AI for several years.

Chess-playing Computers

The game of chess has long been considered to be a benchmark of the achievements of computer intelligence. Chess requires a combination of planning, evaluation, logic, and foresight, is widely played across the world, and is a very complex game but with a few simple very well-defined rules. Chess-playing expertise has long been considered a mark of intelligence. Early in the history of AI there was optimism that computers would soon beat humans. Although, as we have seen, Simon and Newell (1958) predicted that a digital computer would be world chess champion within 10 years, it took considerably longer for computers to reach that level of performance. In 1968, the international chess master (a very strong player) David Levy bet that no computer would be able to beat him within 10 years, a bet he won. (He eventually lost to one in 1989.)

Dedicated chess computers started to be of the same level as competent chess players in the 1980s, but even at that time it was unclear whether they would ever be able to beat exceptionally strong players, known as grandmasters. In 1989, the computer Deep Thought beat the grandmaster Bent Larsen under chess tournament conditions. In Philadelphia, in February 1996, the IBM computer Deep Blue beat Garry Kasparov at chess (see Figure 4.5). The event was notable because it was the first time a computer had defeated a reigning chess champion under chess tournament conditions. Kasparov went on to defeat Big Blue in a six-game match 4–2 (Deep Blue picking up the win and two draws), but a year later in a rematch in New York an updated Deep Blue defeated Kasparov 3 ½ – 2 ½, Deep Blue winning twice. The victory was widely reported and discussed, being seen as hugely symbolic for the advances in AI. (There is a possibility that the first defeat occurred because Kasparov's confidence was shaken, mistaking a move resulting from a bug in the chess program as Deep Thought, and Kasparov was generally suspicious that the computer might be receiving human help (a suggestion IBM strongly denied; Silver, 2012).)

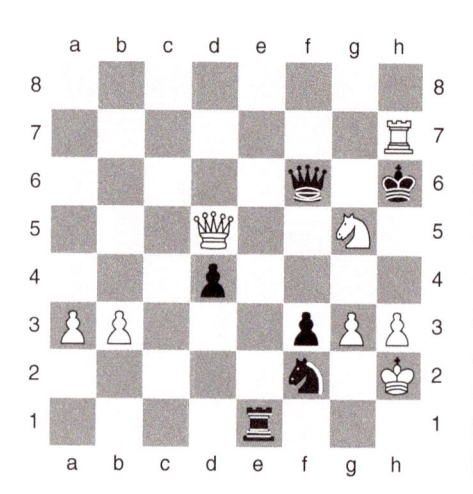

Figure 4.5 Deep Blue v. Kasparov (1996 match, Game 1). The diagram shows the final position, after which with Kasparov lost.

Deep Blue was a supercomputer, with a specialist program running on specialist hardware, but with the progress of time ordinary commercial chess programs running on regular desktop computers became increasingly powerful. In 2002, Deep Fritz drew a series of eight games 4–4 with the reigning world champion Vladimir Kramnik, with Kramnik losing two games. There are two different approaches to reasoning, and both are used by humans in playing chess. An **algorithm** is a routine that follows a rule or series of rules; for example, putting a particular value into a formula such as

$$f(x) = 2x + 1$$

will always deliver the same, correct answer. An algorithmic approach to playing chess is brute force: you examine every possible move and every possible reply and then every possible reply to that reply, and perhaps so on. The problem with brute force is that the number of possibilities grows exponentially, and even for today's computers the number of combinations will be overwhelming, and impossible for a human. Hence humans rely much less on brute force (although a book like Kotov's (1971) *Think Like a Grandmaster* emphasises the importance of calculation in chess mastery at a high level) and more on general guidelines, called **heuristics**, such as in chess 'castle early', 'don't move the pawns in front of your king unnecessarily', and 'centralise your rooks'.

Deep Blue used specially designed computer chips to play by brute force, purely algorithmically, evaluating about 100 million positions a second, searching about 7 moves deep (or 14 *ply* as we say, 7 turns for each player), and to 20 moves deep in some positions (Hsu, 2002). Chess programs no longer rely merely on brute force, now also using heuristics, tables of information about endgame positions, 'books' about opening knowledge, and databases of games that help evaluate positions (Greenemeier, 2017). In general, the way in which positions are evaluated has advanced. Now brute force is too strong for humans to be able to see far enough ahead. Computers are so powerful compared to the human mind in this respect that chess computers no longer need dedicated hardware. From 2005 on, chess programs running on desktop and laptop computers, and even smartphones, have been able to defeat extremely strong players quite routinely. In 2006, Deep Fritz, running on an ordinary desktop computer, beat Kramnik in a six-game match. These days apps running on smartphones will win. As Eschner (2017) puts it, 'the search for a computer that can beat even the best at chess was only really interesting between 1994, when computers were too weak, and 2004, when they got too strong'.

More recently, AlphaZero is a chess-playing program developed by DeepMind, a UK AI company acquired by Google in 2014. DeepMind specialises in developing neural networks, resembling the structure of the brain more than traditional computer programs, that learn (see below for more detail). AlphaZero learns to play chess and improves by learning from its mistakes – by playing against itself. After nine hours of training, AlphaZero was beating Stockfish 8, a 'conventional' chess program, although of course the hardware AlphaZero uses is extremely powerful. Chess grandmasters have commented on the power and style of AlphaZero, noting that it appears to display deep positional understanding with highly aggressive attacking play (Sadler & Regan, 2019; Silver et al., 2018).

These feats might be an impressive sign of computer power, but no one would argue that they are indicative of general intelligence, let alone any marker of consciousness. They have chiselled away at one small part of our conception of ourselves as special, but they have changed chess greatly. Grandmasters use chess programs for developing opening lines and training, and analysis has created many novelties (Rowson, 2019).

> **Box 4.1 Computer Beats Human**
>
> For those of you who know chess and chess algebraic notation, here is Game 1 of the 1996 match between Deep Blue (playing white) and Garry Kasparov, the reigning world champion. It was the first game to be won by a computer against a world champion under standard tournament conditions and time controls (40 moves by each player in 2 hours).
>
> 1.e4 c5 2.c3 d5 3.exd5 Qxd5 4.d4 Nf6 5.Nf3 Bg4 6.Be2 e6 7.h3 Bh5 8.0–0 Nc6 9.Be3 cxd4 10.cxd4 Bb4 11.a3 Ba5 12.Nc3 Qd6 13.Nb5 Qe7 14.Ne5 Bxe2 15.Qxe2 0–0 16.Rac1 Rac8 17.Bg5 Bb6 18.Bxf6 gxf6 19.Nc4 Rfd8 20.Nxb6 axb6 21.Rfd1 f5 22.Qe3 Qf6 23.d5 Rxd5 24.Rxd5 exd5 25.b3 Kh8 26.Qxb6 Rg8 27.Qc5 d4 28.Nd6 f4 29.Nxb7 Ne5 30.Qd5 f3 31.g3 Nd3 32.Rc7 Re8 33.Nd6 Re1+ 34.Kh2 Nxf2 35.Nxf7+ Kg7 36.Ng5+ Kh6 37.Rxh7+ 1–0
>
> Black resigned because he has to play Kg6 and then white has too many simultaneous threats.
>
> Computers playing in a two-player game usually use what is called a minimax algorithm to evaluate a search tree built up of all the legal moves in a position, with each position in the search tree receiving a score; the algorithm then selects the move that maximises the goodness of the end position for them. At the start of the game white has 20 possible moves, as does black in reply, so there are already 400 possible positions after the first pair of moves (a search depth of just 2). There are over 70 000 positions after two moves each, over nine million positions after three moves, and over 280 billion different possible positions after just four moves each. That is why if you're going to evaluate every position you need powerful computers and good evaluation algorithms. There are means of reducing the search space: alpha–beta pruning stops evaluating a move as soon as it is shown to be weaker than the previously considered move. Humans rarely use mental brute force to solve anything, which is good because we're not really very good at it.

The Turing Test

If we have a really smart computer, how could we tell if it is conscious or not? One famous test for the abilities of a computer is the **Turing test**, proposed by the British computer scientist Alan Turing (1912–1954, famous for his work on the Enigma machine and usually held to be the originator of computer science and AI; see Figure 4.6). Turing proposed that, to be deemed intelligent, a machine should show behaviour indistinguishable from that of a human. In practice, this means that a human listening to or looking at the output of a computer would not be able to tell what comes from a person and what comes from a machine.

The problem with the Turing test is that intelligent behaviour is easy to mimic and people are easy to fool. Several very basic computer programs have appeared to be able to trick some people into believing that they are dealing with a person at the other end of a computer terminal (as it was then). One of the most famous was Joseph Weizenbaum's (1966) program ELIZA. ELIZA simulated a Rogerian psychotherapist (named after the psychologist Carl Rogers, who developed a person-centred therapy where the therapist unconditionally empathises with the patient, often by reflecting back what they have said) simply by identifying a few key words in the input provided by the human, applying a few simple rules to transform the syntax (e.g. Turning YOU into I), and equipped with a few stock phrases, in a program just a few hundred lines long. Here is a sample of an interaction between a human and the program.

Figure 4.6 Alan Turing (1912–1954). The British mathematician and pioneer computer scientist whose early electromechanical machines helped crack the Enigma code in World War II. The Turing machine is an abstract model of a general-purpose computer. Turing's work is considered essential for the development of the electronic computer and artificial intelligence. Source: Heritage Images/Hulton Archive/Getty Images.

chatbots because the humans know that the programs are not conscious, or are not real people; there are things you might not feel bad about telling a computer program that you would like to keep even from your therapist.

Of course, being intelligent is a far cry from being conscious, but the idea of the Turing test is easily extendable to consciousness: a computer is doing a very good job of appearing to be conscious if we can't distinguish its output from that of a human. With smart computers we face the same problems as with other human minds – we will never be able to be sure that a computer is conscious, just confident beyond a point of reasonable doubt. There might be a future world inhabited by humans and intelligent robots, and some humans think the robots are conscious, whereas others don't. For some people, the 'conscious' robots are really simply zombies.

> **TRY THIS:** Finding the Computer Program
>
> What questions would you ask to show that ELIZA is a computer program and not a person? Consider only honest respondents, and so ignore the possibility that a person is trying to pretend to be ELIZA.

> **TRY THIS:** Chatbot
>
> Find a chatbot online. The answers to which questions suggest you're not talking to a human? How would you characterise these sorts of questions more generally?

Early AI Models of Psychology

One of the first topics to be approached by AI researchers was language. The idea was to make an interface for computers of the sort we now see with Alexa and Siri. Inputting data and programs into early computers was time consuming and cumbersome, relying on pieces of card with holes punched in them. The work of Noam Chomsky (e.g. 1957), which showed how a limited number of syntactic rules could give rise to an infinite number of sentences resonated with programming language. This linguistic progress contributed to the optimism that psychological processes could be seen as computation and therefore codified in a computer language.

One of the earliest and most influential computer models of an aspect of cognitive processing was a simulation of language comprehension by Terry Winograd at MIT called SHRDLU (Winograd, 1972). The name came from ETAOIN SHRDLU, letters arranged in descending frequency of usage in English and as arranged on some computer keyboards of the time. The simulation operated on a very limited domain – a *microworld* – called BLOCKSWORLD, so called because it comprised simple geometric objects such as large blue block and green pyramids (see Figure 4.7). The program could keep track of simple commands such as putting green pyramids on top of large red blocks. It would also give simple replies, such as 'OK', 'I can't', and 'I'm not sure what you mean by "on top of"'; note that in doing so it uses a set of templates of likely necessary replies rather than generating each reply from syntactic rules. Nevertheless, the accomplishments of SHRDLU were impressive: it maintained a representation of the scene so that it knew where every object was, with some background knowledge such as pyramids can't be put on other pyramids (they're not stable), and that if you had a blue block on top of a red block and were told to put the green pyramid directly on top of the red block you would have to take the blue block off first.

Although at the time SHRDLU was considered an impressive demonstration of the power of AI, it was very limited.

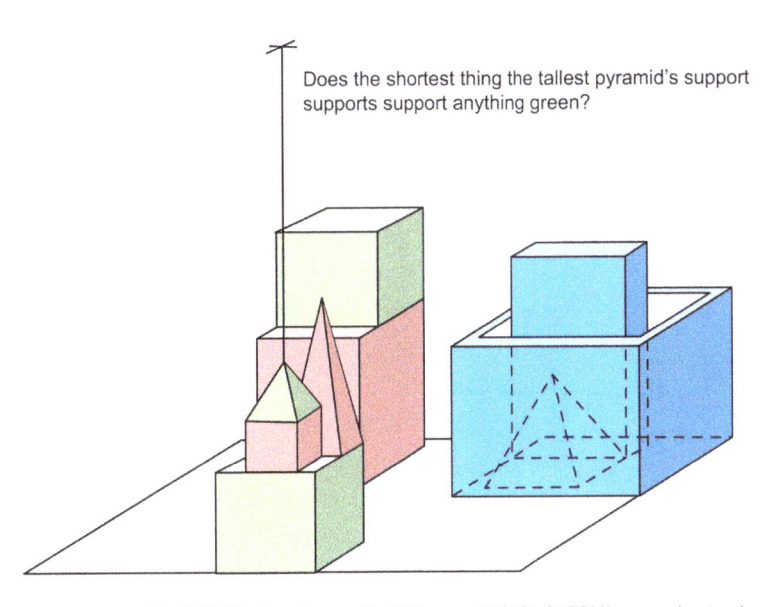

Figure 4.7 BLOCKSWORLD, the microworld of Winograd (1972). SHRDLU can understand questions (shown) and follow instructions to manipulate items in the microworld.

The program could only 'talk' about the object in BLOCKSWORLD; if you asked it about putting a cat on top of a chair, it would be lost. It didn't really understand language in the sense of working out the full syntax of a sentence and assigning word meanings, and it didn't generate sentences using the sort of mechanisms humans do. In summary, SHRDLU was very restricted in what it could do. Ask it about whether dogs have legs and it would be lost.

Such programs illustrated a deeper problem with AI, at least with approaches where the knowledge in the program is supplied or 'hard wired' by humans: they only knew what they have been told, or can work out by making inferences based on what they had been told. You might say the same is true of us, but we know an awful lot; and potentially virtually anything for all that we know can be brought to bear on interpreting a particular statement (Dreyfus, 1992). This problem has been called the *background knowledge problem* or the *frame problem*. It is not easy to abstract features of the world to give effective performance in a microworld because the amount of relevant background information is potentially huge. Humans are different from coded programs because we have developed in the world and have learned over a long period of time. Note that this comparison isn't an argument against all AI, just AI models of a certain sort, those pursued by researchers until fairly recently. Nor is it an argument against the usefulness of these models in what they are trying to do, simply that many of them tell us little about psychology and nothing about consciousness.

How Smart Are Computers Now?

Computers are already smarter than humans in some fields. From the earliest days they have been better at arithmetic computation – that after all is why they were built in the first place. But what about more complex skills? Another milestone was reached in March 2016 when Google's program AlphaGo beat the South Korean Go grandmaster Lee Se-Dol 4–1. The game Go is seen as even more difficult than chess because of its complexity and very large number of possible positions, the computational complexity making it very hard for a computer to succeed at merely by brute computational force. Whereas Deep Blue relied on more or less brute computational force (in addition to a database of chess openings), AlphaGo also uses algorithms that enable it to learn as it plays.

The narrower the field of ability under consideration, the easier it is to specify what constitutes good performance, and the more likely it is a computer will be good at it. Most computer programs are currently bad at generalising. A chess program will be unable to play Go without some modification, and to simulate an accountant carrying out financial tasks requires a completely different program. Humans can switch between tasks, and computers currently cannot, but there is no reason why in principle they shouldn't. The pace of development in hardware at least is very fast. Moore's law states that the number of transistors in an integrated circuit doubles every two years or so, and hence the power of hardware has been increasing exponentially; whether this rate of growth can be sustained, of course, remains to be seen. The American futurologist Ray Kurzweil talks about the accelerating trend in technological development (see Figure 4.8).

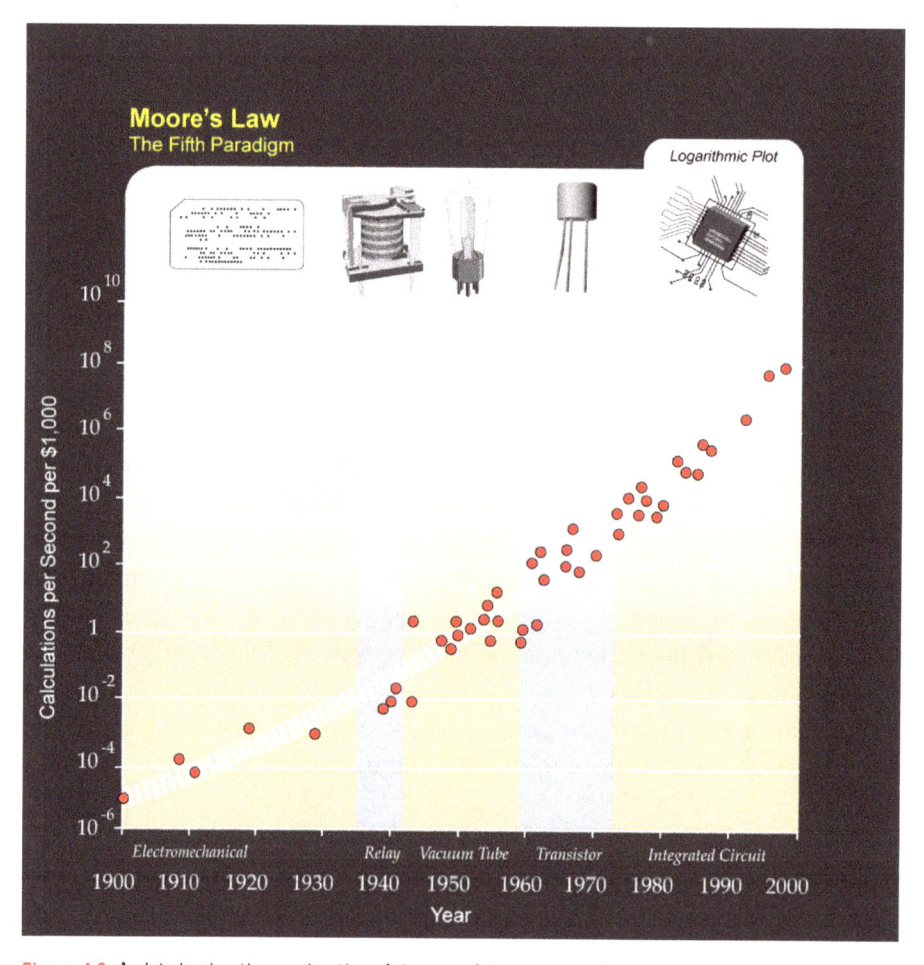

Figure 4.8 A plot showing the acceleration of the rate of development of important cultural and technological events. The times they are a-changin' – faster and faster and faster. Source: Courtesy of Ray Kurzweil and Kurzweil Technologies, Inc. Creative Commons Attribution 1.0 Generic license. Based on Kurzweil (2005).

ARTIFICIAL INTELLIGENCE

One recent trend in computing is the use of techniques based on *deep learning*, where instead of being explicitly supplied with explicit algorithms to solve problems or with knowledge pre-programmed in a database, programs learn information by extracting statistical regularities from large data sets supplied to them. After all, human children are not explicitly taught everything they know; they acquire it from the environment. Deep learning enables computers to learn abstract representations in complex tasks such as speech and object recognition, and is applied to creative areas such as discovering new drugs (LeCun et al., 2015).

Deep learning also means that it is no longer simply true that you only get out of computers what you put in. That once was true, but now many programs can learn. Deep learning is based on an approach called *neural networks* (*connectionism* in psychology), which involves the interaction of many very simple, neuron-like units; these networks can learn and generalise, and operate far more like how the brain works. Approaches involving learning are more promising for understanding consciousness than traditional, 'good old-fashioned' AI.

It is debatable whether these learning algorithms should be seen as 'intelligent' because they simply give a classification based on a statistical prediction learned from data; they have no idea what they are doing, or why, and have no flexibility. In any case, intelligence alone does not make us conscious, and neither does raw computing power. A computer is most unlikely to become conscious just because it has more transistors. The key question is: what is necessary above intelligence and computing power to make a computer conscious? Or maybe, no matter however powerful, no computer could ever be conscious.

The Computational Correlates of Consciousness

The term *computational correlates of consciousness* (analogous to the neural correlates of consciousness) was coined by Mathis and Mozer in 1995. These models seek to understand the processing differences between conscious and conscious systems, and ask what the computational utility of consciousness is. Quite often the proponents of these models state that explaining qualia is beyond the remit of the model. Therefore, although cognitive models are informative, they are clearly limited in being unable to explain the hard problem.

For Mathis and Mozer, computational states enter awareness if they persist for long enough, an idea similar to the neuronal workspace and information integration theories, and which Mathis and Mozer call the persistence hypothesis. They make use of ideas from connectionist modelling such as attractor networks. They show that persistent states exert a larger influence in computer simulations than do transient states.

Cleeremans (2014) focuses on computational principles that distinguish unconscious and conscious states. Representations that enter consciousness are distinguished by their stability, their strength, their persistence, or their stability. These ideas of the computational correlates of consciousness also form part of the global workspace theory.

Although the ideas of examining which sorts of cognitive processes may be important in consciousness and of using explicit computer models to explore the issues are both interesting, this type of research is at a very early stage. Reggia et al. (2016) argue for the importance of studying the computational correlates of consciousness, but conclude that we are some way from understanding them, particularly the correlates of phenomenal consciousness.

LIDA

Is it possible that a computer sitting on a desk in a room could ever become conscious, no matter how many transistors it may have or how clever its software might be? The approach to building an AI without any sensors measuring the outside world is called the *disembodied approach*.

Researchers have thought about what would be necessary for machine consciousness (Gamez, 2008). For example, Aleksander (2005) came up with the following list:

1. Depiction. The system has perceptual states that 'represent' elements of the world and their location.
2. Imagination. The system can recall parts of the world or create sensations that are like parts of the world.
3. Attention. The system is capable of selecting which parts of the world to depict or imagine.
4. Planning. The system has control over sequences of states to plan actions.
5. Emotion. The system has affective states that evaluate planned actions and determine the ensuing action.

This type of design is an example of a *top-down* construction: we specify what properties a consciousness entity should have, and then implement them. The problem is that we don't have a good enough understanding of what consciousness is to guarantee a top-down construction that will lead to the emergence of consciousness. Looking at the list above, for example, is emotion an indispensable precursor of consciousness? Or could we have beings such as the Vulcans in *Star Trek* or the Cybermen in *Doctor Who* that are completely logical and lack emotions, and yet which are still presumably conscious?

One sophisticated set of simulations for modelling cognition in a range of systems is the LIDA (Learning Intelligent Distributed Agent) environment (and its predecessor IDA) created by Stan Franklin at the University of Memphis (Baars & Franklin, 2003; Franklin et al., 2012). Franklin has developed an explicit, computational model of global workspace theory, an approach to consciousness we will cover in more detail in Chapter 8. LIDA is more of an environment for simulating models of consciousness rather than a simple model in its own accord. LIDA is a hybrid model with both symbolic and connectionist aspects. Its basis is an *atom* of cognition, based on a 10 Hz cycle, which is used to build larger cognitive representations. In each cycle, a number of psychological modules deliver an output and interact. In each cycle there is a sensing phase where there is understanding of any new input, an attention phase where the new input interacts with existing memory and the result is added to the workspace, and an action phase where appropriate learning occurs and any necessary action is prepared. The cycle is repeated as a complex model is built up. Consciousness corresponds to activity in the attention phase.

It is difficult to give more than a flavour of this sort of model in a limited space. The attention phase does not produce consciousness though, but is a model of consciousness. Such models have the great virtue of enabling the testing of assumptions and the plausibility of models by forcing people to be quite explicit about their model.

Could a Disembodied AI Ever Be Conscious?

The alternative to top-down is a *bottom-up* approach, where we start with something simple and let the environment mould its development. A parallel is to a newborn baby, which already has a sophisticated brain, but has had very little exposure to the environment (although it does have some exposure to information in the uterus, and clearly has some knowledge and skills partly programmed by its genes). The newborn may be full of possibility, but on our continuum of consciousness, it is some way beneath an older child, and possibly beneath some animals. What expands its consciousness is growth, which occurs through genetic reprogramming interacting with exposure to the environment. It's the two-way interaction with the environment that is an important and probably essential part of cognitive development. The developmental psychologist Jean Piaget (1896–1980) described how children learn by discovering discrepancies between what they expect and what they experience, and resolve these discrepancies using the processes of accommodation and assimilation – what we would now call a feedback loop (Goswami, 2007).

With humans, perception and feedback from the environment are essential for the development of sophisticated consciousness: how can you have a sense of self, for example, if you do not know that there is a distinction between you and the rest of the world, a distinction that can only be learned by interacting with the world? The importance of the body and mind being and located in the world, and interacting with it, particularly the body influencing the mind, has recently come to greater prominence in cognitive psychology, the approach being called **embodied cognition**, *situated cognition*, or *enactivism* (e.g. Noe, 2010; Wilson & Golonka, 2013).

There is no reason to suppose that a highly intelligent computer would be very different from a child, so that a disembodied AI that isn't connected to the world and that can't interact with it – perceive the world, act, and observe the effects of the action – is unlikely to be able to achieve higher levels of consciousness. If so, we have nothing to worry about from SkyNet! (Famous last words perhaps.) My guess is that the best bet for a conscious computer would be an intelligent robot capable of perception and action, and at the moment that is a long way off. I don't think we'll see a conscious robot in 2040, but that's just my 2020 guess. A lot can happen in 20 years.

One might wonder how else could it be. We could imagine how a disembodied computer could be very intelligent (we could train one to take IQ tests, for example), but it is difficult to see how such a thing could ever be conscious, reiterating the importance of the dissociation between intelligence and consciousness. There is more to being conscious than being very clever.

In summary, one possible means of producing a conscious AI is to build a super-intelligent computer, and let it perceive the world, interact with the world, move around the world, housed in a robot, and let it learn. And wait and see what happens.

There is an alternative to an actually embodied agent, and that is a virtually embodied agent. Instead of developing in and roaming around the actual world, the agent is placed within a simulated world with which it interacts virtually. Winograd's BLOCKSWORLD is a simple simulated world. For the agent to be a candidate for consciousness the simulated world would presumably have to be quite a rich world. What sort of virtual consciousness could develop in such a world, and would it be the same as actual consciousness? And if functionalism is correct, given all that matters are functional relations, wouldn't any agent be just as conscious as us? These are clearly fascinating issues, but much remains to be done on them.

Robotics

A robot is a machine controlled by a computer or equivalent that can interact with the world without the direct assistance of humans, and is able to carry out a complex sequence of actions automatically. The term comes from the Czech word 'robota', which means 'forced labour'; it was first used to denote a fictional humanoid in the 1920 play *R.U.R.* by the Czech writer Karel Čapek (1890–1938).

One of the simplest sorts of robot is a device that moves around the ground, avoiding obstacles, and comprises a sensor for detecting objects, a means of moving, a computer processor to host some kind of intelligence to process the input and to decide what to do in response, and of course some kind of power source (Winfield, 2012). Let's not underestimate the size of the problem: moving is a perhaps surprisingly complex task; humans are supremely efficient movers, and although much seems effortless, a great deal of our brain is devoted to processing movement (including a great deal of the cortex, many subcortical structures, and the **cerebellum**). Nevertheless, the intelligence necessary to sense and move is very limited. It is found in commercial robot vacuum cleaners and lawn mowers, and however impressive this technology might be, surely no one would say that these devices are conscious?

Very simple robots first appeared in the late 1930s and '40s, but commercial robots were first widely used in industry in the late 1950s and early '60s. The first of these is generally agreed to be the Unimate, a robot that took castings from an assembly line and welded them on to car bodies at the General Motors plant at Ewing Township in New Jersey in 1961. The robot was primarily a mechanical arm, and followed instructions stored on a magnetic drum. Robots are now ubiquitous in industry, the military, and healthcare, replacing humans on a range of tasks that are repetitive (assembly lines), dangerous (bomb disposal), and require great precision (medicine), not to mention cutting costs by omitting expensive human workers.

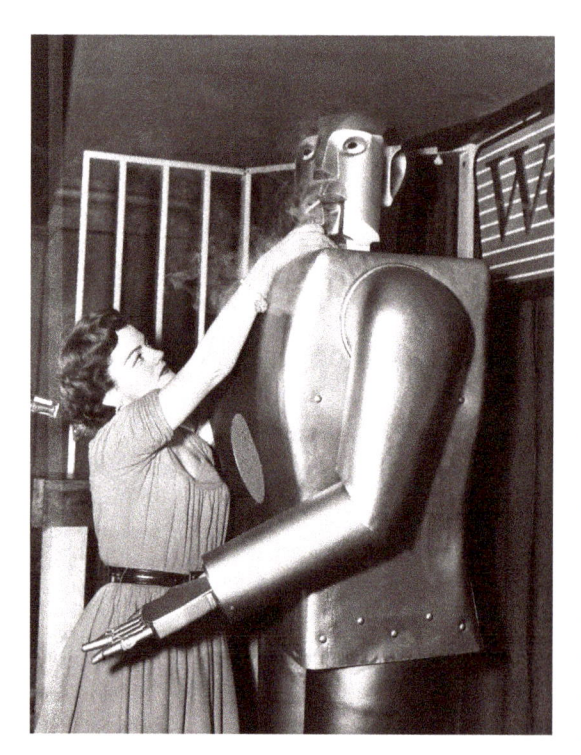

Figure 4.9 Elektro the smoking robot. Of course, he had no robotic lungs to worry about. Source: Bettmann/Getty Images.

Many industrial robots look nothing like us, but robots in humanoid form have captured our imagination and countless have appeared on television, in film, and in advertising (see Figure 4.9). Examples include *Metropolis* (a 1927 movie by Fritz Lang), the Terminators in the franchise of the same name, and Data in *Star Trek: The Next Generation*. Many of these robots have personalities, and some have emotions (at least in the case of Data, when he was given an emotion chip upgrade; eventually though he had the chip removed).

There are a number of reasons for adopting a humanoid form for highly intelligent robots. First, it is a good form, as evolution has demonstrated, suited to a range of tasks. Indeed, it's difficult to imagine evolution coming up with a radically different form for organisms capable of locomotion with several senses and hands. Although we have our design flaws (we are at a high risk of choking, for example, because of the proximity of the oesophagus and trachea), it is difficult to imagine any highly intelligent, indeed conscious, life form looking radically different from us. It is no coincidence that many aliens in fiction generally have humanoid form (see Box 4.2). Second, research shows that we are most comfortable interacting with forms that are similar to us. CRONOS is a robot built in a collaboration between the Universities of Essex and Bristol in the UK, particularly by Rob Knight. CRONOS has a humanoid design, with two arms and legs, torso, head, and one eye. As the constructors point out, although the robot is built with the biological principles of the design of the musculoskeletal system in mind, the biggest problem with making it look more human is skin (see Figure 4.10).

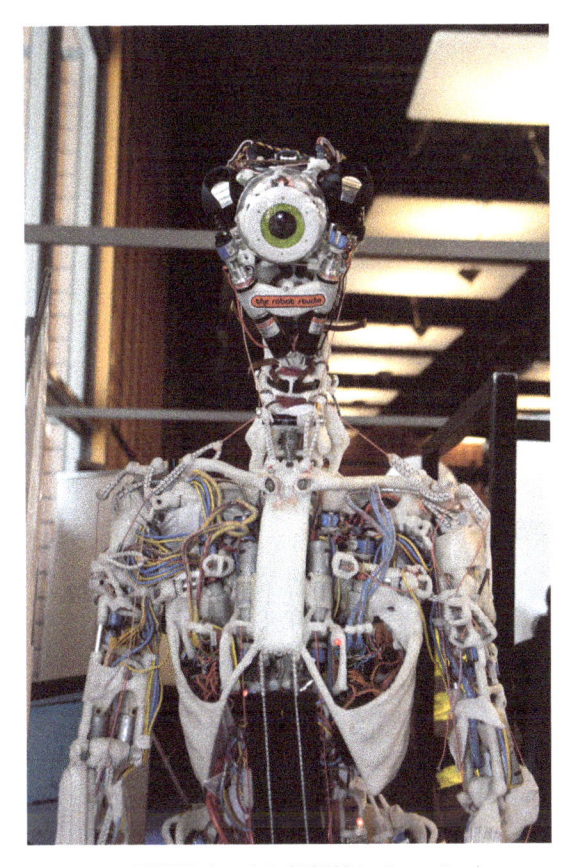

Figure 4.10 CRONOS the robot. CRONOS is also pretty close to everyone's idea of what a robot should look like, but there's no danger of mistaking it for a human. Source: Daniel Santos Megina/Alamy Stock Photo.

More specifically, we like our robots to be either indistinguishable from us (not currently possible), or like us but not too like us. There is a dip in the relationship between our emotional response to a form and its similarity to us if the form is like us but not quite the same; this dip is called the *uncanny valley* (see Figure 4.11). Most people find forms in this region to be disturbing or even creepy (Kätsyri et al., 2015; Mathur & Reichling, 2016). This feeling seems to arise because people attribute to them the ability to feel and sense rather than the capacity to act (Gray & Wegner, 2012).

> **TRY THIS:** An Emotion Chip
>
> In *Star Trek: The Next Generation*, the android Data was given an emotion chip upgrade. How plausible is this idea, particularly when considering what we know about the modularity of the mind and of the brain?

Figure 4.11 The uncanny valley. We're not unsettled if the robot looks nothing like a human, like CRONOS (Figure 4.10) or a perfect replica of a human, but we think that those that stray into the uncanny valley of almost human but not quite are unsettling. Source: Chris McGrath/Getty Images Europe.

Box 4.2 Aliens

Sophisticated artificial intelligences, robots, and aliens have been a very common topic in popular culture since the beginning of at least the twentieth century. Edgar Allen Poe, Jules Verne, and H.G. Wells are often mentioned as the founders of modern science fiction. Aliens invading Earth are usually hyper-intelligent, hyper-technological beings who are all presumably conscious, but how plausible are the forms of these aliens? The well-known Daleks in the British BBC television programme *Dr Who* have a very non-human form, with one eye on a stalk, a plunger for a hand, rolling around without legs, but at least they have the excuse that they were designed and evolved outside their robotic form. The most common forms are humanoids (such as the ubiquitous 'greys'), insect-like forms, and aliens with tentacles (see Figure 4.12); the Martians in H.G. Wells' 1898 novel *The War Of The World*s had tentacle form (as do the Daleks). While clearly humanoid aliens might plausibly have evolved advanced intelligence and consciousness, it is less plausible that insects and tentacles are sufficient for intelligence to evolve. Surely we need binocular vision, mobility, sophisticated manual dexterity, and the ability to communicate? Or perhaps that conclusion is simply a failure of my imagination.

Swarm Intelligence

In the same way that complex 'swarm' behaviour can emerge from the interaction of many individual animals following simple rules, similarly complex behaviour can emerge from the interaction of many simple individual robots. Such complex behaviour is called **swarm intelligence**.

A prominent example is Amazon Robotics (formerly called Kiva Systems), which fulfils orders by collecting items from shelves and placing them on conveyor belts or near humans.

When an item is selected, the central software selects the nearest robot, or bot, to go and pick it up. Items are categorised by barcodes, and bots navigate around the warehouse by barcodes on the floor. Bots are able to lift heavy weights and move around avoiding collisions. It is estimated that Amazon uses more than 100 000 robots in their warehouses, and is investigating extending their use to automated delivery.

In these systems each robot is not particularly intelligent; nevertheless the system as a whole can carry out sophisticated tasks. These robots are still relatively large; a nanobot is a miracle of miniaturisation, where a robot is microscopically small; only slightly larger are their cousins microbots. Currently, nanobots are largely hypothetical, although a few have been created to carry out very simple tasks, such as counting molecules or positioning other molecules, mostly in medicine (Patel et al., 2006). Nanobots and microbots are far too small to be conscious, but what about a swarm of millions of them? Could the swarm be collectively conscious?

Figure 4.12 Aliens with tentacles. Could such a life form really evolve to make spacecraft to travel the universe? Source: Hulton Archive/Handout/Moviepix/Getty Images.

Swarm intelligence of simple robots is reminiscent of several other things we have examined: flocking behaviour, the China brain, and the human brain, in which no individual neuron is conscious, but the brain made out of many neurons is. There is no suggestion that at the moment robot swarms are conscious, but could in the future a swarm behave like a conscious organism? It is difficult to see any reason in principle why it should not be a possibility.

Evolutionary Robotics

Putting aside considerations such as creationism and intelligent design, humans weren't created; we evolved, with primates splitting from other mammals about 65 million years ago, and at some point in our evolution consciousness appeared (of which more in the next chapter). Evolution is an effective way of solving problems associated with adapting to the world without design. Hence it is not surprising that some robotics scientists have taken an evolutionary approach to robot design.

Programming based on evolutionary principles has a long history in computer science, with perhaps the best-known approach being the *genetic algorithms* first developed by the American psychologist and computer scientist John Holland (1929–2015). Genetic algorithms are computer programs that solve problems using principles such as mutation and selection; essentially, the better code is at solving the problem, the more likely it is to survive in the program.

Genetic algorithms have been used in programming the controller modules of robots, the part that interprets the world and controls action, although it is not the only form of genetic programming. Neither is evolutionary programming restricted to the control program; it is possible to 'evolve' the hardware too. Core features of the robot are coded as its genome, and genetic processes operate on that genome to improve the robot's fitness for a particular task or set of tasks (Nelson et al., 2009; Nolfi et al., 2004). One of the most interesting examples of evolving hardware is the Golem Project, a collaboration between Brandeis and Cornell Universities (Lipson & Pollack, 2000). Sometimes the results of the evolution process are surprising, looking nothing like we might expect them to (Winfield, 2012). The form shown in Figure 4.13 was created through an evolution-like process for solving the problem of moving across surfaces

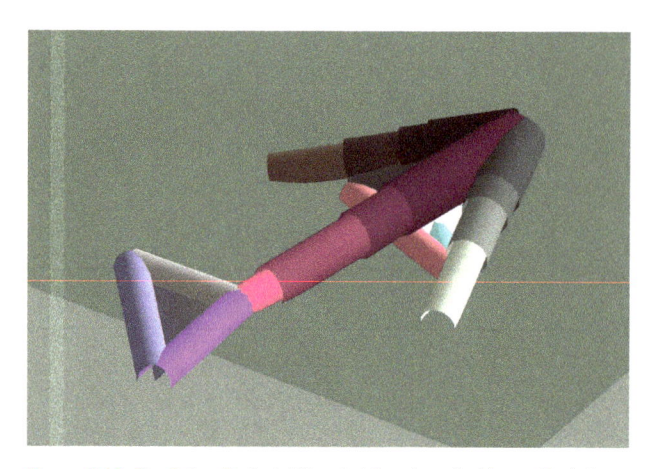

Figure 4.13 The Golem Project; this robot form is called Arrow. Evolution rather than design plays an important role in determining the form of these robots that try to move as efficiently as possible over surfaces. Source: With permission from Hod Lipson.

Robots and Consciousness

Robots are perhaps a better bet than AIs for becoming conscious in the long run because, like us, robots can interact with the world: they take in information, and act upon the world, and then observe the results of that interaction. In that respect, they are capable of possessing a self-model. Interaction with the world and having some concept of one's self are prerequisites for consciousness.

To muddy the waters slightly, many 'robots' are in fact computer simulations of robots. Building a hardware robot is difficult and expensive, and simulating the robot before it is built (indeed if it is ever built) is a means of reducing the cost and time. As robots grow in complexity, so will the simulation. If a robot could be conscious, could a simulation of a robot ever be conscious?

> **TRY THIS:** Simulating Robots
>
> Suppose we manage to construct a robot that most people agree is conscious. What would it take to simulate this robot? Could the simulation be said to be conscious? Could we construct a simulation of a robot that is in principle conscious, and if we don't then actually construct that robot, what is the status of the simulation? To what extent could we simulate its interaction with the environment?

Building a Brain

The AI and robot systems we have considered so far share the characteristic that the emphasis has been on the software, particularly knowledge and learning, and perception and action. Consciousness, if it arises at all, arises from the potential complexity of the software and how it interacts with the world. We haven't been too concerned with the hardware, as long as it is powerful enough to do what we require of it.

There is formal proof from computer science that any hardware equal in computing power to what is called a **Turing machine** can carry out any computation (see Hofstadter, 1979, for an accessible account of the proof). A Turing machine was first described, as its name implies, by the British mathematician and computer scientist Alan Turing (1912–1954). It's a specification of a length of tape upon which symbols can be manipulated according to a set of rules. If the tape is infinitely long, Turing showed that the machine can carry out any computation. It sounds simple, but it provides a formal specification of all computers. A Turing machine is a theoretical construct, not a physical object. It's an abstraction that shows that anything with its power can compute, and that's why we don't care too much about what sort of computer or tablet or smartphone we use, as long as it's sufficiently fast, and the style of the design is to our liking. So if we deem one computer conscious, any other computer running the same software in the same environment should also be capable of being conscious. (One important caveat is that if consciousness depends on the speed of interaction with the world the power of the computer may be important.) In fact, we don't need to restrict ourselves to silicon-based computers: anything equivalent to a Turing machine will do, a notion called **substrate independence** (which is a thesis that is the basis of functionalism, discussed in Chapter 2).

As we have seen, many people don't like the idea that the China brain (see Chapter 2), or a collection of strings and matchboxes forming a Turing equivalent to a computer, could be conscious. Others, like me, have no difficulty with the idea that a suitable future robot could be conscious, but baulk at the matchboxes. Why? Is this belief rational?

Many believe that there is something special about the brain that makes it capable of consciousness, but it is incumbent on those researchers to say what property a brain has that a robot lacks. An alternative approach to top-down AI is that of studying the brain and trying to build one from the bottom up.

Constructing an Artificial Brain

The idea of constructing an artificial brain may sound fanciful, but the possibility has been widely discussed, although initial attempts understandably focused on parts of the brain rather than the whole thing (Eliasmith et al., 2012). One goal of the Allen Institute in the United States (founded by Microsoft co-founder Paul Allen) is to create a complete map of every neuron in the brain as well as all the connections between them, in the same way as the Human Genome Project has mapped out the human genome. It remains to be seen to what extent understanding the brain's mapping will help us to understand consciousness (Regalado, 2014). Of course, we are not limited to creating a brain from organic materials; would transistor simulations of neurons do just as well? Remember our thought experiment in Chapter 2 of replacing a brain neuron by neuron with silicon replicas, wired and functioning in just the same way. At what point, if any, would you say the machine ceases to be human? Presumably, if the experiment were really carried out gradually the being would feel just the same all the way through, and would still feel human, but outsiders might have a different opinion.

Although this research is necessary speculative, the project does have some clearly defined goals. Some believe that constructing a brain is the logical endpoint of computational neuroscience, the field of computer modelling of the neural substrate of behaviour. It is also argued that this research provides a testing ground for ideas in psychology and philosophy. The method of constructing a larger system by working out what each smaller part is doing is sometimes called reverse engineering.

There are two different approaches to building a brain. The first one is *whole-brain emulation*, where the low-level functions of the brain are simulated by another program. A person emulation models a particular brain (Bostrom, 2014; Sandberg & Bostrom, 2008). Simulations capture principles of what is being modelled at a higher level, and need not capture as much detail.

There are two ways of emulating hardware; one is to do it by hardware, so that, for example, we essentially construct a silicon brain, with transistors representing each neuron and its synapses. The other is to do it by software – in the way that programs such as Parallels® and VMware® Fusion emulate a PC on a Mac. Software simulation of the brain though isn't quite as costly as computer hardware emulation, because neurons are relatively slow; although transmission speeds vary greatly, a typical fast transmission is around 100 m s^{-1}. Contrast that with transmission speeds in a silicon chip, which is typically a few per cent of the speed of light (which is 299 792 458 m s^{-1}). So, although chips have a lot to do when modelling a brain, they can do it much more quickly than a brain can.

Eliasmith et al. (2012) describe a simulation of a 2.5 million neuron brain they called *Spaun*. Two-and-a-half million is big, but still much smaller than a human brain. The model is presented with visual images, and draws any response with a robot arm. The architecture of the model is that there are five interacting modules between input and output: information encoding, transformation of input, evaluating reward, information decoding, and motor processing, with access to working memory; all under the guidance of an action selection system. The model illustrates a range of behaviours and psychological principles. It is most unlikely that any such model could be conscious, but it is a significant step along the way to possible machine consciousness.

There is another possible consequence of being able to model whole brains down to individual neurons and the connections between them, and that is the possibility of *uploading*. Uploading is transferring a copy of yourself, your personality, memories, and presumably consciousness, to a suitable host computer. Some enthusiastic press reports say that we should be able to upload our minds to computers by 2045 (Sandberg & Bostrom, 2008). Even if we could emulate a brain, it is possible that continued consciousness depends on continued interaction with the world. Uploading clearly assumes substrate independence.

The second possible approach to building a brain, and one that is more tractable at present, is *part-brain emulation*, which is modelling parts of brains. Fleischer et al. (2007) describe the modelling of the **hippocampus** and surrounding cortical regions in Darwin X!, a brain-based device that comprises a neural simulation guiding a robotic platform that actually moves through a maze. The robot has a camera as well as robotic whiskers for discriminating textures of surfaces. As well as providing a model of behaviour and the neural computations necessary, the simulations lead to insights on how the brain might work (for example, in this model the sensory cortex provided surprisingly little input).

We might one day be able to simulate a brain; it might be conscious; but would this achievement help us to understand consciousness? Understanding complicated computers raises the same sorts of issues as understanding complex humans, but we might be able to use information about how the entity was constructed, and speculate about which parts of the processes involved appear to be critical. However, this discussion is very promissory, even speculative; for all the discussion above, very few people are currently attempting to do whole-brain emulation, because it's too difficult given our current knowledge and technical ability to map the brain. Hence, a date of about 2050 for a conscious computer sounds optimistic. At the moment, we are starting to make progress in thinking about how to emulate the fruit fly (*Drosophila*) brain (Givon & Lazar, 2016).

Playing with possibly conscious entities raises serious ethical issues (Sandberg, 2014): if we make an entity that seems to be conscious, would it then be right to modify it to see which aspects of its construction are necessary for consciousness? I don't think so. Uploading generates perhaps even more ethical issues; what happens after a power outage?

Neuroprosthesis

A **neuroprosthesis** is replacement of a part of or an extension to the brain. The earliest example that could be considered a proper example is a cochlear implant, which is a device used to improve hearing in hearing-impaired individuals by stimulating the auditory nerve directly. Cochlear implants have been used widely since the 1970s. Figure 4.14 shows the structure of the device: a part is implanted inside the ear bypassing the bones of the inner ear and the cochlear, an organ essential for hearing, and sends electrical signals about the sound input directly to the auditory nerve. Deep-brain stimulation (DBS) uses a device called a neurostimulator, which is implanted in the brain, which sends electrical impulses to stimulate specific parts of the brain, and has been used to treat disorders such as Parkinson's disease, depression, epilepsy, and OCD.

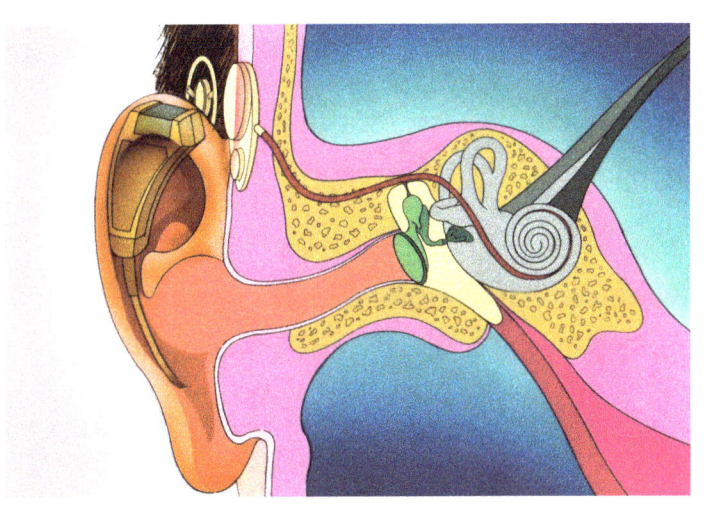

Figure 4.14 The structure of a cochlear implant. These implants enable people with some hearing problems to hear again. Would you accept a neural prosthesis? Source: DeAgostini/Getty Images.

We are now at the stage where brain–computer interfaces are just starting to become reliable and widespread in use, for example, in stimulating the spinal cord in paralysed people to control the movement of limbs. There are now brain-controlled wheelchairs, which use a person's EEG to navigate the environment (e.g. Bi et al., 2013).

Naturally, given the complexity of the tasks they are trying to do, these devices are not always completely reliable, or without side effects, but they represent an astonishing level of technological achievement. Their contribution to our understanding of consciousness is, however, limited, although they might contribute to our understanding of volition, the initiation of movement. More revealing might be neural augmentation, which is improving our mental abilities through prosthetic technology. (The more general term *neuroenhancement* includes cognitive enhancement through pharmacological means.) Some futurologists, such as Elon Musk, think that, if we are to stay safe from future AI technology, we must use enhancement to keep ourselves safe.

Although the idea is presently only science fiction, suppose you could have a module plugged into your brain that increases your working memory capacity, or enables you to carry out mental arithmetic with the facility of a digital computer, or gives you near-instant access to any book ever published, would you accept that module? There are profound ethical issues: all technology comes with a level of risk, and what if most of the population could not afford to pay for the technology?

What would the subjective experience of possessing such a neuroprosthesis be? How would your subjective consciousness change if your working memory were increased, or your general speed of processing increased?

Such questions are likely to remain wildly speculative for the near future. Again we see that, although the technology is of great interest and promise, it is currently very limited in what it tells us about consciousness now.

The Future of AI

Although there is widespread agreement that AI and robotics are topics that should be covered in any book on consciousness, at the moment they tell us very little about it. The previous discussion shows, however, that research in this area might contribute to our understanding in the future. What is the likely future?

The Technological Singularity

What will happen if and when computers are more intelligent than us? As technology and intelligence increase, new avenues of progress open up. Many believe that, when AI reaches a critical point, there will be an abrupt increase in the development of new technologies leading to self-reinforcing runaway technological growth. Technology will develop exponentially providing us with very sudden unimaginable technological advances and changes to civilisation. A very intelligent computer might design an even more intelligent computer; robots might learn and improve themselves. Kurzweil (2005) calls the point at which this growth takes off the **singularity** (or the technological singularity). Of course, technology will continue to improve; the defining characteristic of the singularity is that there will be a discontinuity, a sudden change in the slope of the graph of improvement against time as new technology leads to a dramatic increase in the growth of technology. Not everyone thinks that there will be a discontinuity: others believe that technology will continue to change smoothly and fairly predictably, and that there is no reason to suppose that a sheer increase in computing power will ever lead to significant change (e.g. Searle, 2014).

What is this 'intelligence' that will continue to increase? My favourite definition is the operation one of 'what is measured by intelligence tests'. If we say someone is intelligent, we mean that they know a lot, and are good at solving problems and coming up with solutions to difficulties, an everyday definition that confounds fluid intelligence, crystallised intelligence, and creativity. For now, we will just take intelligence to be the ability to acquire and use information to solve problems; those who need more detail should consult a text such as Maltby et al. (2013).

We can all think of examples of people who are very intelligent, but lack 'common sense', or are very good in narrow domains, such as solving mathematical problems. The extreme example of this narrowness is in savant syndrome, where individuals on the autistic spectrum disorder display remarkable talent in a very specific area, such as arithmetic calculation, giving the day of a week from a date (17 May 1862, anybody?), having exceptional memory, or being able to draw or play an instrument. At the moment, computer programs are very narrow; they're good at tasks that can be reduced to calculation, but that's it. Clearly the ability to calculate quickly doesn't lead to consciousness. Human-level machine intelligence requires much more, so that a computer can do a human job – the occupations most at risk are those where the skills can be codified and learned, such as a lawyer, doctor, or accountant.

Of course, being as intelligent as a human does not mean that such a computer will be conscious. There is much more to being conscious than being smart, although in evolution the two have gone hand in hand. However, as Harari (2016) argues, we are now seeing the decoupling of intelligence and consciousness. As we have seen, computers might be more intelligent in some respects, but are not conscious – yet. The topic of exploring the construction of artificial conscious entities is called artificial consciousness.

Some hope that one consequence of such technological change is that humans might be able to improve their lives and intellects to the point that they can live for ever. The technique of changing and improving our lives through technology is called **transhumanism** (see Box 4.3).

> **TRY THIS:** Building a Reassuring Robot
>
> How would a computer or robot providing a medical service, such as a general medical checkup or enquiry, have to behave to reassure you that it was as capable as, if not better than, a real doctor?

> **Box 4.3** Transhumanism
>
> Transhumanism is the philosophy that we can extend and improve human existence by making use of and developing technologies to enhance our bodies, physiologies, and particularly our intellect. A neuroprosthesis is one possible future method of improving our intellect: suppose a chip could extend our working memory capacity, or make us faster at numerical computation?
>
> At present, though, the methods open to transhumanists are limited. One popular mechanism is enhancement through implanted computer chips that enable people to carry

> **Box 4.3** (cont.)
>
> out at present what are fairly simple tasks, such as unlocking a door. Less invasive methods include trying to extend your lifespan through supplements, or enhancing your intellect through a class of drugs called neural enhancers or *nootropics*. Many of these drugs were originally developed for the treatment of disorders such as Alzheimer's disease.
>
> The ultimate aim of transhumanism is to escape death, either by extending our life expectancy to near infinity, or by uploading our consciousness to some kind of external hardware.

Is AI a Threat?

There are two ways in which AIs or robots might be a threat to us. The first is the only source of danger, at present, and that is a result of human error, either as a result of a programming bug or incomplete knowledge in a database, for a hardware failure. The consequences of a bug could still be catastrophic (an accidental nuclear war would be an extinction-level event or threat, or existential threat). It was feared, for example, that the Y2000 Millennium bug was going to cause widespread havoc, but in the event fortunately very little materialised.

Robots and AIs capable of being a threat as a consequence of their own decisions probably require a sense of self, a sense of self-preservation, and probably need to be conscious. So the second source of threat is that if an AI does eventually become self-aware it could 'choose' to harm us in some way. Humanity does not have a very good record of how it treats species it considers in some way inferior to itself. From the extinction of the passenger pigeon to intensive farming of pigs, we have not covered ourselves in glory. We haven't even been good with dealing with our own species, as history shows. If a computer or robot is more intelligent than us, it might well consider itself superior to us, so why should it be kindly disposed towards us? Malevolent robots and AIs are dominant themes in the science-fiction literature. From the HAL 9000 computer in *2001: A Space Odyssey* (Kubrick, 1968) to SkyNet in the *Terminator* franchise, AI is often portrayed as a threat to humans and humanity.

The science-fiction writer Isaac Asimov (1920–1992) proposed *Three Laws of Robotics* in his short story 'Runaround' in 1942 that he considered should be programmed into robots to ensure that they never threaten humans. The laws are (Asimov, 1950):

> '1. A robot may not injure a human being or, through inaction, allow a human being to come to harm.
>
> A robot must obey orders given it by human beings except where such orders would conflict with the First Law.
>
> A robot must protect its own existence as long as such protection does not conflict with the First or Second Law.'

Would implementing Asimov's Laws help? I think here consciousness is particularly relevant. These rules would prevent a relatively simple general AI or robot from deliberately harming humans, but the situation with more advanced computers is much more murky. Why would a conscious entity be constrained to observe any limitations we might impose from the start? Is not freedom the cost of consciousness? You can lecture me all you like on morality, you can raise me from birth to follow certain rules, I can have love and respect for the sanctity of life of my own species hardwired into me, but there will be occasions when I might decide to override those constraints. If I feel threatened, if I think a loved one is threatened, if I think I could get away with it, if I think it is essential for the species, who knows what conventions could be jettisoned? The illusion (at least) of free will goes with consciousness.

Even if you reject the idea that computers could be conscious, and could pose a purposeful threat to humanity, there are still plenty of reasons to be concerned about technological advance. Increasingly technology is replacing humans in the workforce. Unemployment might increase, and the consequences for the economy are unpredictable. Even unintelligent nanobots could prove an existential threat. Grey goo is a hypothetical end-of-the-world scenario where out-of-control self-replicating but dumb nanobots consume all biomass on Earth. My favourite example is Bostrom's (2014) paperclip maximiser. An AI controlling a robot or factory could be given the simple instruction 'maximise paperclip production'. What could go wrong? At some point a self-improving AI would in its drive to make as many paperclips as possible start doing things that would threaten humans. Why do we need those nice fields to grow food when we could have a big paperclip factory there instead? And so on.

Should we be worried? I think so, if not for us, but for our children or grandchildren. A bug in a computer system controlling nuclear weapons is one thing, but a conscious super-AI with a grudge is another. These are existential level threats. The future is not always necessarily rosy.

Chapter Summary

- Artificial life is the field of study concerned with simulating aspects of life.
- Boids is an early artificial life program simulating the behaviour of a flock of birds whereby complex behaviour arises from three simple rules.
- Intelligence can be decoupled from consciousness; there might be some minimum level of intelligence necessary for consciousness, but possessing high intelligence does not guarantee that the possessor is conscious.
- Artificial intelligence (AI) is enabling computers to do smart, human-like things, and to perform tasks normally requiring human intelligence.
- We should distinguish AIs from robots, which can interact directly with the physical world.
- Computers have been able to beat grandmasters at chess regularly since the late 1990s.
- Computers can now beat humans at the game Go.
- The Turing test is an indication of a computer's ability to exhibit intelligence so that it is indistinguishable from a human.
- Many computer scientists believe that we will build computers exhibiting general human-level intelligence (as opposed to intelligence dedicated to very particular skills),

called artificial general intelligence (AGI), sometime this century, and probably in the first half of the century.
- Swarm robots use a large number of relatively simple robots with decentralised control.
- We need to be wary of possible threats exhibited by AI and AI-bearing robots. There is no guarantee that programming them with Asimov's Laws means they must obey them.
- It is unlikely that a computer could become conscious without exposure to the environment, and particularly perceiving the world, acting upon it, and observing the results, in the same way that a child develops cognitively.
- We can use evolution to drive the process of robot construction. Evolutionary successful robots might not look like we expect.
- We could develop an AI capable of consciousness by constructing an intelligence and letting it develop, building a brain of some sorts, or perhaps by whole-brain emulation.
- A neuroprosthesis is an electronic replacement or enhancement of part of the nervous system.
- Kurzweil states that there will be a technological singularity in the near future when the rate of development increases dramatically; this event is likely when AI systems are able to improve themselves.
- Although of great technological importance to humanity, this research does not currently tell us much at all about consciousness.
- Just because we might construct a conscious computer or robot does not mean that we will be any closer to understanding consciousness!
- Transhumanism is improving the human condition, particularly extending it, using technology.

Review Questions

1. Which, if any, properties of life are essential for consciousness?
2. When does a simulation stop being a simulation and become an implementation?
3. What might constitute a 'Turing test for consciousness'?
4. To what extent is the brain a swarm of neurons?
5. To what extent is the brain's structure necessary for consciousness, and how might an artificial brain develop any necessary structure?
6. Is it possible to implement something at the level of hardware or software that would remove a robot's ability to harm a human?
7. What might we have to fear from a technological singularity?
8. What is transhumanism, and what are the ethical problems associated with it? Would you want to live for ever?

Recommended Resources

General

McFarland, D. (2008). *Guilty Robots, Happy Dogs*. Oxford, UK: Oxford University Press.

RECOMMENDED RESOURCES

Artificial Life
Levy, S. (1993). *Artificial Life*. Harmondsworth, UK: Penguin Books.

Artificial Intelligence
Bechtel, W., and Abrahamsen, A. (2001). *Connectionism and the Mind: Parallel Processing, Dynamics, and Evolution in Networks*. Hoboken, NJ: John Wiley & Sons.

Bostrom, N. (2014). *Superintelligence: Paths, Dangers, Strategies*. Oxford, UK: Oxford University Press.

Kurzweil, R. (2005). *The Singularity is Near*. New York, NY: Penguin Group.

O'Connell, M. (2017). *To Be a Machine*. London: Granta.

Robotics
Winfield, A. (2012). *Robotics: A Very Short Introduction*. Oxford, UK: Oxford University Press. A short work that reviews the complete field of robotics for the beginner.

AI as Threat
See Bostrom and Kurzweil above.

Transhumanism
Kurzweil, R., and Grossman, T. (2004). *Fantastic Voyage: Live Long Enough to Live for Ever*. Emmaus, PA: Rodale Books.

Kurzweil, R., and Grossman, T. (2009). *Transcend*. New York: Rodale.

5 ANIMAL CONSCIOUSNESS

This chapter examines whether consciousness is restricted to human animals. We first examine what non-human animals can do – the topic of animal intelligence – and the particular issue of which animals feel pain. We then consider the mirror test of self-awareness. We examine differences in consciousness between animals. What is it that distinguishes a shrimp from a chimp?

The question then arises of what animals think, if anything, of humans and other animals. When we interact with other humans, we have a model of what others think and believe, and how the beliefs of others determine how they act. How important are these models for consciousness? This question leads to the issue of why consciousness might have evolved. Humans, of course, are unique in naturally using a sophisticated language; what role does this play in consciousness and self-awareness? How did the evolution of language interact with the evolution of consciousness?

Finally, we consider the possibility that consciousness might be very widespread – the idea called panpsychism that not only animals are conscious, but inanimate things too.

Which Non-human Animals might be Conscious?

As we saw in Chapter 1, opinions vary about which other animals might be conscious. On average the people I have talked to draw a line between birds (most people think them conscious) and fish (not conscious); other studies draw the line after ants. We are hampered by a lack of a clear definition of consciousness, and you will probably be inclined to admit degrees of consciousness: we might be self-aware, but my poodle Beau might only be aware (see Figure 5.1).

These are not merely intellectual questions of interest only to philosophers. In the preceding chapter, we considered whether, if a computer is conscious, we should be able to switch that computer off at will. There are more obvious profound moral implications from animal consciousness. If gorillas are conscious, should we keep them in zoos? If cows are conscious, should we breed and slaughter them for food? Should we test beauty products that cause pain and distress on conscious rabbits?

Animals are divided into species, genus, family, order, class, and phylum. For example, wolves are designated with the species *lupus*, from the genus *Canis* (including all dogs, coyotes, and jackals), family Canidae (also including foxes and some other extinct species), order Carnivora (meat eaters including cats, bears, and pandas – not necessarily all strictly solely meat eating!), class Mammalia (mammals feeding mostly live young with milk), and phylum Chordata (having a complex spinal cord). Humans are species *sapiens*, genus

THE MIND OF AN ANIMAL   109

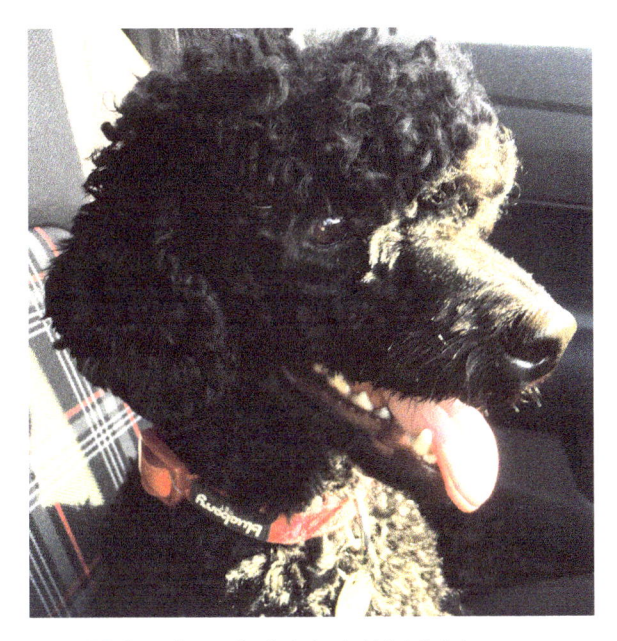

Figure 5.1 Beau the poodle. He is (probably) definitely aware, but is he self-aware?

Figure 5.2 A puffin with fish. Birds have brains that are very different in structure from those of primates yet exhibit complex and intelligent behaviours. And should we feel sorry for the fish? Source: Education Images/Universal Images Group/Getty Images.

Homo, family Hominidea, order primates, and class mammals; there are no other living members of genera in *Homo*, and our closest relatives are chimpanzees and then gorillas. Although there is a strong correlation between when an order appeared and the complexity of the organism, and between duration of time since appearance and the repertoire of behaviours and brain structure and complexity, one must apply some caution. It isn't simply the case that clear evolutionary steps added increasingly complex brain structures. Birds, for example, which pre-date mammals and which are thought to be direct descendants of dinosaurs, have complex brains with very different structures from mammals (see Figure 5.2). It is true that a large **neocortex** is an evolutionary late development limited to higher primates, but evolution has also led to alternative brain structures, which may support complex cognition.

> **TRY THIS:** Which Animals Are Conscious?
>
> Ask people you meet which other animals are conscious. Is the line somewhere between bird and fish, as I have found? Beware: you might get asked what you mean by consciousness.

The Mind of an Animal

I love feeding the birds in my garden. They hop around seemingly with such great purpose that I find it difficult to believe that they are not like me or all other humans, an idea known as anthropomorphism. I have been close to cats, and particularly dogs, and I find it impossible to believe that something isn't going on in there when I look into their eyes. But are they conscious?

When thinking about animals and consciousness there are two important questions. The distributional question is: which non-human animals (if any) are conscious? The phenomenological question is what is the consciousness of a particular animal like: what is it like to be a bat, rat, or cat?

Most people are like me and believe that some animals are conscious to some degree. In July 2012, a group of eminent consciousness researchers, including David Edelman, Philip Low, and Christoph Koch, proclaimed the Cambridge Declaration on Consciousness, concluding:

> The absence of a neocortex does not appear to preclude an organism from experiencing affective states. Convergent evidence indicates that non-human animals have the neuroanatomical, neurochemical, and neurophysiological substrates of conscious states along with the capacity to exhibit intentional behaviours. Consequently, the weight of evidence indicates that humans are not unique in possessing the neurological substrates that generate consciousness. Non-human animals, including all mammals and birds, and many other creatures, including octopuses, also possess these neurological substrates.

The declaration emphasises consciousness in birds (perhaps I'm right about the birds in my garden), particularly the African grey parrot.

Animal Intelligence

We have seen with computers that consciousness and intelligence are to some extent decoupled. How smart are animals? Naturally abilities range greatly, increasing as one moves up the evolutionary ladder, so the most advanced intellectual skills are shown by primates. We often talk about the size and complexity of human brains, but dolphins, elephants, and whales have larger brains, and although the human cortex is highly folded, so are those of other primates, dolphins, elephants, and pigs. The long-finned pilot whale has the largest number of cells in the neocortex, the part of the mammalian brain responsible for higher cognitive functions, of all animals (Mortensen et al., 2014). The brains of some birds, such as crows and parrots, are very densely packed with neurons (Olkowicz, 2016), and although birds don't have a neocortex, they do have a structure called a pallium, which carries out equivalent functions. Although the case is less clear, cephalopod molluscs (such as the octopus) can make sophisticated perceptual discriminations, have good memories, can learn complex behaviours, and although very different in structure from mammals, have complex nervous systems. They are therefore likely to possess conscious states (Edelman & Seth, 2009). Contrary to the belief of at least my students, other commentators have pointed to the strong possibility of consciousness in fish (Balcombe, 2016). There has even been some recent debate about whether insects are conscious (Barron & Klein, 2016; Adamo, 2016). For insects the argument comes down to how exactly should consciousness be defined; is it the presence of brain structures that enable the creation of a representation of the organism's position in space. We should not assume that higher cognition and consciousness depends on the precise characteristics of the primate brain.

Given the complexity of non-human primate brains, it is unsurprising that the ability to recognise ourselves, metacognitive skills that show what we understand about our own thinking, having a model of what other animals are thinking, the ability to empathise, and long-range planning have all been demonstrated in primates, and even some rodents (Smith et al., 2014).

The animal psychologist Irene Pepperberg has worked with African grey parrots for many years, particularly spending 30 years with an individual called Alex (1976–2007) (see Figure 5.3). Alex was able to solve complex problems, including problems in numerical cognition, and use language. It is well known that parrots are excellent mimics of language, but Alex used language to communicate, and to help him reason. Pepperberg argued that at the time of his death Alex had the cognitive abilities of a human five-year-old child, and lived at the emotional level of a two-year-old, although she believed he was still learning and developing when he died (Pepperberg, 2013). Critics argue that the bird just learned responses rather than meaning – it uttered a particular sound in a particular situation to get a reward (e.g. see Hesse & Potter, 2004). In reply, Pepperberg noted that Alex's high accuracy and the types of error he made resembled those of children. Many believe that Pepperberg's work suggests that Alex showed evidence of high-level cognition and language use. Alex also asked self-referential questions, such as asking 'what colour?' apparently referring to himself, suggesting that he had a self-concept and therefore self-awareness.

Figure 5.3 Alex the talking parrot. Irene Pepperberg worked with Alex, an African grey parrot, for over 30 years, arguing that Alex had language and cognitive abilities similar to those of a five-year-old child. Source: Martin Barraud/OJO Images/Getty Images.

There was nothing particularly special about Alex; the ability of birds in the wild, particularly corvids (crows, particularly scrub jays), is remarkable. Some birds behave in a way that is indicative of their having **episodic memory** (Dally et al., 2006). Episodic memory is not just remembering things but knowing that they've remembered. Episodic memory is important because it involves awareness of memory, and, as we shall see in Chapters 7 and 8, is thought to play a central role in cognition and consciousness. Scrub jays also appear to have some model of what other jays know (Shaw & Clayton, 2013), and take counter strategies such as hiding their food caches out of sight to protect them from theft (Clayton et al., 2007). While the brains of birds are different from those of mammals, they are still very complex (Figure 5.4). Rats, too, and presumably therefore many other mammals, may

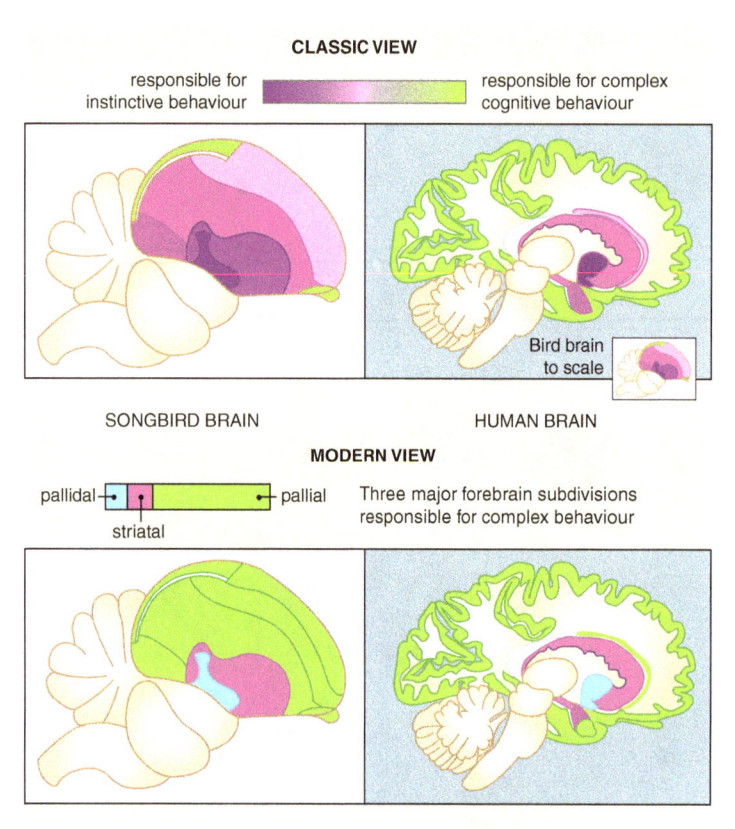

Figure 5.4 Classical and modern views of a typical bird brain. Recent thinking attributes higher cognitive functioning to much of the bird brain. Source: Courtesy of Erich Jarvis/AvianBrain.org.

Figure 5.5 A common raven (*Corvus corax*) performing cognitive experiments. Birds are smart, and crows (of which the raven is one) are particularly smart. Source: Cyril Ruoso/Nature Picture Library/Science Photo Library.

possess an episodic memory, remembering not just specific memories but the sequence in which the events occurred (Babb & Crystal, 2006; Basile, 2015; see Figure 5.5).

Any student of consciousness will soon be told that dolphins and perhaps whales are highly intelligent and probably that they are conscious. It would, however, be premature to draw much in the way of conclusion at the moment. It is often overlooked that it is methodologically difficult to carry out suitable research with active marine animals (Harley, 2013). It is likely that dolphins self-recognise in mirrors (although obviously they cannot touch marks on their heads, making testing more difficult; Marten & Psarakos, 1995). They show some uncertainty about their judgements, which is taken as a sign that not only do they remember things – which would be most unremarkable – but also they remember remembering things (Smith et al., 1995). These signs suggest that dolphins possess awareness and self-awareness.

One method of exploring possible animal consciousness would be if we can find a distinctive **signature of consciousness** in humans using techniques such as fMRI (Barttfeld et al., 2015). Such work is in its infancy, and it isn't easy to get an active wakeful animal into a brain-imaging machine. We can currently distinguish between the resting state of wakeful and anaesthetised macaque monkeys by looking at how active connections are between different parts of the brain, and how integrated different parts of the brain are (Barttfeld et al., 2015). Another line of research is to examine which brain structures are centrally involved in humans in a process hypothesised to signify consciousness, such as which parts of the brain become active on recovery from general anaesthesia, and suppose similar consciousness exists in animals having similar brain structures. Such an argument confirms at least the range of animals thought to be conscious according to the Cambridge Declaration (Mashour & Alkire, 2013; there is more on anaesthesia in Chapter 10).

Occasionally, in movies, you see hyper-intelligent aliens flying sophisticated interstellar starships, and when you eventually see them, these days, the forms are often insect-like beings, worms, or spiders. The Daleks in the television science-fiction series *Doctor Who* have suckers for hands; their ability to manipulate objects must be very limited. Without hands, how could they become that intelligent? Intelligence and consciousness, as we have noted, depend on interacting with the world, and I think it is unlikely that we can interact much without hands suited to grasping and manipulating objects – hands suitable for exploring the world. I do not find these aliens at all plausible. For the same reason, I am sceptical that animals such as dolphins can be exceptionally intelligent – having an intelligence close to that of humans, for example; that doesn't mean that they might not have limited consciousness.

In summary, there are good grounds to suppose many non-human animals might be conscious. We can make a very good guess though based on the similarity of the complexity of their brains and types of processing, such as self-reference, to us. It is also not helpful to restrict consciousness to self-consciousness and thereby by definition exclude virtually all other organisms apart from humans from being in any way conscious (e.g. Humphrey, 1984, p. 48: 'some would say "self-consciousness", although what other kind of consciousness there is I do not know)'. *Self-consciousness*, consciousness of our selves, is a sophisticated sort of consciousness. Most people would agree that we are conscious, of a sort, when dreaming, or when a baby, or that a dog has some kind of consciousness.

> **Box 5.1   Learning Without Neurons**
>
> We should be careful to avoid assuming that things need to be like us in order to carry out the behaviours of complex organisms. In Figure 5.6, French researcher Audrey Dussutour holds a 'Blob', a single-cell organism she is studying, in her lab at the Animal Cognition Research Centre of the French National Centre for Scientific Research (CNRS) in Toulouse, France. This organism is not animal, plant, or fungus, and does not have a nervous system, but can learn to avoid noxious stimuli and grow in the
>
> Figure 5.6 'The blob'. This unicellular organism of course has no neurons but can nevertheless learn. Source: Eric Cabanis/AFP/Getty Images.

Box 5.1 (cont.)

Figure 5.7 A slime mould, close up in its natural environment. These simple organisms display behaviour that we might well describe as intelligent. Source: Stephane de Sakutin/AFP/Getty Images.

direction of favourable environments. The 'blob' is a type of slime mould (*Physarum polycephalum*), one of the oldest organisms on the planet (see Figure 5.7). It will also learn to take the most economical path between food sites in a format similar to human designs, and can even be trained to solve maze-like puzzles (Nakagaki et al., 2000; Tero et al., 2010).

The Mirror Test of Self-recognition

When we see ourselves in a mirror we usually recognise ourselves immediately. Hence the idea that self-recognition, being able to recognise ourselves as distinct from other people, has garnered importance in studies of animal consciousness. You can only be self-aware if you can recognise yourself as a thing separate from others. There was one blue tit (chickadee) that spent hour after hour flying up at his reflection in the glass window of my bedroom. It is unlikely that he was admiring his reflection in the mirror; most likely he was flying to attack what he thought was a competitor. He couldn't distinguish himself from others.

Based on this concept, the American psychologist Gordon Gallup devised the **mirror test** of **self-recognition**, or **MSR** (Gallup, 1970). He would put a red spot of dye on the forehead of an animal, a place that the animal cannot normally see. The animal is then allowed to see its reflection in a mirror. The question is then whether the animal rubs or examines the spot or displays grooming behaviour towards it (Figure 5.8)? It will only be able to groom itself if

Figure 5.8 The mirror test of self-recognition. Using a mirror, I recognise that the red spot is on ME. Can other animals identify themselves as special?

it recognises itself. Many species have 'passed' versions of the mirror test, including many species of non-human primates, dolphins, whales, and magpies (Prior et al., 2008; Reiss & Marino, 2001). The case of elephants is controversial (Povinelli, 1989). Chimpanzees have outstanding performance, even recognising visually inverted television images of their own arms (Menzel, 1985).

Interpretations of results from the mirror test are controversial. With some training, pigeons can pass the test (Epstein et al., 1981), as can rhesus monkeys (Chang et al., 2017). Does the training facilitate the animal's understanding of the significance of a mirror, or just to make certain movements by rote? The mirror test is restricted to the visual modality, but an olfactory analogue suggests that dogs can distinguish their own scent (Cazzolla Gatti, 2015; Horowitz, 2017). That in itself would not be surprising, but in the sniff test of self-recognition (abbreviated to the STR), dogs spend longer sniffing and investigating their own scent when it is modified by overlaying an additional odour on it, suggesting that they can recognise it as being special in some way. So, the mirror test in its original form is too conservative as a measure of self-recognition.

Does self-recognition necessitate self-awareness? It's very easy to get into a very complicated muddle about these things. There are two sources of controversy about the mirror test. The first is whether animals fail the task because of a lack of self-awareness. Gallup originally argued that chimpanzees passed the test, but monkeys failed. As we have seen, first there are methodological details of the test that need to be explored (such as Epstein et al., 1981, showing that pigeons could pass if they have an appropriate training regime), and second, we must not be too anthropomorphic in our expectations of how animals should behave (dogs failing the visual version of the test). Menzel et al. (1985) argue that many animals, particularly some monkeys, fail not because they lack self-awareness, but because they lack specific perceptual-motor skills – an idea supported by the finding that some monkeys succeed on the task with training. Second, what does self-recognition tell us? Does an organism, or even a robot, that recognises itself, have to be conscious? Many people, don't think so (e.g. see Suddendorf, 2013). You might be able to program a computer that recognises its own mirror image (for example, by detecting that the movements it sees are the movements it makes); such a program would have no 'self model'. There is also the issue of whether even a self model necessitates consciousness? Do p-zombies have self models? All organisms might need to pass the MSR test is a concept of their own bodies (Heyes, 1994, 1998).

Our current best bet is that you don't need to be conscious to be able to pass the mirror test, and you can be conscious without being able to pass the mirror test. But it's difficult to see how you can pass the mirror test and not be self-aware. We are also left with the paradox that tasks that we believe are more cognitively demanding, such as awareness of mental states, do not distinguish between

> **TRY THIS: Looking in a Mirror**
>
> Study yourself in a full-length mirror. Pay attention to your face. What do you see? Do you look like what you think you look like? Continue looking. Does anything change?

> **TRY THIS: Animals in the Mirror**
>
> If you have access to a companion animal, put them in front of a mirror. How do they behave?

primates, whereas the cognitively more simple mirror test does. Perhaps the mirror test is simply more of a test of bodily awareness than of self-awareness.

Animals and Pain

We have seen that feeling pain is a hallmark of consciousness, but simply moving away from a noxious stimuli is not (see Chapter 2). The difficulty is in distinguishing responding to noxious stimulus from responding to and feeling pain. Beau, my poodle, ignored my warnings about playing with a bee, with predictable results. As well as jumping away, he yelped, and I find it impossible to believe that the yelp was not associated with feeling pain. We can't be absolutely sure that animals feel pain (but then we have also seen that I can't be absolutely sure that you feel pain like I do, either). Animals obviously exhibit pain behaviour. It is pitiful to behold a non-human animal in pain; the distress is apparent. It would be a brave person to say that a dog or cat is merely exhibiting a behaviour associated with a response to a noxious stimulus without experiencing any pain.

An amoeba will move away from what for it is an unpleasant environment (widely mentioned but rarely cited; see Craig, 2003), but an amoeba is most unlikely to experience the pain consciously. So, how far down the evolutionary ladder does pain likely go? It's a reasonable assumption that to feel pain animals should have a nervous system capable of being aware of pain. All mammals share a similar brain design, so it is not implausible that all mammals both respond to pain in the same way as us and experience pain in the same way. Animal models of human pain make this assumption (Wilcox & Hirshkowitz, 2015), with mice being widely used.

Recall that students at least place the line for conscious–nonconscious around about fish. Do fish feel pain? Opinions are mixed. Some fish at least (e.g. trout) do have nerve cells that resemble nociceptors and that respond to noxious stimuli, such as heat, pressure, and acid, both physiologically and behaviourally (Sneddon et al., 2003). When injected with acetic acid, which is at least an aversive stimulus and potentially would be painful, fish seek out painkillers (e.g. going to part of an aquarium suffused with lidocaine). On the other hand, some researchers point to the absence of a neocortex, and point to methodological flaws in some of these experiments (Rose et al., 2014). Others argue that the absence of a complex cortex is not a sufficient reason for denying that fish can feel pain, and that we are being too anthropomorphic in insisting that creatures must have a human-like brain (Sneddon & Leach, 2016; but see Key, 2015, for the alternative view).

It is widely believed that crabs and lobsters scream when put into boiling water, which is thought to be an effective and humane way of killing them. But these crustaceans do not have vocal cords or lungs, so cannot 'scream' as such; the screaming sound sometimes heard is instead the sound of air escaping from joints. That isn't to say that they don't feel pain, however, but one of the most commonly quoted examples is a myth. We don't know how far down the scale the capacity for feeling pain goes. Lobsters and crustaceans, and many other invertebrates, don't have a brain: they have collections of higher densities of nerve cells at several places in their bodies, or less. One argument is that the absence of complex brain structures means that the creature can't feel pain, but there must be an element of conjecture in that belief.

> **Box 5.2 Do Plants Feel Pain?**
>
> Forest fires have increased in frequency with climate change (Figure 5.9). They can be disastrous events, destroying large areas of woodland, and devastating communities while costing life, but do the trees *feel* anything as they burn? The first response of most is that this is a ridiculous question; how can they? They're plants, not animals. However, there is some evidence that plants can communicate that they are in a stressful environment to other plants. Tobacco and tomato plants that are not watered or have their stems cut emit frequent high-frequency (20–100 kHz) sound; when the plants are not in environmental stress they omit far fewer of these sounds (Khait et al., 2019). One plausible mechanism for generating these sounds is the process of cavitation whereby air bubbles burst in the xylem of the plant. Plants can also emit volatile compounds when stressed by drought, and trees respond to the health of their neighbours.
>
> It's one thing communicating distress or a warning to a similar organism, but quite another to say that the organism is experiencing something, such as pain, while it does so.
>
> Figure 5.9 A forest fire: firefighters work to put out a forest fire on Signal Hill, Cape Town. Are the trees hurting? Source: Rodger Bosch/AFP/Getty Images.

Theory of Mind

Santino is a chimpanzee in Furuvik Zoo in Gävle, Sweden. Either because he wished to display his dominance, was annoyed by tourists staring at him, or was just plain bored, he started throwing stones at the (initially) unsuspecting tourists (Harari, 2016). What was even more interesting was that he showed clear signs of planning ahead: early in the morning he would collect suitable stones and put them in neat piles ready for use when the tourists arrived. Not surprisingly, word got around and the tourists learned to back off when he reached for his pile of stones; clever tourists. Santino then engaged in what can only be described as preplanned deceptive behaviour; he made a pile of hay and hid stones under it so that he could produce them suddenly and throw them quickly at the again unsuspecting visitors (Osvath & Karvonen, 2012).

Why would Santino behave in this way? Because he wanted to throw the stones at people, but he knew that if the people could see the stones they would stay away, so it was necessary to deceive them. Santino had an idea what other people were thinking. Deception is only possible if you have a theory of mind: you need to know what the other person believes, how the other person thinks.

A **theory of mind** is an important component of awareness in social animals. Not everyone is totally convinced by Santino's feats, arguing more research is necessary (see Shettleworth, 2010, for the sorts of arguments based on learning theory employed to be able to avoid ascribing a theory of mind to primates).

There is much research on chimpanzees and theory of mind, starting with a famous paper by Premack and Woodruff (1978), who claimed to have demonstrated the chimpanzees understand human goals. Since then, a debate has raged about the best methodology to use, and how results should be interpreted. The most reasonable conclusion at present is that, unsurprisingly, the answer is complex, and that chimpanzees have some theory of mind, but not in the full manner humans do (Call & Tomasello, 2008). In particular, there is no evidence that chimps understand false beliefs, such as being able to predict what another will do based on what that other knows, when the first chimp knows that what the other knows is in fact wrong. In this way the behaviour of the chimpanzees resembles that of younger children who are still, in Piagetian terms, highly egocentric (Kesselring & Müller, 2011).

Cheney and Seyfarth (1990) explored the minds and society of vervet monkeys, showing that they have sophisticated understanding of other monkeys' social roles. You have to be smart to survive in a complex social group of other smart animals. You are at a great advantage if you can work out the motives of others, and if you can work out if others are trying to deceive you. To be able to do these things you need to work out what the other believes, and sometimes what the other believes you believe. That is, you need a complex mental model of the minds of at least the other close members of your social group. The connection between social intelligence and theory of mind is obvious: to be socially intelligent you need a sophisticated theory of mind. To be able to work out what someone clever is likely to do and decide how to respond to that, you need to be able to mentally simulate their thoughts and actions, and what they will most likely do in response to your actions.

We then have the question of whether you can have a theory of mind without being conscious. Can you imagine a computer program that learns to be prosocial?

These results on the theory of mind in non-human animals are important because it's very difficult to imagine having a theory of mind without a sense of self versus other, and in turn it's difficult to conceive of that without self-awareness and consciousness. So these results suggest that at least animals such as chimpanzees are conscious in a way not wholly dissimilar to us. It is, however, always possible for a sceptic to produce increasingly convoluted alternative explanations in terms of conditioning and associative learning. In the end, you have to decide which you think is the most parsimonious explanation.

The Importance of Social Interaction

A theory of mind is essential for dealing with other clever animals like you. The idea that consciousness serves some social function is widespread. The evolutionary biologist E.O. Wilson sums up this approach in his (2012) book *The Social Conquest of Earth*, when he says that we evolved intelligence to 'feel empathy for others, to measure the emotions of friends and enemy alike, to judge the intentions of all of them, and to plan a strategy for personal social interactions'. The *Social Intelligence Hypothesis*, as this idea is called, might explain why humans had to become so clever, but does it also explain why they were conscious?

A corollary of this approach is that, if a species does not inhabit a complex social network where members need to model others, it has no need of consciousness. But we suspect that at least some, and perhaps many, other social species have consciousness to some degree. Hence, although consciousness may serve a social function in humans, it is unlikely to have developed for that reason alone. We should again distinguish between consciousness and self-consciousness, and argue that the development of self-consciousness depends on high intelligence and belonging to a complex social network.

Prosocial behaviour is behaviour that benefits other people, without necessarily benefitting yourself. When you donate or share something, or volunteer for some unpaid activity, you are engaging prosocially. To do so you also need to know what others will find beneficial, so prosocial behaviour necessitates having a theory of mind (Figure 5.10). There is now considerable evidence that chimpanzees can sometimes act prosocially. For example, if one has access to a tool, such as a straw, that another chimpanzee does not have access to and that would enable that other chimpanzee to achieve some goal that they can't achieve without it (drinking from a spot they can't reach), the first chimpanzee will pass the second chimpanzee the straw. Usually, the first one doesn't get rewarded – the second chimpanzee rarely offers to share the drink with the first (Tennie et al., 2016; Warneken & Tomasello, 2006).

Figure 5.10 A group of chimpanzees at Ngamba Island Chimpanzee Sanctuary, Lake Victoria, Uganda. Chimpanzees live in socially complex networks where social status really matters. Having a theory of mind greatly facilitates social interaction. Source: DEA/G. Cozzi/De Agostini/Getty Images.

There are even suggestions that some chimpanzees engage in ritual behaviour, which supposes a high level of consciousness. Kühl et al. (2016) observed chimpanzees in West Africa accumulating stones in piles at specific sites reminiscent of human cairns. Sites were mainly around trees, and rocks were often thrown into position. Although there are presently other explanations, such as exaggerated display behaviours, they do not cover all the facts, such as the specific locations. The suggestion that the chimpanzees are practising a form of religion is taking the interpretation of the data a bit far, but we must conclude that some animals engage in highly sophisticated behaviour.

The Evolution of Consciousness

If consciousness evolved as a result of natural selection, it must confer some evolutionary advantage. What might this advantage be?

Some researchers argue that organisms capable of some kind of consciousness, possessing a sensory and neural system capable of some kind of representation, appeared in the geological Cambrian period, with fossils possessing these structures appearing from about 520 million years ago (Feinberg & Mallatt, 2013). Edelman (1992, 2003) distinguished primary moment-to-moment consciousness, or simple consciousness, also assumed to be present in many animals, from higher-order consciousness, or self-consciousness, that relies on symbols, mostly language based. Although, of course, we are most unlikely to know for sure when self-consciousness first appeared in humans, there are a few indications of when it did so.

Something very significant in human evolution happened around 60 000 years BP (before present). Modern humans – *Homo sapiens* – evolved in Africa, perhaps as long as 200 000 years ago, although some estimates are more recent (100 000 BP). For tens of thousands of years they lived in Africa doing the same thing millennium after millennium – that is, not very much. Then several things happened very close together: they spread out of Africa and multiplied greatly, they became more aggressive hunters, their tools became much more sophisticated, and there are clear signs of the widespread appearance of art, ritual burial, and therefore religion, and music. This period is sometimes called the *Upper Palaeolithic Revolution* (Diamond, 1997). It is unlikely that all these things appeared independently and coincidentally; it seems obvious that they are related in some way. One possibility is that they are linked to the evolution of language; genetic mutations and changes in the speech apparatus appear around then (Harley, 2014). It is also possible that this change was in some way linked with the evolution of consciousness.

We have seen that social intelligence confers great advantage in rich social networks. The most vociferous proponent of the idea that consciousness is a consequence of sophisticated social intelligence is the Cambridge animal psychologist Nicholas Humphrey (Humphrey, 1984, 2006). Humphrey argues that you can only attain the highest level of the mental simulation of others if you are conscious. Consciousness provides a huge evolutionary advantage, and once acquired by some it was rapidly selected for.

Humphrey thinks that any species with a sufficiently rich social life will develop consciousness, although he is cagey about any other species managing to do so, apart perhaps from the great apes. This view appears to equate consciousness with self-consciousness (Humphrey rather dismisses this distinction, asking what other kind of consciousness there is, but our conclusion has been that the classification of consciousness is complex). The Cambridge Declaration attributes consciousness to several animal species, and many of them do not have social systems as complex as those of primates.

Mithen (1996, 2005) argues that around the time of the Upper Palaeolithic Revolution there was a major change in the cognitive processes of humans that enabled them to think differently. Before this time he argued that the minds of earlier humans and precursor species were highly compartmentalised or modular, with separate and specific domains.

A change combined the ways of thinking into a very fluid, non-modular way exemplifying what Mithen called cognitive fluidity. Cognitive fluidity is an important aspect of consciousness, enabling us to reflect on all of our thinking and behaviour.

Protoconsciousness

Our closest neighbours, Neanderthals (either a separate species, *Homo neanderthalensis*, or possibly a subspecies, *Homo sapiens neanderthalensis*), have a rather bad reputation, as slow, ugly, stupid creatures wiped out (or forced to the margins) by the more graceful and intelligent *Homo sapiens*. This popular image is unwarranted. Like humans, Neanderthals used tools and made fires, and almost certainly used language, made musical instruments, and possibly used ritual burial (Rendu et al., 2016). It is difficult to believe that such achievements are not possible without human-like levels of consciousness.

Allan Hobson describes a state he calls protoconsciousness, which is very like the dream state that occurs in rapid eye movement (REM) sleep (Hobson, 2009). In the great majority of dreams, there is awareness but no self-awareness; impressions and perceptions are jumbled and not integrated. Hobson argues that protoconsciousness preceded self-awareness and full human consciousness in evolutionary terms. Babies and young children also experience a state of protoconsciousness before they mature. It makes sense that some other animals are in a state of protoconsciousness, and, although we cannot be sure, possibly early humans and Neanderthals.

The Importance of Language

As far as we know, only humans have language. Human language uses a finite number of words combined with a finite number of rules for combining words to be able to produce an infinite number of sentences that can be used to communicate about anything, including language itself (Harley, 2014). The key idea is that we can communicate about anything; bees may have an impressive dance that tells other bees about the location of rich nectar sources, but they're limited to communicating about nectar.

Some other species have impressive communication systems. Monkeys have different calls for different threats; the dance of the honey bee is well known; and some dogs seem capable of understanding some aspects of human language, being able to respond to different words. But again they are extremely limited in what they can communicate about.

Many people believe that species such as whales and dolphins use a language. In fact, there is no evidence that they do, at least as 'language' is defined above, although they do possess an impressive range of cognitive, perceptual, and social skills (Figure 5.11). Then we have attempts to teach human-like languages to animals. We have seen that Pepperberg taught Alex the parrot language, and he understood an impressive number of words, and aspects of word order. Most of this work, however, has focused on teaching language to chimpanzees. One famous example is that of teaching an artificial language based on English to a bonobo chimp called Kanzi; her performance is impressive, but researchers still argue over whether her performance has captured the key features of human language (Harley, 2014; Savage-Rumbaugh, 1996; Sundberg, 1996).

Figure 5.11 Dr Louis Herman researches dolphin sensory abilities. Dolphins display an impressive range of cognitive, perceptual, and social skills, and might well be self-consciousness. There is no clear indication though that they routinely use a language. Source: Tony Korody/Sygma/Getty Images.

It is apparent then that only humans are born into a culture that uses language. Why is language so important when thinking about consciousness? Many researchers (e.g. Corballis, 2014, 2017; Mithen, 1996) see the evolution of language as a critical step in human evolution and the development of advanced cognitive skills and consciousness. We can only conceive of ourselves as ourselves, that is be self-conscious, if we have a symbol for ourselves, such as the first-person pronoun 'I' (Gallagher & Zahavi, 2012).

Mithen (1996) argues that the evolution of language was essential for the development of reflexive consciousness. It allowed non-social ideas to be imported into the domain of social intelligence. In Mithen (2005), music took the stage: our ancestors sang and used music to increase group cohesion, and language developed from that. Hence the development of self-awareness sprang ultimately from early attempts to communicate by whatever means in social networks. Needless to say, reasoning about early archaeology is somewhat speculative.

Recursion

The power of human language comes from its ability to generate an infinite number of sentences using a finite number of grammatical rules to combine a finite number of words. As a consequence, we can use language to express any idea. We obtain this immense power with a process known as recursion. Recursion is when something is defined in terms of itself, such as this dictionary entry:

> *Recursion.* See recursion.

We can define grammatical rules in terms of themselves, such as with the linguistic construction known as centre-embedding, where we could carry on, potentially infinitely, embedding new clauses.

> The rat the cat expired.
> The rat the cat the mouse loved expired.
> The rat the cat the mouse the louse sucked loved expired.

In practice, such sentences rapidly become very difficult to understand.

Chomsky (1957) argued that recursion gives human language its great power – in particular its infinite creativity and its ability to express any idea. He later went on to claim that the ability to use recursion is also what makes human language unique (Hauser et al., 2002). The ability to use recursion is what makes humans special.

Corballis (2014, 2017) adopts a broadly similar approach, although he argues that recursive thinking was prior to language, and that language made use of the ability to think recursively. In particular, Corballis argues that language and recursive thought enable us to make use of mental time travel, enabling us to bring past events into consciousness, examine them, and think about the future and what is likely to happen if particular events occur. As far as we can be sure, only humans can make use of mental time travel. We will see later how important mental time travel is in consciousness research (see Chapter 8).

Recursive thinking is also important in sophisticated social intelligence. In many social situations, I might try to work out what you think of me, or even what you think I think of you. We could go on. Recursion is important in deception and lying: you need to be able to work out what I think you think I think …

Language enables us to provide an internal commentary on our mental processes. (We don't just mean internal spoken language; sign language is as powerful as spoken language, and users report an internal sign language.) It is very difficult to envisage how we could answer questions such as 'Am I aware?' or 'Am I aware of being aware?' without some kind of internal language. So, while language might not be essential for lower types of consciousness, it does seem to be so for higher self-reflective types.

The Bicameral Mind

Other researchers have argued that there have been very substantial recent changes in cognition in humans. The American psychologist Julian Jaynes (1920–1997) proposed that there was a significant change as recently as 3000 years ago (1000 BCE). Before that, Jaynes argued, minds were what he called *bicameral*. The left and right

> **TRY THIS:** What Makes a Good Liar?
>
> How effective a liar would one be without the ability to model others and what they think of us?

hemispheres, he proposed, were not fully integrated before this time, so that right-hemisphere brain activity was interpreted by the dominant left hemispheres as 'voices' from God or some other supreme authority. Essentially, early humans were 'schizophrenic', their dominant left hemispheres being perpetually exposed to voices generated by their right hemispheres. Hence, minds were split into two 'chambers', corresponding to the two hemispheres (hence bicameral). Although Jaynes talks about consciousness appearing then, he is using the word to refer to metaconsciousness – self-awareness, the realisation that we are conscious.

The evidence for this idea comes from an analysis of early literature. In Greek myths, such as those portrayed in Homer's epic poems the *Iliad* and the *Odyssey*, about the fall of Troy and its consequences, the gods were always speaking directly to humans, and humans were acting directly upon their instructions. The heroes are described as not having their own motivations, but as following the orders of the gods. At the end of the stories depicted in these poems, the gods withdrew from human affairs. Not long after, we see in Greek civilisation the development of a very rational way of thinking that led to the development of self-reflection and philosophy. Gods were much more distant, and did not speak to humans or interfere in everyday life. Consider also the changes observed in the Old Testament of the *Bible*, where in the early books God is always speaking directly to humans, but as time progresses he becomes much more withdrawn.

Jaynes is talking not just about the integration of different types of information, but about the development of meta-awareness – our ability to examine our own thoughts, our ability to introspect. He talks about the origins of consciousness, but it is really the origins of metaconsciousness; there is no reason to suppose that humans were not aware before this point. He also accepts that sometimes animals appear to be thinking about solving problems (e.g. apes and crows thinking about tool use), but because they lack language this meta-awareness is extremely restricted.

It should be said that these ideas about the bicameral mind are not widely accepted, or even now taken seriously. Clearly, there were changes in the ways of thinking of the Greeks in the first millennium BCE, but there is no evidence that there was revolution rather than evolution. Neither is it the case that the right hemisphere generates internal voices – and that's not the way auditory hallucinations are generated in schizophrenia. Finally, but importantly, what would have been the biological mechanism for the change and its transmission? There is no sign whatsoever of any major relevant mutation around this time. (Jaynes did address this point, arguing that the changes were prompted by the stress of the Bronze Age Collapse, a widespread time of social disorder around the end of the second millennium BCE probably provoked by climate change or a mega-volcano, although how these stressors would provoke the biological change is still unclear.) Note that Jaynes, therefore, places the development of modern consciousness as occurring much later than in all other theories, and tens of thousands of years after the development of language.

Panpsychism

Some think that things other than animals might be conscious too. **Panpsychism** is the view that consciousness is a universal and basic feature of all physical objects – or some views, some physical things. If it turns out that an electron has a physical state, then panpsychism is true. That means that it is like something to be an electron.

To most people this assertion sounds ridiculous. The idea reminds me of the ancient Greeks and Romans, who thought that trees and streams each had an associated minor deity, a nymph. Another currently more respected version of the same idea (called *pantheism*) is that reality is identical to divinity: everything is, or contains, some aspect of God.

Surely there can be nothing less conscious than a stone? Nevertheless panpsychism has remained a respectable philosophical tradition in its attempt to overcome the problem of mind–body duality by shifting the emphasis from the classic division of nature into objects, mind, space, and time, into some other division, such as events (Whitehead, 1933). Note that the basic idea says that everything, even a stone, has some consciousness, but does not imply that a stone has a mind of its own.

Panpsychism is, in fact, one of the earliest philosophical accounts of what we now call the mind–body problem, and its popularity only really started to decline as late as the early twentieth century (Koch, 2014). Panpsychism has made something of a comeback with the work of the neuroscientists Giulio Tononi and Christoph Koch, who argue that consciousness is graded and can appear in very simple systems (Tononi & Koch, 2015). In an idea we will consider in more detail later (Chapter 8), Tononi and Koch say that everything that is the right sort of stuff is conscious. Any complex system has the basic attributes of mind and has a minimal amount of consciousness in the sense that it feels like something to be that system. The more complex the system, the larger the repertoire of conscious states it can experience. They formalise complexity with a measure they call *integrated information*. Not everything can be conscious, but, most controversially, even circuits as simple as a photodiode (made up of a light-sensitive sensor and a little memory) can have a tiny amount of experience (by which they must mean awareness). Some consider David Chalmers to have panpsychic views.

Apart from the question of how an inanimate object could possess any mental property or an element of consciousness, panpsychism suffers from the *combination problem*. Each neuron in the brain might have a degree of consciousness, but how do they then combine to make the whole brain conscious? A parallel problem is why isn't a very large number of rocks as conscious as we are? One solution is that, rather than the micro-consciousnesses simply adding up, they interact in some way under the right conditions so that animal consciousness emerges, although how they interact is unclear. Not everyone agrees that the combination problem is as severe as most take it to be (Harris, 2019).

The *Stanford Encyclopaedia of Philosophy* remarks that most people's reaction to panpsychism is an incredulous stare: how can people get paid for thinking such rubbish? But the history of science and thought is full of ideas that were met with incredulous stares that later turned out to be right after all. In 1895, just eight years before the Wright brothers took off at Kitty Hawk, the renowned physicist Lord Kelvin was supposed to have said 'heavier-than-air flying machines are impossible' (Figure 5.12). So, we should suspend our disbelief and consider the evidence, which is in part that no other account of consciousness is coherent or satisfying to many people.

Another problem is that the theory isn't really a theory because it's not scientific. How should we go about testing it? How could we falsify the notion that a rock has a small element of consciousness?

Figure 5.12 The first controlled, powered, and sustained heavier-than-air human flight, on 17 December 1903, near Kitty Hawk, North Carolina, by the Wright brothers, Orville and Wilbur. In 1895, Lord Kelvin, one of the most noted and respected physicists of his generation, had proclaimed the received wisdom that 'heavier-than-air flying machines are impossible'. We should be a little wary of rejecting alternatives to the received wisdom (such as panpsychism) out of hand. Source: Universal History Archive/Universal Images Group/Getty Images.

But if we accept a physicalist position, as of course most researchers do, then logically there are really only two alternatives (Nagel, 1979; Seager & Allen-Hermanson, 2015): either the mental emerge in some way from the physical, or everything has a mental aspect. So, either consciousness emerges somehow or we adopt panpsychism, and we cannot reject panpsychism out of hand.

Chapter Summary

- The Cambridge Declaration of 2012 states 'that humans are not unique in possessing the neurological substrates that generate consciousness'.
- The distributional question is: which non-human animals (if any) are conscious?
- The phenomenological question is what is the consciousness of a particular animal like?
- Many animals are capable of complex cognitive skills involving superior memory, episodic memory, metacognition, planning, tool use, and deception.
- Tests of self-recognition, such as the mirror test, suggest that several animal species can recognise themselves and have a concept of self.
- However, self-recognition need not be associated with consciousness.
- Experiencing pain, which entails consciousness and awareness, needs to be distinguished from avoiding noxious stimuli, which does not.
- Some argue that fish feel pain.
- A theory of mind is a model we have of what others think, and is essential for tasks that involve taking someone else's point of view or deception.
- Consciousness might have evolved as a result of sophisticated social behaviour, when animals need a theory of mind, and a model of the self and of other's selves.
- One of the major proponents of a social driver in the evolution of consciousness is Nick Humphrey.
- Protoconsciousness is a precursor of consciousness, proposed by Allan Hobson, and experientially rather like the dream state.
- Only humans are born with the ability to use language.
- Language enables us to communicate an infinite number of ideas using a finite system of words and grammatical rules.
- Only humans appear to have the ability to reason recursively, and recursion gives human language its great power.
- Recursion plays an important role in theory of mind and social intelligence.
- The bicameral mind hypothesis is that humans developed meta-awareness when the left and right hemispheres became fully integrated only a few thousand years ago.
- Panpsychism is the idea that consciousness is distributed widely in the universe. Some argue that even some very simple systems can have a modicum of experience.

Review Questions

1. In psychology, a double dissociation is observed when one person can do one thing but not another, while in another person the reverse pattern is found. For example, some patients with brain damage can produce language but not comprehend it, while others can comprehend it but not produce it. Are intelligence and consciousness an example of a double dissociation?
2. What would a suitable version of the mirror test be for organisms such as bats that make use of echolocation more than vision?
3. Animals in distress appear to be in pain – they are exhibiting pain behaviour. What arguments could you muster to support the proposal that appearances are deceptive, and that there is no experience of pain?
4. Which social behaviours could be said to be 'easier' to carry out if the animal is conscious?
5. When and why did self-awareness evolve?
6. Which animals are likely to be conscious, and which self-conscious, and what in their biology explains this difference?
7. What are the ethical implications of panpsychism?
8. Many arguments about consciousness in other animals, computers, or even in other people, are based on analogy: if a person or animal acts like me in a particular situation, they are probably like me and therefore probably conscious. If a dog looks to be in pain, he is probably experiencing pain and, therefore, is at least aware. How reasonable is this argument? How scientific is it? How philosophically sound is it?

Recommended Resources

The Mind of an Animal

Balcombe, J. (2016). *What a Fish Knows*. London: Oneworld.
Waal, F. De (2016). *Are We Smart Enough to Know How Smart Animals Are?* London: Granta.
Godfrey-Smith, P. (2016). *Other Minds: The Octopus and the Evolution of Intelligent Life*. London: William Collins.

The Evolution of Consciousness

Humphrey, N. (1984). *Consciousness Regained: Chapters in the Development of Mind*. Oxford, UK: Oxford University Press.
Humphrey, N. (2006). *Seeing Red: A Study in Consciousness*. Harvard, MA: Harvard University Press.
Humphrey, N. (2011). *Soul Dust: The Magic of Consciousness*. London: Quercus.
Mithen, S.J. (1996). *The Prehistory of the Mind: A Search for the Origins of Art, Religion, and Science*. London: Thames and Hudson.
Mithen, S.J. (2005). *The Singing Neanderthals: The Origins of Music, Language, Mind and Body*. London: Weidenfeld & Nicolson.
Renfrew, C. (2007). *Prehistory: The Making of the Human Mind*. London: Phoenix.

Panpsychism

Harris, A. (2019). *Consciousness*. New York: Harper. A popular science account of consciousness arguing for panpsychism.

Koch, C. (2012). *Consciousness: Confessions of a Romantic Reductionist*. Cambridge, MA: MIT Press.

Strawson, G. (2006). *Consciousness and its Place in Nature*. Exeter, UK: Imprint Academic.

PART II

THE WORKINGS OF CONSCIOUSNESS

6 LOOKING AT OUR OWN MINDS

This chapter examines introspection, and why its results are not always reliable. We begin with the nature of introspection and the process of trying to study our own consciousness, called phenomenology. We then look at what we believe about the world, and how unreliable these beliefs can be. The unreliability of these beliefs can be exacerbated by brain damage, most strikingly in a state called denial. Although the private nature of consciousness sets its study apart from the rest of science, you'd think that there would be a positive side: at least we can study consciousness by looking into our own minds. This process of looking into our own minds is called introspection. Introspection sounds easy enough: we report on what we are thinking now. However, it turns out that we do not know ourselves very well. We think we know why we act as we do, but our behaviour is influenced by many small things in the past, and we do not have easy access to all of them. Introspection turns out to be of very limited use.

How much of our minds are we conscious of now? How much are we in principle capable of being conscious of? Are there parts of the mind that are mostly hidden from consciousness? We next examine the unconscious, particularly the psychodynamic views of Freud and Jung. We conclude by looking at how what is outside consciousness might affect our consciousness without our realising it, a process commonly known as subliminal perception.

We will see that in general it is questionable whether it makes sense to talk about 'reality', and that our sense data is not necessarily veridical. In particular, my view of the world might not be the same as yours.

A further problem is that our view of the world is not reliable. We do not have reliable access to the causes of our behaviour. Our behaviour is influenced by many things of which we might not be aware. We forget things. We might be deluded. These difficulties make introspection, which is the most obvious means of gathering data about ourselves and our own behaviour, very unreliable. All we can report is what we currently believe.

The Contents of Consciousness

We have noted before that we are always conscious of something, but what is that something? What kind of things do we think about? And what methods do we have available for exploring the contents of consciousness?

The Stream of Consciousness

Our impression is that the contents of our consciousness seem to be a continuous stream of mental chatter and perceptions. William James used the term the **stream of consciousness** to refer to the flow of thoughts, feelings, ideas, and impressions in the conscious mind (James, 1890). We can add music to this list, particularly the annoying 'ear worm' when a tune can get stuck and play seemingly clearly time and time again, becoming immensely annoying (Beaman & Williams, 2010). James was impressed by the stream's apparent continuity; he argued that, although we are only aware of one mental event at any one time, they merge together seamlessly to give the impression of a fast-flowing stream. Each 'object' of consciousness is linked in some way to the external world or what has gone before. We can though only be conscious of one object at a time, and we may decide to pay attention to one of these objects. James believed that introspection, the process of looking at the contents of our own minds, was limited as a tool for studying consciousness because, at best, we can freeze this stream in one moment and are limited to reporting just that. Other researchers go further, and argue that the stream itself is an illusion, not in the sense of not being real, but not being what it seems (Blackmore, 2002). We don't watch a rich stream of visual information, or listen to a perpetual soundtrack whether internally or externally generated. Our representations of the world are rather impoverished, as the phenomena of **change blindness** and **inattentional blindness** show.

But who is the 'we' observing the stream of consciousness and choosing to pay attention to part of it? We run into the problem of the homunculus again. Blackmore (2002) argues that the stream of consciousness is another illusion – not in the sense that it doesn't exist, but that it isn't what it seems to be. The stream of consciousness is not a succession of rich and detailed experiences, but of nothing much at all. Bernard Baars also argues that the stream of consciousness is illusory in the same way as watching a movie, when it is in fact (usually) 24 distinct pictures, or frames, a second. We assemble continuity from discrete events, and we can only be conscious of one thing at a time, as studies of ambiguous figures show (Baars, 1997; Elitzur, 1997).

My impression is that the stream of consciousness is only there when I look for it – it only exists during introspection. A moment's impression is that whenever we look something will be going on, and that we can only detect the stream when we are looking in some way. A lot of the time, I am not thinking about very much, so in that sense it is an illusion.

Part of the aim of Buddhist meditation is to quieten our inner voice and the stream of consciousness (Blackmore, 2002).

TRY THIS: Your Stream of Consciousness

Pay attention to your stream of consciousness. What is it comprised of? How detailed is it? Would you describe it as a continuous stream? Can you switch it off at will, and, if so, for how long? Research Buddhist meditation, and give it a try. To what extent would you conclude that the stream is a rich picture displayed on a screen with an observer watching it, or would you describe it in some other way?

The Process of Introspection

At first sight we are in a privileged position when studying consciousness: all we have to do is ask ourselves what we're conscious of just now. Introspection is the process of the examination of the contents of our own minds. What are you thinking right now? How do you feel? What are you conscious of right now? There, you've just introspected. Whereas **phenomenology** is a philosophical approach, introspection is a psychological act.

At first sight introspection is a splendid thing: we have a method suitable for the systematic investigation of our private states. In 1890, William James (Figure 6.1) wrote that 'introspection observation is what we have to rely on first and foremost and always ... everyone agrees that we there discover states of consciousness' (p. 185). But by definition introspection can't tell us about what is not conscious. We might be able to shift some material from unconsciousness to consciousness, for example by recalling something, but at any one time most of what we know is out of our reach, and must necessarily be so by the limited capacity of consciousness.

We can think of introspection as turning our attention inwards to our minds. This formulation is also problematic: who is turning their attention, and what is being examined? I find there is the possibility of an infinite regress here. As soon as I start paying attention to my mind, the focus of my attention shifts, from what I was previously paying attention to, to the act of paying attention, and then the act of paying attention to that act of attention ... and so on. At the very least, when we introspect what we observe is not just a sensation (say), but a sensation interacting with the act of observing. There is also the additional complication that observing the mind's contents changes those contents in some way. The French philosopher Auguste Comte (1798–1857) put it this way: 'the thinker cannot divide himself into two, of whom one reasons while the other observes his reason' (James, 1890).

Figure 6.1 The philosopher and psychologist William James (1840–1910). Among many other achievements, James was the first to set up an educational course in psychology, and is called 'the father of American psychology'. He was the brother of the novelist Henry James and diarist Alice James. William James coined the phrase 'stream of consciousness', a continuous flow of thoughts, impressions, and feelings. Source: Universal History Archive/Universal Images Group/Getty Images.

Farthing (1992) distinguishes three types of introspection: *analytic*, *descriptive*, and *interpretive*. Analytic introspection attempts to describe our experience in terms of its constituents. You have to be careful when carrying out analytic introspection to avoid committing what the psychophysicist Edward Titchener (1867–1927) called the *stimulus error* (Farthing, 1992). So, when I report what I'm looking at, I am not looking at a desk, but at quadrilateral shapes with quadrilateral columns (drawers to you) underneath, coloured grey, shading from light grey nearer the window to dark grey further away – add as much detail as you like. According to Titchener, I do not 'see' a desk. This assumption is highly questionable, and indeed it isn't really clear what I 'really' see, so this method has been called into disrepute. It was also problematic that analytic introspection is unreliable, because even observers trained in the method report 'seeing' different things (and, having tried it, I report I see different things at different times). But perhaps even worse, it isn't at all clear what this sort of method tells anyone about anything.

Descriptive introspection, also called phenomenological introspection, asks simply, 'What do I perceive, think, or feel?' Descriptive introspection reports our immediate experience, but is necessarily one step removed from it (Farthing, 1992). People use everyday language and categories ('I see a table' is permitted), but do not interpret what they introspect. We are, perforce, limited to what we can describe in language, and we can only describe one thing at a time.

Interpretive introspection attempts to discover the causes of our thoughts and feelings: not just what do I think, but why do I think it? The distinctions here are not always clear: if I say I am feeling love for someone, is that a description or an interpretation of the contents of my consciousness (Farthing, 1992)? As we shall see, although we might give a reason for doing or believing something, the reasons we report might not be correct.

People differ in what they report about the contents of consciousness, although it is not clear whether we differ in how we perceive our contents or just in how we report them. Strawson (2018) reports that he does not perceive a continuous stream of consciousness at all, but rather a series of repeated 'launches', as though consciousness gets rebooted every time he looks. Any period of true continuity is very different from the ones going immediately before and after. (This report is closer to my own experience.)

TRY THIS: Introspecting

Try introspecting. Look at a person or an object (for example, Figure 6.2). What are you seeing? Can you shift what you are seeing from, say, a face, to eyes and mouth, to the coloured circles of the eyes? What if anything is the importance of this process? Try analytic, descriptive, and interpretive introspection. And what is the difference, if any, if you recall a face rather than looking at it?

Figure 6.2 Types of introspection. Try each of analytic, descriptive, and interpretive introspection while looking at a human face.

As can be seen, simply thinking about what we're thinking about isn't as simple as it might first appear.

Phenomenology

Phenomenology is the philosophical study of experiences from the *first-person point of view*: we analyse the contents and structures of our own consciousness. Phenomenology is concerned with the proper description and understanding of experiences and how they are related to other experiences. Introspection is a tool used in phenomenology, but phenomenology is a much wider philosophical approach than the use of that tool. Phenomenology originated in Continental Europe with the ideas of such philosophers as Heidegger, Husserl, Merleau-Ponty, and Sartre. In contrast to our own first-person viewpoint, most of science puts aside our own experiences and beliefs and takes the supposedly neutral third-person viewpoint. (The second-person viewpoint would be talking about another, you.) Even then the distinction is not as clear cut as the average scientist might believe; for example, the validity of observations made looking through a telescope depends upon beliefs such as the accuracy of the observer's visual system and the construction of the optical device.

The blurriness of the distinction is shown if we reflect on even apparently simple psychology experiments. Suppose we ask a participant to press a button when a light comes on and measure that reaction time. What exactly are we measuring (Gallagher & Zahavi, 2012)? How does the participant know that the light has come on – are they introspecting and looking for an awareness of the light, or is there some simpler explanation that bypasses awareness? Such issues are rife in psychology, and indeed in the study of the psychology of language a huge literature has developed on the apparently simple task of people recognising words (Harley, 2014).

The discipline of phenomenology was founded by the German philosopher Edmund Husserl (1859–1938). Husserl's first key claim is that we should distinguish consciousness from what consciousness is directed at; he took from Brentano (1874) the idea that consciousness is intentional, that is that it is always directed at something, what he called the *intentional object* (Husserl, 1973 [1913]). We are always conscious *of* something, even if it is our own thoughts.

Husserl further asked how we should try to observe consciousness. He wanted to know how we observed objects in the world free of preconception. He said that knowledge of essence of things could only be possible if we 'bracket' all assumptions about the existence of an external world, while trying to remove all cognitive processes from perception; he called this procedure *epoché*. It involves trying to look at an object without preconception of what it is or how it appears, as though we can by effort abolish our interpretation of our sense data to get to the sense data itself. In an epoché, we try to suspend our usual attitude to what we perceive and instead of taking it for granted focus on what we experience. The phenomenologist will try to capture the experience as it is, as well as how perception of an object, say, differs from imagining or remembering that object (Gallagher & Zahavi, 2012).

Husserl's account of phenomenology contained a *transcendental ego*, the real self, which underlies all human thought and perception. A transcendental ego sounds rather like a homunculus, the ultimate inner little creature perceiving the world as it really is. Is there a real self watching the perceptions? And then the distinction talk about real perceptions stripped of cognitive processes doesn't fit well with what we know about cognitive processing; we can't remove cognitive processing at will, and it doesn't make much sense to talk about perceptions as they really are.

More recently, Daniel Dennett has used the term *heterophenomenology* to describe the scientific approach to the study of consciousness (Dennett, 1991). We take into account what a person reports, but do not take their claims as necessarily reliable. For, as we shall see, people are often wrong about themselves, but it takes a third party to know it. It is not the contents of the reports that are the data, but the reports themselves (Gallagher & Zahavi, 2012). So, heterophenomenology is the study of the phenomenology of another person.

> **TRY THIS: Finding a Raw Percept**
>
> Introspect by looking at a natural scene. Can you get to the raw percepts – the lowest-level sensory data? Can you change what you see? If you can't get to the real world just now, use Figure 6.3. Can you see objects as anything other than objects? Can you isolate individual sensory features, such as shape and colour in the absence of others? How does the scene correspond to qualia?
>
> Figure 6.3 A landscape of rainbow and tree. Can you get to the raw percepts, or can you see a rainbow only as a rainbow and a tree only as a tree? Source: Craig Roberts/Photographer's Choice/Getty Images Plus.

Experience Sampling

One way to find out what people think about is to ask them, and the most commonly used method is called the **experience sampling method (ESM)**. Participants carry a timer (now most likely to be a smartphone app) that makes a sound at predetermined or random intervals, and the person has to stop immediately and note what they were thinking just then. The ESM has applications to many areas where we want people to think about what they're doing, such as in education, when dieting, when trying to get sufficient exercise, and undergoing medical treatments (Myin-Germeys et al., 2009; Zirkel et al., 2015). ESM is also a useful method for studying mental illness; for example, it has shown that people with a major depressive disorder tend to think of ideas or memories associated with a positive affect less often than members of a control population (Telford et al., 2012).

What do people report they are thinking about when asked? Perhaps unsurprisingly, the variation is enormous and depends on the circumstances. One 'result' from ESM has entered urban folklore, the idea that men think about sex every 7 seconds (or every 15 seconds, or every 3 minutes, depending on the website you read). There is, in fact, very little research to back up any of these figures, as most studies ask people to estimate the frequency of thoughts retrospectively. Many attribute this claim to the Kinsey Reports (Kinsey et al., 1948, 1953) of the American sexologist Alfred Kinsey (1894–1956), who in fact just reported that '54% of men think about sex every day or several times a day, 43% a few times per month or a few times per week, and 4% less than once a month' (Kinsey Institute, 2020). A more recent ESM study of 283 college students found that men thought about sex 19 times a day, on average (and women 10 times a day), but that they thought about food and sleep more often (Fisher et al., 2012). Also the variation between people is enormous.

One important finding from experience sampling is that people do not always think about what we think they are thinking about: our minds wander from the task that should be at hand (nearly half, at 46.9%; Killingsworth & Grant, 2010). How many times have you sat in a class or meeting and found that you're not thinking about the class or meeting at all, but something completely different? We'll look at mind-wandering in detail later. About half the time we are thinking about what we are currently doing, and we think about the future more than the past (Busby Grant & Walsh, 2016).

The Limits of Introspection

The problems with interpreting what people report they are conscious of at any one time can be divided into problems with the accuracy of introspection and problems with attributing reasons for our behaviour.

The major limitation of introspective methods is that people obviously can only describe what they can put into words and what they can remember. Remembering might be a curious difficulty given people are asked about their immediate experience, but many ideas and impressions are very fleeting. I am often thinking of something only to know an instant later that I have forgotten it. Farthing (1992) describes other problems: putting things into words may distort ideas; people may reconstruct thoughts rather than describe them directly; and observing a mental process may change it. In addition, people may censor what they report, and people's reports cannot be independently verified. Someone might be reluctant to own up to thinking about sex so

> **TRY THIS:** Experience Sampling
>
> It's possible to try experience sampling on yourself. Just set up a series of alarms, for example, on your smartphone, to go off at several random times through the day, and note down what you were thinking about at the time they go off. How would you summarise your day's thinking?

much, for example. So what people report may not always be an accurate description of what they have thought.

We also have surprisingly poor access to the reasons why we act as we do. The classic paper on the problem of using verbal reports of mental processes as data is Nisbett and Wilson (1977). The main problem they identify is that we get into big trouble as soon as we start asking people why they are doing or have done something because people don't always really know why they have acted as they have. We don't explain our behaviour simply on the basis of sensory data, but instead we resort to theories about why people, including ourselves, behave as they do. As such, we are influenced by many types of cognitive bias and distortion.

An example of difficulty in attributing correct explanations to our behaviour is shown in the phenomenon known as *cognitive dissonance*. Goethals and Reckman (1973) provide a classic demonstration of this effect. They surveyed groups of students about their social attitudes, such as racial integration and bussing students into segregated schools. There then followed a discussion session, where a confederate had been planted in the audience who was extremely well versed in the arguments in favour and against bussing, and whose goal was to counter the prevalent belief of the group. Goethals and Reckman measured the attitudes of the students after this group. It is perhaps not surprising that the students shifted their attitudes in the direction encouraged by the persuasive argument; what is surprising is that, when then asked to describe their original opinions, the students were poor at doing so, and expressed their original beliefs as being very similar to their final beliefs. So, if they changed their minds in favour of bussing, they thought they had always been in favour of bussing. We cope with the cognitive dissonance of having to change our views by believing that they haven't been changed at all because we have always believed what we now believe.

Cognitive dissonance is a powerful and widespread phenomenon. In another unpleasant-sounding experiment, Zimbardo et al. (1969) made participants eat insects. Surprisingly, all the participants did, but some were asked to do so by a rude, bullying experimenter, and others were asked very nicely by a polite experimenter. Only the group asked to do so by the rude experimenter claimed that they had enjoyed eating the insects. Those with the nice experimenter could presumably account for their compliance by telling themselves they were just doing it to be nice. Those with the rude experimenter couldn't do this and had to find some other explanation why they had complied – and what could be easier than just believing you enjoyed the taste of munching on those crunchy legs. For example, we might hypothesise that when we decide to carry out some simple task, such as lifting a finger, the order of events is: conscious decision to act, planning the act, and execution.

So asking people what they're thinking about and why they're thinking or believing it are both fraught with difficulties.

Your Beliefs

We make statements about our *beliefs*. We use the verb 'believe' to express various degrees of tentativeness, from 'I believe Dhaka is the capital of Bangladesh' to 'I believe you love me'. One might now quibble and say that everything is really a belief, so that when I say 'it is sunny' I should really say 'I believe it is sunny'; there are after all some contrived ways in which my belief might be false, but in general we use 'believe' for statements about which we might have some doubt. In all cases when I say 'I believe x', I mean that I think x to be true.

I know I make mistakes, and I accept that some of my beliefs about the world might be wrong. I think my erroneous beliefs are peripheral, though. I can never remember that the capital city of Canada is Ottawa; I keep thinking it's Montreal (or perhaps Toronto). Such a mistake (and I apologise to all Canadians, particularly residents of Ottawa) doesn't matter that much to me. I accept perception isn't always totally veridical. We are fooled by visual illusions, for example. Figure 6.4 shows a Kanizsa triangle, which is a type of optical illusion demonstrating illusory contours. There appears to be a bright white triangle in the middle with real edges and contours making it stand out from the other white areas. These edges are illusory. We do not see what we think we see. We think, however, that our view of our immediate surroundings, and our beliefs about the here and now, are basically correct. But they are beliefs about the way the world is, rather than facts.

Figure 6.4 A Kanizsa triangle. There appears to be a bright white triangle in the middle with real edges making it stand out from the other white areas, but these edges are illusory. We do not see what we think we do. Source: Yuriy Vlasenko/Shutterstock.

So, pragmatically, we often say that we believe something to flag a degree of uncertainty. 'I believe my grandfather was born in Southampton, England' – I think it's true, but I am by no means absolutely certain.

'Beliefs' are a special kind of thing; we can't just believe, we have to believe something. In the same way, we can't just think, we must think something. Statements like 'believe', which exhibit the phenomenon of intentionality, 'about ness', are called *propositional attitudes*.

So, when I think about my beliefs, rather like a less sceptical and less disciplined Descartes, I can rate how firmly I believe them, or how certain I am that they are right (that is, correspond with a world I believe to be right), and all my beliefs fall on a continuum of certainty.

How wrong can we be about our beliefs?

The Reliability of Beliefs

Finally, some people are very sceptical about the world (Box 6.1). We don't need to go to these extremes to see that some of our beliefs are questionable. People have different beliefs about religion, morality, and politics, which can lead them to have very different value systems. People may say that someone else's beliefs are wrong, but it can be extremely difficult getting someone to change their beliefs, as you will know if you have ever had a serious political disagreement with someone clever and articulate. Beliefs such as these are built on other beliefs, and to get two

> **TRY THIS: Your Beliefs**
>
> Choose some beliefs and rate them on a 1–7 scale for certainty. Try to make the beliefs you rate as disparate as possible. Is there any pattern in your ratings? How difficult did you find it simply to choose statements you would consider to be beliefs?

> **Box 6.1   Solipsism, Anti-realism, and Deceiving Devils**
>
> *Scepticism* is the philosophical doctrine of questioning; we are particularly interested in being sceptical about knowledge. René Descartes questioned what he could be certain of; he concluded that he could only be absolutely certain of his existence (as questioning our own existence can only be done by something that exists, giving rise to his famous statement 'I think, therefore I am' ('je pense, donc je suis' in French and 'cogito, ergo sum' in Latin). The philosophical doctrine that we can only be sure that the only thing that exists is our own mind is called *solipsism*. We cannot be sure that the external world and other people exist beyond inside our minds. Because this view is counterintuitive to most people, it is often described as *anti-realism*.
>
> And yet ... why do we have these illusions of an outside world if, in fact, there is no such thing? A number of fanciful ideas have been proposed. We might be brains in vats bathed with the necessary nutrients and information supplied to our sensory systems by mad scientists (see Box 9.1), or we might be the creation of fiendish devils to provide their amusement, or we might even be the results of some sophisticated simulation, rather like in *The Matrix* series of films (The Wachowskis, 1999). In fact, Nick Bostrom argues that either the human species is likely to become extinct before it reaches a 'post-human' stage, or any post-human civilisation is unlikely to run simulations of their evolutionary history, or we are living in a computer simulation (Bostrom, 2003). David Chalmers has reportedly put the probability that we are living in a simulated universe at 20%. Therefore, we should take the idea that we are living in a simulation seriously. How can we tell whether or not we're living in a simulation? First, it is unlikely that the universe is completely simulated because simulating everything is likely to require too much computing power. Second, the simulation may well contain bugs. Hence, we should be on the lookout for presumably small glitches in reality, perhaps at the quantum level.
>
> Solipsism, anti-realism, deceiving devils, and simulations are all depressing hypotheses, and in general most people don't accept them. Such approaches get us nowhere. Even most solipsists act as though the outside world both exists and is as it appears to be. I've never met a solipsist who will let me punch them on the nose. We think that there is something out there that causes us to perceive the world and act in a particular way, which in turn changes the way the world appears. Just saying that our consciousness is some kind of illusion doesn't explain how that illusion arises, or why it feels like the way it does to be me.

apparently rational people to agree may involve stripping back layers of belief in a way few of us usually have time for.

Sometimes we are less rational than we think we are. We can suffer from mistaken beliefs that we refuse to change in the light of further evidence.

Could any of my beliefs about the world be wrong? Surely not. Yours maybe, but not mine. When a person has a persistent incorrect belief about the world, we say they have a delusion. Now I might believe that the capital of Tajikistan is Tashkent, but a better-educated person than me may point out that it is, in fact, Dushanbe. Even if I'm sceptical I would go to Wikipedia and there indeed it confirms that it's Dushanbe. Grudgingly admiring of my friend's superior general knowledge, I admit he's right and change my belief. I haven't been delusional here, simply wrong.

We also, when it comes to social behaviour such as stereotypes and prejudice, might not know what we think. Some of our beliefs are implicit, not explicit: we might deny vociferously that we are prejudiced, but, rather worryingly, act as though we are (Greenwald et al., 2002; Nosewk et al., 2009).

Delusions

I might persist in arguing that really the capital of Tajikistan is Tashkent. Wikipedia is wrong. After all, I'm told it occasionally is. Perhaps my friend has edited it to deceive me. My friend, getting frustrated, sends me a book on the history of Uzbekistan. I claim the book is a fake. Eventually, to settle it once and for all we fly to Tashkent and Dushanbe and speak to the people there. I say they are all involved in a giant conspiracy to try to fool me. Now I am no longer just wrong, I am *delusional*. You would worry about my mental health.

Delusions, along with hallucinations, characterise schizophrenia. One of the most common types of schizophrenia is *paranoid schizophrenia*, defined by the presence of paranoia,

---

Box 6.2 Schizophrenia

Schizophrenia is a type of psychosis, a severe type of abnormal state of mind defined as 'losing touch with reality', and therefore of obvious interest to consciousness researchers. Schizophrenia is a severe and distressing mental illness marked by hallucinations (particularly *auditory verbal hallucinations*, or *AVHs*), delusions (particularly paranoia, the belief that one is being watched or victimised, and megalomania, the belief that one is particularly important), problems with thinking and planning, and sometimes problems with emotional regulation, motivation, and social interaction. The cause – or causes – of schizophrenia are not known, although there is a large genetic component, and several environmental causes stressing the developing foetus and child are known, such as oxygen starvation, childhood trauma or abuse, and early recreational drug abuse. It has been hypothesised that genetic predisposition interacting with environmental stressors results in abnormalities in neurotransmitter levels, including dopamine and glutamate, although the links are not simple. There are also structural differences between the brains of people with and without schizophrenia, although the direction of causality is not clear. Schizophrenia tends to first occur in late adolescence or early adulthood, and is often marked by periods of remission followed by relapses.

Fortunately, the development of antipsychotic medications has greatly improved the life quality of people with schizophrenia. However, like most medications antipsychotics have side effects, which can be severe and may affect compliance (whether or not people take the drug). The mechanisms of action of these drugs are not always fully understood. The most widely used typical antipsychotic, Haloperidol, reduces dopamine levels in the brain, although it has other effects too.

the delusional belief that someone in particular or people in general are out to get or deceive the person (see Box 6.2).

There are also neurological syndromes where a person's beliefs about the world and particularly other people appear to be very wrong. Here are some of the more dramatic examples.

The **Capgras delusion** (or syndrome) is the delusional belief that a friend or family member (or even number of people, but often the person's partner) has been replaced by impostors. These impostors look identical, but the person refuses to acknowledge that they are the same. The person will attribute the impostor to the activity of the secret service, robots, clones, or even Martians. Curiously, the patients do not express much interest in what has happened to the 'real' person; some are even very friendly to the supposed impostor. Capgras syndrome has been observed in people with brain injury, dementia, and schizophrenia, but is most commonly associated with parietal-temporal lesions (Ellis & Lewis, 2001; Stone & Young, 1997). Capgras syndrome is named after Joseph Capgras (1873–1950), a French psychiatrist who described the case of Madame M., a woman who claimed her husband and other loved ones had been replaced by doubles.

Lucchelli and Spinnler (2007) describe the case of Fred, a 59-year-old well-educated man who developed severe frontal dementia. Early on, Fred's wife Wilma reported that for over a year he had been seeing her as a 'double'. In the first event, he returned home and asked her, Wilma, where Wilma was. He denied that she was Wilma, that he knew very well who the real Wilma was, and concluded that the real one had gone out and would be back later.

Capgras delusion is thought primarily to be a disorder of face processing. (Face-processing disorders are known as prosopagnosia.) In particular, people cannot access the units that store information about people (called person identity nodes) as normally happens in face recognition. Although the person is activating the correct face recognition unit, they do not get the emotional arousal that normally goes with well-known faces. The delusion arises from an attempt to reconcile the lack of emotional activation with the perceptual recognition (Corlett et al., 2010; Ellis & Lewis, 2001; Ellis & Young, 1990). Some argue that there is an additional problem with reasoning so that some people are biased to thinking that the mismatch is with others, leading to Capgras, while others are biased to thinking that the problem is with them, leading to Cotard's (see below, Stone & Young, 1997). Hirstein and Ramachandram (1997) propose a similar type of explanation, arguing that connections from the face-processing region of the ***temporal*** lobe to the limbic system have been damaged.

The *Fregoli delusion* is another delusional disorder of person recognition in which people believe that two or more people are the same person in disguise, often persecuting the sufferer (Langdon et al., 2014). This can be explained at the functional level using the same sort of face-recognition model, but this time postulating that different face-recognition units are erroneously attached to the same person identity node. Once again there are several physical causes, including trauma to the brain, prolonged use of the drug L-DOPA (used to treat Parkinson's disease), and psychopathological disorders such as schizophrenia. However, the detailed mapping between psychological explanation in terms of a face recognition model and the range of damaged brain regions is again not perfectly understood. The disorder is named after the Italian actor Leopoldi Fregoli (1867–1936), who was famous for his ability to change his appearance quickly.

Fregoli and Capgras syndromes are types of delusional misidentification syndromes. We also rarely find *subjective doubles syndrome* (where a person thinks that they have a double, or doppelgänger, with different personality characteristics, who is leading their own life), and also intermetamorphosis, where a person believes they can see another person changing into someone else.

These delusions are bizarre, but *Cotard's delusion*, commonly known as the walking corpse syndrome, is even stranger: a person believes they are already dead, or do not exist (Debruyne et al., 2010). It is difficult to imagine what it would be like to be a sufferer of Cotard's delusion. There are less extreme versions where the person thinks they are missing a body part, or blood, or are putrefying, or are dead but in heaven or hell. Cotard's is a severe delusion of negation, and appears to be related to severe depression and self-loathing.

Charland-Verville et al. (2013) describe the case of a patient who following an episode of depression attempted suicide by self-electrocution, and was left with severe brain damage. Eight months later he told his doctor that his brain was dead, that he did not need to eat or sleep, and that he was coming to the doctor's to prove that he was dead. He admitted that, if he could still speak, hear, and so on, his mind was still alive, and he could not explain this observation given that his brain was dead. The researchers examined his brain activity using positron emission tomography (PET). There was hypometabolism (greatly reduced metabolism) across a wide region of the brain, suggesting **bilateral** (on both sides of the brain) lesions of the **fronto-parietal cortical network**, especially parts of the dorsolateral frontal lobes, the posterior parietal lobes, **precuneus**, and the anterior cingulate cortex. The authors note that other research has shown that these regions are critical for conscious awareness (Vanhaudenhuyse et al., 2011), and contain key parts of the default mode network, which has key responsibility for integrating the self (Buckner et al., 2008; Northoff & Bermpohl, 2004). We will consider these idea and brain regions later, but for now all we need note is that some delusional disorders are disorders of consciousness, and that intact consciousness depends on particular areas of the brain, particularly the fronto-parietal network.

Mass Hysteria

Sometimes more than one individual is affected by the same delusion, a phenomenon we call *mass hysteria* (or in DSM *mass psychogenic illness*). In October 1965, over a hundred schoolgirls at a secondary school in Blackburn, northern England, complained of dizziness, and many fainted; 85 were taken to hospital. No organic factors could be identified, and the most likely cause was identified as a mass hysteria leading to over-breathing (Moss & McEvedy, 1966). The authors describe how the hysteria is spread by a social 'contagion'; and in most cases there is a 'trigger', with some germ of truth, that gets things going (such as some actual cases of fainting in an earlier assembly, and a polio epidemic earlier in the year, in the Blackburn case).

A web search will reveal many other hypothesised cases of mass hysteria, not always as well documented as the Blackburn case, with glorious names such as the Tanganyika laughter epidemic of 1962, the Portuguese Morangos com Açúcar Virus (strawberries with sugar) soap opera virus of 2006, and the widespread and repeating *koro*, the shrinking penis panic (now listed in DSM; see Mattelaer & Jilek, 2007). A succession of pop stars, from The Beatles to David Cassidy and Donny Osmond to the Bay City Rollers, have prompted mass hysteria, with young fans swooning and crying when they see their idols (Figure 6.5).

Mass hysteria can either be positive or negative. A positive mass delusion is an enthusiasm for something, such as aliens, yeti, or The Beatles; a negative mass delusion is fear of something, such as witches, shrining penises, or toxic fumes (Bartholomew & Hassall, 2015). *Moral panics* are further examples of mass psychogenic illness when people come to believe that there is some threat to society, an example being satanic child abuse (see Box 6.5).

Confabulation

In all these cases of delusion, there is often a lack of insight into the person's condition. Some people

Figure 6.5 Beatles hysteria: fans at a performance by The Beatles at Shea Stadium, New York City, 15 August 1965, crying and fainting. The phenomenon was called Beatle mania, but The Beatles were not alone among pop stars in facing such adoration. Source: Everett Collection Inc/Alamy Stock Photo.

Box 6.3 The Tanganyika Laughter Epidemic of 1962

On 30 January 1962, three girls in a mission school for girls in Kashasha, a village near Bukoba on the western coast of what was then Tanganyika (and is now Tanzania), started laughing. The laughing reportedly became uncontrollable and started spreading, affecting 95 out of the 159 pupils, but none of the staff. All of the girls were between 12 and 18. Several of the girls lived in the nearby village of Nshamba, to where the 'epidemic' spread. By the end of May, 217 young people had had uncontrollable attacks of laugher typically lasting a few hours but up to 16. It took 18 months for the outbreak to die out completely, affecting in total around 1000 young people; the laughter was sometimes accompanied by other symptoms, such as crying, screaming, difficulty breathing, fainting, and flatulence. A similar but much smaller outbreak occurred around the same time near Mbarara, in Uganda, about 100 miles north of Bukoba (Rankin & Philip, 1963).

There are several theories as to why mass hysteria occurs and, of course, they might not be in conflict. Some say these incidents are either hoaxes or are greatly exaggerated. They often occur at times of uncertainty and social change. Independence from Britain had only

> **Box 6.3** (cont.)
>
> been declared on 9 December 1961. Many of the adolescents affected reported that they were afraid of something, but could not say what. Another hypothesis is that the hysteria was caused by a conflict between the more liberal youth and the more conservative older generation who had endured World War II. It is perhaps no coincidence that Beatle mania happened around the same time. Teenagers.

report that they know that what they believe is odd or fantastic, but by no means always. Often, to explain the bizarre beliefs people need to make up stuff – 'they must be doubles', 'they must be robots', 'they've implanted a receiver in my skull'. This process of manufacturing or distorting ideas and memories and providing complex fantastic explanations is known as **confabulation**. Confabulation is found in many disorders, including schizophrenia, dementia, and neurological conditions such as denial. Some consider confabulation a kind of filling in: the person is asked for information, so supplies it.

There are three messages to take away from these bizarre delusions. The first is that we can have very firmly held beliefs that are just wrong. The second is that illness or damage to the brain can change our belief system very specifically, so that we can hold beliefs that might have been thought to be incompatible with everything else we know. The third message is that the mapping between the brain and cognitive processes is obviously present, but is very complex. Capgras and Fregoli syndromes are very specific, but it is not the case that they result from very narrowly circumscribed damage to the brain, a pattern that we shall see repeated.

Denial

One of the characteristics of these delusional disorders is that, by the nature of the symptoms, the person affected denies that they are deluded, or have any symptoms of psychopathology. This denial of illness is fairly common in these types of syndrome. **Denial** is particularly common in spatial and attentional disorders such as neglect, which we will come to later. Denial as a neurological disorder is called **anosognosia**. Anosognosia is clearly another case of a disorder of self-awareness.

One of the most striking examples of anosognosia is the *Anton–Babinksi* syndrome (also known as Anton's syndrome, cortical blindness, or visual anosognosia). Patients with Anton–Babinksi suffer from damage to the **occipital lobe** of the brain where a great deal of high-level visual processing takes place (see Figure 6.6). These patients are cortically blind, which is easily demonstrated with the standard tests of vision, and which means that their eyes

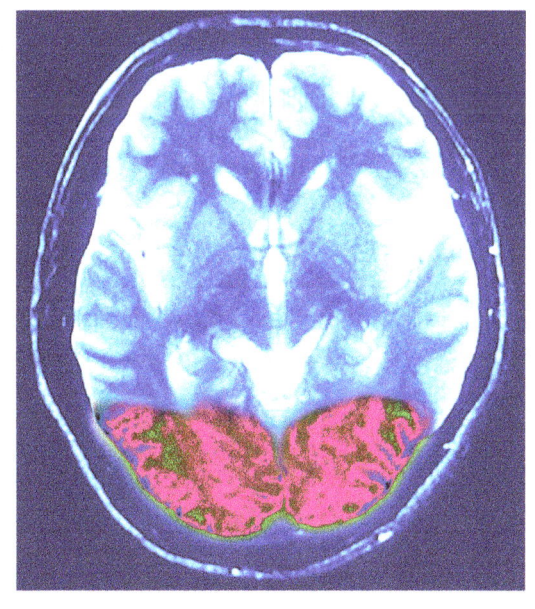

Figure 6.6 The occipital lobe of the brain. In this image of a slice through the brain the eyes would be towards the top. The occipital is towards the back of the head and is almost completely dedicated to relatively early visual processing.
Source: BSIP/Universal Images Group/Getty Images.

and optic nerves are completely normal. However, those with Anton–Babinksi deny that they are blind, arguing that they can see perfectly well. The denial is necessarily accompanied by much confabulation, as patients are forced to explain the mismatch between their behaviour and abilities and their beliefs. At first, it is not always obvious that the person has lost their sight because they do not report any problems; it is only when they knock into things and do things such as walking into closed doors that suspicions are aroused. Maddula et al. (2009) describe the case of a 83-year-old woman who suffered a stroke causing **bilateral** (affecting both sides of the brain) occipital lobe damage. Although unable to see anything, she said her vision was normal, providing answers to questions about what she could see (such as the colour of the doctor's tie); needless to say, her answers were completely wrong. These patients obviously need much care.

The exact causes of the behaviour of Anton–Babinski patients is not clear. There must be damage to other cortical areas in addition to the occipital cortex, or at least dissociations between the occipital cortex and other parts of the brain; one possibility is a disconnection between the **visual cortex** and language areas of the left hemisphere (Prigatano & Schachter, 1991), although much remains to be clarified about such an explanation.

Anosognosia is found in a range of neuropsychological problems, most commonly in neglect, and in this case is usually marked by damage to the right parietal lobe and the right fronto-temporal-parietal area (Moro et al., 2011). These patients usually deny that one of their limbs belongs to them, which is sometimes known specifically as **asomatognosia**.

> **Box 6.4** Dementia and Alzheimer's Disease
>
> As life standards and medicine advance, the population ages, and age-related illnesses that were once relatively uncommon become much more widespread, including *neurodegenerative diseases* that involve degradation of the nervous system, including the brain. *Dementia* is the general term for a broad range of symptoms, including loss of memory, problems with language, loss of ability to plan, personality changes, emotional problems, and many others; the diseases are *progressive* meaning they get worse with time, eventually, if the person lives long enough, leading to problems with motor control and death.
>
> There are several diseases that result in dementia, but the most common and best known is Alzheimer's disease. It is usually seen in people over 65, although *early onset Alzheimer's* can start much earlier. We think it affects about 5% of people over 65. The first symptoms are increasingly obvious memory lapses, with then difficulty planning, mood swings, and disorientation. Behaviour may include confabulation, as the person tries to explain their lapses. The brains of people with Alzheimer's disease are characterised by plaques and tangles of proteins and dead cells. The exact cause is unknown, although there is a clear genetic component, and factors such as depression, head injury, and high blood pressure play a part.
>
> Currently, there is no cure for Alzheimer's, although a healthy lifestyle can reduce the onset and severity, and certain drugs (that mostly act on the **acetylcholine** system) look promising, at least in the earlier stages.

Anosognosia is also often found in Alzheimer's disease (Box 6.4), where sufferers again deny that there is anything wrong with them or their memories. Anosognosia is unsurprisingly accompanied by confabulation.

Anosognosia is a complex phenomenon and probably comprises several different but similar deficits (Heilman et al., 1998; Moro et al., 2011). The underlying problem is one of synthesising different types of information. Consciousness involves the coming together of information, and the processes that are responsible for this coming together can be selectively disrupted. The affected person is unable to integrate sensory information with their current temporal-spatial model of the world and their spatial model of their own body. Hence, anosognosia is a disorder of self-monitoring (Berti et al., 2005).

Is Anything Unavailable to Consciousness?

In contrast to the limited amount of information of which we are aware at any one time, there is a massive amount of information outside momentary awareness. How is this material organised?

We should distinguish between processes that are outside of consciousness and content that is outside consciousness. If I ask you what the capital of France is, you will say 'Paris'; the name is brought into consciousness. but where was it before? We should further distinguish between material that could be brought into conscious and material that can't (called **unconscious**). When you are looking at an object or retrieving a name, some of the material that can be brought into consciousness but isn't yet is called *preconscious*. We also have material that is just beneath some threshold of conscious awareness, and which might influence the content of consciousness, called subliminal processing, discussed in more detail later in this chapter. Hence, we have several types of processing which turn out to be served by different systems in the brain (Dehaene et al., 2006).

Whereas unconscious cognitive *processing* is uncontroversial, unconscious *content* requires much more consideration. It is uncontroversial that we cannot access the earliest stages of visual processing, say; it is controversial that you have repressed early childhood memories.

Freud and the Unconscious

According to Freud's 'iceberg' model, the mind has three levels, and we are conscious of only one small part at any one time (Freud, 1924; Wilson, 2004b). At any one time, we are paying attention to what is at hand. We have seen that an important aspect of consciousness is its selectivity: we are not aware of very much right now, and we are not even aware of much we are doing right now. Then there is the preconscious – material of which we are not aware just now but which could be brought into awareness, if required. You probably weren't thinking of your breakfast just now, but now I ask you what you had, you can (I hope) remember; you have made the preconscious conscious.

The bulk of Freud's metaphorical iceberg is the unconscious (see Figure 6.7). Freud's theory of the unconscious was a complex one that changed over time. Whereas the *preconscious* contains material that could be brought into consciousness, but just isn't at a particular

Figure 6.7 Freud's iceberg model of the mind. Most of the iceberg is hidden beneath the waterline – part of what makes them so dangerous to shipping. For Freud the conscious mind is just the tip of the iceberg: much mental content is hidden away in the unconscious. Source: brainmaster/E+/Getty Images.

Figure 6.8 A Rorschach test item. What do you think of when you look at this image? Filthy. Source: zmeel/E+/Getty Images.

time, the unconscious contains material that we are not able to bring into consciousness. According to Freud, the material in the unconscious is so unpleasant to us that we actively repress it. It is a repository of memories and wishes, desires, and impulses.

In Freud's model, the unconscious is not just a passive repository of information: it is knowledge, memories, and desires actively kept from consciousness. How can we explore the contents of the unconscious? Freud believed that on occasion our guard would fall and the unconscious would break through in some way. This happens most frequently in dreams, when the contents of the unconscious break through in disguise, as we shall discuss later. The unconscious can also be manifest in what Freud called the psychopathology of everyday life (Freud, 1905). Slips and mistakes were for Freud very revealing, not occurring by accident but by the unconscious breaking through. These errors are called **Freudian slips**. A simple example Freud describes is that of an occasion when the President of the Austrian Parliament was contemplating a very difficult session, and instead of announcing, 'I declare this session open', he said, 'I declare this session closed'. Modern cognitive psychology explains the majority of errors in terms of mistakes being made in information-processing models (Harley, 2014).

Other more interventional approaches ask people what their associations are to a particular stimulus. The best-known example is called free association, and simply involves asking people to say what is the first thing that comes into their minds in response to, say, a word, or perhaps a dream fragment. The process can then be repeated with the response acting as the new stimulus. Free association is often combined with dream interpretation.

A similar type of method is the *Rorschach inkblot test*, where people are asked to describe what they see in an essentially random pattern (Exner, 2002; see Figure 6.8). The test is named after its creator, the Swiss psychologist Hermann Rorschach (1884–1922), and is the most commonly used projective personality test, where people's emotions and hidden conflicts are revealed by their interpretation of ambiguous stimuli. For measuring personality, objective tests based on questionnaires are now greatly preferred; as a means of therapy, it is limited by the efficacy of the scoring system or means of interpretation and the underlying theory the analyst uses. If we don't actually have a repressed conflict with our father, then no amount of interpreting inkblots will reveal one.

Some people believe in the existence of repressed memories that can be uncovered by appropriate therapy, such as hypnosis. The idea is that some memories, such as of childhood sex abuse, are too horrendous to remember, and so are repressed by a Freudian-like process. One mechanism might be that the person might be in a dissociated state while being abused, so that the memory is later difficult to recall. This topic is very controversial. There is evidence that people can deliberately forget items in a list of words in an experimental paradigm (MacLeod, 1975), but, in spite of much investigation, there is no systematic evidence that people widely repress unpleasant memories (McNally, 2007). What is more, attempts to 'recover' repressed memories through 'recovered memory therapy' can be unreliable or dangerous, because we know from extensive research on eyewitness testimony that false memories can be created by directed and leading questioning (Loftus & Ketcham, 1994). It is worth noting that both the APA (American Psychological Association) in the United States and the British Psychological Society in the UK have produced statements saying that occasionally a forgotten memory from childhood may be remembered, but often there is then no way of telling whether it is true or false without other evidence (Wright et al., 2006; see Box 6.5). It is true that we cannot remember many memories from early childhood, and none from infancy, but this is most likely because of the structure of

Box 6.5 Satanic Child Abuse

Stories of child abuse by satanic cults first emerged from the United States in the 1980s, and spread around the world. The reports seem to have started with the publication of a book in 1980 by the Canadian psychiatrist Lawrence Pazder called *Michelle Remembers* about his patient (and later wife) Michelle Smith. Pazder used hypnosis to help Michelle recover memories of abuse as a child by a group of Satanists. Pazder believed Michelle's case was just one involved in a conspiracy. More cases followed, one of the earliest being the McMartin Pre-school (based in Manhattan Beach, California), investigated in 1984–1987. The case came to trial, but ended in 1990 with no convictions obtained, and all charges being dropped; the investigation resulted in the most expensive criminal trial in US history. This pattern of accusation, investigation, and no charges being brought or convictions made was repeated across the world. Cases such as the Orkney child abuse scandal of 1991 resulted in children being taken temporarily from their parents.

Satanic child abuse reports have many similarities with stories of witchcraft, which were particularly common in the seventeenth century, but have been reported throughout history. Examples include the Salem witch trials in Massachusetts in 1692 and 1693, where hundreds of people were accused of witchcraft, with 19 people, mostly women, executed, and the witch hunts under the self-professed 'Witchfinder General' Matthew Hopkins in England

> **Box 6.5** (cont.)
>
> around the time of the English Civil war (1642–1651), which led to a few hundred executions, again mostly of women. Incidents of satanic child abuse and witchcraft are further examples of mass hysteria, or mass psychogenic illness (see earlier in this chapter). They are particular examples of moral panics when people come to see a particular threat and find evidence to support their perceptions. The trigger for the investigation is usually small (in one example a child having painful bowel movements), the investigation widespread and involving apparently ridiculous accusations (a teacher flying), and absurd items being taken as evidence (a video recording of a popular television programme). It is easy to view events with the wisdom of hindsight, but at the time consciousness is distorted by the pressure of public opinion.

memory and the means of encoding (Tustin & Hayne, 2010), rather than repression as Freud argued, and we are unlikely to be able to retrieve true memories from this period of childhood amnesia with out assistance.

Although the Freudian unconscious has an important role in folk psychology, there is little scientific evidence for it. There is also little evidence that we systematically repress our desires and memories. We now know the mind is much more complicated than Freud envisaged. In a way, Freud happened to be right, because cognitive psychology shows that a great deal of processing is inaccessible. For example, a face-recognition or word-recognition module may not be accessible to consciousness, but does it make sense to talk of it as being in the unconscious? As we learn skills, processing becomes automatic, but again does it

> **TRY THIS:** Keeping an Error Diary
>
> Keep a slip and error diary. Over a period of a week, record all the slips, mistakes, speech errors, and forgetting you make. How would you explain each one? Do you see any evidence of Freudian repression?

> **TRY THIS:** Free Association
>
> Try free association: here are six words – free associate to each of them. Do you notice any blocks? Can you draw any conclusions:
>
> Lettuce
> Rocket
> Elephant
> Leg
> Mother
> Death

make sense to talk of automatic processing? The parts of the iceberg below the water are cognitive processes, not memories, and we can only be conscious of the outcome of most of these processes, not the processes themselves.

Jung and the 'Collective Unconscious'

The Swiss psychoanalyst Carl Jung (1875–1961) further developed Freud's idea of the unconscious by proposing that beneath the personal unconscious there is a **collective unconscious**, which is shared across humanity. It contains shared symbols common to all people called *archetypes* (Jung, 1969; he first used the term in 1919); these archetypes can be recognised in dreams, art, and myth (see Figure 6.9). Archetypes are modified by an individual's experience, including the experience of all people sharing a particular culture. Examples of archetypes include the archetypal figures (with self-explanatory names, such as the Devil, Hero, Wise Old Man, Wise Old Woman) and archetypal motifs (such as the Flood and the Apocalypse).

Many are fascinated by the idea of a collective unconscious, and some say it is useful in therapy. Perhaps sadly though, Jung's theory of the collective unconscious is not a scientific theory, and there is no experimental evidence for it. For example, there is no agreement about what is an archetype and what isn't; you will come across different lists.

It's certainly the case that themes recur across cultures and stories. Booker (2004) describes what he calls the seven basic plots, and argues that all significant works of literature across the ages derive from one of these plots. (The book is written from a Jungian perspective.) It is also clearly the case that certain types of symbolic and religious figures recur across time and cultures. But do we need to posit a collective unconscious to account for these? And what about stories that don't appear to fit these seven basic plots – are these stories not really literature? But humans have similar brains and live in broadly similar environments, so it would be a surprise if certain ideas didn't recur across cultures, myths, literature, and history. We don't need to construct a collective unconscious to explain these observations.

Figure 6.9 Jungian archetypes revealed in the major arcana of the Tarot. Jung argued that tradition and culture might reveal universal aspects of the collective unconscious. For example, the High Priestess is the anima and Death is the shadow, although several interpretations are possible. Source: De Agostini Picture Library/Getty Images Plus.

Subliminal Processing

The idea of **subliminal** suggestion is a powerful one that has entered the popular imagination. In 1957, in Fort Lee, New Jersey, USA, during a screening of the movie *Picnic* (Logan, 1955) starring William Holden and Kim Novak, a subliminal message was flashed on the screen exhorting the audience to 'Eat popcorn' and 'Drink Coca-Cola' (see Figure 6.10). James Vicary, the vice president of the company responsible, said that sales of popcorn and Coca-Cola surged; however, he was exaggerating for the sake of his company. The ploy made no difference. Later, he said that the whole thing was a hoax. Although we should be very sceptical as to whether or not the advertising ploy could work, people were quite rightly outraged by the ethics of the trick.

Figure 6.10 Subliminal advertising using a scene from the 1957 movie *Picnic* with the actress Kim Novak. It's not clear that subliminal advertising has any effect at all, and most would now consider it to be highly unethical. Is it just accidental that the supermarket is full of that nice smell of freshly baked bread? Source: Walter Daran/The LIFE Images Collection/Getty Images.

'Subliminal' means under the threshold of conscious perception. Can stimuli presented at an intensity such that they do not reach conscious awareness still influence later behaviour? In 1983, the British psychologist Anthony Marcel (1983a, b) published two large papers called perception without awareness. Marcel reported five experiments, and we shall examine the fifth here. It is well known that seeing a word like DOCTOR immediately before a word related in meaning (semantically related), such as NURSE, speeds up the recognition of the second word, relative to an unrelated control word (such as BUTTER). Marcel used a paradigm known as *masking* whereby if a word is followed quickly enough by another word-like stimulus, called a mask, participants can no longer identify the first word. Indeed, if the mask comes quickly enough after the target word, participants can't even tell if a word was present or not. Marcel showed that words that were masked still primed subsequent words. That is, even if a person didn't know whether or not they had seen a word, let alone that it was DOCTOR, they were still faster to identify NURSE. His findings were problematic for then current models of word recognition and perception because they violate the idea that perception is linear: we can only access properties of a word after we have consciously identified it.

Marcel's results were controversial at the time and in particular a critique by Daniel Holender was very influential (Holender, 1986). Holender argued that it was very difficult to perform experiments such as Marcel's and ensure that the mask was totally effective on every trial. However, later experiments by Merikle and Cheesman (1987) and Greenwald et al. (1995) provided support for Marcel's conclusions (although it should be noted that there is still some argument; see Holender & Duscherer, 2004).

Perhaps we shouldn't be too surprised that stimuli that do not enter consciousness can influence processing; remember the cocktail party effect?

One of the most worrying uses of subliminal processing is to influence our buying decisions. We have already seen that things can affect our behaviour even when we are not aware of them (see Chapter 3). Why do you think supermarkets smell of fresh bread and have shiny products near the entrance?

Another area where subliminal priming is occasionally thought to be effective is in education. Many people believe that if they listen to tapes with subliminal messages on them they can learn or effortlessly self-improve. Unfortunately, there is no evidence to support the idea that we can learn without effort. Pratkanis et al. (1994) performed an experiment where participants were given tapes with subliminal messages aimed at improving either memory or self-esteem. Participants listened to these tapes daily. After five weeks, participants believed their performance had improved, although objective measures showed no difference between before and after. Ingeniously, Pratkanis et al. had deliberately mislabelled half the tapes so that half the participants who thought they were getting subliminal messages improving self-esteem were getting messages about memory, and vice versa. Again these participants thought they had improved consistent with the label rather than the actual message, although the objective measure still showed there was no improvement (or deficit). Unfortunately, it seems you can't learn without effort.

One clear conclusion is that nothing is clear! Subliminal advertising does not work, but supermarkets try to influence our decisions by what is positioned at the door. We can deliberately forget things, but there is no evidence for repressed childhood memories. Social priming is controversial, but we can nudge people's behaviour.

Chapter Summary

- Introspection is the examination of the contents of our consciousness.
- We can introspect analytically, descriptively, or interpretively.
- Introspection has many limitations as a method, including forgetting, being forced to verbalise our thoughts, and censorship.
- In addition, the contents of introspection might be unreliable. We are particularly poor at being able to explain the reasons for our actions.

- Phenomenology is the philosophical study of experience from the first-person point of view.
- The experience sampling method (ESM) is a means of collecting data about what people are thinking about at any one time by issuing a reminder at random intervals.
- Mental illnesses such as schizophrenia and Alzheimer's disease can lead to floridly incorrect beliefs called delusions.
- Delusions may be accompanied by confabulation as a means of explaining away discrepancies between what the delusions predict and the way the world 'really' is.
- Several neurological disorders can generate false beliefs, including among others Capgras, Fregoli, and Anton–Babinksi delusions (or syndromes).
- These disorders are often accompanied by a denial that there is anything wrong (anosognosia).
- Freud divided the mind into conscious, preconscious, and unconscious.
- Freud argued that the contents of our consciousness were the 'tip of the iceberg' and that we have an extensive unconscious full of repressed desires and memories.
- There is no scientific evidence for an unconscious full of repressed memories.
- The mind has a much more complex structure than that proposed by Freud.
- There is little evidence that there is an unconscious store of actively repressed wishes and memories.
- Much of cognitive processing is not available directly to consciousness.
- Jung argued that we also have a collective unconscious of culturally shared material and symbols (archetypes).
- There is little evidence for a collective unconscious in the way that Jung conceptualised it.
- Nevertheless, our behaviour can be influenced by things of which we are not aware (subliminal processing).

Review Questions

1. Husserl's approach to phenomenology was based on the idea of an *epoché*, trying to get rid of our interpretation of sense data to get to the sense data itself – getting rid of the cognitive processes in perception to leave us with the basic percept. Given what you know about research on cognition and perception, is this process possible?
2. Nisbett and Wilson's classic paper on the illusion that introspection provides accurate insight into our mental states was published in 1977. What has changed since then? Do their conclusions still hold?
3. To what extent does experience sampling give a reliable measure of the contents of consciousness?
4. To what extent are neurological disorders of belief disorders of consciousness?
5. Compare and contrast Freud and Jung's conceptions of the unconscious.
6. Discuss the status of recovered memories.
7. Evaluate the evidence for subliminal processing. To what extent does it occur outside laboratory conditions?
8. How would you use psychology to help you sell something?

Recommended Resources

Introspection

Farthing, G.W. (1992). *The Psychology of Consciousness*. Upper Saddle River, NJ: Prentice Hall. Dated but still a good introduction to introspection and its dangers.

Gallagher, S., and Zahavi, D. (2012). *The Phenomenological Mind*. London: Routledge. The best overall introduction to the philosophy and practice of introspection and phenomenology.

Mass Hysteria and Popular Delusions

Bartholomew, R.E., and Hassall, P. (2015). *A Colourful History of Popular Delusions*. New York: Prometheus.

Neuroscience of Belief

Hirstein, W. (2006). *Brain Fiction: Self-Deception and the Riddle of Confabulation*. Cambridge, MA: MIT Press. The neuroscience of confabulation.

The Psychoanalytical Unconscious

Freud, S. (1905). *The Psychopathology of Everyday Life*. Harmondsworth, UK: Penguin. Freud's original work on how the unconscious can break through into everyday life is still very readable.

Tallis, F.R. (2012). *Hidden Minds: A History of the Unconscious*. New York: Arcade. The story of the idea of the unconscious in psychology.

The Psychological Subconscious

Eagleman, D. (2011). *Incognito: The Secret Lives of the Brain*. New York: Pantheon. Popular science account of subconscious processing.

Loftus, E., and Ketcham, K. (2013 [1994]). *The Myth of Repressed Memory: False Memories and Allegations of Sexual Abuse*. New York: St. Martin's Griffin. Loftus is a leading researcher on the unreliability of eyewitness testimony.

Packard, V., and Miller, M. (2007). *The Hidden Persuaders*. New York: Ig Publishing. Landmark work, originally published in 1957, on the role and secrets of advertising in American society.

Sunstein, R.H., and Thaler, C.R. (2009). *Nudge: Improving Decisions about Health, Wealth and Happiness*. London: Penguin. Much talked-about book on how to influence people and society by 'nudging' them towards making small changes.

7 SELF AND IDENTITY

The late, great comic Peter Cook once quipped, when he had offended someone and the rather pompous person asked if Cook knew who he was: 'Is there a psychiatrist in the house? We have a man here who doesn't know who he is.'

Who am I, and what makes me distinct from everyone else?

In this chapter we are concerned with the self and personal identity. The self is the inner eye we think of as running ourselves, the thing perceiving the world, the thing making choices. Needless to say that, if things were really this way, the self would just be a homunculus, and we are faced then with all the problems the homunculus introduces. Integrating all the information about ourselves necessitates that we examine ourselves – that we take a first-person perspective to ourselves (Vogeley & Fink, 2003).

We first look at models of the self, at this idea of recursion, and look at the neuroscience of the self. We then consider the two broad theories of the self, ego and bundle theories. We examine the importance of the apparent continuity of existence for our self, and the role our memories play in maintaining ourselves. What happens when we lose these memories in amnesia and dementia?

Which parts of the brain are involved in generating a model of ourselves? We look at how our self model can be affected by brain damage. In particular, we examine split-brain patients: can a brain house two selves? We then examine the physical boundaries of the self, and how they can be manipulated. Do we always equate our selves with our bodies? We conclude with considering the idea that the self is yet another illusion.

The Self

I have a sense of being a person that exists in space and time. There seems to be a 'me' in my head, looking out at the world. I am the same person wherever I am (although I might behave slightly differently on the beach than at graduation). I think of myself as having continuous existence over time; I think of myself as being the same person I was when I was ten. A key part of me is my store of memories; they help form my identity and define myself over time. Myself is my *self*. The self is the individual person as the *object* of our consciousness: it only seems to be there when we are looking.

Our sense of *self-identity* has both a psychological and physical aspect (Gillihan & Farah, 2005). I think of myself as a person: the same person who wakes up in the morning that went to bed at night. I identify myself with my physical body. I think both my mind and body are unique, and my body belongs to me.

I think of my self as existing in a particular place at a particular time, and I have a sense of having existed, reinforced by my memories, since birth. These memories contribute to my sense of self as distinct from others; only I have these memories. I have my own distinct personality, partly shaped by my past experiences. My self is located in my body, which is discrete in space and time. We think we are unique.

What makes us unique and constant? At first sight, this is a stupid question. A quick answer might be our bodies, our awareness, and our experiences. But a few thought experiments should convince you that the question isn't quite as trivial as it might first appear.

How do you know you are the same person waking up this morning that went to bed last night? Of course I am, you might say, but it is conceivable that you were brought into existence this morning, complete with your memories. It is not inconceivable that you are a computer simulation that an advanced civilisation started running this morning (or whatever corresponds to their morning), complete with fabricated memories of your life up to now. There is no way to be absolutely certain, however unlikely you think it might be.

Think back to when you were five, or ten, or some other early age you can remember well. Would you say you're the same person now as you were then? Most people would say yes, but physically you were very different. Your memories would be very different; you have experienced a vast amount since then, and then you could remember many things you presumably can't remember now. More importantly perhaps, your intellectual and cognitive abilities would have been vastly different from what they are now, and your brain and nervous system much less mature. We think we're the same person because there is continuity of physical presence (the same body) and mental experience (the same mind), but there are many gaps in the record.

We can also imagine ourselves in the future, or in counterfactual situations where something could have been otherwise (what would have happened to me today if I hadn't gone to the gym this morning?). This type of awareness is sometimes called **autonoetic consciousness**. We shall see in Chapter 8 that it might have a particularly important role in consciousness. For now, the main point is that not only do we see our selves extending from now into the past, but we can also envisage them extending into the future.

> **TRY THIS:** Who Is Looking at Your World?
>
> Presumably you have a sense of looking out on the world. Who is looking? How would you describe that feeling of being in the world?

The 'Self Model'

We each appear to have a model of ourselves that when we think about ourselves appears to tell us who, where, and when we are. I am Trevor, sitting in a chair as the sun rises low over the Scottish hills in winter. I can think back to my breakfast (prawns on gluten-free bread), and I can remember having to learn Latin at school when I was 11. I think of myself as an academic and writer, and as an introvert who likes a laugh. And so on.

I am very confident about the memories I've mentioned, but I have several 'memories' that on closer analysis must be wrong. I can remember a pile of our furniture on our front lawn. (It's a long story.) But when I think about the dates, we weren't living in the house whose lawn I remember when that event actually happened (if it ever happened after all). My memories must be inaccurate and incomplete. And there's nothing particularly poor about my memory as studies of memory outside the laboratory have shown.

I enjoy reading accounts of crime in the local newspaper. One of the most common defences offered is that 'the accused is guilty but in mitigation they acted right out of character', as though the propensity to knock someone on the head occasionally is not at all part of their character.

We think we have a model of ourselves, even if it is less complete than we might first think. We have seen in our discussion of introspection that we do not know very accurately why we act as we do (Chapter 6): our beliefs about why we act as we do can be very wrong (Nisbett & Wilson, 1977).

There are also different levels of the self introduced as we think about ourselves. We can think about ourselves thinking about ourselves, introducing a meta-self. This process is recursive: we can think about ourselves thinking about ourselves thinking about ourselves. This ability to think about what we are thinking about is the source of our self-awareness, and this ability might be what sets us apart from most if not all other animals. The infinite regress of the homunculus argument is not wholly convincing. We are very happy to accept statements like 'I am watching television'; we don't say that the experience of watching television is illogical. At the very least, the infinite regression argument needs some discussion about why the regression is infinite.

> **TRY THIS:** Describing Yourself
>
> How would you describe yourself? In the same way that intelligence tests intelligence, personality tests measure personality. The output is a diagram showing your score on several factors such as extraversion, neuroticism, openness to new experiences, agreeableness, and conscientiousness, or more. Such diagrams are readily available online. Score yourself by completing one of these diagrams. Then take the personality test and see how that output matches up with your self model. For even more hours of endless fun, ask your friends and relatives to score you too.

> **TRY THIS:** Thinking About Yourself Thinking About Yourself
>
> Think about yourself. Think about yourself thinking about yourself. Think about yourself thinking about yourself thinking about yourself. Can you actually do this? If so, how far can you go? Can you appreciate why the regression might or must be infinite?

Ego and Bundle Theories

There are two main theories of the self, ego theories and bundle theories (Parfit, 1984, 1987).

The **ego theory** says that there is a single, unified me that observes and experiences the world. Our continued existence only makes sense in the context of the continued existence of a subject of experience, the ego (similar to Freud's ego). Our consciousness is unified at any one time because only one person, my ego, is having all these experiences. My life is unified because there's only one person who has had all these experiences over a lifetime. René Descartes' famous statement 'I think, therefore I am' draws attention to the ego as the only thing we can be sure about. The ego and homunculus ideas are the same: there is an inner, persistent self. It's what most people who haven't studied consciousness are likely to think about the self.

The **bundle theory** says that we cannot explain the unity of consciousness or the unity of a whole life by referring to a single thing that experiences. There is no ego. Instead, our mental experience is made up from a long sequence of many different mental states, events, and thoughts. Each series of experiences is like 'a bundle tied up with string': each series of mental events is unified by how one experience causes another, or our later memories of them. Similarly in Buddhism there is no self (a doctrine called *anattā*); it is an illusion. In the eighteenth century, Scottish philosopher David Hume (1738) said that all we see are bundles of properties (Figure 7.1); there is nothing more to an object, no 'whole object' over and above these features. We group these perceptions together to perceive objects and we think that there is a self perceiving them. In a similar way, if we pay proper attention to our consciousness, there are only perceptions, thoughts, and ideas; we do not find any independent self. Of course, we talk about I, me, and we, but these pronouns do not correspond to anything real; the self is nothing more than a linguistic construct.

Of the two approaches, the ego theory is surely the more intuitive: surely I have a self, myself; it is experiencing the world right now, reading this book, becoming increasingly frustrated because how could it possibly be otherwise? We each have our own personal identity. The first-person identity, where we refer to ourselves, gives us our sense of ourselves.

The British philosopher Derek Parfit (1942–2017) described a number of thought experiments designed to show that there is no stable self (Parfait, 1984). Let's begin with the most famous, the *teletransporter paradox*. The teletransporter will be familiar to anyone who has ever seen any of the *Star Trek* franchise or movies: beam me up, Scotty! Let's describe the simplest version, which

Figure 7.1 The Scottish philosopher David Hume (1711–1776). Hume argued that all we perceive are bundles of features, such as shape, colour, and texture. There is nothing over and above this bundle that makes an object. In the same way, we are just a bundle of sensations, thoughts, and feelings; there is no 'self' or 'ego' over and above these things. Source: De Agostini Picture Library/De Agostini/Getty Images.

is more or less the classic *Star Trek* transporter: you enter a big machine, the machine breaks you down into constituent atoms, reading their exact positions and states, then relays all that information at the speed of light to Mars, where another machine receives the information and reconstitutes you, atom by atom from locally available atoms, extremely quickly, so that you are an atom-for-atom copy of the original. What do you think of that? Would you be happy to travel that way? The transporter problem has been around in different forms for a long time. The ancient philosophers Heraclitus, Plato, and Plutarch speculated about the *Ship of Theseus*: the ship has been around for a long time, and repaired many, many times, plank by plank, nail by nail, so that after a while it has no material in common with the original ship. Is it still the same ship?

I would be happy to be teletransported, and so would everyone else I have asked (although in the original *Star Trek* series 'Bones' McCoy was suspicious of the transporter and was reluctant to travel that way). The experience would presumably be one of going into a machine, blinking, and appearing the next moment somewhere else. I would still be me and feel like me. But the physical body would be very different from the original me – the atoms would be completely different. We clearly then don't think that the exact atoms we're made of matter very much.

Now let us consider the situation of our intrepid space explorer in the face of a number of possible malfunctions of the transporter. In the next version, the device produces the copy of you perfectly well, but fails to disassemble you, so there is a you on Earth and a you on Mars. Which is the real you? Presumably both of them are thinking that they are the real you. In another variant, the device produces two copies of you on Mars. Which of them is the real you? What will they think when they look at each other in the receiving machine? In the example called P-transporter 4, the sending machine malfunctions so that you arrive on Mars OK, but the original you gets mangled and dies a horrible painful death. Should the new you be particularly upset about that?

There aren't any obvious answers to these questions. Parfit says that there is nothing in addition to the thoughts and relations between thoughts to determine identity; there is no one self over and above our experiences.

Imagine getting an operation where individual cells in your brain and body were replaced with exact duplicates. Are you the same person when only 2% of your cells have been replaced? What about 50%? Or 95%? Is there a point in a 100% transplant surgery where you stop being you and become something new? Is there a critical point when you stop being you? Natural beliefs lead us to think that there is some critical point in the replacement surgery where you stop being you and become your replica. Parfit thinks that if we believe in the bundle theory we should discard these natural beliefs because you are not a separately existing entity. There aren't two possible outcomes, but two different descriptions. The problem arises because of our language: it's a 'mere choice of words' (Parfit, 1987: 23).

Although at first sight the bundle theory might appear to be counterintuitive, it is difficult to pin down what is wrong with these thought experiments, and consequently it is very popular with consciousness researchers.

THE SELF

> **Box 7.1 Face Transplants**
>
> The first full-face transplants were carried out in Spain and France following a series of partial face transplants beginning with Isabelle Dinoire in France in 2006. A face transplant is an immensely complex operation, involving transplanting skin, mucous membranes, bones, blood vessels, and nerves from an organ donor. The transplant involves a lifetime course of immunosuppressant drugs, which leaves the recipient open to a much higher probability of life-threatening diseases, such as cancer. In addition to physical rejection, however, there is also the danger of *psychological rejection*. Although we see our own face only infrequently in reflections, we take it as one of the defining characteristics of our appearance and of our selves. Perhaps surprisingly, psychological rejection doesn't turn out to be a problem in practice. The reasons for this lack of rejection include psychological counselling and that patients immediately seem to take ownership of their new faces, integrating their new appearances with their selves by feeling that they have gone from 'disfigured' to 'normal'.
>
> Psychological rejection of transplants is not unknown, however. In 1998, Clint Hallam was the recipient of the world's first hand transplant; in 2001, he asked for it to be amputated, saying that it never felt his own. Even then the situation was complex because he was not taking the necessary anti-rejection drugs, and had great problems with motor control of the new hand.

The Knower and the Known

There is one other account of the self we should consider in detail, one that makes a distinction between a *central self* and a more *peripheral self*. The distinction has a long history: William James (1890) distinguished between the self as knower and the self as known. One way of putting it is that I can think about me. There seems to be a core self that is our awareness, and we can be aware of our self; for James, the self is made up of both the knower and the known. A similar distinction is between a *minimal* and *narrative* self (Gallagher, 2000), and between a *core* self and an *extended* self (Damasio, 1999).

For Gallagher, the minimal self is the 'I' that experiences the 'now', with everything else stripped away. The minimal self has a sense of agency (it is I that initiates my actions), and a sense of ownership (I belong in my body), although we cannot normally distinguish between these two senses. The extended self is what persists over time: it has a past of autobiographical memory, and it can think about itself in context and in the future. The narrative self is the story we tell ourselves about ourselves.

Damasio's Three Levels of Self

The neuroscientist Antonio Damasio proposed that there were three levels of selves, based on evolution, animal psychology, and neuroscience, corresponding to different types of consciousness (Araujo et al., 2013; Damasio, 1999, 2010). The proto-self is not aware; it exists in even quite primitive organisms. The organism can be described as having a proto-self that responds to the environment. Such organisms may have feelings (such as pain) but not emotions (fear of having pain). Core consciousness emerges when the organism has emotions in response to changes to its internal state; for example, when an organism feels fear, then responds on the basis of those emotions (for example, by fleeing). Extended consciousness depends on having autobiographical memory, where the sense of awareness extends over time, leading to a sense of identity (Damasio, 1999).

The proto-self is a nonconscious state shared by many animals, which consists of some moment-by-moment representation of the organism's internal state. The creature might be hungry, or experiencing an aversive stimulus, or representing its location in space. The proto-self isn't really a self in the sense that we think of it, but a prerequisite of any experiencing self is that it has information about the state of its body. The proto-self depends on evolutionarily older regions of the brain such as the brainstem, **hypothalamus**, and **insula** (insular cortex) that are involved in *homeostatic* mechanisms of regulation, such as hunger, thirst, movement, feelings from the body, and emotion. In some ways, the proto-self resembles Freud's concept of the Id. The proto-self represents the body and our emotions. The brainstem plays an important part in its formation, although in healthy humans the insular cortex, an area we have seen is suspected to play an important role in self-identity, is also involved. Damasio's account has the virtue of explaining what role the insula plays, but also why it is not essential to the constant self. The lower portions of the brainstem receive information from the heart, and digestive tract, while the higher portions construct an image of the musculoskeletal body. Damasio states that a proto-self may be present in many non-human animals too. The proto-self is an interconnected and temporarily coherent unconscious collection of neural patterns representing the state of the organism, moment by moment, at multiple levels of the brain.

The core self is the self that is aware of the body and through perception the outside world. For Damasio, consciousness is the feeling of knowing a feeling. Again, a sense of ownership is important: an organism distinguishes between itself, as represented by the proto-self, and the outside world. The core self is closest to the everyday conception of self and is conscious in the way a lay person would consider. When considering the self and the role of introspection, we have come across several instances of brain damage where the self and consciousness are greatly changed by the damage; nevertheless, we would not wish to deny that the person is conscious. Damasio proposes that in these people the core self is still intact. The core self is produced whenever an object of any kind modifies the proto-self. The core self does not change much throughout our lifetime, and we are conscious of it. Hence, we can speak of core consciousness. Core consciousness is supposed to continually regenerate in a series of pulses, which seemingly blend together to give the stream of consciousness. Damasio connects his conception of core consciousness with the view expressed by a variety of earlier thinkers such as Locke, Brentano, Kant, Freud, and William James. Finally, there is extended consciousness. The core self is the momentary self. It exists in 'pulses'. It comes into existence when the proto-self perceives objects and how those objects relate to the body. Is the object food? A predator or some other kind of threat? Another body like ours? Something else? Core consciousness is raw experience: there is no reflecting on the feeling of knowing a feeling, no language, and no past or future. Damasio hypothesises that the main coordinator of the core self is the **thalamus** (see Figure 7.2), but other areas are involved, including the brainstem, the thalamus, and the cortex.

THE SELF

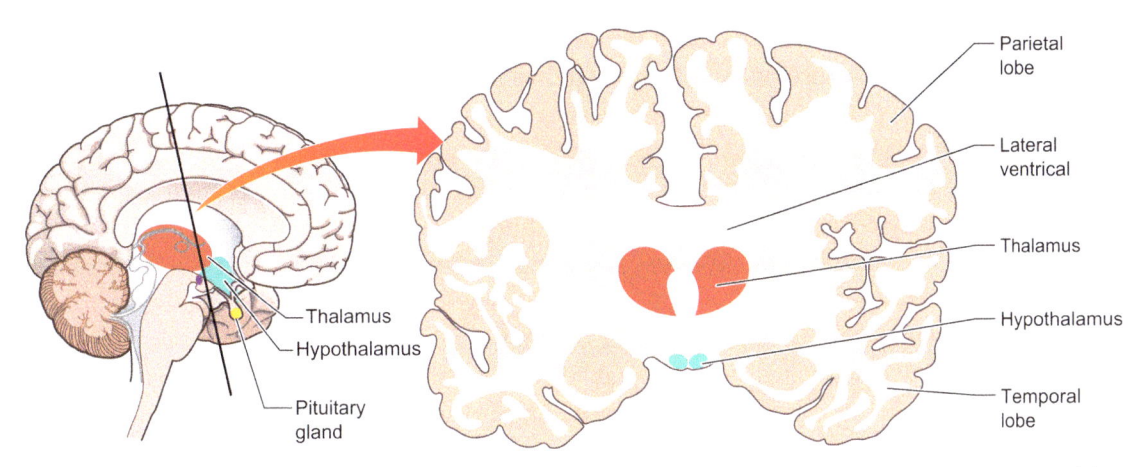

Figure 7.2 Location of the thalamus. The thalamus is a relatively large subcortical structure that connects to many other parts of the brain, and acts, among other things, as an important hub relaying information from the senses and different parts of the brain.

Reflection, or self-awareness, only comes with extended consciousness, which gives us self-awareness and an autobiographical sense of our past and future. While many animals may have a core self, only humans and perhaps a few other animals have an extended self, and we are distinguished by the neural mechanisms that implement these higher-level processes, such as highly developed frontal lobes. The extended or autobiographical self is based on memory and also on anticipations of the future, and develops gradually throughout life. You must have a core self in order to acquire an autobiographical self, but the converse is not true; there are cases in which people lose their autobiographical self, temporarily or permanently, while maintaining their core consciousness. The core self addresses primal first-person experience, the state of a self experiencing perceptions and what those perceptions immediately mean to the self, to the body. Perhaps more accurately, it is addressing the feeling of first-person experience. The autobiographical self permits the existence of a much richer form of consciousness, which Damasio calls extended consciousness.

The core and extended selves are dissociable (Damasio, 1999). We find impairments to the extended self in amnesia and Alzheimer's disease, but the core self is always intact. There isn't a double dissociation though because we can't have an extended self without a core self, although there are times that the core self might be temporarily absent (such as during sleep or an epileptic absence). Cotard's delusion (see Chapter 6) gives an inkling of what it might be like to possess an extended self without a sense of agency or ownership, although some self-awareness must still be present.

Damasio attaches great importance to the role of emotion, which he takes to refer to internal changes in body state (chemical, visceral, and muscular) and also the accompanying changes in the nervous system. Emotions are not conscious. But when they are induced (for example, by the sight of an external object) they may give rise to 'feelings', which provide the stimulus for action. Feelings may be accessible to consciousness.

Types of Self and the Executive Self

There are several aspects of what we consider to be our self. Regardless of how Parfait's thought experiments might query the notion, we do think of ourselves as being the same person as we were before we went to sleep last night or when we were five. We possess a continuity of existence, which, because it depends so much on memory, we can call our mnemonic self. We think of ourselves as having fairly consistent beliefs and traits that constitute our personality. We have a feeling that we are in control of our actions, that we make decisions, and plan for our future. We have seen (Chapter 3) that it is questionable whether we consciously choose to act, but the illusion that we are in charge of our destiny is a powerful one. We can call this aspect the *executive self*. Decision making, planning, reasoning, and thinking about our selves and our cognitive abilities (a skill called *metacognition*) are all examples of what are called *executive processes*. Executive processes are instantiated in the frontal lobes of the brain, particularly the prefrontal cortex, with different regions associated with different types of executive process (Alvarez & Emory, 2006).

Unsurprisingly, damage to the frontal lobes leads to impaired executive processing. One of the most famous case studies in psychology is that of the American railroad worker Phineas Gage (1823–1860). By all accounts, Phineas Gage was a very pleasant chap, and a conscientious and skilled worker until in 1848 an accidental explosion drove a large iron sleeper right through his head, severely damaging his left frontal lobes (see Figure 7.3). Astonishingly, he was able to seek medical help (as we are ever being reminded the brain itself has no pain receptors, but there are plenty around the rest of the head, and that could not have felt good). After the accident, his friends noted that he was no longer the same person, becoming coarse, vulgar, capricious, and indecisive. The damage had affected his personality and executive processing. Although the details of this famous historical case are necessarily sparse, the basic findings about personality, executive processing, and localisation of function have been replicated many times. Brain damage can change aspects of our selves.

Figure 7.3 Reconstruction of the wound to Phineas Gage and the iron rod that caused it. After the 1848 accident and damage to his left frontal cortex, Gage was by all accounts a changed man. Source: Martin Shields/Alamy Stock Photo.

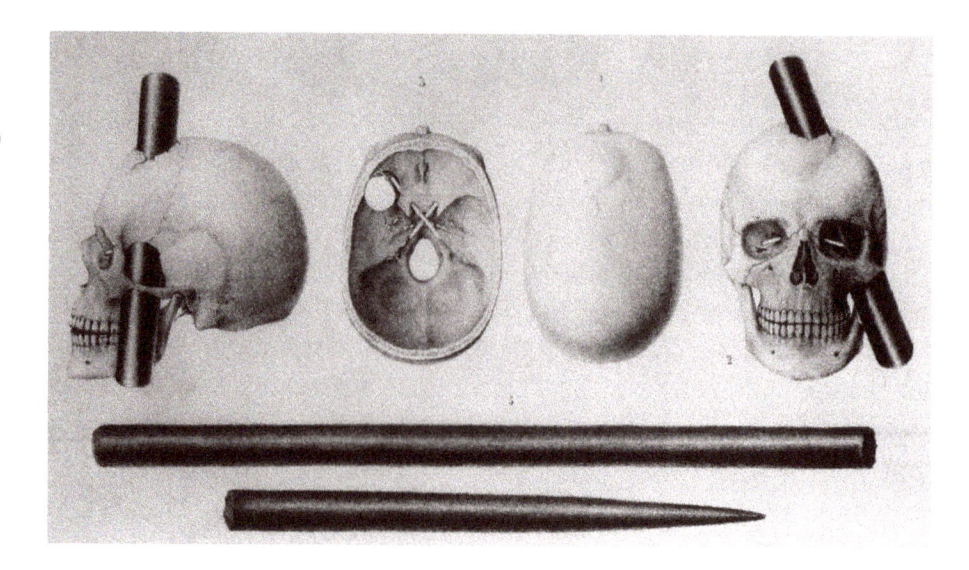

The Continuity of Existence

We have a strong sense that we have been the same person for as long as we remember. Even though our consciousness is periodically interrupted by sleep, and occasionally perhaps by anaesthesia or concussion, we believe ourselves to be just that – the same self. We call this phenomenon *continuity of existence*.

We believe that we are the same person because of our memories. We can remember what we were doing five minutes ago and before we fell asleep. Think what it would be like to come into existence with no memories or previous experience; we might be conscious, but it would be difficult to envisage having any sense of self. The system of memory that stores information about our selves and our personal experiences is called **autobiographical memory**. Our autobiographical memories are, however, incomplete; in particular, there is a *recency effect*, which means that more recent events are remembered better. I can remember what I had for breakfast today but not for this day last week. The further back we go, the less complete our autobiographical memories are.

Our memories are particularly poor for early childhood, and nonexistent for when we were very, very young. Typically we cannot remember anything before we were three or four, although some can remember things as young as two, and for others it's a bit later. This phenomenon is called childhood or *infantile amnesia*. There is no evidence for Freud's psychoanalytic theory of the origin of childhood amnesia, which states that we do not remember early childhood because we have repressed the memories because they are too traumatic (Freud 1899, 1905). There are several possible far more plausible reasons why we might not be able to remember very early memories. We do not have language when very young (Harley, 2017), and our cognitive structures are very different (Piaget, 1990), so memories might be encoded, stored, and retrieved differently (Hayne, 2004). Young rats show a version of infantile amnesia (Feigley & Spear, 1970), suggesting that human language and self-awareness are not important in the origin of early amnesia. The fragility of early memory is most likely due to structural and neurochemical differences in the basis of memory (Li et al., 2014). Nevertheless, we do not doubt that we are the same person as that baby we see in family photographs. So, we are willing to accept breaks in our memory and personhood as long as the veracity of the continuousness can be attributed in some way. Few would deny that young children and babies are conscious, even self-aware at the upper age range of childhood amnesia. Even though we were conscious then, we are incapable of recalling that consciousness later.

Autobiographical memory comprises memory for life events; the question of whether it is a separate memory system (from other facts, say) need not detain us (see Conway & Pleydell-Pearce, 2000, for a review and discussion). Autobiographical memory is the source of our sense of continuity of self. Note that memory alone doesn't make us conscious; my laptop has a memory, yet it isn't conscious. Consciousness is associated with a particular type of memory.

> **TRY THIS:** Your Earliest Memories
>
> What are your earliest memories? To what extent do you think you are the same person then as now? How reliable do you think your early memories are? Can you check them against objective records, such as reports from family members, photographs, or videos?

Amnesia and the Loss of Memories

Cognitive psychology distinguishes between semantic memory, our memory for general knowledge, and episodic memory, our memory for specific events (Eysenck & Keane, 2015). If I ask you what the capital of France is you access semantic memory, and if I ask you what you had for breakfast you access episodic memory. Episodic memory is particularly important because it involves the awareness of memory. It enables *mental time travel*, where we can revisit events in our past (Tulving, 2002). Our autobiographical memory is made up of episodes encoded by episodic memory.

We routinely forget a great deal, particularly as time passes, but nothing is comparable to the loss of memory experienced in amnesia. **Amnesia** is loss of memory and the ability to learn new information, and organic amnesia results from damage to the brain, particularly the medial temporal lobe (including components of the limbic system, the hippocampus and mandala) and the mammillary bodies (often classified as part of the thalamus). There are two different types of amnesia, which usually co-occur: *retrograde amnesia*, which is problems with recalling events that happened before the onset of amnesia, and *anterograde amnesia*, which is the inability to learn new information and recall events after the onset of amnesia (Shimamura, 1992).

Autobiographical memories are gradually lost in (mostly) elderly individuals suffering from types of dementia, most commonly *Alzheimer's disease*, a progressive degenerative neurological disorder.

One of the most famous cases of organic amnesia is a patient referred to as HM, who in 1953 underwent surgery to remove *bilaterally* the *medial temporal lobes* in an attempt to improve his severe epilepsy. The epilepsy did improve, but for the rest of his life he suffered from severe anterograde and retrograde amnesia (Scoville & Milner, 1957). HM (whose real name was Henry Molaison) died in 2008, and was one of the most studied individuals in psychology (Squire, 2009). Unless he rehearsed it constantly, most new information would quickly slip away. He found it nearly impossible to retain new episodic information. He met researchers frequently, but had no idea who they were. He had no knowledge of current affairs.

Oliver Sacks describes the case of Jimmie G., who into the early 1980s still believed it was 1945, denied ever having met the doctor before ('I'd remember that beard!'), and is shocked by his appearance in the mirror (Sacks, 1985). Jimmie G. suffered from Korsakoff's syndrome, sometimes found in very severe long-term alcohol abusers. Severe alcohol abuse may go with malnutrition, leading to prolonged deficiency of vitamin B1 (thiamine), which, along with the toxic effects of the alcohol, leads to the destruction of the medial temporal lobes, which are particularly susceptible to the buildup of the chemical toxins without B1 to clear them away. Korsakoff patients tend to confabulate, making up stories and information (Kessels et al., 2008).

One of the most well-known cases of organic amnesia is that of Clive Wearing (Wearing, 2005; Wilson & Wearing, 1995). Clive Wearing (b. 1938) was a highly respected musician and musicologist, who fell ill in March 1985 with an exceptionally severe headache. The illness was due to herpes encephalitis; in very rare cases the *herpes simplex* virus (the cold sore virus) can attack the central nervous system (see Box 7.2). (Encephalitis is an inflammation of the brain with sudden and unexpected onset.) Later investigations showed that the virus destroyed much of his hippocampus (along with some other regions

THE CONTINUITY OF EXISTENCE 167

of his brain, including the frontal lobe; see Figure 7.4). From the time of his illness, he has been unable to form new memories; he suffers from retrograde and severe anterograde amnesia.

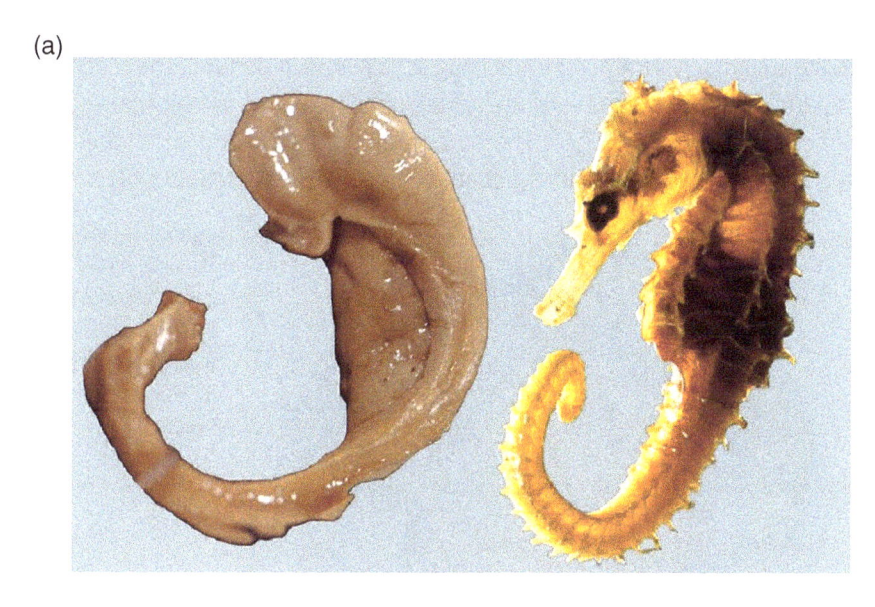

Figure 7.4 The hippocampus, and the seahorse from which it gets its name (genus Hippocampus), and its location in the brain. Several brain structures are involved in encoding memories, but the hippocampus is particularly important. It is part of the limbic system, which was once thought to be involved primarily with emotion, but we now know its role is much more complex. There is one hippocampus in each hemisphere.

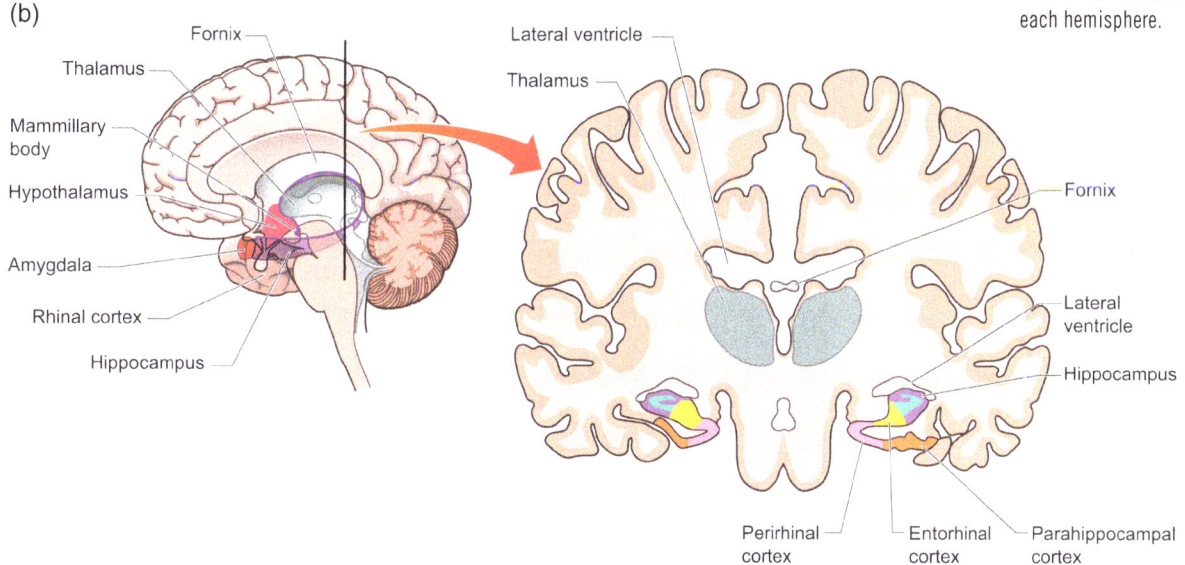

Box 7.2 *Herpes simplex* Encephalitis

Herpes simplex **encephalitis** is a viral infection of the brain (see Figure 7.5). It affects about one in half a million people a year. *Herpes simplex* is the same virus (HSV-1) as that which causes cold sores. More than half the population have been exposed to the virus, but for

Box 7.2 (cont.)

some unknown reason (although stress has been implicated), in some people the virus spreads along a nerve axon to the brain. People over 50 are particularly prone to the disease. The main symptoms are an excruciating headache accompanied by confusion. Immediate treatment with the antiviral drug acyclovir is important. The mortality rate is about 70%, and survivors display varying degrees of neurological damage caused by the resulting inflammation (see Figure 7.6). The hippocampus, limbic system, and temporal lobes are particularly susceptible to damage (Sabah et al., 2012; Whitley, 2006).

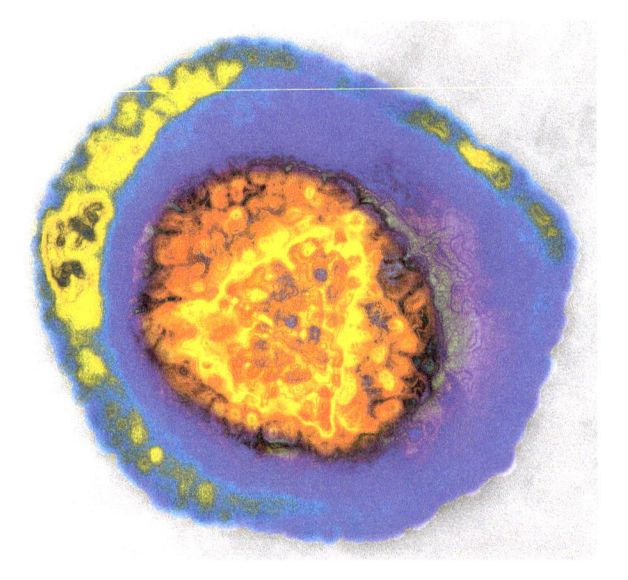

Figure 7.5 The *Herpes simplex* virus. The same virus is responsible for giving cold sores on lips and severe brain damage following encephalitis (inflammation of the brain). Source: BSIP/Universal Images Group/Getty Images.

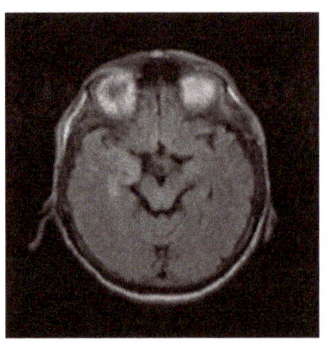

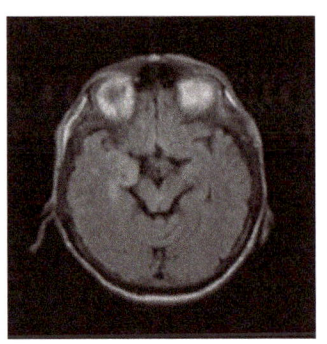

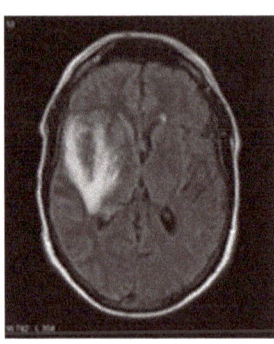

Figure 7.6 Examples of lesions to brain following a *Herpes simplex* encephalitis infection. The limbic system and hippocampus are particularly susceptible to damage. Source: (Top and bottom left) Case contributed by Assoc Prof Frank Gaillard, rID: 9164 and rID: 10644; (bottom right) Case contributed by RMH Core Conditions, rID: 34113, Radiopaedia.org.

Clive Wearing's memory is limited to between 7 and 30, typically 20, seconds; virtually everything before that window is lost. He says that he has just woken up, or that he is conscious for the first time, or that he has just woken from a coma. He keeps a diary, and makes a note of his continual awakenings, but he then crosses out the earlier entries, denying that he wrote them. Clive's case shows what it is like to have a consciousness that exists only in a window of now. An analogy is that his consciousness has to be rebooted every 20 seconds or so. Some of his skills remain – procedural information, which is how to do something – and he does remember a few autobiographical facts from before his illness (he knows he has children, but cannot remember their names). Is he still the same person as he was before? Many aspects of his personhood – his love of music and his wife – remain unchanged, and indeed frozen since 1985 (Sacks, 2007). Although Clive Wearing's personality was affected by the brain damage (he became more aggressive), he was still recognisable as the same person. He still had the same pleasures and loves. He still knew he was conscious, even though this consciousness came newly into being every few seconds or so.

These studies of severely disrupted episodic memory also show us that continuity of existence is not essential for at least some sense of self. In all these cases, we could say that core self is intact, but the extended self is damaged as a result of damage to the brain systems serving it.

The Neuroscience of the Self

Given the complexity of the self, the self model, and what is involved in maintaining the extended self, it will be no surprise that many brain regions are involved in doing all this. The **prefrontal cortex** plays a major role in tying everything together (Vogeley & Fink, 2003; Vogeley et al., 1999). Damage to the frontal lobes leads to changes to personality, and in disorders such as schizophrenia, dysfunction of the prefrontal cortex leads to disruption of the self model (Vogeley et al., 1999).

An area of the brain known as the insula (or *insular cortex*, a region of the cortex folded deep in the lateral **sulcus,** which is the fissure separating the temporal from the parietal and frontal lobes) plays a particularly important role in representing the self (see Figure 7.7). fMRI shows that the insula is highly active when we engage in self-reflection (in this case deciding whether statements such as 'I am a good friend' or 'I am attractive' are true; Modinos et al., 2009). On the other hand, Philippi et al. (2012) describe a patient who had extensive damage to his insula on both sides of the brain, as well as surrounding areas, as a result of a *herpes simplex* infection of the brain. Although he had several severe impairments, including profound memory loss and difficulty recognising objects, his self-awareness was intact. He could recognise himself in mirrors, in photographs from various periods in his past, knew when he was touching himself compared with being touched by others, and could describe his own personality, among other measures. He did show some minor impairments, such as remembering more recent autobiographical memories, but it is clear that there was no significant damage to self-awareness, which should be the case if the insula is central to maintaining our identity. Philippi et al.'s findings reiterate that our

Figure 7.7 The insular cortex, or insula, is a fold in the cortex in the lateral sulcus. It is thought to play an important role in representing the self.

(a)

Insular cortex

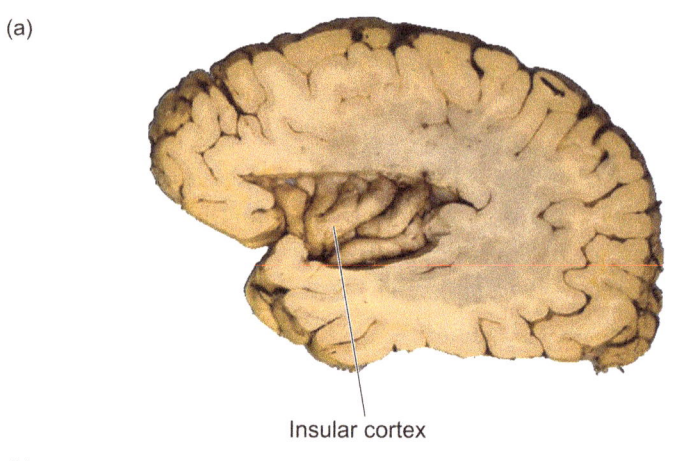

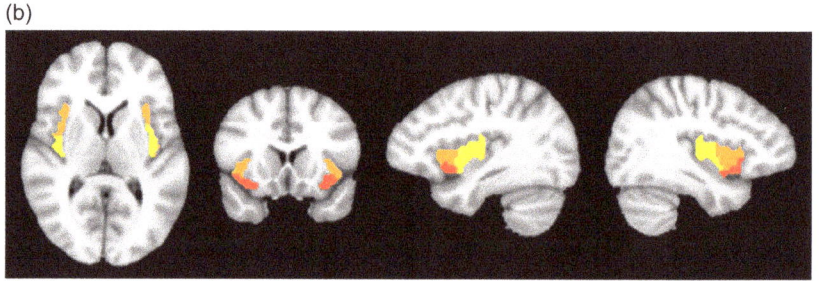

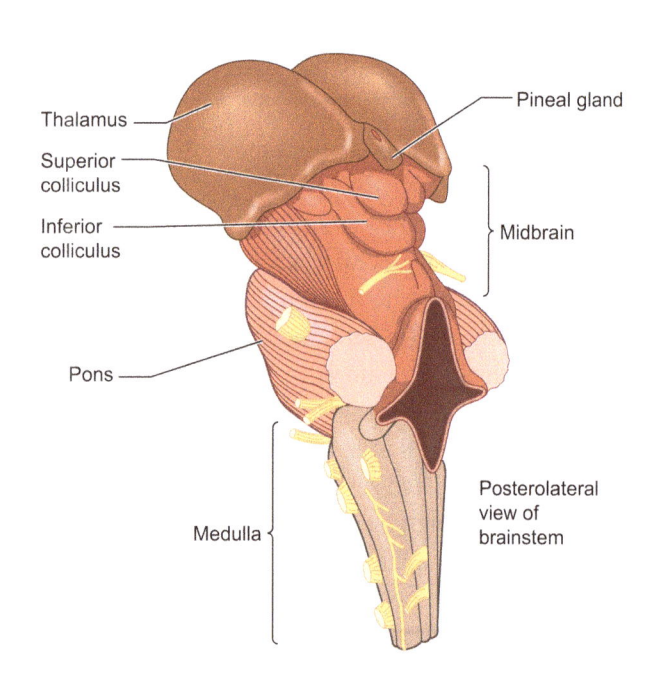

(b)

Figure 7.8 The brainstem. A small region of the brain between the spinal cord and the upper regions of the brain, responsible for many essential functions including breathing, heart rate, and sleeping.

Thalamus
Superior colliculus
Inferior colliculus
Pons
Medulla
Pineal gland
Midbrain
Posterolateral view of brainstem

sense of ourselves comes from the interaction of networks distributed across large portions of the brain, even including the thalamus and brainstem (Figure 7.8). This conclusion is supported by a meta-analysis showing that, when we are selectively processing information about the self, many of the brain regions already mentioned, including the ventromedial prefrontal cortex, **anterior** cingulate, and several other regions including the bilateral anterior insula, left **striatum**, right thalamus, and amygdala become activated (Northoff et al., 2006).

The insular cortex also becomes activated when we make judgements about our body, such as estimating our heart rate (Critchley et al., 2004) and making a judgement about the intensity of our emotional experience (Zaki et al., 2012).

Disorders of the Physical Self

We identify our psychological selves with our physical selves. Your body is just yours, and you locate your self and consciousness in it. It's located where you are. You look out of your eyes and you can see the front of your torso, arms, and legs, and just about your nose. If you look in a mirror, you can see the rest of your face including your eyes.

Another case where the psychological self becomes detached from the physical self is the out-of-body experience, which we will consider in Chapter 11 on altered states.

Split-brain Studies

The brain comprises two cerebral hemispheres, left and right, which are connected by a bundle of nerve cell fibres called the *corpus callosum* (Figure 7.9). These fibres enable information to be transmitted very quickly between the two hemispheres. In the early 1960s, the American psychologist Roger Sperry (1913–1994), with his PhD students, including Michael Gazzaniga (b. 1939), investigated split-brain patients. The split-brain procedure is an operation on the brain called a **callosotomy**, or more particularly a *corpus callosotomy*, and involves cutting through the corpus callosum (as distinct from the earliest version of the procedure known as a **commissurotomy**, which involved cutting through other brain structures such as the thalamus as well). It was a rare treatment for extremely severe epilepsy, the idea being to prevent the spread of epilepsy from one hemisphere to another. The first patient they studied was Patient W.J., who underwent a full corpus callosotomy in 1962. W.J. was a paratrooper who had suffered head injuries in 1944 in World War II; as a result, he suffered a series of convulsions that at one time went on for several days. The operation greatly improved his condition (Gazzaniga et al., 1962). There are only a handful of such split-brain patients suitable for testing; from the late 1970s less radical treatments, including better drugs or more refined surgery, meant that a full corpus callosotomy was no longer necessary. Roger Sperry was awarded the Nobel Prize in Physiology for Medicine in 1981.

It is widely known that there is substantial hemispheric specialisation, with the majority of people showing localisation of many language functions in the left hemisphere. The widespread view of the left hemisphere as analytic and the right hemisphere as responsible for spatial holistic processing is not very far off the mark (beware, though, of anyone claiming they are a right-brain person). The body is wired contralaterally, so that information from the left side of the body goes initially to the right hemisphere, and vice versa. For example, the right ear projects initially to the left hemisphere, and the right motor cortex controls the left side of the body. The situation with the eyes is a bit more complex, with the left-hand side of the entire visual field going to the right hemisphere, and the right-hand side to the left.

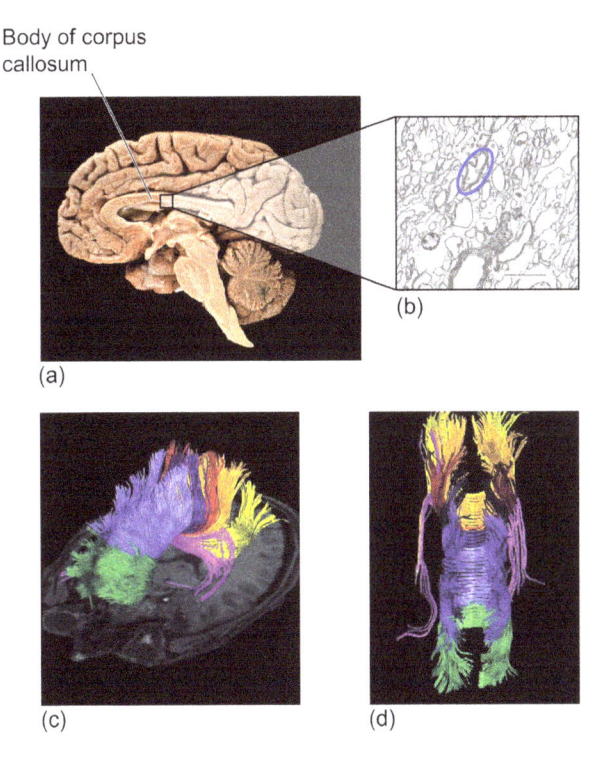

Figure 7.9 The corpus callosum. The corpus callosum is the tract of fibres connecting the two cortical hemispheres.

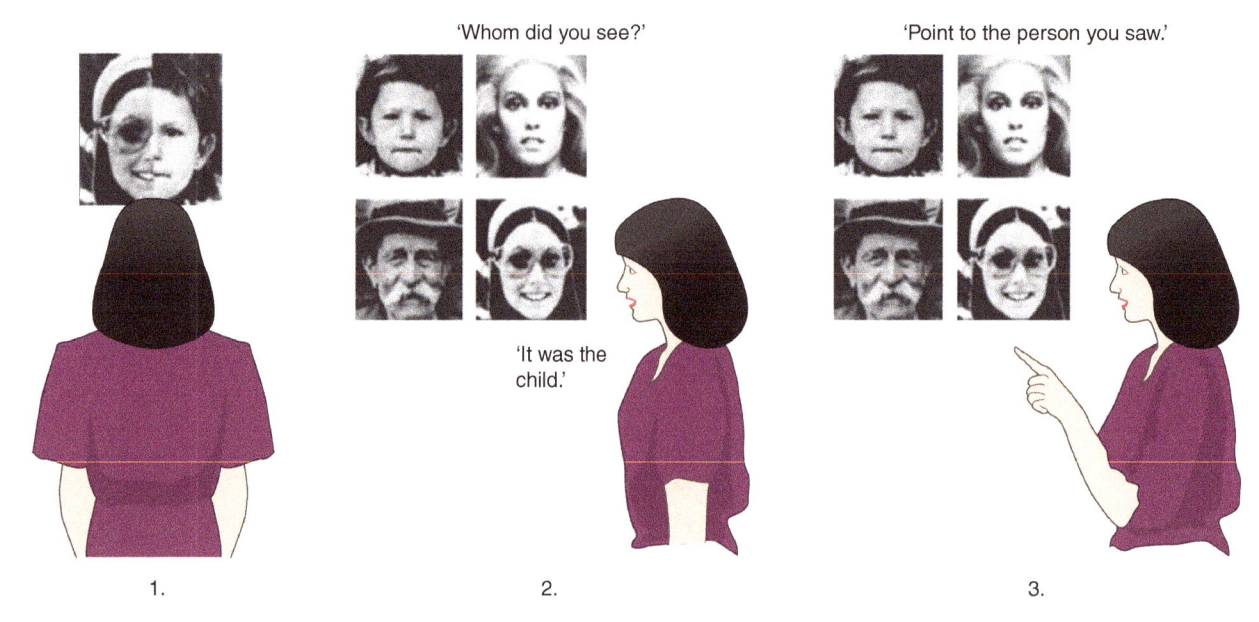

Figure 7.10 Split-brain testing setup. Information can be presented to each hemisphere either consistently or in conflict.

Normally information is transmitted relatively quickly from one hemisphere to the other so that relatively sophisticated experiments with sensitive timing measurements are needed to detect these differences. With split-brain patients, however, the severed corpus callosum means that with, an appropriate setup (as in Figure 7.10), information can be presented selectively to either hemisphere (Gazzaniga, 2005; Wolman, 2012). The results of doing so are often striking. The 'left hemisphere' can name an object presented to the right visual field, but the right hemisphere cannot name one presented to the left visual field; it can, though, draw a copy. One early study of a teenage boy whose 'right hemisphere' was asked to name his favourite girl at school was unable to do so; he could though indicate her with gestures by his left hand. Some argue that the left and right hemispheres have different concepts of self, the future, culture, and history. For example, when they asked the right side of patient P.S.'s brain what he wanted to be when he grew up, he replied 'an automobile racer'. When they posed the same question to the left, however, he responded 'a draftsman' (Brogaard, 2012).

Which aspects of consciousness are split in these split-brain studies? The only answer that makes sense is phenomenal consciousness (Bayne, 2008). One possibility is that phenomenal experience is restricted to the left hemisphere, and the right, without language, maintains some *zombie-like state* (a model proposed, but not supported, by Bayne), with split-brain behaviour resulting from automatic processing. This model gives too much prominence to language, and in any case the right hemisphere supports some linguistic processing.

Others argue that the left and right hemispheres are independently conscious. We appear to ourselves to have unified consciousness because of left-hemisphere dominance (Agrawal et al., 2014). Furthermore information transfer between the two hemispheres is also very important in 'normal' people. We call this account the *two streams of consciousness model* (Tye, 2003). The surgical operation splits a unified consciousness into two.

Alternatively, each hemisphere might normally support its own phenomenal consciousness, but in everyday life the streams of consciousness are the same because they are receiving the same contents, and it is only in laboratory conditions that the streams are different.

Another possibility is that there is only phenomenal consciousness at any one time but it switches hemispheres depending on the demands of the current task and what is most in focus as the result of the task (Bayne, 2008).

Parfit (1984) argues that the conclusion that there are two streams of consciousness in these split-brain patients can only be explained by there being two selves is implausible. He argues that the bundle theory gives a more natural account because the split-brain cases are simply an extension of our everyday experience, where all that there is a succession of sensations, experiences, and states of awareness, crucially, often overlapping. Rather than duplicating entities as in the ego theory, the bundle theory just means there are more disparate overlapping experiences. Pinto et al. (2017) agree, arguing that, although perceptual streams are divided, consciousness is not.

It is difficult to choose between these alternatives. The split-brain data are complex, and after callosotomy (but not commissurotomy), the two hemispheres are still connected in a slow and roundabout way through deep-brain routes. Furthermore, these patients can learn to observe the effects of the actions of each hemisphere so that, over time, as is the case with most neurological impairments, performance improves. People learn to adjust. So, although the effects described above are found with experimental testing, in actuality the effects of the corpus callosotomy might be ameliorated.

Dissociative States

A dissociative state is state where the person feels detached from reality in some way. It can range in severity from very mild to very severe, and be transient or long persisting. People can be detached from their immediate surroundings, or in more severe cases feel detached from their body, emotions, and environment. The most common dissociative state is daydreaming or **mind-wandering**, which we will discuss in more detail later.

Many people experience occasional states known as *derealisation* and *depersonalisation* (Hunter et al., 2017). With derealisation, people feel detached from reality, perhaps as though they are living in a movie. The surroundings seem unreal or distorted in some way; when I temporarily experience derealisation, it is as though I am separated from the world by a thick sheet of glass or Perspex, which affects both sound and vision, a common finding. The world might appear drained of colour and emotional potency. With depersonalisation, the most frequent symptom is anomalous body experience. People feel like they are detached observers of themselves, or not really there, and the world feels less real and becomes more dream-like. They feel like their body does not belong to them, or that they are not in control of themselves in some way. Some people say they feel like a robot. Emotional responses might be flattened or altered in some other way. Depersonalisation is very common, with only anxiety and depression occurring more frequently as psychological symptoms. It also occurs commonly in life-threatening states, with 50% of people reporting it in events such as earthquakes and car accidents. In general, depersonalisation is most associated with anxiety. Depersonalisation also occurs relatively frequently with migraine and temporal lobe epilepsy.

Derealisation and depersonalisation often go together, and in more extreme cases depersonalisation–derealisation disorder is recognised as a pathological disorder by the APA in DMS-5. The symptoms can be provoked by a very wide range of circumstances, including anxiety, trauma, sleep deprivation, jet lag, too much caffeine, too much alcohol, **psychoactive** drugs, and drug withdrawal, to name just a few (e.g. Baker et al., 2003; Raimo et al., 1999; Stein & Uhde, 1989).

As ever, there are probably several different things going on in different instances of depersonalisation and derealisation. Imaging studies reveal over-activation in the prefrontal cortex and large changes in activation in the sensory association cortex; at the same time the *serotonergic*, endogenous **opioid** and *glutamatergic NMDA* pathways are involved (Simeon, 2004). EEG studies show that slow waves (theta waves) are abnormally present during some episodes (Raimo et al., 1999).

Dissociative fugue (in incarnations of the APA Diagnostic and Statistical Manual of Mental Disorders prior to 5, it is called fugue state) is a condition where a person has a loss of memory for autobiographical information, usually as a result of a severely stressful event, for a short period of time, usually a few hours or days (although longer periods have also been reported). During the fugue, the person might travel and assume a new identity. Some loss of memory can be induced by psychoactive drugs, body trauma, or delirium, but these are not counted as psychiatric in origin. On recovery, the person may be surprised to find themselves in unfamiliar surroundings. After recovery from the fugue, there might be a more permanent loss of memory for the precipitating stressful event (called dissociative amnesia).

There are several famous instances of people with fugue states. The first widely discussed case was that of Ansel Bourne (1826–1910; if his name sounds familiar it's because Jason Bourne took his name from him). Bourne was a preacher from Greene, Rhode Island. He planned a trip to visit his sister in Providence on 17 January 1887. However, he instead withdrew his savings and went to Norristown, Pennsylvania, where he opened a shop under the name Albert J. Brown, starting a new life. When he woke on the morning of 15 March, he reported that he had no idea where he was, he became confused when people told him that his name was Albert J. Brown, stating it was still 17 January and he was Ansel Bourne. He had no memory of the previous two months. Later, under hypnosis, he could assume the identity of Albert Brown. At least this story had a happy ending: he lived the rest of his life as Ansel Bourne (Rieber, 2006).

It is not always easy to verify the identities of people returning from fugue states if a longer period of time elapses. One of the most famous instances was the Bruneri–Canella case, when an Italian man, Professor Giulio Canella, a philosopher, somewhat ironically, went missing during the Great War in 1916 on the Macedonian Front, and then reappeared in 1926. His wife, seeing a newspaper photograph, visited a man in hospital who claimed to have no memory of his past and who had forgotten his identity, and identified him as her lost husband. However, an anonymous letter instead claimed that he was actually Mario Bruneri, an anarchist and petty criminal. Eventually, he was legally identified as Bruneri, but 'Canella' and his 'wife' fled to Brazil, where he died in 1941. If nothing else, the story shows the complexity of cases of lost identity and of proving that a person who claims to have no memory is a particular person after a great deal of time has elapsed. (It would probably be easier now with DNA testing.)

As with many of these more bizarre states, there is always some controversy about them. The reporting of any condition that is wholly dependent on self-report is always open to some doubt.

> **Box 7.3 Derealisation: A Case Study**
>
> Across 15 years of prolonged and severe derealisation, I have only experienced punctuated moments of 'touching reality' approximating about 30 minutes in total. This 'popping in and out' of existence contrasts with the detachment I feel from the world. It can't be easily described without some reference to what processes might be involved. It's as if somehow all the sensory information fails to merge and form a unified sense of the world, but is rather disharmonious and fragmented. People and the objects around me seem somewhat distanced and unreal; not within my reach, presenting as a decoupage of objects, people, and scenery. And from behind/within this machinery I am flooded with internal information from my viscera (increased heart rate, decreased temperature, etc.), which further contributes to a sense of disconnectedness from the outside world. There was a significant qualitative difference in my experience of the world after a traumatic event. The change occurred within a few minutes – like a drunken state. This has persisted since then, apart from those moments of sobering up. I don't question whether I'm different from other people; I compare my experience of reality to what it was like before.
>
> (My colleague Anna Z., 2019.)

Dissociative Identity Disorders

Even most non-psychologists have heard of 'multiple personality', known properly now as **dissociative identity disorder** (DID, and never to be confused with schizophrenia). 'Multiple personalities' have been documented and written about in fiction throughout history, but it remains a controversial topic. The most notable recent case was that of Chris Costner Sizemore (1927–2016), initially given the pseudonym of 'Eve' (Thigpen & Cleckley, 1954, 1957). The book was made into a film, also called *The Three Faces of Eve*, starring Joanne Woodward, and also released in 1957 (Johnson, 1957). Thigpen and Cleckley argued that Eve had developed multiple personalities in response to childhood trauma, although Sizemore herself thought that the personalities had always been present. She said that, in fact, over her life she had 22 personalities, not 3 (Bernstein, 2016; Sizemore, 1977). Her three commonly portrayed characters were described as Eve Black (an impetuous and reckless barfly), Eve White (a mousey housewife), and her true self (Jane).

There is much scepticism among psychiatrists and psychologists about DID and what it means, with some believing that the phenomenon is as described, but others believing that the symptoms are invented by people with personality disorder, or even implanted, perhaps accidentally, by therapists (Brand et al., 2016; Gillig, 2009; McAllister, 2000). There does seem to be some consensus emerging that DID is a real if complex disorder, and, in fact, may not be that uncommon. People with DID are usually highly hypnotisable, suggesting a strong tendency to dissociation, and systematically have a history of childhood trauma. If we accept the existence of dissociative fugues, then accepting DID does not seem much of a leap further, and some researchers have found physiological differences accompanying the different states (Reinders et al., 2006), supporting their existence.

It is nevertheless difficult to know what to make of DID. The most obvious interpretation is that the whole 'self system' is duplicated, triplicated, or more. If we examine the differences between the personalities we can begin to see what is involved in a 'self': a personality, of course (being a predisposition to act and evaluate the world in certain ways in particular situations), and a set of memories (as one personality does not always remember the existence of other personalities). The bundle theory accounts for the personalities as different bundles that cohere closely. The ego theory would have to presuppose the existence of two or more egos, which seems more problematic.

The Boundaries of the Self

One of the key factors that individuates our sense of self is the way in which the self is located in our body, and the body is located in physical space. It's my body. My sense of self is particularly located (for me) in my head between my eyes, but I look down and I also think of my fingers as part of me. If I hold someone else's hand, intertwining our fingers, I can still differentiate my fingers from those of the other. How does the brain assign ownership to our body, and can it get things wrong?

Unsurprisingly, perspective-taking in space relies on those parts of the brain that support spatial processing, most importantly the right *parietal cortex* (Vogeley & Fink, 2003). The insula, which we have met before in the context of the self, is thought to play a role in representing our own body (Craig, 2009), and involved in locating our body as the source of our actions (Farrer & Frith, 2002; Tsakiris et al., 2007).

Phantom Bodies

Patients whose physical and psychological selves become decoupled are said to be experiencing **autoscopy**, or *autoscopic phenomena*. In an autoscopic hallucination, the person sees their physical body in a different location but continues to experience themselves located in their original, proper location. It is like seeing a double of yourself, which is presumably where the idea of a doppelgänger comes from. In **heautoscopy**, people shift their psychological self so that it is with the translated body image so they seem to be experiencing themselves and the world at another point in space. Autoscopic phenomena are rare illusory visual experiences in which a person perceives their body from a different perspective in external space. They consist of an out-of-body experience (OBE, see Chapter 11) and autoscopic hallucination, occasionally present in epileptic attacks and schizophrenia (Blanke & Mohr, 2005). In heautoscopy, the person perceives a duplicate of their body. The present lesion analysis suggests a predominant implication of the right hemisphere in these patients. For example, Patient B.F. suffered damage to her occipital cortex and basal ganglia during childbirth, and saw a translucent mirror image of herself about 1 m in front of her (depending on where she was looking). It behaved in the same way as herself, seeing actions happening to it (Zamboni et al., 2005). These disorders of perceiving one's body arise from damage or disruption to the more posterior regions of the brain, on either or both sides, a diagnosis that sounds infuriatingly imprecise. The phenomena happen because the disruption leads to the generation of ambiguous or conflicting sensory information, which cannot be properly integrated into one coherent self image (Blanke & Mohr, 2005). This model is supported by findings from experiments in which states resembling these disorders can be induced by a variant of virtual reality in which participants are given conflicting visual-somatosensory input (Lenggenhager et al., 2007).

Phantom Limbs and Phantom Pain

Our sense of the properties of our body can be misled. One of the best-known examples is that of **phantom limbs**, where a person feels that an amputated or severed limb is still attached, and particularly still feels pain in the missing limb. It was originally thought that the pain originated from pathological changes to the nerves in the stump of the remaining limb, but evidence now suggests that the pain originates in the central nervous system (Flor et al., 2006). For example, the phantom limb pain is not stopped by local or epidural anaesthesia (Baron & Maier, 1995). There are cases of people reporting a phantom limb, such as an arm, even when that limb has been missing from birth (La Croix et al., 1992; Saadah & Melzak, 1994).

Phantom limbs and their implications have been most extensively explored by the Indo-American neuroscientist Vilayanur (V.S.) Ramachandran. Ramachandran explains the sensations in terms of neural plasticity, so that after the loss of the limb the body's image is remapped in the somatosensory cortex (Ramachandran et al., 1992). The motor cortex is one of the few areas of the brain that is very clearly topographically organised, so that parts of the body that are close to each other are mapped to physically close regions in the motor cortex. As the neural map of the body is reorganised, areas nearby become involved in the function of the limb or body part loss.

One consequence of this remapping is that space in the somatosensory cortex previously occupied with representing the missing limb is reallocated to remaining parts of the body, which results in some confusion interpreted as sensation (and pain) in the missing limb (although as ever there are dissenting voices arguing that the phantom pain results from 'bottom-up' exaggeration of random noise from the severed nerves; see Vaso et al., 2014). Ramachandran developed a mirror box system to treat phantom limb pain, in which a pair of mirrors is used so that the mirror image limb is seen in place of the lost limb. The person then moves their remaining limb. The person can then to some extent learn to control the corresponding missing limb so that they can move it out of what is perceived to be a painful position or spasm (Ramachandran et al., 1995).

In summary, the generation of a physical self image, and identification of our self with our body is a complex process, which can be partially disrupted.

> **TRY THIS:** A Mirror Box 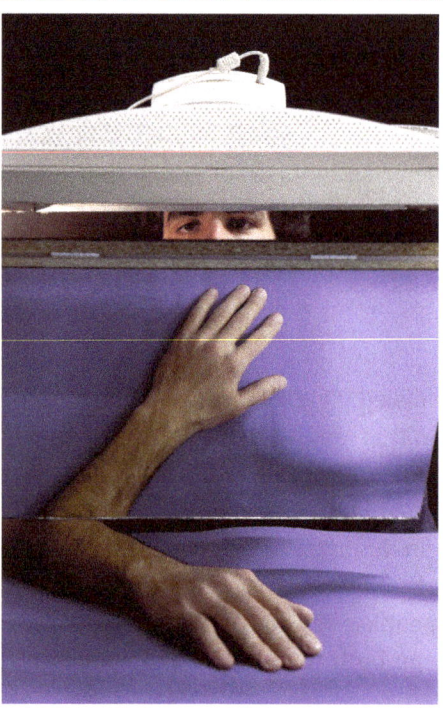
>
> Build your own mirror box system and use it to examine the consequences of giving input to your right arm or leg when you see it as your left. Designs are widely available online. You will need two mirrors of reasonable size (see Figure 7.11).
>
> Figure 7.11 The mirror box setup. The setup enables the mirror image limb to be seen instead of the missing limb, enabling the person to 'control' the movement of the missing limb. Source: Pascal Goetgheluck/Science Photo Library.

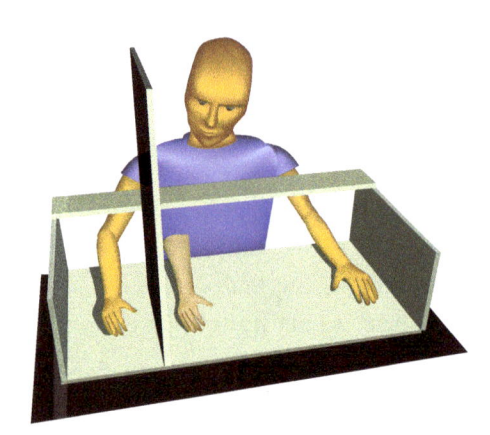

Figure 7.12 The rubber hand setup. After a while some participants 'feel' the sensation in the rubber hand. Source: Rohde, Di Luca, & Ernst (2011).

The Rubber Hand Illusion

Distortion of our body image is not restricted to pathological delusions. Our perception of our body parts is not accurate, and we can easily be misled about the extent of our body.

In the **rubber hand** illusion paradigm, participants sit with, say, their left hand hidden from their sight. They see a lifelike rubber left hand in front of them. The experimenter strokes both the person's hidden left hand and the visible rubber hand with a brush (see Figure 7.12). If the two hands are stroked simultaneously and in the same way, participants gradually start to experience the rubber hand as their own. They start to feel that the tickling is located in the rubber hand. For example, when asked to point to their left hand with their right, they usually point to the rubber hand rather than their own left hand (Botvinick & Cohen, 1998; Ehrsson, Holmes, & Passingham, 2005; Ehrsson, Spence, & Passingham, 2004). The illusion takes about 11 seconds to kick in. When the experiment was carried out with participants in a fMRI

THE BOUNDARIES OF THE SELF

scanner, in this initial period there was activation of the parietal cortex; around 11 seconds there is enhanced neural activity in the region of the motor cortex corresponding to their hidden hand. If the stroking of the real and rubber hand was not coordinated, this activation did not occur. So, the parietal cortex appears to be involved in integrating visual and touch information, and the premotor cortex is involved with the sense of ownership of the hand.

It's possible to go further and generate a similar illusion for the whole body. Petkova and Ehrsson (2008) reasoned that if perspective is important in assigning ownership to the body – from the point of view of eyes in our heads we always see our arms, torso, and legs in the same way – it should sometimes be possible to fool the brain by manipulating our perspective. Petkova and Ehrsson gave headsets to participants to wear so that they see a mannequin from the perspective of their head (see Figure 7.13). They were given synchronised visual and tactile stimuli (they could see the right abdomen of the mannequin being stroked while their own stomachs were brushed in the same place). Participants soon reported illusory sensations being located in the alternative body, claims supported by physiological measures. Similar results can be obtained using virtual reality (Slater et al., 2010).

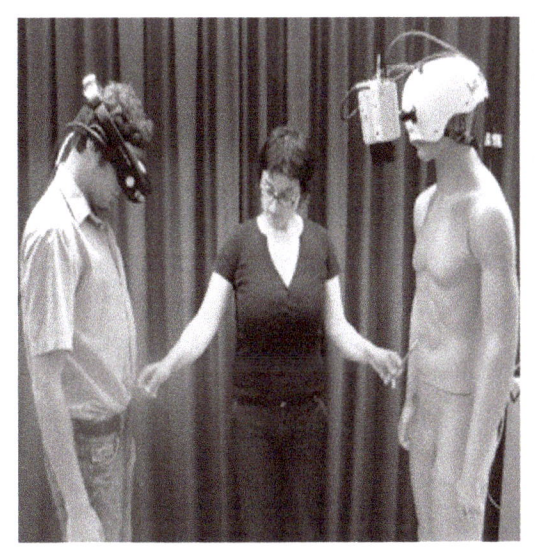

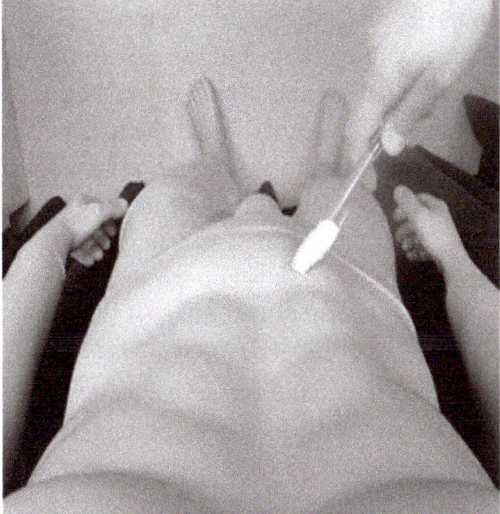

Figure 7.13 The Petkova and Ehrsson person-swapping setup. This paradigm extends the rubber hand to a whole body so people report sensations that are located in the mannequin. Source: © Petkova et al. (2008).

These studies show that the brain can be fooled by appropriately misleading visual and tactile information. Bottom-up perceptual mechanisms can override top-down knowledge, and we can be tricked into locating our body self image outside our body.

> **TRY THIS: Your Rubber Hand**
>
> The rubber hand illusion is easy to demonstrate if you can find a willing accomplice. Model hands can be found surprisingly cheaply on the internet.

Awareness of Motor Control

Blakemore et al. (2002) propose a model of motor control based on achieving a desired state (such as grasping a cup) derived from a goal (drinking your tea), through a series of intermediate steps, which continually reduce the discrepancy between target and actual state as we make the movement. Some of the stages of this model, such as formulating the goal and observing the final step, are available to awareness, but some (such as the fine-grained control of motor movements and the operation of feedback) are not. Blakemore et al. argue that the model can account for all disorders of motor control. For example, phantom limbs appear because of discrepancies between any motor commands issued to the limb, prediction of the limb's position, and the absence of feedback. Some people with schizophrenia report that they are not in control of their movements, and attribute control to some external agency, such as aliens; in this case the prediction mechanism and belief systems are both faulty so abnormal sensations are attributed to external control. In patients with alien hand syndrome, representations of the hand are activated inappropriately. The goal of reaching for a cup, for example, is activated by the sight of the cup even though it is not consistent with the person's current goals.

Is the Self Restricted to the Body?

Is the self limited to my body? Some authorities talk about the *extended self* or **extended consciousness**. The British philosopher Andy Clark, in particular, has championed the extended mind hypothesis (Clark, 2010, 2013).

Clark starts from the idea known as embodied cognition (*enactivism* means much the same). Embodied cognition emphasises the way in which cognitive processing is deeply influenced by how it is embedded in the world: cognition depends on the perceptual and motor systems and our interaction with the world (Shapiro, 2017). It hardly sounds a very controversial hypothesis, and the debate is often in the detail of exactly what experimental results show. There are though several, perhaps surprising, findings. One consequence is that when we simply think of moving our hand, say, the motor cortex associated with the hand might be activated to some extent. Simply seeing someone carry out a motor action such as lifting a cup is enough to engage the appropriate motor parts of your own frontal and parietal cortices (Rizzolatti & Sinigaglia, 2007). The meaning of words is grounded in motor actions and perceptual features; activating the meaning of a tool, such as 'hammer', activates the parts of the cortex associated with tool use (Kemmerer, 2015). The body and environment can influence our thoughts: in one well-known experiment, exposure to a dirty room or noxious smell makes people more severe in their moral judgements, while exposure to a clean room makes them less severe (Schnall et al., 2008).

Clark goes further, and argues that the tools we use – pens, smartphones, paper, the internet even – are part of our cognitive environment so that some objects can be seen as extensions of our mind. There is some evidence for this claim in that, as we become very skilled with a tool, our body representation changes as though we have incorporated the tool into our body schema (Maravita & Iriki, 2004). For example, the receptive field of the body of a skilled tennis player changes to include the tennis racket – it is truly as though the racket becomes an extension of the arm.

Although these observations are interesting, it is stretching it to say that my tools are part of me. If you were to lose your smartphone, you would be temporarily bereft, but it can be replaced; the same cannot be said of our amygdala. My hand is somewhere in between; if it were severed, it might be possible to attach it back, or even give me a hand transplant, but it is unlikely to recover the full range of movement, and for a while I might view it as an alien hand – not quite my own. Indeed, some hand transplant recipients have difficulty adapting to their new hands, and such problems are likely to increase as the range of transplants increases. Face transplants, for example, are likely to challenge our self concepts, and give rise to psychological rejection as well as immunological rejection (Bluhm & Clendenin, 2009). Isabelle Dinoire, who had the first face transplant, said of her new appearance such things as 'it will never be me' and 'I am not sure who I am'.

The biggest change in extending our consciousness was the development of writing. Writing enables us to remember much more than we could otherwise; writing enables us to store and pass on cultural information. Writing enables us to make and share plans. Writing enabled the development of shared mathematical information and hence the development of physics. A culture with writing is much better placed to predict the future.

It is likely that we are currently going through another period of being able to extend our consciousness as computing devices become so small and cheap. A smartphone is a prime example of a device that enables us to have more information to hand and provides us with an easy means of storing our thoughts.

While not wishing to deny that our tools are extremely important, the extent to which you view the idea of extended cognition as useful will depend upon the extent to which you view our boundary of skin and brain (or even neural sheath) as arbitrary.

Is the Self Just Another Illusion?

The saying is 'know thyself' – but what if there isn't a self to know?

Is the self then just another item on our increasingly lengthy list of illusions? Even if it is an illusion, then it is a useful one. We talk about our selves a great deal.

But folk psychology and our beliefs are, as we have seen, unreliable guides to what is really happening in the mind. Several authors talk about the myth of the self. In fact, what they mean is that the ego theory of the self is wrong. The German philosopher Thomas Metzinger has been arguing this point for years (2004, 2010). Again, for Metzinger, constructing a model of the world and our place in it is central. Sophisticated organisms don't just model the world, they model themselves in it – they have a self model. Our self model is constructed by the prefrontal cortex. The model of the world is so good that we routinely mistake it for the real thing. There's no such thing as a self, a persisting entity, just our experience of the model. Slightly confusingly, he talks about the phenomenal self, as they appear to us in our model. We have a virtual self in a virtual model of the world, and it's all impoverished relative to the 'real' world. It's a subtle distinction.

Clark (2016) emphasises the idea that humans are concerned with prediction. In a world that's constantly changing, taking time and effort to build a detailed model would be a waste of time; we might spend so long processing the perceptual input and constructing the model that we would never be able to do anything. Instead, we do the minimum we need, 'just in time'. Think again about what you're conscious of right now: we focus on what we're doing and at any one time our model is comparatively impoverished. The advantage of predictions is that we can ignore predictions about the world that are verified and focus on discrepancies, which are more likely to be important. Similarly, Chater (2018) argues that, contrary to many of our beliefs, the mind is 'shallow': not that much is going on (often very true in my case). Often we only do the minimum processing necessary to get by. There are several complex models of how we derive grammatical structure from language we hear and read, but maybe much of the time we just pick up on one or two important words.

The underlying idea here is that much less is going on than our folk psychology leads us to believe. We have seen that many researchers argue that the self is an illusion. John Locke found that, when he introspected, there was no self, just his bundle of feelings and perception. Susan Blackmore and Daniel Dennett are most vociferous in their denials of the existence of the self. Dennett (1991) argues that it is merely a narrative, a story we tell ourselves (ha) and others to explain the coherence of our experience.

In case you think believing in a self is essential to negotiate the world, consider Cotard's delusion. Individuals with Cotard's delusion believe themselves to be missing a body part, to be dead, or no longer existing, or to have no self. As with all these bizarre delusions, its origin is not clear. It might be related to Capgras delusion. It is not, though, without consequence; denying the self leads to self neglect and prevents the person making sense of reality, leading to severe psychosis. The delusion has many different causes (Debruyne et al., 2010).

The self is the observer of experiences and the initiator of actions. I find it very difficult to think of the self as just yet another illusion. I think of myself at the centre of the universe. Does saying that this self is merely an illusion and a narrative I've constructed make it any less real?

Not everyone agrees, and the self view does have some support. Sui and Humphreys (2015) argue that the self reference is necessary to bind perception and memory into a coherent whole. Hence, not only does the self exist, but it serves an important psychological function. The research has generated some interesting debate as to the nature of the self (is self-reference the same as telling a story?) and the role of neuroscience data in resolving conceptual issues (Lane et al., 2016; Sui, 2016). It is well known that our memory is better for things that are related to ourselves than to other people (Symons & Johnson, 1997). If the self is a fiction, it is a very powerful one, believed in by most people. We have to ask what is the point of the fiction, and still need to explain the details of how the fiction arises and how people negotiate it (Gallagher & Zahavi, 2012).

Chapter Summary

- The self is the owner of our experience, the 'me' in my head.
- Ego theory says that there is an ego observing the world, and this ego can be identified with my self.
- Ego theory may suffer from a problem of infinite regress.
- Bundle theory states that all that there is to the self is a series of perceptions and thoughts that can be tied together at any one time.
- Bundle theory says that this series of thoughts and perception merely gives the illusion of our self.

- Damasio distinguishes between the proto-self, core self, and extended self.
- The core self is consciousness in the now.
- The self is based on homeostatic mechanisms in the body, shared by many organisms.
- The extended self has autobiographical memory and self-reflection.
- The self arises from widespread coordinated action across the brain, including the frontal lobes.
- The insula plays an important role in maintaining our sense of self.
- Autobiographical memory provides us with continuity of existence.
- Infantile amnesia refers to the inability of adults and older children to access memories from when we were very young.
- Severe instances of amnesia show what happens when this continuity of existence is lost.
- Split-brain patients exhibit behaviour that could be interpreted as having two selves, located in each hemisphere.
- Dissociative states show that not all memories and aspects of processing might be available to the self at all times.
- Dissociative identity disorder ('multiple personality') shows that the self can be fragmented.
- Some people who have lost limbs report phantom limbs, and particularly pain in the lost limbs.
- Phantom limb pain results from cortical changes.
- We can be mistaken and misled about the boundaries of our selves.
- The rubber hand illusion provides an example of how we can be tricked into being wrong about the boundaries of our selves.
- According to embodied cognition, cognitive processes only make sense if we realise they are situated in the world, and that the body can influence our minds.
- The distributed self is extended or distributed in space; a laptop enlarges our cognitive repertoire.
- We have many effects on the world, but that is not to say that these effects are in any way conscious.
- Many argue that the self is an illusion, and that it is merely a narrative we construct to make sense of our experiences.
- Anattā in Buddhist theology is the doctrine that there is no permanent self or essence.
- Even if the self is an illusion, we need to explain the cognitive processes involved in the creation of the illusion, and how individuals use, talk about, and respond to it.

Review Questions

1. If we are limited in how far we can go in thinking about ourselves thinking about ourselves, is the self truly recursive?
2. Do models of the self such as Damasio's address the hard problem of consciousness?
3. What makes you the child that you were aged five?
4. How is your consciousness distributed in space?

5. What do phantom limbs tell us about consciousness?
6. Is the self just an illusion?
7. Discuss phenomena that suggest that we do not identify our selves with our bodies.
8. Some medical researchers claim that one day head transplants will be possible. What are the likely consequences for the sense of self for such hypothetical patients?

Recommended Resources

General
Gallagher, S. (ed.) (2011). *The Oxford Handbook of the Self*. Oxford, UK: Oxford University Press.

Ego and Bundle Theories
Parfit, D. (1984). *Reasons and Persons*. Oxford, UK: Oxford University Press.

The Neuroscience of the Self
Damasio, A. (1999). *The Feeling of What Happens*. New York: Harcourt Brace & Company.
Damasio, A. (2010). *Self Comes to Mind: Constructing the Conscious Brain*. New York: Pantheon.
Gazzaniga, M.S. (2015). *Tales from Both Sides of the Brain: A Life in Neuroscience*. New York: Ecco Press.
Ramachandran, V.S. (1998). *Phantoms in the Brain*. London: Fourth Estate.
Ramachandran, V.S. (2012). *The Tell-Tale Brain*. London: Windmill Books.

Amnesia and Fugue States
Kring, A.M., and Johnson, S.L. (2013). *Abnormal Psychology* (12th ed.). Singapore: Wiley.
Wearing, D. (2005). *Forever Today: A Memoir of Love and Amnesia*. London: Corgi Press.

The Distributed Self
Clark, A. (2010). *Supersizing the Mind: Embodiment, Action, and Cognitive Extension*. Oxford, UK: Oxford University Press.
Hofstadter, D. (2007). *I Am a Strange Loop*. New York: Basic Books.

The Myth of the Self
Hood, B. (2013). *The Self Illusion*. London: Constable.
Metzinger, T. (2010). *The Ego Tunnel: The Science of the Mind and the Myth of the Self*. New York: Basic Books.

8 COGNITION AND CONSCIOUSNESS

How are cognitive processes related to consciousness? This chapter will examine some models that have their focus primarily in cognitive issues. We begin by looking at the role of language in consciousness and self-awareness. What is thinking, and the stream of thought that appears to fill our mind – a kind of perpetual internal flow we have called the stream of consciousness? Most of us hear some kind of internal voice when we think – what is this inner speech, and where does it come from? And how do we form pictures, called mental images, in the mind?

Attention is a bottleneck in mental processing, and we consider it next. We look at the structure of the attentional system and how it is related to the brain. We examine the idea that there are two types of attentional process, focused and unfocused, and particularly examine the default mode network, the idea that when nothing important is happening our mind starts to wander. What is the neuroscience of this network, and why is it so important for consciousness? We then look at two very different models of consciousness that place great emphasis on attention and cognitive processes, the global workspace model of Baars and the multiple drafts model of Dennett.

We then turn our attention to the importance of constructing a model of the world, and the role consciousness plays in constructing and maintaining this model. What is the role of consciousness in thinking about the future, and in thinking about our own mental processes, metacognition? Is thinking about ourselves, recursive thinking, central to consciousness? We then examine those accounts of consciousness that consider it to be an emergent process. Next we look at how consciousness develops across childhood.

We conclude by looking at a conception of consciousness that says that consciousness emerges from quantum mechanical processes.

Consciousness Is About Limitations

We know that one important aspect of consciousness is that it is limited – we aren't conscious of very much at any one time. What about what is outside consciousness, what Freud called the preconscious? Clearly, there is a great deal of stuff we could be aware of if we wanted to. You are unlikely to be thinking about:

The capital city of Germany

until I mention it.

At that point Berlin will hopefully 'pop' into your consciousness. Where's it been all that time? In a way, it's been nowhere; it's always stored in memory, but somehow it's been brought into focus – to our **attention**. Attention is another somewhat slippery term for the bottleneck that occurs in processing – we can't do everything at once. To what extent are consciousness and attention related? Are they even the same thing?

Several other concepts much studied in cognitive psychology are relevant to our discussion of consciousness. We have touched on the role of language and the importance of recursion in the evolution of consciousness. What other roles does language play in consciousness? Thinking is another of those folk psychology terms that we use all the time, but that proves difficult to pin down. It's the expression of an idea, and directed towards something. We can't have a thought in isolation; we can only think about something. Problem solving on the other hand can be conscious or unconscious – we can think as we try to solve a problem, but sometimes the solution appears when we haven't been thinking about the problem, a process known as incubation.

Language and Consciousness

'The limits of my language mean the limits of my world' commented the philosopher Ludwig Wittgenstein (1961).

A **language** is a system of a finite number of rules for combining a finite number of words to generate an infinite number of sentences. It's obvious that spoken language isn't necessary for consciousness in humans: people with hearing impairments use sign language, which is as rich and as complex as spoken language (Harley, 2014). Few would want to deny that infants at the prelinguistic stage of development are in some way conscious, and there are occasional instances of feral children who have grown up without any apparent exposure to language who also are presumably conscious. As we have seen, most people believe that at least some non-human animals, who do not naturally use a language, are conscious. So, a formal language isn't necessary for consciousness. What about self-consciousness though? It's difficult to imagine how an entity could reflect upon its own existence without a means of expressing the concepts necessary – a language in some form.

Some researchers think that language is of paramount importance in consciousness. MacPhail (1998) argues that language is essential for the development of the self, and that a self-concept is essential for consciousness. It follows that non-human animals cannot be conscious. This position is too extreme. First, we have seen strong evidence of consciousness in many non-human animals. It also seems perverse to deny consciousness to infants and children before they start acquiring language, at around 18 months. What about people who for whatever reason don't use language, or use an alternative form, such as sign language? Nevertheless, language may play a role in facilitating symbolic representation, and may make some tasks easier.

Language and Culture

There is a story, sadly almost certainly apocryphal, that, when various native peoples met people from the west for the first time (take your pick of Native Americans seeing Columbus's

LANGUAGE AND CONSCIOUSNESS

ships, or Indigenous Australians coming across Captain Cook's ship *The Endeavour*), they were unable to 'see' the ships, because they had no conception of such constructions – the ships were so alien to them that they were invisible. The story seems to come from the lack of interest from people on the shore when Cook's ships sailed near to the coast.

Although there are no such gross differences in perception and thought between cultures, there are nevertheless more subtle differences. We don't all perceive the world in quite the same way; the details of the form of our consciousness depend on our experience.

The idea that the form of our language affects the way in which we think has been around for some time. The idea was developed by the American linguist Benjamin Lee Whorf (1897–1941). Whorf was a chemical engineer who worked in fire prevention, but he was also interested in linguistics. He was responsible for formulating what is known as the *Sapir–Whorf hypothesis* (Harley, 2017). The Sapir–Whorf hypothesis combines two ideas called linguistic relativism and linguistic determinism, which say that different languages dissect the world in different ways, and these differences have consequences, so speakers of different languages perceive and categorise the world in different ways.

This type of research is methodologically quite difficult to do. There has been a great deal of work on colour perception: not all languages have names for all the basic colour terms, and the hypothesis is that speakers of these languages will find it more difficult to remember colours for which they do not have names. The Dani people of New Guinea, for example, only have two colour terms, distinguishing between light and dark colours (see Figure 8.1). The Pirahã people of the Amazon basin only have words corresponding to 'one', 'two', and 'many' in their language, and their numerical cognition is affected by the lack of a more sophisticated counting system. If they are dealing with more than three objects their performance on a range of tasks, particularly involving memory, is poor (Gordon, 2004). So the way in which we perceive and categorise the world, the contents of our consciousness is affected by the form of our language. The consensus is that, while there is little support for a strong version of the Whorfian hypothesis, language helps understanding a great deal (Frank et al., 2008), and the availability of language terms affects cognitive processing, thus supporting a weak version of the Sapir–Whorf hypothesis (Winawer et al., 2007).

Figure 8.1 Members of the Dani people of Papua, New Guinea. There has been much research on how the Dani people perceive and remember colours because they only have two basic colour terms: 'mili' for cool, dark shades, and 'mola' for warm, light shades. Source: 12MN/iStock Editorial/ Getty Images Plus.

Visual perception has also been shown to be sensitive to cultural differences. The *Muller–Lyer illusion* is one of the best known and most pronounced examples of a *visual illusion*. The illusion shows three lines that are the same length, but the middle one looks longer than the surrounding two (see Figure 8.2). We can't help but see the lines of different lengths, even when we know they're not. But there are clear cultural differences in

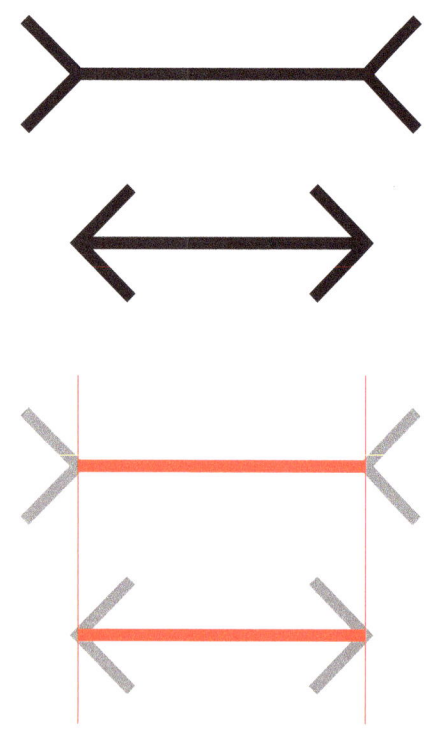

Figure 8.2 The Muller–Lyer illusion. The two horizontal lines in the top half of the figure are of the same length (as demonstrated by the figure beneath). The arrows cause the lines to appear to us to be of different lengths. Source: bobmadbob/iStock/Getty Images Plus.

susceptibility to the illusion, with people from western cultures most sensitive to it. There has been considerable debate as to the reason – is it because of differences in pigmentation in the eye, or because of the differences in experience with straight lines (e.g. see Jahoda, 1971)? It is suggestive that there are differences between urban and rural dwellers from the same culture and race (Ahluwalia, 1978), which supports the idea that it's exposure to straight lines that matters. The idea that sensitivity to the illusion is caused by exposure to the straight lines, right angles, and corners that dominate the built-up industrial environments is called the *carpentered world* hypothesis.

Thinking

Fernyhough (2016) notes that there are two related uses of the word 'thinking'. In its broadest sense, 'thinking' is used to stand for everything the conscious mind does. The other use is that 'thinking' is some form of inner speech, where our thoughts are internalised language. Fernyhough prefers this narrower meaning of thinking as a conscious, active process that is almost conversational; it is quintessentially linguistic – verbal for those who use speech, and visual or gestural for those who use sign language.

The idea that thinking involves some sort of language has been quite popular across the years. Consider those statements like 'I believe that the Earth is flat', 'I wish you would give me all your money', and even 'I think that my poodle is more intelligent than most people'. First, as we have noted, you can't just believe, or whatever, you have to believe something (if only that you believe that you believe). These sorts of structures are called propositions, and they are expressed as verbs (I believe) and complement clauses (that I believe something). They also have a *truth value* – either the statement 'I believe that the Earth is flat' is true or false, and hence these mental states held by people towards propositions are sometimes called propositional attitudes. The British philosopher Bertrand Russell spent considerable time worrying about them (Russell, 1912). I can, of course, say something I know not to be true (in fact, I don't really think the Earth is flat), and we call such statements lies. The important point is such statements can only be described in language-like terms. We need something corresponding to verbs, and we need something that these verbs express. That is, thought has a syntax.

For this reason, many scholars have concluded that thought is couched in language. The *Language of Thought Hypothesis* says that thought and thinking take place in a mental language, sometimes called *mentalese* (Fodor, 1975). Thinking consists in syntactic operations combining internal representations of the world. A language of thought helps us to explain a number of characteristics of thought, such as its *generativity*, which means that just like overt language it can express any concept by combining a finite number of words with a finite number of syntactic rules to generate an innate number of concepts, so can our internal language enable us to express a potentially infinite number of thoughts from finite, limited experience. Recursion, rules defined in terms of themselves (see Chapter 4), plays a central role here. This approach, of language manipulating concepts representing states of affairs, and thinking being the transformation of one mental state into another, is called the *Representational Theory of Mind* (Fodor, 1975). We have used the word representation rather blithely, in its everyday sense, up to now. In cognitive science, a representation is a **symbol** that stands for something else. For example, on a map, a church symbol stands for a church in the real world. The degree to which the symbols resemble what they represent is an important undecided question in psychology, but there is no reason why in principle symbols could not be very abstract. In language, words are symbols representing objects in the world (among other things); the symbol 'church' bears nothing but a totally arbitrary relation to the object in the world it stands for.

Note that the internal language of thought and the external language of communication do not have to be the same thing, but an obvious step is to say that they are.

We also use thinking in the sense of 'solving a problem' – 'that's something to think about'. Problem solving is a complex process, which modern researchers conceptualise as an example of a dual-route process, where one route is conscious and the second not (Evans, 2010). You may have experienced the phenomenon of trying to remember something, or solve a problem, but you cannot: however, you find that you do something else and the solution comes to you later. This process of background, unconscious thinking is called incubation, and has been the topic of much research (Sio & Ormerod, 2009).

Inner Speech

Experience sampling methods (ESMs) show that we are all talking to ourselves quite a lot of the time: *inner speech* takes place at any one time in about a quarter of all samples (Heavey & Hurlburt, 2008). But there is a great deal of individual variation.

Developmental psychologists have debated the role of inner speech in cognitive development. For Chomsky, language is a separate module that develops independently of cognition; for Piaget, cognition was primary and drives language acquisition. In the 1930s, the Russian psychologist Lev Vygotsky argued for a more complex picture of linguistic, social, and cognitive development (Vygotsky, 1934). Vygotsky noted that before the age of three or so children produce *monologues* – speech that is not socially directed at anyone, but instead appears to be thinking out loud. Indeed, he believed very young children can only think out loud. Around the age of three these monologues disappear. Vygotsky argued that they didn't really disappear – they became internalised to become inner speech. At this point children's overt language is directed towards being social, whereas our thinking becomes linguistic and more rational.

How like overt speech is inner speech? Does inner speech use the same mechanisms in the brain as when we speak out loud? How rich is the code we use? Vygotsky (1934) believed that inner speech is 'thinking in pure meanings', although it is a bit unclear what that means. More recent research suggests it is more complex than that. The key question is how detailed is the representation of sound in inner speech? Is it abstract (called phonological) or detailed (called phonetic)? The general paradigm that has been used is to give participants difficult phrases, such as tongue twisters ('she sells sea shells on the sea shore') to repeat internally, and ask the people to report the internal errors they make. Phonological inner speech would show a lexical bias effect but not a phonemic similarity effect; phonetic inner speech would show both. Lexical bias is the outcome that speech errors tend to result in words more often than non-words than you would expect by chance; phonemic similarity is when similar sounds (e.g. t and d) get confused more often. After some debate (Corley et al., 2011; Oppenheim & Dell, 2008, 2010), a reasonable conclusion is that inner speech is flexible – it is primarily at the phonological level but can sometimes involve phonetic information. Although we know introspection is flawed, this conclusion does seem to chime with experience; we sometimes sound words out in some way, and the level of detail appears variable. Inner speech is clearly more detailed than simply the activation of word meanings.

Despite its variability among individuals and across the life span, inner speech appears to perform significant functions in human cognition, including reasoning, planning, problem solving, control of behaviour, and memory rehearsal (Alderson-Day & Fernyhough, 2015). A large meta-analysis of functional neuroimaging studies shows that areas such as the left **inferior frontal gyrus** (LIFG; **Broca's area**, see Figure 8.3), which are active when we speak out loud, are also active during inner speech (Morin & Hamper, 2012). Furthermore, disrupting the activity of this region using brain stimulation techniques can interrupt both overt and inner speech. Activation of the LIFG is particularly high when people are self-reflecting or retrieving autobiographical information, pointing to the importance of inner speech not just to thinking, but to tasks involving self-awareness.

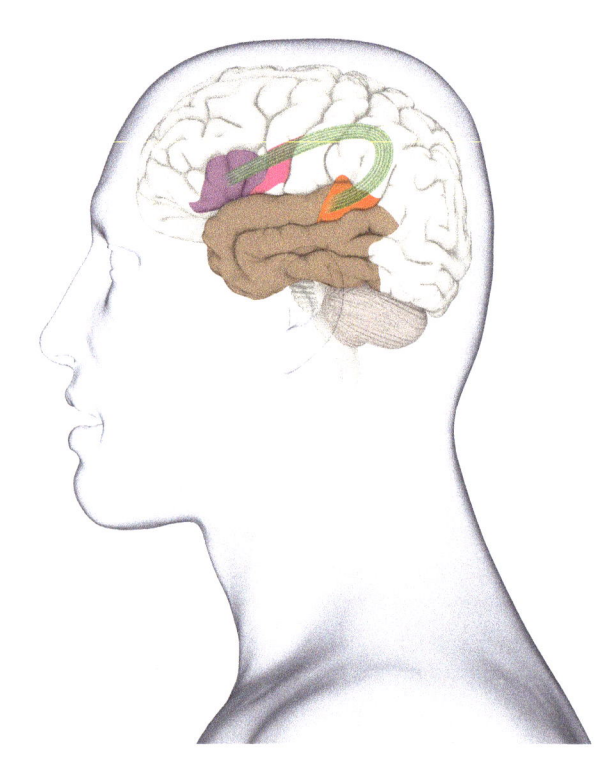

Figure 8.3 Broca's area. The most important language-processing areas in the left hemisphere, with Broca's area shown in purple. Broca's area is involved in sequencing language units, such as sounds to produce words and words to produce sentences. Source: Dorling Kindersley/Getty Images.

It's possible that the auditory hallucinations of schizophrenia arise at least in part by an inability to distinguish between inner speech and external stimuli. Speech that we hear that arises internally but whose source is attributed to be external, a failure of *source monitoring* (being able to identify where something comes from), is called an **auditory verbal hallucination (AVH)**. Although relatively common in schizophrenia, they are not limited to it, and also occur in a significant minority of the general population (Moseley et al., 2013). They are relatively common when falling asleep and waking up (see Chapter 11).

Inner speech has also been implicated in disorders as diverse as bulimia and anorexia, social anxiety, sexual dysfunction, and depression; although, of course, it is difficult to disentangle cause from symptom (Baumeister et al., 2011; Scott et al., 2014). There is no harm in trying to improve our self-talk; such an approach is advocated for, among other things, improving athletic performance (Hardy, 2006).

> **TRY THIS:** Your Inner Speech
>
> Observe your inner speech. How much is it like listening to external speech? Can you detect variations in the details of the sounds you produce in your mind? When are you most likely to be talking to yourself?

Mental Imagery

Clearly, not all mental activity takes the forms of words and inner speech. We also have (or appear to have) **mental images**, the most striking and common of which are, for most people, visual images.

It might seem obvious that these visual images are indeed pictures in the mind, but in cognitive psychology nothing is obvious. There has historically been considerable debate as to the nature of these images. On the one hand, the spatial representation theory was championed by the psychologist Stephen Kosslyn (e.g. Kosslyn, 1996). This theory holds that visual images are like pictures, and that we can carry out operations on the pictures themselves. On the other, we have the propositional theory that holds that mental images are really coded in the same abstract representation that represents languages, called *propositions*, a theory most identified with the Canadian philosopher Zenon Pylyshyn (1973, 2002).

The imagery debate is one of the longest-running and indeed most bitter debates in the history of cognitive psychology. It began with Pylyshyn's (1973) famous critique on the dual-code theory of Allan Paivio (e.g. Paivio, 1986). *Dual-code theory* states that we need linguistic and pictorial codes to represent the world; Pylyshyn argued that we can do everything with a linguistic-type code. Very soon though Kosslyn became most identified with the pictorial side, and a long series of papers ensued. Kosslyn argued that there are many situations where we appear to solve problems by using the pictorial properties of images. If I ask you to visualise a map of the United States and then tell me which is closer to Denver – San Francisco or Boston, you have the experience of seeming to answer the question by forming an image of the map and inspecting it to see which is closer. Kosslyn showed that behavioural measures such as reaction time depended on visual characteristics of images, such as how far points were in the pictures and maps. Pylyshyn replied that these results had alternative explanations, including the effect of the way the experiments were set up (the experimental demand characteristics). Our mental maps are by no means always accurate: ask yourself which is further west, Reno or Los Angeles in the United States, or Edinburgh or Liverpool in the UK?

Pylyshyn pointed out that one of the major problems with visual images is, once more, the homunculus problem: who is doing the looking? Isn't there going to be an infinite regress? You might say that you have the experience of looking at visual images – but who is this 'you'? And when I think about my visual images, they're pretty sketchy, and I'm hard pressed to say that they really are a picture. If the behavioural data can be explained either way, what conclusion can we draw? Pylyshyn also argued that we're not saying that the pictures are encoded linguistically, but in *mentalese*, in the language of thought, and we don't know what format that has.

One of the central arguments was whether the representation was analogue or propositional: analogue representations maintain some of the physical properties of what is being represented, such as the way a map maintains the relative distance between points. But eventually analogue representations become non-analogue: maps become pixels or dots of print, television pictures become pixels. The debate started to dry up.

More recently, though, the embodied cognition approach has livened things up again. Parts of the brain involved in perceptual processing become activated when we start thinking about pictures (Kosslyn et al., 2001). Although suggestive that forming mental images does involve elements of perception, it is by no means conclusive, as it is not clear that this activation is not just a side effect rather than playing any causal role in processing.

One final issue concerning mental images is whether we experience qualia when we form a mental image. If you visualise a red rose, do people get the quale of redness in the same way as if we actually look at a red rose? I'd say I do, but more fleetingly and not as intensely as when I see the real thing, which then raises the interesting issue of can we have degrees of qualia?

> **TRY THIS: Your Mental Images**
>
> Form a mental image of something – anything. Say a red rose. What is your experience of having the image? How like the red is the red that you visualise? If you think you can experience the qualia of red in a visual image, then consider how accurately you can visualise pain.

Attention

Many people think of attention as being like a spotlight, something that brings some things (aspects of mental processes) into focus, hence giving rise to the name **selective attention**, emphasising the point that we only pay attention to some things because we have limited processing capacity. We therefore have to select what information we process more deeply. So attention is the cognitive mechanism that allows some information to be more thoroughly processed than other information. The nature of attention is one of the most important questions about A-consciousness (access consciousness; Block, 2005, 2011).

Early approaches to attention thought of it as a bottleneck, and the main question was what was it that decided what got through the bottleneck and what didn't. Think of how much information our brains are receiving at any one time; in addition to continual input from our five senses (sight, hearing, touch, taste, and feel), the brain is receiving a great deal of information from the body, such as a sense of where our body parts are, not to mention any pain. Within vision and hearing, in particular, there are many competing stimuli. Yet, we seem to be aware of relatively little at any one time, which is where attention and the bottleneck come in. Broadbent (1958) proposed that all incoming sensory information is stored in a sensory buffer; we then pay attention to some of these stimuli on the basis of their physical properties, such as which ear the message was played to, or the type of voice. In particular, semantic processing can only take place after the filter has selected the stimulus, or *channel*, to which to pay attention. This point is particularly problematic given the *cocktail party effect* (Cherry, 1953). If you are at a party listening to what the person over the wine glass is telling you, you might think you are completely focused. It's noisy and you're paying attention. You can't hear anything else (indeed being able to hear every other conversation that was going on in the room would be a distracting and unpleasant experience). Then you hear your name mentioned across the room. 'I never really liked that Trevor.' You orient to it, so we must be monitoring the environment all the time, and processing it to a sufficient depth that we can orient to it if necessary. Treisman (1964) therefore proposed that information from the unattended channel is attenuated rather than completely eliminated.

Exactly what is 'attention' in these and similar models? Is it the process that selects among stimuli, or the outcome of being in the 'spotlight' of attention? The latter doesn't make much sense, so attention is generally thought to be the process of selectively focusing on aspects of the perceptual input. We then have the familiar problems: who or what is directing attention? How are the decisions being made? Is attention a thing, a process, an outcome, or what? Of course, we can observe parts of the brain lighting up as stimuli are selected for further processing – but is this all attention is? A view similar to this position was outlined by Anderson (2011) in a paper provocatively entitled 'There is no such thing as attention'. (The idea that attention is unnecessary in psychological explanation was first proposed as early as James in 1890; and if you are now worried that you thought you knew what attention is, but are no longer sure, James also said 'everyone knows what attention is'.) The fallacy of treating an abstraction as something real is known as *reification*. When researchers say that they manipulate attention, they don't, directly: instead, they manipulate variables such as the interval between cues and targets, or spatial location, or channel (Anderson, 2011). Things to which we are paying attention are in some kind of selective focus, but do we need to posit anything else?

It is also a reasonable guess that awareness and attention are related, so that what selective attention selects is what we're aware of – that is, attention determines the contents of our consciousness. However, most researchers believe the opposite: attention and awareness are *doubly dissociable* in that you can have either without the other (Cohen et al., 2012; Koch & Tsuchiya, 2007; Lamme, 2003; Mole, 2008, Tononi & Koch, 2008). Hence, for example, imaging studies suggest that a distinct brain network is involved in feature selection, whereas other areas are involved in higher-level processes and self-reflection (Koch & Tsuchiya, 2007; Lamme, 2003). Studies on patients with blindsight (see Chapter 10) show that orientation and attentional cues do not necessarily lead to visual awareness. And we can orient (pay attention) to 'invisible' (sub-threshold) objects (Tsushima et al., 2006), so that you can orient towards a stimulus and select it for awareness without its actually reaching awareness.

Some think that the above summary is an exaggeration, and that, although we cannot have attention without awareness, there is no robust empirical support for awareness without attention (Cohen et al., 2012). Cohen et al. argue that attentional selection is necessary but not sufficient for consciousness. These experiments are controversial because of the methodological difficulty of demonstrating consciousness without attention.

> **TRY THIS:** Shifting Your Attention
>
> Play with shifting your attention around you. Experiment with all the senses, and also shift it inside you as well around the outside world. How would you describe what is happening?

We must be careful here, again, in thinking about exactly what is meant by attention and awareness (Koivisto et al., 2009). The experiments discussed above all concern perception (usually visual perception) and externally presented stimuli. Little is known about how internal material is made conscious. It is conceivable that something could be made conscious without conscious selection (e.g. when we are reminded of something and something pops into consciousness from memory). The deeper one delves, the more confusing awareness, attention, and selection become.

Visual Attention

Most work has been carried out on visual attention, on the processes whereby visual stimuli are selected for further processing, reach awareness, and on the capacity limitations of the visual system.

The research literature on visual attention is enormous. One clear conclusion is that there isn't a clear conclusion. The cognitive system and brain structures implementing visual processing are highly complex. Visual processing involves several modules, and several cortical and subcortical systems that run in parallel.

The Default Mode Network

As the old joke goes, I was trying to daydream, but my mind kept wandering.

I find it very difficult to stay focused. My mind is always wandering. I started writing this section and before I knew it I was thinking about having to weed the garden. I've got this far, and I'm thinking about lunch. Surely, everyone is familiar with this phenomenon of mind-wandering. When our *minds wander*, we stop being focused, we start thinking about things we have to do, things we should do, things we would like to do, and sometimes we find ourselves in a reverie without being sure how we got there – we also call this daydreaming. We call these intrusions *task unrelated thoughts* (TUTs for lovers of acronyms).

Our minds wander all the time. In a sample of 2250 people who reported what they were doing at any time, using a smartphone to ask them at random times (experience sampling), people reported that they were thinking about something else other than what they should have been doing 46.9% of the time (Killingsworth & Gilbert, 2010). (The only activity in which people did not report mind-wandering was sex.) We do not always enjoy it when our minds wander. In their study, Killingsworth and Gilbert (2010) found that people are less happy when their minds are wandering than when they are focused. People do not even feel happier when they are thinking about pleasant things. The amount of mind-wandering is related to working memory capacity (Kane & McVay, 2012) and is associated with the loss of executive control over our thoughts (Smallwood & Schooner, 2006). People with lower working memory capacity are more likely to have mind-wandering. They're more likely to make mistakes too. It's difficult to tease apart causality here, although Kane and McVay argue that a third variable, attention-control capability, underlies both working memory capacity and TUT rate. There are individual differences in how prone people are to daydreaming: the personality trait in which a person becomes absorbed in their mental imagery and fantasies is called **absorption**. Absorption is measured by the Tellegen Absorption Scale, which asks questions such as 'When I listen to music I get so caught up in it that I don't notice anything else' and 'I can be deeply moved by a sunset'. Perhaps unsurprisingly, when their minds wander, people tend to make more mistakes on the tasks on which they should be focusing (Smallwood & Schooner, 2015).

Mind-wandering sounds bad, and to some extent it is if we should be doing something else, but does it always have a cost without a benefit? Baars (2010) notes that some, perhaps much, creative work and planning in the arts, sciences, and mathematics happens in mind-wandering time. It would be most surprising from an evolutionary point of view, he notes, if such a large allocation of mental resources were to have no useful adaptive function.

Mind-wandering is what happens when you stop focusing on the task at hand. In recent years, neuroscientists have come to recognise the importance of what has been called the default mode network (DMN) or **default network** (**DN**). The default mode network is a network of brain regions that are highly active together, and distinct from other regions and networks in the brain, and active when a person is 'doing nothing' (which is the default): when the brain is in wakeful rest, daydreaming, thinking about others, or thinking about the future (Buckner et al., 2008; Raichle et al., 2001). All are distinct from the opposite mode, which is staying focused on a particular task. I have just spent two minutes before trying to write that sentence, getting my thoughts together, staring into the distance, and soon I found I was thinking about what I should do in the gym and whether I should have breakfast tomorrow, totally unrelated to what I should have been thinking about. My mind had wandered and presumably my default mode network had become very active. It's called 'default mode' become the system becomes activated when we're not engaged with a particular task or perceptual processing. Instead, the DMN handles self-generated thought. Now I'm back to concentrating on writing, the default network is off.

The default network comprises a number of **hubs** associated with specific brain regions responsible for different types of processing (Buckner et al., 2008; Andrews-Hanna et al., 2014). Outside of the hubs and the parts onto which they're connected, there's not much of the brain left! Clearly, these regions are involved in processing a great deal of what we consider to be important in being conscious. Changes to the functioning of the DMN are observed when we fall asleep (Picchioni et al., 2013), and when we meditate (Xu et al., 2014). Damage to the DMN is associated with a range of pathologies, including autistic spectrum disorder, Alzheimer's disease, depression, schizophrenia, and post-traumatic stress disorder, among others (Buckner et al., 2008). The default network brain regions deactivate when we engage with a task.

Is it that surprising that the brain is active when we appear to be doing nothing at all? We know that it is virtually impossible to keep your mind completely empty (we are always conscious of something), and hence we are always thinking of something, and thinking is an activity. The importance of the DMN is in showing how specific brain regions are related, in that this background activity has a use (e.g. in planning future activity), that the brain has a natural resting state from which it moves only when there is some external demand, and how damage to the network can give rise to a range of deficits. Not everyone is, however, convinced that the brain has one natural resting state, which should act as a baseline. It might also be that the energy-consumption measures upon which these conclusions are based are more complex than first appear (Morcom & Fletcher, 2007). Clearly, though, doing nothing and thinking about nothing in particular are more complicated than you might first think.

The DMN isn't just activated when we do nothing; it is actively involved when we plan life events, reflect, and daydream. Hence, it has an active component, daydreaming and mind-wandering, and a negative component, stopping or carrying on doing nothing. Active mind-wandering involves the part of the **pons** in the brainstem known as the *locus coeruleus* and the neurotransmitter norepinephrine (Mittner et al., 2016). The neuroscience of the DMN is shown in Box 8.1.

Box 8.1   The Default Mode Network

Regions involved in the **default mode network** (DMN) include (see Figure 8.4):

- **Frontal regions of the brain** – involved in information regarding the self.
- **Angular gyrus** – connects perception, attention, and action, and involved in the recall of episodic memories.
- **Medial prefrontal cortex** (mPFC) – involved in decisions about self processing such as personal information, autobiographical memory, future goals and events, and decision making.
- **Posterior cingulate cortex** (PCC) and **precuneus** – combines information from memory and perception. The lower (**ventral**) part of the PCC is involved in tasks relating to the self, others, remembering the past, and thinking about the future, and processing concepts plus spatial navigation, while the upper (**dorsal**) part of the PCC is involved with involuntary awareness and arousal.
- **Dorsal medial subsystem** – involved in thinking about others.
- **Dorsal medial prefrontal cortex** (dmPFC) – involved in determining the purpose of other people's actions.
- **Lateral temporal cortex** – involved in the retrieval of social semantic and conceptual knowledge.
- **Temporo-parietal junction** (TPJ) – involved in processing 'theory of mind' information.
- **Medial temporal subsystem** – involved in autobiographical memory and future simulations.
- **Hippocampus** – responsible for the formation of new memories.
- **Pons** – involved in regulating active mind-wandering.
- **Posterior inferior parietal lobe** (pIPL) – the junction of processing auditory, visual, and somatosensory information and attention.

ATTENTION

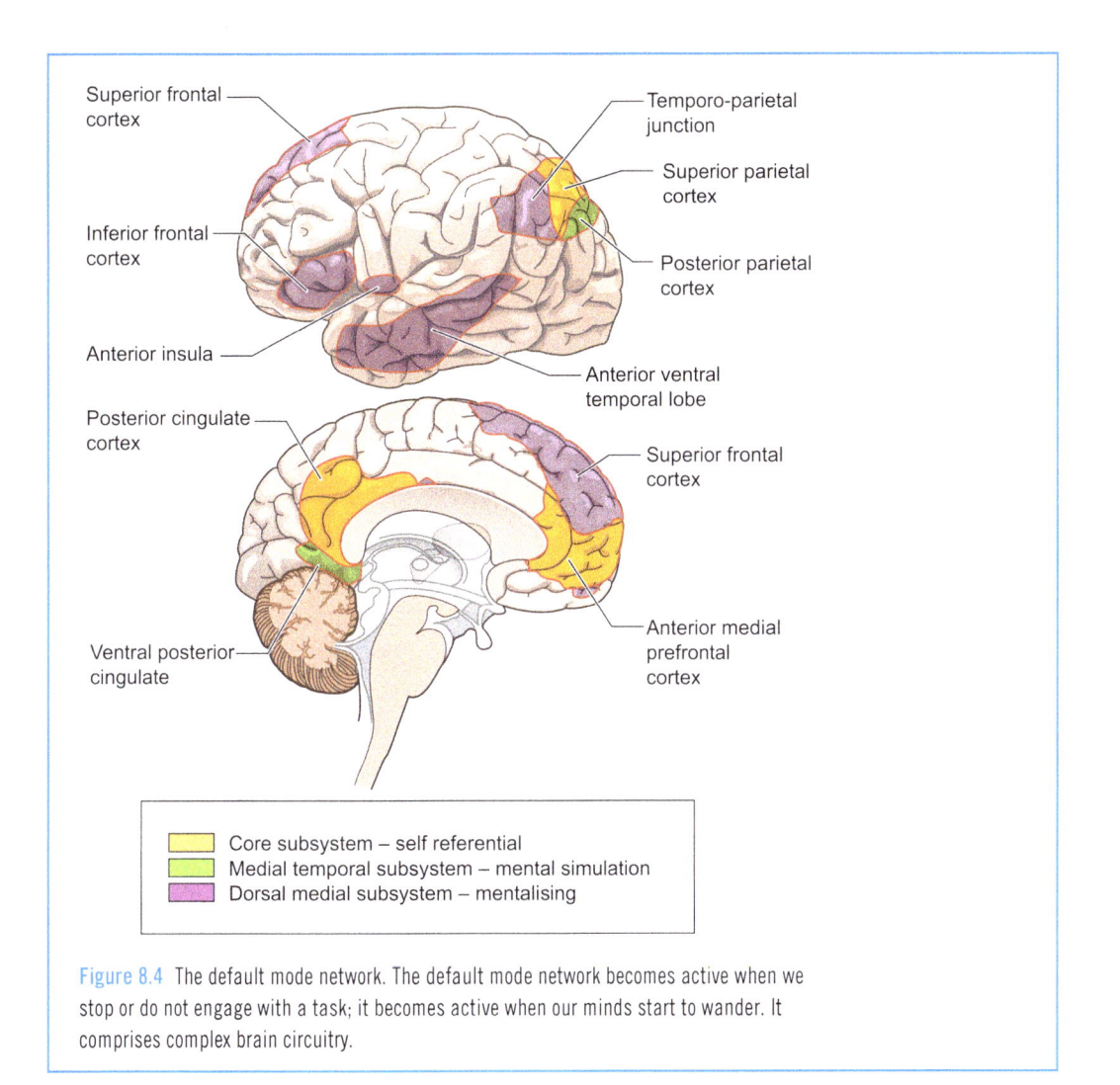

Figure 8.4 The default mode network. The default mode network becomes active when we stop or do not engage with a task; it becomes active when our minds start to wander. It comprises complex brain circuitry.

> **TRY THIS:** Your Wandering Mind
>
> Here is a nice easy one: sit back and let your mind wander. Give yourself two minutes. What did you think about? How did the thoughts flow into one another? Was the stream of consciousness smooth or were there sudden jumps? Can you notice a stream of consciousness when you are not introspecting? Does that question even make sense?

Global Workspace Theory

Over recent years, the psychologist Bernard Baars has developed a notable and influential model of consciousness called the **global workspace theory** (**GWT**; Baars, 1983, 1988, 1993, 1997, 2002; Baars & Geld, 2019). GWT can best be thought of initially as a theatre with a stage illuminated by a beam. The beam is directed by the cognitive processes corresponding to attention, and it lights up the current contents of working memory. We're conscious of what is illuminated just now. The model comprises a global workspace, a set of input assemblies for making the results of perception available, and output mechanisms for action of the appropriate sort.

The advantage of GWT is its simplicity and intuitive appeal. If an educated lay person were to formulate a model of consciousness, it would probably be something like GWT.

The model is much more fleshed out than described above. For example, anything on the stage can be brought into consciousness by moving the spotlight appropriately, but there is much behind the scene comprising cognitive machinery that is always out of reach. We can't be conscious of the processes, such as executive processes, themselves, only of what the searchlight lights up. There is an audience, of sorts, but not an inner person that looks at what is illuminated. Instead, there are structures such as long-term memory; for example, seeing a person's face, and being conscious of that face, might remind us of what we were doing with them when we last saw them. Shallice and Cooper (2011) support the global workspace approach, emphasising the importance of *supervisory processes*. Supervisory processes control other processes, and are greatly involved, among other things, in metacognitive processes.

GWT explains several important features of consciousness, such as its limited capacity, its sequential nature, and its ability to trigger many unconscious cognitive processes. The cognitive model integrates well with the neuroscience data. And it is explicit enough to be computationally modelled, with the simulations enhancing our understanding of cognition (Franklin et al., 2016).

GWT is currently one of the most popular approaches to consciousness, and recently its neural bases have been explicated (see below). Nevertheless, it is not without criticisms. One is that it is a glorified Cartesian theatre, but Baars refutes the allegation that GWT is an homunculus-based theory because, he says, although there is a theatre with objects in the spotlight, there is no audience to watch them. It is the activation of the contents of working memory that determines consciousness, not something being observed.

Another drawback is that it is not clear that GWT addresses the 'hard problem'. Where do qualia come from? Elitzur (1997) makes this point, but concedes that Baars constrains the range of possible theories and does address how cognition and consciousness are related. In particular, Baars attempts to explain why there are no conscious experiences accompanying all brain states. Nevertheless, it is difficult to escape the conclusion that, in common with virtually all cognitive and neuroscience models, GWT is a model of A-consciousness but not P-consciousness.

The Neuronal Workspace Theory

The neuronal workspace theory has been developed in a series of papers by the French neuroscientist and psychologist Stenislas Dehaene in a variant known as the **neuronal workspace theory** (NWT). This model is complex and provides a comprehensive and detailed account of where processes related to integration and attention occur in the brain (Dehaene et al., 1998; Dehaene & Naccache, 2001). It extends the concepts of GWT.

As part of this work, Dehaene has been concerned with whether the brain shows a particular characteristic pattern when we are conscious – does consciousness have a signature?

A neural signature of consciousness, if reliable, could have many implications. It would enable us to tell if a person in a coma is conscious, and if animals shared similar patterns we might wish to conclude that they too are conscious in the same way as us.

Current methods of imaging are limited by either relatively poor temporal or spatial resolution; neither fMRI nor magnetoencephalography (MEG) can tell us exactly where something is happening at any precise time. And, of course, conventional techniques in experimental psychology, such as reaction time experiments, tell us nothing about where in the brain the complex processes studied are happening. To sidestep these methodological problems, Dehaene combines these techniques with a sophisticated mathematical analysis that enables us to look more accurately in space and time as we carry out aspects of particular tasks – not just did a part of the brain light up when a participant was given a stimulus, but which part, and when; for example, when did the participant first become aware that the stimulus in a particular location was a digit rather than a letter. Dehaene and colleagues showed that a particular 'brain wave' associated with the perception of a novel stimulus, the *P300*, is associated with conscious processing. The P300 is so called because in EEG it occurs about 300 ms after the presentation of the stimulus and has a positive voltage; the P300 occurs mostly over frontal areas of the brain.

Dehaene (2014) argues that this signature of consciousness arises when perception 'breaks free' of the initial modular processing of perceptual information, enabling the sharing of information across modules and the brain. When we become conscious of information it becomes *globally available* to a highly interconnected system, and low-level data becomes integrated into a single percept – a process Dehaene calls *ignition* (and is presumably the same as getting into the spotlight in Baars' account).

The distinction between *modular* and *liberated* processing is reflected in the results of an analysis of a masking paradigm experiment, in which a stimulus is partially obscured by another pattern. Early processing produces linear activation patterns, but then at a certain point we observe a nonlinear pattern; it's at this point that ignition takes place, in more frontal regions of the brain. Ignition occurs when preconscious sensory data coalesces into an integrated percept. The preconscious data may be incomplete, ambiguous, and self-contradictory, but the conscious percept is a single, coherent, and unambiguous thing. We never perceive ambiguous stimuli in both states simultaneously. Sensory awareness occurs when this coherent representation forms following the activation of corresponding sensory projection areas of the cortex. The **sensory cortex** can be activated internally, as well as externally, resulting in conscious inner speech and imagery. Once a conscious sensory content is established, it is broadcast widely to the audience of other networks along **cortico-cortical** and **cortico-thalamic fibres**. Dehaene and Changeux (2004) postulate a widely dispersed set of reciprocally connected neurons with long-distance axons linking most of the cortical and thalamic regions. These regions carry out further processing on the conscious percept, including evaluation and an assessment of the importance of the percept for the self.

The long connections enable information to be transferred across the brain and for feedback between regions. Consciousness depends on re-entrant processing (or recurrent processing), with feedback from later levels of neuronal processing to earlier in the cortex being essential for consciousness to develop.

On Dehaene's account the role of consciousness is to provide a stage or blackboard that allows the processing of a number of independent modules to cooperate and share information). This approach is compatible with a number of other proposals (Baars & Geld, 2019; Crick, 1984; Crick & Koch, 1990; Damasio, 1989; LaBerge, 1997; Gazzaniga, 1996; Ramachandran et al., 1995; Edelman, 1989; Llinás & Ribary, 1992; Newman & Baars, 1993; Shallice et al., 1996; Posner, 1992). The model bears similarities with others. The Colombian neuroscientist Rodolfo Llinás (b. 1934) argued that the main purpose of the nervous system is prediction. Events come into focal consciousness in sophisticated brains because of the simultaneous activation of different locations in the brain through long-distance neural connections becoming simultaneously active through electrical oscillation (Llinás, 2002; Llinás & Ribary, 2001). Taken together, GWT and NWT provide an emerging consensus among many researchers on how consciousness and other cognitive processes are realised, and how this relationship is implemented in the brain.

One prediction of GWT/NWT is that we are only conscious of an object after extensive processing – that is, consciousness is an *all-or-nothing phenomenon* in that we should either be able to report all features of an object or none at all (Sergent & Dehaene, 2004). However, we are conscious of more detail than we can report at any time; our perceptual experience seems to *overflow* that which can be accessed (Block, 1995, 2005; Lamme, 2010). For example, we can be conscious of a colour that we have seen without being able to identify the object with which it is associated. Using an **attentional blink** paradigm, where rapid serial presentation makes it very difficult to identify a second target presented very quickly after a first, Elliott et al. (2016) showed that there can be a severe impairment in conscious access to one feature of an object, while another feature is correctly accessed (such as the identity of a letter and the colour in which it is presented). Such results support the notion that consciousness is not all-or-nothing. These results can be reconciled with GWT/NWT by the *partial awareness hypothesis*, which states that consciousness of different levels of representation can occur independently so that people can be aware of features of an object without being aware of the entire object (Kouider et al., 2010). However, awareness of any one feature still seems to be all-or-none.

One criticism of the model is that it doesn't explain the nature of phenomenal consciousness, and doesn't really solve the hard problem.

> **Box 8.2** The Neuroscience of the Neuronal Workspace Model
>
> Dehaene et al. (1998) argued that five brain circuits are involved in consciousness:
>
> - **prefrontal cortex** and **premotor** regions for planning
> - **infero-temporal cortex** for high-level perception
> - **amygdala**, **cingulate cortex**, **orbito-frontal cortex** for evaluation
> - **hippocampal** and **parahippocampal** regions for long-term memory
> - **posterior parietal cortex** for attention orientation.
>
> These five circuits are interconnected so that any new stimulus can readily be evaluated and acted upon as appropriate. There is then feedforward excitation until top-down

> **Box 8.2** (cont.)
>
> processing is engaged, which leads to *ignition*: ignition occurs when top-down and bottom-up processing meet. Ignition is all-or-none so activation from a stimulus either ignites the global neuronal workspace or it quickly dies out. The outcome of ignition is to make a representation globally available by activating long-range *cortico-cortical* and re-entrant or recurrent connections (Lamme & Roelfsema, 2000).
>
> Conscious representations are globally available in the way that nonconscious ones are not. An ignited representation inhibits competitors, which leads to an attentional bottleneck and phenomena such as inattentional blindness. The *frontal cortex* is involved in active maintenance of an ignited representation.

The Multiple Drafts Model

The philosopher Daniel Dennett has been particularly scathing about models that imply the existence of a homunculus that watches what he calls the Cartesian theatre, a giant multisensory cinema screen where the contents of consciousness are displayed. For Dennett, many models of consciousness, including GWT, are of this type, although we have seen that Baars and others strongly resist this claim. Dennett asks, where is this homunculus? Presumably there is another smaller homunculus inside its head, and so on, with an infinite regress? He says that such models are implicit dualist theories because the regress can only be saved by an observer that is in some way different. Instead, Dennett (1978a, 1991, 2013) denies that consciousness comes together in one place, which is why the search for neural correlates of consciousness has proved so elusive. He proposes instead a **multiple drafts model** (**MDM**). At any one time, many things are going on in our brain, running side by side, but what matters most is our memory of events. There is no privileged consciousness processing in the sense of the Cartesian theatre or a workspace happening at the time; instead, things are reconstructed if necessary from the drafts after the event has happened.

Dennett describes a very simple visual illusion, the **phi illusion**, in which a series of still images are perceived as moving. In one variant of this illusion, two coloured lights, coloured blue and red, are placed close together, and alternately quickly flash on and off (Figure 8.5).

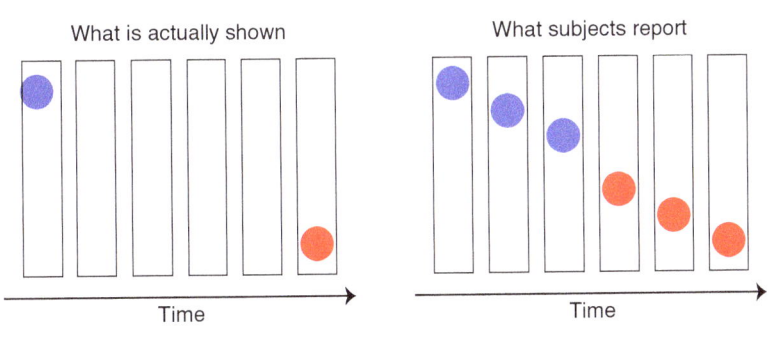

Figure 8.5 The phi illusion. What is actually presented: two images presented in strict succession. What a person sees if the duration is short enough: the stimulus moves and appears to change colour halfway through. What is more, people report the colour changing before it does so, which is of course impossible. A person's experience in the phi illusion must therefore be constructed.

If the interval between the flashes is less than a second, the first light appears to move to the position of the second light, changing colour as it does so. So we see the blue light change colour before the red light is switched on. How can this be?

Dennett proposes that the standard explanations of the phi illusion are of two types, which he calls *Orwellian* and *Stalinesque*. In the Orwellian version, history gets rewritten (as happens in Orwell's novel *Nineteen Eighty-Four* (1949)): the participant changes their memory in the light of the second light. In the Stalinesque version, there's a show trial, with the events reconciled prior to entering consciousness. In the MDM, none of this happens because we don't construct any detailed representation. The same event is interpreted at different times (hence the multiple drafts) and it is only when we try to remember what happened that events are crystallised.

In later versions of the model, consciousness corresponds to 'fame in the brain' (Dennett, 2001, 2015). Getting items into consciousness is a competitive process. Contents of consciousness are those states that have at that time won the competition by being strong and stable, as defined by the pattern of activity in neurons associated with that state.

For Dennett, there is no hard problem of consciousness, and indeed, there aren't really any problems of consciousness. We are conscious of whatever is most active in the brain at any one time. We need a suitably complex information-processing system, which is why computers aren't conscious at the moment, but there is no principled reason why they shouldn't be. Consciousness is 'just' an illusion.

There are several criticisms of the MDM. Dennett argues that consciousness, qualia, the self, and so on are all illusions, but for many these are the real issues about consciousness (Chalmers, 1996). Has Dennett really constructed a model of consciousness, or has he just side-stepped what it is?

Modelling the World

We have seen that even primitive organisms maintain a balance with their environment, a process called homeostasis. Indeed, even a thermostat responds to the temperature of the environment. It would be pushing it to argue that it is a representation of the world. Nevertheless, my poodle Beau has a representation of his world; he knows where his toy bag is, what it is, that it's the same thing if I move it, which toys are in it, and which are elsewhere in the house with an accuracy that amazes me. He clearly has a model of the world. When I watch him exploiting his model of the world, I can see that he is conscious. Of course I can do the same, and more; my model of the world must be very rich.

Mental Models

A **mental model** is a type of representation that we construct to represent the world around us. A mental model goes by a variety of alternative names, including a situation model, but mental model is the one we will use here. The idea was primarily developed originally in the context of understanding text or conversation as it unfolds (Harley, 2017). The model helps us to make predictions, solve problems, and make inferences from what we hear (Johnson-Laird, 1983). For example, from their perspective, Mary is on the left of Jane and Roger is on the right of Jane; as you look towards the three who is on the right? You probably solve this picture by forming some kind of mental picture. (Let's not worry about whether the underlying form of that picture is pictorial or propositional.) We can easily extend this idea to propose that at any one time we have a model of the world around us that determines how we act. I might turn to my left and say to you, 'It's a lovely day' because in my model you are to my left and last time I looked through the window it was a lovely sunny day. The model is a representation of everything we know about the world around us. We don't have to worry too much here about how detailed the model is at any time. I have a surprisingly good representation of where books are in the apparently random ordering in my study, but as I sit at the computer writing this passage I'm not thinking about them. I am thinking about the keys on the keyboard though. So we might want to distinguish between active (in focus) and background components of the model, but again we need not get into the details of how the models work. The important part here is that we have some kind of model of the world around us, and we use that model to govern our behaviour and make predictions about what's likely to happen (Clark, 2013, 2016).

Included within mental models of the world are our mental models of other organisms – a theory of mind of our colleagues and tribe is a mental simulation, a specific type of mental model. A model of another person is a sophisticated model; we need to be able to predict the responses of others, consider the possibility that others are deceiving us, and model what they would do if we did one thing or if we did another. The cognitive demands of these tasks can be quite heavy, but do they necessitate our being conscious? It is possible to construct computer simulations of aspects of the world, although they fall way short of the complexity of the natural world. Is there something about complexity? Does a model become conscious when it's sufficiently plausible? It doesn't seem intuitively appealing that consciousness depends on the complexity of what is being modelled. As we have seen (Chapter 5), Humphrey (1984, 2006) argues that consciousness is particularly important for modelling the mental states of other people.

Mental Time Travel

One reason humans have been so successful is because of our ability to plan for the future. Some animals prepare for lean times by hiding acorns (squirrels) or nuts (scrub jays), but no other species comes close to our ability to plan for the future. Planning is a complex cognitive skill that necessitates having a model of the present and being able to work out how different actions will change that model. We have seen that autonoetic consciousness is the term used to refer to our ability to place ourselves in the past or future (**mental time travel**) and other *counterfactual* situations where the world would be other than it is (Schacter et al., 2007). For example, I can imagine (just about) a world in which Beau is not always by my left side. Such thinking would appear to require self-awareness and the ability to think about our own thinking (metacognition).

With mental time travel, also called *chronesthesia*, we can imagine ourselves in the future (and the past), and we can run simulations of what might happen in the future, and of conditional futures and counterfactual pasts (if only I had done that …). What if I say that to her if it's raining outside and if she says that back to me, what then would I do?

Sometimes the ability to mentally place ourselves elsewhere is called autonoetic consciousness. I find it difficult to imagine being able to construct models such as this without being aware. Mental time travel was first described by the memory researcher Endel Tulving; it allows us to be aware of the past and the future in the sense that we can think about and plan the future, think about possible outcomes, and select among them for ones we want (Suddendorf & Corballis, 2007; Suddendorf, Addis, & Corballis, 2009; Tulving, 1985). Mental simulation is useful for understanding the perspectives of others in social interaction, for exploring options in complex decisions, and for replaying past events (both literally and counterfactually) in order to be able to learn from them (Baumeister & Masicampo, 2010).

The machinery for mental time travel is shared with that for episodic memory. Brain scanning shows that the left parietal cortex is important, with activation highest there if we think about ourselves, at a medium level if we think about our best friend, and lowest if we think about the Queen of Denmark (Lou et al., 2004). Furthermore, **transcranial magnetic stimulation (TMS)** of this area reduces the ease with which we can retrieve adjectives describing ourselves. Profoundly amnesic patients (such as Clive Wearing, see Chapter 7) are unable to imagine the future as well as being unable to remember their past (Hassabis et al., 2007; Suddendorf et al., 2009), showing that similar brain regions must be involved in mental time travel in both directions. Nyberg et al. (2010) conclude from imaging studies that many regions of the brain are involved in *chronesthesia*, particularly the *left parietal cortex*, but also regions of the *frontal lobes* and *cerebellum*. The hippocampus plays a role in storing the content of what we're imagining, but not, apparently, in manipulating it in time (Nyberg et al., 2010; Squire et al., 2010). As mental time travel also involves examining our thoughts, it is to some extent a metacognitive ability; these ideas are not exclusive.

There has been debate as to whether mental time travel is a uniquely human ability; Suddendorf et al. argue that there is no unambiguous evidence that non-human animals are capable of this type of planning. The difficulty is being able to show that animals have true episodic memory rather than semantic or procedural: does a bird that has hidden a nut remember actually hidden, or does it simply know where it is hidden? For example, we know when we were born (we have semantic knowledge for this information), but do not remember it (we do not have episodic knowledge). They also argue that language evolved for the sharing of past events and plans about the future because mental time travel needs us to be able to remember and refer to different points of time (past, present, and future), which only language can enable us to do effectively.

There does then seem to be something special about mental modelling of conditional futures and mental modelling of the future actions of other complex organisms. However, the argument that I find it difficult to imagine being able to do these things without being conscious is hardly the most convincing or the most sound of arguments. It's a promising line of research, but there is much work to be done, and it isn't clear how such an approach will relate to the hard problem.

Perhaps it isn't consciousness in general that is necessary for this sort of thinking, but self-consciousness in particular; we need to be able to think about our position in time and space. Edelman (2003) drew a distinction between primary consciousness, which is a simple awareness that includes perception and emotion, and which should be ascribed to most animals, and secondary consciousness, which is an individual's ability to access their history and plans. It depends on and includes such features as self-reflective awareness, abstract thinking, and metacognition.

Metacognition

Metacognition is our ability to reflect on and manipulate our cognition. It's thinking about thinking. If you're thinking about how to solve a problem, how best to learn something new, or what you can and can't remember, then you're thinking metacognitively. Metacognitive skills vary between people, with better learners having stronger metacognitive skills (Sternberg, 1986). Metacognition is often described as 'thinking about thinking', but in fact it is a complex skill. It is difficult to see how one could think metacognitively without awareness; indeed, some researchers define metacognition as awareness of one's mental states or cognitive processes (Smith et al., 2016). Some researchers distinguish between monitoring and control (Dunlosky & Thiede, 2013). Monitoring is making judgements about our memories and knowledge – how strong is a memory, how accurate is it, when did it happen or when did we learn it, and control is using that knowledge to influence our actions. Metacognition is largely the domain of the prefrontal cortex (Fleming & Dolan, 2012; see Figure 8.6). Judgements can be prospective, thinking about how we're going to do, and retrospective, reflecting on how we have done.

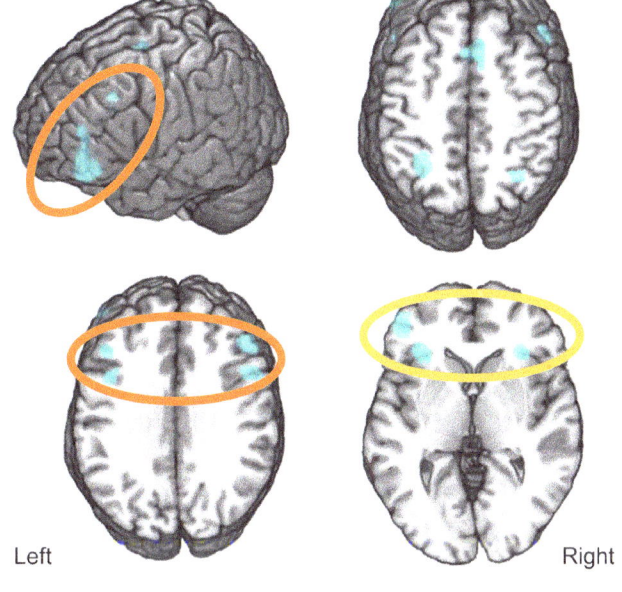

Figure 8.6 The brain and metacognition. Metacognition is thinking about cognition, and involves executive processing, high-level processes such as thinking and reasoning that govern behaviour. The figure shows areas of the brain that are particularly active in verbal and nonverbal reasoning.

There has been some debate about whether non-human animals can employ metacognitive processing. Can they monitor their own mental states? The German psychologist Wolfgang Köhler (1897–1967) was stranded on the island of Tenerife during World War I, while carrying out work on problem solving by chimpanzees. He placed bananas out of their reach, and found that they did things like stacking wooden crates on top of each other, and getting sticks to poke through the bars. They didn't solve the problems immediately, but instead appeared to try mental simulation (not his phrase) resulting in insight (his phrase). He reported his work in a famous book called *The Mentality of Apes* (Köhler, 1917). Insight and evaluation require some level of metacognitive processing. There is also some evidence that monkeys can monitor their behaviour and use past learning to inform decision making (Middlebrooks & Sommer, 2011). These studies usually examine how uncertain the monkey is, with uncertainty hypothesised to be based on a metacognitive judgement. Part of the problem here is that analysing metacognition is tied up so much with language, which restricts examining that aspects of it to humans. The consensus of much research on many species of animals, including apes and dolphins, is that some non-human species have at least an analogue of metacognition. Some animals do seem able to monitor their own cognitive processes (Smith et al., 2016).

Things are complicated by a lack of agreement over definitions and, as ever in psychology, the complications arise because we are using words to name things we can't see. If we take the Smith et al. definition of metacognition as awareness of our mental states, our lives are simple and there isn't much more to say. Metacognitive states are a subset of all our mental states: we are always conscious of metacognitive states, but there is plenty more we can be conscious of at any one time.

But not everyone defines metacognition in terms of awareness of mental states. Indeed, Smith et al. also define metacognition as 'the capacity to monitor mental states or cognitive processes', which doesn't seem quite the same thing. Several authors deny that metacognitive processing necessitates awareness. Hence, Kentridge and Heywood (2000) don't formally define metacognitive processes, but argue that all that is required for the control of our own processing is a feedback loop, and a feedback loop does not necessarily entail consciousness. This argument is part of a wider debate about awareness, metacognition, feeling of knowing, memory retrieval, and the nature of metacognitive judgements (e.g. see Koriat & Levy-Sadot, 2000, for a brief introduction and discussion of the issues involved).

Clearly, reflecting about our own awareness is what it means to be self-aware. However, the precise relationship between metacognition, consciousness, and cognitive processing is complex and dependent on definitions and exactly what is happening when we monitor and change our cognitive processes. We don't yet have a theory of micro-cognition. So, clearly, we cannot simply say that consciousness arises from metacognition, and it is incorrect to say that consciousness and metacognition are the same thing.

Perhaps metacognition is another thing like attention: researchers think they have identified a set of processes that go together and then give that set a name. The set becomes reified into a thing. It should also be noted that metacognitive theories are not exclusive of some other approaches. For example, Shea and Frith (2019) argue that the global workspace model needs metacognitive processes to carry out the cognitive work involved in the workspace, particularly making *confidence estimates* of information from different sources so the information can be effectively combined in the workspace.

Representational Theories

Representations play a central role in cognitive psychology. A representation is something that stands for something else; for example, on a map the little church symbol *represents* a map in that location in the world.

The American philosophers Fred Dretske (1995) and Michael Tye (1991, 1995, 2002) have developed what is called a **representational theory of consciousness (RTC)**, or *representationalism*. There are several varieties of representational theory, but they all share the idea that qualia are representations of some kind.

We have met the idea of intentionality, the idea that mental states are about something, before (Chapter 1). Intentional states represent objects (which don't have to be real), or more complex states of affairs, again which might be only hypothetical. Representational theories extend intentionality to consciousness. Our cognitive representations determine the phenomenal character of our experiences: it isn't correct to say that qualia are not part of representational content. Pain and colours are representations, so that the sensation of pain represents actual (or at least potential) damage to the body where the pain is felt.

RTC isn't easy to explain or understand. The key idea is that everything is considered part of a representation, including things that many thought could not be (such as qualia, emotions, and pain). This change is thought to make all mental phenomena more tractable.

Recursion (Again)

We have seen that not only are we conscious of mental states, we can also be *self-conscious* – conscious of being conscious of mental states. A development of RTC is *higher-order thought theory* (HOT; Rosenthal, 2006). In HOT, the relevant state upon which the model is based is the representation not of a perception but of a second-order thought. A first-order mental state is the basic perception. A second-order mental state or thought operates on the first-order state so that it is being like something to be that person. A third-order state is limited probably only to humans and operates on the second-order state and corresponds to a process of introspection or reflection. The phenomenal quality doesn't change from the first-order mental state, but what we do with it does, from experiencing states to reflecting on the experience. At this point, metacognitive processes are engaged and recursion becomes an issue.

According to this view, it is one thing to have a first-order mental state, like a percept, but organisms only start being conscious when they have mental states about these mental states. We call the states like the original percepts, or internally generated mental images, first-order mental states. Higher-order representational theories deny that having first-order mental states is sufficient for self-consciousness. It is only when we observe lower-level processing that we can become conscious of it (see Lau & Rosenthal, 2011, for a review, although these ideas date back to Kant and Locke).

This ability to think about our own thinking seems to set humans apart from computers (at least at the moment) and most animals. A robin might be aware, but we have no evidence, and consider it unlikely, that it can think about its own consciousness. It's possible that some animals, such as chimpanzees, are capable of this type of thought, but at the moment it's very difficult to tell (we might in the future discover a neural signature of this type of thought). Higher-order theories also enable us to make sense of some of the neuropsychological data, where what might be lost is the ability to think about our mental states. For example, what might be lost are concepts like the idea of seeing – so the first-order states might be intact, but some of the higher-order states lost.

We call awareness of our own awareness *meta-awareness*, and it is a particular type of metacognition (the ability to think about our own cognition). Given that consciousness is an intentional state, in that we are always conscious of something, we sometimes talk about *metaconsciousness*. We can also be aware of our being aware of being aware, and we could in principle carry on being aware like this infinitely.

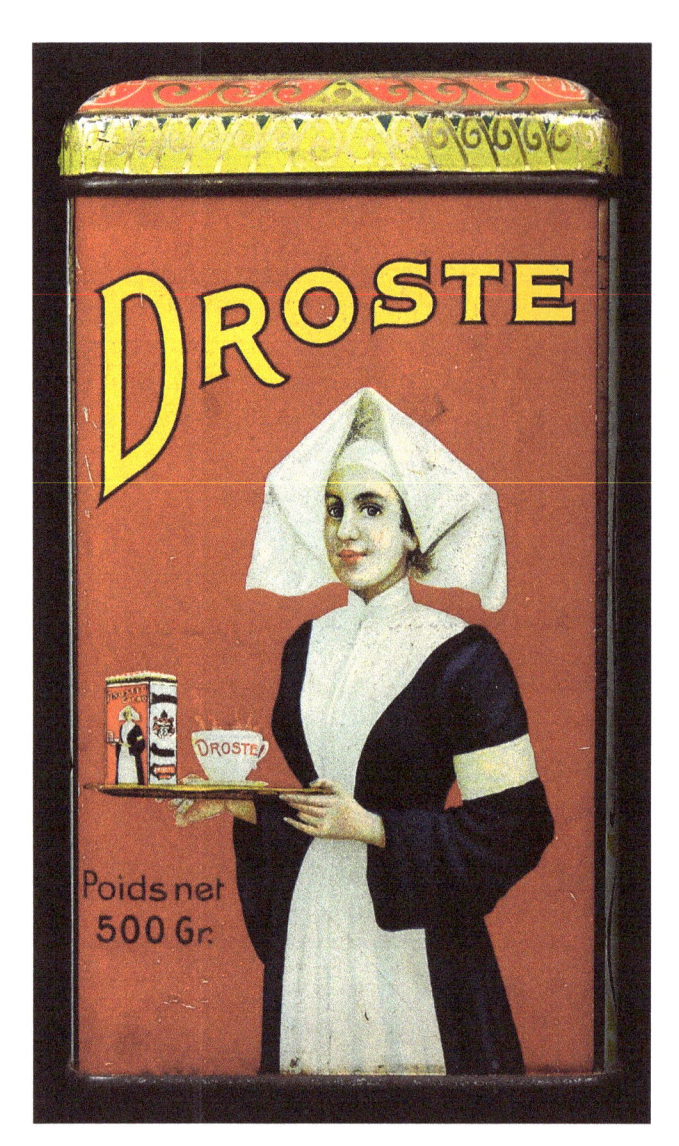

Figure 8.7 The Droste cocoa tin, 1904 design, illustrating recursion. The cover is an example of recursion: it shows a woman holding a tin of Droste cocoa, on which there is a woman holding a tin of Droste cocoa, on which …

As we have seen, we call this technique of a process calling itself, potentially indefinitely, recursion (see Chapter 4). Recursion is illustrated by the Droste effect (also known as *mise en abyme*), where a picture is shown containing a picture of itself (see Figure 8.7). This effect is also called self-reference. Or try arranging mirrors so that you can look into the reflection of a mirror directed at you and a mirror reflecting that scene. The mind has the same ability: we can watch ourselves, which means our watching ourselves, and so on, for ever. We have already discussed recursion in the context of grammatical rules, Chomsky's idea that recursive thinking is what makes humans special, and in modelling sophisticated social interaction (see Chapter 5).

The idea of recursion plays an important role in the work of Hofstadter (1979, 2007), who sees the idea of the self and consciousness arising from strange self-referential or *strange loops*. Hofstadter is fond of using visual analogies, such as comparing the origin of consciousness to the way in which pointing a video camera at the screen to which it is connected generates bizarre and complex structures. Consciousness arises in some way from this self-monitoring. Hofstadter also points out that, when networks are very tangled, it doesn't always make sense to talk about 'higher' and 'lower' levels of representation.

Surely Hofstadter is correct in that self-reference plays an important role in consciousness, and must be essential for self-consciousness. Strange loops probably play some role too. It is difficult, though, to see how this approach provides much more than a framework for understanding consciousness, and therefore it is unclear how detailed phenomena can be explained by the approach. And, of course, there is no real indication of how strange loops solve the hard problem.

It is also impossible to think about self-consciousness without accepting that we can be aware of our own mental states, and that this awareness plays some important role. It is another step though to distinguish between first and higher-order mental states, and to say that the latter make the former conscious. Hence, this approach appears to say that animals who cannot form higher-order thoughts (as we have seen, almost all of them except perhaps chimpanzees and dolphins) must lack phenomenal consciousness, not just self-consciousness (Tye, 1995). Debate about this point has generated a large and messy literature. Another objection is that higher-order thoughts may not explain the properties of phenomenal consciousness. It is conceivable that we could have mental states that are subject to higher-order thoughts, but still not be conscious of them (Chalmers, 1996). The model doesn't explain why phenomenal consciousness arises.

> **Box 8.3   What Is a Complex System?**
>
> A **complex system** is one composed of many subsystems that interact to make the behaviour of the whole system very difficult to predict. They are also marked by the appearance of some kind of order – to choose a fairly non-controversial system, cyclones and depressions emerge from turbulent air to form weather systems. Examples include the weather, society, the brain, and cities, although there are many more.
>
> Complex systems are marked by many associated features, including:
>
> **Chaos.** In chaotic systems, small initial differences are magnified so that very small differences in starting conditions can make the outcome very quickly completely unpredictable even for the most powerful computers of the foreseeable future. This is where the butterfly effect comes in – a term coined by the American mathematician Edward Lorenz, who gave the example of the course of a weather system being affected by the flapping of a butterfly's wings on the other side of the globe some weeks before. **Chaos** makes weather forecasting so difficult! Note that unpredictable doesn't mean non-deterministic. Those with some mathematical background should read up on the logistic map function.
>
> **Nonlinearity.** A small change in an input results in a large change in the output.
>
> **Feedback loops.** The output of one process is fed back as the input to another process. We've talked about strange loops in the main text.
>
> **Adaptation.** Complex systems are resilient. You damage one transistor on the logic board of a computer and the whole thing stops working. Your neurons are dying all the time and you don't notice. You damage a termite mound and the little blighters will repair it.
>
> **Emergence.** See the main text for this controversial subject. The idea is that new behaviour unpredictable from the analysis of the lower levels of the system can emerge.

Emergence

Hofstadter (1979, 2007) argues that consciousness emerges from the behaviour of strange, *tangled loops*, in the same sort of way that termite swarm intelligence enables them to build and maintain complex mounds when each individual termite is pretty simple (and probably unaware of the larger enterprise being undertaken), or birds and fish produce complex large-scale flocking behaviour when each individual is engaged in purely local behaviour (see Chapter 4). The idea of **emergence**, or **emergentism**, is that something new arises from the interaction of many simple things that isn't present in the simple things: flocking and birds, swarm intelligence and termites. The example is often given of water; it feels wet to the touch, flows, has high surface tension, dissolves many other substances – yet how can we explain all this from the properties of its constituent atoms of hydrogen and oxygen? The properties of liquid water emerge from individual water molecules, not one of which is liquid. The whole seems to be more than the sum of its parts. Emergence is the name given to the phenomenon of novel structures from the self-organisation of complex systems.

The *emergence* theory of consciousness says that consciousness is a novel structure that somehow emerges from the behaviour of a very complicated, self-organising complex system. A complicated system is simply one with many parts that can therefore interact in many ways; a complex system is one that is very sensitive to the starting conditions (the fluttering of the proverbial butterfly's wings in the Amazon basin starting a storm in the Atlantic being an example). Often, mention of fractals and phrases like 'the edge of chaos' are dragged into this type of theorisation. The idea that consciousness is an emergent phenomenon is currently very popular among psychologists. It all sounds good – but what does it actually mean?

There are two types of emergence, weak and strong. Essentially, if we can simulate it on a computer, at least in principle, it's weak emergence. We can reduce the higher-level behaviour to the lower-level constituents. Hence the flocking behaviour of birds in Boids (see Chapter 4) is weak emergence; it is clearly easily simulated by a computer program, and it is also clear how the complex behaviour emerges from the lower-level behaviour. It is, however, not at all clear how consciousness could emerge from the interaction of millions of neurons in this way.

Strongly emergent properties are not reducible to their constituents; a whole new level emerges from the interaction of many simple units. The new level is not predictable from the laws governing the behaviour of the simpler units. It cannot therefore be simulated on a computer (although it might be possible for a suitably powerful computer to show this type of emergence). That means that the emergence of the complex phenomenon is not predictable from the laws of physics. Obviously, this proposition sounds unsatisfactory and many people don't like the idea, and indeed many reject it.

Exactly how are the lower-level components combined so that mental states and consciousness emerge? Many researchers don't like the idea of emergence because they think it doesn't really solve anything. How can something come out of nothing? How can just combining things in a clever way cause a completely new level of thinking to emerge? How can you get something that is not predictable from the laws of physics?

Representation and Consciousness

One conclusion from this chapter is that consciousness is not readily uniquely identified with any one cognitive process. Concepts such as attention and metacognition are closely related to consciousness, but cannot be identified with it. In case you think this is obvious, I have heard many seasoned psychologists saying things like 'consciousness is the same as metacognition'.

Although ideas such as recursion, mental models, higher-order thought, and mental time travel do not in themselves solve any of the problems of consciousness, they are clearly important concepts that play some role. I find it particularly difficult to imagine that a system that can model the future and consider and evaluate alternative outcomes involving other complex organisms could be anything other than conscious, but a limitation of imagination on my part is proof of nothing. These ideas do tie in with the evolutionary theories that say consciousness has evolved as a consequence of highly intelligent, highly social organisms having to interact with each other.

The GWT is probably currently our best bet as a model of consciousness, integrating attention, perception, and metacognition with a secure neuroscientific underpinning. Its main failing is that it doesn't deal with the hard problem.

We are also faced with what appears to be a rather unappealing but strictly logical binary choice between consciousness either somehow mysteriously emerging at a certain level of complexity, or being there all along, to some extent, so that even a single atom is a tiny bit conscious (panpsychism). This argument does seem to be unimpeachable logically. Either way, it suggests that something fundamental is missing from our understanding of the universe. If anything, the mystery deepens.

In this section, we are left with the impression that mental modelling, mental time travelling, recursive thinking, and loops of thoughts and sense impressions are important concepts in consciousness research, but these ideas don't yet add up to a coherent whole. Higher-order thought is clearly important, but it isn't clear how an explanation of qualia fits in. Hofstadter's writings on consciousness are fascinating and influential, but it isn't really clear what his model of consciousness is, or how it solves the hard problem.

Free Energy

Over several papers, the British neuroscientist Karl Friston has developed a model of consciousness based on the principle of *free energy* (Carhart-Harris & Friston, 2010; Friston, 2009, 2010, 2018). The central idea is *optimisation*: living things try to optimise the value of something, such as the value to the organism, or minimise surprise. The principle of free energy says that systems optimise the level of reward: essentially, if you think there's going to be a big payoff, you're willing to put in a lot of effort. Organisms reach a state of equilibrium with their environment and try to resist disorder. (If you have any background in the physical sciences, you will recognise terms such as free energy, disorder, and entropy, and their use in this framework is not coincidence.) The brain creates an internal model of the world, which it tries to optimise on the basis of its sensory inputs. We see optimisation on many levels – individual animals will put in a lot of effort to avoid a predator or find a rich food source. In the coronavirus crisis of 2020, societies were willing to make enormous changes and sacrifices to minimise the number of deaths.

The theory is mathematical and technical, but consciousness emerges as a result of specialisation. While the general tendency in the universe is for disorder (entropy) to increase, living things in their effort to optimise act against entropy, increasing order. This tendency leads to hierarchical organisation, specialisation, and processes, such as attention, which focus attention on what is essential. The brain becomes an 'inference energy', making inferences in an attempt to predict what is going to happen in the world. Consciousness comes with the development of attention.

It is too early to evaluate free energy as an explanation of consciousness, but this field is likely to be one to watch. One much-discussed application of free energy is using its ideas to help construct a conscious AI.

Quantum Consciousness

We need to consider another possibility that is popular in certain circles, but is difficult to fit in anywhere else, and that is the idea that consciousness is associated with quantum mechanics. Quantum mechanics is the approach of physics to matter and energy at the very small, subatomic scale. Energy is hypothesised as being in very small packets, or quanta, and the laws of physics at this very small scale are probabilistic rather than deterministic. What on earth could these ideas have to do with macroscopic matter and processes, such as brains and neurons firing?

Several theorists, mostly physicists and mathematicians (e.g. Bohm, Dyson, Penrose, and Wigner), have argued that classical physics cannot explain consciousness, and that we therefore have to draw upon ideas from quantum mechanics. Most notably, the British mathematician Roger Penrose (1989) has pursued this line of argument, resulting in a model called quantum consciousness. The corollary of this argument is that conventional computers can't be conscious because they don't possess the quantum properties that brains do.

The Oxford mathematician Roger Penrose and American anaesthesiologist Stuart Hameroff have developed an account of consciousness over several years (Hameroff, 1998, 2006, 2007; Penrose, 1989, 1994, 1997; Hameroff & Penrose, 2014). The theory is called orchestrated objective reduction, or 'Orch OR'. They suggested that quantum vibrations were 'orchestrated' (hence the name) by synaptic inputs and memory stored in microtubules. *Microtubules* are major components of the cell structural skeleton (see Figure 8.8). Microtubules play an important role in the theory. A microtubule is a tube made out of proteins that forms the inner skeletons of cell (the cytoskeleton) and helps move materials about inside the cell, as well as some other functions involving movement. The idea then is that these particular structures enable quantum computations from which consciousness arises. They argue their model can account for a range of additional phenomena, including the binding problem, and anaesthesia, by identifying ways in which anaesthetics 'erase' consciousness by effects on microtubules (rather than, say, on neurotransmitter levels).

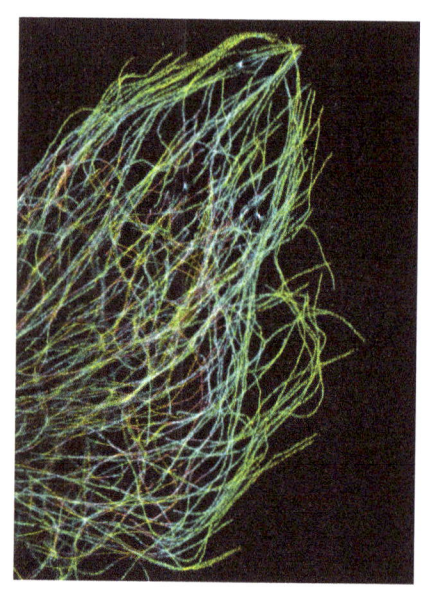

Figure 8.8 Microtubules at the edge of a cell. Microtubules provide a scaffold to give the cell support and structure, but are quantum effects in them also responsible for generating consciousness? Source: National Institutes of Health (NIH)/Public domain.

The quantum consciousness account has many critics. Many researchers are understandably dismayed by the notion that we need to reject our current understanding of the laws of physics to understand consciousness, believing instead that consciousness is completely compatible with these laws (although uniformly failing, as this chapter has demonstrated, to show how). On the other hand, it isn't clear that quantum consciousness fares any better: where in the model does the feeling of being like me arise? How do extremely small vibrations in tubes of protein turn into a feeling of pain? Quantum consciousness introduces new machinery but still faces the same old problem.

I cannot pretend that I understand the details of this account, and I also admit that I have met no psychologist who is convinced by it. If there is a gulf in the sciences, it is between those who are mathematically literate and those without advanced mathematical skills to whom a part of the world is denied. Without advanced mathematics, we cannot understand some concepts properly, let alone evaluate them. A mean comment on quantum models of consciousness is that quantum mechanics is deeply mysterious, and consciousness is deeply mysterious, so they must be related.

One point worth taking from this line of argument is that neurons are usually seen as simple accumulators or electrical switches (most obviously in connectionist modelling of behaviour). They are much more complex than most accounts suggest, and it is possible that this complexity plays some additional role in generating consciousness.

Box 8.4 Quantum Mechanics

The classical laws of physics were discovered by Sir Isaac Newton in the seventeenth century. They show how the behaviour of all matter in the universe is determined by three simple laws. The few anomalies remaining were thought to be minor.

Lord Kelvin was famously reported to have said around 1900: 'There is nothing new to be discovered in physics now. All that remains is more and more precise measurement.'

There were a few puzzles though. The first was the photoelectric effect, whereby ultraviolet light causes electrons to be emitted from some metal surfaces. The particular puzzle was that the energy of the electrons emitted depended on the frequency of the light, not the amplitude (see Figure 8.9). It sounds a small thing, but the explanation motivated a huge change in our understanding of the physical world. The second was the way black bodies emitted radiation (when you heat something up before it starts to glow); the pattern couldn't be explained by classical physics. The third was the way in which light sometimes appeared to act as a wave, and sometimes as a collection of particles.

Quantum mechanics says that at very small distances (e.g. light) Newton's laws no longer apply. There are two main ideas. The first is that everything comes in small packets, or is quantised. Nothing is in between, nothing is continuous at these extremely small distances and levels of energy. Even light, which appears to us to be continuous and act mostly like a wave, comes in tiny parcels called photons. Einstein first demonstrated this with the photoelectric effect.

The second idea is that at the quantum scale events are probabilistic. In Newton's scheme, the universe is like a giant pool table, with events precisely determined by prior events. In quantum mechanics, electrons don't have precise locations around atoms: instead, there is a probability distribution of where they are. Indeed, there are limits to knowledge: Heisenberg's uncertainty principle says that the more accurately we know a particle's location, the less accurately we know its speed (technically its momentum).

There are many strange ideas in quantum mechanics. It is worth spending a little time reading about *Schrodinger's cat*, the *many worlds interpretation*, and *action at a distance*. However, quantum mechanics is not just an abstract idea: it has several important applications. The quantum computer (see Figure 8.10) allows states other than 0 and 1 (the basis of the bit), hence immensely increasing the speed and power of a computer (which might be necessary for any computer modelling of consciousness).

Box 8.4 (cont.)

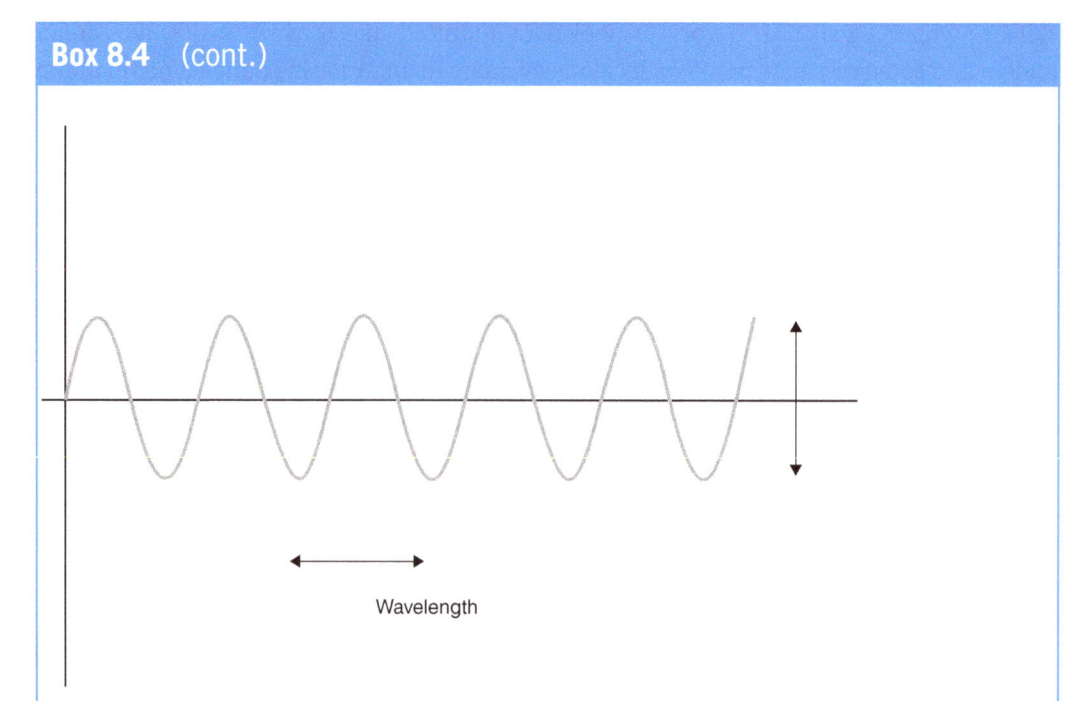

Figure 8.9 A wave. The amplitude is the height of the wave, and the frequency is how many times the wave happens in a set period. In quantum mechanics, quantum entities such as electrons and photons can be described both as waves and particles, depending on the circumstances.

It is remarkable that, in 1905, Einstein published four scientific papers: one on the photoelectric effect demonstrating through the photoelectric effect that light came in small

Figure 8.10 A quantum computer: the IBM Q System One. Although quantum computing is in its infancy, it is clear that it could lead to much more powerful computers. Rather than the binary bit, it uses the qubit, which can hold much more information. Source: Misha Friedman/Getty Images News/Getty Images.

> **Box 8.4** (cont.)
>
> packets called photons; one on the motion of small particles in water (Brownian motion) effectively proving the existence of atoms; one considering what happens to bodies moving at the speed of light and hence introducing the theory of special relativity; and one, almost as an afterthought, showing the equivalence of mass and energy ($E = mc^2$). Not bad for one year for someone previously largely unheard of. It is called Einstein's 'Annus Mirabilis', and I consider it one of humanity's greatest achievements. If you consider zombies to be plausible, you must consider the possibility that Einstein could have achieved all this without being conscious (see Figure 8.8).

Chapter Summary

- The Sapir–Whorf hypothesis says that there are differences in the way in which languages of different cultures carve up the world.
- These differences affect the way in which speakers of those languages perceive and categorise the world, and hence think.
- The carpentered world hypothesis is that sensitivity to visual illusions is caused by lifelong exposure to the straight lines and right angles that dominate the western built-up environments.
- A language of thought is a representational system that mediates perception and action, and in particular is the format in which we think.
- Although language-like, a language of thought need not be identical to any spoken language.
- Much thinking occurs in some form of inner speech and its analogues.
- The level of the detail of the sound representation is variable and more work needs to be done to clarify its format.
- We can also form and think in terms of visual images.
- Whether or not these images have an underlying pictorial or propositional representation has been the subject of considerable debate, and is still unresolved.
- William James formulated the idea that there is a stream of consciousness, a continuous flow of sensations, idea, thoughts, and impressions.
- Many now believe this continuous stream is an illusion.
- Attention is how we select particular elements for further processing given limited resources. It is not the same as consciousness.
- The default mode network is a brain circuit that is active when we are not engaged in focused thinking.
- The global workspace theory (GWT) of Bernard Baars is a comprehensive and coherent model of consciousness that can be related to underlying brain structures.
- Baars argues that there is no 'hidden observer' of the multisensory screen that is at the centre of GWT theory.
- The neuronal workspace theory (NWT) of Dehaene extends GWT, in particular showing how it is implemented in the brain.

- Daniel Dennett argues that models such as global workspace suffer from the fatal flaw of being disguised homunculus models that just shift and hide the issues that need to be addressed.
- Dennett talks of a Cartesian theatre as a multisensory cinema screen on which sensory data is played – but in such models what interprets the data?
- Dennett proposes an alternative approach called the multiple drafts theory.
- In multiple drafts theory, nothing is in charge, and several streams of processing are occurring in parallel. It is only when we remember events that a record becomes fixed and the illusion of consciousness is generated.
- As yet, no model answers the 'hard problem', although researchers disagree on how important this failure is.
- The ability to form sophisticated mental models is an important characteristic of human thinking.
- Mental time travel is an important feature of human thinking.
- We can form models of complex counterfactual social events, and these are cognitive tasks that might necessitate awareness.
- Metacognition is the ability to monitor and manipulate our own cognitive processes.
- The extent to which a particular ability is associated with awareness depends on the exact definition we give that ability.
- Saying that metacognition is awareness of our cognitive abilities is very different from saying that metacognition is the ability to manipulate cognitive abilities.
- Recursion is the ability to define, call, or use a process that calls itself. In terms of consciousness, we can imagine ourselves being aware of ourselves being aware of ourselves, and so on, and on, and on …
- According to emergence theories, consciousness is an emergent property of a complex system.
- Emergence can be weak or strong.
- Consciousness develops throughout childhood, and is associated with cognitive and linguistic development.
- Penrose and Hameroff propose a quantum mechanics model called quantum consciousness where consciousness is generated by quantum gravity effects in microtubules in neurons.
- Quantum mechanics models can be difficult to evaluate, and it is still not clear how they address the hard problem.
- Either consciousness somehow mysteriously emerges at a certain level of complexity, or it is there all along, to some extent, so that even a single atom is a tiny bit conscious (panpsychism).

Review Questions

1. When consciousness researchers talk about things being an illusion, what do they mean? Do they simply mean things don't exist?
2. How might consciousness differ between people using just spoken language and people using just sign language?
3. Compare and contrast the global workspace and multiple drafts models of consciousness.

4. To what extent are the details of the locations of brain structures and processes in the neuronal workspace model important for understanding phenomenal consciousness?
5. How could a (nonconscious) computer be programmed to anticipate and plan for the future? How does memory retrieval in a computer differ from human episodic memory?
6. What is a representation, and why is the concept important for understanding consciousness?
7. What is emergence, and what might consciousness emerge from?
8. How would you answer Question 8?

Recommended Resources

Language and Consciousness
Fernyhough, C. (2016). *The Voices Within: The History and Science of How We Talk to Ourselves*. London: Profile Books.

Harley, T.A. (2017). *Talking the Talk: Language, Psychology, and Science*. Hove: Psychology Press. My own introduction to language with some emphasis on language and thought and the Sapir–Whorf hypothesis.

Mental Imagery
The Stanford Encyclopaedia of Philosophy. 2020. Mental imagery. Website. https://plato.stanford.edu/entries/mental-imagery/.

Kosslyn, S.M., Thompson, W.L., and Ganis, G. (2006). *The Case for Mental Imagery*. Oxford, UK: Oxford University Press.

Tye, M. (1991). *The Imagery Debate*. Cambridge, MA: MIT Press.

Attention
Montemayor, C., and Haladjian, H.H. (2015). *Consciousness, Attention, and Conscious Attention*. Cambridge, MA: MIT Press.

Raichle, M.E. (2010). The brain's dark energy. *Scientific American*, 302, 44–49.

Searle, J.R. (1997). *The Mystery of Consciousness*. New York: The New York Review of Books.

Modelling the World and Higher-level Models
Carroll, S. (2016). *The Big Picture: On the Origins of Life, Meaning and the Universe Itself*. London: Oneworld.

Gennaro, R. (2017). *Consciousness*. London: Routledge.

Hofstadter, D. (1979). *Godel, Escher, Bach: An Eternal Golden Braid*. New York: Basic Books. I have suggested this brilliant book more than once.

Quantum Consciousness
Penrose, R. (1989). *The Emperor's New Mind: Concerning Computers, Minds, and the Laws of Physics*. Oxford, UK: Oxford University Press.

9 PERCEPTION AND CONSCIOUSNESS

Seeing is believing, according to an old saying.

We can divide the contents of consciousness into top down and bottom up: top down is about thinking, and how our brain can change the world, and bottom up is about the mass of sensory data coming into the brain. If we have learned one thing so far, it is that such divisions can be misleading because self-consciousness seems to depend on some giant loop of data, processing, and more data. Nevertheless, it is difficult to overestimate the importance of incoming information to consciousness; it is difficult to imagine that any entity could be conscious without at least having had a large amount of incoming information at some time.

Psychology texts distinguish between the sensing of the environment through sight, sound, touch, smell, and taste, and perception, which is the interpretation of these data. Most of the work we'll examine comes from vision, partly because for most people it is the dominant sense, but also because it is the easiest sense to study. There has been a large amount of work on vision, so much so that it is easy to think that some have equated consciousness with visual awareness. We should bear these points in mind.

As we have seen, self-report is often unreliable, and self-report described by someone else other than ourselves can be even more difficult to interpret. Consider the inverting glasses pioneered by the American psychologist George M. Stratton (1865–1957). When you put these glasses on, the world appears to be turned upside down. Now, within a few days people are able to adjust to them – that is, they manage not to get run over. But that is not the same, as I have seen claimed, as people learning to see the world upside down. We begin with an examination of empiricism, the idea that our knowledge comes primarily from sensory experience.

How do we become aware of perceptual information? What can go wrong with these processes? We look at visual illusions and visual attention. In particular, we look at how the Necker cube has been used to study consciousness.

We then consider what can go wrong with visuo-spatial perception, and how brain damage can affect these processes. We focus on the conditions of blindsight and neglect.

We then look at how we come to bind things together so we see those patches of orange and black in different places together and associate it with that roaring sound so that we see a tiger in front of us instead of constituent parts and colours? This binding problem is a fundamental one in consciousness research. Finally, we consider the possibility that perception is yet another illusion.

Empiricism

What do we know of the world? If I pause my frantic typing on my laptop, just now I can see a tree in autumnal colours against a blue morning sky, with a small white cloud floating above it, and the Scottish hills in the distance. But is that really what I see, rather than just how I interpret what I see? Starting with the sky, I don't really see it at all: I see an expanse of uniform light blue (because light of a particular frequency falls in a particular pattern on my retina). The cloud is a patch of white against it adopting a particular shape. The tree is more complicated: what I am seeing are apparently connected patches of brown, green, black, and yellow, together appearing to form a shape I have come to know as 'a tree'. Similarly, the hills are nothing more than patches of green and brown colours. Is then what I think I'm seeing what I'm really seeing? Does it make any sense to talk of 'really seeing' at all? Can I even trust my senses?

The idea that we can only gain knowledge through our senses is known as **empiricism** (in contrast to **rationalism**, where reason is held to be the source of knowledge), and, for most people, there's little surprising in that idea. But exactly what knowledge are we gaining through our senses? As we've just noted, we don't really see trees, we see patches of colour and shape. And what is colour? We know that certain colours correspond to particular wavelengths of light, but as we have further seen in our discussion of qualia, what we experience is a sensation that is private and that we have no way of sharing with anyone else. The yellow of the leaves in my tree might arise from light with a wavelength around 500 nm (a nanometre, nm, is a billionth of a metre), but I have no way of knowing that the colour you are experiencing is the same as the colour I am experiencing. Indeed, as we have also seen, such questions might be outside the scope of our science. Consider another example from a different sense. The laptop on my lap: it feels very solid to me, but we know that atoms and molecules are mostly empty space, so perhaps the feeling of solidity is an illusion. Even my impression of the distinctness of objects – the laptop now resting on the table – is a result of my constructing the visual scene and of subtle physical forces at work.

So the external world doesn't really 'look' the way I perceive it. In a sense, much of what we call reality doesn't look like anything at all: what colour is the sky when no one is looking at it? (The question 'If a tree falls in a forest and no one is around to hear it, does it make a sound?' is an old experiment along these lines.) The sky might scatter light at around a wavelength of 475 nm, but as we now know it makes no sense to talk about the light itself containing sensation. Indeed, as the sky comprises many gaseous molecules, what is this thing called sky that we are looking at? The idea that physical objects don't exist in themselves, but only as a set of sensory stimuli located in a particular place and time is called *phenomenalism* – familiar to us as the bundle theory (see Chapter 5). It's a radical form of empiricism most associated with philosophers such as John Stuart Mill, David Hume, and particularly Immanuel Kant: we can never know the 'real' objects, and therefore it makes no sense to talk about them; all we know about are bundles of associated sense data or properties. This view doesn't mean that there is no external reality, just that talking about it is meaningless.

Are You Dreaming Now?

There are other, perhaps seemingly more fantastic, grounds for being sceptical about what we know. How do you know that you're not dreaming right now? I'm pretty confident that I'm not dreaming, and you probably are too. My current experience contains a degree of ability and reflection that is absent from my dreams; however, as we shall see later, there are some borderline states. I not infrequently have false awakenings: I dream I'm waking up, and then wake up a bit later to realise that I was in fact still asleep at the time. Some people have lucid dreams, a phenomenon that we discuss in detail later (see Chapter 13), where they are dreaming and are aware of doing so. The categories of dreaming and waking experience do bleed into each other, to some extent. 'Reality' might not be what it seems.

In one thought experiment, a brain is disconnected from its body by an evil scientist and bathed in a vat of nutrients that keeps it alive and healthy. Its sense nerves are connected to an artificial input by the scientist, so that the brain is provided with a virtual reality. After all, what a person sees is just a pattern of electrical impulses travelling down the optic nerves from the stimulation of cells on the retina; there is no reason in principle why we could not simulate this electrical pattern and provide it artificially. If we did so, we would 'see' what that pattern corresponds to. In principle, we could supply a complete life to a brain in a vat (see Box 9.1).

Box 9.1   The Brain in a Vat

This *brain in a vat* thought experiment dates from Descartes, who talked about an evil demon fooling us into thinking that we are perceiving a 'real' world, when in fact the demon is providing a complete illusion for us. The idea was given new form by speculating that an evil scientist has turned you into a brain in a vat of nutrients with wires providing the sensory inputs (Harman, 1973; Putnam, 1981). Other wires might be connected to the output parts of the brain reading your intended actions so that the scientist can take your interaction with the world into account. Or to give the thought experiment a more modern twist, how do you know that you're not currently in a very good virtual reality simulator?

How do you know that you're not a brain in a vat? 'Ridiculous nonsense,' you reply, but of course a brain in a vat would also say that. Or think that. We are left with the view that we cannot completely reject these ideas; that view is called **scepticism** – you cannot be certain of anything (see Box 6.1). Our grounds for trusting that reality is as we think it is are shaky, and we take a lot on faith. Some argue that if we're living in a simulation the program might have small bugs in it, and we should look for the effects of those bugs, but then again the program running our simulation might be bug-free.

Normal Visual Perception

It is well known that there are five senses: vision, hearing, taste, smell, and touch (and the 'sixth sense' discussed in Chapter 10), but by far most research has been carried out on the processes of vision, followed by those of hearing. We have quite a good understanding of perceptual processing, what happens from the sense organ (such as the eye) to the brain, and the routes and regions of the brain involved in perceptual processing (see, for example, Harris, 2014; Ward, 2015). Scepticism teaches us that the output of these processes might not always be reliable.

Filling in

We seem to have a complete view of the world. If I look around I can't see any gaps in the world; if I look ahead I am aware of a complete visual world. But we know this cannot be right because of the existence of blind spots, where the optic nerve makes contact with the retina of the eye; there aren't any light detection cells, the rods or cones, there, so we can't be seeing anything at those points. Yet we don't see gaps in our visual field; our brain must be **filling in** those gaps. We blink on average 15 times a minute, with each blink lasting 200 ms or more, yet most of the time we are not aware of the world flickering in and out of existence. Filling in also occurs with some visual neurological deficits; patients don't always report gaps in their visual fields, instead filling in those regions.

There are two possible explanations for filling in. First, we could simply ignore the absence of something. Second, we could instead actively construct a spatially isomorphic or similar representation from the surrounding information through a process of neural computation so that we really do fill in. Most neuroscience evidence supports this second more active explanation, although the 'simply ignoring the absence' position has its supporters (Dennett, 1991). For example, we observe negative afterimages in these filled areas (such as after seeing a bright coloured light), which could only plausibly occur if we construct a representation from surrounding information (Komatsu, 2006).

We *blink* to protect the eyes by removing debris from their surfaces. Blinking is semi-autonomic in that we can blink at will, but we also routinely involuntarily blink 15 times a minute, with each blink lasting more than 100 ms, so that in any minute our eyes are typically shut for over 2 seconds – and most of the time we don't notice (Bristow et al., 2005). Bristow et al. used fMRI to show that the act of blinking suppresses activity in the visual, parietal, and prefrontal cortices that are usually associated with awareness of change in the environment. Blinking isn't completely unnoticed however, because it affects our sense of time, so that the more we blink the more quickly we think time passes (Grossman et al., 2019). Nevertheless, we do not observe the world as punctuated by regular darkness; we normally stitch these stretches of unbroken visual awareness together to a seamless whole.

Whatever the explanation, filling in is yet more evidence that our impression of the world is not what it seems.

Bistable Figures

A **bistable** object is one that has two stable configurations (also called *multistable* figures, particularly if there are more than two stable configurations). The Necker cube is one of the best known of this sort of ambiguous figure, being first presented by the Swiss crystallographer Louis Necker in 1832 (see Figure 9.1). It

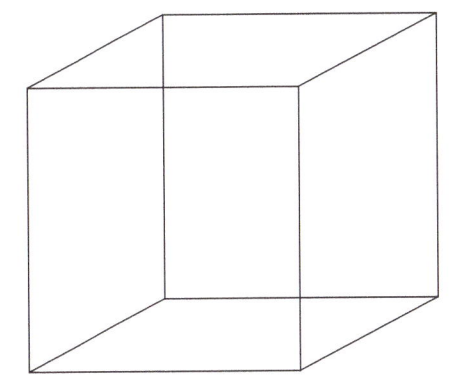

Figure 9.1 The Necker cube. Can you see both interpretations? Can you switch at will? Source: grebeshkovmaxim/iStock/Getty Images Plus.

Figure 9.2 A bistable figure: which way up are the stairs? A perspective reversal optical illusion called the Schroeder stairs. Wooden object which may be perceived as a downwards-leading staircase, from left to right, or turned upside down. I find this one harder to reverse at will. Source: PeterHermesFurian/iStock/Getty Images Plus.

is sometimes called a visual illusion, but really it's simply ambiguous. There isn't enough information in the drawing for us to be able to tell which is the front face of the cube and which is the rear, and if you look at it a while you will notice that your interpretation switches between the two. You can usually force one interpretation by a seeming effort of will. A second example is the stairs in Figure 9.2. There are several other well-known good examples of bistable figures, including the young girl–old lady figure (Figure 9.3) and concealed figure in Figure 9.4. An example from an artwork is Salvador Dali's 1940 painting *The Slave Market with the Disappearing Bust of Voltaire* (see Figure 9.4).

Notice though that, in line with the argument that you can only really be aware of one thing at once, you can't be conscious of both interpretations at the same time; it is one or the other. That observation poses the question, what happens when we switch?

The switch is often called a reversal. In particular, are there any neural correlates of a reversal? EEG shows a reversal positivity at 120 ms in the occipital lobe, which is early in processing, although earlier and later signals are also shown. This sort of result suggests that spontaneous reversal is largely a bottom-up phenomenon (Kornmeier & Bach, 2005). Later research showed that reversals could be 'primed' by a context of prior exposure to unambiguous figures, suggesting that both top-down and bottom-up processing takes place, consistent with the observation that by effort we can often force a reversal (Intaite et al., 2013). These neurological markers are correlates of events in consciousness.

Concealed figures are similar to bistable figures, where an object is cunningly concealed in a figure. It took me a long time to see the object in this figure (see Figure 9.5), but once seen it is difficult to un-see. What changes when we see the object? Presumably the low-level processes of perception are unchanged, so it must be our interpretation of the figure that alters.

Binocular Rivalry

Each eye receives a slightly different image of the world, and we usually combine these images seamlessly and without thinking. Difficulties can be provoked in combination, observed as

Figure 9.3 The young girl–old lady figure. A famous bistable figure: once you've seen it this one should be fairly easy to change at will. Source: Universal History Archive/Universal Images Group.

NORMAL VISUAL PERCEPTION

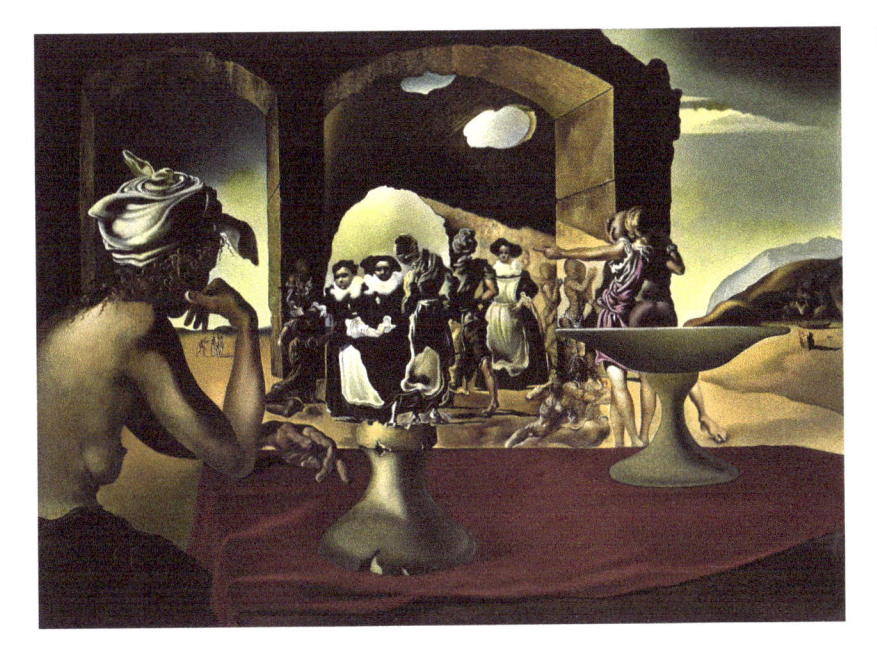

223

Figure 9.4 'The Slave Market with the Disappearing Bust of Voltaire', by Salvador Dali (1940). Look carefully at the statue of the head, which contains hidden figures. Or perhaps a hidden statue. Source: Bridgeman Images.

the phenomenon known as *binocular rivalry*, in which awareness of perception alternates between different images presented to each eye. We don't see the images superimposed on top of each other, but see one image from one eye clearly for a short duration before it switches to the other, and then back, and so on; the images are in competition. The switches are not instantaneous, like one slide being replaced by another, but occur in a wave-like fashion spreading from one end of one picture to the other, with the time determined by the precise physical properties of the picture (such as how close lines are together; Wilson et al., 2001). Hence, binocular rivalry is a test of visual awareness in the same way as ambiguous figures are; we are only aware of one thing at any one time (Crick & Koch, 1998). The same questions arise: what determines the switch, and are there any neural correlates of the switch?

As with ambiguous figures, there are no simple answers, even using brain imaging and modern electrophysiological techniques (Blake & Logothetis, 2002). At least, we have convergent evidence: different mechanisms at different levels of the visual processing hierarchy are involved in maintaining images and determining switches. Imaging suggests that spontaneous switches are associated with heightened activity in several cortical regions, including the right **fronto-parietal** regions, associated with spatial attention

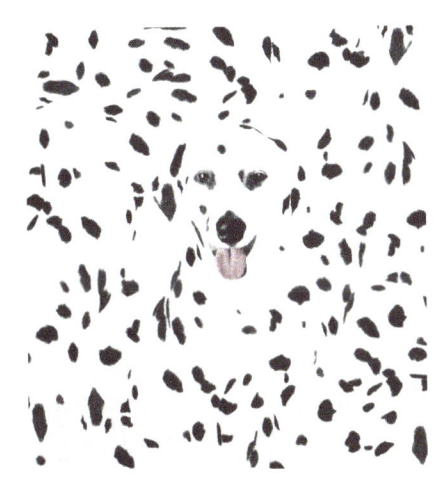

Figure 9.5 A concealed figure. The shape of a Dalmatian is hidden but revealed with surprisingly little information. Source: Mark Burnside/Stone/Getty Images Plus.

TRY THIS: The Necker Cube

Examine the Necker cube in Figure 9.1. Do you see any reversals? Can you learn to reverse at will?

(Blake & Logothetis, 2002). One study presented a picture of a face and a building, and observed activity in the **fusiform gyrus**, a region usually associated with face recognition, and part of the **parahippocampus** (grey matter surrounding the hippocampus), known to be sensitive to the presentation of buildings and spatial locations. Importantly, the heightened activation occurred in phase with the image that the viewer reported to be dominant at the time (Tong et al., 1998). To get this pattern of selective activation of alternating precise regions of the brain, the visual system must have settled on a precise interpretation earlier in processing; we don't see both regions active and some higher-level centre must then select between them. Studies of epilepsy patients undergoing neurosurgery with electrodes implanted in their brains suggest that internal changes in the contents of perception are signalled by medial frontal activity two seconds before the switch, and a highly specific activation of the medial temporal lobes one second before; this selective activity can be as selective as a single neuron (Gelbard-Sagiv et al., 2018).

These studies suggest that visual awareness is a complex process with several mechanisms and sites involved. There is no one region associated with determining what we are aware of. Top-down feedback neural loops from the parietal and temporal cortex also seem to play a role in stabilising the activity of neurons early in visual processing, again demonstrating the importance of feedback loops in consciousness (Logothetis, 2006). Indeed, the complexity of the processes involved in generating rivalry suggests that we should distinguish perceptual awareness from subjective consciousness (Giles et al., 2016). One key piece of evidence for this conclusion is that stimulus features that are invisible to participants can generate rivalry (Zou et al., 2016). Perceptual awareness involves creating a representation that enables participants to be able to make discriminations, whereas subjective consciousness enables participants to make valid verbal reports, a distinction also observed in blindsight (see below). Current thinking is that binocular rivalry might not involve subjective consciousness (Giles et al., 2016).

Change Blindness and Inattentional Blindness

The complexity of the perceptual representations we construct usually seems impressive, sometimes amazing. Look at a rich visual scene or listen to some complex music; there appears to be so much there. The amount of information is almost overwhelming. However, two much recently studied topics in vision research show that most of the time we perceive surprisingly little.

One of the more tedious pastimes I remember as a child was 'spot the difference' pictures in magazines and annuals where you had to spot the minor differences between two seemingly identical pictures. It could be surprisingly difficult. This idea of failing to spot changes is the basis of change blindness; change blindness is a phenomenon in perception in which some very large changes in a visual scene occurring in plain sight are not noticed (see Figure 9.6).

In the first detailed experimental studies of change blindness, participants viewed detailed, full-colour everyday visual scenes presented on a computer screen while their eye movements were recorded (McConkie & Currie, 1996). The computer was programmed to make changes in the scene depending on where the person was looking, and a change was made in the picture, such as removing a window from a building. McConkie and Currie found that, when the change occurred during a *saccade* (an eye movement), quite large changes could be made without people noticing them. Rensink, O'Regan, and Clark (1997) used a variant of this technique when the change was made during a brief (under 80 ms) flicker on the screen, and found the same pattern of results. Subsequent transcranial magnetic stimulation (TMS) studies showed that, when the *posterior parietal cortex* (PPC) is inhibited, people are significantly slower at detecting changes between successive pictures (Tseng et al., 2010). The PPC is important for maintaining visual images in short-term working memory. Although the earliest studies used static photographs, similar effects have been found with motion pictures (Simons & Levin, 1997).

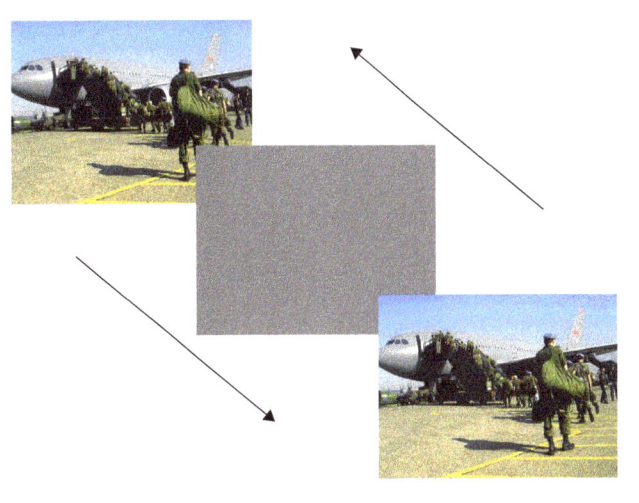

Figure 9.6 Stimulus used in change blindness experiment. The two pictures are changed until the participant detects the difference. It can take several seconds even for relatively large changes to be noticed, as here. (No, work it out for yourself.) Source: Le Moan et al. (2018). © 2018 Elsevier Inc. All rights reserved.

Detecting changes in pictures is one thing, but asurely everyone would notice a gorilla walking right in front of them? Apparently not. *Inattentional blindness* occurs when a person fails to recognise an unexpected stimulus that is in plain sight – such as watching a video of baseball players in action in which a person in a gorilla suit walks slowly across the screen, even stopping to wave (see Figure 9.7). If the participants are engaged in some other task, such as counting the number of throws of the ball, about half of them do not notice the unexpected event (Simons & Chabris, 1999). Inattentional blindness has been observed in a variety of settings (Mack & Rock, 1998). There are competing theories about why inattentional blindness occurs, with much debate about how much perception happens unconsciously (Mack, 2003).

These results support the idea that our representation of the visual world is not as rich as we might think. Although we must be careful about drawing too strong a conclusion (such as we never encode very much in the first place; see Simons & Rensink, 2005), it is safe to conclude that we do not always have close to as much a rich visual representation of the world as most of us think we do. The apparent richness of the visual world is yet another illusion.

Visual Illusions

We cannot rely on perceptual information for an accurate picture of the world. We are easily deceived, as the study of perceptual illusions, particularly visual illusions, shows.

Figure 9.7 Stimulus used in inattentional blindness experiment. Can you see the gorilla? A surprising number of people can't when paying attention to something else that is demanding, such as counting the number of passes. Source: Simons & Chabris (1999).

Visual illusions tell us a great deal about the processes of visual perception (see Wade, 2006), and we have mentioned them a few times before as a tool with which we can help understand consciousness, but our emphasis here is what they tell us about visual awareness (see Figure 9.8). The existence of visual illusions confirms that what we think is out there needn't necessarily be so. Lines are not of the lengths we might think, areas are not of the brightness we might think, and things do not magically appear and disappear at the periphery of our vision. We can conclude that our awareness is misleading us about the world.

Illusions are not confined to the visual modality. The charmingly named cutaneous rabbit illusion is evoked by tapping two separate regions of a person's skin in very rapid succession. It is best to use an area such as the arm; try the wrist and elbow. Often you will have the sensation of taps in between, taps hopping up the arm, even though none has been applied there (Geldard & Sherrick, 1972; Miyazaki et al., 2010). The explanation is far from clear, and needs a complex mathematical model. We hear words or even phrases in meaningless sounds, apparently because we don't (or should that be the brain doesn't?) like random noise (Deutsch, 2003). Then there is the Shepard tone, an auditory analogue of the

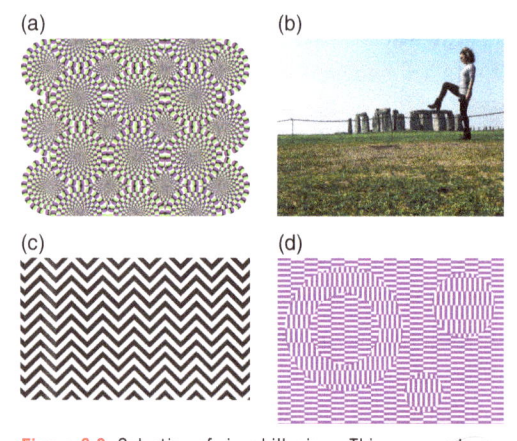

Figure 9.8 Selection of visual illusions. Things are not what they seem. Source: BSIP/Universal Images Group/Getty Images; Alexandra Seres/EyeEm Getty Images; saulgranda/Moment/Getty Images; BSIP/Universal Images Group/Getty Images.

never-ending Escher staircase (also called the Penrose stairs). After a while, one starts to believe that no input can be trusted.

No-report Paradigm

Most studies of consciousness have relied on people reporting what they see, particularly in perceptual research reporting when they see a stimulus. Recently, a different approach, called the *no-report paradigm*, has become popular (Tsuchiya et al., 2015), particularly for studying how perceptual awareness is based in the brain. No-report involves using some alternative measure other than verbal reports. Such a technique involves making use of some other measure assumed to correlate with consciousness. For example, studies of binocular rivalry might make use of changes in pupil size or eye movements to measure aspects of visual awareness. The advantage is that no-report avoids making the assumption that consciousness is limited to what can be reported verbally; the disadvantage is that we have to assume that some measure that is not available to verbal report does indeed measure consciousness (Overgaard & Fazekas, 2016).

> **TRY THIS:** Phantom Words
>
> Search online for the Deutsch phantom words and Shepard tones. Try them. Also follow the instructions for the cutaneous rabbit – you'll have to be fast though.

Disorders of Visuo-spatial Perception

Neurological damage can lead to a range of perceptual deficits. For example, agnosia is a problem with visual object recognition; there are several types, depending on exactly where in the brain the lesion lies. Prosopagnosia is a problem with face recognition, and alexia with recognising words. Although these deficits impinge on everyday life, and affect the quality of experience, they do not tell us about consciousness itself.

On the other hand, there are deficits that do. The first two we consider, blindsight and neglect, are not simply deficits of visual perception: they involve awareness of space, too, and for that reason are called visuo-spatial deficits.

Blindsight

One of the most striking demonstrations that vision and awareness can be dissociated is the phenomenon known as blindsight. **Blindsight** follows as a result of damage to the occipital cortex leaving a person cortically blind in at least part of the visual field (an area called a *scotoma*). Yet, nevertheless, they can retrieve some information from the visual field. A person with blindsight will deny that they can see, but when asked to guess – for example, the location of a flash of light, whether an object is at position A or B, or the colour of an object – they perform significantly better than chance. They also make appropriate saccades to moving objects in their blind area. Perception of motion is most likely to be preserved in blindsight. Research on blindsight was pioneered by Larry Weiskrantz (1926–2018), who for many years was head of the Department of Experimental Psychology at the University of Oxford (Weiskrantz, 1986, 1997). Much of our understanding of blindsight in humans comes from studies with patient D.B. in London. D.B. had had his right occipital cortex removed to treat a brain tumour, and carried out a series of experiments first explored on monkeys (Cowey, 2004; Weiskrantz, 1986).

Blindsight can be contrasted with Anton–Babinski syndrome (see Chapter 6), where people think they can see, but who are in fact cortically blind. If sufferers from Anton–Babinski syndrome have kept the idea of seeing while losing the ability to see, sufferers from blindsight have lost the idea of seeing without losing the ability to see.

Blindsight is further confirmation that, contrary to our everyday assumptions, visual stimuli do not need to reach awareness to influence behaviour. It shows that the well-known route of visual processing in the brain from optic nerves to the *occipital cortex* is not the only visual processing pathway. My undergraduate model of the brain is wrong. In fact, we now know that there are several branches in the visual processing system, involving the **lateral geniculate nucleus** and **superior colliculus**. Indeed, Ward (2015) states that it is currently believed that there are ten visual processing routes – doubtless the number will be different by the time this book is published (see Figure 9.9).

The primary visual route, leading to what most of us think of as visual awareness of objects in a scene, is called the **retinal–geniculate–striate pathway** (Pinel & Barnes, 2017). We have some vision in blindsight because of pathways that ascend from subcortical structures directly to the secondary visual cortex surrounding the primary cortex but not passing through it. A completely different explanation is that the **striate cortex** is not completely destroyed. At present, it is not clear which is the best explanation, and indeed both might pertain (e.g. Gross et al., 2004).

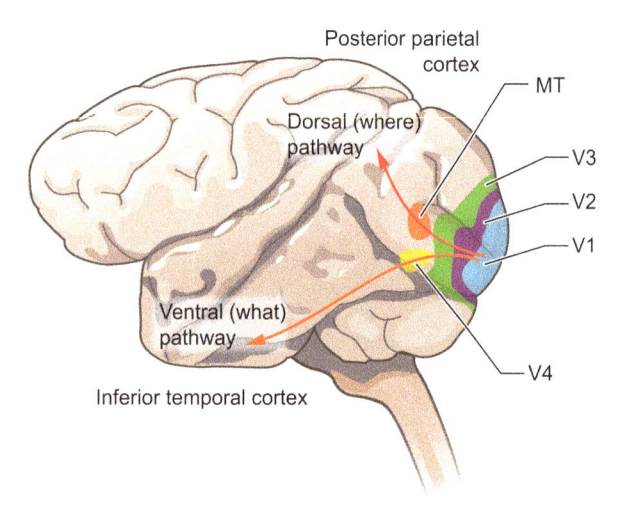

Figure 9.9 The dorsal and ventral visual streams in the brain. Essentially the ventral is the 'what' stream, the dorsal the 'where'. These are the two main routes from eye to perception, but others have been proposed. V1 to V4 refer to visual areas; MT is the middle temporal visual area, sometimes also called V5.

Evidence for the best-known secondary pathway comes from a distinction between pathways for object recognition and an unconscious pathway associated with action (Goodale & Milner, 1992; Westwood & Goodale, 2011). The inspiration for this distinction comes from a classic study of patient D.F., who had profound agnosia but was able to grasp and manipulate objects. So she was unable to recognise a letterbox or letter, yet was able to post the letter through the slit, whatever angle the slit was set to, even though she was unable to say anything about the slit. The two-visual-systems hypothesis (also called the perception–action hypothesis) states that the *dorsal–ventral* anatomical split of the visual cortex should be interpreted as the neural substrate of two independent functional modules: vision-for-perception (the ventral pathway) and vision-for-action (the dorsal pathway). The ideas are related to the work of Ungerleider and Mishkin (1982) on two visual processing pathways in monkeys, a dorsal stream processing spatial location, called the 'where'

DISORDERS OF VISUO-SPATIAL PERCEPTION

pathway, and a ventral stream processing visual feature, called the 'what' pathway. Milner and Goodale extended this work, arguing that the dorsal pathway is concerned with action, and that people only have conscious access to the 'what' pathway. Although the actual situation in humans might be more complex (Freud et al., 2016), it does seem to be the case that there are multiple visual processing pathways in the brain with varying degrees of accessibility by consciousness.

Spatial Neglect

Spatial or visual **neglect** is a disorder where a person appears not to notice part of their visual space (see Figures 9.10 and 9.11). In the most extreme case, they neglect all but one side of their visual space, so the disorder becomes known as *hemispatial* neglect. When asked to draw a clock, they might draw only one side, or compress all the numbers into one side; when asked to copy a picture, they might copy only one half; and they even tend to avoid looking into the neglected space (Li & Malhotra, 2015). Neglect leads to some bizarre behaviour: a person might dress only half their body, or eat only one side of a plate of food.

Figure 9.10 How the world appears to people with spatial neglect. The details and severity of how much information is lost will depend on the precise size and location of the lesion. Source: Li & Malhotra (2015).

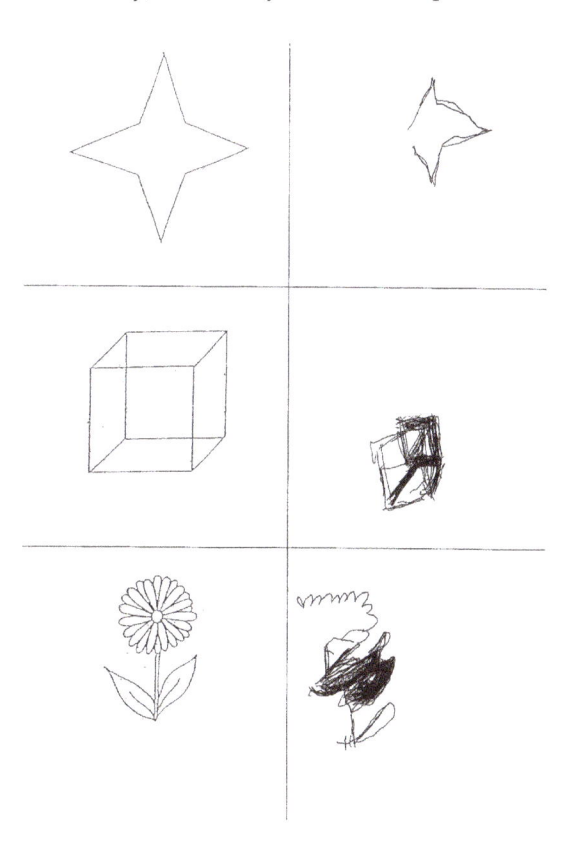

Figure 9.11 The copying task and spatial neglect. Again, how much can be copied depends on the details of the lesion. Patients tend to omit the left side or parts of the left side. Source: Li & Malhotra (2015).

It is therefore unsurprising to learn that neglect is accompanied by anosognosia (denial) and confabulation. Bisiach et al. (1990) describe the case of a patient who attributes their arm to another person, thereby concluding that they must have three hands.

Neglect is not simply a perceptual disorder, but is *attentional*. This idea is most clearly illustrated by an experiment where two patients from Milan were asked to imagine the view of the cathedral square, the Piazza Del Duomo, in Milan from the cathedral steps; they could describe only one side, but when asked to then imagine it from the opposite end of the square they would be unable to describe what they had just recalled, but would be able to describe what they had just omitted, showing that the deficit was not simply visual, and that the information that cannot be produced must be present (Bisiach & Luzzatti, 1978).

Neglect arises from damage to the *parietal lobe*, and is usually, but not invariably, associated with right-hemisphere damage leading most often to left spatial neglect. Blindsight and neglect show us that our representation of the world can be severely restricted.

Synaesthesia

Synaesthesia is a phenomenon in which activation in one sense leads to activation in another – for example, a person might hear a particular sound when seeing a particular colour, or feel a particular shape when tasting a particular food. People who report a lifelong history of such experiences are known as *synaesthetes*. One common form of synaesthesia is grapheme–colour synaesthesia, where letters or numbers are always perceived as coloured (Cytowic & Cole, 2008; Cytowic & Eagleman, 2011; Ward, 2008). Synaesthetes often find some commonalities across letters (for example, the letter A is likely to be seen as red). Synaesthesia is not uncommon (at least 1 in 2000 people, perhaps as commonly as 1 in 20), and tends to run in families (Baron-Cohen et al., 1996; Ramachandran & Hubbard, 2001a, b). It can also be produced by damage, and is also often induced by hallucinogens in those not normally predisposed to it.

Synaesthesia arises when there is crosstalk between brain areas, a condition known as hyper-connectivity. The experience of seeing colour when looking at graphemes might be due to crosstalk between the letter recognition area of the brain and the nearby regions involved in processing colour called V4 and V8 of the visual cortex. Grapheme–colour synaesthetes are often able to give the appropriate colour of a grapheme in the periphery of their vision even when they cannot identify its shape (Ramachandran & Hubbard, 2001a, b).

A different theoretical approach to synaesthesia is that based on synaesthesia really being a form of *ideasthesia*. In ideasthesia, concepts activate particular percepts. According to this account, synaesthesia is a phenomenon mediated by the extraction of the meaning of the stimulus. Thus, synaesthesia may be fundamentally a semantic phenomenon – to do with meaning – it isn't the sensory properties of the stimulus that give rise to the synaesthesia but its meaning (Dixon, Smilek, Duffy, Zanna, & Merikle, 2006). Naturally, it is difficult to tease these apart, but studies have examined ambiguous stimuli where the meaning is influenced by the context. Therefore, to understand neural mechanisms of synaesthesia, the mechanisms of semantics and the extraction of meaning need to be understood better (Gray et al., 2006).

Grossenbacher and Lovelace (2001) describe a neurobiological model of synaesthesia based on hierarchically arranged cortical sensory pathways where there is crosstalk between normally independent processing modules. Crosstalk arises either from side-to-side links between modules or top-down information flow after perceptual pathways have converged.

Proprioception

Proprioception is our sense of our own body and the effects of moving parts of it. The sense is provided by special neurons called proprioceptors in muscles and tendons.

When he was 19, Ian Waterman had a severe bout of gastric flu. Normally, gastric flu, although most unpleasant, passes quickly without side effects, but he developed a very rare auto-immune disorder, which attacked his nervous system, leaving him with the permanent side effect of losing all sense of proprioception (Cole, 1995, 2016). Although he was able to move normally, he had no idea where his limbs were unless he could see them. He could still feel pain and temperature, showing these systems must be distinct. His movement was unsurprisingly highly uncoordinated.

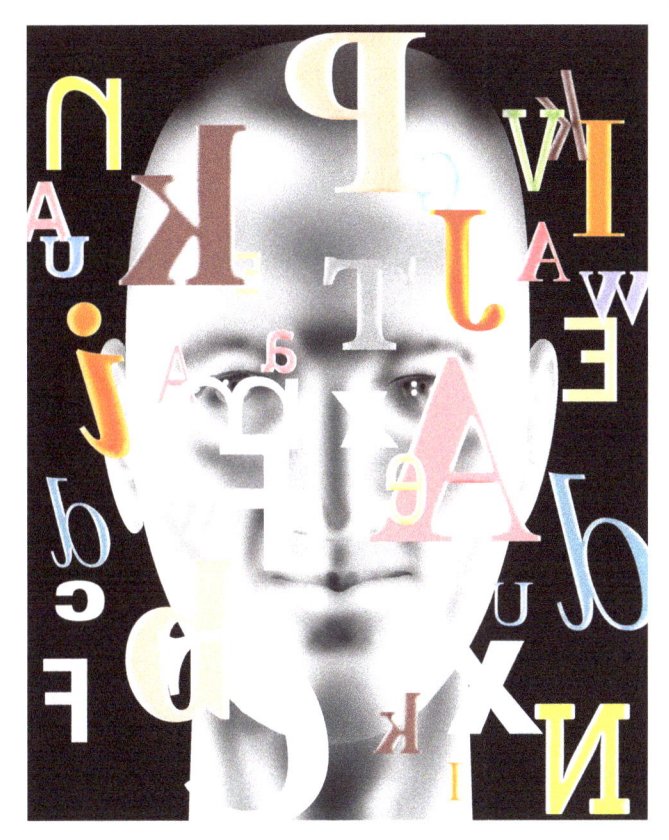

Figure 9.12 Representation of colour–letter synaesthesia. In one of the more common types of synaesthesia, particular letters or digits are associated with specific colours. Source: Fort Worth Star-Telegram/Tribune News Service/Getty Images.

Proprioception information is integrated across the brain and eventually represented in the *parietal cortex* (Ehrsson et al., 2005).

The Binding Problem

When we see a tiger, we don't see a head, a patch of orange, black stripes, teeth snarling in empty space – all these things are bound together. We see a face, not a series of lines. And when it roars, the roar comes from the tiger, not a point in space. All these features get integrated in some way – but how? The **binding problem** is how do different sensations get bound together to form a unitary percept so that we perceive one thing with all the associated emotions? Binding involves within modality (so that we recognise one object with everything in the right place) and across modalities (the roar goes with the sight of the tiger). It involves the selection or segregation of data within a modality (visual, say) so that we form distinct objects. It also involves aggregation of data across modalities so that we experience objects as wholes and as a unitary experience. After all, it is the whole object we are aware of, not individual features (unless we choose to focus on them). Crick and Koch (1990, 2003) outlined highly influential ideas in this area, arguing that perceptual binding occurred through neural binding mechanisms that underlie the apparent unity of consciousness.

The brain might use one of two methods to bind different stimuli into one object by location (there are patterns of cells that correspond to a particular object, such as seeing a tiger), or by time, so that a pattern resonates together.

Do perceptual pathways in the brain converge on a group of cells or even a single cell that represents a conscious perception? The classic example of this is a grandmother cell – one cell that is activated when we see our grandmother (or a giraffe, or whatever). Such an arrangement would solve the binding problem, but is very unlikely because, if we lost that one neuron (and neurons are being lost all the time), we would forever lose our grandmother. Much more likely are groups of cells. Although the brain has many parallel circuits, it does display a certain form of convergence as one moves farther from the primary areas of the cortex and closer to the 'associative' ones. Many areas of convergence have been identified in the frontal cortex, the anterior temporal cortex, and the *inferior* parietal cortex. We find that there are certain neurons located at the top of the hierarchy in the visual cortex that respond specifically to faces, and even to faces seen from a certain angle (Chang & Tsao, 2017).

The alternative to perceptions being bound by place is that they are bound by time, in which case features relating to the same object 'fire together' in some kind of synchrony.

Milner (1974) suggested that features of individual objects are bound via the synchronisation of the activity of different neurons in the cortex. Later in processing objects represented in the visual cortex are represented by assemblies of neurons that fire simultaneously (Engel & Singer, 2001). It is thought that **gamma waves** play a special role in temporal binding. Gamma waves are fast waves with a frequency of about 30–100 Hz, most typically around 40 Hz. They play an important role in synchronising and binding information (Box 9.2), and thereby giving rise to visual awareness and the unity of consciousness (Baldauf & Desimone, 2014; Crick & Koch, 2003; Engel et al., 1999; Gold, 1999; Gregoriou et al., 2009). Neurons involved in perceiving an object oscillate synchronously at around 40 Hz, even though they are not directly connected to each other. It is only when perceptual features become bound by the synchronised firing that we can be visually aware of the stimulus – or perhaps when features become bound we automatically become aware. Hence, the binding problem and perceptual awareness are closely linked (Crick & Koch, 2003).

> **Box 9.2** Gamma Waves
>
> Gamma waves are a type of neural oscillation detected by EEG in the 25–140 Hz range, most typically around 40 Hz. They crop up all over the place in consciousness research, and seem to have some unifying effect of bringing together stimuli or aspects of stimuli. They are observed when we engage in a range of cognitive phenomena, including tasks that access

> **Box 9.2** (cont.)
>
> working memory, involve attention, or involve perceptual grouping. In particular, they are thought to be involved in perceptual binding (Chapter 9): features that oscillate together bind together. They are disrupted in epilepsy (Chapter 11), schizophrenia, mood disorders, and Alzheimer's disease, although as ever we should be cautious about claiming any direction of causality from a correlation. One effect of meditation (Chapter 16) is to enhance gamma wave oscillation.
>
> Gamma waves are observed across large areas of the brain, but it is thought that the thalamus, which we know plays a significant role as a switch for consciousness, and in gating and relaying information between different parts of the brain (this chapter), is important in initiating them. Gamma waves are important in synchronising activation across structures in the thalamo-cortical loop, in which feedback structures play an important role, with thalamo-cortical feedforward and cortico-thalamal feedback connections making recurrent loops.

Gamma waves appear to be involved in both the segmentation and selection of visual features to form distinct objects (Fries, 2009). Different objects in a scene will cause synchronisation at slightly different frequencies. Gamma waves of 40 Hz are seen during REM sleep but not during non-REM sleep, presumably because in dreams aspects of imagined visual scenes still need to be bound. When features are synchronised, a 'wave' passes though parts of the brain. The wave originates in the thalamus, and sweeps across the brain to the frontal cortex 40 times a second, bringing different neural circuits involved in perceiving an object into synchrony with each other. This pattern is called *thalamo-cortical resonance* (Llinás et al., 1998). The thalamus and cortex are richly interconnected, with feedback loops from the thalamus to cortex and back again. Llinás and Ribary (1993) argued that the thalamo-cortical resonance is modulated by the brainstem, and is given extrinsic content by sensory input in the awake state and by intrinsic activity during dreaming. Crick and Koch state that, if two neurons are oscillating synchronously in the gamma frequency range (around 40 Hz), then they are contributing to the same, conscious representation.

Not all researchers are convinced that gamma waves are central in binding. Gamma waves are observed in anaesthetised rats, which are not consciously perceiving anything (Vanderwolf, 2000). Of course, rats might be different from humans, and it is possible that gamma waves serve more than one function, but it is curious that something thought to be central to consciousness is just as apparent in an anaesthetic state.

What would a failure of binding look like? We occasionally mis-parse a visual scene, perhaps attributing an arm to the wrong person. The rare *Balint's syndrome* is a neurological disorder where the primary visual cortex V1 is intact, but the person is functionally blind. Balint's syndrome results from damage to both inferior parietal lobes. It's so rare because the person has to be unfortunate enough to suffer damage to the same locations in both hemispheres by two strokes. The primary symptom of interest here is *simultagnosia*, where in Balint's the person can see the individual details of the scene, but not the whole. So they might be able to identify the glass in your hand, but not your hand or arm. In addition, the person's perception of body space remains intact, but the person cannot react to the world and objects in it. The most obvious explanation of this disorder is a failure of binding. The person can perceive individual features, but is unable to bind them and therefore cannot form a coherent representation of the world.

Generally, the experimental evidence shows that consciousness is associated with at least high-level integration of information (Mudrik et al., 2014). We normally become aware of stimuli when they are bound together. Such integration obviously involves connections across brain regions: for example, to perceive a strongly scented red rose you need to access information from the visual and olfactory brain areas.

Microconsciousness

The British physiologist Samir Zeki, working within visual perception and just visual consciousness, argues that there is not just one consciousness, but 'multiple consciousnesses' organised in a hierarchy, with a single unified consciousness (that of myself as the perceiving person) sitting at the apex (Zeki, 2003). Zeki uses the term *microconsciousness* to denote consciousness for individual attributes of any one percept.

According to the microconsciousness account, consciousness is distributed in time and space in the brain. The theory is based on the finding that the motion of an object may be perceived at a slightly different time than its colour. Colour is perceived in area V4 in the visual cortex and motion in area V5. Damage to V4 leads to achromatopsia and to V5 to akinetopsia, distinct and dissociable disorders. Furthermore experiments show that colour is perceived before motion by 80 ms (Zeki, 2003). This temporal asynchrony and spatial dissociation in visual perception reveal plurality of visual consciousnesses that are asynchronous with respect to each other. In effect, each module in the visual brain (Zeki & Bartels, 1998) generates its own consciousness, a microconsciousness. These are then put together through binding into a macro-consciousness, awareness of a percept. At the top of the hierarchy is the unified consciousness, which gives rise to our sense of ourselves as a person. Of necessity, one level depends upon the presence of the previous one.

Some believe that TMS (transmagnetic stimulation) evidence argues against a distributed view. TMS disruption of visual processing shows that activity in the V1 area is essential for visual awareness. So each perceptual module cannot independently generate a 'microconsciousness': you cannot get awareness in the movement module alone without V1 activity (Cowey & Walsh, 2000). The microconsciousness theory was also criticised by Cohen and Dennett (2011), who argue that the idea of dissociating consciousness from cognitive processing, in that unified consciousness is put together post-experientially, is incoherent. It makes no sense that the unified person is having conscious states (such as of motion and colour alone) of which they are not aware.

Visual Awareness

We have seen that because visual awareness is so easy to measure there has been considerable research on the topic. Recent research has shown that there are individual neurons that respond to single concepts (famously the actress Jennifer Aniston; see Box 9.3). In fact, activation of single neurons in the **anterior medial temporal lobe**, particularly the amygdala, corresponds to visual stimuli being identified and reaching visual awareness. Using an attentional blink procedure, where the second of two stimuli presented in close succession often goes consciously unnoticed, Reber et al. (2017) tested a population of surgical patients with micro-wires used to measure individual neurons. They found that these neurons need to reach a certain level of activation before the participant would report seeing, the target, suggesting that neural events correlate with consciousness in a graded fashion. There was also a gradient of awareness from the front to the back of the medial temporal lobe to the amygdala. The amygdala, in addition to its many other functions, therefore seems to play an important role in visual consciousness as well (Fu & Rutishauser, 2018).

> **Box 9.3** The Jennifer Aniston Neuron
>
> Early in the history of neuroscience, it was speculated that cells involved in visual processing were connected together in a hierarchy so that eventually one specific cell would fire when it recognised an individual person. The cell was dubbed the *grandmother cell* – it would only fire if your grandmother was present in the visual field. The idea lost favour in part because of lack of evidence, and in part because it seemed infeasible – what happened if that one cell died? Would you ever be able to recognise your grandmother again?
>
> Working with open brain surgery, Fried and colleagues found specific individual cells in the human hippocampus, entorhinal cortex, and amygdala (taken together forming the *medial temporal lobe*) that fired when presented with pictures of famous people such as Jennifer Aniston, Halle Berry, and Bill Clinton (Kreiman et al., 2000). These cells are believed to sit on top of a hierarchy of processing, each representing an agglomeration of specific features (such as blonde hair, hair style, blue eyes, and characteristic jaw bone). Note that, although an individual cell might fire in response to a particular person, there might be more than one such cell, providing a degree of redundancy. Hence, these studies strictly support the notion of *sparseness* rather than the concept of a grandmother cell (Quiroga et al., 2007).

The Grand Illusion

We are tempted to think that we have a rich and detailed representation of the world, but like much in consciousness research, this belief is wrong, so much so that Noë (2002, 2010) talks about the *grand illusion* of perception and reality. Our representation of the world is not like a multisensory movie.

Perception involves many processes running in parallel in the brain, both within and across modalities. At some point we have to bring them all together; the binding problem is how these parallel processes are synchronised. We never 'perceive' objects unbound, but whether this happens because we are conscious of them, or before we are conscious of them, is not clear. Although we think we are conscious of a lot (for example, that the visual scene I 'see' is very rich), in fact, we seem to see remarkably little. The contents of our consciousness are more impoverished than we first think.

When I was an undergraduate in the mid-1970s my model of visual processing and the brain was a very bottom-up one: early processing neural circuits fed into increasingly complex and later circuits (light and dark into edges, edges into shapes, shapes into 3D, 3D into objects, objects into things with association, and finally meaning and hence consciousness – not that that word was allowed); we know that the brain is full of feedback loops. Feedback loops – or, as Douglas Hofstadter would say, strange loops – are central to consciousness.

Hoffman (2019) argues that as all that matters is that we survive, so that our genes get carried into the next generation, the results of perception do not have to be veridical, but they do have to be effective. Hoffman gives the example of an icon for a computer file – we interact through the icon because it's simple and effective. We wouldn't be able to manage interacting directly with the series of 0 and 1 bits stored in memory. Hoffman goes further, and says that, given this argument, it doesn't make sense to talk about what the outside world is 'really' like. Indeed, it doesn't make sense to talk about reality at all. In the end, Hoffman argues, for a modern version of idealism – all there is is in the mind.

Chapter Summary

- Empiricism says that we obtain all knowledge through our sensory experiences.
- How do you know that you are not a brain in a vat, connected up to sensors that provide perceptual information, and other sensors that provide the illusion of control and movement?
- Visual illusions show that the world is not always as it seems.
- We do not see our blind spots where the optic nerve meets the retina; instead, we must fill in or complete the visual scene.
- We cannot be conscious of ambiguous figures in both states simultaneously; we can only be aware of one state at any one time.
- Similarly, we can also only perceive the Necker cube in one way at any one time.
- There is no simple neural correlate marking a reversal when we swap from perceiving the Necker cube in one way to another; both bottom-up and top-down visual processes appear to be involved.
- Studies with binocular rivalry support the conclusions from the Necker cube. There is no one region of the brain in which we 'become aware' of the visual scene.
- Feedback loops in the brain play an important role in visual awareness.
- Change blindness is the phenomenon in which we are not aware of quite large changes made in the visual scene at some moment of transition, such as during an eye movement.
- Inattentional blindness is our inability to detect large 'surprise' events if we are paying attention to some other aspect of the scene.
- Change and inattentional blindness suggest that much visual processing may be unconscious, or even that our representations of the visual scene can be quite sparse.
- Blindsight is a neurological condition where people are consciously blind, yet can still detect information from parts of scenes even though they report they are not aware of them.

- There are (at least) two visual processing routes, and maybe as many as ten.
- These visual processing routes have differing degrees of access to consciousness, with the what (visual features) being the one with most.
- Neglect is a disorder of attention where people lose the ability to direct their attention towards one side of the visuo-spatial world.
- Synaesthesia is a sensory confusion whereby some people experience some sensory stimuli in terms of other senses, such as always hearing a particular sound or hearing a particular colour when they see a number.
- We have a model of proprioception.
- Somehow we bind features together to form a representation of a single object so that we are aware of the whole object rather than its separate components.
- Binding can be either by brain location or temporally.
- The grand illusion is the idea that we do not have a detailed perceptual representation of the world most of the time.
- Hoffman argues that our perceptual representations enable us to survive, and might be nothing like 'reality'.
- Talking about reality might be meaningless.

Review Questions

1. If suitable visual analysis hardware and software existed, could a robot be vulnerable to a visual illusion?
2. Suppose you have a very powerful computer. What is the minimum you would have to add to it to enable it to recognise a dog?
3. What do disorders of perception tell us about normal perception?
4. What is visual neglect, and what does it tell us about normal consciousness?
5. What is the origin of synaesthesia? Could synaesthetes be said to see the world 'wrongly'?
6. What is perceptual binding, and when does it occur?
7. What is meant by the perceptual world being an illusion? And is this claim true?
8. To what extent is perception the result of evolutionary processes, and therefore what does it mean to say that perception is veridical (that is, sees the world as it really is)?

Recommended Resources

The Perceptual System

Harris, J. (2014). *Sensation and Perception*. London: Sage.

Pinel, J.P.J., and Barnes, S.J. (2017). *Biological Psychology* (10th ed.). Harlow, UK: Pearson.

Disorders of Vision and Space

Weiskrantz, L. (2009 [1986]). *Blindsight: A Case Study and Implications*. Oxford, UK: Oxford University Press.

Harrison, J. (2001). *Synaesthesia: The Strangest Thing*. Oxford, UK: Oxford University Press.

Cole, J. (2016). *Losing Touch: A Man without his Body*. Oxford, UK: Oxford University Press.

The Binding Problem

Koch, C. (2004). *The Quest for Consciousness: A Neurobiological Approach*. Englewood, CO: Roberts & Co.

The Grand Illusion

Chater, N. (2018). *The Mind is Flat: The Illusion of Mental Depth and the Improvised Mind*. London: Penguin.

Frith, C. (2007). *Making Up the Mind: How the Brain Creates Our Mental World*. Oxford, UK: Blackwell.

Noë, A. (ed.) (2002). *Is the Visual World a Grand Illusion?* Charlottesville, VA: Imprint Academic.

10 CONSCIOUSNESS AND THE BRAIN

Where are the processes that generate consciousness located in the brain? Materialism implies that consciousness is dependent on the brain, but is that the whole brain, or a particular part of the brain, or something going on in the brain?

In this chapter, we are concerned with the search for the neural correlates of consciousness (often abbreviated to NCC). The neural correlates of consciousness are the minimum neural mechanisms that are sufficient for one conscious percept, thought, or memory (Tononi & Koch, 2015). We know that consciousness doesn't depend on a whole brain, because we know that people can survive substantial trauma to the brain (such as by an injury or stroke) resulting in a great loss of brain matter, but depending on the extent of the damage they carry on living and clearly remain conscious. So, is there a particular part of the brain that is responsible for consciousness?

This chapter looks at the relationship between mind and brain, asking where consciousness might be located. Consciousness could correspond to a location in the brain (or system), or a process, or both. We first look at the electrophysiology of the brain, asking if there are patterns of activity associated with consciousness. We consider the evolution of the brain, examining the timeline of the evolution of structures that might support consciousness. We then examine the development of consciousness within an individual, particularly considering cases where the brain fails to develop normally. We then examine how anaesthetics work, asking if there is a switch or simple mechanism that they affect, drawing particular attention to the thalamus. We conclude with some models of consciousness that pay particular attention to brain structures and processes, especially Tononi's integrated information theory.

It seems obvious to us now that our consciousness is associated in some way with our brains, but at other times some people have thought otherwise. The Stoic philosophers of Ancient Greece thought that the mind was in the heart; for them the job of the brain was to cool the heart. The Ancient Greeks though were reluctant to dissect the human body, which limited their knowledge of how the body works. For most of history, however, the command centre of behaviour was associated with the head and brain. The early Egyptians knew, for example, that damage to the head and the brain led to changes in behaviour.

Our understanding of the brain and the NCC has progressed rapidly over the last few years thanks to huge advances in techniques for examining the living brain (see Box 10.1).

> ### Box 10.1 Studying the Living Brain
>
> X-rays enable us to view most of the soft organs of the body, but the brain is carefully protected by a large bone, the skull. Brain imaging enables us to see the structure of the brain. *Functional imaging* gives us a real-time picture of the brain as it is working. Imaging techniques have different *spatial* and *temporal* resolutions, both of which have been improving over the last few decades. Modern techniques are mostly *non-invasive* (do not involve surgery), but a few are *invasive*, involving placing electrodes in or on the brain.
>
> A **computed tomography (CT) scan**, formerly known as a computerised axial tomography scan or a CAT scan, combines X-ray measurements taken from different angles to produce cross-sectional (*tomographic*) images (virtual 'slices') of the brain.
>
> **Positron emission tomography (PET)** is a functional imaging technique that is used to observe metabolic processes in the brain. The subject is given a radioactive tracer (most commonly fluorine-18, harmless in low doses) which is used in metabolic processes. PET scans measure the emission of electromagnetic waves (gamma rays), enabling the system to build up an image of functional activity in the brain.
>
> **Electroencephalography (EEG)** is an electrophysiological monitoring method that records the brain's electrical activity. Electrodes are placed on the scalp at specific locations. EEG measures voltage fluctuations across the brain.
>
> **Electrocorticography** is an invasive version of EEG with electrodes placed in the brain.
>
> **Magnetic resonance imaging (MRI)** uses strong magnetic and radio waves and, making use of a phenomenon called nuclear magnetic resonance, builds an image of the tiffs of the brain.
>
> **Functional magnetic resonance imaging (fMRI)** extends MRI and enables us to build up a coloured picture of what is happening in the brain as we carry out a task. fMRI makes use of changes in blood flow (what is called the *haemodynamic response*). The basic idea is that parts of the brain that are working harder require more oxygen from the blood, and fMRI measures the BOLD (blood oxygen level dependent) contrast. fMRI is now the most widely used technique in cognitive neuroscience.
>
> **Transcranial magnetic stimulation (TMS)** uses a powerful magnet to influence electrical activity in targeted locations in the brain, so we can see what effect the manipulation has on a person's reported experience.
>
> **Magnetoencephalography (MEG)** measures changes in magnetic fields caused by electrical activity in the brain. MEG makes use of many very sensitive magnetometers called SQUIDs (superconducting quantum interference devices).
>
> **Optogenetics** is a technique for using light to control neurons that have been genetically modified to make them light sensitive. The technique enables us to identify the role of particular neurons and neuronal assemblies in networks, as well as enabling us to generate some spectacular images.

The Neural Correlates of Consciousness

The **neural correlates of consciousness** are which parts of the brain are involved in generating aspects of consciousness, and how? The problem is a set of closely related issues. How does the brain give rise to consciousness? Are there particular brain structures we can identify that are active when we engage in certain sorts of processing? How does brain damage affect consciousness? Why does the cerebral cortex appear to give rise to consciousness, but not the cerebellum, even though it contains more neurons and is just as richly interconnected? Where do you think you are? I don't mean are you reading this book in your living room or in a coffee shop – where are you in your body? I think I'm between and behind my eyes, and definitely in my head. Everyone knows that the brain is the organ of the body that controls behaviour and processes information. In some way, 'I' am in my brain. NCCs are measured by an imaging technique of some sort while a person's state of consciousness changes – from awake to sleep, from conscious to anaesthetised, or when an object changes from seen to unseen.

There are two types of NCC: a location in or part of the brain, or a type of activity, such as a particular electrical pattern. Of course, there is also the possibility that both are necessary – consciousness corresponds to a particular activity at a particular location.

Although we cannot point to any one small part of the brain and say that's where consciousness is located, it is equally clear that some parts of the brain are more involved with maintaining consciousness than others. The cerebellum, the part of the brain towards the rear responsible for coordination and the control of the movement, can suffer massive damage, with drastic consequences for behaviour, but leaving consciousness unaffected. We have seen how damage to different parts of the brain can leave consciousness unaltered or change aspects of it (see Chapter 7). On the other hand, a pathway in the brain called the **thalamo-cortical system** is closely involved in maintaining consciousness, and severe damage to it will lead to loss of consciousness. The thalamus is a relatively large region of the brain near the centre that acts as a relay for sensory and motor signals and in maintaining alertness, and is richly connected to the cortex.

The brain is to varying extents electrically active all the time. How does the pattern of activity differ when we are alert and awake from when we are in non-dream sleep, under anaesthetic, or comatose? We discuss the several ways in which these states differ.

The 'Astonishing Hypothesis'

The central puzzle of consciousness is how can the objective, physical processes of the brain give rise to subjective, mental experiences? (This question is just another way of asking the 'hard question'.)

The British biologist Sir Francis Crick (1916–2004) was the co-discoverer of the structure of DNA. He later moved to California and pursued what he called the *astonishing hypothesis* – the idea that consciousness and the behaviour of humans arises just from the behaviour of neurons. You might conclude that the hypothesis isn't that astonishing, because as we have seen there isn't really an alternative; it is astonishing though how it happens. As the philosopher Noë observed, what is astonishing about the 'astonishing hypothesis' is how astonishing it isn't. Perhaps more astonishing is Crick's idea that only specific groups of neurons are involved in generating consciousness (Crick, 1995), and hence his research programme was the search for the neural correlates of consciousness. It should be said the research is very focused on vision and the visual cortex.

There are two ways in which it's astonishing, First, throughout most of history most people have believed in a soul, an immaterial essence that is us. Indeed, many people still believe in them. It is easy, as a psychologist, to get hardened to accepting that all we are is our brains, but, in western societies, most people of religious faith accept the existence of souls as something apart from our brain. We'll be looking at the relationship between the brain and the mind in the next chapter. But even if you don't believe in souls, and accept that the brain is all there is, it's astonishing that a pulsating mass of grey matter made up of relatively simple cells gives rise to the complexity of us, and particularly that somehow it gives rise to consciousness, to sensation, to the feeling of being me.

As when we talk about consciousness generally, we can consider consciousness in its wider meaning – those psychological processes such as attention, visual binding, the representation of the self in space, and so on – and consider what are the neural correlates of those processes – which parts of the brain are involved in attentional processing, for instance. Or we can take a stricter definition of consciousness, considering only core consciousness, and asks where that takes place. Finally, there is the issue of what does it even mean to talk about consciousness taking place anywhere at all.

Mind Reading: Finding Internal Content from the Outside

There have been several reports in the press of researchers being able to tell what a person is thinking by looking at the brain's activity. For example, Norman et al. (2006) reviewed the use of a technique called *multi-voxel pattern analysis (MVPA)*, which uses large amounts of fMRI data to build a detailed picture of the pattern of activity present in the brain at any time. MVPA is a very sensitive technique. Haxby et al. (2001) showed that patterns of activity in the ventral temporal cortex could be used to tell whether a person was looking at a face, shoe, bottle, or other object. Similar studies have been used to predict the orientation of an object a person is looking at, or whether a person is looking at a picture or object (Norman et al., 2006). Haxby et al. call this use of imaging mind reading, as analysis of imaging data tells us what a person is thinking (or at least looking at). It doesn't matter whether the stimuli are endogenous or sensory input (Kanwisher, 2010).

This research is of more than scientific interest. One applied goal is to assist communication with people with severe mobility impairments, such as motor neurone disease and *locked-in syndrome* (see later this chapter).

The Electrophysiology of Consciousness

Electrophysiology is the study of the electrical activity of the nervous system. The technique was first studied systematically by the German psychiatrist Hans Berger in the early 1920s. We call a representation of the electrical activity an EEG, and we record the electrical activity by placing a number of electrodes over the human scalp (see Figure 3.7). We

THE ELECTROPHYSIOLOGY OF CONSCIOUSNESS

observe that the activity of the brain isn't random, but instead we can see synchronised patterns in the form of waves – colloquially called brain waves (see Figure 10.1). Brain waves result from groups of neurons in the brain pulsating together.

Waves are classified depending on their frequency (how many times things happen a second). The pattern of waves observed depends upon what we are doing; in general, the more alert we are the more high-frequency waves we observe. Berger called the larger amplitude, slower frequency waves that appeared over the posterior scalp when a person's eye are closed alpha waves, and the smaller amplitude, faster frequency waves that replace alpha waves when a person opens their eyes he called beta waves. However, it turns out there are several types of brain wave; many of these wave types are observed roughly in sequence when we move from an alert state to deep sleep. These types of wave are given in bands based on cycles per second, with Hz as the symbol for the unit of frequency Hertz, and 1 Hz being one cycle a second (see Box 10.2).

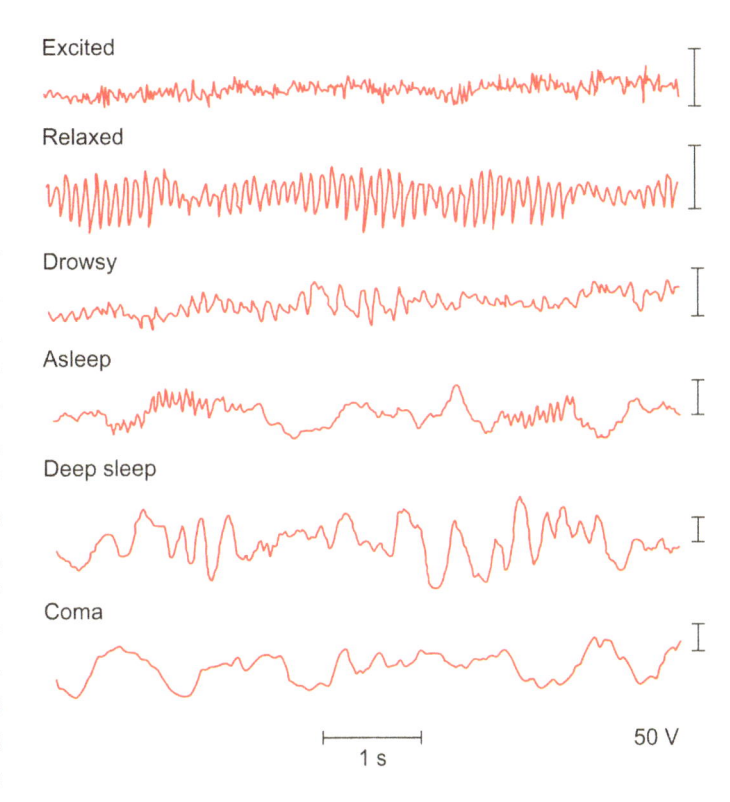

Figure 10.1 Examples of EEG output. Characteristic EEG activity during various mental states. Is there any pattern of progression from the alert waking state through sleep to coma?

Box 10.2   Brain Waves

Gamma waves (30–100 Hz). These very fast waves are involved in the coordination of information across different brain regions. Gamma waves might play some special role in binding aspects of perceptual phenomena together and consciousness. A frequency of around 40 Hz is most typical. Because of the way in which they coordinate information across the brain, and in doing so might bind together aspects of a percept, they have long been thought to play a special role (Gray, 2006).

Beta waves (12.5–30 Hz). We observe these relatively high-frequency waves when a person is alert with their eyes open, and can be said to characterise normal waking consciousness.

Alpha waves (8–12.5 Hz). These waves tend to be larger amplitude and appear over more posterior regions of the scalp when a person's eyes are closed. These are found when people are calm but awake, usually with their eyes shut.

Theta waves (4–7 Hz). Found in deep sleep and some meditative states.

> **Box 10.2** (cont.)
>
> **Delta waves (0.5–3 Hz)** are very slow and often of high amplitude. They are observed in deep, dreamless sleep and in deep meditative states in very experienced meditators.
>
> **Infra-slow (<0.5 Hz)**. These very slow waves are difficult to detect and very little is known about them. It has been suggested that they are involved in overall timing of brain activity.

We have seen that an NCC could be a location or activity (or both): are there any EEG patterns that correspond uniquely to being conscious? As we shall see, there are several candidates, but we must be cautious when evaluating them (Tononi & Koch, 2015). What looks like an NCC could instead be a signature of perceptual processing leading up to our becoming aware of a percept, or even simply of reporting or reflecting on the percept. So, as ever, interpreting the EEG data is more difficult than it first seems. Some researchers have proposed that high levels of activation of the **fronto-parietal cortex** in the gamma range (35–80 Hz, centred around 40 Hz) are a signature of consciousness, as might be an EEG event known as the P300, a wave marked by a positive deflection occurring 300 ms after a stimulus (Dehaene & Changeux, 2011; Koch, 2004; Tononi & Laureys, 2009). But we observe consciousness without frontal involvement, gamma activity without awareness during anaesthesia, and consciousness without a P300 when dreaming (Cot et al., 2001; Engel & Singer, 2001; Goldberg et al., 2006; Murphy et al., 2011).

The Evolution of the Brain

We have seen that most people only attribute consciousness to relatively later evolutionary creatures. We should remember that when taking this line of argument we can never know for sure which animals are self-aware, which are aware, and what it is like to be a rat or bat or cat. Nevertheless, in general, the complexity of the brain, as measured by total number of neurons, number of distinct brain regions, and degree of connectivity, increases with the lateness of the date at which an animal first appeared. So, terrestrial lizards have more complex brains than fish, and mammals have more complex brains than lizards, although we should remember that there are many differences in animal brains that are related to their environment and mode of life. What does comparative neuroanatomy, the study of the structure of the brain across different types of animals, tell us about consciousness (see Figure 10.2)?

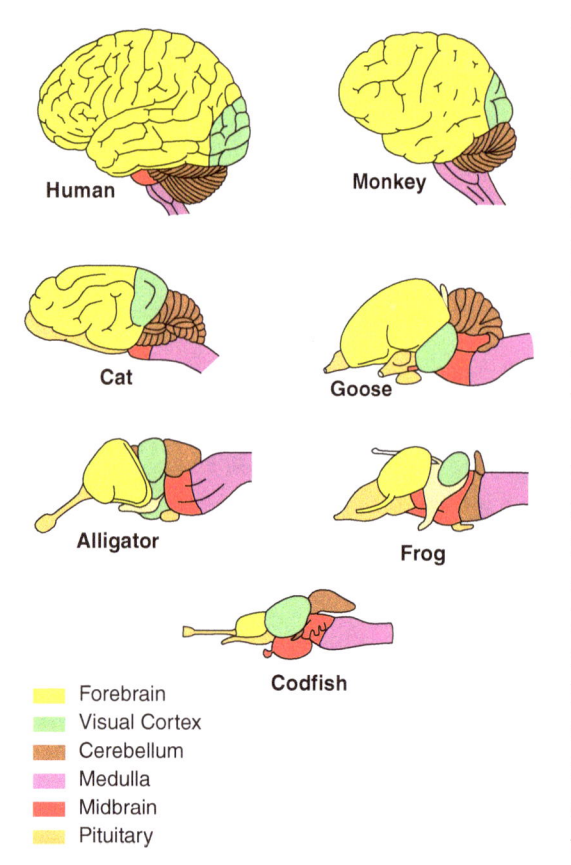

Figure 10.2 The evolving brain (not to scale). Basic similarities remain, but the amount of frontal cortex increases as we move 'up' the evolutionary scale. Different animals evolve to fit different environmental niches and the demands on their brains are consequently very different and they evolve to reflect that.

- Forebrain
- Visual Cortex
- Cerebellum
- Medulla
- Midbrain
- Pituitary

Popular psychology books often talk about the 'lizard brain' as that part of our brain that controls basic behaviour, the 'limbic brain' as controlling emotion, and the neocortex as controlling planning, thinking, language, and other higher behaviour, with self-help involving learning how to use the neocortex to control our more primeval urges. The inspiration for this work comes from a simplified view of evolution, and the work of MacLean (1990) on the triune brain. The triune brain has three parts. The reptilian complex contains the basal ganglia and similar deep-brain structures, and is involved in mating rituals, aggression, and territoriality. The *paleomammalian* complex comprises the **limbic system**, including the cingulate cortex, and is responsible for emotion. It arose early in mammalian evolution. The *neomammalian* cortex arose late in evolution in higher mammals, and comprises the outer cortex including the *occipital*, *parietal*, *temporal*, and *frontal* lobes. The *frontal* lobes are particularly developed in higher primates, especially the prefrontal cortex, particularly humans. More recent research in comparative neuroanatomy shows that the situation is much more complicated than the triune brain suggests: for example, reptiles engage in more than ritual behaviour, as we have seen birds can be remarkably intelligent, and a form of the neocortex appeared very early in mammalian development.

It is difficult to draw anything other than very general and speculative conclusions from comparative neuroanatomy. It seems likely that in primates the prefrontal cortex is associated with self-awareness. Consciousness in the sense of awareness is likely to be present to some degree in all mammals. But we cannot exclude the possibility that other brain structures are involved in other animals, and therefore that some non-mammal animals (particularly birds) possess some degree of awareness.

The Development of Consciousness

Most people believe that a newborn infant is not as conscious as an older children. The research on the development of consciousness is even more speculative than most consciousness research, and largely depends on generalisations from the development of neural pathways hypothesised to be associated with consciousness in adulthood. For example, minimal consciousness is thought to develop during the third trimester of prenatal development, about 24–30 weeks, as neural fibres linking the thalamus to the sensory cortex develop. At around this time, the foetus displays EEG patterns characteristic of sleep and dreaming, with the proportion of REM increasing with time (Okai et al., 1992). Around this time, the foetus responds to external stimuli (for example, the heart rate increase in response to sudden sound), and even makes facial expressions associated with external stimuli. These findings should not necessarily be interpreted as demonstrating the presence of waking consciousness as they are all consistent with responses generated by unconscious reflexes (Lagercrantz & Changeux, 2009). This issue is particularly important because of the discussion of whether a foetus can feel pain, with the consensus being not before 24 weeks, while some researchers argue for slightly earlier. The **thalamo-cortical** connections necessary to feel pain are not developed until that time (Lee et al., 2005).

Although the newborn infant appears to be awake, it is likely that their consciousness is very different from that of adults, probably more akin to many animals, because they have no

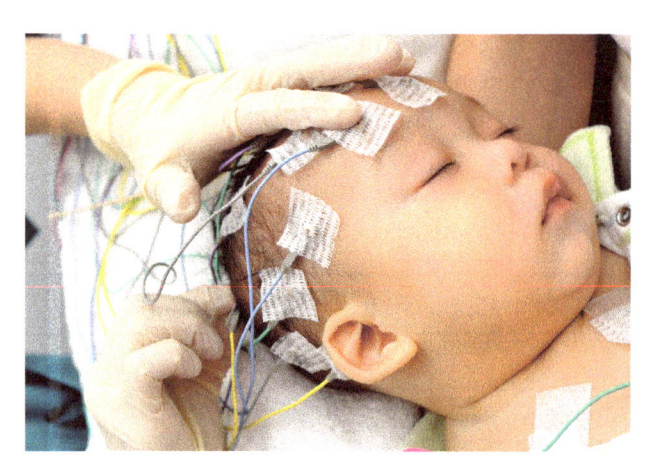

Figure 10.3 An infant being tested with EEG. The principles of testing an infant with using EEG are similar to testing adults. Source: dblight/E+/Getty Images.

language, poor perceptual abilities, and their brains are still very different from adult brains. Kouider et al. (2013) examined the EEG of infants of different ages when they viewed pictures of adults (see Figure 10.3). Even 5-month-old infants showed the same characteristic late slow wave as adults, but it was weaker and earlier than that of 12-month-olds. So indications of conscious visual perception are present early, but the mechanisms associated with them continue to develop. A great deal of brain maturation occurs in the first 12–18 months, with language starting to emerge towards the end of this period. The development of language is likely to be of great importance to the development of consciousness, aiding metacognition and the explicit manipulation of a self symbol labelled 'I' and 'me'.

Higher-order theories of consciousness emphasise the importance of being able to represent representations (Rosenthal, 2006). You need to have beliefs about your own mental states and a subjective perspective on an independent reality. Given young children do not have these, self-consciousness does not develop until relatively late, perhaps as late as age four.

Our ability to analyse our own consciousness continues to develop as our metacognitive skills develop (Piaget, 1990). It is likely that childhood amnesia is related to these structural and corresponding cognitive and metacognitive changes; perhaps we can't remember 'our' experiences if we have no proper 'I' to have them in the first place. It is possible to tell a coherent story here, although much remains speculative.

Incomplete Brains

Unfortunately, occasionally children are born with devastating brain damage. *Anencephaly* is a disorder of the embryonic development of the neural tube, the structure that turns into the spinal column and brain, such that much of the brain and skull fails to develop at all. In particular, anencephalic children are born without most of the **cerebrum** (cortex, hippocampus, **olfactory bulb**, and basal ganglia); some children may be born with only a brainstem. Many of these children usually do not live long, but they are of interest here for what they can do – which is very limited. *Hydranencephaly* is a neural tube defect where upper brain structures fail to develop, being replaced with cerebrospinal fluid (CSF), sometimes due to the pressure of the CSF. (The causes of these disorders are complex, several, and unclear.) Some patients can live surprisingly long, the oldest patients being 35 (Aleman & Merker, 2014). Damasio supports his theory of protoconsciousness with hydranencephaly. He argues that these children have a kind of proto-sentience somewhat similar to normal newborns, although they are never able to move beyond that cognitive stage. Yet they appear to enjoy sensations, music, have favourite caregivers, and generally have a sort of primal existence.

Hydrocephalus is the condition commonly known as 'water on the brain', and is defined by an accumulation of CSF, the clear fluid that protects and bathes the brain and spinal column, in and around the brain (see Figure 10.4). Although it can occur at any age, it can have severe consequences when it is a developmental disorder. It is not uncommon, affecting more than 1 in 1000 births, and now can be fairly easily treated by the surgical implant of a shunt to relieve the fluid pressure. If not treated, however, it can have dramatic and severe consequences, with the pressure of the fluid filling and enlarging the ventricles of the brain, and pushing brain matter to the edges. The skull may become enlarged *macrocephaly* and distorted.

There are two main issues here. The first is the role of the cortex in consciousness. The second is the range of behaviours that can be achieved with limited brain matter.

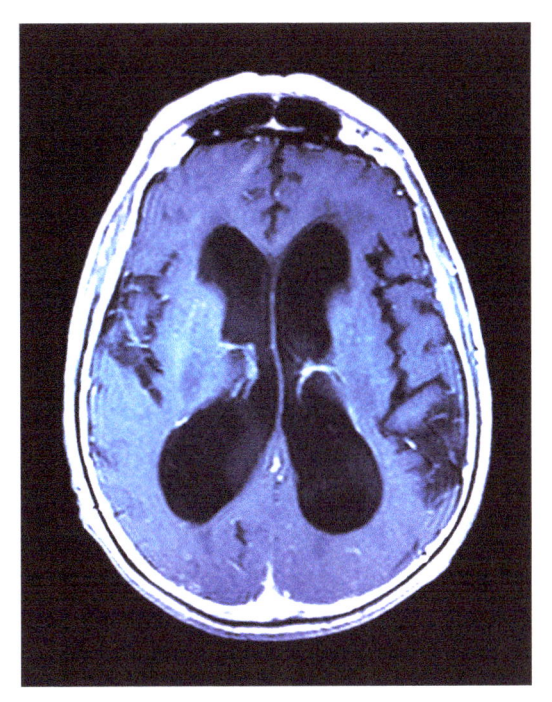

Figure 10.4 Hydrocephaly scan. In hydrocephalus, cerebrospinal fluid accumulates in the brain and causes pressure. In infants and children, if not treated early enough, it can distort the shape of the skull. The pressure can also distort the shape of the brain. Note that the brain may be compressed and not necessarily smaller. Source: Living Art Enterprises, LLC/Science Photo Library.

General Anaesthesia

One obvious way of finding neural correlates of consciousness is to compare brain activity when we're conscious with when we're unconscious. Given that we are not reliably unconscious in sleep (see Chapter 12), a suitable candidate to study is when a person is anaesthetised.

There are several types of anaesthetics. Many people are unfortunately familiar with the local injection that is used to reduce pain when dental work is being carried out. Here, though, we are concerned with general anaesthetics, which are interesting from our point of view because they appear to knock out consciousness. How do they do this? Is consciousness like a switch that can be turned on and off, and if so how does it operate? A general anaesthetic induces a state with an absence of consciousness, like dreamless sleep, with the obvious difference that when asleep a knife slicing open our stomach would very quickly wake us. Hence, although the friendly anaesthetist might say, 'I'm putting you to sleep', that clearly isn't what happens.

Unsurprisingly, there was considerable effort spent on finding anaesthetics; along with analgesics and antiseptics that make modern surgery possible. The pain of operations and amputations without a general anaesthetic is unimaginable. Early attempts to sedate involved drugs such as opium and alcohol, but the first recorded successful public use of an anaesthetic for surgery was dental extraction under the influence of inhaling nitrous oxide (laughing gas) by Horace Wells in New York in 1844 (and possibly earlier). Unfortunately, nitrous oxide alone is unreliable at inducing general anaesthesia, and there were cases of people waking and crying out in pain in the middle of the operation. James Young Simpson used inhalation of chloroform for an operation in Edinburgh in 1847, and chloroform was widely used until its toxic effects on the heart and liver were apparent. The principles of anaesthesia were now though clearly established, and there was rapid progress in improving drugs and technique. In particular, intravenous administration is now preferred in adults because it is possible to be very precise about the dose. The first intravenous anaesthetic was sodium thiopental (1934), and now several reliable ones are available, among which *propofol* is one of the most popular.

Note that general anaesthetics do have risks associated with them, including death (they may be used in execution by lethal injection, and the anaesthetic propofol was a constituent of the cocktail of drugs responsible for the death of Michael Jackson in 2009), which is why it is so difficult to get a general anaesthetic at the dentist these days.

Box 10.3 The History of Anaesthetics

For much of history, operations and amputations were relieved by a slug of brandy and the hope of passing out from what was called 'the terror that surpasses all description'. There is historical evidence of plant preparations being used – some Sumerian artefacts from 4000 BCE depict the opium poppy. A little later, there is evidence that surgeons in India used cannabis vapours around 600 BCE and, a little later still, Assyrians used compression of the carotid artery to interfere with blood flow to the brain and produce temporary unconsciousness. In 1525, the Swiss physician and astrologer Paracelsus (with the splendid full name Philippus Aureolus Theophrastus Bombastus von Hohenheim, c. 1439–1541) observed that ether put animals to 'sleep'. Ether (ethyl ether) is an organic compound with a distinctive structure. The British chemist Humphry Davy (1778–1829) observed the anaesthetic effect of the gas nitrous oxide ('laughing gas'). Soon after, there was a craze for ether frolics, playing with ether or nitrous oxide to produce mind-altering effects for entertainment.

The first substantiated accounts of using a general anaesthetic to produce unconsciousness during surgery was by the American dentist William T. Morton (1819–1868), who used ether to anaesthetise a patient while a tumour was removed from the neck of the patient in a public demonstration at Massachusetts General Hospital on 16 October 1846. News of the success of the surgery spread quickly. However, anaesthesia with ether was not without risk, and gradually chloroform, first used by the Scottish obstetrician James Young Simpson (1811–1870), replaced ether as the preferred anaesthetic. The use of anaesthetics in surgery was popularised when Queen Victoria received chloroform in 1853 for the birth of her eighth child, Prince Leopold. These anaesthetics were used as gases, but in 1934 the first intravenous anaesthetic, sodium thiopental, was synthesised. Since then, several others have been discovered. The technology of accurate delivery has clearly transformed medicine.

Remember to distinguish anaesthesia, the loss of feeling, from analgesia, the relief specifically of pain. The distinction is a little blurred with local anaesthetics and topical analgesics. General anaesthetics render a person unconscious.

How Do General Anaesthetics Work?

Originally, medics thought that anaesthetics had a simple effect on a single locus (such as the lipid membrane of neurons). Unfortunately, there is no single effect with response to pain and consciousness being decoupled: decerebrate rats (rats whose cerebrums have been disconnected) need exactly the same dose of anaesthetic to prevent a movement response to a painful stimulus as a cerebrate rat, suggesting that the prevention of a motor response (which operates at the spinal-cord level) is independent of the perception of pain (which operates at the level of the brain; Rampil, 1994). We now know that anaesthetics must act in a more complex way than simply activating a 'consciousness off' switch.

Anaesthetics switch off consciousness very quickly, regardless of our will – you can't will yourself to stay conscious after an anaesthetic has been administered to you. At first sight then, understanding their mechanism of action should be very useful for understanding the biological basis of consciousness. Unfortunately, things are never simple with consciousness, and there are a number of problems. The first problem is that we have a very poor understanding of how anaesthetics work. The second problem is that drugs are used in combination and so isolating the effects of one is difficult. Third, suppose anaesthetics work like a switch. What happens if you switch off your television set at the electricity mains? The picture goes out immediately. Yet very little of the apparatus responsible for generating the picture is present in the power switch, and if we were somehow scanning the electronic workings of the television, we would see that electrical activity was changed across the set.

With those caveats in mind, we do know a little about the biological effects of anaesthetics. Propofol does several things, mainly involving binding to receptors of the inhibitory neurotransmitter GABA, and thereby making GABA more available. It also stimulates a system known as the **endocannabinoid system**, a biological system sensitive to chemicals related to cannabis. Perhaps together, these neurotransmitter effects reduce the brain's electrical activity, particularly in the gamma band, implying that the brain's ability to integrate information is reduced (Kotani et al., 2008; Lee et al., 2009). We know something about how EEG changes as patients become unresponsive: loss of consciousness is marked by an increase in low-frequency EEG power (under 1 Hz), the loss of coherent occipital alpha oscillations (8–12 Hz) in the occipital lobe, and the appearance of frontal alpha oscillations (Pardon et al., 2013). Frontal alpha and very low-frequency oscillations are also observed in some **coma** states.

This type of research is in its early stages and much is still unknown about the mechanisms involved and what they mean. An attempt to interpret the findings has been made by the American neurosurgeon George Mashour. Mashour (2013, 2014) argues that consciousness is marked by the presence of perceptual binding; if we see and hear a dog barking, we recognise them as belonging to the same object, that the dog is black and there isn't just a patch of blackness moving around independently of the shape. Unconsciousness is marked, he says, by cognitive unbinding; stimuli don't get integrated and make it to consciousness. We will return to binding later, but for now note that consciousness is marked by a pattern of electrical and presumably therefore chemical activity that marks coherence, binding, and integration of incoming stimuli. Mashour and Hudetz (2018) point out that as general anaesthetics do not have an effect on the sensory pathways, but do on the parietal-frontal and top-down networks, sensory processing in itself is not sufficient for consciousness (Crick &

Koch, 1995). What are important are the feedback loops, and general anaesthetics interfere with these. Tagliazucchi et al. (2016a) show that propofol reduces connectivity in the brain, particularly activation in long-range connections.

Ching et al. (2010) provide a computational model showing how propofol might act via **GABA** by reducing the strength of thalamo-cortical loops to produce this abnormal alpha activity, which in turn reduces the cortical input to the thalamus. These models point either to the role of the thalamus as an 'on–off' switch or limiting its efficiency at allowing signals up to the cortex; in either case, the thalamus plays a central role in general anaesthesia and therefore consciousness.

In summary, we now know that anaesthetics cause loss of top-down information in the thalamo-cortical loop resulting in a failure to be able to integrate sensory information.

Post-operative Recall

Although in most cases the right dose of anaesthetic will induce complete unconsciousness, about one in five patients do afterwards report having had dreams (Miller et al., 2014).

One of many people's worst fears is being aware under general anaesthesia but because of the paralysis unable to do anything about it, a phenomenon called *post-operative recall*. Reports after operations of such cases are very rare (about 0.2%; Sebel et al., 2004). Without wishing to stoke people's fears, there might be a much higher incidence of awareness under anaesthesia than post-operative reports suggest. The isolated forearm technique involves inflating a cuff around the forearm before the drugs are injected so that the hand can move when the rest of the body is paralysed. People are asked to squeeze their fingers if they are awake. Russell and Wang (2001) detected movements in 7 out of 40 participants. People are right to fear it: people who undergo the experience report that it is one of the most horrific and traumatic experiences imaginable. More worryingly, some people report having awareness of the operation while anaesthetised, and even feeling the pain, but unable to communicate this awareness because they are completely paralysed. There are two variants of this state, awareness without later recall (as the amnesic effects of the drugs still work), and awareness with later recall (Crick & Ghoneim, 2001); it is possible that the incidence of the first category is underestimated because the patient has to convey signs of awareness somehow, which is very difficult if they are still effectively paralysed. Surgeons may now monitor awareness through such means as EEG; as you might object, having read this book, whether such means are wholly effective is highly debatable.

> **TRY THIS: Consciousness Scales**
>
> The Bispectral Index Scale is a scale developed for use in anaesthesia, and is shown on a special monitor during surgery. The scale gives a number, ranging from 0 (equivalent to EEG silence) to 100; the desirable value for surgery is between 40 and 60 – any higher and there is a risk of some awareness during surgery. As a student of consciousness studies, what do you think of such a scale? What would you expect a score of 100 to correspond to? What number would you give your consciousness now?

> **TRY THIS: Forget the Pain**
>
> I once was given a very minor surgical procedure. Beforehand, the specialist gave me this helpful explanation of how the drug worked: 'This drug doesn't stop the pain; it just stops you remembering it. It might hurt at the time, but you won't remember a thing when you come round.'
>
> Would you be apprehensive if offered that type of drug?

> **TRY THIS: Imagining a Painful Operation**
>
> Here is a thought experiment. You are told that you have to have an operation that will be extremely painful. Fortunately, the surgeon will be able to give you an injection that will make you forget all the pain and everything about the operation. The surgeon tells you that it will be done Wednesday or Thursday evening, and when you wake up you will be completely normal. On Thursday night, though, the surgeon leaves the paperwork beside your bed and you can look to see whether or not you had the operation the night before. Do you care? Most people prefer the outcome where they've already had the operation. Given you will remember nothing, is this preference rational?

The Thalamus and Thalamo-cortical System

The thalamo-cortical system is a set of neural pathways that connect the thalamus, to the cortex, and back again. The thalamus is a relatively large structure near the centre of the brain that acts as a relay between subcortical and cortical regions, in effect 'deciding' what gets through from these lower regions of the brain to the higher. The thalamus also plays an important role in regulating attention and arousal. We have seen that researchers believe that it plays an essential role in consciousness, by generating 40 Hz gamma waves that synchronise inputs from other parts of the brain. In particular, this loop may bind different percepts together to provide a unified percept. Early models of anaesthetics proposed that they worked by 'switching off' the thalamus, by changing the pattern of its electrical activity, but we now know that their effects are much more complex.

Almost all anaesthetics (as well as sleep) reduce electrical activity in the thalamus, suggesting that some minimum level of activity is necessary to maintain consciousness. Results of damage to the thalamus (by reduced blood supply in a stroke) confirm that it has an important role in consciousness. First, patients with thalamic lesions often suffer from chronic pain (called thalamic pain syndrome). Second, damage can affect arousal and attention (Srivastava et al., 2013) and sleep, particularly causing insomnia (Tinuper et al., 1989). Imaging and lesion studies also suggest that central portions of the thalamus are involved in mediating arousal and attention (Portas et al., 1998; Schiff, 2008). Some researchers argue that comparatively small (1 cubic centimetre) bilateral lesions of the thalamus (particularly central and dorsal portions known as the **thalamic intralaminar nuclei**, which are connected to the ascending reticular system) can completely knock out all awareness (Bogen 1995a, b; Edelman et al., 2011). In a similar vein, some argue that conscious awareness arises from synchronised activity in the thalamus, even going so far as to specify the dorsal thalamic nuclei, called the *thalamic dynamic core* (Ward, 2011). Ward argues that, while the cortex computes the contents of consciousness, the thalamus displays them, and thus 'experiences the results of those computations'. A similar proposal has been made by Tononi and Edelman (1998, 2000), who proposed that the large, brain-wide population of synchronously firing cortical neurons that are associated with conscious awareness of a stimulus forms a dynamic core of neural activity. However, the dissociative drug ketamine increases global levels of metabolism at the doses at which it causes loss of consciousness, so the explanation must be a bit more complicated. It's possible ketamine simply scrambles the signals in the thalamo-cortical circuits rather than just reducing them.

Are NCC Frontal or Posterior?

However, many believe that the thalamus plays an enabling role in consciousness, and does not generate the content, which is the role of the cortex. It is the difference between the power supply to the television and the parts that generate the picture. In general, the anatomical neural correlates of consciousness are mostly cortical. There has been disagreement about whether the anterior (front) or posterior (rear) regions of the cortex play larger roles. The balance of evidence of lesion studies and brain imaging of different tasks requiring different levels of access to consciousness suggest that phenomenal consciousness is associated with posterior regions of the brain including cortical sensory areas (Boly et al., 2017; Koch et al., 2016). The fronto-parietal network involved in task monitoring and reporting plays a less important role. For example, frontal lesions lead to subtle impairments of the executive self (see Chapter 7), while posterior lesions lead to profound alterations in consciousness (see Chapters 7 and 9).

Clearly, both frontal and posterior cortical regions have been thought to be important in generating consciousness. One resolution is that posterior regions are concerned with P-consciousness, while frontal areas are concerned with A-consciousness.

Re-entry and the Dynamic Core Hypothesis

Gerald Edelman (1929–2014) won the Nobel Prize for his work on the immune system. This work influenced his ideas on consciousness, which emphasise the importance of feedback connections in the thalamo-cortical system. He called this feedback system *re-entrant*. Edelman bases his ideas on natural selection and the development of the immune system, and pulls them together under the label of *Neural Darwinism* because patterns of neuronal activity are competing against each other, a process called *neuronal group selection*. Only one pattern can win: we can be conscious of only one thing.

Re-entry makes use of the circuits that are present in the thalamo-cortical loop: consciousness depends on long-range and massively parallel connections from one brain area to another, characterised by the bidirectional exchange of signals along reciprocal axonal fibres linking two or more brain areas (Edelman & Gally, 2013). These structures allow for widely distributed groups of neurons to achieve integrated and synchronised firing (Edelman & Tononi, 2000). Each separate area functions to process a distinctive feature of the overall conscious scene, and synchronous firing binds these features together (Engel & Singer, 2001). Clearly, the thalamus plays a central role in maintaining awareness, but it is not the same as saying it is the seat of consciousness. We see again, though, the importance of circuits in the brain, particularly involving the cortex and thalamus, and that it is particularly important that these circuits have feedback connections. Feedback in the brain clearly plays a vital role.

The **dynamic core** and **global workspace models (GWM)** share a great deal (Edelman et al., 2011). The dynamic core hypothesis (DCH) proposes that conscious experience arises from re-entrant neural activity in the thalamo-cortical system, while global workspace shows how the limited capacity of momentary conscious content interacts with the huge capacity of long-term memory. This shifting assembly of spiking neurons throughout the forebrain becomes synchronised using the re-entrant feedback connections to form the dynamic core. The global–neuronal workspace model and DCH are two of the most promising lines of consciousness research. They differ in other key respects: DCH argues that the NCC begin relatively early, while GWM argues that they begin relatively late. The DCH proposes that the NCC involve fairly localised thalamo-cortical re-entry loops, particularly in sensory areas, while GWM favours widespread cortical connections, particularly in frontal and parietal regions. GWM favours simple content to consciousness, while DCH proposes that the content of consciousness can be richer. Pitts et al. (2018) argue that these differences can be reconciled. Although details remain to be clarified, they argue that key insights will follow when we have fully explicated the relation between attention and consciousness.

The Claustrum

Another region that has received considerable interest in recent consciousness research is the **claustrum**. The claustrum is a sheet of neurons that lies beneath the inner surface of the cortex near the insula, near the centre of the brain (see Figure 10.5). Although small, it is important in that it receives input from most regions of the cortex and projects back to most regions of the cortex, as well as to the amygdala, caudate nucleus, and hippocampus (Crick & Koch, 2005). It is important because we have seen that the need to rapidly integrate and bind information in neurons that are situated across distinct cortical and *thalamic* regions is vital for consciousness. Crick and Koch (2005) argue that the claustrum appears to be in an ideal position to integrate the most diverse kinds of information that underlie conscious perception, cognition, and action. They propose that it is the plausible location of something that acts like the conductor of a Cartesian theatre in that different attributes of objects, both within (such as colour and motion) and across modalities (such as visual form and sound location), are rapidly combined and bound in the claustrum. They also compare the claustrum to the conductor of an orchestra, referring to its regulatory role in consciousness and cognition.

Figure 10.5 The location of the claustrum. The claustrum is a thin sheet of neurons lying beneath the cortex. It acts as another important neural hub, more important in terms of mixing different sorts of information than the thalamus. The thalamus is the large lower central mass. Source: (b) Copyright © 2014 Gattass, Soares, Desimone, & Ungerleider.

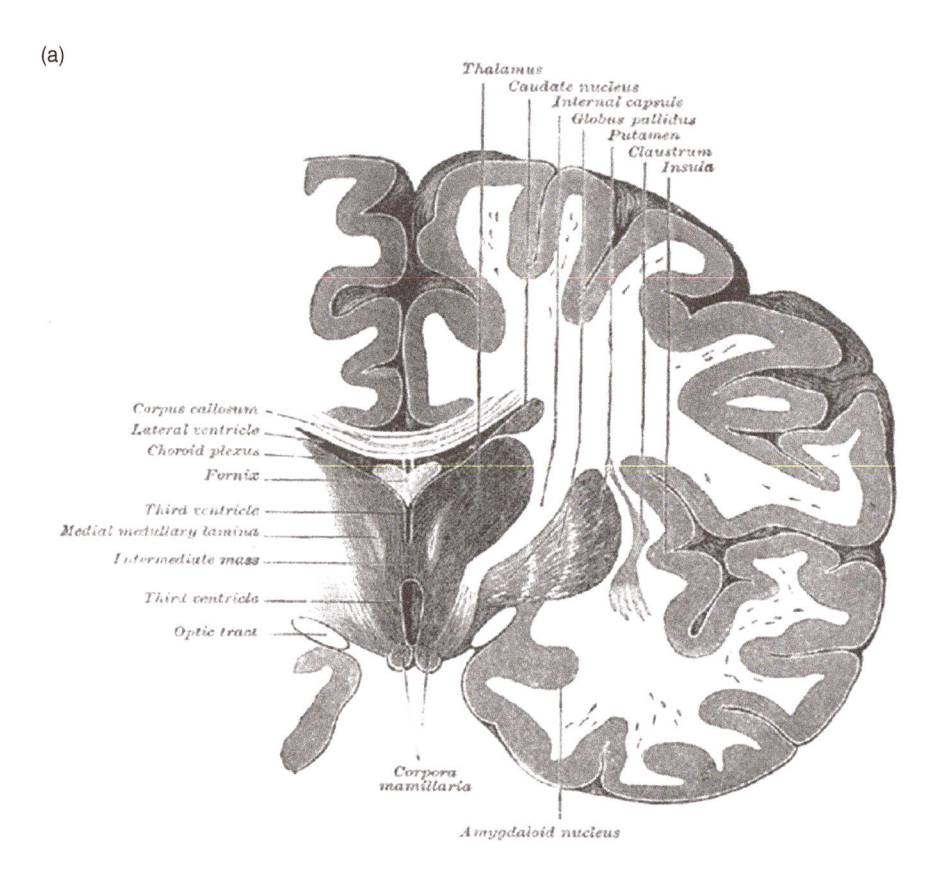

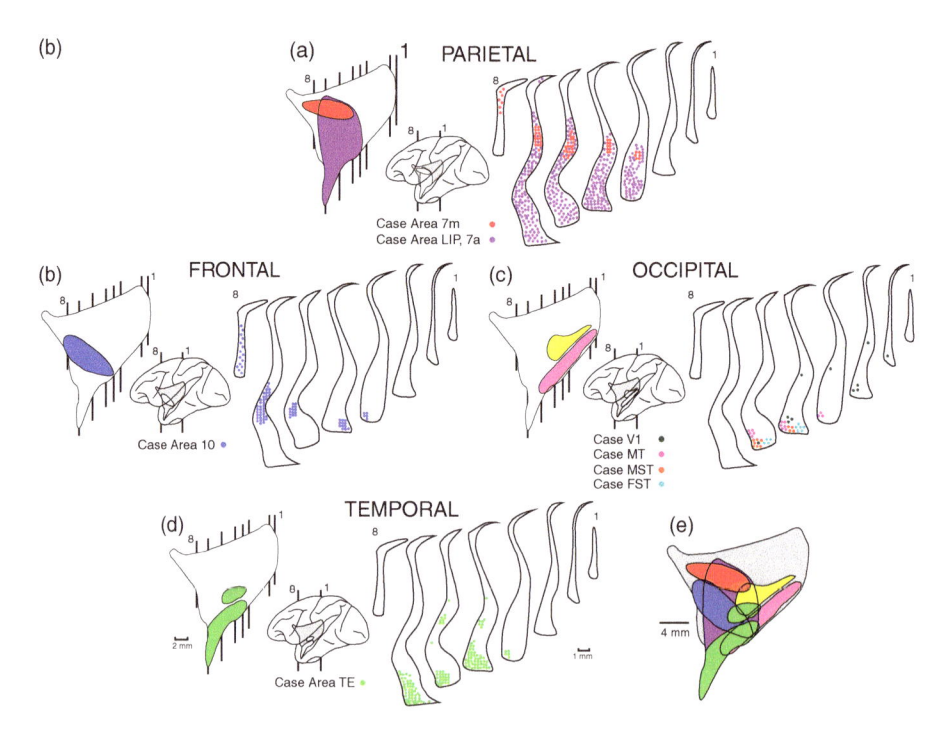

This postulated intra-claustrum mixing of information differentiates it from the thalamus, which also has widespread and reciprocal relations with most cortical regions, but which does not possess any obvious mechanism to link its various constitutive nuclei.

Patru and Reser (2015) argue that the claustrum is involved in delusional states. It is involved in interpreting sensory information and carrying out 'reality testing'. Dysfunction in the claustrum results primarily in disruption of higher behavioural and cognitive functions, rather than a specific, unitary deficit. On the other hand, Patru and Reser point out that removal of the claustrum when necessitated for tumour treatment, with all its associated problems, did not cause any simple cognitive or perceptual deficit. However, these operations were **unilateral**.

Recent research on mice suggests that as few as three very large neurons project from the claustrum and effectively connect the whole brain; one neuron alone covers the whole cortex (Bray, 2018; Reardon, 2017). This research, based on work by Christoph Koch, needs to be evaluated in more detail in time, but it shows the importance of large-scale connectivity, and the role that structures such as the claustrum and thalamus have as hubs. These structures clearly play a central role in consciousness.

The Role of Anterior Cingulate

One region of the brain that has received a great deal of interest is the anterior cingulate cortex (ACC, or just anterior cingulate; see Figure 10.6). This structure is another hub responsible for relaying information from different areas of the brain. It is the front part of the cingulate cortex, part of the limbic system, surrounding the corpus callosum, the bundle of fibres that connects the two cortical hemispheres, and connects the limbic system, thalamus, and cortex. The functions involved link motivation to carry out tasks, emotion, and learning. The ACC is involved in reward-based learning, particularly in detecting errors, where there is a mismatch between prediction and occurrence (Bush et al., 2002). Crick (1995) argued that the ACC plays an important role in awareness and free will – indeed, he argued that it is the location of free will. Patients with damage to the ACC have disordered free will, such as alien hand syndrome (see Chapter 6). It is worth noting that the ACC is also involved in registering pain, and particularly emotional responses to pain. This finding makes sense if the ACC has some central role in consciousness (Price, 2000).

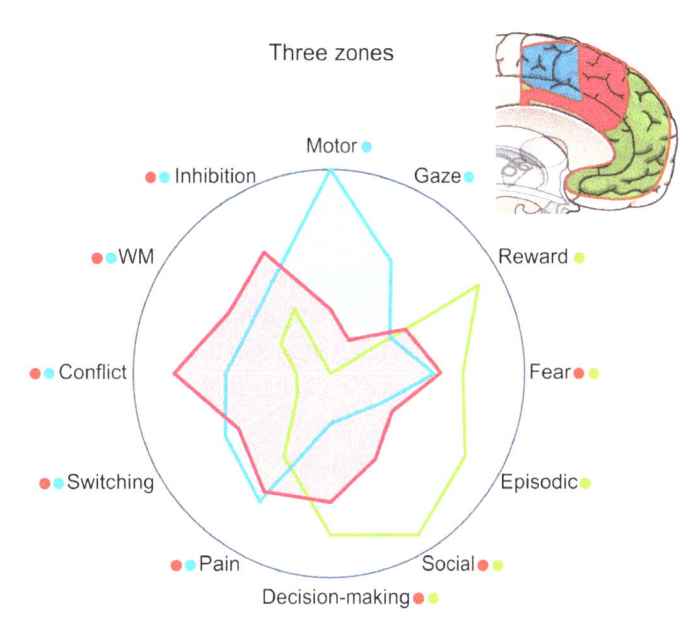

Figure 10.6 The location of the anterior cingulate. Yet another important hub thought to play an essential role in maintaining consciousness, and that plays an important role in free will – whatever 'free will' means.

Integrated Information Theory

Tononi and Koch (2015) argued that we can best start to understand consciousness by thinking about the essential properties of consciousness, and then ask what kinds of physical mechanisms could support them. They conclude that **integrated information theory** (**IIT**; Tononi, 2008, 2012; Hoel et al., 2013; Tononi & Edelman, 1998) best accounts for what is conscious and what is not. *High integrated information* means that the system cannot be subdivided into two independent systems – the future state of system A depends on the current state of system B and conversely.

Tononi and Koch note that consciousness has the following properties: it exists, it is structured (we can distinguish a book, the colour red, and a red book), it is specific (any particular experience is comprised of a particular set of features), it is integrated (we don't perceive the left side of the visual scene from the right, even though they come from different visual pathways), and certain things are excluded from consciousness (I might be perceiving a red book, but I do not directly perceive my blood pressure as I do so).

IIT introduces a new notion of information called *integrated information*, which can be measured as 'differences that make a difference' to a system from its intrinsic perspective, not relative to an observer. Tononi argues that a novel notion of information is necessary for quantifying and characterising consciousness as it is generated by brains and other things (Tononi et al., 2016). IIT specifies a set of postulates that any physical system must have to be able to explain these essential properties of experience. On this account, qualia are conceptual structures that are maximally irreducible intrinsically. Information becomes integrated in the thalamo-cortical system, which is ideally suited as the physical seat of this integration because it contains a large number of discrete but richly interconnected elements.

One consequence of this approach is panpsychism, so even simple electronic devices that process information may not be completely unconscious. Animals are of course conscious, but so also is any kind of system, living or not, that has high 'integrated information' (named Φ or '**phi**'). Tononi presents a detailed mathematical explanation of phi, which is beyond the scope of this text. Unlike classical panpsychism, not all physical objects have a phi that is different from zero: only integrated systems do. So a brain does, but a group of disconnected neurons in a dish, or a galaxy of stars, do not.

Critics of IIT argue that conscious awareness is more than anything that can be concluded from accounts of information alone. There are also concerns about the measure phi and how it is computed. In addition, many do not like the conclusion about panpsychism, and the predictions that certain things are conscious that are generally thought not to be (Doerig et al., 2019). Maybe integrated information theory does not solve the hard problem, but then what does? It is undoubtedly a fascinating and coherent account that unifies a great deal of consciousness research.

Radical Plasticity

Cleeremans (2011) proposes that we are not born conscious, even though we have the necessary neural hardware. Although necessary, it is not sufficient, because our neural system has to learn to become conscious, an idea Cleeremans calls radical plasticity. Cleeremans too maintains that *prediction* plays a central role in processing. He suggests that not only does the brain have to learn to predict its effects on the world through feedback, and learn to predict the effects of the environment on ourselves, but it also has to learn about the consequences of neural activity in one region of the brain on other regions. In doing so, we eventually develop meta-representations – representations of lower-order representations and ourselves. Consciousness hence develops from learning, neural plasticity, and the development of metacognition. Cleeremans states that the conscious mind is the brain's implicit theory about itself. He also stresses the role of emotion in making us aware that some states are more important than others.

Radical plasticity combines ideas about prediction with some from neural and cognitive development, metacognition, and higher-order representational theory. This approach is consistent with others we have considered that make use of these ideas, but emphasises the role of learning, particularly a system learning about itself, and emotion, so that the system cares about what happens to it. Later work extends these ideas, exploring the roles of agency and embodiment (Caspar et al., 2015).

What Is Death?

Benjamin Franklin famously observed that there are only two certainties in life, death and taxes. Taxation is too complex for this book, so let's talk about death.

At first sight, this question might strike you as one of the most stupid of the many stupid questions in this book. *Death* is what happens when we die, of course!

In fact, death is in many cases far from clear cut. How do we define death? When the brain stops working? Death might be very clear in some cases of extreme trauma (e.g. when the body is almost destroyed in an explosion), but in most cases it isn't easy to say when the brain has stopped working (see Figure 10.7). The brain is a complex organ with many components and functions and components don't necessarily all stop at exactly the same time.

We have talked about the search for the neural correlates of consciousness (see Chapter 10). Such a search is relevant here because if we could reliably identify such a pattern we could be able to tell if people in borderline states do have any awareness. It would be particularly important with types of coma where the person appears to be unconscious, but their neural signature shows otherwise. It would not, however, be a reliable indicator of death because, as we shall see, there are states where a person is not conscious but we would not

Figure 10.7 Death is not always instantaneous, in the same way that a deciduous tree does not change immediately from its summer to winter appearance. Just because the heart has stopped beating doesn't mean the brain is yet dead. And loss of consciousness is not necessarily the same as brain death. The correspondences are unclear. Source: Lorna Wilson/Taxi/ Getty Images Plus.

want to terminate their life-support systems. And who would want to be declared dead when they are asleep? So, the issue of defining death is of practical importance as well as theoretically significant.

Death is presumably like nothing – rather like the deepest phase of your sleep. It is a core belief of many religions that there is some kind of afterlife, where we are resurrected in some form and presumably conscious again. Faith is beyond the scope of a book about science. Some people are attempting to bypass death by having their bodies cryogenically frozen so that they can be brought back to life at some point in the future when science has solved the problems. Some are even just freezing their heads, recognising that the brain is the important part, and that the problems concerning the rest of the body can be sorted out later.

After the body has rotted, or been cremated, or destroyed in some other way, and the brain destroyed, we are unarguably dead (religious beliefs aside). But is there a clear moment of death? What happens when someone 'dies peacefully in their sleep'? Is death really the all-or-none phenomenon that we first assume it is?

As far as we can tell, only humans have knowledge of death and its certainty. It's one thing that seems to set us apart from other animals. Is knowledge and fear of death the price of meta-awareness?

Death and loss of consciousness are not the same thing. People often lose consciousness (as measured by a lack of response to stimuli) before brain death, and it is possible that some form of consciousness might persist briefly after death according to some definition has occurred.

It is revealing to plot the level of consciousness (arousal or wakefulness) against the contents of consciousness (our awareness of our self and environment), as in Figure 10.8.

Figure 10.8 Awareness plotted against arousal. Plotting degree of arousal against degree of phenomenal consciousness gives a two-dimensional space in which varying states and disorders of consciousness can be located. Death corresponds to being permanently at the origin. Source: Ward (2011).

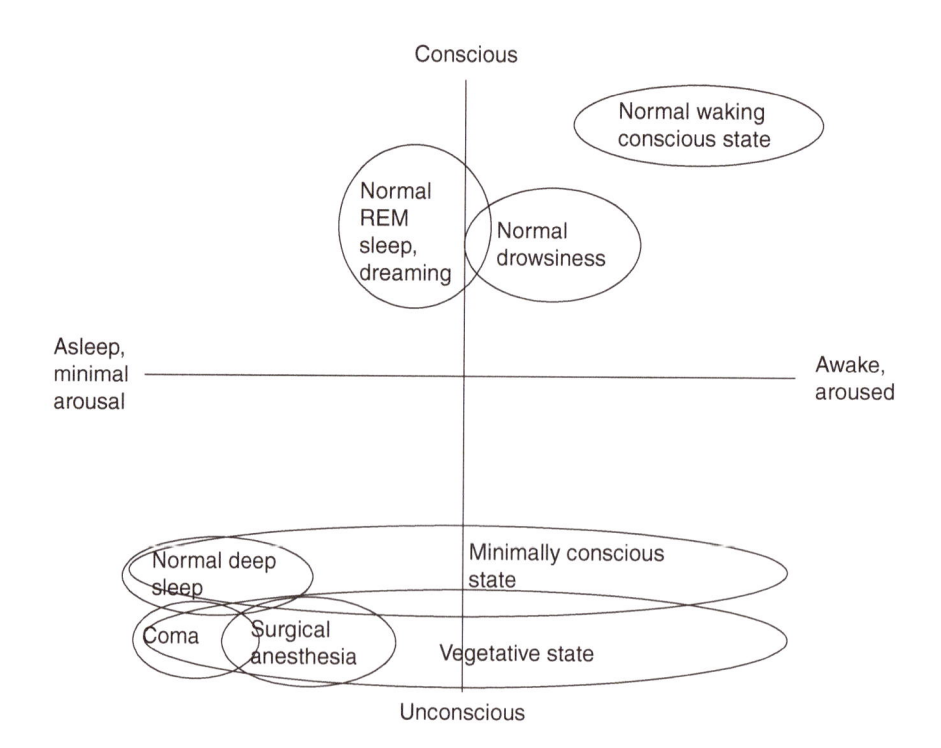

In the normal waking state, arousal and awareness are positively correlated. The more aroused we are, the more aware we are of our environment. Dreamless sleep is a region of low awareness and low arousal. Death corresponds to a permanent stay at the origin – no arousal and no awareness. Coma-like states and general anaesthesia are states of low arousal and very low awareness near the origin. The points of low awareness but high arousal are called vegetative states. Minimally conscious states are between vegetative states and normal wakefulness.

Death as Loss of Higher Functions

You might think death is one of the easiest of all things to define: it is when everything stops working. However, when we are dying, usually everything does not stop working at the same time, so what measure of cessation should be taken? In fact, things are sufficiently unclear for different countries to use different criteria.

There are two types of criteria: one is *cardiorespiratory failure*, when the heart stops beating and the person stops breathing, the other neurological. The problem with defining death as cardiorespiratory failure is that with modern medicine it is possible to 'resurrect' patients who have suffered failure for some time. We can also keep people on cardiorespiratory support almost indefinitely. The brain starts to die after 3–4 minutes of oxygen starvation. Hence, we now measure neurological death by the cessation of electrical activity in the brain. The problem here is that, in many cases, electrical activity does not stop across the whole brain at the same time. We cannot define death as the permanent and irreversible loss of consciousness. As we have seen, we have no universally agreed neural correlate of consciousness; and there are likely to be problems with universal acceptance of 'irreversible', too. It is clearly inadequate to take death to be the cessation of higher functions in the neocortex. Although this definition captures the importance of cognitive functioning for human life, it excludes patients who are in coma and vegetative states (Laureys, 2005).

Recent research has shown that it is possible to halt cell death in a large mammalian (pig) brain using a procedure combining surgery, perfusing the brain with chemicals, and *cryogenics*, maintaining the brain at a very low temperature (Vrselja et al., 2019). While this research is potentially of great practical importance, in the first instance treating stroke victims, there are no immediate implications for consciousness research. While the research shows that it is possible to extend brain cell life by several hours, it doesn't currently show that it is possible to sustain the pattern of electrical activity and brain function necessary for awareness.

Disorders of Consciousness

Frith (2019) distinguishes level of consciousness (whether we are awake or asleep or in a coma, and how aroused we are) from the specific contents of conscious experience, from metaconsciousness, our ability to reflect on our subjective experiences. In this section, we look at level of consciousness. There are several related neurological conditions that are called consciousness disorders because lack or apparent lack of consciousness is the most apparent symptom. In all disorders of consciousness, the brain's metabolic activity is reduced; consciousness cannot be sustained when the brain's metabolic activity falls below 40%, and the depth of coma is correlated with the level of metabolic reduction.

Coma and Coma-like States

A coma is often described as a state between life and death. Coma occurs in the immediate aftermath of a severe acute brain injury, although it can be induced by anaesthetics to aid recovery. In a coma, a person is unconscious and cannot be wakened. They show no signs of arousal in that there is no response to stimuli such as spoken commands, light, or pain, and show no sign of a sleep–wakefulness cycle. Coma-like states are of particular interest for the student of consciousness studies because they are at the margin of normal consciousness, and might reveal something about the neural correlates of consciousness. In a coma (at first sight at least), the brain is keeping us alive, but we are not conscious. Coma-like states and general anaesthesia are states of low arousal and very low awareness near the origin. The points of low awareness but high arousal are called vegetative states.

As the individual starts to recover from the brain injury, the coma resolves into one of a number of other states: persistent vegetative state; chronic coma (which is very rare); minimally conscious states; normal consciousness.

These states can be mapped in a 2D space with axes of degree of arousal and degree of awareness.

Persistent vegetative state (PVS) is a disorder of consciousness in which patients with severe brain damage are in a state of partial arousal rather than true awareness. After four weeks in a vegetative state, the patient is classified as in a PVS. This diagnosis is classified as a permanent vegetative state some months (three months in the United States and six months in the UK) after a non-traumatic brain injury or one year after a traumatic injury. Nowadays, some doctors and neuroscientists prefer to call the state of consciousness an *unresponsive wakefulness syndrome*, primarily for ethical questions about the word 'vegetative'.

PVS patients fall in a range of different levels of consciousness. Some level of consciousness means a person can still respond to some stimulation. PVS patients may open their eyes in response to feeding, whereas patients in a coma subsist with their eyes closed (Emmett, 1989). Individuals in PVS are seldom on any life-sustaining equipment other than a feeding tube because the brainstem (which of course governs heart rate and rhythm, respiration, and gastrointestinal activity) is relatively intact (Emmett, 1989). In a vegetative state patients may open their eyes, and make involuntary movements. There is no real awareness and no sleep–wake cycle. A person might gradually recover from a vegetative state, or they might stay in it for several months, PVS, for which the prognosis is very poor. The chances of recovery depend on the extent of injury to the brain and the patient's age – younger patients having a better chance of recovery than older patients (Jennett, 2002). Misdiagnosis of PVS is not uncommon.

Whether or not there is conscious awareness in a vegetative state is a prominent issue. Three completely different aspects of this issue should be distinguished. First, some patients can be conscious simply because they are misdiagnosed and are in fact not in a vegetative state. Second, a patient may be examined during the beginning recovery.

A **minimally conscious state (MCS)** is between a vegetative state and normal wakefulness. There is some awareness – much more than vegetative states – but not persistently so, and the person will be unable to communicate reliably. Unlike PVS, patients with MCS have partial preservation of conscious awareness. They will show some evidence of consciousness of the self and environment. They might be able to verbalise or gesture yes and no, make purposeful movements, smile or cry appropriately in response to linguistic or visual emotional stimuli, make appropriate eye movements, or follow simple commands. Responses may be inconsistent. The MCS was only formally accepted into medical use as late as 2002, and the prognosis is usually much better than for PVS (Giacino et al., 2002). MRI imaging shows that patients in MCS demonstrated some evidence of preserved speech processing, with there being more activation in response to sentences compared to white noise (Coleman et al., 2007). One of the more common diagnostic errors involving disorders of consciousness is mistaking MCS for a vegetative state, which can lead to serious consequences for medical management.

These disorders of consciousness show that there is a range of states governed by arousal and awareness. Furthermore, in general there is activity across all or parts of the brain, rather than disorders being linked to very specific brain locations.

Definitions of Death

Total brain death, permanent cessation of all electrical activity in all of the brain, is a sufficient but not necessary criterion for death (Sarbey, 2016) in that many regard such a definition as too stringent. It is, however, the baseline definition in the United States, and is one of the two ways of determination of death, according to the Uniform Determination of Death Act of the United States (the other way of determining death being 'irreversible cessation of circulatory and respiratory functions'). It differs from PVS, in which some autonomic functions remain. So, in the United States, death is defined as necessitating brainstem death. Individual states may have their own definitions, with New Jersey ruling that individuals can prevent official declaration of death defined on neurological grounds alone, so that brain-dead individuals on life-support machines can be declared still alive. A similar picture applies in the UK, where the definition is just as confused. In the UK, the Royal College of Physicians, in 1995, proposed that death is defined as the irreversible loss of brainstem function alone.

Some regard death as the permanent loss of higher functions, permanent cortical death because it 'is the irreversible loss of that which is essentially significant to the nature of man' (Veatch, 1975). However, such a definition is in conflict with those that say that death involves brainstem death.

Locked-in Syndrome

Locked-in syndrome (LIS) is a state where a person cannot move, but is fully conscious. They are awake but unable to move any muscle, although some people can communicate by eye movements. The French writer and journalist Jean-Dominique Bauby (1952–1997) suffered a major stroke at the age of 43, after which he could only move his left eyelid. Using partner-assisted scanning, when a partner shows the person letters one-by-one with the person blinking at the right letter, Bauby mentally composed and then dictated letter-by-letter the book *The Diving Bell and the Butterfly* (1997), later made into a film (Schnabel, 2007), describing his life before and after the stroke. He died unexpectedly two days after the book was published.

In total or **complete locked-in syndrome (CLIS)** the eyes are paralysed too. In LIS, EEG is normal. LIS shows us what it is like to be conscious in the almost complete absence of motor output. LIS patients can live, with support, for several decades, their quality of life now being greatly enhanced by means of computer-assisted communication. Four patients with *amyotrophic lateral sclerosis* (ALS, also known as Lou Gehrig's disease or motor neurone disease, the condition affecting the physicist Stephen Hawking, and which for unknown reasons leads to the death of neurons controlling voluntary action) with CLIS were able to learn to generate 'yes' and 'no' answers using a brain–computer interface using a technique called functional near infrared spectroscopy (fNIRS). This technique measures oxygen levels in the cortex and hence neuronal activity (Chaudhary et al., 2017).

LIS is caused by a number of disorders, including motor neurone disease and catastrophic strokes, which leave the brainstem damaged but upper brain intact. Some snake bites (such as that of the southeastern krait) and curare (an alkaloid plant extract) can cause temporary muscle paralysis mimicking LIS.

Can We Escape Death?

Is it possible to escape death and exist for ever? If you are religious and believe in a soul and some kind of afterlife, such as resurrection or reincarnation, you will believe that we can.

Unfortunately, nothing in science leads us to expect (let alone hope for) an afterlife. The brain and mind are intimately connected, and when the brain is (completely) dead, so is our mind. However, we have seen that it is not always clear when the brain is dead, and what happens in this hinterland between partial and total brain death is uncertain, but in all cases there will come a speedy end to consciousness and existence.

One way we could live if not for ever but for a very, very long time is by extending the human life span through science. The American futurologist Ray Kurzweil is the major proponent of this idea (Kurzweil & Grossman, 2004). In the not-too-distant future, he argues, death will largely be abolished by medicine (apart from a few tragic accidents where the body is completely destroyed). We will have cured all disease, prevented cancer, and be able to use organ replacement and nanotechnology to keep our brains and bodies forever young. All we have to do is live long enough to survive into this golden age. Kurzweil discusses an extensive anti-ageing programme based on diet, exercise, wise and healthy living, and supplementation (see Box 4.3 on transhumanism).

A second way is if we could 'upload' our consciousness to some external device, such as an external brain or a computer. After all, if functionalism is correct, the substrate doesn't matter, and a computer is as good as anything else. This technology is currently in the realms of science fiction, and whether it will ever be possible, even in principle, is controversial. But if in the future we have a sufficiently powerful computer (which might be quantum or biologically based), and it is connected and can interact with the world (otherwise life might not be worth living), why not?

We do live on in some way after our death through our actions and 'genes and memes'. Our children, if we have any, perpetuate our memory for a while, the ideas, fame, or notoriety of some might be perpetuated in society for some time, and all of us do things that ripple out from us changing the world for ever. Hofstadter (2007) takes this idea that we live on in some sense in the memories of other people in his idea that our selves are in part 'distributed' over others. Hofstadter (2007) points out that everything we do has a consequence on the world; our actions leave 'ripples' that spread out from us, having widespread and unpredictable effects. He also argues that these external effects are part of us, and therefore to some extent our identities exist independently of us and persist after our deaths. He was particularly concerned with the tragic death of his wife, and how she in some sense lived on in the world by her effects on it while living. Black (2018) makes a similar point: the memory of us, and therefore to some extent our memories, live on for a while in our relatives, on average for three generations or so. Some teachers live on by their effects on their pupils, and some live on for a while through their artefacts. My books will outlive me, but probably not by much. A few historical figures persist in cultural memory for much longer: the plays of Aeschylus (born around 525 BC) are still critically acclaimed.

It is, of course, true that we affect the world, but it matters less to me if I am not there to observe it. It is difficult to see this sense of 'living on' as being anything other than metaphorical.

Chapter Summary

- The triune brain model divides the brain into three parts.
- The reptilian brain (based on the basal ganglia) is responsible for ritualistic behaviour such as mating rituals, aggression, and dominance.
- The paleomammalian brain (characterised by the limbic system) is responsible for emotional behaviour.
- The neomammalian brain (characterised by the neocortex) is responsible for higher cognitive functions and is associated with awareness and self-awareness.
- However, we should not deny awareness to other types of animal with different types of brain.
- EEG measures the brain's electrical activity.
- Gamma waves (30–100 Hz) are involved in the coordination of information across different brain regions and might bind aspects of perceptual phenomena and bring them into consciousness.
- Beta waves (12.5–30 Hz) are observed when a person is alert with their eyes open, and can be said to characterise normal waking consciousness.
- Alpha waves (8–12.5 Hz) appear over more posterior regions of the scalp, when a person's eyes are closed and are found when people are calm but awake.
- Theta waves (4–7 Hz) are found in deep sleep and some meditative states.

- Delta waves (0.5–3 Hz) are observed in deep, dreamless sleep and in deep meditative states in very experienced meditators.
- The neural correlates of consciousness (NCC) are the structures and processes in the brain that give rise to and accompany consciousness.
- Hydrocephaly shows that there is not just one functioning type of brain organisation, and that consciousness can arise after profound changes to brain structures.
- Although the details of the ways in which anaesthetics work are not fully understood, they function by interrupting the coherence normally associated with consciousness in the thalamo-cortical loop.
- Integrated information theory is an important account of consciousness proposed by Tononi and others, which stresses the way in which information is brought together to give consciousness.
- Phi is a measure of the informational complexity of the system that says which systems will be consciousness.
- Radical plasticity emphasises the roles of learning, plasticity, and prediction in the development of consciousness.
- Death can be defined in different ways and the definition has varied across history and location.
- Heart death and brain death occur at different times.
- Defining brain death is complicated because electrical activity in different parts of the brain might shut down at different times.
- Coma is a loss of consciousness when the brain is still by some criterion alive.
- We have distinguished between full consciousness, minimal consciousness, coma, and persistent vegetative state.
- In locked-in syndrome, the person is fully conscious but unable to move.

Review Questions

1. To what extent would brain imaging of different types of everyday consciousness enable us to locate the neural correlates of consciousness?
2. What does knowing where something is happening in the brain tell us about what is happening?
3. How do general anaesthetics work?
4. Which brain structures are essential for consciousness?
5. What is the function (or functions) of brain waves?
6. What is phi, and how does it explain consciousness?
7. How is death best defined?
8. In what circumstances should we turn off life-support machines?

Recommended Resources

The Brain and Consciousness

Dehaene, S. (2014). *Consciousness and the Brain: Deciphering How the Brain Codes Our Thoughts*. New York: Viking Press.

Edelman, G.M. (1992). *Bright Air, Brilliant Fire: On the Matter of the Mind*. New York: Basic Books.

Edelman, G.M. (2004). *Wider than the Sky*. London: Allen Lane.

Laureys, S., Gosseries, O., and Tononi, G. (2016). *The Neurology of Consciousness*. New York: Academic Press.

Shallice, T., and Cooper, R.P. (2011). *The Organisation of Mind*. Oxford, UK: Oxford University Press. See mainly Chapter 11.

Integrated Information Theory

Massimini, M., Tononi, G., and Andersen, F. (2018). *Sizing Up Consciousness: Towards an Objective Measure of the Capacity for Experience*. Oxford, UK: Oxford University Press.

Tononi, G. (2012). *Phi: A Voyage from the Brain to the Soul*. New York: Pantheon.

Defining Death

Bauby, J.-D. (1997). *The Diving Bell and the Butterfly*. Glasgow: HarperCollins.

Owen, A. (2018). *Into the Grey Zone: Exploring the Border Between Life and Death*. Cleveland, OH: Guardian Faber.

PART III

OTHER STATES OF CONSCIOUSNESS

11 ALTERED STATES OF CONSCIOUSNESS

So far we have focused on normal waking consciousness. Normal waking consciousness is what most of us experience most of our lives, but we all experience variants of consciousness, and some report experiencing some very odd states indeed.

Some significant changes in consciousness – naturally occurring ones brought on cyclically by sleep, including dreams, and those induced by hypnosis, meditation, and drugs, warrant chapters of their own. In this chapter, we'll look at some other altered states of consciousness (ASCs) experienced by some of the people some of the time. We look first at the general characteristics of ASCs. We then examine forms of sensory deprivation, and its uses. Some people have experiences where their sense of self appears to leave their body, a phenomenon called an out-of-body experience (OBE). A significant minority of the population suffer from migraine headaches or epilepsy, which can produce perceptual distortions as well as distortions in the way people experience the world. Finally, we examine the effects of a curious disease called *encephalitis lethargica*.

What Is an ASC?

We need first to think a little more about what an **altered state of consciousness (ASC)** might be, and the term raises the question about what is 'altered'. What is the unaltered norm (NSC, normal state of consciousness) to which it is referring?

One simple definition is that 'altered' is contrasted with 'normal waking consciousness'. However, even then, some caution is necessary. A cup of coffee provides caffeine, which changes our neurotransmitter levels, which changes our level of arousal. Would we say that a caffeine-induced high is an ASC? Most of us live with some traces of caffeine in our bodies; the half-life of caffeine is about 5.7 hours (Statland & Demas, 1980). That means that if you have an average cup of coffee, which contains about 100 mg caffeine, at 3 pm, there will still be 50 mg in your body at 9 pm. Does coffee promote an ASC? What about differences between people – is my normal today your normal?

Charles Tart (1990) preferred a subjective definition of an ASC as a qualitative change in consciousness – if an individual thinks their consciousness is significantly altered, it's an ASC. A slightly more formal approach is to say that an ASC is a qualitative change characterised by some objective marker. One such marker is an EEG pattern that shows differences from a normal alert waking beta rhythm (Ludwig, 1966; see Figure 11.1). It can, however, be difficult to find an objective marker for every altered state, or the available biological

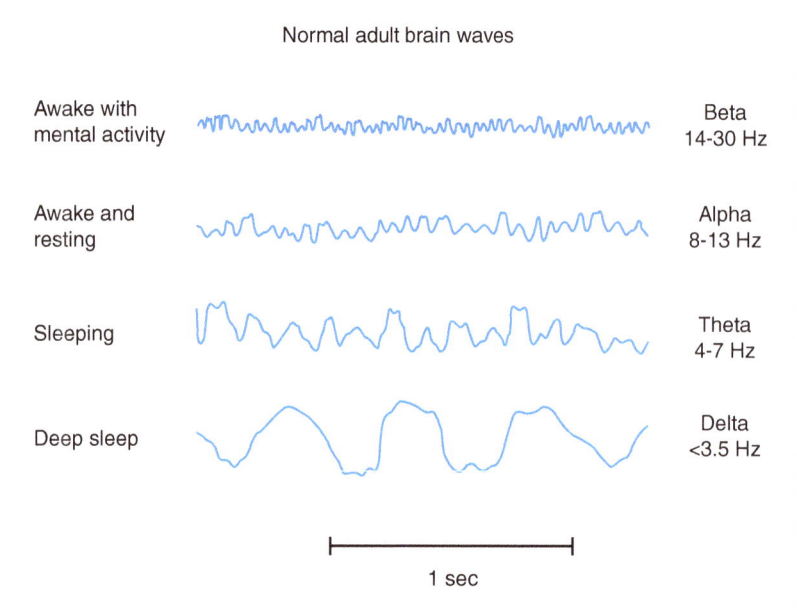

Figure 11.1 Normal waking state and some other states as revealed by EEG. The graph compares beta (awake), alpha (basically awake but resting), theta (light sleep), and delta waves (deep sleep).

Normal adult brain waves

- Awake with mental activity — Beta 14–30 Hz
- Awake and resting — Alpha 8–13 Hz
- Sleeping — Theta 4–7 Hz
- Deep sleep — Delta <3.5 Hz

1 sec

markers may show no difference, and often in practice they are very difficult to implement – you don't know when somebody is going to have a spontaneous out-of-body experience, and it is difficult to hypnotise people or make them sleep in noisy fMRI scanners. Hence, researchers currently tend to prefer the subjective definition (Blackmore & Troscianko, 2018; Farthing, 1992).

We all experience sleep, where we are almost unconscious, and dreaming, which is a very distinctive state of consciousness. We can modify our consciousness deliberately (by taking certain drugs, or allowing ourselves to be hypnotised, among other methods), or can sometimes be put involuntarily into a different type of consciousness (for example, with an out-of-body experience, or a profound religious experience). Some consider a sexual orgasm to be a significant change in consciousness.

We can also call these variants of consciousness ASCs. Looking at how consciousness can change might tell us a great deal about normal consciousness. The aim is to relate the phenomenology of the ASC (how it feels to us) to the cognitive mechanisms involved and their biological underpinnings; while this aim is a noble one, it is as yet rarely achieved. ASCs are also important because, in part, so many people think they are important. In some cultures, ASCs have much greater importance than they do in the west. Some people deliberately seek ASCs to explore their consciousness and nature; such people sometimes call themselves *psychonauts*.

If we can't give a proper definition of consciousness, then it is hardly surprising that we struggle with the idea of an ASC. For now, I will assume that, if you know what an NSC is, you know what an ASC is too.

What is the nature of the alteration? Revonsuo et al. (2009) suggest that the difference between an ASC and an NSC isn't caused by a change to consciousness, but by a change to the relation between representations, the world, and consciousness. The details will depend on what is causing the change.

Box 11.1 Psychonauts

Psychonaut is the name given (usually by the person themselves) to people dedicated to exploring consciousness and altered states of consciousness for spiritual or research purposes, or just for self-exploration and self-understanding. It is reasonable to suppose

> **Box 11.1** (cont.)
>
> that they have been around in some form or other for nearly as long as humans have been practising religion and making works of art. Some of the Romantic poets can be seen as psychonauts: Samuel Coleridge was addicted to opium in the form of laudanum, a tincture of the whole opium head containing all the active alkaloids dissolved in alcohol. He famously wrote the poem *Kubla Khan* under its influence, although its initial construction was notoriously disturbed 'by a person on business from Porlock'. Whether the opium actually had a beneficial effect is debatable, and most scholars believe the work of writers addicted to opium, such as Coleridge, suffered rather than benefitted from the drug.
>
> One of the most famous psychonauts was the American academic and writer Timothy Leary (see Figure 11.2), who preached the value of LSD in changing society. After an early career as a clinical psychologist at Harvard, Leary came to believe in the therapeutic potential of LSD (an idea now seen as respectable – see Chapter 15). Leary was fired from Harvard in 1963. He coined such phrases as 'think for yourself and question authority' and, most famously of all, 'turn on, tune in, drop out'.
>
> Psychonauts use many of the methods discussed in this section of the book, including drugs (particularly bold – see Chapter 15), meditation, sensory deprivation, and habituation, particularly with the ganzfeld, brain-wave entrainment through such means as listening to binaural beats, ritual, types of singing (*Icaro* is a 'magic song' sung in the South American ayahuasca ceremony, discussed further in Chapter 15), hypnosis, dream recall and analysis, and lucid dreaming. It is difficult to evaluate the results: the definition of success is a completely personal matter.
>
> Perhaps transhumanists (see Box 4.3) can be seen as their most modern incarnation. What better way of exploring your consciousness than by extending it?

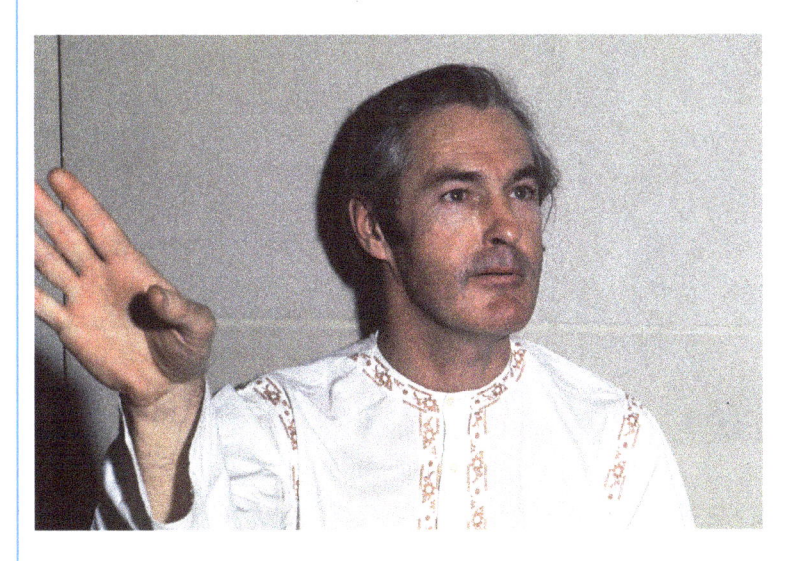

Figure 11.2 Timothy Leary (1920–1996). Leary was an American psychologist and writer famous for his advocacy of mind-altering drugs, particularly LSD. Source: Bettmann/Bettmann/Getty Images.

Types of ASC

We will briefly examine some less common ASCs. Vaitl et al. (2005) survey the complete field of ASCs. They argue that a phenomenological analysis shows that ASCs can be classified along four dimensions: level of activation, awareness span, degree of self-awareness, and whether sensory dynamics are increased or decreased. For example, **near-death experiences** are marked by increased self-awareness and increased sensory dynamics, and extreme drowsiness by reductions along all dimensions. Strong ASCs are mainly brought about by a compromised brain structure, transient changes in brain dynamics resulting in disconnection between areas of the brain, and changes in neurochemical and metabolic processes, while less pronounced ASCs can be produced by environmental stimuli, mental practices, and techniques of self-control. In a similar vein, Cavanna et al. (2018) argue that ASCs arise from changes to the dynamic core (see Chapter 9); that is, changes to the patterns of connectivity in the brain.

Sensory Deprivation

Orfield Laboratory's anechoic ('echo free') chamber in Minneapolis is listed in the *Guinness Book of Records* as the quietest place on Earth. It is reported that very few people can bear to be in it for more than 45 minutes, no one has lasted an hour, and many ask to leave after just a few minutes (Figure 11.3). The sounds of people's own bodies start to sound very loud. After a while, some people start to hallucinate sounds. The brain doesn't like the complete absence of sensory input; indeed, the brain doesn't like constant sensory input, being attuned to change.

We are usually bombarded with sensory information. **Sensory deprivation** is the removal of some or as much of this perceptual information as possible (Figure 11.4). One standard way of diminishing sensory input is to put the person in a tank full of saline water calibrated so that the person floats (hence avoiding feeling the effects of gravity). Whether or not the person likes or dislikes the following state depends on many factors, such as the feeling of security, duration, and how much choice the person has in terminating the state. Sensory habituation is the provision of a constant sensory field (such as red light and a uniform sound rather than darkness and

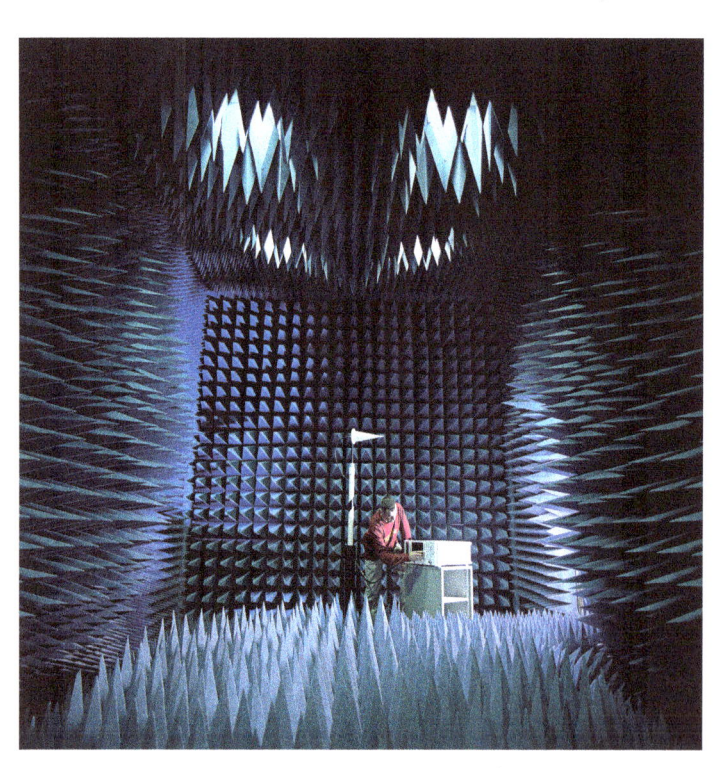

Figure 11.3 A quiet place: inside an anechoic chamber. The chamber both greatly reduces noise from the inside and reflects sound from the inside. Source: Jeff Corwin/Photolibrary/Getty Images Plus.

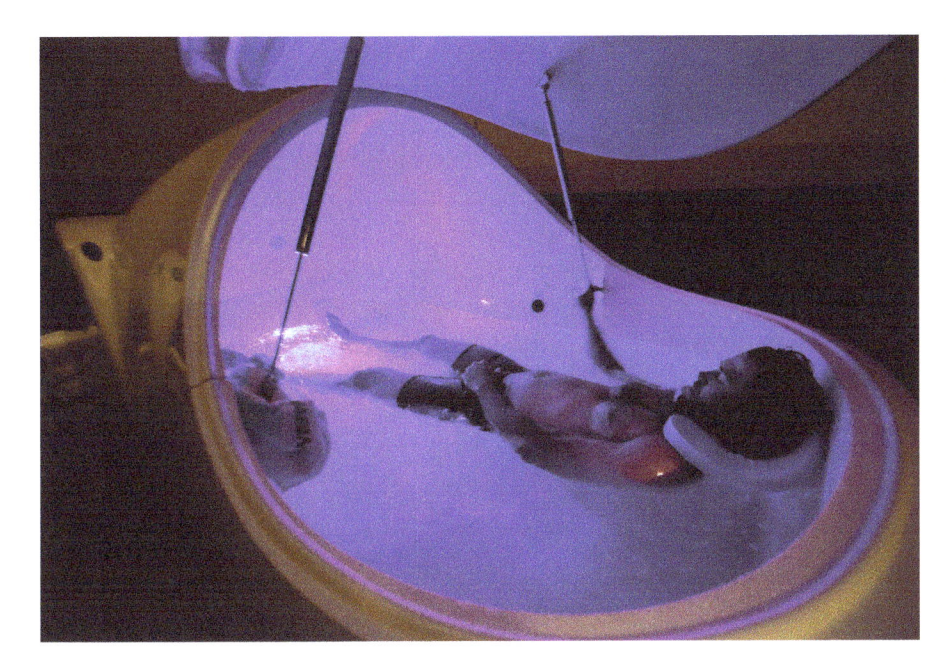

Figure 11.4 A salt-water sensory deprivation tank. People float to reduce tactile sensation and the pull of water, and are visually and acoustically isolated. People find short periods in the tank pleasant, but longer periods, particularly when the duration is not under the participant's control, are often perceived as being unpleasant. Source: MediaNews Group/Bay Area News via Getty Images.

silence), and people seem to prefer habituation to deprivation. The effects of short-term voluntary sensory habituation are pleasant with similarities with sensory deprivation but also similar to meditation and relaxation exercises (Wackermann et al., 2008). The effects of long-term involuntary sensory deprivation are unpleasant and include a loss of sense of time and high levels of anxiety and hallucinations, so much so that sensory deprivation has been (and probably still is) used as a method of psychological torture.

It is cheap and easy to produce a form of sensory deprivation using just a simple hood thrown over the head or eye masks and earmuffs. The technique was reportedly used by British security forces in Northern Ireland and American security forces for the interrogation of suspected terrorists.

When used beneficially, these techniques are sometimes given the umbrella term **restricted environmental stimulation therapy (REST)**. REST can be used for relaxation and behaviour modification; one study suggests REST is highly effective in helping people stop smoking (Suedfeld & Baker-Brown, 1987). Electrophysiological studies suggest that critical changes occur after about 30–40 minutes, with a general reduction of electrical activity in the brain along with occasional bursts of alpha and particularly theta waves. These bursts may correspond with the experience of hallucinations (Iwata et al., 1999, 2001). The changes seen are very similar to those observed with experienced meditators.

The Ganzfeld

Many people find sensory deprivation unpleasant even for short durations, and intolerable for longer periods. We tend to prefer sensory *habituation* to deprivation; in habituation people are presented with a uniform sensory field with a technique known as the **ganzfeld** (German for 'uniform field'). You can carry out a simple form of the ganzfeld experiment using headphones playing white or pink noise (the random hiss you used to be able to get out of analogue detuned televisions and radios, but there are plenty of samples on the web) and shining a red light through half ping pong balls (padded to avoid nasty cuts), which provide a uniform pleasant red visual field (see Figure 17.6). The technique induces a state ranging from relaxation to states with intense dream-like imagery, particularly with pronounced visual images. Wackermann et al. (2008) showed that EEG patterns in the ganzfeld were very different from those of sleep-related states, with pronounced alpha waves.

Out-of-body Experiences

Some people report that sometimes they are located temporarily 'out of their bodies' – an experience we call an **out-of-body experience (OBE)**. The following is a typical example, taken from the Out of the Body Experience Research Foundation; it is Richard F.'s experience, posted on 20 July 2016:

> I had been sitting in a hard wooden chair meditating for about 90 minutes. At the time I couldn't get away from the fact my ass was really hurting and I wanted to move but was trying my best to ignore it. I just thought of this my hands were feeling like wooden. Out of nowhere and completely unexpected I found myself with my back to the ceiling and I was pushing against it. The ceiling was about 15 ft high. While I was pushing against the ceiling (with my back to the ceiling it was more like spreading my arms against ceiling) I became aware of where I was and that my body was still sitting there and I knew my ass was still hurting but I didn't feel it. Then before I had time to analyze more I was back in my body with my seat hurting. I felt euphoric. I can't tell you if I had sight while out of my body or not. It all happened pretty fast 2 or 3 seconds.

In an OBE, your sense of self is moved out of your body. People sometimes have the sensation of floating above their bodies; sometimes they can see their bodies from another point of view (a phenomenon called autoscopy, and as we have seen in Chapter 6 sometimes found in rare neurological disorders of spatial attention), typically looking down on them from above.

Spontaneous OBEs occur when people are falling asleep, at times of severe trauma or extreme effort, in near-death experiences (see Chapter 17), with the use of drugs (particularly dissociative hallucinogens, such as ketamine), and occasionally for no apparent reason. An estimate is that 5% of the population have experienced OBEs (Blackmore, 1982).

A quick search of the web will show many sites full of suggestions on how you can have an OBE. I think I have tried all of them, without the slightest bit of success. All of the techniques involve relaxation, almost to the point of falling asleep, accompanied by some kind of visualisation. One well-known technique is imagining yourself climbing up a rope, stairs, or a ladder, focusing on the feel of the rope and the climbing action as much as possible. You imagine yourself climbing up in the dark, and after having climbed for a while, you 'open your astral eyes'. It's this bit that gives me difficulty, which is perhaps why it's never worked for me. Alternatively, you can visualise the details of the space around you, and then imagine what your room looks like from another point of view in the room, trying to shift your perspective to that point. Or you can try forming a double elsewhere in the room and then shifting your attention to that point.

Spontaneous OBEs are interesting and we can infer something about what is happening from their descriptions. As with all field studies, the conclusions we can draw are limited because of the lack of control. It's also difficult to get data such as imaging data because of their rarity and lack of predictability. There have been several attempts to induce OBEs in the laboratory using a variety of methods (see Box 11.2).

Box 11.2 Laboratory-induced OBEs

Numerous methods have been tried to promote OBEs in the laboratory, although none will work with 100% reliability. Very strong acceleration forces, i-forces (such as you experience when a fast car zooms off from being stationary, or on some fairground rides) can cause them; they sometimes accompany a phenomenon known as G-LOC (*gravity-induced loss of consciousness*) in fighter pilots in simulations in centrifuges (Typ Whinnery is the name most associated with this research; see for example Whinnery & Forster, 2013), sensory deprivation, and electrical and magnetic stimulation of the brain (Saroka et al., 2010). Some claim that binaural beats (different rhythms presented to each ear so they are slightly out of phase) can facilitate OBEs; like many other claims, there is a lot of material on the web, but a dearth of scientific evidence.

In one study, the participant sits wearing a pair of head-mounted video displays (Ehrsson, 2007). These displays show a live film recorded by two video cameras placed beside each other 2 m behind the participant's head, with each camera presented as a live feed to each corresponding eye, but the participant sees them merged as a stereoscopic. In effect, they see their own back as seen from the perspective of someone sitting behind them. The researcher then stands beside the participant and uses two plastic rods to simultaneously touch the participant's actual and illusory chests. Participants reported that they experienced sitting behind their physical body and looking at it from that location. Studies such as these confirm that there is nothing mystical about OBE, and that they arise because of conflicts while integrating aspects of our representation of our body in space.

Explaining OBEs

There is no need to postulate the existence of a soul that moves through 'astral projection' in order to be able to explain OBEs. Even so, some of the psychological theories now seem overly complex, if not just rather strange: for example, the astronomer Carl Sagan suggested that they are some kind of rebirth fantasy. OBEs are a form of dissociative state, and there is obviously some misalignment of our model of the world so that our considered and actual positions do not coincide, generating the hallucination that 'we' are located elsewhere other than our body. Blackmore (1992) expanded this basic idea, stating that in an OBE we remain conscious, but temporarily lose contact with at least some sensory input. In this respect, OBEs share some features of lucid dreaming.

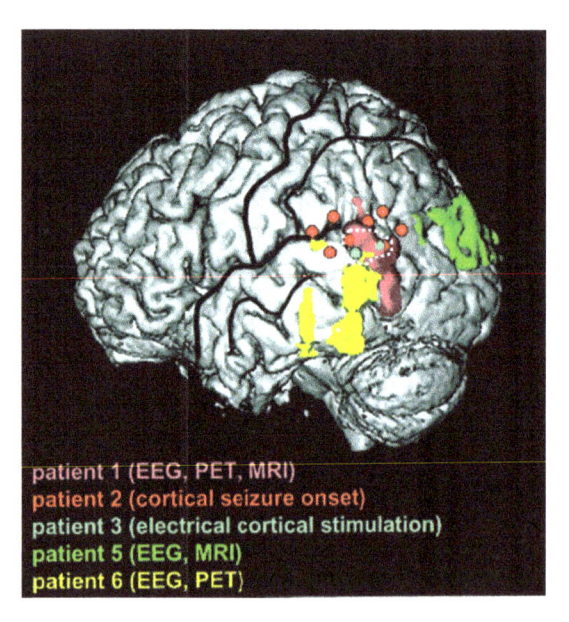

Figure 11.5 Lesions affecting the sense of self in space leading to OBEs. The figure shows overlap in lesion sites in the left hemisphere of five patients prone to OBEs and related (autoscopic) phenomena. Note these sites cluster around the TPJ (temporo-parietal junction). Source: Blanke et al. (2004). © 2004, Oxford University Press.

OBEs are hallucinations created by a mismatch between sensory data and our model of our location in space, and resemble disorders of the self such as autoscopy and heautoscopy (see Chapter 7). This idea is supported by brain imaging and stimulation studies. Some of the best-known work is that of the Swiss neuroscientist Olaf Blanke (Blanke & Mohjr, 2005; Blanke et al., 2002, 2004). These studies show that OBEs can be caused by electrical stimulation (in a patient undergoing surgical treatment for epilepsy) of the **right angular gyrus**. The patient also experienced distortions of her perception of her arms and legs (Blanke et al., 2002). Blanke et al. hypothesise that the **vestibular cortex**, which is located close to the right angular gyrus, is also involved, explaining the sensations of levitation and the body feeling light that are commonly reported in OBEs. The source of the experience is abnormal activity at the **TPJ** (**temporo-parietal junction**; see Chapter 7), although we still need to explain the source of that abnormal activity (see Figure 11.5).

Guterstam et al. (2015) used a multisensory virtual reality system based on the rubber hand illusion (see Chapter 7) to create an OBE illusion while participants were being scanned in fMRI. They found similar results to Blanke et al., and argued that self-consciousness of the body comprises two components: the feeling that the body is part of the self, called body ownership, and the experience that the body is located somewhere in space, called self-location. These two components can be dissociated, where in asomatognosia limbs can fail to be recognised as part of the self, in OBE the self-location is detached from the body. Brain imaging shows that body ownership is associated with activity in the **premotor** and *intraparietal* areas, while self-location depends on the hippocampus and *intraparietal* areas. The two systems are normally mediated by the posterior cingulate cortex.

The important point is that there is nothing mysterious about an OBE. It is not your soul travelling elsewhere; severing a cord between your astral and physical body will not cause you to die; and OBEs are not evidence for dualism. Instead, they reflect pathological brain activity, and this explanation fits in well with what we know from studies of lesions affecting the sense of self in space.

TRY THIS: OBEs

Try some OBE induction techniques. A search of the web will give you more detailed instructions. Some people suggest *binaural* beats, where sounds of beats of different frequencies are played to each ear; apps for presenting binaural beats are found easily. Around 4 Hz is suggested.

> **TRY THIS: OBEs** (cont.)
>
> One of the easiest techniques is mental induction by visualisation. One of the classic techniques is to lie down, shut your eyes, and try to imagine floating out of your body, adopting the point of view of the floating body, imagining looking down on yourself. (People who talk about *astral projection*, the technique of moving yourself elsewhere, will tell you to imagine a cord between the heads of the true and visualised bodies. You are implored to ensure the cord is never broken, or you will die, an injunction you can ignore. Probably.)
>
> The *Monroe technique* is based on physical and mental relaxation. First, you relax your body with progressive muscle relaxation and deep, slow breathing. Second, try to enter the state bordering sleep – Phase 1 sleep or the hypnagogic state (Chapter 12). One way is to hold up your arm as you fall asleep; when you do sleep, your arm will fall, and you wake. You practise this technique until you can enter light sleep without waking without needing to raise your arm. Another possibility is to concentrate on an object. Try to inhabit this state without thinking about anything. You then try to deepen how relaxed you are. Some people report 'vibrations', or tingling sensations, or electric shocks throughout the body; you then need to practise controlling these vibrations. You can then either think about yourself lifting out of your body, floating up, getting lighter and lighter, or trying to rotate your mental body image, so you roll into a mental body that's in a different position from your physical body. At the end, don't forget to merge your physical and mental bodies.
>
> I've never got any of them to work, but you might; good luck!

Migraine and Epilepsy

Many people are unfortunately familiar with *migraine* headaches; it's estimated that 15% of the population get them at least occasionally. The pain of the headache is often preceded by signs involving a change of consciousness: first, there may be a *prodrome phase* hours or even days before the headache, with numerous symptoms including nausea, constipation, irritability, depression, inability to concentrate, sensitivity to light or smells ... the list is long. It can last 24–48 hours and affects 80% of sufferers, or *migraineurs*. In my case, the most interesting symptoms are feeling light headed and 'not quite real' (derealisation). Many people then experience a *visual aura* (Sacks, 1970): mine is typical, starting with a blind spot, from which zigzag lines start to radiate, expanding to fill the visual field, before being pushed away to the margins, at which point the pain begins (see Figure 11.6). Some people experience a *post-drome* phase after the headache, in which they may be tired, experience mood changes, feel depressed, have an upset stomach, or they may feel exhilarated, almost manic.

Migraine then can involve changes to consciousness, as well as headache pain. The causes of migraine are still poorly understood: there is clearly a genetic component, as twin studies suggest around 50% heritability (Plane et al., 2007); and several environmental triggers are reported, including foods such as cheese, red wine, or chocolate, as well

Figure 11.6 Migraine aura. A typical migraine might start with a prodrome phase, marked by physiological and psychological changes, followed by an aura. A typical aura might start with a central blind spot and jagged coloured lines working out from it to the edge of the visual field. Source: smartboy10/DigitalVision Vectors/Getty Images.

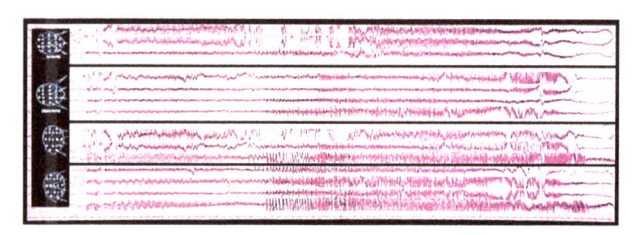

Figure 11.7 EEG during an epilepsy seizure. In focal seizures abnormal electrical activity is detected only around a specific brain region; in a generalised seizure changes are widespread. The EEG may appear to 'go wild'. Some abnormal electrical activity might also be detected outside a seizure. Source: BSIP/UIG via Getty Images.

as less specific triggers such as stress, fatigue, and hunger. As a teenager, I worked out that I got a migraine every Sunday after my weekly cheese-eating Saturday night; it didn't prevent me, though, from the stress of having to mow the lawn. The mechanisms whereby genes and triggers interact to generate the symptoms and pain are also poorly understood. Some argue that blood flow to the brain is important, with constriction and expansion of the blood vessels leading to psychological changes and pain; others argue that patterns of neuronal activity in the brain are more important, with receptors for the neurotransmitters **NDMA** and **serotonin** being particularly important. The brainstem seems to play an important role in initiating the symptoms (Akerman, Holland, & Goadsby, 2011; Dodick & Gargus, 2008; Olesen et al., 2009; Shevel, 2011). The spread of the visual aura from the centre of the visual field can be traced as activation spreads across the visual cortex (Sacks, 1970).

Epilepsy also involves the spread of abnormal neuronal activity across the brain, but with more dramatic and dangerous consequences. In an epileptic *seizure*, there is a burst of excessive electrical activity in the brain corresponding to sudden discharging of neurons; how it affects the person depends on how much of the brain, and which specific areas, are affected (see Figure 11.7). Epilepsy is less common than migraine, but still affects around 1 in 100 people.

The most obvious signs of epilepsy are the seizures (Duncan et al., 2006). About 60% are convulsive; about two-thirds of them begin from a focal point in the cortex, spreading to the rest of the cortex, and the rest start as generalised seizures affecting both hemispheres. These seizures (commonly known as grand mal seizures) begin with strong muscle contractions on both sides of the body. The person loses consciousness completely and takes some time to regain it, with a *postictal* state where the person is unresponsive and deeply asleep, and is deeply confused on waking. Convulsive seizures result from epileptic activity starting in the motor cortex.

The other 40% are non-convulsive seizures, the most dramatic being the absence seizure, where for several seconds the person has a greatly reduced level of consciousness (perhaps not appearing to 'be there'; hence the name). Absence seizures are also called petit mal seizures. The person quickly returns to normal, and is not confused. Seizures starting with a focal point in the occipital lobe give rise to visual disturbances, coloured patterns, and hallucination. Seizures focused in the parietal lobe give rise to disturbances in bodily sensation, OBEs, and complex disorders of cognition and experience, including memory confusions and intense emotional states.

Again, like migraine, seizures may be preceded by auras, also involving hallucination of sensory phenomena, such as smells, and automatisms, which are simple repetitive movements like smacking the lips.

> **TRY THIS:** Your Migraine Aura
>
> If you are unfortunate enough to suffer from migraines and auras, sketch your aura. Time how long it takes for the aura to move across your visual field. What is the temporal relationship between the cessation of the aura and the commencement of the pain?

As with migraine, the cause of most cases of epilepsy is unknown. Some cases occur as the result of brain injury, stroke, brain tumours, infections, and traumatic birth, but for around half of the sufferers there is no obvious cause. As with migraine, there is a genetic component, with twin studies suggesting a heritability of around 50% (Pandolfo, 2011). In the past, surgery was often needed for severe epilepsy (rarely necessitating severing the corpus callosum), but now epilepsy can usually be controlled by anti-convulsant drugs, such as sodium valproate.

Consciousness is invariably lost during a seizure. Generalised seizures involve greatly increased neuronal activity in frontal-parietal networks and associated subcortical structure such as the thalamus, while others involve greatly decreased activity in the same areas (Blumenfeld & Taylor, 2003). Nevertheless, the outcome is the same, consistent with the conclusion in Chapter 9 that activity in this thalamo-cortical circuit is essential for maintaining consciousness.

Near-death Experiences

When close to death, some people report particular experiences, which often have much in common. There are examples from people in surgery, or suffering a cardiac arrest, who later report that they heard voices, saw things, and felt euphorically happy and at peace, and without fear of death. Often people report travelling down a tunnel of light, and meeting deceased loved ones, and then entering darkness or entering the light. These experiences are called near-death experiences (NDEs). NDEs are not uncommon; one estimate is that 13% of Americans report having them (Mobbs & Watts, 2011). Although most people report that NDEs are very pleasant, not all are – there are descriptions of a small number of frightening near-death experiences, characterised by dread and fear.

The term NDE and the original description of the phenomena was first reported by Moody (1975), who surveyed 150 people who nearly died. He described nine elements usually commonly found in an NDE: peace and painlessness, a strange sound, an out-of-body experience, a tunnel experience, rapidly rising into heaven, seeing people or light, the sense of a divine being, a reluctance to return, and a life review. Some people who have an NDE report afterwards that in that state they suddenly recalled many memories of people and life events – the fabled 'life flashing before your eyes', called the *life review experience* (LRE). LREs often run in chronological order, and although they are most usually found in NDEs, they are also observed at other times of great stress (Katz et al., 2017). About 13% of NDEs contain LREs (Van Lommel et al., 2001).

Ring (1980) summarised the experiences of NDE by arguing that they fall into five successive stages: a feeling of great peace, a feeling of separation from the body, entering darkness, seeing light, and entering the light. He stated that, while most people in an NDE experienced stage 1 (feelings of peace and contentment), only 10% experienced stage 5 ('entering the light').

Some awareness can continue for some time after the heart stops beating because lack of oxygen takes a while to affect the brain (Parnia et al., 2014), so there has been a great deal of work on cardiac arrest survivors. Parnia et al. carried out a large study of 2060 people surviving cardiac arrest. Almost 50% of the survivors reported memories from the period of the arrest, with seven major themes recurring in these memories: fear, bright light, meeting family members, animals and plants, violence and persecution, deja-vu, and recalling events after the arrest happened. Of the survivors, 9% reported NDEs, while 2% described awareness with 'seeing' and 'hearing' actual events related to the resuscitation. One patient had a verifiable period of conscious awareness during which time cerebral function should have ceased (for up to three minutes).

Of course, an NDE isn't the same as dying and coming back from death; the person never fully died (although admittedly it depends how we define death). Lack of clarity on this point leads to the generation of extraordinary newspaper headlines, such as: 'There IS life after DEATH: Scientists reveal shock findings from groundbreaking study' (*Daily Express*, UK, 16 August 2016) – as a description of the Parnia et al. (2014) study above. Don't believe everything you read in the news.

Box 11.3 How NDEs Reduce Fear of Death

A search of the web shows anecdotal evidence of how profoundly an NDE can change lives: if the descriptions are to be believed, alcoholics stop drinking, criminals become model citizens, atheists embrace God, and people stop fearing death. Only a minority of people (1 in 5) report that the NDE does not change them in some way (Atwater, 2007). Not all changes are for the better; divorce and suicide rates and problems at work increase following an NDE, perhaps because after changing for the better people become more open and trusting to the point of becoming naive following the experience, with some people becoming disillusioned (Atwater, 2007; Shermer, 2018).

We shouldn't be too sceptical. After all, a single experience with a hallucinogen such as LSD can profoundly and permanently change a person's life (see Chapter 15). Clearly, some single significant experiences can in principle change a person's life, but our understanding of how is currently limited. Our understanding of the mechanisms involved in long-term change is particularly poor. The drug evidence suggests that single events can result in long-term psychopharmacological change, and perhaps something like that is happening here.

> **Box 11.3** (cont.)
>
> On the psychological level it might simply be that having a pleasant NDE shows you that the process of dying will not be unpleasant and indeed may be pleasurable (note the reluctance to return characteristic). Finally, many people following NDEs become more spiritual and think there is some form of existence after death. It should also be noted that not everyone who has an NDE loses their fear of death.

NDEs are often *transformational* in that the recovered person undergoes major changes in the way they view their lives and a loss of fear of death (van Lommel, 2011). NDEs induced by virtual reality can reduce fear of death (Bourdin et al., 2017).

Biological Explanations of NDEs

Few scientists accept that NDEs are caused by the person's soul travelling towards death and coming back, although they are often interpreted in that way (see above). EEGs are never completely flat in NDEs. Some argue that NDEs are not actual memories of what happened but instead stories created on waking. There is evidence against this idea: the stories told by people who reported NDEs and those asked to make them up on recovery are very different, and people in NDEs can access information about events that occurred while they were in that state (Sartori, 2008).

Instead, we favour an explanation in terms of the brain starting to die or being placed under extreme stress – the brain's physiology at such a critical juncture causes the features of the ASC that the person later reports. Sue Blackmore's *dying brain hypothesis* says that the phenomenology of NDEs can be explained by the physiological changes accompanying the start of brain death and particularly changes caused by lack of oxygen (Blackmore, 1993). As the body is starved of oxygen, the levels of CO_2 (carbon dioxide) increase. For example, the image of going into a tunnel of light can be explained by the reduction in blood flow to the visual cortex.

Some argue that the euphoria and hallucinations in NDEs are explained by the brain being flooded with N,N-dimethyltryptamine (*DMT*), an endogenous hallucinogen (Strassman, 2001). There are strong resemblances between NDEs and states induced by DMT (Timmermann et al., 2018), including a sense of transcending one's own body and communicating with entities. However, the pineal gland would be unable to manufacture enough DMT in the very short time available (see Chapter 16 and Kingsland, 2019, for a review). Instead, the body does release natural painkillers, endorphins, which create the sense of euphoria. There could also be a sudden large increase in binding to a type of serotonin receptor, 2A, in the cortex; psychedelic drugs, such as LSD, also bind to these receptors, and one of the long-term effects of psychedelic drug use is decreased fear of dying (Kingsland, 2019). The link is rather tenuous but plausible.

What explains the presence of LREs when people's 'lives flash before their eyes'? A variety of explanations have been proposed. Given the speed with which these events occur, it is likely that some biological explanation underlies their occurrence. One possibility is that oxygen starvation leads to neuronal disinhibition starting in the visual cortex, so that many neurons start firing at once, and altered activity in the parts of the brain responsible for hosting autobiographical memories (Blackmore, 1993; Greyson, 1998; Katz et al., 2017; Mobbs & Watts, 2011).

Not all researchers accept that neurophysiological models account for all aspects of NDEs (Greyson et al., 2012). NDEs are uniformly reported as being pleasant, while electrical stimulation of the temporal lobe usually produces a very disturbing and frightening experience (Gloor, 1990). The blood oxygen levels of NDEs are the same as or even higher than control patients (Parnia et al., 2001). NDEs are also unlike hallucinations in other neurological conditions, being more realistic, more pleasant, and involving all the senses (Greyson et al., 2012). Some of these objections have in turn been questioned (Mobbs, 2012), so the jury must stay out. It is difficult to collect neuroscience data for NDEs because of their rarity and unpredictability.

Encephalitis Lethargica

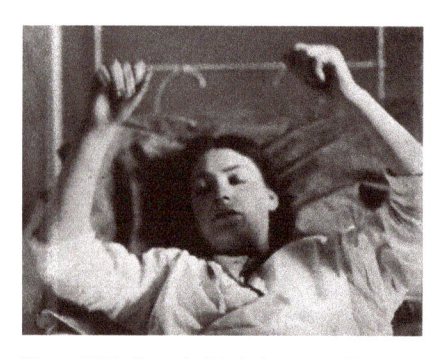

Figure 11.8 *Encephalitis lethargica* sufferer. The patient appears to be in a sleep-like state. Also called sleeping or sleepy sickness, *encephalitis lethargica* should not be confused with the disease transmitted by tsetse flies. First observed in 1916, its cause is still uncertain. Source: Stern (1928).

Encephalitis lethargica was a disease that emerged in the first part of the twentieth century. It was also called 'sleepy sickness' (but should not be confused with the parasitic disease 'sleeping sickness' transmitted by the tsetse fly in tropical Africa). Encephalitis lethargica affected around 5 million people across the world between 1915 and 1925, although most cases were reported from Europe and North America (see Figure 11.8). It was first described in 1917 by the noted Austrian–Romanian neurologist and psychiatrist Constantin Freiherr von Economo (1876–1931); von Economo also produced a detailed early atlas of the cellular structure of the brain. The disease was rather mysterious, initially producing the usual encephalitis symptoms of high fever, severe headache, sore throat, confusion, seizures, impaired and double vision, along with a striking lethargy; some entered a coma, and about a third of the patients affected died in the acute phase. It is estimated that initially hundreds of thousands of people, perhaps more, were affected to some degree.

Many of the patients who survived the acute phase never fully returned to normal, and in particular their level of consciousness was often affected, with some degree of lethargy (Sacks, 1973). In the more extreme cases, people would be left apparently aware, but unable to initiate movement, so they became 'living statues', not moving or speaking, and lacking in any kind of energy. Some patients persisted in this state for decades.

The cause of the disease remains uncertain. No similar outbreak has been reported since, and the tools of pathology were nowhere near as sophisticated at the time of the original outbreak as they are now. At first, the disease was associated with the 1918 Spanish flu epidemic that was raging around the world after the Great War, but when von Economo autopsied the brains of the two types of patients, he found that they had different types of lesions, with the patients who had been comatose before their deaths having lesions in the posterior hypothalamus or the upper part of the **midbrain**. Von Economo was the first scientist to use the term 'wakefulness centre' to refer to these two parts of the brain. Patients who experienced *sleeplessness* before dying had brain lesions in the anterior hypothalamus, so that came to be known as the 'sleep centre'. It has been suggested that some flu patients developed an auto-immune response to the flu; however, the encephalitis lethargica outbreak commenced a few years before we think the Spanish flu pandemic started (which was in late 1917). Analyses have not detected consistent evidence of the presence of any kind of flu in these patients, although over the time involved these techniques are unreliable (McCall et al., 2009). One strong candidate for the cause of the disease is an enterovirus, transmitted through the intestines, of which polio is the best-known example (Dourmashkin et al., 2012); another possibility is a diplococcus bacterium, such as *Streptococcus*, associated with the condition known as 'strep throat'. Whatever the ultimate pathogen, the effect was to damage deep-brain structures, particularly the basal ganglia (Dale et al., 2004). But the precise cause of the disease and how it produced its dramatic effects remain unknown (Vilensky, 2011).

In the late 1960s, there was some hope that treatment with the drug L-DOPA would 'awaken' these patients, who by then had been 'asleep' in care in some cases for about 50 years. The drug worked in the short term in many patients, but most then fell back into their original torpor. This process is documented in Sacks's famous (1973) book *Awakenings*, and the film of the same name (Marshall, 1990).

Encephalitis lethargica is relevant to our study of consciousness because it left so many people in such a strange state for so long. The original epidemic occurred long before the advent of modern imaging and electrophysiological techniques, so we cannot be sure what changes the disease effected in brain networks and on correlates of consciousness, but it does reiterate the importance of the brainstem in maintaining normal consciousness. While we mostly can only speculate on the phenomenology of what it must have been like to be a sufferer, Sacks's readable and watchable account gives some idea.

Other Types of ASC

There are many other instances of ASC with varying degrees of frequency of occurrence and intensity. We could mount an argument, for example, that the state of intense romantic love (sometimes called *limerence*) is an ASC: it's marked by distortions of reality, obsession, and intrusive thoughts, and it's claimed in the popular press that it involves high levels of dopamine and oxytocin and lower than normal levels of serotonin. There is though an absence of peer-reviewed research in this area, although some of these claims are not implausible.

Illness-induced fevers can produce a state of delirium that is clearly not a normal state of consciousness, and, as the name implies, is similar to that caused by deliriant hallucinogenic drugs (see Chapter 15).

These considerations lead us back to the definition of an ASC: how altered does a state of consciousness have to be for a researcher to want to label it altered? There is no objective measure.

Chapter Summary

- An altered state of consciousness (ASC) is a marked change in the quality of consciousness.
- An ASC can be defined objectively or subjectively (qualitatively).
- It is not always possible to find an objective marker of an ASC.
- Sensory deprivation is an ASC brought on by prolonged reduction in levels of sensory input.
- The effects of short-term voluntary sensory deprivation are pleasant and similar to meditation.
- The effects of long-term involuntary sensory deprivation are unpleasant and include high levels of anxiety and hallucinations.
- The ganzfeld is a state of reduced sensory input created by sensory habituation to a uniform input; most people find the state dream-like and relaxing.
- In OBEs, or out-of-body experiences, people find themselves located outside their body, often looking down on it.
- OBEs are caused by a mismatch between sensory data and our model of our location in space.
- Migraines are headaches preceded by changes in consciousness, including changes in awareness and visual hallucinations.
- Epileptic seizures may also be preceded by changes in consciousness, including hallucinations.
- People close to death sometimes experience near-death experiences; these experiences can be explained physiologically, although there is no agreement over the details of the explanation.
- Encephalitis lethargica was a disease of unknown aetiology prevalent 1915–1925 that left many patients in a sleep-like state with profound difficulty in initiating movement.

Review Questions

1. What is altered in an altered state of consciousness?
2. Do all ASCs depend upon altered psychopharmacology?
3. What are the beneficial effects of ASCs, if any?
4. What changes in an out-of-body experience?
5. What causes epilepsy?
6. What can be learned from the study of the encephalitis lethargica epidemic?
7. Is love an altered state of consciousness?
8. What cases near-death experiences?

Recommended Resources

What Is an ASC?

Kingsland, J. (2019). *Am I Dreaming? The New Science of Consciousness and How Altered States Reboot the Brain*. London: Atlantic Books. An excellent review with emphasis on how ASCs, including drugs, can help people, particularly those with mental illness.

RECOMMENDED RESOURCES

Sensory Deprivation and the Ganzfeld
Taylor, K. (2016). *Brainwashing: The Science of Thought Control*. Oxford, UK: Oxford University Press. Goes beyond isolation and deprivation to cover the neuroscience of all aspects of attempts to brainwash people.

OBEs
Nicholls, G. (2012). *Navigating the Out-of-Body Experience: Radical New Techniques*. Woodbury, MN: Llewellyn Publications. If you ignore the New Age aspects, this book has a good coverage of techniques.

Migraine and Epilepsy
Sacks, O. (1992 [1970]). *Migraine*. New York: Vintage Books.

Near-death Experiences
Blackmore, S. (2017). *Seeing Myself: The New Science of Out-of-Body Experiences*. Philadelphia, PA: Robinson Press.

Encephalitis Lethargica
Sacks, O. (1973). *Awakenings*. London: Duckworth. The classic work, which inspired the film of the same name.
Vilensky, J. (2010). *Encephalitis Lethargica: During and After the Epidemic*. Oxford, UK: Oxford University Press.

12 SLEEP

We spend nearly a third of our lives asleep. Sleep is the altered state of consciousness in which we spend much of our time, yet, by its very nature, we remember very little of it. Dreams, imagery of some sort while asleep, and which some of us remember with varying degrees of clarity, are an important component of sleep. Everyone dreams – those who claim not to just don't remember them. When we're asleep we're very vulnerable; we retreat to our comfortable beds in our darkened, heated bedrooms, while our ancestors would huddle together in a cave.

Why is the study of sleep so important (Figure 12.1)? One reason is because it is defined by the absence of consciousness; however, unlike other states marked in the same way, such as coma and death, we easily and routinely move out of it to normal waking consciousness. Perhaps then the study of the differences between normal waking consciousness and sleep can tell us what it is about the brain that marks consciousness. So, what are the neural correlates of sleep? And given we spend so much of our time in unconscious sleep, what is its purpose? Why do we seemingly have to be regularly unconscious for long periods to maintain periods of normal waking consciousness?

We need to qualify the above by reminding ourselves that some of the time we are asleep we are not unconscious, but in a peculiar state of limited awareness we call dreaming. Dreaming is so interesting that it merits a chapter of its own. Dreamless sleep and dreaming are the most common ASCs in our lives.

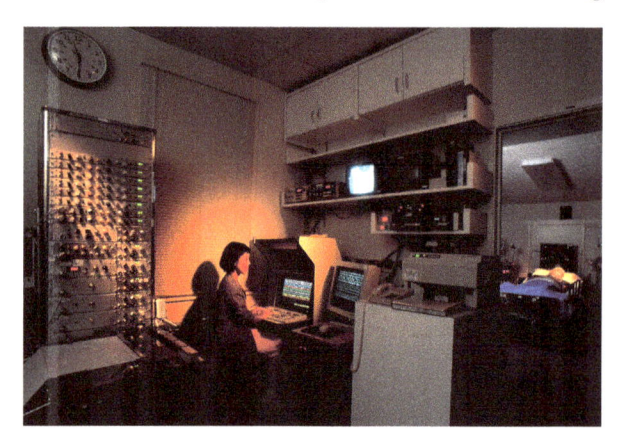

Figure 12.1 A typical sleep laboratory. The Sleep Disorder Testing Lab in Honolulu. The more measures from the sleeper the better. But the more things attached to the sleeper the harder sleep might be to find. Source: Gary Hofheimer/Photolibrary/Getty Images Plus.

What Is Sleep?

Sleep can be defined as a state characterised by reversible unconsciousness, particular brain-wave patterns, sporadic eye movements, and alterations in muscle tone. It's obvious that we have two types of sleep, dreaming and non-dreaming sleep.

It is also obvious, if you observe someone sleeping for a period of time, that there are two externally different types of sleep. These are named after whether or not there are eye movements during sleep: **REM (rapid eye movement)** and **NREM (non-rapid eye movement)** sleep. REM sleep is also characterised by muscle paralysis (low muscle tone), so that only the eyes and vital muscles can move, and a high proportion of dreams are reported if the person is woken. REM sleep is also known as paradoxical sleep because, whereas the person gives the appearance of being deeply asleep, the brain is very active. In NREM sleep, there is no eye movement, the muscles are not paralysed, and if the person is woken during NREM sleep they report dreams much less frequently.

Sleep occurs in cycles of approximately 90 minutes, with this rhythm called the *ultradian sleep cycle*. Sleep proceeds in cycles of NREM followed by REM, usually four to six such cycles a night. NREM sleep dominates sleep at first, with some REM occurring after 90 minutes. The duration of REM sleep increases through the night, with most occurring as we get closer to waking. The proportion of REM sleep varies with age: in healthy young adults NREM comprises about 75–90% sleep time.

For most people, falling asleep is a gradual process. Sometimes we note a distinct state called the **hypnagogic state** as we fall asleep, characterised by lucid if strange thoughts, feelings of falling, sudden muscle jerks, particularly with the legs, and vivid imagery or hallucinations, including vivid auditory imagery (Schachter, 1976). Some people sometimes hear their names called or a doorbell ringing.

The need for sleep decreases as we age. Newborn children can sleep as much as 18 hours, while school-aged children need 9–11 hours, and 6–8 hours in old age, often with poorer quality of sleep and less time in deep sleep.

We sometimes experience a similar sort of transition to the hypnagogic state between sleeping and waking, called the *hypnopompic state*, although waking is often determined by external events such as alarms.

Do All Animals Sleep?

It is obvious observing an animal like a cat or a dog that they sleep a great deal, and they even appear to have periods when they are dreaming. All animals and birds sleep, although the amount and nature of sleep varies enormously. Horses and giraffes sleep only 3 hours a day, pigs and humans about 8 hours, cats sleep 15 hours, the tree shrew 16 hours, and the North American little brown bat nearly 20 hours a day. Clearly, there isn't a strong relationship between size and predator status and the amount of sleep needed, but in general smaller animals, who tend to have higher rates of brain metabolism, tend to require more sleep, while larger animals tend to need less. Some animals, such as horses, can even sleep standing up (they

> **TRY THIS:** Keep a Sleep Journal
>
> Keep a sleep journal. When do you fall asleep? How long do you take to get to sleep? What time do you wake up? When do you use an alarm? How long does it take you to wake up? Is there any relationship between your mood and energy levels and your pattern of sleep?

> **TRY THIS:** Exploring Your Sleep
>
> For a few nights, explore your sleep. What phases and events can you distinguish? How many states would you say comprise your sleep?

Figure 12.2 A manatee sleeping on the sea floor. Animals have to sleep in what we consider extreme conditions, in the air and in the ocean. Source: Jonathan Bird/Photolibrary/Getty Images Plus.

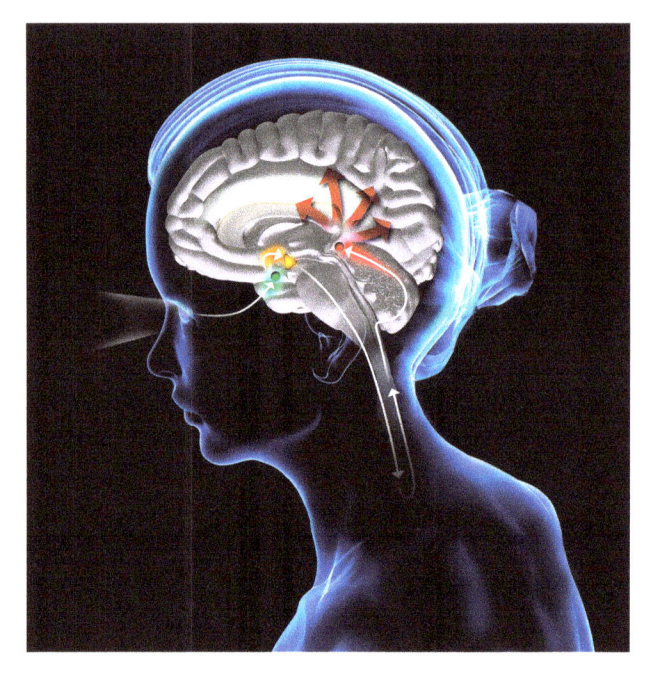

Figure 12.3 Melatonin production. Melatonin is a hormone secreted by the pineal gland at night. It regulates the body's daily biological rhythm depending on luminosity. Light regulates its secretion via a path involving the suprachiasmatic nucleus and the paraventricular nucleus, a structure in the hypothalamus. Source: Ernando da Cunha/Science Photo Library.

take a long time to stand up, which is an obvious disadvantage if you are sleeping when predators are around). Some birds, such as swifts and albatrosses, appear to sleep while on the wing. Many animals show evidence of both REM and NREM sleep, although the proportions vary enormously. And, of course, some animals sleep underwater (see Figure 12.2). As we shall see, studies of animal sleep inform us about human sleep and sleep disorders (Ballie, 2001).

The Biology of Sleep

We go to sleep when we're tired; sometimes we distinguish between physical and mental tiredness. What changes when we sleep? Which parts of the brain are involved, and what regulates our sleep–wake cycle?

Circadian Rhythms

Our energy levels and the desire for sleep do not remain constant throughout the day. Our body follows a rhythm, called a **circadian** rhythm. In humans it's not exactly 24 hours; we can tell from people removed from external cues that it's rather longer, at least 24.2 hours. However, when exposed to environmental stimuli, called *zeitgebers*, such as light and temperature, the rhythm becomes entrained to the 24-hour cycle. All animals, plants, and fungi have circadian rhythms of some sort.

Primitive animals show evidence of circadian rhythms, suggesting that sleep-like states have very early evolutionary roots. The nematode *Caenorhabditis elegans* is, evolutionarily, a very early animal that shows periods of lethargy or relative inactivity. Earthworms are less active in the dark, and consume less oxygen in these less active phases, evidence of cyclicality in periods of activity. Marine worms (*Platynereis dumerilii*) make light-catching proteins to switch **melatonin** (a hormone that plays an important role in regulating sleep and wakefulness) production on and off, so producing melatonin at night. Melatonin governs the depth at which they swim (going deeper in the daytime to avoid predators and harmful ultraviolet (UV) rays). These results may explain how sleep cuts us off from the world. When we're awake, signals from

THE BIOLOGY OF SLEEP

our eyes and other senses pass through the thalamus, a gateway in the brain. Given these findings, we can conclude this sort of mechanism has been around for at least 700 million years (Tosches et al., 2014). Melatonin is important across the animal kingdom for governing active–inactive cycles (see Figure 12.3).

Many fish show periods of inactivity in which they appear to become less responsive to external stimuli (e.g. Titkov, 1976, for an early report). Birds show REM and NREM sleep. So, virtually all creatures have periods of relative inactivity, all animals appear to have periods of sleep, and all birds and mammals dream. Some species, particularly birds and marine mammals, such as dolphins, sleep with only one cerebral hemisphere asleep at any one time, a phenomenon known as *unihemispheric sleep*. Unihemispheric sleep enables the animal to fly or swim and remain alert to threats while sleeping. Such sleep has only been observed with slow-wave sleep.

Alekseyeva (1958) observed that conjoined twins, who share a circulatory system, have independent sleep–wake cycles, showing that sleep and wakefulness are not simply regulated by a chemical in the blood. Mammalian circadian rhythms have three markers: body temperature, levels of the stress hormone **cortisol** in plasma, and levels of melatonin, secreted by the pineal gland in almost all vertebrates (see Figure 12.4). Cortisol levels typically rise throughout the night, peak in the awakening hours, and diminish during the day. Melatonin shuts the thalamus down by causing its neurons to produce a regular rhythm of bursts (Tosches et al., 2014). Melatonin is used as a treatment for some sleep disorders, helping with entrainment, and hence if taken correctly helping with jet lag. Some people believe it helps with insomnia, although the evidence is mixed (Srinivasan et al., 2009). Melatonin levels are governed by exposure to light. Blue light, principally around 460 to

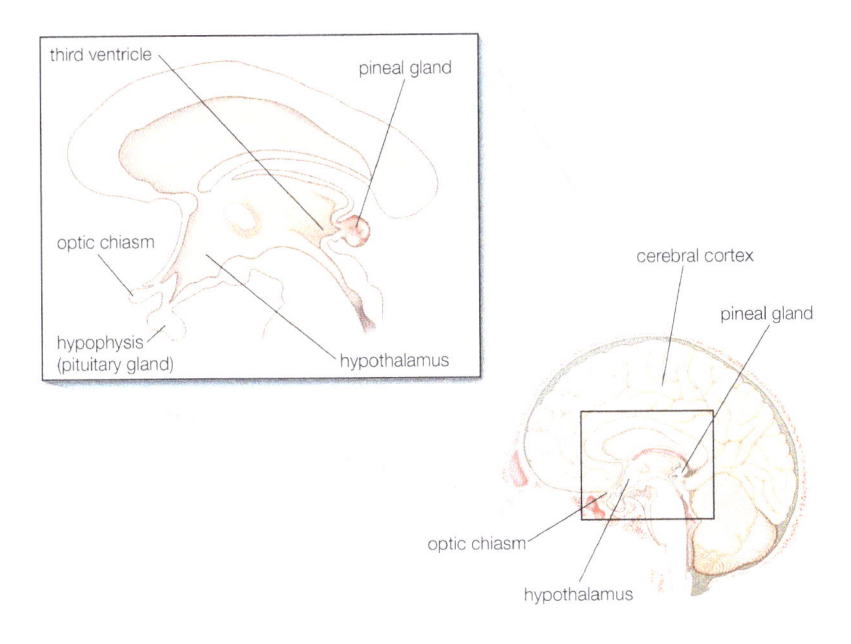

Figure 12.4 The location of the pineal gland. Descartes thought it was the seat of the soul, because of its position. Almost all vertebrates possess a pineal gland. Source: Encyclopaedia Britannica/Universal Images Group/Getty Images.

480 nm, suppresses melatonin, proportional to the light intensity and length of exposure. Exposure to light stimulates a nerve pathway from the retina in the eye to the hypothalamus where the **suprachiasmatic nucleus (SCN)** initiates signals to other parts of the brain that control hormones and body temperature.

The Electrophysiology of Sleep

For a long time, it was thought that 'sleep' was a single state, or at least that the differentiation between dreamless sleep and dreaming would suffice to capture the range of sleep states. It wasn't until Eugene Aserinksyn and Nathaniel Kleitman studied the EEG of sleep that the true variety of sleep states was known (Aserinsky & Kleitman, 1953). The pioneering work was continued by Kleitman's student William Dement (b. 1928), who emphasised the association between REM and dreaming, and the pattern of EEG across sleep. Dement originally proposed that there were four NREM stages of sleep, although now just three are thought to be necessary to capture what happens (Dement & Kleitman, 1957; Dement, 1974; see Figure 12.5).

Figure 12.5 Brain activation in sleep. It is immediately obvious that the waking state and REM sleep are very similar, and very different from mostly dreamless slow-wave sleep. Source: Yves Forestier/Sygma/Getty Images.

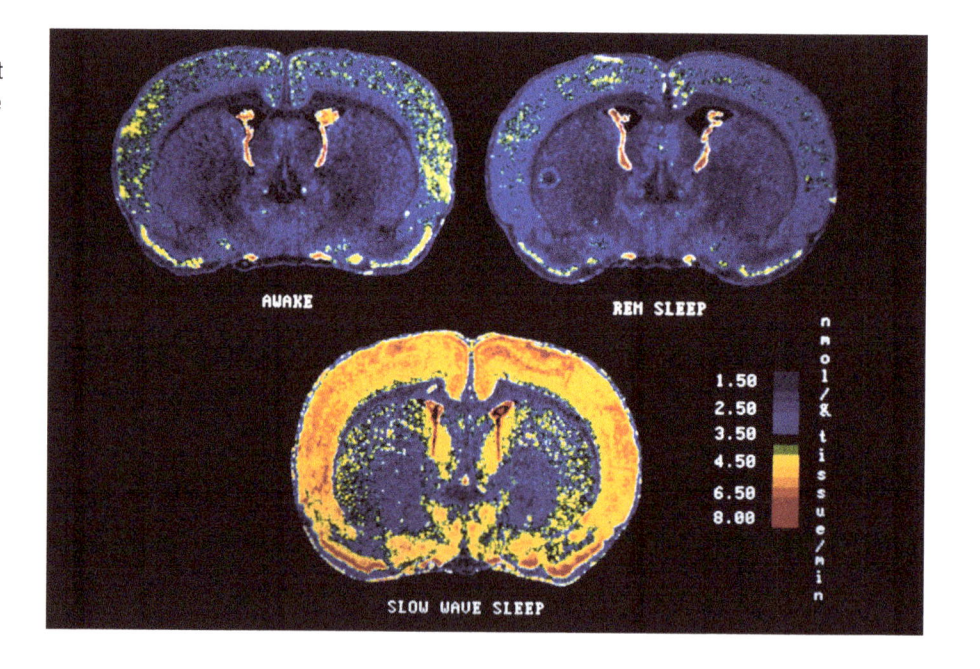

Stage 1 is somnolence or drowsy sleep, and includes the later processes of falling asleep and initial sleep. There is hypnagogic imagery and any thoughts recalled in this stage are strange. There are slow rolling eye movements to the side. In the EEG there's a gradual drop out of alpha, more beta, more centro-frontal theta, and POSTS (*positive occipital transients of sleep*) at around 5 Hz.

In Stage 2 sleep, there is unsynchronised beta and gamma to synchronised alpha (8–13 Hz), moving to theta (4–7 Hz), which on the whole is the predominant frequency in a night's sleep.

THE BIOLOGY OF SLEEP

Stage 3 sleep is deep sleep. It is characterised by at least 20–50% delta waves, and because of these slow waves is often known as slow-wave sleep (SWS). Initially, stage 3 was followed by stage 4 sleep, characterised by more delta waves, but in 2008 the American Academy of Sleep Medicine concluded that stages 3 and 4 were not clearly differentiable, and discontinued the use of stage 4 (Schulz, 2008). Stage 3 EEG also shows the presence of K complexes and sleep spindles. High-amplitude, widespread sleep spindles have a frequency of 12–16 Hz (typically 14 Hz) and are maximal in the central region (vertex), although they occasionally predominate in the frontal regions. Most sleep disorders, parasomnias, occur in this stage. As noted there are dreams in this stage, but they aren't as vivid or memorable or bizarre, more 'thoughts'. Non-REM dreams are usually shorter, less vivid, and less bizarre than REM dreams, but this might be because non-REM dreams are shorter or are less well remembered.

The imminence of NREM sleep is indicated by the presence of **ponto-geniculo-occipital** (thankfully abbreviated to PGO) **waves**. These waves traverse much of the rear of the brain, originating in the pons, moving to the lateral geniculate nucleus of the thalamus, and then to the visual cortex. PGO waves were first observed in non-human animals (cats and rats) using electrodes implanted in their brains; although their presence was inferred in humans, it was some time before they were measured directly in human patients receiving DBS for Parkinson's disease (Lim et al., 2007). PGO waves are most prominent at the onset of eye movements in REM sleep. Hobson et al. (2000) argue that they mark the onset of dreaming. In the **activation-synthesis model**, PGO waves are the signal for the brain to start recalling experiences from the previous day for processing.

Massimini et al. (2005) used transcranial magnetic stimulation (TMS) of the premotor area. When quiet, wakefulness activation cascades across the cortex. When in REM, TMS provokes a stronger initial response but then dies out and does not cascade across the cortex. The fading of consciousness during certain stages of sleep may be related to a breakdown in cortical effective connectivity.

> **TRY THIS: Falling Asleep**
>
> What happens when you fall asleep? Try to observe the process. What happens to your thoughts? How do they change? How does watching yourself fall asleep change things? (Note that you might find it keeps you awake, in which case you will have to discontinue the project after a while. Good luck getting to sleep after that.)

The Neurology of Sleep

We now know a great deal about the biology of sleep, thanks particularly to advances in understanding the electrical activity of the brain, and advances in neuroanatomy.

The earliest substantial work on the neurophysiology of sleep was carried out by the Belgian neurologist Frédéric Bremer (1892–1982). His earliest research was on how the cerebellum controls muscle tone (the resistance of muscle to stretching), which he extended to how the brain controls the body during sleep. He performed a series of cuts, called

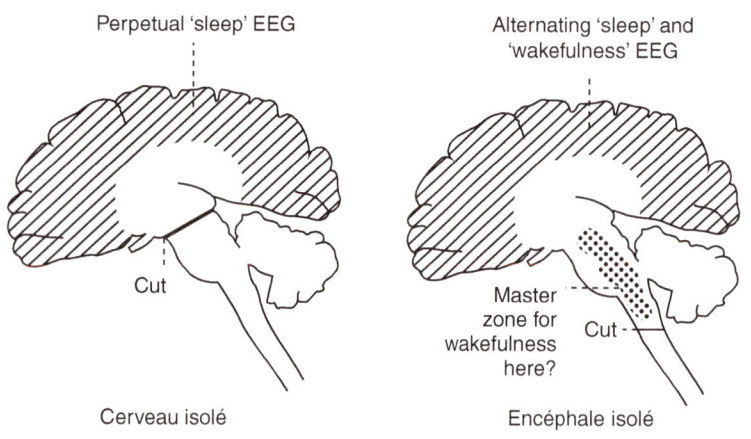

Figure 12.6 Brain transections. The work of Bremer showed that the two transections known as the cerveau isolé and encéphale isolé have very different effects, leading to the identification of the brainstem and structures such as the reticular activating system as playing an essential role in sleep–wakefulness.

Figure 12.7 EEG of a cat. Cats have been widely used in sleep research. The EEGs of all mammals are broadly similar. Source: Library Book Collection/Alamy Stock Photo.

transections, at different levels of the brains of cats. First, he observed that lesioning the hypothalamus caused sleepiness in cats. He is most remembered for showing in particular the very different effects of two transections he called the *cerveau isolé* and *encéphale isolé* (see Figure 12.6).

The cerveau isolé transection isolated the forebrain from the rest of the nervous system, cutting through the midbrain, and resulted in the cat entering a state of perpetual deep sleep, as though the animal were drugged eternally on barbiturates. Bremer hypothesised that sleep was caused by the deprivation of sensory input from the lower brain spinal column, leaving only visual and olfactory input intact, an idea called the *deafferation sleep hypothesis*. That is, the higher brain needs continual input from the body; deprive the body of this stimulation, and we fall asleep. In contrast, the encéphale isolé transection isolated the whole brain, leaving the animal paralysed, but with normal sleep–wake cycles. (Describing these experiments leaves me queasy and feeling a little guilty.)

The deafferation hypothesis was soon rejected – after all, the brain was still receiving visual and olfactory input, and why was there no sign of dreaming? – but the work did show the importance of structures in the mind–brain and brainstem for maintaining sleep-wake cycles and arousal.

Moruzzi and Magoun (1949) demonstrated the importance of a structure called the **reticular activating system** in the brainstem for maintaining awareness and arousal (see Figure 12.7). (The reticular activating system is now often called the *brainstem neuronal populations*.) The reticular activating system (named after its superficial resemblance to a net) projects to many higher areas in the brain. Moruzzi and Magoun showed how electrical stimulation of the reticular activating system had widespread effects on arousal. Stimulating the structure produced wakefulness in cats. They proposed that wakefulness depends on continual background activation from the reticular activating system. Reduced activation, either naturally as part of the sleep–wake cycle, as the effect of sleeping drugs such as barbiturates, or through injury, such as with Bremer's experiments, leads to normal sleep, anaesthesia, or pathological somnolence. Countless autopsies subsequently showed that when a person's brainstem is damaged, whatever the cause, that person falls into a coma. The brainstem clearly then plays some essential role in maintaining the state of

THE BIOLOGY OF SLEEP

wakefulness (see Figure 12.8). The reticular formation in the brainstem then became the prime contender for the title of the 'wakefulness centre'. In subsequent experiments, the application of electrical stimuli to the thalamus of cats while they were awake caused them to fall asleep, thus demonstrating that sleep is not simply a passive process, in which being deprived of sensory inputs was what caused people to fall asleep, but rather involves interactions between the thalamus and the cortex. In particular, a region of the brainstem called the **mesopontine tegmentum** is thought to contain a flip-flop switch for controlling whether we are in REM or non-REM sleep (Lu et al., 2006). The mesopontine tegmentum contains two regions that are mutually inhibitory (by means of the inhibitory neurotransmitter **GABA**), with the REM-on area projecting with excitatory glutamate neurons to the base of the forebrain to control REM EEG and to the medulla and spinal cord regulating loss of muscle tone in REM sleep. As ever, the main issue is the poorly understood mechanisms by which these brain processes translate into experience.

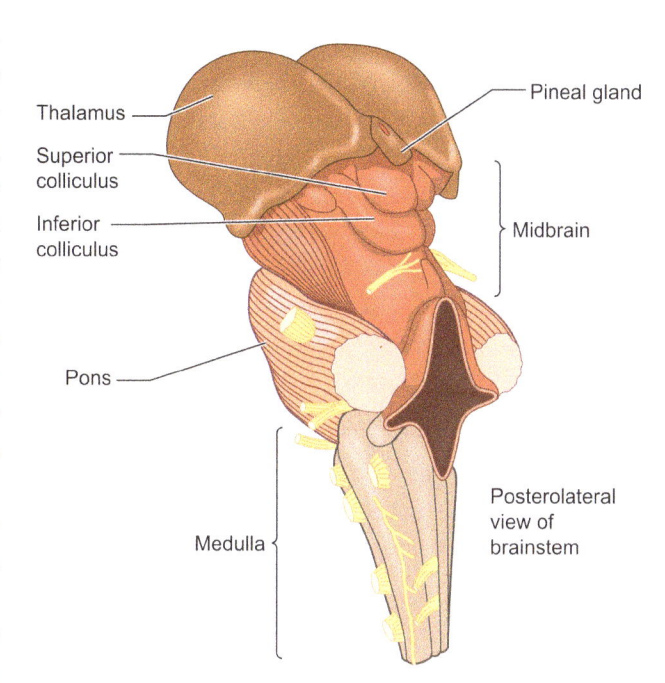

Figure 12.8 Brainstem structures. Although relatively small, the brainstem plays an essential role in maintaining life, in maintaining cardiac and respiratory function, as well as arousal and the sleep–wakefulness cycle.

We cannot conclude that consciousness is located in the reticular activating system, any more than we could conclude that a television picture resides in the television's plug. Nevertheless, these brainstem structures play an essential role in the picture.

The Neuropharmacology of Sleep

Levels of neurotransmitters vary systematically during sleep. Neurotransmitters are substances that act as messengers in the nervous system (see Box 12.1).

Box 12.1   Neurotransmitters

A neurotransmitter is a chemical messenger that plays an essential role in the nervous system enabling communication between neurons. Although transmission within a neuron is electrical, most transmission between neurons is chemical. The brain houses a large number of neurotransmitter systems. Some neurotransmitters are loosely associated with brain structures, such as the dopaminergic system. They are not confined to the central nervous system: famously there is more serotonin in the gut than in the brain. The German pharmacologist Otto Loewi (1873–1961) was the first to discover a neurotransmitter, acetylcholine, in 1921, using beating frog hearts.

Box 12.1 (cont.)

Neurotransmitters can be excitatory (ones that increase activation in the target neuron) or inhibitory (reducing activation in the target neuron). When I was a student, we only talked about a handful of neurotransmitters; we now know that there are over a hundred, and possibly many more, including gases such as nitric oxide and even hydrogen sulphide.

Neurotransmitters can be grouped by the similarity of their chemical structures. For example, monoamine neurotransmitters are neurotransmitters containing an amino group connected to an aromatic ring. Examples are dopamine, epinephrine, and norepinephrine (these three being further grouped together as catecholamines), and serotonin.

For our purposes some of the most important are:

Acetylcholine (ACh). Parts of the brain or body that are affected by acetylcholine are called cholinergic. In the brain acetylcholine plays a role in arousal, attention, memory, and motivation. In the body it is essential for muscle movement (and nerve agents block its action). A lack of acetylcholine is associated with Alzheimer's disease, and cognitive enhancers and anti-dementia drugs work primarily on the cholinergic system.

Dopamine (DA). The brain has several dopaminergic pathways. One pathway is central to reward and motivation, so dopamine plays an important role in the psychology of addiction. Damage to the dopamine-secreting neurons of the substantiated nigra in the midbrain leads to the degenerative disorder of movement Parkinson's disease.

Epinephrine (also known as adrenaline). Epinephrine can be classified as a neurotransmitter and hormone, and is also an important medication, central in modulating the body's sympathetic and parasympathetic systems. Threats lead to the release of adrenaline, stimulating the sympathetic nervous system, preparing an animal for fighting or fleeing; the parasympathetic system reduces these symptoms afterwards (also called 'rest and digest').

Gamma-aminobutyric acid (GABA). The most common inhibitory neurotransmitter. Drugs such as barbiturates and benzodiazepines work on the GABA system and reduce the arousal of the brain.

Glutamate. The most widespread excitatory neurotransmitter in the brain.

Norepinephrine (NE, also called noradrenaline). NE prepares the body for action in the 'fight or flight' response. It generally increases arousal and alertness.

Serotonin (5-hydroxytryptamine, 5-HT). Associated with mood and emotion regulation and numerous other functions, and often considered to play a central role in virtually all mental illnesses. SSRIs, for example, are a class of drugs that are selective serotonin re-uptake inhibitors, thereby increasing the amount of serotonin in the brain.

THE BIOLOGY OF SLEEP

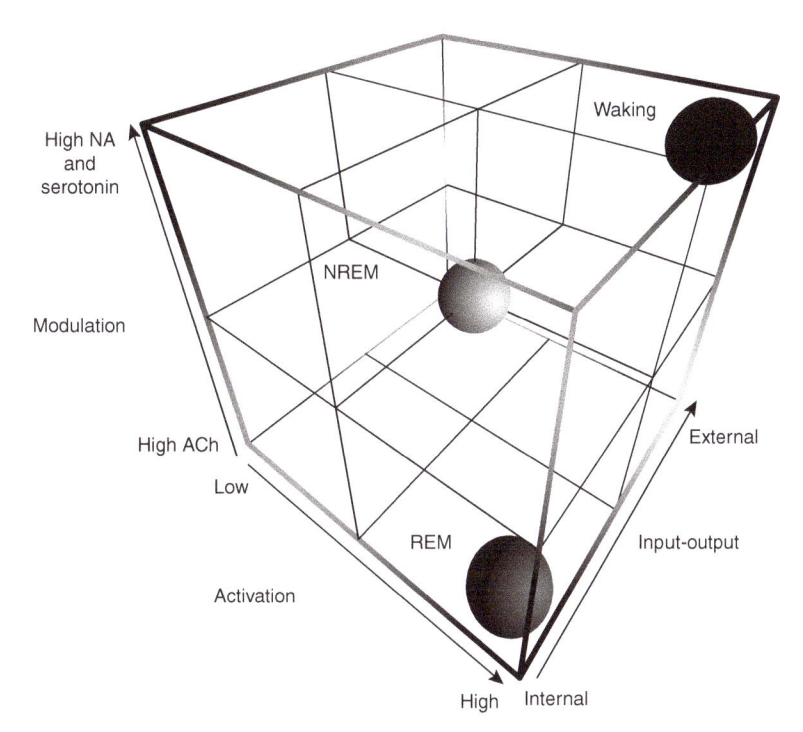

Figure 12.9 Hobson's AIM model of consciousness. Different states of consciousness can be mapped onto a three-dimensional space with axes activation (how aroused the system is), input-output gating (how much information is being transferred from the outside world), and modulation (the amount of aminergic neurotransmitters arising from the brainstem).

The AIM Model of Sleep and Dreaming

Harvard University psychiatrists John Allan Hobson and Robert McCarley first proposed the activation-synthesis hypothesis of dreams in 1977 (Hobson & McCarley, 1977), although it has been updated several times. Their general model of sleep and dreams is called **Activation input modulation model (AIM)**. The model uses a three-dimensional structure to determine the different states of the brain over the course of the day and night (see Figure 12.9).

The three dimensions of the model are *activation*, *input*, and *modulation*, giving the AIM model its name. The level of activation in the brain reflects the rate of information processing, and is determined by the brainstem and reticular activating system. It is measured by EEG. Input is the source of information, gated between external, that is sensory and motor input and output, particularly in the waking state, and internal, when we are dreaming. Modulation is achieved by mixing different types of neurotransmitters released from the brainstem, particularly the balance of aminergic (such as serotonin) and cholinergic (such as acetylcholine) neurotransmitters, determining whether we remember mental activity (waking versus most dreaming) and whether thought associations are close and logical (waking) or loose (dreaming)

The triggering of REM sleep is complex. An **agonist** is a substance that binds to a particular type of neurotransmitter receptor in the nervous system and therefore activates the response of that type of receptor (the opposite is an **antagonist**). The injection of cholinergic agonists (such as a substance called carbachol) in a dorsolateral part of the mesopontine tegmentum, part of the pons, induces REM sleep in rats and cats (Semba, 1993). This region of the pons contains two cholinergic nuclei that project widely throughout the brain, and are involved in attention, arousal, learning, limb movement. Pontine waves (P-waves, or ponto-geniculate-occipital waves) are brain waves generated in the pontine tegmentum.

Sleep Disorders

Not everyone puts their head on the pillow and falls asleep immediately, to wake up naturally seven and a half hours or so later feeling completely refreshed, having had a pleasant undisturbed night's sleep. Like every other psychological process, sleep can go wrong in many ways. Disorders of sleep are called parasomnias.

The most common sleep disorders are problems getting to sleep and staying awake when you don't want to. Everyone has bad nights, trouble getting to sleep sometimes, and days when they feel very tired and sleepy. For most people sleep isn't instant, with the average person taking 10–20 minutes to fall asleep, a period called *sleep latency*.

Getting to Sleep and Staying Awake

Insomnia is a prolonged problem with being awake when a person wants to be asleep. Mostly this means trouble getting to sleep, although many also wake in the night and cannot get back to sleep. Lack of sleep leads to other problems, such as tiredness during the day, low mood, difficulty concentrating, and an increased probability of making errors. Insomnia is very common, and has many causes. Pain, digestive problems, too much caffeine before bed, anxiety, external noise, and many other factors can all cause difficulty sleeping, but often there is no obvious external factor leading to the problem. At any one time, 10% of western adults suffer from some sort of insomnia. Insomnia is more common in women and the elderly (Qaseem et al., 2016). For a diagnosis of *chronic insomnia disorder*, patients must have symptoms that cause clinically significant distress or impairment, be present for at least three nights a week for at least three months, and not be an obvious result of other medical disorder or treatment.

The prevalence of poor sleep varies across the world, with 32% of a sample from Belgium reporting poor sleep, but under 20% from Brazil (Thompson, 2020). There is no simple explanation; however, people from Austria report even better-quality sleep than people from Brazil. Factors such as industrialisation, length of daylight, use of artificial light, method of sleeping (bed or futon or hammock?), family structure, and use of afternoon napping are all likely to have effects, as are sources of stress in societies and how sleep problems are perceived.

The first line of treatment of insomnia is proper sleep hygiene: going to bed at the same time and place every night, trying to keep regular hours, avoiding coffee and other stimulants well before trying to rest, avoiding alcohol (which, although a depressant, interferes with sleep), avoiding bright light, and avoiding too much stimulation. Other options involve looking at flowing images (Figure 12.10). Further treatment involves cognitive behavioural therapy (Qaseem et al., 2016). Another option is the use of drugs. Psychoactive drugs that cause sleepiness are known as *hypnotics*. (In lower doses, these drugs sedate, so the class of drugs is sometimes called sedative-hypnotic.) The earliest effective hypnotics were barbiturates, such as phenobarbital, but these drugs quickly cause dependence and are highly dangerous in an overdose. There have been many cases of suicide or death by accidental overdose, including those of Judy Garland, Jimi Hendrix, Abbie Hoffman, and Marilyn Monroe. Hence, short-term benzodiazepines now are preferred, although a new class of non-benzodiazepine hypnotics, called *Z-drugs* (such as zolpidem – Ambien), are also widely prescribed (Ramakrishnan & Scheid, 2007). These drugs act on the neurotransmitter GABA receptors and increase the availability of GABA in the brain, with the effect of decreasing neuronal excitability. These drugs should not usually be used for more than four weeks because otherwise the patient starts to become dependent, and the drugs actually interfere with sleep in the long term. They decrease slow-wave sleep and delay the onset of REM sleep.

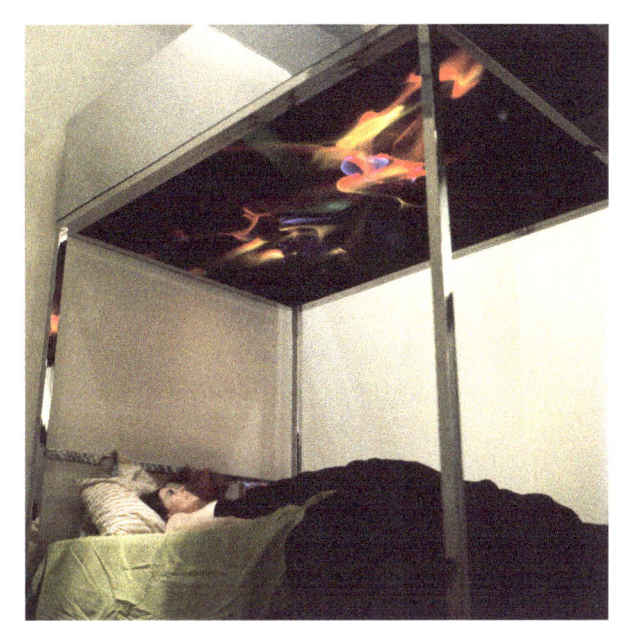

Figure 12.10 Non-drug treatments of insomnia. Lack of sleep is more than annoying: it can be dangerous. Many treatments exist; here sufferers are watching relaxing patterns generated above them. Source: F. Roy Kemp/Hulton Archive/Getty Images Plus.

Narcolepsy is a pathological inability to control the sleep–wake cycles so that a person feels excessively sleepy in the day, and indeed falls asleep for short periods ranging from seconds to several minutes. Most people affected by narcolepsy also suffer from sudden loss of muscle tone (catalepsy). A few suffer from vivid dreams or hallucinations on waking up. Again, the exact causes are not well understood. There is a family history of narcolepsy in some sufferers, and, in some cases, trauma, excessive stress, or infection may play a role. One theory is that narcolepsy is an auto-immune disorder resulting in abnormally low levels of the neuropeptide *orexin*. (*Neuropetides* are relatively small proteins related to hormones used by neurons to communicate with each other; they differ from neurotransmitters in not persisting in their form in the intersynaptic space.) Orexin regulates appetite, sleep, wakefulness, and arousal. A mutation in the gene responsible for orexin receptors causes narcolepsy in dogs (Lin et al., 1999). Estimates of the incidence of narcolepsy are very wide because of the difficulty in defining a disorder with so many causes, without any biological marker, and where the incidence is self-reported: if I have a few days where I am excessively sleepy and fall asleep during the day, will I report myself as having narcolepsy? Estimates range therefore from 2 to 6000 per million (Goswami et al., 2016). Narcolepsy is a serious and dangerous disorder, with sufferers more likely to be involved in accidents, with the consequences of falling asleep while driving obvious.

Problems During Sleep

There are also sleep disorders in people who can get to sleep. Some disorders are found in particular stages of sleep. Stage 3 disorders include talking and walking in our sleep, and bedwetting (particularly in younger people). Most of us sometimes talk in our sleep (see Box 12.2). A few years ago, I recorded my dreams every night using a sound-activated recorder. I would typically say something in my sleep once a week or so. On one occasion, I let out a blood-curdling scream, and then said something totally mundane – 'I must make a cup of tea'. I had no memory of it in the morning.

Box 12.2 Talking in Your Sleep

Dion McGregor (1922–1994) was an American songwriter better known for talking in his sleep, so much so that his nocturnal speech was turned into minor hit records, particularly *The Dream World Of Dion McGregor* (1964a) and accompanying book (1964b). Samples of his sleep talking are easily found online. His sleep talking was much more than the occasional phrase, comprising diatribes and descriptions, often shouted. His most famous 'hit' was 'Has anyone got the mustard?', where he talked a great deal with repeated questions about the whereabouts of the mustard. His sleep talking was curious in that it appeared to be narrative descriptions of his dream content, descriptions called *somniloquies*. Although bizarre, the dreams described seem less incoherent than many other dreams. Four stars, well worth hearing, particularly for the description of the martini eyewash.

Unfortunately, little is known about the mechanisms likely to give rise to such descriptions, or the sleep state while they were produced. To my knowledge, McGregor was never formally tested by a sleep scientist. Cases such as McGregor's are extremely rare, but he is not unique. In England, Adam Slavick-Lennard's wife took to recording his sleep talking (including the phrase 'Enough with the cheese. Enough!' – what is it with sleep talking and food?) and followed a blog with a book, *Sleep talkin' man* (Slavick-Lennard, 2013). It's noted that about 5% of adults talk regularly in their sleep. Sleep talking seems to occur in all sleep stages, but is more understandable in stages 1 and 2. Note that even the sweetest person can become extremely foul-mouthed in their sleep.

Some years ago, my partner went through a phase of screaming during through the night. Typically it was around 3 a.m., and she would start with a whimper, muttering, building up to a crescendo of screaming for several seconds. She would then sit upright, eyes open. She didn't always wake up (although I did, heart racing). At first, I would wake her to tell her everything was all right, but later I learned to let her be. (The consensus is that it is indeed best not to wake a person during an attack, and in any case the person can be difficult to wake as they are near to deep sleep.) She would have no memory of the event in the morning and after six months or so these *night terrors*, as they are called, stopped. When I did wake her, she would report some alarming and very frightening image – the one I remember was that she said a tall figure with wild hair and six arms (rather like the Hindu deity Vishnu) was staring at her; this was accompanied by an extremely strong feeling of dread. Heart rate can increase enormously, pupils become very dilated, and the person may sweat profusely. Night terrors usually occur relatively early in the night in Stage 3 or 4 NREM deep sleep. They are more common in children (with a childhood incidence of about 6.5%, compared with 2% in adulthood; American Psychiatric Association, 2013), peaking at around 3½ years. There is no association between night terrors and psychiatric disturbance in childhood, but there is with adults, particularly anxiety disorders, post-traumatic stress disorder, depression, and some personality disorders (e.g. Szelenberger et al., 2005). (My partner had bipolar disorder.)

Night terrors are different from *nightmares*, which are emotionally unpleasant dreams (with a story) that are also accompanied by feelings of dread and fear. Night terrors are relatively rare, whereas nightmares are relatively common; most people have them occasionally. Night terrors occur in NREM sleep, while nightmares occur in REM sleep; therefore, night terrors tend to occur relatively early in the night. However, night terrors are still relatively poorly understood. In a night terror, a person might sit upright suddenly and start wailing and screaming. They can be inconsolable.

There is some evidence that delta wave sleep is abnormal in people prone to night terrors, with the consequence that the person is unable to sustain slow-wave sleep (Szelenberger et al., 2005). There is a strong genetic basis for night terrors, and they are more common among women than men (Schredl, 2011).

Night terrors may be associated with sleepwalking, or *somnambulism*, and both may run in families. Sleepwalking is more common in children. Sleepwalking occurs towards the beginning of the night in Stage 3 slow-wave NREM sleep. Sleepwalkers usually have their eyes open, and may perform tasks while walking around. Around 5% of children have sleepwalked in the last year, but only 1.5% of adults (Stallman & Kohler, 2016). Some people act out actions in their sleep, sometimes with disastrous results (see Box 12.3).

Box 12.3 Murder in Your Sleep

How responsible should a person be for a crime committed in their sleep, or for carrying out actions they would not normally do? There are occasional stories in the press of people murdering their partners in their sleep. In 2009, 'devoted husband' Brian Thomas (aged 59) strangled and killed his wife Christine while he was having a nightmare about an intruder in their camper van while they were on holiday. The prosecution dropped the case and the jury were formally directed to acquit. Thomas was said to be devastated at the death of his wife of 40 years.

The incidence of *homicidal sleepwalking* is disputed. It is, of course, a convenient excuse. We are talking about dozens of cases in recent times, although presumably it has occurred across history. The first time the defence of acting while sleepwalking was successfully used in American legal history was in the case of Albert Tirrell, who was found innocent of the murder of Maria Bickford in Boston in 1846, being under the influence of 'the insanity of sleep'.

In 1987, Kenneth Parks was found innocent of murdering his mother-in-law in Ontario, Canada (Broughton et al., 1994). Parks was found to have an abnormal EEG where a pattern showed a shift from deep SWS directly to waking, without passing through stage 1 or 2 or REM sleep first. It is thought that the person gets stuck between sleep and wakefulness. Of course, not everyone with this parasomnia then goes ahead to murder people, and the further factors involved are not understood.

Sleep Deprivation

Figure 12.11 Randy Gardner. Randy Gardner has set the world record for sleep deprivation of 11 days and 25 minutes. In this photograph William Dement and Randy Gardner examine data from sleep deprivation. Source: Don Cravens/The LIFE Images Collection/Getty Images.

If sleep is essential, then depriving an organism of sleep should have observable effects – and it does, in humans and non-human animals; these include death. Sleep deprivation is so unpleasant that it is used as a form of torture. Sleep deprivation can be acute (staying awake for a long period of time) or chronic (consistently going without enough sleep every night).

We know a great deal about the effects of acute sleep deprivation through brave volunteers. You won't catch me depriving myself of sleep; when I was young, I took part in a sleep deprivation experiment where we skipped one night's sleep, and that was bad enough. By 9 a.m., everyone was nauseous and spoiling for a fight. The world record for sleep deprivation is held by Randy Gardner, a student in San Diego, who, in January 1964, went 264.4 hours (11 days and 25 minutes) without being observed to sleep (Figure 12.11). Early on, his cognitive performance suffered so that on Day 2 he had difficulty focusing, his eyes became heavy, he became irritable, and his speech was less clear. He had headaches. By Day 6, his speech was almost incoherent and he reported extremely vivid daydreams. On Day 9, he could not complete sentences, his thoughts were fragmented, he was suffering delusions, and became paranoid. He used cold showers and walks to stay awake. When he finished, he slept for 15 hours, and most of his symptoms disappeared. He took an extra 4 hours sleep the second night and 2.5 hours extra the third night. He then seemed fully recovered (Boese, 2016).

Rats that are sleep-deprived by making them stay on little rotating discs over water die after 21–35 days without sleep (Rechtschaffen & Bergmann, 1995). Curiously, the proximal cause of death is hypothermia – the rats have difficulty controlling their internal temperature, although the exact mechanisms that lead to death remain unclear. Acute severe sleep deprivation is just as bad for humans: it causes hallucinations and a gradual progression towards psychosis with increasing time awake (Waters, Chiu, Atkinson, & Blom, 2018), and presumably sleep deprivation would eventually kill us too.

There is a long list of ill effects for chronic deprivation, from everything including bags under the eyes to headaches, increased risk of disease, to hypertension, obesity, and increased chance of type II diabetes (Gottlieb et al., 2005). In the longer term, it may increase the probability of neurodegenerative disorders such as Alzheimer's disease. Of course, we need to be careful when we find a correlation – perhaps one of the earliest signs of Alzheimer's is disrupted sleep. However, as we shall see, there is a possible causal link in the way sleep clears injurious compounds from the brain, such as the neuropeptide orexin (also called hypocretin; Kang et al., 2009; Xie et al., 2013).

It is though a balance; regularly sleeping too much produces a list of symptoms that looks just like regularly sleeping too little! Although we think of sleep as essential for good mental health (and it is), paradoxically sleep restriction might help treat depression (Riemann et al., 2001; see Box 12.4).

> **Box 12.4** Sleep Deprivation for Depression
>
> Finding the right amount of sleep involves finding a balance. We know that insomnia is one of the symptoms of clinical depression. It's something of a vicious circle: you worry and feel depressed, which stops you sleeping, which makes you more irritable and anxious. You feel fatigued, and fatigue might make you less likely to exercise, and we know that exercise helps with depression.
>
> On the other hand, several studies have shown that sleep deprivation can lift mood and improve symptoms in patients with clinical depression (Dallaspezia & Benedetti, 2015). A meta-analysis suggests it's effective for about 50% of patients (Boland et al., 2017). It has the advantage of being a *rapid-onset treatment* – it works quickly, unlike antidepressant medication. Deprivation of REM sleep is particularly effective (Vogel et al., 1975).
>
> On the down side, symptoms recur quite quickly if you stop treatment, for some the next day, and then there is the problem that long-term sleep deprivation is bad for other aspects of your health. The mechanisms involved are not well understand: as we shall see, sleep involves many neurotransmitter systems, and perhaps some of these are disrupted; sleep is involved with learning, and maybe it's the disruption to that which is key. One suggestion is that the disruption to learning and the motivation and reward system means that people are able to find things pleasurable again (Gujar et al., 2011). We don't know. And why doesn't the treatment work for everybody? Is an interaction with specific genes involved? Clearly, more work needs to be done here to understand why sleep deprivation works as an antidepressant and to find an appropriate balance.

Why Do We Sleep?

The common-sense view of sleep is that it refreshes us, and restores mental and physical energy. Is this lay view correct?

Evolutionary Functions of Sleep

Why did sleep evolve? Sleep is universal: every organism has periods of activity alternating with inactivity, and every animal has a period that could be labelled sleep, even if its manifestation is different from ours.

One evolutionary suggestion is that it keeps us out of the way of predators and safe and immobile in the dark. This proposal though doesn't account for how restorative sleep appears to be, and the many bad effects of sleep deprivation. Sleep is clearly involved in the regulation of brain plasticity underlying cognitive processes because sleep deprivation impairs performance on cognitive, motor, and perceptual learning and tasks (see

Wang et al., 2011, for a review). Given that sleep deprivation has such clear consequences, it is clear that sleep serves some important function – or more likely functions.

Another idea is that sleep is involved in getting rid of waste products from the brain. The *glymphatic system*, which clears waste products from the brain, is more effective when we sleep. The position in which you sleep affects the rate at which potentially toxic waste matter can be drained from the brain (at least from a rat brain – Lee et al., 2015; Xie et al., 2013), with sleeping on your side being more effective. In particular, the compound amyloid β, which may be involved in Alzheimer's disease later in life, is excreted more effectively from the brain at night. Therefore, sleep facilitates clearing waste, which is one reason why disruption to sleep may be associated with an increased likelihood of dementia later in life.

The *synaptic homeostasis hypothesis* states that plastic processes occurring during wakefulness result in a net increase in synaptic strength in many brain circuits. We can't go on just increasing synaptic strength because the brain would eventually consume too much energy, so sleep is seen as a mechanism for resetting and lowering the synaptic strength to a baseline level that is energetically sustainable, makes efficient use of grey matter space, and is beneficial for learning and memory. Neural plasticity is increased in SWS (Tononi & Cirelli, 2006). In addition, most of the synapses that strengthen during memory are based on glutamate. Glutamate is the most common neurotransmitter in the brain, and it's also a popular flavouring (MSG, monosodium glutamate). In the brain, too much of it is toxic, and sleep helps us clear excess. Further evidence comes from the finding that, in non-human animals, synaptic strength and density is increased in sleep-deprived animals, compared to recently rested ones. For example, sleep deprivation makes the frontal cortex more excitable to the effects of TMS as shown in EEG (Huber et al., 2013). Along very similar lines, sleep may be involved in pruning synaptic circuits (Wang et al., 2011). The synaptic homeostasis hypothesis brings us to the role of sleep in learning, which we review in the next section.

Sleep and Learning

There has long been a fascination with being able to learn during sleep. You might have seen adverts for systems that help you learn while you sleep, such as exposure to a foreign language while you sleep. There is no evidence that these systems help at all. The idea that sleep (and dreaming) are involved in learning and memory is the most widely accepted and experimentally supported hypothesis explaining our need for sleep.

We know that in the rat the hippocampus plays an essential role in episodic and spatial memory, enabling the rat to replay or self-generate neuronal sequences associated with particular paths. Early animal learning models proposed that the memory traces laid down during the day were transient, and *consolidated* or made permanent at night in SWS (see Pfeiffer, 2018, for a review). Then it was believed that different types of sleep were associated with different types of learning, culminating in a dual-process model with SWS being important for the formation of explicit, declarative memories (for events and facts), and REM sleep being important for the consolidation of non-declarative, procedural, and emotional memories (Ackermann & Rasch, 2014). Although it is agreed that many animal and human studies demonstrate the importance of SWS for explicit memory, it is now believed that the role of SWS extends to consolidating procedural memories, while the purpose of learning in REM sleep is much less clear. REM sleep seems to be involved with the processing of emotional memories, but then so is SWS sleep. In contrast, Stage 2 sleep is associated with simple motor learning. Spindles in the EEG seem to play an important role in memory formation, particularly the integration of new memories with existing knowledge (Tamminen et al., 2010). In non-REM sleep, neurons activated during motor learning during the day are reactivated, leading to the formation of new dendritic spines (Yang et al., 2014). Disruption of REM sleep did not impair spine formation and motor learning.

In summary, non-REM sleep is essential for learning, while the role of REM sleep is more mysterious. However, not only is sleep necessary for memory formation, sleep deprivation is implicated in the creation of false memories (Frenda et al., 2014). In a recent integrative review, Diekelmann and Born (2010) conclude that SWS supports the consolidation of memories relative to other memories, while REM sleep supports synaptic consolidation. During SWS, slow oscillations, spindles, and low levels of the neurotransmitter acetylcholine coordinate the reactivation and redistribution of memories from the hippocampus to the cortex. During REM sleep, high cholinergic and theta wave activity accompanies the subsequent synaptic consolidation of these memories in the cortex. It is clear that we know the basics of how sleep plays an essential role in memory consolidation, but it is just as clear that much remains to be clarified.

Chapter Summary

- Sleep is a state of reversible loss of consciousness.
- It is marked by characteristic EEG patterns.
- All organisms have some periods of inactivity among periods of activity.
- All animals sleep in varying amounts.
- Our bodies follow a circadian rhythm close to, but not exactly, 24 hours long governing our arousal level.
- Light levels, the pineal gland, and melatonin play an important role in feeling sleepy.
- Sleep can be divided into four stages depending on the pattern of electrical activity.
- Sleep is divided into REM and non-REM, with most dreams occurring later in the night in REM sleep.
- The cerveau isolé and encéphale isolé show the importance of the brainstem and reticular activating system in arousal and making us sleep.
- Neurotransmitter levels vary from wakefulness to sleep, and vary during sleep.
- The AIM model of Hobson, activation–input–modulation, shows how sleep, dreams, and wakefulness depend on activity along three dimensions.
- Sleep can be disrupted by many disorders, or parasomnias, including insomnia, sleepwalking, narcolepsy, night terrors, and talking during sleep.
- Sleep is essential, as shown by the serious effects of even mild sleep deprivation.
- Sleep clearly serves several evolutionary functions.
- Sleep and dreaming are involved in learning and memory consolidation.

Review Questions

1. Why do we sleep?
2. What is the role of sleep in learning?
3. How do neurotransmitters vary throughout an average night's sleep, and why?
4. What happens when we fall asleep?
5. Describe the range of sleep disorders found, and explain why they occur.
6. What are the effects of sleep deprivation, both in the short and long term?
7. Are we conscious when we sleep?
8. Are different parts of the brain involved in different phases of sleep?

Recommended Resources

Introductory Books on Sleep

Horne, J. (2006). *Sleepfaring: A Journey Through the Science of Sleep*. Oxford, UK: Oxford University Press.

Lewis, P.A. (2013). *The Secret World of Sleep*. New York: Palgrave Macmillan.

Martin, P. (2003). *Counting Sheep*. London: Flamingo.

Randall, D.K. (2012). *Dreamland: Adventures in the Strange World of Sleep*. New York: Norton.

Walker, M. (2018). *Why We Sleep: The New Science of Sleep and Dreams*. London: Penguin.

Sleep Texts and Sleep Disorders

Moorcroft, W.H. (2013). *Understanding Sleep and Dreaming* (2nd. ed.). New York: Springer.

Morin, C.M., Espie, C.A., and Akerstedt, T. (2012). *The Oxford Handbook of Sleep and Sleep Disorders*. Oxford, UK: Oxford University Press.

AIM Model

Hobson, A. (2017). *Conscious States: The AIM Model of Waking, Sleeping, and Dreaming*. Scotts Valley, CA: CreateSpace.

13 DREAMS

It is likely that nearly everyone dreams every night, even if we don't remember many of our dreams. On average we spend seven years of our lives dreaming.

What is going on in the precious time that we spend dreaming such that we are forced to devote seven years to it? What function, if any, does dreaming serve? And do dreams mean anything? This chapter will attempt to answer these questions. We begin by asking is our experience of dreams, that they have happened in preceding sleep, verifiable, and ask what a dream is. We then examine the phenomenon of lucid dreams, when we know we are dreaming, and sometimes able to influence activity in our dreams. We examine how accurate our memory for our dream is. We look at the differences between REM and non-REM (NREM) sleep.

We then examine what we dream about, and why we dream as we do, and why we dream at all. We look at nightmares, dreams with negative emotional content, and recurring dreams. We ask if dreams are a way of dealing with threat, and whether they are involved in creative processes. We conclude the chapter by discussing psychoanalytic theories of dreaming, and the mechanisms Freud argued we use to manufacture dreams.

Are Dreams Real?

First, we need to question whether dreams can be taken at face value. The American philosopher Norman Malcolm argued not. A sceptic could argue that we don't dream at all, but make up the experience when we wake. Even if we accept that a dream did happen, we only have the dreamer's word that the content of dreaming is as reported (even if it is reported in good faith). Everything about dreaming appears to be *unverifiable* (Malcolm, 1959).

This extreme sceptical position is now contradicted by neuroscience data that provides a coherent account of what is happening while we are dreaming (Windt, 2015). It is, however, true that we don't have direct access to the dream itself; we only have access to our memory of the dream. Usually our memory of dreams fades very quickly, and it is only by rehearsing the dream that we can maintain our memory of it. This artefact applies particularly to trying to recall dreams the morning after. We might have a better record if we wake during the night and try to note them immediately, but even then we are reliant on recalling the dream. Perhaps recalling the dream distorts it? When I remember my dreams, I am often worried that I am imposing more order and plot than might have really been there.

Nevertheless, there is no research to make us doubt that dreams are at least mostly as we report them. We can accept the assumptions that dream reports pretty much faithfully reflect core elements of dream experiences as plausible, and that our reports are transparent (Windt, 2013, 2015). It appears that many other animals, at least mammals, dream because they show similar markers of REM sleep as humans (Frith et al., 1999). Cats with lesions to the brain that remove the paralysis normally associated with REM sleep move as though acting out dreams (Jouvet, 1979). Animals also show similar patterns of neurotransmitters as humans, with high levels of acetylcholine during REM sleep (Stickgold, 1998). This conclusion will not come as a surprise to anyone who is a companion to an animal such as a dog, as they will often notice something of their little doggie dreams in progress (Figure 13.1).

Figure 13.1 Beau asleep. How similar is Beau's sleep to mine? Does he have little doggie dreams full of doggie phallic symbols?

Box 13.1 Zhuangzi's (Chuang-Tzu's) Butterfly Dream

One of the most famous symbolic dreams is that of the Taoist philosopher Zhuangzi (also transcribed as Chuang-Tzu, 369–286 BCE). The dream can be summarised as:

> Once, I, Zhuangzi, dreamt that I was a butterfly, fluttering around. I was conscious only of my happiness as a butterfly, unaware that I was Zhuangzi. Then I woke up, and then I was myself again. Now, I do not know whether I was then a man dreaming I was a butterfly, or whether I am now a butterfly, dreaming I am a man. Between a man and a butterfly there is necessarily a distinction.

> **Box 13.1** (cont.)

Figure 13.2 Zhuangzi's butterfly dream. I dream I am a butterfly and then I wake; but how do I know I am really awake? The photograph shows a red postman butterfly. Source: Susan Walker/Moment/Getty Images.

What is illusion and what is reality (see Figure 13.2)? How do we know when we're dreaming and when we're awake? When I wake up, am I really waking up to 'reality', or am I just waking up to another level of dream (as sometimes does happen)? We cannot be sure of anything.

We can also see the transition from butterfly to man as a metaphor for self-awakening and the transformation of the self to one with greater insight and understanding. The transition represents enlightenment.

What Is a Dream?

A dream is a series of thoughts, images, ideas, and emotions, often connected into some kind of story, that we have while asleep. We're aware of these ideas and images, but we are rarely self-aware during the dream.

I find there are few things quite as tedious as having to listen to somebody else's dream, but here is one of mine, chosen at random from my dream diary:

> I'm watching and involved in a remake of 'Bewitched', set in California. First of all, there's Darren the husband. You can see him driving a small, if not tiny, train along the beach next to the sea. A naughty boy from the neighbourhood makes the train crash into something. Lots of dogs escape from the train. No one is hurt, but there's a bit of a mess, and dogs are running about everywhere. Samantha is having a party and Darren is going to be late. Samantha comes to the rescue and clears up the mess and dogs, and punishes the boy. We can see the incident from a wonderful house looking down at the train, coast, and accident, from a house in the cliffs. I'm at the party with all the other guests. We're discussing the house and saying how good things are. I say something like, 'Excuse me, but this is the best house I've ever seen.' We run out of champagne. I think about going out to buy another two bottles. I vaguely wonder why Samantha doesn't just use her powers to bring more champagne for the party. I have this sense that my mother is there too. It's a lovely day, with sunshine and deep blue skies.

My dream illustrates many of the features of dreams. First, many dreams are bizarre. My dream has many bizarre elements: picture a man riding a tiny train that when it crashes spills a load of full-sized dogs. Dreams don't obey the laws of physics. Second, there is a story of sorts, but it doesn't really make much sense as a linear story. It jumps about a lot, and one thing follows from another, rarely referring back to early story elements to form a coherent narrative. Third, the point of view keeps on changing. Sometimes I'm involved, sometimes I'm just watching, sometimes it's as though I'm another participant in the dream. Finally, there's no reflection on what is happening. I don't stop to think: 'big dogs spilling out of a tiny train; wait, that isn't possible'. The dream carries on without any meta-awareness.

As you might expect, specific visual dream content is associated with the activation of the same areas of the brain as the visual cortical activity pattern associated with stimulus representation (such as humans or scenes) to the extent that it is possible to predict what people might be dreaming about given the pattern of their cortical activation (Horikawa et al., 2013).

It is a mistake to equate dreams with **REM** sleep (Solms, 2000). Dreams are more common in REM sleep, but they do occur in **NREM** sleep too. Dreams in REM sleep tend to be longer and more bizarre; NREM dreams tend to be shorter and sometimes more like isolated thoughts than long complex stories (Hobson, 2009). Note that it is more difficult to detect dreams in NREM sleep as there are fewer overt markers (such as, by definition, eye movements), so we almost certainly do not know as much about NREM dreams. Perhaps the greater memorability of REM dreams is an artefact. We do know that dream reports are associated with an increase in high-frequency activation in posterior cortical regions, called the *parieto-occipital hot zone*, while an increase in low-frequency activation in these regions is associated with an absence of dream experience (Siclari et al., 2017). It follows that REM sleep deprivation is not quite the same as dream deprivation.

We have seen (Chapter 1) that one definition of consciousness is that it is what is lost in dreamless sleep. One problem with this definition is the concept of 'dreamless sleep' rather begs the question of what dreams are (Windt et al., 2016). Do all manifestations of consciousness disappear in dreamless sleep? If we define dreams as hallucinatory experiences in sleep, does sleep thinking and sensation of movement constitute a dream? What about sleep walking and sleep talking (the latter not always corresponding to any mentation reported afterwards)? Hence we should treat the notion of 'dreamless sleep' with some caution.

> **TRY THIS: Keeping a Dream Diary**
>
> Keep a dream diary, at least for a few weeks. The easiest version is simply to use a notepad to record your dreams when you wake up. Slightly more sophisticated, and in my experience giving much better results, is to use a voice recorder on a smartphone. I obtained the best results with a voice-activated recorder; these devices can be bought fairly cheaply.

How Well Do We Remember Our Dreams?

We don't ordinarily remember dreams at all well. Often, on waking we remember a dream, but within a few minutes we are unable to remember anything much about it at all. Very soon the topic of the dream will have gone, a feature of dreams known as *dream amnesia*.

Occasionally, I do remember a particular dream very clearly, with the dream lingering into the day, and it's not always a wholly pleasant experience. Such events make me rather glad that I don't remember all my dreams perfectly. You could end up confused and distressed. There also appears to be a great deal of individual variation in how well people remember their dreams. I am very interested in my dreams, and put more effort into noting and recording them than most people, so am more likely to have relatively good memory for them.

Other factors determine how well people remember their dreams in addition to how interested we are in them. A tendency to wake frequently through the night will lead to better recall. Personality variables such as high openness to experience, higher scores on creativity measures, and absorption scores (see Chapter 14 on hypnosis) correlate with better dream recall (Ruby et al., 2013; Schredl, 2008; Watson, 2003). It is possible that these differences are underpinned by neurophysiological differences. Ruby et al. (2013) showed that people with good dream recall showed a more sustained decrease in alpha activity when they heard first names embedded in a string of tones than people with poor dream recall, suggesting that the names are processed more deeply. A decrease in alpha corresponds to the release of inhibiting processes and increased excitability. This tendency could be reflected in people with better dream recall waking briefly more often during sleep.

Windt (2015) reviews work showing that better dream recall is associated with particular brain states that are different from brain states associated with waking episodic remembering. The **temporo-parietal junction (TPJ)** and parts of the medial prefrontal cortex (mPFC) are particularly important for dream recall (Eichenlaub et al., 2014); we saw in Chapter 7 that the TPJ is particularly important in generating our sense of self, particularly in space. Taken together, all these findings suggest that dreams are different from other forms of cognition. Dreams appear to be the products of particular brain systems, which are periodically activated during sleep, and differences in the processes involved in making them lead to some people recalling them better than others (see Figure 13.3).

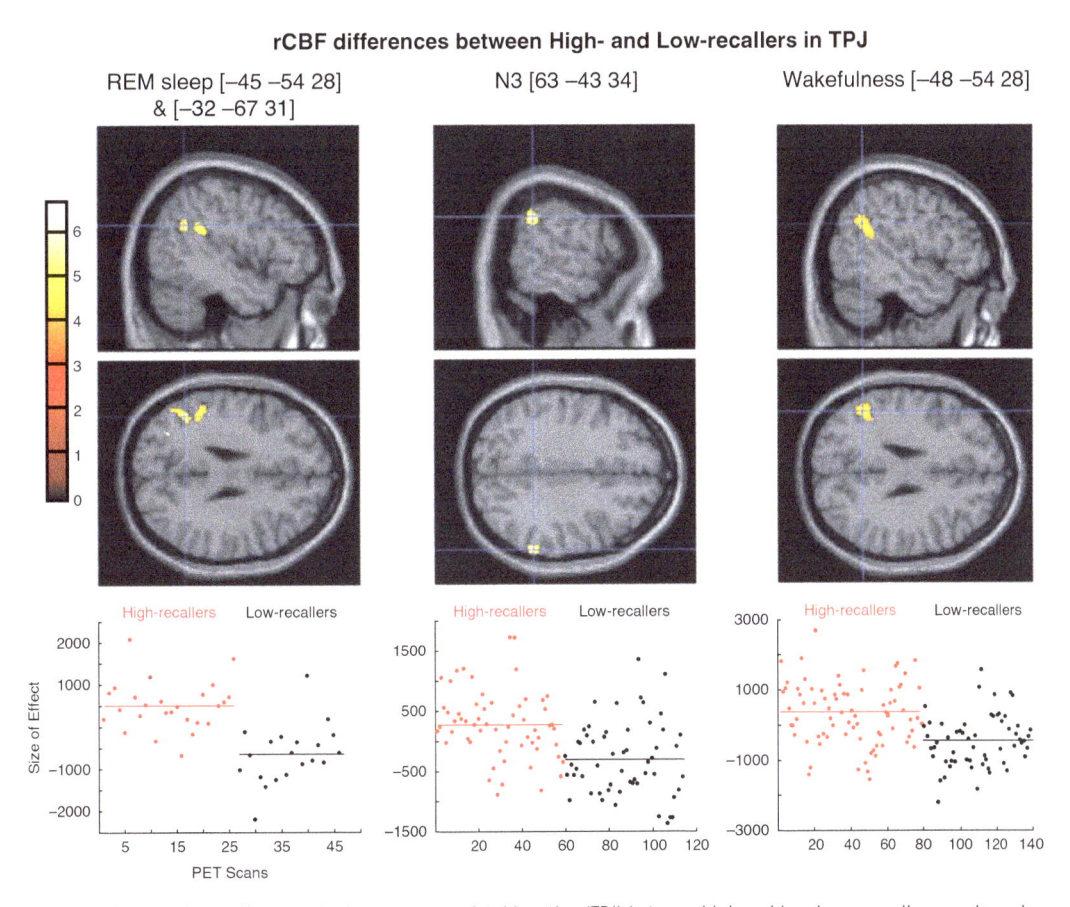

Figure 13.3 Blood flow differences in the temporo-parietal junction (TPJ) between high and low dream recallers as shown by average PET scans. rCBF is regional cerebral blood flow. Data is shown for REM sleep, wakefulness, and N3 (deep slow-wave sleep). Source: Eichenlaub et al. (2014).

Lucid Dreams

Most of the time, most of us are not aware that we are dreaming. A dream in which we are aware we are dreaming is called a **lucid dream**. Surveys suggest that about half the population have a lucid dream at least once in their lives (Blackmore, 1991). There are varying degrees of lucidity, from full-blown knowledge that one is dreaming to nothing more than a hint of awareness that something is different. Many people, on realising that they are dreaming, then attempt to control their dreams, although they are not always successful. Some have argued that this element of attempting to control and influence the dream is so ubiquitous that it should be part of the definition of lucid dreaming (Tart, 1988). One of the most popular activities attempted in lucid dreaming is flying. (I only have occasional semi-lucid dreams, and perhaps because of this, I go no further than levitating around the room a little.) Some dreamers are reliably cued that they are dreaming by noticing aberrant features of the dreamscape. One dreamer noticed that the paving stones outside his house were the wrong way round, and entered a prolonged and detailed lucid dream (Fox, 1962). Others are prompted by a feeling of wrongness in the dream that it isn't reality.

Levels of REM activation are exceptionally high in lucid dreams, probably because of activation of the dorsolateral prefrontal cortex (Kahn & Hobson, 2005). This observation is important because this brain region is usually deactivated while sleeping and is important for executive processing. The conclusion is that lucidity is associated with executive functions that are usually missing from sleep being involved (see Figure 13.4).

There are numerous techniques for attempting to promote lucid dreams, as well as commercially available devices. Generally the standard of methodology of studies examining methods for inducing lucid dreams is low, and no method induces them consistently and reliably (Stumbrys et al., 2012). The most successful methods include some form of external stimulation, and a cycle of intention, imagining being asleep, and autosuggestion.

Lucid dreaming is associated with gamma activity (25–40 Hz) in the frontal and temporal regions. Voss et al. (2014) demonstrated a causal relationship using a system known as *tACS* (transcranial alternating current stimulation) to stimulate the brain at different frequencies; as predicted, only 25 and 40 Hz stimulation was associated with a

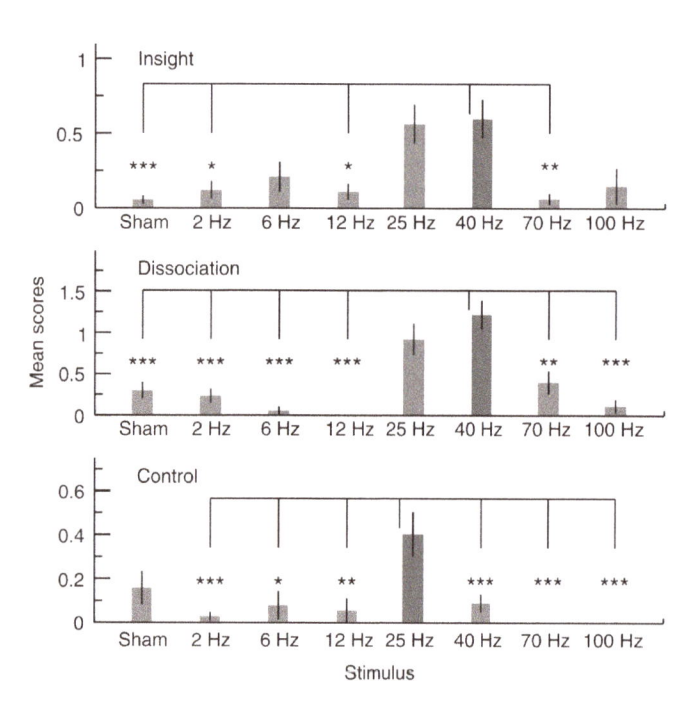

Figure 13.4 Stimulation at 25–40 Hz of the frontal and temporal regions increases dream lucidity. This gamma wave range stimulation increases reports of insight, dissociation, and control, all associated with lucidity. Source: Voss et al. (2014).

LUCID DREAMS

significant increase in the number of lucid dreams reported (see Figure 13.5). Although the neuroscience of lucid dreaming is in its infancy, there is some evidence that frontal and parietal areas are more involved than in non-lucid dreaming (Baird et al., 2019). A word of caution: as yet, there is only a single case study of fMRI and lucid dreaming.

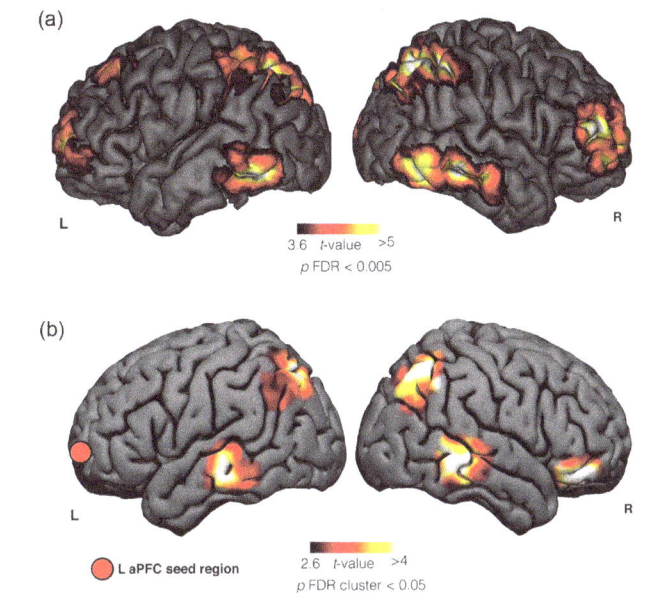

Figure 13.5 Frontal and parietal areas are more involved in lucid dreaming than in non-lucid dreaming. The top diagrams show a single case study of a lucid dreamer, and the lower differences between the lucid dreamer and non-lucid dreamers. Increased activation is seen in the anterior prefrontal cortex (aPFC) and the medial and lateral parietal cortex. Source: Baird et al. (2019).

TRY THIS: Have a Lucid Dream

There are numerous books and websites dedicated to having lucid dreams. Stumbrys et al. (2012) list and evaluate all methods. I have tried many of them without success, but perhaps I just lack the perseverance that is supposed to be necessary. You can also buy lucid dream machines; no one I know has ever had great success with them, but a few have reported a few lucid dreams. Try some of the techniques you find. Do they give you lucid dreams? Does the lucidity of your dreams improve with practice? Note that some people caution against trying to have lucid dreams more than once every three days.

TRY THIS: Dream Enhancers

I am most reluctant to suggest that you should take any sort of drug, but I have experimented with choline and lecithin late at night. Note that these are supplements that are completely legal and widely available without prescription online. Choline is a water-soluble vitamin of the B group and the body easily disposes of excess in the urine. I have also tried sage leaf

> **TRY THIS:** (cont.)
>
> extract and galantamine (found naturally in snowdrops). Galantamine is a cholinesterase inhibitor (it builds up the level of the neurotransmitter acetylcholine in the brain by inhibiting the chemical that normally breaks it down) and has been shown to be effective in increasing the frequency of lucid dreams (Sparrow et al., 2018). When self-experimenting alone, it is very difficult to control for a placebo effect, but I believe my dreams are slightly more vivid with choline. You might experiment with taking a small additional dose of a multivitamin B an hour before bedtime.

Dream Content

What do we dream about, and why? The morning I wrote this section, I had a complex dream where I travelled back in time to help the Prime Minister, Harold Macmillan, win World War II, because something had gone wrong and the Russians were going to rush ahead on the eastern front because they had just lost the tank battle at Kursk (in fact, they won). The narrative was amazingly complex and almost plausible. It is obvious to me, at least that such a dream cannot be wholly randomly generated. The dream also contained a few references to what I had been doing earlier that day (I had been reading an article on spies), but not enough to be able to explain the whole dream.

You will notice if you keep a dream diary that we do incorporate fragments of the previous day's events. These fragments are called the *daily residue*. But we clearly dream about much more than that day's events. We also dream about past events, but not as you might suppose the most recent events; material from days 2 to 4 before the dream is less likely to be incorporated into a night's dreaming than material from days 5 to 7, an effect called the *dream lag* (Blagrove et al., 2011; Nielsen et al., 2004). The likely explanation is that there is a weekly (*circaseptan*) rhythm to memory consolidation, although the details are currently unclear.

The content of dreams resembles the content of daydreams, suggesting that the DMN may be involved in dreaming; in both states, content is drawn from current concerns enhanced by associated memories, and is largely audio-visual and emotional in content. Fox et al. (2013) argue that daydreams and night dreams are on a continuum, with dreaming being more visual and more immersive, and dreaming involving even less prefrontal cortex than daydreaming,

There are also cultural patterns and developmental differences in dream content. Animals appear more frequently in children's dreams and dreams of people from hunter-gatherer societies. The nature of dreams changes as we grow up (Foulkes, 2002). The earliest dreams, up to age five, have no plot and no dreamer participation. Social interaction starts to appear between five and seven, and self participation increases between seven and nine, and finally different emotions and novel characters appear from age nine on.

> **Box 13.2 Dream Content**
>
> G. William Domhoff, an American psychologist, along with Adam Schneider, is one of the founders of The DreamBank, an online collection of over 20 000 dreams (Domhoff & Schneider, 2008). The bank has sophisticated search facilities, and can be used for studying hypotheses about dreams that can only be tested against large datasets.
>
> For example, Domhoff (2003, 2017) analysed large sample of dreams for the number of times people dreamed about particular categories of things:
>
> characters (animals, men and women, friends, strangers)
> activities (thinking, talking, running)
> emotions (happy, sad, embarrassed)
> social interactions (aggression, friendliness, sexuality).
>
> Domhoff found that the proportion of dreams of these categories were stable across time within people. He notes that about 70% of dreams are about personal concerns in the past, present, and future, and that people do not dream about politics, religion, or economics. The more concerned we are about a topic the more we dream about it.
>
> Many of the dreams in the bank are dream diaries deposited by non-researchers. People have many different reasons for recording their dreams. Some see it as a means to personal growth, some for dealing with trauma, and some for keeping memories of the deceased. There is something curious and touching about reading other people's dreams.

Nightmares

Nightmares are dreams that are associated with strong feelings of terror, fear, and distress that wake the sleeper. The sleeper will have emotional responses on waking, might be drenched with sweat, and might wake talking or screaming. Their mood might be affected for some time afterwards, and they might have difficulty returning to sleep. Children reportedly have more nightmares. Most adults have nightmares from time to time, but some people experience them more frequently; if they are frequent enough to bother the person, they are labelled as suffering from *nightmare disorder* in DSM-5. Nightmare disorder is a parasomnia that is distinct from night terrors.

Another relatively common source of unpleasant dreams is the intruder experience, that someone has entered your room, or perhaps is lurking outside, or looking at you with malevolent intention. I often dream that I look outside and someone is looking in my window; a variant is that I come home to find the door open, house burgled, and invariably, my stereo speakers stolen. These sensed presences are often followed by auditory hallucinations, such as voices or footsteps. I once experienced hearing footsteps coming up the stairs, the stairs creaking very realistically, accompanied by low voices, and another bedroom door being opened and shut. I was so convinced that I had experienced this sequence that I burst into the other room with a poker, only to find it, of course, deserted, at which point I concluded that I had simply had a very realistic dream. Such experiences are best described as not uncommon.

People who are suffering from ill health or mental illnesses may tend to have more frequent nightmares. Hartmann (1998) suggests that the nightmares are a way for people to work through their problems, a belief widely held, although it should be pointed out that many studies have not found any such relationship. Stress, anxiety, and mental illness are all thought to be associated with nightmares. In a not dissimilar vein, Nielsen and Levin (2007) argue that nightmares are associated with problems with fear, particularly as a result of a failure of the usual fear extinction function of dreams. Some researchers have suggested that it is the severity of the nightmare rather than the frequency that is associated with psychopathology (Barrett, 1996). The one thing that is clear here is that much is unclear, and more work needs to be done.

There are probably several causes for occasional and frequent nightmares. Frequent nightmares are associated with post-traumatic stress disorder (PTSD), and may involve the sufferer reliving the traumatic event (Pagel, 2000). PTSD dreams are associated with problems with *fear extinction*, meaning that people continue to be afraid of something they need no longer be afraid of (Nielsen & Levin, 2007).

Nightmare disorder can be treated by a variety of psychoactive drugs, none of which is wholly effective, but the most effective of which for PTSD is *prazosin* (Kung et al., 2012). Prazosin doesn't seem to work for non-PTSD nightmares. Although prazosin blocks the action of the 'stress hormone' norepinephrine in the brain, how that affects dreams isn't currently understood.

Box 13.3 Sleep Paralysis

Sleep paralysis is a state where a person wakes and finds themselves paralysed; it can happen when people are waking from falling asleep. People sometimes hallucinate voices and noises, such as bangs as they wake. (In the rare instances it has happened to me, I have hallucinated the sound of the doorbell ringing; I try to get up but can't.) Sometimes people also dream that they are being held or grabbed; often this is accompanied by a feeling of intense fear. Sleep paralysis results from the muscle paralysis of REM sleep persisting briefly into waking. The reasons why this persistence happens are unclear. People with recurrent sleep paralysis tend to show a pattern of more fragmented REM sleep (Walther & Schulz, 2004). Paralysis might be occasional or persistent, and if necessary can be treated with cognitive behavioural therapy and antidepressant drugs.

These episodes occasionally involve something sitting on the person's chest, which is stopping them from moving (Hufford, 1989). The manifestation of the object is culture specific, being labelled as the Old Hag of northeastern US folklore, or an incubus in western

DREAM CONTENT

> **Box 13.3** (cont.)
>
> legend and romantic art. An incubus is famously portrayed in Fuseli's (1802) painting *The Nightmare* (Figure 13.6). Mercutio talks about the Hag pressing on maids in dreams in Shakespeare's *Romeo and Juliet*.
>
> **Figure 13.6** 'The Nightmare' (1802) by Henry Fuseli. A classic depiction of a nightmare, with vision and an incubus sitting on the woman's chest preventing her from breathing properly – conveying the idea of paralysis on waking from the nightmare. Source: Heritage Images/Hulton Archive/Getty Images.

Recurring Dreams

For decades, I had a *recurring dream* where I would turn up to an end-of-college exam to discover I had done no revision or preparation. More recently, the dream has morphed into turning up to give a presentation only to find I had no slides and hadn't prepared at all. Talking to other people, I have found that such recurring exam dreams are quite common, and intuitively are provoked by anxiety. Other common recurring dream themes are losing control of a car, being late, being attacked, being unable to find a toilet (for obvious reasons), and finding something is novel or wrong about your home.

An internet search will throw up many suggested meanings for recurring dreams, usually with little evidence to support the contention. One common suggestion is along the lines that our unconscious is trying to give us a message that we are refusing to hear. Freud talked about recurring dreams; he speculated that men who repeatedly dreamed about their hair or teeth falling out were suffering from castration anxiety (Sulloway, 1979). I have never dreamed about my hair or teeth falling out (so far).

Several explanations have been proposed for why we dream about some things repeatedly. In Revonsuo's (2000) *threat simulation theory*, recurring dreams are naturally a means of simulating particular concerns. Around 66% of recurring dream themes contain at least one threat (Zadra et al., 2006). The same study found that often the dreamer does not succeed in resolving the threat. If recurring dreams are a way of coping with threats, why do they fail to resolve the threat? On the other hand, perhaps recurring dreams represent attempts to resolve threats that are proving stubborn to resolve. More research is needed here. Recurring nightmares are also observed in PTSD (Davis et al., 2007). Freud (1899) thought that recurring themes showed particular neurotic traits, and as there was an underlying problem the dream would recur until the problem was resolved.

Recent research suggests that dreams of failing an exam can be correlated with better performance on the test. Researchers collected dream reports from medical students on several nights before an important exam and found that dreams about the exam on the nights before predicted proportionally higher scores, even though the dreams generally were perceived to be negative (Arnulf et al., 2014). Perhaps dreaming of the exam, even negatively, reflects a stronger desire and motivation to succeed, and maybe the dream helps consolidate memories relevant to what has to be learned (Wamsley et al., 2010). So negative recurrent dreams may serve a positive function.

Introspecting, my sense is that, when I dream about certain things a few times, they become part of the *daily residue* and an attractor in cognitive space, as it were. I have several recurring dreams (a jet falling out of the sky, a nuclear explosion, being burgled, being in *Dr Who* or *Star Trek*), as, it seems, do most people. The dreams don't have any great significance other than that, once I've dreamed the same dream a few times, I'm more likely to do so again in the future. We dream about what we think about.

There is no agreed explanation for why we have recurring dreams, and it is likely that there is more than one reason.

Why Do We Dream?

As is the case with sleep, dreaming might have evolved to satisfy more than one need, so the ideas discussed here need not be in competition. We will consider several explanations. There is less clarity about the purpose of dreaming than there is about the purpose of sleep.

Some researchers argue that dreams do not actually serve any purpose and have no significant influence on our waking actions at all, but are just a random by-product of REM sleep. In the activation-synthesis model, Hobson and McCarley (1977) proposed that dreams are caused by the random firing of neurons in the cortex during REM, and the consequent random activation of memories turned into a narrative. This theory helps explain the irrationality of the mind during REM periods, as, according to this theory, the forebrain then creates a story in an attempt to reconcile and make sense of the nonsensical sensory information presented to it. The peculiar nature of dreams is therefore attributable to certain parts of the brain trying to piece together a story out of what is essentially random information presented to it by the release of acetylcholine from the brainstem during REM sleep. This theory explains both why dreams are so bizarre and why dreams are usually so difficult to remember.

Some researchers point to a similarity between daydreaming and night dreams and argue that the default mode network is involved in dream generation. Domhoff and Fox (2015) take this line, arguing for the additional involvement of the visual and sensor-motor cortices. This idea is supported by imaging studies that show that the hubs involved in the DMN are more active in REM sleep than when we are at rest (Chow et al., 2013; Fox et al., 2013; see Figure 13.7). The central idea is that dreaming is more or less 'daydreaming at night' (Domhoff, 2011).

Dreaming and Creativity

There is a common belief that dreaming is related to creativity and problem solving in that people have good ideas and solve problems in their sleep. It is indeed well known that resting from solving a problem can facilitate finding a solution, a process known as incubation.

There are certainly many anecdotes about people solving problems in their sleep. The German-born physiologist Otto Loewi (1873–1961) won the Nobel Prize in Physiology or Medicine in 1936 for his work on the chemical transmission of nerve impulses. The idea for the key experiment on detecting chemical transmission in frogs came to him in a dream.

One of the most famous anecdotes is the story of the German chemist Friedrich August Kekulé. In 1890, he told the story of how he worked out the structure of the benzene molecule 25 years earlier. The structure had been perplexing chemists for some time; it was known that the molecule contained six carbon atoms, but how were they arranged? He told the story of how, while thinking about the problem, he started to fall asleep, and dreamed of seeing the atoms dancing around until they formed an image of a snake, which then formed a circle by swallowing its own tail (an ancient symbol known as ouroboros). On waking, he realised that the structure of benzene involved the six carbon atoms forming a ring (see Figures 13.8 and 13.9).

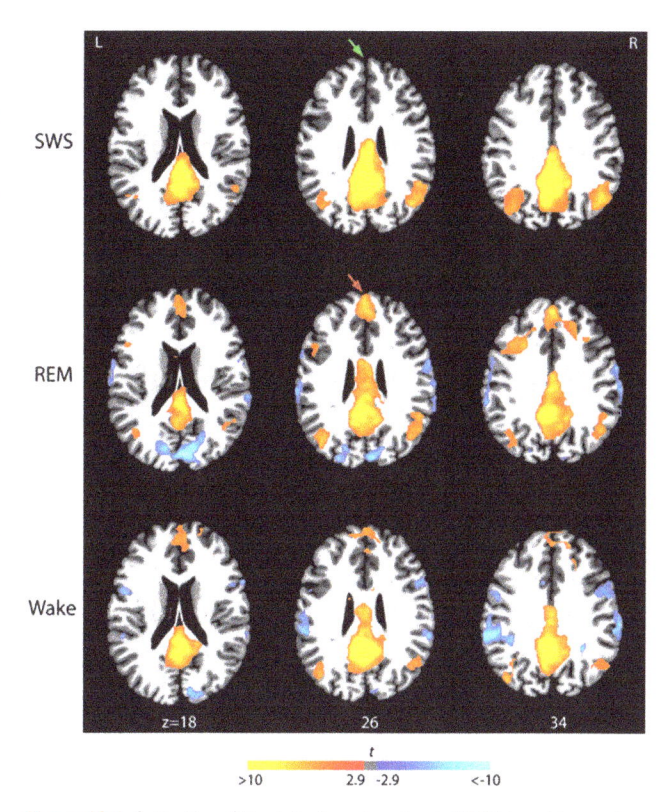

Figure 13.7 Activation of the default mode network (DMN) in waking and REM states contrasted with slow-wave sleep (SWS) as shown by fMRI. The anterior and posterior regions of the DMN are connected in REM and wakefulness but decoupled in SWS. Source: Chow et al. (2013).

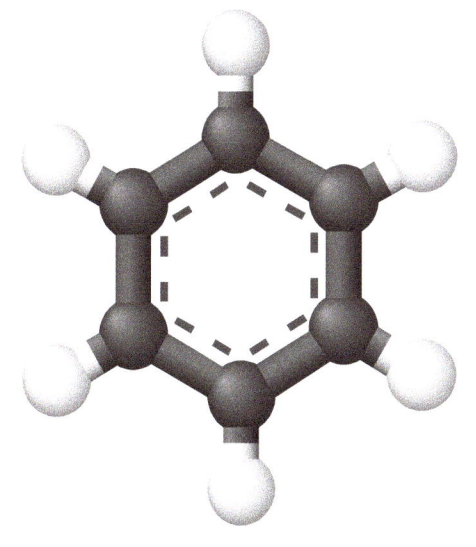

Figure 13.8 The structure of benzene. The chemical formula of benzene is C_6H_6; it forms a ring-like structure.

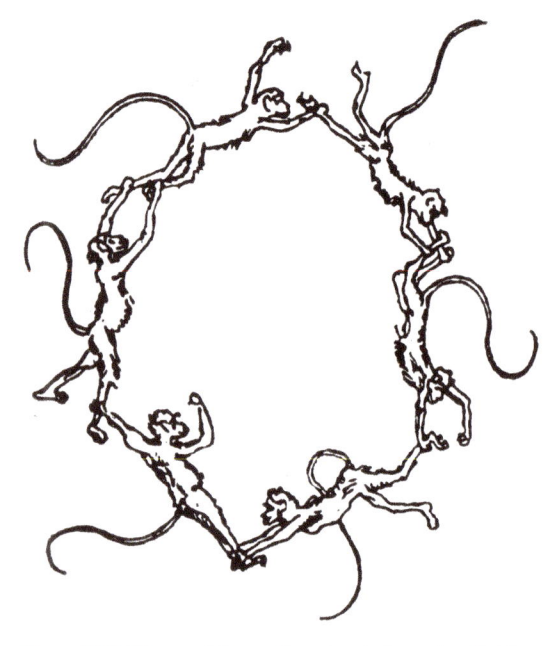

Figure 13.9 'The round dance of monkeys': six monkeys holding hands and paws. An inspirational way of representing the structure of benzene, supposedly by Kekulé himself. Source: Interfoto/Alamy Stock Photo.

Notice the story of the dream was told much later, and also we know that dreaming mostly occurs later in the night. Some sources refer to the dream as a 'reverie', and in some accounts Kekulé talked about seeing six monkeys holding hands, rather than a snake, although Kekulé did describe another dream involved in working out the structure. It all goes to show the problem of drawing conclusions from anecdotes, especially ones reported long after the event.

There are so many anecdotes concerning scientific discovery alone that we should be reluctant to dismiss the idea as having no grounding. The Russian chemist Mendeley attributed his discovery of the structure of the periodic table in 1869 to a period of incubation while falling asleep after thinking about the problem. The Indian mathematician Srinivasa Ramanujan reported that many of his proofs were presented to him by a Hindu goddess while he was dreaming. The inventor Thomas Edison said that when he had a problem to solve he would sit in a comfortable chair with a metal ball in his hand; as he drifted off to sleep he would drop the ball, and the solution to his problem would be there.

Llewellyn (2013, 2015) ascribes a central role to creativity in dreams, and sees dreams as a way of rehearsing possibilities without coming to any harm. For her, dreams are involved in encoding episodic memory, in particular, elaborative encoding of memories where associations are made. Dreams are *hyperassociative* in that normally associations with a particular idea are further reaching and more bizarre than in waking life.

Are Dreams a Way of Dealing with Threat?

One influential theory is that dreaming is a way of dealing with threat. The **threat simulation theory of dreaming (TST)** (Revonsuo, 2000) says that dreams are an ancient biological defence mechanism selected by evolution for its capacity to repeatedly simulate threats. In a dream, we can safely try out different ways of escaping a threat. The dreaming brain is particularly suitable for this role because it generates a conscious experience while being isolated from both sensory input and motor output, meaning that we can't come to any harm.

TST predicts that real threatening events we encounter during wakefulness should lead to an increased activation of the threat system, a threat simulation response, and therefore to more and more severe threatening events in dreams. Valli et al. (2005) tested this hypothesis by analysing the content of dream reports from 122 severely traumatised and less traumatised Kurdish children and 82 non-traumatised Finnish children. The results supported TST. The severely traumatised children reported significantly more dreams and their dreams included a higher number of threatening events, and the threats were judged to be more severe.

Children tend to have many nightmares, and what are called 'primal' dreams, dreams similar to the kinds of dreams humans might have experienced millennia ago, about very basic threats such as being attacked by animals. As children get older, these dreams tend to fade, and their dreams become based more on the subject matter of modern adult life.

Although some dreams clearly deal with threats, it is difficult to cast all dreams as them. Hence, TST is probably just one dream-creation mechanism, albeit an important one.

Psychoanalysis and Dreams

How, most readers will wonder, can a book about consciousness leave a discussion of psychoanalysis and dreaming until halfway through? Sigmund Freud's ideas on dreaming have entered the popular imagination and are considered by some to be at the heart of twentieth-century thinking about humanity. In 2001, *Time Magazine* called Freud one of the most important thinkers of the twentieth century. Yet, as we have seen in his thinking about the unconscious (see Chapter 6), psychologists and neuroscientists see nothing apart from historical value in Freud's work. There is little evidence to support Freud's psychoanalytic theory of the origin of dreams.

> **TRY THIS:** Are There Threats in Your Dreams
>
> Examine your dream diary. Could every dream be construed as dealing with some kind of threat? If not, what proportion?

Freud's ideas about the purpose of dreaming was elucidated in many books and lectures but primarily in *The Interpretation of Dreams* (1899). There are two main ideas: that dreams are a *defence mechanism*, and that by analysing them we can understand the unconscious. Dreams occur as a result of the activity of the unconscious during sleep, with the basic idea of the dream expressing the fulfilment of some *wish*, such as the Oedipal drama of murdering your father and sleeping with your mother. The unconscious content is too unpalatable and might well wake us, so the dream process disguises the true dream content. Hence, the dream has a hidden *latent content* and its actual *manifest content*, and the task of the analyst is to help the patient understand the latent content through discussion and free association. Note that Freud explicitly argued against the contention that all dreams were necessarily sexual in their underlying nature.

The dream process uses several mechanisms to disguise the latent content. *Displacement* is disguising one idea with another, such as dreaming of a partner when the target is the mother. *Condensation* is the combination of two or more ideas into one, such as dreaming of an ambiguous person. The most famous mechanism, however, is through the use of *symbols*, such as a cigar representing a penis or a rocket launching representing sex (see Figure 13.10).

Carl Gustav Jung (1875–1961) began his psychoanalytical career as a close follower of Freud – indeed, Freud saw Jung as his psychoanalytical heir. They split, however, when Jung concluded

Figure 13.10 Dream symbols. *The Flying Scotsman* by a tunnel, belching white smoke. We leave the reader to guess for what this might be a symbol. Source: Lenki/500px/500Px Plus/Getty Images.

that Freud put too much emphasis on sex. Jung instead stressed a person's spiritual development, a process he called *individuation*. Jung also believed that they contained symbols ripe for interpretation in helping people to overcome trauma and to advance spiritually. In contrast to Freud, Jung believed that dreams revealed, while Freud argued that they concealed. He also believed that dreams show us the archetypal symbols of the collective unconscious (see Chapter 6). He argued that occasionally we have *big dreams* that are particularly important in helping with individuation.

The problem with both approaches is that there is no evidence that these processes are happening when we dream, while there is plenty of evidence that other things are happening. To accept the psychoanalytic approach to dreams, you also need to buy into the whole psychoanalytic theory, for which, again, there is no hard evidence. Nevertheless, a large industry has been built up on interpreting dreams, and listing dream meanings and symbols. It is most unlikely that everyone dreaming about going up stairs is doing so because they have decided to put more effort into their life goals.

Alfred Adler (1870–1937) also originally worked with Freud, being a core member and the first president of the Vienna Psychoanalytic Society, although he also split with Freud over a disagreement about the importance of psychosexual development. Adler developed many important ideas about success, achievement, and one's feelings about oneself. He developed the idea of the inferiority complex, where a person's feelings are affected by their sense of worth, particularly a sense of inadequacy, which can lead to aggressive behaviour in compensation. Adler was impressed by the importance of dream interpretation, but he downplayed the sexual element, instead stressing social factors and a person's sense of self worth (Adler & Brett, 2009). He also did not think that we and our dreams are ruled by our unconscious. Dreams are about solving external and internal problems people face in everyday life, and reveal strong feelings, the things that people are really concerned about. Dreams are also a way of compensating for what we consider our inadequacies in waking life. A person worried about being a poor public speaker might have a dream in which they give a wonderful speech, for example. Adler thought that people could learn from what their dreams were telling them, and that they might cast light on how we can solve our problems. In many respects, I think this approach is close to what many lay people think about dreams: they are telling us something, they're not all about sex, and we can learn about something.

TRY THIS: Dream Symbols

Record dreams for a few nights. Find a dictionary of dream meanings or symbols – there are many available freely online. Analyse your dreams according to a dictionary. How plausible is the interpretation? Look at your dream diary from the earlier activity. Does it ring true in any way?

Post-analytic Dream Theories

Several dream interpreters since Freud and the other early psychoanalysts have worked in a broad tradition that goes well beyond the ideas of Freud, and are hence called *post-analytic*.

Calvin Hall (1953) adopted a systematic approach to dream interpretation. He asked participants to log thousands of dreams, and then searched for regularities in those dreams using a coding system. Hall argued that you cannot analyse dreams unless you know the sorts of things a person tends to dream about: the people, the settings, the actions of the dreamer and others within a dream, objects, and the outcome. For Hall, the goal is not to understand the dream, but to understand the dreamer. The sociologist G. William Domhoff worked with Hall and developed his content analysis approach to dream interpretation (see Box 13.2). Domhoff (2001, 2003, 2017) proposed a *neurocognitive* approach to dreaming in which dreaming depends upon the maturation and maintenance of a specific network of forebrain structures. He argues that the output of this dreaming neural network is guided by a *continuity principle* linked to current personal concerns and a *repetition principle* rooted in past emotional preoccupations.

David Foulkes also stresses the importance of the development of dreaming, having studied the dreams of children aged 3–15. Foulkes (2002) proposes a cognitive theory of dream origin where dreams form connections between knowledge already stored in the brain. Understanding a dream resembles solving a puzzle.

Dreams and Learning

We have seen that REM sleep and therefore dreaming plays an uncertain role in learning and memory, contrary to what was thought by researchers just a few years ago. It is possible that dreams are more involved with forgetting than remembering. On this account, dreams are involved in pruning memories. Crick and Mitchison (1983) hypothesised that synapses activated during dreams become weakened rather than strengthened. According to this theory, the content of our dreams has little real significance; instead, we dream about the waste products of our experience. While dreams might be involved in memory pruning, some dreams do have the feel of being important, and about important events and ideas.

Chapter Summary

- A dream is a series of images, ideas, and emotions we have while we are sleep.
- Although we might misremember dreams or have incomplete recall of their content, dreams are real sleep experiences.
- In lucid dreams, we are aware that we are dreaming, and may be able to influence their plot.
- There are several techniques for inducing lucid dreams.
- Dreams have a varied content, and are linked to life events.
- Nightmares are dreams with strong negative emotional content.
- Nightmares are more common in PTSD and can be treated with the drug prazosin.
- There are several reasons why we dream and the theories need not be in conflict.
- The activation-synthesis model sees dreams as essentially random, with the forebrain trying to make sense of random neural fire and turn random neural activity into a story.
- Dreaming is associated with memory pruning.
- Some dreams inspire creative thought.
- Dreams are a way of dealing with threat by being able to practise responses to threatening events safely.

- There is little evidence for the Freudian notion that dreams are disguised wish fulfilment.
- Freud proposed several mechanisms that disguised the latent content of dreams, including displacement, condensation, and symbolism.
- Jung proposed that dreams are concerned with individuation.

Review Questions

1. Why do we dream?
2. Evaluate Freud's psychoanalytic theory of dreaming. How does Freud's account differ from those of Jung and Adler?
3. What is special about lucid dreams, and what do they tell us about consciousness?
4. What is a nightmare, and why do we have them? Why do some people have more nightmares than others?
5. How does PTSD affect dreaming? Should we treat the effects of PTSD, and, if so, how?
6. What is happening in the brain when we dream?
7. How does the nature and content of dreams change from being very young to very old, and what do these differences mean?
8. How essential is dreaming for memory?

Recommended Resources

General

Flanagan, O. (2000). *Dreaming Souls*. Oxford, UK: Oxford University Press.
Windt, J.M. (2015). *Dreaming*. Cambridge, MA: MIT Press.

The AIM Model and Dreams

Hobson, J.A. (2015). *Psychodynamic Neurology: Dreams, Consciousness, and Virtual Reality*. Boca Raton, FL: CRC Press.
Hobson, J.A. (2017). *Conscious States: The AIM Model of Waking, Sleeping, and Dreaming*. Scotts Valley, CA: CreateSpace.

Lucid Dreams

LaBerge, S., and Rheingold, H. (1990). *Exploring the World of Lucid Dreaming*. New York: Ballantine.
Love, D. (2013). *Are You Dreaming? Exploring Lucid Dreams*. Enchanted Loom Publishing.

Psychoanalytic Theories

Freud, S. (1991 [1899]). *The Interpretation of Dreams*. Harmondsworth, UK: Penguin. The essential work on dream interpretation.
Jung, C.G. (1995). *Memories, Dreams, Reflections*. London: Fontana Press.
Jung, C.G. (2014). *Dreams*. London: Routledge.

14 HYPNOSIS

Hypnosis for many people brings forth images of strange men holding a swinging watch in front of someone's eyes, telling them they are feeling drowsy, until the subject shuts their eyes. They can then be made to run around a stage on all fours barking like a dog or mooing like a cow. On apparent awakening, they can be made to do unexpected things on the cue of the hypnotist, which they are then unable to explain. Hypnosis is generally agreed to be a state of highly focused attention and reduced awareness of peripheral stimuli. The term hypnotism is used interchangeably with hypnosis, although hypnosis is now the preferred term.

How accurate is this image of hypnotism? This chapter begins by looking at the history of hypnosis. We then look at the process of hypnosis, asking how hypnotists induce the hypnotic state, and examine individual differences in ability to be hypnotised, as well as whether it is possible to learn to be more hypnotisable.

We then examine whether hypnosis is indeed an altered state at all, or whether subjects just follow orders. We also examine dissociation in this context. Does brain activity change in any way when a person is hypnotised?

We then consider some of the many effects and applications of hypnosis. Can people follow suggestions after the hypnotic trance has apparently finished? Can people be made to hallucinate during or after a trance? Can people really be made to forget what happened during a trance? We look at hypnotic anaesthesia, the use of hypnosis to stop pain, even enabling surgical operations to be carried out. We then consider the efficacy of the use of hypnosis as a method of therapy. Finally, we ask whether it is possible for a person to hypnotise themselves.

The History of Hypnosis

Although knowledge of the practice of **hypnosis** has been around for a long time, the German medic Franz Mesmer (1734–1815) was the first to use hypnosis on a grand public scale (see Figure 14.1). He explained the phenomenon in terms of the transfer of a special sort of energy he called animal magnetism; for a while, the process of hypnosis was known as *mesmerism*. His original interest was in astronomy, and his early work was on the influence of the planets and tides on the human body. He investigated using magnets with patients to induce artificial tides, but soon developed a version of the practice we now recognise as hypnotism.

James Esdaile (1808–1859), a Scottish surgeon who worked for the East India Company in Bengal, was the first person to use hypnosis systematically to induce analgesia (pain

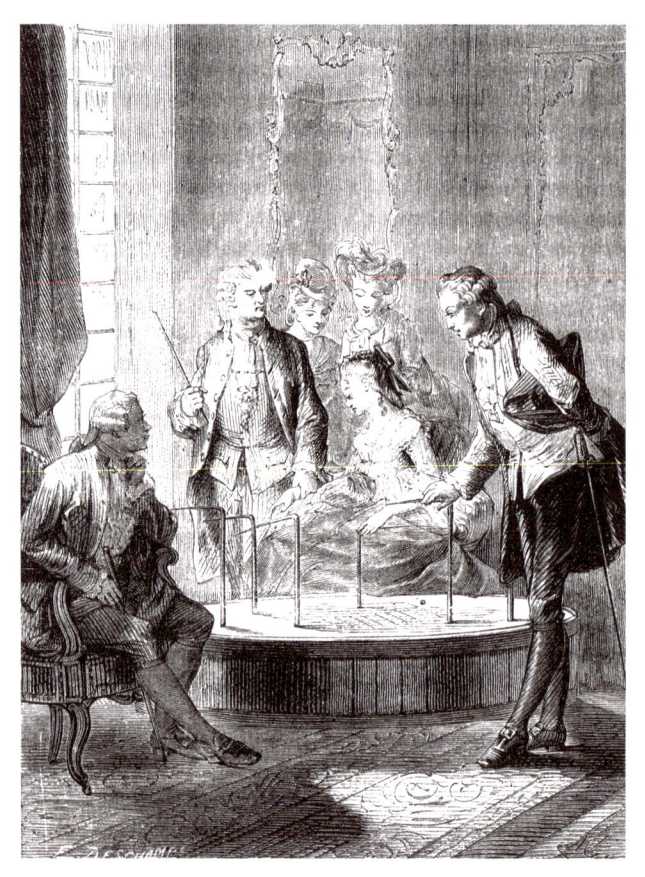

Figure 14.1 Franz Mesmer (1734–1815). Mesmer (right) was a German doctor interested in astronomy, and thought that energy could be transferred between animate and inanimate objects. Hypnotism is still sometimes called mesmerism. Source: Print Collector/Hulton Archive/Getty Images.

relief) in patients so that he could then operate on them. At this time, no effective chemical anaesthetics were available. Hypnosis was also very poorly understood, and Esdaile induced analgesia in a long exhausting process involving shaping his hands into a claw and passing them repeatedly close to the patient's body. He was particularly successful in removing scrotal tumours without anaesthetic. James Braid (1795–1860), a Scottish surgeon who worked in Manchester, England, became interested in 'animal magnetism' after attending a stage performance. He realised that magnetism had nothing to do with the process, and he believed that hypnotism (which he called 'neurohypnology') produced a change of state in some ways similar to sleep. He was the first to explore the mechanisms and uses of hypnotism scientifically. He also performed *self-hypnosis*, or auto-hypnosis (see later in chapter), showing that it produced a similar state to hypnotism, and therefore the hypnotiser was not an essential component of hypnosis, that no energy passed between people, and that special skills such as exceptional charisma were not necessary. Braid later used the word hypnotism; the word hypnosis was first recorded in France in the 1880s. By then, hypnosis was taken seriously and considered amenable to scientific analysis.

Freud studied hypnosis in France under Charcot (see Box 14.1), and used it early in his career with Joseph Breuer to investigate *hysteria* (Breuer & Freud, 2004 [1895]). Hysteria was a general term used at the turn of the century to cover a range of psychological disorders to which we would now give more specific labels, particularly somatisation disorders where symptoms of neurosis are revealed through the body (such as an arm that can't be moved when there is no physiological explanation). Theoretical considerations as he developed psychoanalysis, along with considerations of time and the difficulty he had in hypnotising some people, led him to prefer psychoanalytic discussion, free association, and dream analysis.

> **Box 14.1** Freud, Charcot, Hysteria, and Hypnosis
>
> Attitudes to mental illness have changed over the years, from the view that they were the result of possession or witchcraft, to our relatively enlightened modern view. In the late nineteenth century, a diagnosis of *hysteria* was common. Hysteria was an emotional disorder, often accompanied by what we now call somatisation, where the mental illness affects part of

Box 14.1 (cont.)

the body. The disease was thought to affect only women (hence the name, derived from the Greek for 'uterus'). Early in his career, Sigmund Freud visited the renowned French neurologist Charcot (see Figure 14.2) and his Salpetriere School. Charcot had begun by thinking that hysteria was a physiological disease, but became convinced that it was psychological in origin. Charcot was using hypnosis to treat hysteria, making particular use of suggestion to help the patient to improve. Charcot thought hysteria and hypnosis were inextricably linked, in that the hysteria was a form of hypnosis, so only hysterics could be hypnotised. For Charcot, hypnosis was a symptom as well as a means of treatment, which worked by getting the disturbed state to work against itself. Charcot also argued that, contrary to prevailing thought, hysteria was also relatively common in men. On his return to Vienna, Freud also began using hypnosis, but found it difficult and time consuming, so started pursuing other techniques, leading to the development of psychoanalysis.

Figure 14.2 Jean-Martin Charcot (1825–1893). A French neurologist who pioneered work on hypnotism as a treatment for 'hysteria'. Freud studied with him, but found hypnotism difficult and time consuming, developing the new methods of psychoanalysis as an alternative treatment. Source: Contributor/Universal Images Group/Getty Images.

The Process of Hypnosis

Stage hypnotists have the advantage that they can triage the audience for susceptible people by starting with a very general task ('raise your arm in the air; it is very heavy and you find it impossible to keep it raised', and noting whose arms fall). Hypnotherapists working with individuals don't have that luxury. The process of putting a person into a trance, **hypnotic induction**, is broadly the same, however, whatever the goal.

Hypnotic Induction

In hypnosis, the hypnotist *induces* a *trance* in an individual. There are many ways of doing this, and many individual differences in responses to the induction process. It is useful to distinguish the stage and clinical settings as broad categories of when hypnosis might be carried out because the induction process is likely to differ, although of course hypnosis might be carried out in other settings. In the stage setting, the hypnotist will most likely begin with a triage of the audience with a simple command to everyone, perhaps carrying out further triage until they are left with one or two highly susceptible subjects (see Figure 14.3). The clinician does not have the luxury of triage and has to work with the individual presenting themselves.

Figure 14.3 Group hypnosis. Stage hypnotists often start with suggestions to a group of people and continue working with only the most suggestible. Source: Michael Rougier/The LIFE Picture Collection/Getty Images.

Every hypnotist will have their own preferred method of induction. The traditional image of hypnosis is, for once, not too far off the mark. The hypnotist (usually with a moustache) swings a brightly lit watch in front of the subject, telling them to focus upon it, and not look at anything else. 'Your eyes are getting heavier …' This technique makes sense because in those conditions a person's eyelids will naturally get heavier, and the participant will interpret this natural sensation as the first signs of being hypnotised. It is by no means necessary, however. Modern induction simply involves getting the person to be still, relax, and focus only on the voice of the hypnotist. The early stages of induction involve progressive muscle relaxation. Note that the phrasing of instructions is important. It is good to be forceful, telling a person that 'your hand will rise' rather than giving them an element of choice as with 'you will raise your hand'; such instructions reduce the participant's sense of agency (Terhune et al., 2017). A typical hypnosis session might then continue with the hypnotist telling the subject that they are feeling increasingly sleepy and falling into an increasingly deep hypnotic trance as they count backwards from ten. This process might then be repeated several times to deepen the trance.

After the session, the hypnotist will bring the participant out of any trance, often by a speeded version of the induction but in reverse – counting the numbers in the opposite direction while telling the subject that they feel increasingly alert and awake, for example.

Theodore X. Barber (the X stood for the excellent name Xenophon), often described as a 'critic' of hypnosis, argued that the induction process wasn't really necessary for inducing hypnosis other than that participants believed it was necessary: it was an expected cultural context (Barber, 1969; Chaves, 2006).

The Hypnotic Trance

As the hypnotist continues the induction, the participant hopefully falls into a trance, although the depth of trance varies depending on the person, the hypnotist, and the circumstances. A trance is characterised by the person being in a state of focused attention, consequently with reduced peripheral awareness. The person is more open to suggestion, and may later have poor memory of what happened in the trance. There are four depths of trance, although it is not clear whether they are distinct categories or on a continuum.

The lightest is called light trance, followed by apparent somnambulism, true somnambulism, with the deepest being a state of deep relaxation with attention focused on what the hypnotist is saying. This state is widely attainable. Apparent somnambulism is so called because it resembles sleep; it is possible to induce anaesthesia in this state. True somnambulism is a yet deeper state characterised by complete physical and mental relaxation, so that the participant is in a state of what is called *blank nothingness*. In this state, it is considered that hypnotists can give participants effective suggestions that act post-hypnotically (because there is no censor that can override suggestions). It is possible to carry out surgical procedures in this state.

The deepest hypnotic state is coma, sometimes called the *Esdaile state* (after James Esdaile a noted Scottish surgeon, 1808–1859), which can be attained by only a small proportion of the population. It is reported that the subject feels complete 'bliss', and it is possible to carry out major surgical procedures on them (see below).

Individual Differences in Hypnotisability

People vary in the extent to which they can be hypnotised. We know some of the characteristics of people who make good hypnotic subjects (who tend to be more hypnotisable). Such people are more suggestible than others, a trait that is measured by the *Stanford Suggestibility Scale*. They tend to be involved with nature, more religious, more imaginative, believe themselves to be spiritual, have a fantasy-prone personality, and had more vivid childhood play, including imaginary friends (Tellegen & Atkinson, 1974; Wilson & Barber, 1983). Good subjects tend to score higher in absorption on the *Tellegen Absorption Scale* (Kingsland, 2019; see Table 14.1). People prone to dissociative symptoms, often because of childhood trauma, are easier to hypnotise (Bell et al., 2011).

Table 14.1 Stanford Hypnotic Susceptibility Scale (modified by Kihlstrom, 1985), in approximately increasing order of difficulty, with some possible measures

Eye closure	Eyes closed and at what stage
Hand lowering	Hand lowered by at least six inches
Moving hands apart	Hands more than six inches apart
Mosquito hallucination	Any grimace or acknowledgement
Taste hallucination	Sweet and sour tastes, how strong
Arm rigidity	Amount of bending in 10 s interval
Dream	Recording dream and amount of detail
Age regression	Regression to around age 10 and details
Arm immobilisation	Unable to move arm in 10 s
Anosmia	Inability to smell strong odour
Auditory hallucination	Orients to speaker of hallucinated voice
Negative visual hallucination	Failure to see items
Post-hypnotic amnesia	Three or fewer items from list recalled
Post-hypnotic suggestion	Moves to chair or stands up as instructed

It should be said that these characteristics are neither necessary nor sufficient for high hypnotisability, and the correlations involved are low. Some people argue that hypnotisability is a trait, such as anxiety or sociability or any other fundamental attribute of human personality. But if so, and if it doesn't reliably correlate with anything else, why should such an attribute arise (Heap et al., 2004)?

> **Box 14.2** Categories of Question in the Tellegen Absorption Scale
>
> 1 Is responsive to engaging stimuli.
> 2 Is responsive to 'inductive' stimuli.
> 3 Often thinks in images.
> 4 Can summon vivid and suggestive images.
> 5 Has 'cross-modal' experiences (e.g. synaesthesia).
> 6 Can become absorbed in own thoughts and imaginings.
> 7 Can vividly re-experience the past.
> 8 Has episodes of expanded (e.g. ESP-like) awareness.
> 9 Experiences altered states of consciousness.

Can We Learn Suggestibility?

Is the degree to which we're suggestible fixed, or can we learn, or be trained, to become more suggestible? There is evidence that we can learn to become more suggestible. One well-known way of being able to do so is by following the Carleton Skill Training programme (Fellows & Ragg, 1992; Gorassini & Spanos, 1986).

This training essentially makes a person feel more positive about hypnosis and increases a person's motivation to be hypnotised and respond appropriately. It stresses the importance of mental imagery and encourages people to respond positively to suggestions (such as a person must actually lift their hand while imagining that it is rising by itself). Some studies suggest that 50% of low-hypnotisability people taking the training still count as 'high hypnotisability' over two years later, while others suggest that, while the training does work, gains are modest and are not maintained at follow-up (Bates et al., 1988). It's possible that the differences between results can be explained by the demand characteristics of the programme: those told that the training programme leads to improvements in hypnotisability show more gains. Improving rapport with the hypnotist also leads to improvements (Gfeller et al., 1987).

What Makes a Good Hypnotist?

The would-be hypnotist obviously has to learn the basic skills of hypnosis, but are some people better than others? There has been much less research on what makes a good hypnotist than on what makes a good hypnotic subject. Anecdotally, it is important for the hypnotist to be empathic and to instil confidence, and there is evidence showing that empathy is involved in hypnosis (Wickramasekera, 2015). Additionally, fMRI evidence shows that charismatic religious speakers have the ability to inhibit frontal lobe function in people receiving intercessory prayer, so maybe the perceived charisma of the hypnotist is important after all, and charisma works by suppressing prefrontal lobe function in the listeners (see Figure 14.4). Stage hypnotists and hypnotherapists will, of course, have some different skills, although clearly both need to be effective hypnotists!

Figure 14.4 Charismatic speaker: The evangelical preacher Billy Graham (1918–2018). Some people are better public speakers than others, and some are highly charismatic. They are convincing, engaging, and make the listeners feel special. They work by inhibiting prefrontal lobe function in listeners – the same applies with good hypnotists. Source: Keystone/Stringer/Hulton Archive/Getty Images.

Box 14.3 Snake Charmers and Horse Whisperers

To the western eye, one of the more exotic images of India and southeast Asia is that of the snake charmer (see Figure 14.5). Snake charming is the practice of charming or 'hypnotising' a snake, often a cobra in a basket, with a wind instrument called a *pungi*. The

> **Box 14.3** (cont.)
>
> practice has largely died out in India owing to wildlife protection laws. There is no hypnotism involved: the snake is simply visually following the movement of the pungi, to which it is responding as a predator or prey. The practice of worm charming is a slightly less dramatic means of interacting with wriggly animals.
>
> Horse whisperer is the name given to horse trainers who appear to have exceptional training abilities, and an ability to work with recalcitrant animals. The preferred term is now 'natural horsemanship'. Again, no hypnosis is involved, but some trainers are clearly more gifted than others, skilfully using a range of conditioning techniques, and making use of their calm, tranquil manner. Of course, such skills aren't restricted to horses; some people are better dog trainers than others. (Given the problems I had with Beau, all my own fault, I would definitely not call myself a dog whisperer.) Although these skills do not involve hypnotising the animal in the sense of inducing a special state of suggestibility (we assume), they do involve keeping the animal relaxed and at ease.
>
> Figure 14.5 A snake charmer. Are charmers such as these hypnotising the snake? Source: SM Rafiq Photography/Moment/Getty Images Plus.

Is There a Special Hypnotic State?

There are two very different views of what happens in hypnosis, with the central issue being the extent to which hypnosis really is an altered state of consciousness (ASC). The *state* view says that it is; the *non-state* view says that it isn't.

Dissociation

At the heart of hypnosis as an ASC is the idea of dissociation. Dissociation is when things that are normally connected together become separated, or dissociated, often as a result of excessive stress. We split a part of ourselves off, or ourselves from the environment. Dissociation is found in some types of psychopathology, when some experiences cannot be integrated with the normal sense of self, and the person feels disconnected from themselves or the world in some way. Dissociation can take many forms. For example, we sometimes observe emotional numbing in some instances of PTSD; a person has no emotional response to something that they should find extremely upsetting. Of particular relevance are instances where a person feels taken over by a particular feeling, or does something they would not normally do, without any obvious explanation. In dissociative amnesia, a person is unable to remember certain events, such as prior abuse. In fugue states, people 'go absent', perhaps literally, and may later find themselves in a strange place with no memory of how they got there. In depersonalisation, a person has a sense of not being themselves, of being detached from their own body, and, in derealisation, a person thinks that reality lacks certain qualities, such that they might feel like they are watching a film rather than experiencing reality, or that they are observing the world from behind glass. Many of the 'hysterical' disorders Freud studied would now be labelled dissociative disorder; Anna O., for example, was unable to move the right side of her body, even though there was nothing physically wrong with her (Breuer & Freud, 2004 [1895]). Even more extreme forms of dissociation involve loss of identity. Dissociative identity disorder (DID) is naturally a type of dissociation.

Dissociation may be a natural form of hypnosis, and shares many characteristics with it. Hypnosis can be seen as a way of creating an artificial dissociative state, and then making use of the dissociation.

The US psychologist Ernest Hilgard (1904–2001) first proposed *neodissociation theory* in 1973 as an extension of the idea of dissociation (see also Hilgard, 1977). He argued that hypnosis was a special state of consciousness in which consciousness was divided with the hypnotised person and a *hidden observer*. The hidden observer sits in the background and maintains some degree of objectivity about the situation; Hilgard later specified that it shouldn't be taken too literally, and was most certainly not a homunculus, but instead represents a high degree of cognitive functioning not accessible to awareness, and is why people are unable to act against their 'true' wishes and moral codes under hypnosis. Under hypnosis, there are different levels of awareness that operate independently. So, in analgesia, caused by hypnosis, the hypnotised person is unaware of the pain, but the hidden observer is aware of it, and with amnesia caused by hypnosis, the person who has been hypnotised is unable to recall what happened under hypnosis, but the hidden observer can.

The 'hidden observer' remains a controversial idea in hypnosis research (Kallio & Revonsuo, 2005). It isn't clear exactly what is going on in hypnosis, and it isn't clear that the theory is completely logically coherent.

Non-state Theories of Hypnosis

It's easy to make sense of the state theory because that is probably most people's view of hypnosis: that induction makes a person enter a special state called a trance. Non-state theorists reject the idea of a trance state. The subject is still in control. Non-state theorists interpret the effects of hypnotism as due to a combination of several task-specific factors, such as social-role perception and favourable motivation (Sarbin & Coe, 1972), active imagination and positive cognitive set (Barber, 1969), response expectancy (Kirsch, 2011), and the active use of task-specific subjective strategies (Spanos, 1983, 1986, 1989). All of these essentially say that the hypnotised is being compliant, playing along with being hypnotised, as it were. Other critics say that hypnotic and non-hypnotic experiences are too complex to be divided into special state or non-state categories, and depend on many other variables, such as what people are told, their expectations, and security (Lynn et al., 2015). Furthermore, although we observe changes to brain activity during hypnosis, there is no one particular neural signature corresponding to hypnosis (Lynn et al., 2015; see Figure 14.9).

The three most commonly raised objections to non-state theories are hypnotic analgesia and anaesthesia, post-hypnotic amnesia, and hypnosis-specific changes in the brain during a trance. How can these all be simply due to suggestion? In all cases, the non-state theorists say that they can be, or at least appear to be. The distinction between state and non-state theories is now thought to be not so clear cut; for example Kihlstrom (2014, 2018) argues that hypnosis is an altered state of cognition where the hypnotist and participant interact to produce the changes.

Effects of Hypnosis

Hypnotism is of course much more than a scientific curiosity. It is used on stage to entertain and in counselling as a means of therapy. Hypnotherapy has many specific uses, from helping people achieving goals, such as stopping smoking, to the treatment of anxiety, phobias, and other psychological problems. Both entertainment and therapy depend on the use of suggestions administered during the hypnotic trance.

Hypnotic Suggestions

Suggestions are given in a hypnotic trance for a person to act upon later. They may be therapeutic, such as stopping smoking (see Figure 14.6), or they may be for entertainment, in which case there might be an element of amnesia too (you don't want the person to remember that they've been told to hallucinate that there's a lion on the stage). Nevertheless, there is plenty of evidence that hypnotic suggestions are effective, and accompanied by brain changes detectable by fMRI (Oakley & Halligan, 2013).

Suggestions are easy for the non-state theory to account for: the subject is just being compliant and following instructions. While that sounds very plausible for short-acting suggestions, it sounds less plausible for changing problematic behaviours, such as giving up smoking, and implausible for hypnotic anaesthesia (discussed in detail below). There are many different hypnotic techniques for stopping smoking; for example, the therapist might suggest that the cigarette tastes foul, or leaves the mouth extremely dry and unpleasant. On the other hand, according to the state theories, suggestions work because the changed mental state under hypnosis is conducive to enacting behavioural change. Hypnotherapy for smoking is highly effective, perhaps more effective than nicotine-replacement therapy (Hasan et al., 2014).

Figure 14.6 A group of smokers trying hypnosis to kick the habit. Hypnosis is very widely used to change behaviours such as smoking. The hypnotist (not shown) is Dr Steven Rosenberg, who uses a technique called aversion therapy: Rosenberg hypnotises smokers into believing that cigarettes taste like vomit. Source: William Thomas Cain/Stringer/Getty Images News.

Hypnosis and Memory

One particular type of suggestion is to forget something – such as to forget being given the suggestion, a phenomenon called *post-hypnotic* **amnesia**. Post-hypnotic amnesia was first discovered by Marquis de Puységur in 1784: when working with his subject Victor, Puységur noticed that when Victor came out of hypnosis he would have amnesia for everything that had happened during the session. Puységur soon began treating those who were ill with deliberately induced amnesia. Clark Hull (1933) carried out some of the earliest experimental studies on hypnosis in general and on post-hypnotic amnesia. Hull's work showed that there was dissociation between explicit memory and implicit memory in hypnosis. He also worked on studies on *proactive interference* and *retroactive interference* (Hull, 1940), techniques that are based on old information interfering with learning new, or new information interfering with retrieving old. Hull had to stop working on hypnosis when he moved to Yale University because of fears that it was dangerous. Nevertheless he established that people could be made to selectively forget information under hypnosis.

More controversial is the possibility that people can recall material when in a hypnotic trance that they otherwise cannot recall. Of course, it isn't impossible that people in a very relaxed state, with appropriate cues, might be able to remember stuff they could not previously, but on the whole we should be sceptical about the use of hypnosis to 'recover' lost memories. The idea is very dubious, but controversial and indeed dangerous, because many do believe in it. It has destroyed families. Dubious recovered memories are not limited to childhood; alleged alien abductee Betty Hill reproduced details of travels with aliens under hypnosis (see Figure 14.7). Along with her husband Barney, Betty claimed they were abducted by aliens from rural New Hampshire from 19 to 20 September 1961.

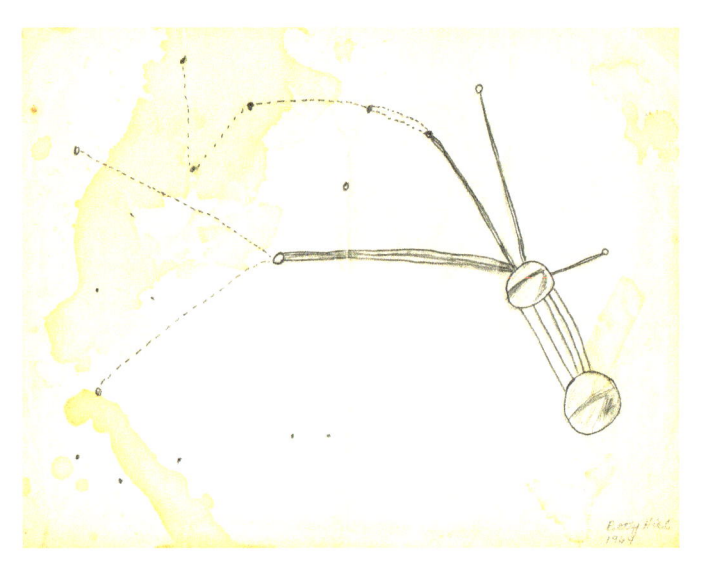

Figure 14.7 Betty Hill's star map. Map depicting an alien star system, with lines and dots to illustrate trade routes, drawn by alleged alien abductee Betty Hill following a hypnosis session with Benjamin Simon, 1964. Source: University of New Hampshire/Gado/Archive Photos/Getty Images.

In general, we know that memory is extremely unreliable. People misremember things, get details wrong, and their memories can be influenced by the way the questions are asked. Eyewitness memory is surprisingly poor (Loftus, 1996); pertinent here is that they can 'remember' things that never happened. There has, unsurprisingly, been much research on such a controversial but important topic (see also Chapter 6). A recent meta-analysis, where results from several independent studies are combined, has shown that nearly half the population are susceptible to creating 'false memories' that have been suggested to them; some people will even embellish the memories with extra details of their own (Scoboria et al., 2017). Generally, leading memory researchers are scathing about the idea that memories of trauma are repressed and can be recovered later by hypnosis or therapy: 'the idea of "recovered memory" is ... a dangerous fad' (Loftus & Ketcham, 2000; see also Conway, 1997).

Even more bizarre and unlikely is the idea that hypnosis can enable us to remember previous lives. There is absolutely no evidence for the idea that people have lived past lives, as we shall see in a later chapter. People who claim that they were Cleopatra, or slaves in Cleopatra's retinue, or a British druid put to death by the Romans are wrong. Nevertheless, people do report past lives in hypnosis; they must be fabricating their past histories, perhaps unconsciously.

Box 14.4   Is Hypnosis Dangerous?

One of my favourite short stories is very short – about a fairground act where a hypnotist levitates a volunteer. Unfortunately, soon after the person starts to rise, the hypnotist dies suddenly, and the volunteer, horizontal in a trance, continues to rise ...

In literature and films, people are occasionally hypnotised and then made to do things against their will, which they then forget, thanks to a suggestion of post-hypnotic amnesia. There is no evidence that anything like this kind of thing has ever been done. Indeed, there is little evidence that hypnosis is dangerous, but plenty that it can be useful.

What about stage hypnotists making people run around barking like dogs? It is most unlikely that the participants really carried out these acts against their will. The non-state theory says that they wanted to please the hypnotist and the audience, and might well have actually enjoyed their performance. The label of hypnosis gives them an excuse to behave in a disinhibited way.

Box 14.4 (cont.)

Nevertheless, some participants have reported side effects after hypnosis. Some people report intruding thoughts or heightened anxiety (Machovec, 1988). Machovec lists around 50 side effects. Some hypnotists bring participants out of trances too quickly, leaving the person sleepy or dizzy – which is possibly dangerous if they're going to drive immediately afterwards. Side effects are more common with poorly or untrained hypnotists. Some hypnotists report that following hypnotherapy the main symptom might subside, but later become manifest in some other way: Kleinhauz and Beren (1984) describe a patient who was treated for smoking but later became severely depressed. Of course, we have no way of knowing whether the hypnosis played a causal role here.

We can conclude hypnotherapy is generally very safe, but as with most treatments, there might be occasional side effects.

Hypnotic Anaesthesia

One of the most impressive uses of hypnosis is to produce *anaesthesia* – an apparent immunity from pain. The use of hypnosis to produce anaesthesia so that a person can be operated upon is called *hypnosurgery*. A quick search of the internet will throw up many videos illustrating it in action. Some of the most impressive include a video of dentistry, and a man being treated with invasive surgery for a hernia.

It is hard to believe people are just being compliant; I think few people would lie there with the agony of the surgeon's knife cutting their flesh (and it is apparently excruciating) simply to please the hypnotist, or to play along with the theatre of it all just for fun. At first sight, the successful application of hypnosurgery supports the state theory of hypnosis.

There are though issues that need to be considered. First, there is a dearth of sound reviews and controlled experiments on hypnosurgery (Wobst, 2007). One difficulty is the ethical one of carrying out surgery on a control group without hypnosis or anaesthesia. Second, the definition of hypnotic anaesthesia and the procedures used are not always as clear cut as one would imagine: Defechereux et al. (2000) define it as 'hypnosis, local anesthesia and minimal conscious sedation'. A search of the internet shows that a number of demonstrations involve local anaesthetics in addition to the hypnosis (see Figure 14.8). In such a situation, it is of course difficult to say what role hypnosis alone has in producing anaesthesia. So, although there is some evidence that hypnosis might reduce post-operative pain and improve outcome and recovery rates after anaesthesia (Häuser et al., 2016), it is not clear that there is much to explain other than some analgesia for local relatively low levels of pain, such as with some dental work.

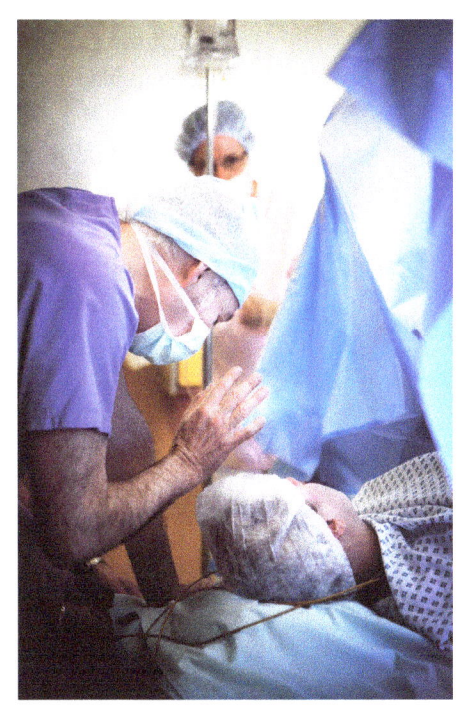

Figure 14.8 A Caesarean operation carried out under hypnosis in the maternity ward of Saint-Gregoire hospital in Rennes, France. The anaesthetist combines hypnotism with spinal anaesthesia. Source: BSIP/Universal Images Group/Getty Images.

In any case, non-state theories find effects of expectancy in how people deal with pain. The experiments that have been carried out on analgesia use broadly the same paradigm (Spanos, 1986): a hand or limb is immersed in very cold water and a baseline measurement of pain or tolerance to pain is measured, and then participants are assigned either to control or suggestion groups and the measurements taken again. Spanos pointed out that there are many cognitive strategies that people can use to reduce pain (such as telling themselves that 'this isn't too bad', or distracting themselves) that do not involve state change or hypnotic induction. Hypnotic and cognitive analgesia produce the same size of effect, suggesting nothing else is involved in hypnosis. Spanos also showed that participants who were expecting to be hypnotised gave higher pain ratings to the water before testing, which would leave more room for improvement after hypnosis, suggesting that expectancy was playing a large role here (Stam & Spanos, 1980).

The Neuroscience of Hypnosis

Imaging techniques, such as *fMRI* and EEG reveal consistent differences between hypnotised and non-hypnotised brains. In hypnotised brains, there is a breakdown in functional connectivity (the flow of information) among anterior frontal regions, which we know are involved in monitoring processing, as well as between frontal and posterior cortical regions (Egner & Raz, 2007; Landry et al., 2014). The default mode network becomes less activated in highly hypnotisable individuals, suggesting an increase in focus and goal-directed activity (McGeown et al., 2009).

TMS applied to the **dorsolateral prefrontal cortex (DLPFC)** increases hypnotic suggestibility (Dienes & Hutton, 2013). We have seen that good hypnotists have the ability to inhibit prefrontal function. These effects target an area of the brain involved in executive functioning, particularly metacognition.

Wide areas of the brain, particularly the anterior cingulate cortex, are involved in hypnosis and hypnotic analgesia, such as when a person holds their hand in uncomfortably hot water (Rainville et al., 1999, 2002). The anterior cingulate is particularly activated during hypnotic induction (Oakley & Halligan, 2010). There is also increased activity in regions that are also active when engaging in mental imagery tasks over much of the brain but particularly the *frontal lobes*, **cingulate gyrus**, and thalamus (Faymonville et al., 2006).

At first sight, these imaging differences appear to support the idea that the hypnotic 'state' is indeed a true altered state, but this point has been debated (Kirsch, 2011). Mazzoni (2013) argue that the changes observed in hypnosis need not be attributable to a special state but to peculiarities of the design of these experiments. For example, many studies have tested only participants scoring high on suggestibility scales. It's also entirely possible that imaging might be showing changes associated with suggestion rather than with an altered state. There is consensus that 'words change physiology' and our consciousness, but the existence of a special trance state is not an essential part of that explanation (Bloom, 2004; Lynn et al., 2015).

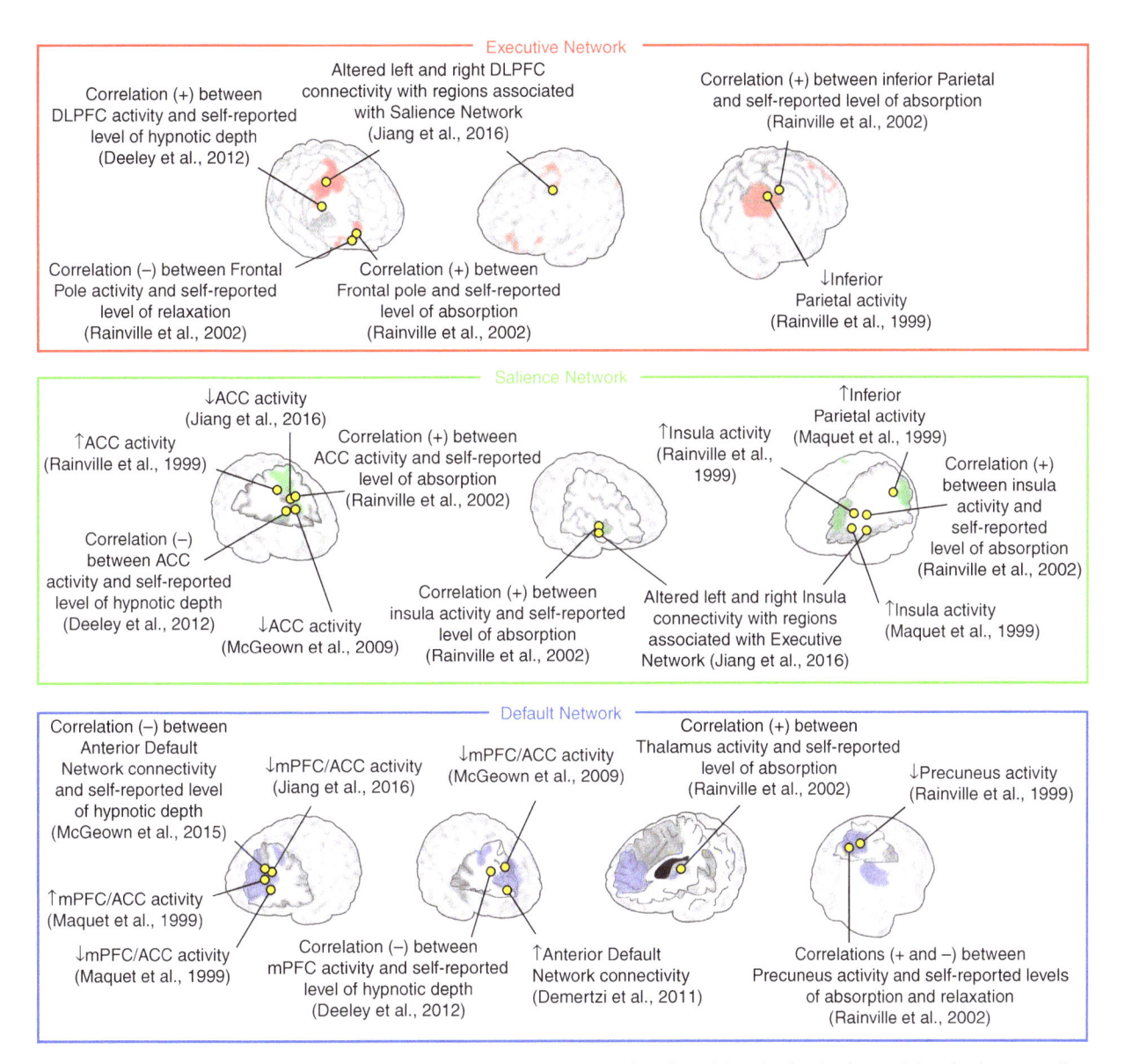

Figure 14.9 Neural correlates of hypnotic induction. The figure summarises several studies, with regional activations and deactivations, as well as changes in functional connectivity within the central executive, salient, and default networks. ACC = Anterior Cingulate Cortex. DLPFC = Dorsolateral Prefrontal Cortex. mPFC = Medial Prefrontal Cortex. Source: Figure 4 from Landry et al. (2014).

Self-hypnosis

Traditional hypnosis involves a hypnotist inducing the trance, but it is possible to induce *self-hypnosis*. The technique is really one of guided visualisation, where a person follows a script to enter a relaxed state and then gives themselves a suggestion. For example, you might visualise being on a very pleasant desert island, relaxing to the sound of gentle

> **TRY THIS: Self-Hypnosis**
>
> Self-hypnosis sessions are easily available online, for free and for purchase. Try one or two. They will be aimed at doing something specific such as relaxing or using autosuggestion to achieve a goal such as stopping smoking or learning better. Evaluate them. Did they work? What would a suitable control be for evaluating their efficacy scientifically?

waves breaking on a beautiful beach, feeling the warm sun on your body. You then find a treasure chest, which contains the suggestion you have previously decided upon. You then visualise yourself successfully enacting the suggestion.

There has been much less research on self-hypnosis than on hypnosis, but there is some evidence that it can work. For example, children prone to migraine taught self-hypnosis report fewer headaches than a control group (Olness et al., 1987). Initial research showed that self-hypnosis could shorten labour and make it more pleasant (Davidson, 1962), although this research has not been replicated (Freeman et al., 1986). It isn't clear whether self-hypnosis works in a similar way to hypnosis, whether the same brain mechanisms are involved, or whether processes that bring out anxiety reduction are involved.

What Hypnosis Tells Us About Cognition

As with much of consciousness research, the study of a consciousness-related phenomenon tells us much about cognition. Hypnosis has made a particularly notable contribution (Kihlstrom, 2014). For example, the phenomenon of *source amnesia*, the finding that people can learn information without remembering where they learned it, was first discovered in the context of hypnosis research (Evans, 1979). The way in which perception can be altered in hypnosis tells us about the extent and limitations of executive process involvement in controlling lower-level processes, and even the way in which automatic processes can be 'de-automatised'. Hypnosis has also informed personality research and social psychology, with information about compliance and the extent of demand characteristics in experiments.

Chapter Summary

- The process of hypnosis has been known about for much of history, and has gone under several different names, such as mesmerism and animal magnetism.
- In hypnosis, a hypnotist induces a trance in an individual.
- There are often thought to be four stages of trance.
- There are individual differences in hypnotisability with more suggestible subjects having identifiable characteristics.
- There are also differences in how good people are as hypnotists.
- There has been a big debate about whether or not the hypnotic trance is a special state of consciousness or whether behaviour under hypnosis can be explained sufficiently in socio-psychological terms such as expectancy effects.

- The alternative explanation is that the hypnotic trance is a special state of consciousness involving dissociation.
- Hilgard proposed that hypnosis involves dissociating the objective observer from a hidden observer.
- There are clear and systematic changes to the brain when a person is hypnotised.
- A hypnotist can implant suggestions during the trance that the person acts upon out of trance.
- There is no evidence that a person can be made to do anything against their wishes under hypnosis.
- Loss of memory of the hypnotic state is called post-hypnotic amnesia.
- Although there is little clear evidence as yet for the success of hypnosurgery without any other form of anaesthetic, hypnosis does change the reported perception of levels of pain, although the reasons for these changes are debated.
- There is no evidence that hypnosis can be used to regress us to earlier lives or to access hidden memories in childhood.
- We can induce a hypnotic-like state in ourselves with self-hypnosis.

Review Questions

1. What are the essential components of hypnotic induction?
2. If there is not a hypnotic state, are people with hypnotic anaesthesia just faking it?
3. What makes a good hypnotic subject?
4. Does self-hypnosis involve the same processes as hypnosis induced by another?
5. How do hypnotic suggestions work?
6. Is it possible to make someone do something they don't want to do when under hypnosis?
7. How does hypnosis differ from relaxed and meditative states?
8. Which brain regions are involved in hypnosis, and why? Does the involvement of specific areas mean that a hypnotic trance is an altered state of consciousness?

Recommended Resources

General
Nash, M.R., and Barnier, A.J. (2008). *The Oxford Handbook of Hypnosis: Theory, Research, and Practice*. Oxford, UK: Oxford University Press. The best general reference on hypnosis.

History of Hypnosis
Waterfield, R. (2002). *Hidden Depths: The Story of Hypnosis*. London: Macmillan.

Hypnotic Induction
Hand, K. (2017). *Magic Words and Language Patterns: The Hypnotist's Essential Guide to Crafting Irresistible Suggestions*. San Francisco, CA: Remind.

Hunter, C.R. (2010). *The Art of Hypnosis: Mastering Basic Techniques* (3rd ed.). London: Crown House.

Hypnotherapy

Brann, L., Owens, J., and Williamson, A. (2015). *The Handbook of Contemporary Clinical Hypnosis: Theory and Practice.* Oxford, UK: Wiley-Blackwell.

Fulcher, R.Z. (2014). *The Beginner's Guide to Hypnotherapy.* Scotts Valley, CA: CreateSpace.

Jaloba, A., and Nicholson, F. (2014). *The Hypnotherapy Handbook.* Scotts Valley, CA: CreateSpace.

Lynn, S.J., Rhue, J.W., and Kirsch, I. (eds.) (1993). *Handbook of Clinical Hypnosis.* Washington, DC: American Psychological Association.

Self-hypnosis

Eason, A. (2013). *The Science of Self-Hypnosis: The Evidence Based Way to Hypnotise Yourself.* San Diego, CA: Awake Media. Widely praised comprehensive guide to self-hypnosis.

15 DRUGS AND CONSCIOUSNESS

A drug is a substance that has a physiological effect when it enters the body. We are concerned with psychoactive drugs, which produce effects on the brain by crossing the blood–brain barrier, leading to changes to our mental state, either in the short or long term; although some psychoactive drugs may have other effects, such as promoting neuron growth. Some psychoactive drugs perceptibly change our consciousness in some way. Drugs work by affecting the brain's chemistry and interfering with the way in which neurotransmitters work. Some drugs (such as alcohol and heroin) take their effects by mimicking neurotransmitters and locking directly to the receptors on the other side of the synapse, while some (such as cocaine and amphetamines) block the re-uptake sites on the synapses so that neurotransmitters cannot be reabsorbed and so the brain experiences a surge in their levels (Nutt, 2012).

This chapter examines what psychoactive drugs tell us about consciousness. We begin with a classification of psychoactive drugs. We then look at the effects of one of the most commonly used substances, cannabis. We move on to the class of stimulant drugs, and look at amphetamine and cocaine. Next, we examine opioids, the class of psychoactive drugs related to opium, including morphine and heroin, that bind to opioid receptors in the brain. We then spend some time with the most notably psychoactive of all drugs, hallucinogens, including naturally occurring hallucinogens and artificially produced LSD.

There is an enormous number of psychoactive drugs that produce effects on consciousness to varying degrees, and we will only be able to survey the most significant ones. They all have their effects by changing the brain's chemistry in some way. Their mechanisms of action are understood in different degrees of depth, but the way in which this translates into changes in the phenomenology of consciousness is much less well understood. In addition, because most of these substances are illegal in most countries for some time it has been difficult to carry out much research.

> **TRY THIS:** Exploring Drugs
>
> Most psychoactive drugs are illegal, and many can be dangerous, so experimental opportunities with them are limited. However, a drug such as alcohol is legal and widely available in most countries. If you are over the appropriate age, and have no moral qualms, what does a small amount of alcohol or caffeine do to you? Exactly how does it change your mental state? And would you say that it changes your consciousness in any way?

A Classification of Psychoactive Drugs

Many drugs have therapeutic uses, and many therapeutic drugs affect the brain and mind; such drugs are called psychoactive. There is a range of drugs used to treat anxiety disorders (including benzodiazepines) and depression (e.g. *selective serotonin re-uptake inhibitors* or SSRIs, such as citalopram, fluoxetine, and sertraline). One difference between drugs used for therapy and drugs used for recreation is that the latter are short acting: they take effect very quickly, and their effects soon fade, often leaving you wanting to take more, and sometimes with unpleasant side effects. Drugs that work on disorders such as depression can take weeks or even months to begin to work. Sadly, there is nothing safe we can take that will make us feel immediately happier that is widely available at the moment. We can kill physical pain, but not mental pain. Then there are drugs that affect arousal, mood, and cognition, but not in any pronounced way. Caffeine, in coffee, is a psychoactive drug: it affects the mind and behaviour. In particular, it is a stimulant. Alcohol has pronounced psychoactive effects, and is a depressant.

There is a huge number of psychoactive drugs. Some have only small effects. In this chapter, we survey the breadth of drugs and discuss some of the more important ones. In each case, we can ask, how do the physiological effects of the drug (which are not always very well understood) relate to the phenomenological effects on consciousness (which are quickly and directly perceived)? Some users also combine drugs to balance or accentuate effects; most notable (and among the most lethal) being the speedball, a combination of cocaine and heroin.

For our purposes, recreational psychoactive drugs have three main effects: they affect arousal (how alert someone feels), mood, and perception. We can divide psychoactive drugs into six broad categories (Farthing, 1992, p. 450), as in Table 15.1.

Table 15.1 Drugs classified by neurotransmitter (Nutt, 2012)

Type	Drug
Central nervous system stimulants	Caffeine; nicotine; amphetamine; cocaine
Central nervous system depressants	Alcohol; sedative-hypnotics and anti-anxiety drugs, including barbiturates and benzodiazepines (minor tranquillisers)
Narcotic analgesics	Opiates, including codeine, morphine, and heroin; synthetic opiates, such as methadone
Antipsychotic agents	Chlorpromazine (major tranquillisers)
Antidepressants	Tricyclics, monoamine oxidase inhibitors, SSRIs (fluoxetine, citalopram, paroxetine), SNRIs (venlafaxine)
Psychedelics	Minor, such as cannabis, MDMA (ecstasy)

There are several caveats that should be noted about this classification scheme. First, the list is far from complete. Second, effects are dose dependent; a large dose of cannabis can act as a major psychedelic. Finally, and most importantly, most drugs have more than one effect. Ecstasy (and to a lesser extent cannabis) can produce hallucinations, enhance perception, alter the sense of time, promote relaxation and reduce anxiety, produce *euphoria* (exceptionally high mood), and generate a sense of inner peace; in social settings, such as parties, it can increase motor activity, and increase positive emotions, self-confidence, sociability, and empathy – all helping to explain why it has been so popular at raves.

The British psychiatrist David Nutt was sacked by the British government in 2009 from his role as chair of the Advisory Council on the Misuse of Drugs for attempting to contextualise the relative dangers of psychoactive drugs. Famously, he said in the press that recreational drug taking was no more dangerous statistically than horse riding, and that alcohol and tobacco produce more harm to society than LSD or cannabis. Nutt has produced several thoughtful analyses of psychoactive drugs and how they affect the brain (e.g. 2012). He classifies drugs in terms of their effects and how they affect the brain through the primary neurotransmitters affected. We should note, however, that we do not fully understand how drugs affect neurotransmitters, and are even less clear how those changes lead to changes in cognition, states of consciousness, and behaviour.

Psychoactive drugs do have severe negative consequences, which for most people outweigh the seemingly attractive list of effects above. Overdoses lead to death, and the amount of drug needed to produce an overdose depends on the purity of the drug, experience, and individual biology. Many drugs are addictive and thereby ruin lives. And, of course, most are illegal in most countries.

People take psychoactive drugs for many reasons. Those addicted simply crave more to avoid the crash; some take them under peer pressure; most take them because they want to 'feel good' in the short term. A few, sometimes called psychonauts, take drugs (particularly psychedelics) to explore consciousness and to experience higher states.

Cannabis

Cannabis is one of the most commonly used and widely available psychoactive drugs. It's the third most popular recreational psychoactive drug in the world, after alcohol and nicotine. Cannabis use is not illegal everywhere, and there has been a recent trend towards liberalisation, with some US states, from California to Washington, recently legalising cannabis for recreational use. Some countries, such as Canada, the Netherlands, Spain, Portugal, and Uruguay, allow personal consumption of cannabis with varying degrees of restriction. Several other US states and countries have legalised cannabis for restricted medical use. Cannabis is extracted from the cannabis or hemp plant *Cannabis sativa*, which originally grew in Central Asia. Marijuana comprises the dried leaves and other parts of the plant, particularly the resin, which can be smoked as 'weed', or taken orally (see Figure 15.1).

Cannabis produces several dose-dependent effects on consciousness, which, as with all psychoactive drugs, can vary from person to person and situation to situation. It can

Figure 15.1 A cannabis plant. The major psychoactive ingredient of cannabis is tetrahydrocannabinol (THC), which can be extracted from the plants in several ways. Cannabis plants grown in an indoor planting area at the Medicinal Cannabis Research Institute at Rangsit University in Bangkok, Thailand. Source: Lauren DeCicca/Getty Images News/Getty Images.

produce alterations in mood, particularly euphoria, changes to the sense of time so that the passing of a few minutes can seem like the passing of hours, enhancement of perception, particularly with colours seeming brighter, synaesthesia (most noted with movements), and changes to cognition. The cognitive and physical impairments are so severe that activities such as driving are highly dangerous and unsurprisingly illegal. A very high dose can lead to anxiety, panic attacks, hallucinations, and very rapid heartbeat.

The major psychoactive ingredient of cannabis is **tetrahydrocannabinol (THC)**, although cannabis may include hundreds of related *cannabinoids*, some of which complicate the effects of cannabis. The action of THC is complex, but it acts an agonist for the *cannabinoid receptor* CB_1, as well as to a lesser extent opioid receptors. CB_1 is a receptor in the *endocannabinoid* system of receptors, and endocannabinoid neurotransmitters. The exact function of this system is currently not well understood, but it is involved in the regulation of appetite, mood, motor learning, memory, and cognition (Grotenhermen, 2003).

> ### Box 15.1 Medicinal Use of Cannabis
>
> It is now generally agreed that cannabis has several medical uses, treating pain, inflammation, mood, sleep, and numbness resulting from nerve damage. It is used, for example, in treating pain, epilepsy, and multiple sclerosis. Users report that it provides relief superior to other treatments, if indeed there are any other treatments.
>
> While the psychoactive ingredient of cannabis is THC (tetrahydrocannabinol), the medically active ingredient is CBD (cannabidiol). CBD is derived from cannabis and makes up a large proportion of the plant extract. CBD has a low affinity for the cannabinoid receptors that make THC psychoactive, but has many effects across the brain, particularly in the basal ganglia.
>
> Because cannabis is widely illegal, it has been difficult for patients to obtain CBD. Restrictions are being lifted, and, for example, the Food and Drug Administration (FDA) in the United States approved the drug Epidiolex based on CBD for the treatment of epilepsy. It is claimed that THC also has therapeutic effects, although its use is more controversial. It is now legal in many countries to buy CBD oil, usually with some stipulation that it is not advertised as a medicine and does not contain more than a trace of THC. The difficult with many of these products is that it's not clear what you're getting, and how much CBD there is in it.

Amphetamine and Other Stimulants

Stimulants increase the arousal of the central nervous system. Arousal levels range from deeply asleep to normal waking consciousness to highly aroused, and is mediated by several neurotransmitters, including acetylcholine, norepinephrine, dopamine, and serotonin. Arousal increases excitatory cortical activity and results in greater alertness, vigilance, and processing efficiency.

The most widely used stimulant is caffeine, present in drinks such as tea and coffee. Caffeine reduces fatigue (to the point that it can prevent us from sleeping), improves vigilance, concentration, and cognitive performance in general, and improves motor performance. It has physical effects, increasing blood pressure and decreasing the width of blood vessels, and increases the speed with which material passes through the gut.

You can have too much of a good thing. Higher doses can cause anxiety and panic attacks, and the physical effects become more pronounced. Caffeine has withdrawal symptoms: stop drinking coffee, and you will experience withdrawal symptoms, particularly headaches, irritability, and even depression.

Caffeine works by antagonising *adenosine* receptors – it binds to the adenosine receptors in the brain, and as adenosine has an inhibitory effect on the central nervous system, caffeine has the effect of increasing arousal and reducing drowsiness (see Figure 15.2).

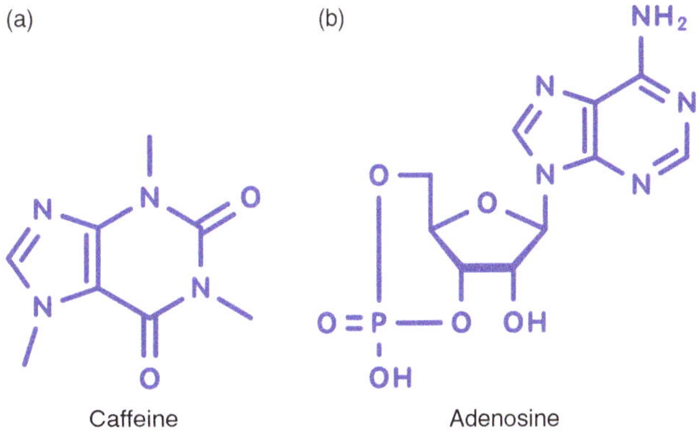

Figure 15.2 Caffeine and adenosine. The key parts of the structure are similar, so caffeine molecules from tea and coffee can bind to the adenosine sites. Source: Molekuul/Science Photo Library/Getty Images.

Amphetamine

Amphetamine is the best example of a stimulant. It increases arousal in the form of increased wakefulness and alertness, increased strength and improved reaction times, and increases in motivation, including sex drive, and improves memory recall and mood, even causing euphoria in higher doses.

It is used medically to treat a range of disorders, including attention deficit hyperactivity disorder and narcolepsy (problems with staying awake; see Chapter 12). It is a tightly controlled prescription drug in most countries because of many and varied short-term side effects (such as difficulty in sleeping, increased heart rate, and effects on blood pressure), the high risk of addiction, and long-term side effects arising from excessive use, particularly *amphetamine psychosis*, a condition resembling schizophrenia (see Box 15.2). Addiction also leads to increased tolerance, meaning abusers take yet larger doses. Addiction and amphetamine psychosis are rare in medicinal use, but recreational doses tend to be significantly higher (Bagot & Kaminer, 2014). Large doses also have paradoxical effects, making people *less* alert and causing muscle breakdown.

> **Box 15.2** Amphetamine Psychosis
>
> Amphetamine or, more generally, *stimulant psychosis* is an organic brain disorder that results from the long-term abuse of amphetamine or other stimulants. It can also occur on withdrawal. Some people are more susceptible than others, implicating the involvement of genetics. The prognosis is variable, with some people improving in a few weeks, while others may experience the symptoms for much longer. In many ways, stimulant psychosis resembles schizophrenia, and indeed some people transition to permanent schizophrenia. Symptoms include hallucinations, involving all senses, paranoia, disturbed thought, and delusions. People also suffer from anxiety and mental and physical agitation. In general, the longer the duration of the euphoric stage, the more likely a drug is to lead to psychosis: hence, amphetamines, where the euphoric effect can last hours, are more likely to cause problems than cocaine, where the euphoria generally fades after half an hour. Anti-psychotic medications are effective (Henning, Kurt, & Espiridon, 2019).
>
> Stimulants result in long-term changes in the brain. They block the re-uptake or stimulate the production of dopamine and norepinephrine, and therefore cause changes to the dopaminergic pathways. This, in turn, leads to increased activity of the mesocortical, mesolimbic, and nigrostriatal systems, which are involved with cognitive functions such as working memory, motivation and reward, and movement. The excess of dopamine might have knock-on effects, such as producing excessive amounts of the excitatory neurotransmitter glutamate, which in large amounts can be neurotoxic. As you might expect, the detailed mapping between these physiological changes and the details of the symptoms requires further research.

Methamphetamine is related to amphetamine, and indeed it initially metabolises into amphetamine. It is used as a recreational drug because of its euphoric, stimulant, and aphrodisiac effects. It is though highly addictive and has many unpleasant and dangerous side effects. Crystal meth is a particularly potent form, and is responsible for widespread addiction and health problems, particularly in the United States, where the term 'crystal meth crisis' has been in use since the latter part of the twentieth century.

Stimulants do have important medical uses – in addition to keeping us awake. *Methylphenidate*, more commonly known under the brand name Ritalin, is a stimulant used to treat narcolepsy and ADHD (attention deficit hyperactivity disorder), particularly in children. Ritalin also gives modest gains in general cognitive performance, such as improving working memory and inhibitory control (Ilieva et al., 2015). As with all stimulants, Ritalin is addictive and has a similar lengthy list of physical and psychological side effects. Because of these factors, the prescription of Ritalin is very tightly controlled.

As you might expect, amphetamine takes effect by increasing the effects of excitatory neurotransmission in the brain. It increases levels of the neurotransmitters dopamine and norepinephrine, particularly in neural pathways projecting to the frontal cortex.

Cocaine

Cocaine ('coke', 'snow', 'blow', and many more names) is a stimulant widely used as a recreational drug, taken usually by snorting into the nose (traditionally through bank bills, explaining why a large proportion of bills are contaminated with low levels of cocaine) or rubbing along the gum line, and occasionally by injection. It is now almost universally illegal, and is the most widely used illegal drug (after cannabis, where cannabis is illegal). It occurs naturally in the leaves of the Coca plant in western South America, with a content of about 0.5% of the plant (see Figure 15.3). Cocaine is prepared from the leaf by a chemical process involving solvents; it was first extracted by the German chemist Albert Niemann (1834–1861) in 1859. (He died young, probably as a result of lung damage caused by his research.) For a while, cocaine was widely used. Freud experimented with it as a treatment for depression and impotence. Cocaine was even added to the drink Coca-Cola, although it was removed in 1903. The dangers of the drug became apparent as it was widely used, and it was made illegal in the United States through acts in 1914 and 1922.

Figure 15.3 Coca plant fields in Yungas, Bolivia. The coca plant is the source of cocaine. Source: Jeff Rotman/Photolibrary/Getty Images Plus.

Cocaine is a psychoactive alkaloid. Alkaloids are a group of chemicals with a particular structure, widely occurring in nature and all with a bitter taste; many have effects on animals. It is a stimulant that produces an intense feeling of euphoria (happiness and well-being), although accompanied by agitation in some people. If inhaled it takes a few seconds or minutes to work, and the effects last from 5 to 90 minutes (Pomara et al., 2012). It increases heart rate, dilates the pupils, and increases sweating; it also acts as a local anaesthetic.

Cocaine has many adverse effects, which increase with prolonged use. It destroys the lining of the nose, and with prolonged use destroys the septum (the piece of cartilage up the middle) of the nose. It can cause heart problems, and an overdose can cause dangerously high blood pressure. It also causes sleep disturbances, depression, brain damage, hallucinations, paranoia, itchiness, a belief that the skin is crawling with insects (called formication) ... the list goes on. It is also very addictive because of the effects it has on dopamine levels and the brain's reward system. The drug is a white powder usually 'cut' (diluted) with other white powders to increase the profit margin, and some of these may pose additional health risks. Prolonged use leads to tolerance, so that a higher dose is needed to produce the same effect. Because it is addictive, stopping cocaine use leads to withdrawal symptoms.

Like all psychoactive drugs, the way in which cocaine works is very complex. It affects several neurotransmitter systems, particularly by inhibiting the re-uptake of norepinephrine and serotonin as well as dopamine (the surge in dopamine interfering with the reward system).

Crack cocaine can be smoked, and offers a particularly intense high of euphoria. It is particularly addictive and associated with social deprivation.

Opiates and Opioids

An opiate is a drug derived from *opium*, a substance derived from the opium poppy (*Papaver somniferum*) seed head. Opioid is the more general modern term for the class of drugs that bind to *opioid receptor*s in the brain, peripheral nervous system, and gut, having among others and to differing extents the psychoactive effects of analgesia (pain relief) and euphoria. You can think of receptors as locks: when the right key is inserted into the lock, the site fires, activating that neuron and the pathway in which it is involved. All opioids lead to *tolerance* (you need an increasingly larger dose to get the same effect) and *dependence* (you need to keep taking them or you will develop increasingly extremely unpleasant withdrawal effects). They also have many side effects, including lowering of blood pressure, lowering of the production of sex hormones, constipation, sedation, and, most seriously in the short term, depression of respiratory function. Dependence and activation of the reward system lead to *addiction*.

Opioids can be naturally occurring or artificially manufactured, called synthetic opioids. Synthetic opioids tend to be much stronger, more addictive, and more dangerous. In recent years, the number of synthetic opioids manufactured for pain relief has increased with drugs such as tramadol, fentanyl, hydrocodone, among others. Their widespread prescription, particularly in the USA, with addictive properties, has led to talk of an *opioid epidemic* (McGreal, 2018).

Morphine

Laudanum is a tincture of opium (around 10%) and alcohol, and was used widely in Europe and the Americas until the twentieth century. Opium contains several opioids, including codeine and morphine. The sale of drugs began to be regulated in most countries in the early twentieth century, and the sale of opioids became greatly restricted with laws passed in many countries, including the USA in 1914 and UK in 1920.

Morphine was first isolated around 1805 by the German chemist Friedrich Sertürner in what was probably the first isolation of an active ingredient from a plant. It is mostly taken intravenously. Morphine is one of the most tightly controlled drugs, but synthetic opioids such as heroin are much more commonly used as a recreational drug.

OPIATES AND OPIOIDS

Morphine was the first opioid to be shown to bind to opioid receptors. The first detailed explication of the operation of these sites was by Pert and Snyder (1973), who used *naloxone*, a substance that blocks the action of opioids. Activation of the receptors was shown to lead to analgesia, the reduction of the sensation of pain, but there are several types of receptors, each having subtly different effects, with some leading to a feeling of euphoria, hence accounting for the range of effects shown by opioid drugs (see Figure 15.4). Like many recreational drugs, opioids also lead to a large sudden increase in levels of dopamine, providing a sudden sense of pleasure and reward.

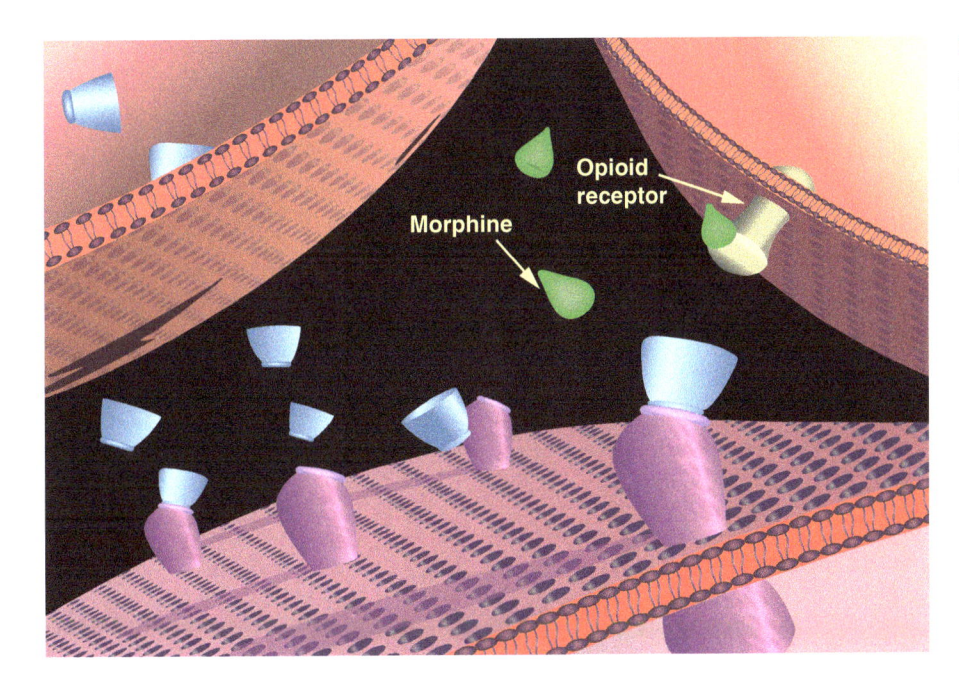

Figure 15.4 Morphine opioids activating receptors. Morphine binds to the μ-opioid receptors (MOR) in the nervous system, giving rise to analgesia and euphoria.

Morphine is an example of an *endogenous* opioid because it can be manufactured by our own bodies, particularly by white blood cells, and hence provides pain relief. This process accounts for anecdotes of people with horrific injuries reporting feeling no pain, and sometimes being euphoric.

Heroin

Of all the hard drugs, heroin is the hardest. As the Velvet Underground say in their wonderful but utterly depressing song 'Heroin', 'Heroin, be the death of me; Heroin, it's my wife and it's my life' (Reed, 1967). Heroin addiction is all-consuming misery punctuated by a few highs of relief.

Heroin produces a sense of extraordinarily strong state of euphoria. It is usually injected (thereby also introducing a danger of contamination of blood-borne diseases by shared needles) to obtain the effects as rapidly as possible and to get the immediate 'rush'. The euphoria can last for a few hours. Because of the intense high, heroin is highly addictive, with users rapidly craving a repeat sensation. However, in addition to the psychological dependence, heroin quickly also causes physical dependence – withdrawal from the drug after just a few hours produces highly unpleasant effects, including anxiety, depression, very runny nose, cramps, chills, and sweats, which are quickly abolished by more heroin. Worse, users become increasingly tolerant of the drug, necessitating higher and higher doses, increasing the severity of the craving and the withdrawal symptoms, and so the addicted user soon spirals out of control. These reasons are also why withdrawal from heroin is so difficult.

Heroin also comes with a risk of overdose, the lethal dose depending on the tolerance of the user. Long-term use also leads to a number of physical side effects including respiratory and cardiac diseases. An overdose usually kills by causing respiratory failure. A large number of rock stars have died as a result of either accidental or deliberate heroin overdose (and, without a suicide note, it is difficult or impossible to determine which it was), including Tim Buckley, Pete Farndon, Janis Joplin, Dee Dee Ramone, Sid Vicious, and Mikey Welsh. Kurt Cobain shot himself while high on heroin.

Heroin is closely related to morphine, and is also called diamorphine. It was first synthesised in 1874 by the English chemist Charles Romley Alder Wright, paradoxically in the search for a non-addictive alternative to morphine as a strong painkiller. Some users claim it produces the most intense euphoria of any opioid. The brain quickly turns heroin into three metabolites, including morphine. Although the other metabolites might be psychoactive, and might enhance the effects of the morphine, the effects are essentially the same as morphine (Martin & Fraser, 1961).

Hallucinogenic Drugs

Hallucinogens are a class of drugs that cause changes in consciousness by altering neurotransmitter levels resulting in distortions of perception, emotion, and aspects of cognition. In particular, they cause *hallucinations*, although they might be better called pseudohallucinations because they don't involve the generation of something out of nothing (seeing or hearing things and being unable to distinguish those visions from reality), but mostly involve distortions or exaggerations of perceptions. Hallucinogens also tend to be *empathogenic* in that they foster feelings of love and affection to other people and the natural world. Some are also **entheogens**, creating feelings of mystery and awe, religious feelings, and even ideas that the person is meeting God. Hallucinogens are particularly important drugs in consciousness research because of the magnitude of the change they cause in consciousness.

Hallucinogenic substances are fairly widespread through the natural world, mainly in plants and fungi (although the cane toad secretes bufotenin, a hallucinogen, along with several other toxic compounds, making toad licking a dangerous pursuit). They are bitter, alkaloid substances. There are three broad types of hallucinogenic drug: deliriants, dissociatives, and psychedelics. These hit different psychopharmacological pathways, although the effects are not always clearly distinguishable, and most naturally occurring hallucinogens produce many effects, if to differing degrees.

Deliriant Drugs

Deliriants (such as belladonna, henbane, and mandrake) produce confusion and an inability to control actions. There are also usually profound (and normally unpleasant) physical symptoms, such as racing heart and excessive sweating. Deliriant drugs produce confusion and delusions. They have a long history of shamanic and magical use – alcohol is the only mind-altering drug that has been used longer. They produce out-of-body experiences, the idea of flying and soaring, and changing form (think of witches at sabbaths changing into cats and flying on broomsticks). Deliriants are alkaloids, such as scopolamine, and are found in plants of the nightshade (or *Solanaceae*) family, including deadly nightshade (*Atropa belladonna*), the mandrake (*Mandragorum officinarum*), and jimsonweed (*Datura stramonium*). In spite of their ritual use, these drugs are not widely used recreationally because the effects and side effects, including headache, depression, amnesia, increased heart rate and body temperature, and loss of motor control, are so unpleasant and, as implied in the name deadly nightshade, overdosing has fatal consequences. The drugs are anticholinergic – they work by blocking the action of the neurotransmitter acetylcholine.

Dissociative Drugs
Dissociatives (such as ketamine, nitrous oxide, and salvia) produce more of a sense of detachment (dissociation), along with catalepsy, amnesia, and analgesia. Dissociative drugs induce a sensation of dissociation. Dissociation, as we have seen, covers a range of psychological states all involving detachment.

Dissociatives include phencyclidine (*PCP*, or angel dust) and ketamine. PCP can be taken in any form, and is a *NMDA N*-Methyl-d-aspartic acid receptor antagonist, blocking the action of the excitatory neurotransmitter NMDA. It is addictive. Ketamine induces a strong dissociative state. It also provokes hallucinations. It can have a number of dangerous side effects, including effects on blood pressure and provoking strong anxiety. It also has a number of dangerous interactions with other drugs. Its use as an anaesthetic is limited because of the side effects, particularly the hallucinations. Ketamine works primarily as an NMDA receptor antagonist (but also on the monoamine and opioid systems). The effects of ketamine are relatively short lasting. It is taken in a number of ways, with injection of course being the fastest acting. It takes effect in minutes, with the hallucinations typically persisting an hour or two. It produces feelings of dissociation and detachment, particularly depersonalisation and derealisation. The degree of dissociation and the vividness of the hallucinations is dose dependent; very high doses produce what is known in slang terms as the K-hole, a feeling of extreme dissociation that has been likened to catatonic schizophrenia, NDEs, and out-of-the-body experiences (see Chapter 11), with euphoria, loss of bodily awareness, loss of time perception, and a sense of floating in space. The session ends with the user confused and sometimes with amnesia (with the result that ketamine has a reputation of being a date rape drug).

Ketamine has been used as an anaesthetic, although its use is restricted because of the numerous side effects. However, there is some evidence that ketamine may be useful for elevating mood very quickly, and therefore may be of use as a short-term treatment in depression, particularly as antidepressants take weeks or months to start working (Caddy et al., 2014). The regulation of ketamine for recreational users is tightening in the UK as the result of the increasing number of deaths attributable to its use.

Psychedelic Drugs

Psychedelics produce an alteration of cognition and perception. They produce enhancement of colours, synaesthesia, hallucinations in the sense that colours and shapes are moving, impairments of memory, and the drawing out of time. People think magically, associating unassociated things and events. In higher doses, there might be *ego dissolution*, where the person stops thinking of themselves as an individual and has some sense of cosmic unity.

Peyote

Peyote (or peyotl, *Lophophora williamsii*) is a small cactus found in the Chihuahuan Desert of the southern United States (especially Texas) and north Mexico (see Figure 15.5). Like all plants, it contains a mixture of substances, those of the most interest being psychoactive alkaloids, found in the largest concentration in the cactus buds. Alkaloids are a group of organic compounds with a broadly similar chemical structure where nitrogen atoms play a prominent role. Many alkaloids have pharmacological effects, and are poisonous in large doses. The most important alkaloid in peyote is **mescaline**.

Figure 15.5 The peyote cactus. A source of mescaline. Source: Sinisa Kukic/Moment/Getty Images.

Mescaline is found in several other American cacti, including the San Pedro cactus (*Echinopsis pachanoi*), and the Peruvian torch cactus (*Echinopsis peruviana*), and in some beans in small amounts. Like other hallucinogens, its precise effects are dose dependent, distorting and exaggerating sensations and changing cognitive processing. Mescaline produces similar effects to other hallucinogens, but with more alteration to thinking processes and a more altered sense of time and self-awareness. Colours are accentuated, flat shapes appear three dimensional, and there may be synaesthesia. The person tripping may become euphoric. The effects last about 10 hours and are often characterised by the person having deep insight (at the time) into the nature of reality.

Mescaline was first synthesised in 1919 by the German chemist Ernst Späth. It has been used to explore creativity, and as an entheogen. An entheogen is a hallucinogenic drug that generates a religious or intense spiritual state, and therefore which is used in some religious processes. It's illegal to use peyote in the United States, but an exception is made for the Native American Church ceremonies.

Aldous Huxley famously described his experience with mescaline in the book *The Doors of Perception* (1954). In 1955, the British politician Christopher Mayhew took mescaline under psychiatric supervision for the BBC television programme *Panorama*, although the results were deemed too controversial to broadcast. Mayhew, however, thought very highly of the experience, calling it 'the most interesting thing I ever did'. Jean-Paul Sartre apparently had a bad trip with it in 1929, in which he saw many crabs that started to follow him (*New York Times*, 2009); he decided that they were symbolic of his sense of isolation. His trip affected

HALLUCINOGENIC DRUGS

his description of the world in his novel *Nausea* (1938). There are many other literary and popular descriptions of mescaline being used to explore creativity or the nature of reality.

Mescaline has the chemical structure 3,4,5-trimethoxyphenethylamine. As with all hallucinogens, the precise pharmacological effects are unknown, and the way in which they alter behaviour and cognition is even less clear, although all mimic the brain's naturally occurring neurotransmitters. Mescaline is known as a serotonergic psychedelic, interacting with the neurotransmitter serotonin by binding to serotonin sites across the brain; in particular, it activates the serotonin 5-HT2A receptors (and is hence a serotonin agonist). It excites the serotonergic pathway in the brain, making neurons in the prefrontal cortex especially hyperactive. The gap in our knowledge between our understanding of neuroscience and the profound changes in consciousness is enormous.

Psilocybin

Magic mushrooms are a group of small brown or grey mushrooms found across the world, often on damp grass (see Figure 15.6). Magic mushrooms contain psilocybin, which, while it does nothing much itself, soon breaks down in the body to psilocin, which is a potent hallucinogen.

Brain imaging using fMRI shows that psilocybin decreases in the coupling between the mPFC and PCC (medial prefrontal cortex and posterior cingulate cortex). This means that there is decreased activity and connectivity in the brain's key connector hubs. The PCC is closely associated with the default mode network (DMN, see Chapter 8). Essentially the **default network** is switched off (Nutt, 2012). The DMN is associated with self-reflection, daydreaming, the self, and ego concept (Carhart-Harris & Friston, 2010; Gusnard et al., 2001; Raichle, 1998).

Figure 15.6 Magic mushrooms. 'Magic mushrooms' are actually a group of many fungi that contain psilocybin and psilocin. One of the most common is *Psilocybe semilanceata*. Shown are *Galindoi* variation of *Psilocybe mexicana* mushrooms, two middle, and *Psilocybe cubensis* mushrooms, left and right. Source: The Washington Post/Getty Images.

DMT

DMT (or more properly N,N-DMT, short for N,N-dimethyltryptamine) is a substance derived from the alkaloid tryptamine, which in turn is related to the amino acid tryptophan, which in turn is a precursor of serotonin (and other substances, including melatonin). DMT is found in many tropical plants, such as the shrub *Mimosa tenuiflora* of northeast Brazil and the vine *Diplopterys cabrerana* of the Amazon basin (see Figure 15.7). It is particularly noted for its role in spiritual and religious ceremonies, so much so that Strassman (2001) dubbed it the 'spirit molecule'.

DMT can be inhaled, injected, or taking orally in a drink. It has a short onset of action and is relatively short lived. However, for the oral form to become available it must be accompanied by a substance known as monoamine oxidase inhibitors (MAOIs), which inhibit the activity of the enzyme monoamine oxidase responsible for the breakdown of the monoamine group of neurotransmitters that includes dopamine, serotonin, and epinephrine. DMT acts as an agonist for serotonin receptors, particularly 5-HT2A, but, as is common with all these drugs, it also affects other systems, such as acetylcholine, dopamine, and glutamate receptors.

It can be seen that the conditions for the effective use of DMT are more complex than with other hallucinogens. The drink ayahuasca makes the uptake of DMT relatively easy because it is a brew of several plants, including the vine *Banisteriopsis caapi*, which contain all the ingredients for effective oral uptake. Forms of ayahuasca are brewed across the Amazon basin, have a variety of names, and are used as entheogens. The drug plays an important role in several shamanistic religions in South America, and is also used as a medicine (see Figure 15.8). It's been shown that one-off ayahuasca consumption in these ceremonies can improve mental health, life satisfaction, mindfulness, and thinking skills for at least a month (Uthaug et al. 2018).

Figure 15.7 Plant source of ayahuasca from the Amazonian basin in Peru. Ayahuasca is rich in DMT, among other substances. Source: Alison Wright/Corbis Documentary/Getty Images.

Figure 15.8 Ayahuasca ceremony in Yarinacocha, in the Peruvian Amazon, 2018. Led by a shaman, many westerners who attend the ceremonies describe them as 'life changing'. Proper ceremonies will screen the health of participants. Source: Manuel Medir/Stringer/Getty Images News/Getty Images.

DMT produces physical effects on blood pressure, heart rate, and temperature, and, psychologically, it produces euphoria, a sense of calm, and pronounced visual hallucinations (Strassman, 2001). As expected, given it is an entheogen, DMT produces a feeling of awe and intense spirituality, and particularly the feeling of the presence of a god.

DMT is also interesting because it is thought to occur naturally (endogenously) in small amounts in animals. It has been noted in small amounts in rat brains and in human cerebrospinal fluid and the pineal gland (Smythies et al., 1979), and therefore has been hypothesised to occur in small quantities in the human brain. It has been speculated that larger than normal quantities of DMT might play a role in generating hallucinations in schizophrenia (Wyatt et al., 1974).

It has also been speculated that it might play a role in spiritual, paranormal, and religious experiences, although the current evidence for this speculation is very limited. Indeed, more recent thinking suggests that the serotonergic effects of endogenous DMT might foster a calm, relaxed state and suppress rather than promote psychotic symptoms. Because it is found endogenously, there has been a surge of interest in DMT, partly due to the work of the American psychiatrist Richard Strassman (2001), who argues that the brain is flooded with endogenous DMT in circumstances such as birth, death, near death, some moments of extreme stress, and some extraordinary spiritual events. He calls DMT the 'spirit molecule'. For example, Strassman (2014) argues that visions promoted by DMT were responsible for at least some of the events described in the Old Testament.

The problem with emphasising the role of endogenous DMT is that it has, so far, only been found in extremely small amounts, and if it is produced by the pineal gland, the pineal gland is too small to be able to produce rapidly the amounts of DMT needed to produce hallucinations and peak experiences (Nichols, 2017).

LSD

Lysergic acid diethylamide (LSD) is a synthesised compound in the ergot line family of alkaloid compounds, which are found in a variety of plants, including morning glory and the ergot fungus. LSD is extremely potent: 20 micrograms (mcg) are enough to have an effect, although the average 'good quality' blotter contains around 100 mcg (see Figure 15.9). With an oral dose, euphoria and dizziness begin 20 minutes or so after ingestion. Hallucinations peak after 3–4 hours, and fade out after 6–15 hours. Usually, all effects are gone after a night's sleep.

A larger dose can produce an intense spiritual experience. Any drug used for 'religious' effects and to seek transcendental experiences is called an entheogen, and, with LSD, users typically take a very large dose in search of such experiences. In general, whether trips are good or bad depends on prior mood (set) and setting.

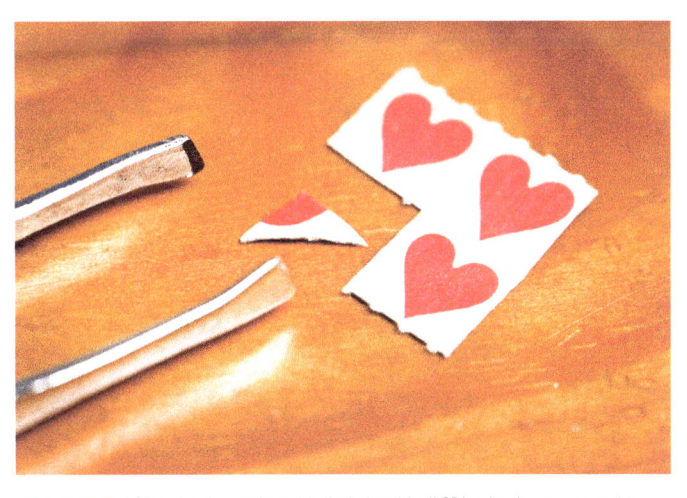

Figure 15.9 LSD tabs. Lysergic acid diethylamide (LSD), also known as acid, is the most famous of all hallucinogenic drugs. It is most often sold on blotting paper. It is extremely potent. Source: RapidEye/E+/Getty Images.

With anything above a very small dose, the phenomenology of an LSD trip is intense. There are visual and auditory hallucinations, usually with sensations being exaggerated and distorted rather than seeing imaginary things, at least at lower doses. Shapes and colours seem to shift of their own accord, and senses are mixed with synaesthesia, most obviously if people listen to music. Many people report seeing fractals, shapes that are similar, perhaps reflecting the organisation of the visual cortex (see Figure 15.10). People get an altered sense of time so that a few seconds can seem to last for an eternity.

Figure 15.10 Representation of fractals in a psychedelic LSD experience. Fractals are shapes that are self-similar at every scale. They are frequently reported in trips, which might reflect the organisation of the visual system. Source: oxygen/Moment/Getty Images.

LSD is not addictive and has relatively low toxicity. Some people do report long-term flashbacks, where hallucinations that occurred during the experience recur much later, a condition known as *hallucinogen persisting perception disorder* (HPPD). There is, in fact, little evidence that flashbacks occur, except in some special circumstances (Goldman et al., 2007). There are though many myths about drug use, particularly hallucinogens (such that there is a Wikipedia page devoted to them; see Box 15.2). There is little evidence that hallucinogen use worsens mental health or that use is associated with long-term psychosis (Krebs & Johansen, 2013). In fact, as we shall see, hallucinogen use is probably beneficial for mental health.

Box 15.3 Urban Myths and LSD Use

There are many exaggerations and distortions of information about LSD. Persisting stories are often most unpleasant and include:

> The man who saw such horrible things he pulled out his own eyes.
> The tripping babysitter who put the baby in the microwave.
> The man who permanently thought he was a glass of orange juice such that he could never bend over again.

> **Box 15.3** (cont.)
>
> Strychnine is used to mix LSD.
> People have gone blind looking at the sun with their naked eyes while tripping.
>
> There is no evidence that any of these things ever happened. When I was young, people would regularly tell of 'friends of friends' who had deliberately jumped off buildings, thrown themselves out of high-up windows, or plucked their own eyes out (one that particularly disturbed me) while hallucinating under acid. While I can find no account of people doing these things deliberately, there are accounts of people having fatal accidents, such as falls, while tripping. And, of course, people with suicidal ideation might act rashly. Substances as strong as LSD should always be respected, and should be avoided by people with medical conditions or mental illness unless taken under strict medical supervision, and should never be taken alone.

The History of LSD Use

LSD was synthesised by the Swiss chemist Albert Hofmann (1906–2008; yes, he was 102 when he died) on 16 November 1938, while he was researching lysergic acid for circulatory and respiratory stimulants. He put it aside until 16 April 1943. He must then have absorbed some through his fingertips. He later said:

> I was affected by a remarkable restlessness, combined with a slight dizziness. At home I lay down and sank into a not unpleasant intoxicated-like condition, characterised by an extremely stimulated imagination. In a dreamlike state, with eyes closed (I found the daylight to be unpleasantly glaring), I perceived an uninterrupted stream of fantastic pictures, extraordinary shapes with intense, kaleidoscopic play of colours. After about two hours this condition faded away.

He later described LSD as 'my problem child' (Hoffmann, 2018).

Probably no other substance has had such a dramatic and widespread cultural effect as LSD on the culture into which it was introduced. Many artists used LSD as a way of boosting creativity. Western art is full of references to LSD and its effects from the 1950s onwards. The Beatles discovered LSD in 1965, supposedly when John Lennon and George Harrison's dentist added LSD to their coffee. By the end of 1966, all of The Beatles had tried it or were regular users, with Paul McCartney declaring, 'it opened my eyes … it made me a better, more honest, more tolerant member of society' (Brown & Gaines, 2002). Hallucinogenic drugs, particularly LSD, were the motivation for a new type of rock music, psychedelia, noted for its weird lyrics and long, drawn-out instrumental solos, and occasional use of non-western instruments, which aimed to recreate the hallucinogenic experience in music (as well as be suitable for listening while influenced). Do yourself a favour and try some early Pink Floyd or Jefferson Airplane. Although psychedelic music faded away in the early 1970s, as LSD was less widely available and used less, its influence on modern rock music is profound.

There were several well-known experiments with LSD, mescaline, and psilocybin in the 1950s and '60s, with famous pioneers including Alfred Hubbard (1901–1982, known as 'Captain Trips') and particularly Timothy Leary (1920–1996), who coined the phrase 'turn on, tune in, drop out'. Ken Kesey (1935–2001), author of the novel *One Flew Over the Cuckoo's Nest* (1962), used the royalties to fund an acid-inspired bus trip (pun intended) across the United States fuelled by LSD to promote its benefits and turn culture into counter-culture. The United States made LSD illegal in 1967, which corresponded with the 'Summer of Love' (Box 15.4).

Box 15.4 The Summer of Love

The 'Summer of Love' was the peak of the social changes in the 1960s. It was a culmination of many factors, including the post-war 'baby boom', the anti-Vietnam war protests, the influence of the Beat Generation, the development of feminism, civil rights, the availability of the pill – and the availability of LSD. The Summer began in February, at the Human Be-In event at the Golden Gate Park, San Francisco, where Timothy Leary famously pronounced 'turn on, tune in, drop out'. The main event was during the early summer of 1967 when large numbers of 'hippies' converged on San Francisco (see Figure 15.11), centred on the Haight Ashbury area. Psychedelic drug use was abundant, although the focus was on using LSD to explore consciousness rather than drug use itself.

Figure 15.11 The Summer of Love, 1967. Hippies gather in Golden Gate Park in San Francisco, California, to celebrate the summer solstice, 21 June. The Summer of Love was mainly a Californian phenomenon, particularly around San Francisco, although the ideas, partly fuelled by LSD, changed the world.

The Summer of Love also saw significant changes in rock music, with the release of albums such as The Beatles' *Sgt. Pepper's Lonely Hearts Club Band*, Jefferson Airplane's *Surrealistic Pillow* (with its very obviously hallucinogen-inspired hit 'White Rabbit', and

> **Box 15.4** (cont.)
>
> Love's *Forever Changes*, with its obviously psychedelic cover, among many others. Indeed, psychedelic rock, with its notable cover art, directly inspired by LSD dates from this period.
> In 1968, there was widespread rioting, particularly in Paris, and the 1960s are generally agreed to have ended with the death of Meredith Hunter at a Rolling Stones concert at the Altamont Free Concert on 6 December 1969.

Less salubrious uses of hallucinogens include the Concord Prison experiment (1961–1963), when Timothy Leary gave psilocybin to prisoners at Concord State Prison, Massachusetts, in the hope, or expectation perhaps, that it would make the prisoners more social and less likely to offend. Although Leary claimed that the experiment worked, later analyses found significant problems with the original design and analysis (Doblin, 1998). Project MKULTRA was a CIA-sponsored research programme into mind control (1953–1973), including control by hallucinogens, such as LSD. The aim was to extract confessions and information from suspects, and to brainwash subjects into changing their behaviour. Many of the CIA experiments were illegal at the time.

> **Box 15.5** The Good Friday Marsh Chapel Experiment
>
> One of the most famous experiments of in the field is known as the Good Friday experiment, also known as the Marsh Chapel experiment (Pahnke, 1966). The experiment was carried out in 1962 by a graduate student, Walter Pahnke, under the supervision of Timothy Leary, then of Harvard (those were the days: no ethics committees then) on Good Friday at Boston University's Marsh Chapel. Walter N. Pahnke, a graduate student in theology at Harvard Divinity School, designed the experiment under the supervision of Timothy Leary and the Harvard Psilocybin Project. Twenty divinity students were divided into two groups in a double-blind study, one group received psilocybin and the other a control, the vitamin niacin. Members of the experimental group reported profound religious experiences. Several reported some years later that it was still one of the most profound mystical experiences of their spiritual life (Doblin, 1991). A later replication produced similar results, again with the participants commenting on the intensity of the experience (Griffiths et al., 2006). This study suggests first that some hallucinogens can act as entheogens, producing profound religious states, and second that the origin of mystical experiences might well share the same pharmacological pathways as those drugs.

The Neuroscience of Hallucinogens

Hallucinogenic drugs show that disruption to the brain's neurotransmitter systems can have profound effects on consciousness. They have a number of psychopharmacological effects, but the detailed way in which they work to produce the phenomenology is complex and far from fully understood. In particular, we know that they activate a subset of serotonin receptors of the 5-HT2A type; hence, hallucinogens are *5-HT2A agonists*. The class of widely prescribed drugs called SSRIs also increase the levels of serotonin in the brain, but do not lead to hallucinations. SSRIs work very slowly, taking weeks or even months to give therapeutic benefit (although levels of serotonin start to rise relatively quickly in the brain), whereas hallucinogens cause a large and sudden increase in the availability of serotonin. This connection between hallucinogenic and therapeutic use is an important one to which we will return.

One suggestion is that activating the 5-HT2A receptors leads to the excitation of neurons in the prefrontal cortex, but how this leads then to the hallucinatory experience is unclear (Béïque et al., 2007). A possibility is that activating these 5-HT2A receptors leads to a release of the excitatory neurotransmitter glutamate downstream in the **thalamo-cortical system**. Another possibility is that the prefrontal circuits become disrupted without any release of glutamate (Béïque et al., 2007; Vollenweider & Kometer, 2010). But it is still a long step from this type of explanation to explaining the phenomenology of the psychedelic state.

Imaging studies using fMRI show that psilocybin, the active ingredient of magic mushrooms, causes a decrease in blood flow, and therefore presumably activity, in what are the hub regions of the brain, such as the thalamus and anterior and posterior cingulate cortex (ACC and PCC; see Carhart-Harris et al., 2012; see Figure 15.12). Hubs occupy central positions in a network; they are not associated with very specific tasks (contrast the occipital cortex, for example), but act as relays, connecting different regions of the brain and allowing information to be integrated and relayed to other areas (van den Heuvel & Sporns, 2013). Hence, psychedelic drugs may decrease activity and connectivity in the brain's key connector hubs, which then enables a state of 'unconstrained cognition' (Carhart-Harris et al., 2012). Reduced blood flow to the PCC and mPFC was observed under the administration of psilocybin. Hallucinogens also reduce the number of alpha waves generated by the PCC; the decrease in alpha waves correlates with the amount of ego dissolution and increase in magical thinking the person reports. These two areas are considered to be the main nodes of the DMN. One study on the effects of LSD demonstrated that the drug desynchronises

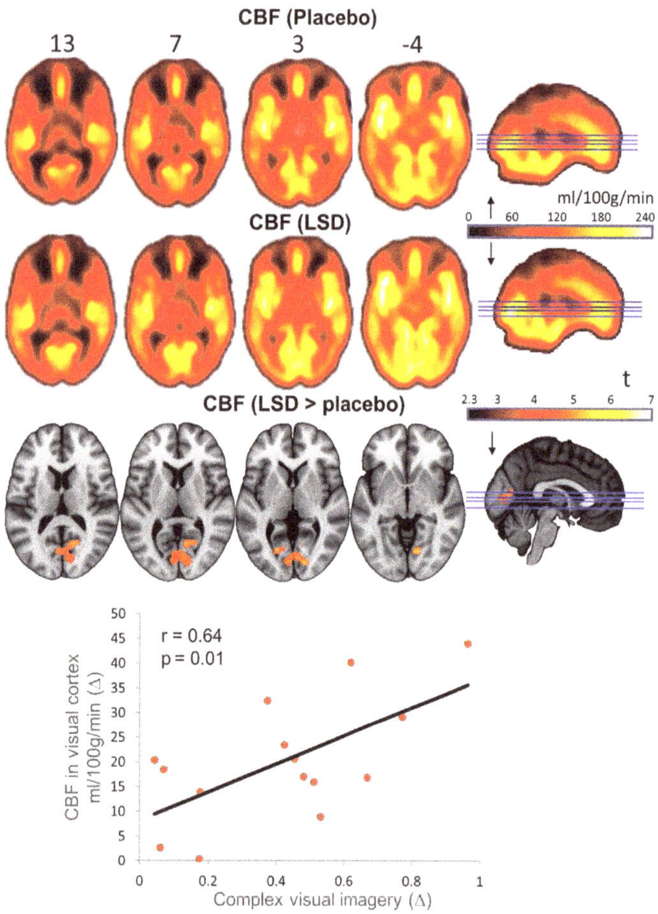

Figure 15.12 Imaging the hallucinating brain. The key part of the illustration is the difference in cerebral blood flow (CBF) between the LSD and no-LSD (placebo) conditions. Notice the blood flow is particularly high in the visual cortex. Source: Figure 1 from Carhart-Harris et al. (2016).

brain activity within the DMN; the activity of the brain regions that constitute the DMN becomes less correlated.

One of the most profound effects of LSD is *ego dissolution*, the sense of loss of the self and the loss of barriers between the self and the outside world. fMRI imaging studies show that ego dissolution with LSD is accompanied by an *increase* in global connectivity, particularly areas associated with the DMN and thalamus (Tagliazucchi et al., 2016b). Furthermore, the brain regions showing increased activation correspond to those regions with the highest serotonin 2A receptors. LSD seems to increase communication between normally distinct brain networks.

The Social Context of Drug Use

Psychoactive drugs should always be seen in a physiological, psychological, and cultural context. While some are used for medical treatment, many others of those that we are discussed are illegal in many countries. Although there is general agreement that hard drugs such as heroin are dangerous, there is still debate over whether criminalisation of users is the best policy. Arguments about the legality of drug use are particularly prominent with cannabis. Hallucinogens have been used by several cultures for self-exploration, religious ceremonies, and initiation rites throughout recorded history. In addition to their perceptual effects, hallucinogens have been taken deliberately to 'explore the mind' and 'the nature of reality'. They are often taken for religious purposes.

The Dangers of Cannabis

How dangerous is cannabis? First, the effects of smoking forms of cannabis such as 'weed' are unsurprisingly not dissimilar to the well-known negative effects of smoking tobacco, and we know how bad smoking is for you. Second, there is the fear that people who are 'stoned' are more likely to commit self harm and crime. Third, there is some concern that cannabis can act as a trigger for schizophrenia. We should distinguish here between inducing schizophrenia in people completely undisposed to it, for which there is little evidence, and bringing about an onset or earlier onset in those disposed to it, and for which there is some evidence. It might even be that people with schizophrenia take cannabis because it provides some relief from the psychotic symptoms (Nutt, 2012), although the current evidence that THC and CBD are effective for treating mental illness is weak (Black et al., 2019). Fourth, there is related concern that cannabis can have detrimental neurodevelopment effects for young users. Fifth, long-term cannabis use seems to lead to changes in brain structure, particularly brain volume in the orbito-frontal cortex and increased neural connectivity, perhaps as a compensation (Filbey et al., 2014).

Finally, there is concern that cannabis is a *gateway drug*, leading users to take harder drugs. You might start off smoking a few joints, but in a few years you end up a heroin addict.

In all of these, it can be very difficult to distinguish cause from effect; perhaps people with a tendency to developing schizophrenia are more likely to want to take cannabis than those without any such tendency, and perhaps people with addictive personalities inclined towards hard drug taking are more likely to start with cannabis when young. Perhaps crime and drug taking form a cluster of risk-taking behaviours.

Against this backdrop, cannabis has many medical uses, including pain relief where other drugs don't work, treating severe epilepsy, and improving quality of life for sufferers of diseases such as cancer and multiple sclerosis, as well as some mental illnesses. The positive effects come from the largely non-psychoactive constituent *cannabidiol* (CBD) rather than THC, and it is now possible to obtain CBD in many places in an oil. CBD does have side effects, such as gastric problems and fatigue.

Nutt (2012) ranks cannabis relatively low on the scale of dangerous drugs, arguing that many of the above dangers have either been misinformed or are based on dubious evidence. Number one on his list of dangerous drugs is alcohol.

Cultural Diversity in Drug Use

Perhaps the best-known account of the use of hallucinogenic drugs in religious practices is a series of books on the training of a shaman by the anthropologist Carlos Castaneda, starting with *The Teachings of Don Juan* (1990; see Figure 15.13). There has been considerable debate as to whether these books should be filed under fact or fiction, or just partly fictionalised fact. The books describe his apprenticeship with a Yaqui shaman in the Sonora Desert of Mexico in the early 1960s, making widespread use of hallucinogens including peyote, jimson weed, and psilocybin. After making considerable money from the books, Castaneda withdrew to a large house in California to work on his inner development, which is something I would really like to do.

Figure 15.13 Some of the writings of Carlos Castaneda (1925–1998). Castaneda was author of *The Teachings of Don Juan* (1968), describing his training in shamanism, and its sequels. The books were originally treated as non-fiction, but are now regarded as largely fictional. Source: www.pqpictures.co.uk/Alamy Stock Photo.

Different cultures have different views on psychoactive drugs. It is in part historical accident that caffeine and alcohol are acceptable in the west, while cannabis is not, when arguably the former are more dangerous (Nutt, 2012). Across the world different drugs are tolerated, even venerated in spiritual practice. For example, *khat* is a shrub found in the horn of Africa whose leaves contains *cathinone*, a stimulant and euphoric. The leaves are chewed. Similarly, the leaves of the *coca* plant, which contain cocaine, are chewed by indigenous peoples in South America for its stimulant effects. The *betel* or areca nut is widely chewed in South Asia, again for its stimulant effects. *Ayahuasca* is a potent psychedelic brew used in religious and spiritual ceremonies in South America, rich in DMT and MAOIs.

Therapeutic Use of Hallucinogens

There has been a surge of interest in the use of hallucinogens, particularly LSD and psilocybin, as a treatment for a range of physical, mental, and existential problems. In addition to normal doses, there has also been research into the use of *micro-doses*, quantities so small that they do not have any overt effect. This kind of research is difficult to do because the political stigma associated with hallucinogens makes getting the proposed research past ethical review committees very difficult. Most of the research has been carried out by the

British medic David Nutt and neuroscientist Robin Carhart-Harris at the Centre for Psychedelic Research at Imperial College, London.

The range of disorders with which hallucinogens helps is impressive, including schizophrenia (although LSD may also precipitate acute psychosis in *susceptible* individuals; Passie et al., 2008) and particularly mood disorders.

The wider therapeutic benefits of hallucinogens are reviewed by Kingsland (2019). There is some evidence that small doses of LSD can improve the quality of life of terminally ill cancer patients; LSD may help with cluster headaches; ketamine might be a very fast-acting antidepressant; and, although not strictly a hallucinogen, ecstasy has been considered as a treatment for PTSD; LSD and psilocybin can help with depression (Carhart-Harris et al., 2016) and alleviate anxiety and depression in patients with terminal illnesses. They can help alcoholics and people trying to stop smoking. In summary, they help with anxiety, depression, addictions, and helping people find meaning in life.

Carhart-Harris and Nutt (2017) propose that the two serotonin receptors, 5-HT1A and 5-HT2A, work in different ways, with the 5-HT1A system involved with passively tolerating a source of stress, while active coping and changing behaviour is mediated by the 5-HT2A system. They further argue that the 5-HT1AR pathway is enhanced by SSRIs (drugs such as Prozac), but the 5-HT2AR pathway is enhanced by psychedelics.

We have seen how drug mixtures such as ayahuasca are used in shamanic ceremonies in the Amazonian basin. There is now western interest in attending these ceremonies for self-exploration, releasing creativity, and engendering permanent psychological change for the better (Kingsland, 2019; Pollan, 2019). There are anecdotal stories in the press about how hallucinogens and the ayahuasca ceremony might also enable us to cope better with fear of death, with terminally ill cancer patients reporting that the ceremony removed all anxiety about their impending death. These ideas about death transcendence, among other positive life changes, are backed up with research on psilocybin (Griffiths et al., 2018).

Chapter Summary

- A psychoactive drug changes our mental state by crossing the blood–brain barrier.
- Psychoactive drugs affect neurotransmitter levels and change behaviour in the short or long term, but might have other effects.
- Psychoactive drugs can be therapeutic and recreational.
- Recreational drugs affect arousal (alertness), mood, and perception.
- Very high good mood is called euphoria.
- Cannabis is the third most popular recreational psychoactive drug after alcohol and nicotine.
- Cannabis produces several dose-dependent effects, including changes to mood, time perception, cognition, motor control, and perception.
- Its psychoactive ingredient includes tetrahydrocannabinol (THC), which is an agonist for the cannabinoid receptors.
- Amphetamine is a stimulant that affects several neurotransmitter levels.

- Excessive amphetamine use leads to amphetamine psychosis.
- Cocaine is an alkaloid, which is a stimulant that also produces euphoria.
- Opiates and opioids such as heroin and morphine act as painkillers.
- Hallucinogenic drugs are widely occurring naturally and have deliriant, dissociative, and psychedelic effects.
- LSD was the first and most widely used hallucinogen, and affects serotonin receptors.
- LSD use was associated with widespread social change in the 1960s.
- Naturally occurring hallucinogens include peyote cactus, magic mushrooms, and ayahuasca.
- DMT is also found endogenously, but almost certainly in too small amounts to have much effect.
- Naturally occurring hallucinogens are involved in many religious ceremonies across cultures.
- Hallucinogens that give rise to a sense of awe, a feeling of the presence of God, and feelings of insight into the meaning of life are called entheogens.
- Psychoactive drugs are illegal in many countries, although cannabis has been legalised in some parts of the west.
- Psychoactive drugs are banned because they are seen as dangerous to individuals and society, particularly developing adolescents and young adults.
- Recent research has shown that hallucinogens in large and small (micro) doses might be an effective treatment for mental illness, particularly depression.
- Hallucinogens can increase creativity, and use is associated with long-term changes to people's sense of purpose and meaning.
- The evidence on whether cannabis is a gateway drug is mixed.
- Many psychoactive drugs are illegal in many countries, but the evidence that criminalisation is best is complicated.

Review Questions

1. What are opioid receptors, which drugs bind to them, and what effects do these drugs have?
2. How can psychoactive drugs be classified?
3. How do psychoactive drugs have their effects, and what is the relationship between cognitive and other psychological changes and any psychopharmacological change?
4. Might hallucinogens have any therapeutic effects, and how might these effects occur?
5. What do hallucinogenic drugs tell us about 'normal' consciousness?
6. Why might so many psychoactive drugs occur naturally?
7. What role have psychoactive drugs played in the development of cultures across the world?
8. Should LSD remain banned?

Recommended Resources

General

Nutt, D. (2012). *Drugs Without the Hot Air*. Cambridge, UK: UIT Cambridge Ltd.

RECOMMENDED RESOURCES

Cocaine
Markel, H. (2011). *An Anatomy of Addiction: Sigmund Freud, William Halstead, and the Miracle Drug Cocaine*. London: Vintage.

Hallucinogens
Hofmann, A. (2018). *LSD My Problem Child / Insights/Outlooks* (trans. J. Ott, reprint edition). Oxford, UK: Beckley Foundation Press.

Lee, M.A., and Shlain, B. (1985). *Acid Dreams*. New York: Grove Press.

Cultural Context of Psychoactive Drug Use
Castaneda, C. (1990). *The Teachings of Don Juan: A Yaqui Way of Knowledge*. Harmondsworth, UK: Penguin.

16 MEDITATION AND TRANSCENDENTAL EXPERIENCES

Our normal waking state of consciousness is characterised by moderate arousal, orientation to the external environment, particularly for most of us to the visual world, and is defined by a prevalence of beta waves. If we are not oriented towards a particular task – and often when we are! – the default mode network kicks in and often against our will our mind starts to wander.

This chapter examines ways of improving on this everyday state. Is it possible to become more focused and less prone to distraction? First, we examine mindfulness, trying to pay complete attention to what we are doing, and being aware of our surroundings. We move on to the process of meditation, focused attention in the relaxed state. How do we meditate? What are its benefits? And how might meditation change the brain? We move on to other 'higher' altered states, and examine whether it is possible to have a state of consciousness that in some way is 'better' than normal. In particular, we look at varieties of religious experience, spending some time on Buddhism and Zen Buddhism as examples of different ways of looking at consciousness and the self. We conclude with an examination of religious practices, including prayer and ritual.

Meditation

When I was younger, many people saw meditation as at best a curiosity carried out by a few weirdos, and at worst a form of eastern quackery. Now, it is widely practised and accepted as beneficial. Meditation and mindfulness are similar. **Meditation** is a practice that leads to focused attention in a relaxed state. There are many different types of meditation, but they all have in common focusing on something. The most common types of meditation are breath and mantra meditation. All forms involve sitting fairly comfortably, back upright, often with crossed legs on the floor, but not so comfortable that one falls asleep. The meditator focuses on the rise and fall of their breath, or the words of their mantra, or the mantra combined with the breath. In breath meditation, you do not try to change the pattern of the breath, but accept it as it is. You focus on the breath, and if other thoughts arise, you let them be. There is no failing at meditation: it is what it is.

We can even meditate on the nature of consciousness itself (Blackmore, 2011). What am I doing now? Where do thoughts and actions come from? Can I spot the origin of thoughts and decisions to act?

Most people choose to meditate first thing. A typical meditation session lasts 15–30 minutes, although some people meditate twice a day, and some for much more. The historian and author Yuval Harari (author of *Sapiens*, 2014) practises *vipassana meditation* for two hours every day, as well as a one- or two-month silent meditation retreat every year. Vipassana meditation is also called insight meditation, where the aim is to see things as they really are. Harari attributes his ability to focus and write on his meditation practice.

The Physiological Effects of Meditation

Many benefits are claimed for meditation, both psychological (including being less anxious, calmer, feeling reduced effects from stress, an improved ability to focus, and resilience against pain) and physiological (having generally improved health, improved heart health, improved immunity, reduction of cortisol levels from the effects of stress, and increased longevity), bearing in mind that the physiological–psychological distinction is not always clear cut. The list sounds magical, and a search on the web reveals further benefits building up a miraculous list including almost every aspect of health you can think of. Nevertheless there is empirical support for many of these claims.

Baird et al. (2014) found that a two-week meditation programme significantly enhanced introspective accuracy as measured by meta-memory judgements. The results suggest that the capacity to introspect is plastic and can be improved through training. And although highly skilled meditators with thousands of hours of practice show the most profound changes, some changes in novice meditators are evident after just a few hours. An extreme example of physiological change is that Benson et al. (1982) found that practitioners of gTum mo yoga could increase the temperature of their fingers and toes by up to 8.3 °C (see Box 16.1).

Box 16.1 Raising Body Temperature Through Meditation

Shaolin kung fu is one of the oldest types of kung fu, combining martial arts with Chan Buddhism. It is widely reported that Shaolin monks can perform extraordinary mental and physical feats. They can crouch or balance in uncomfortable positions for many hours, bang their heads against each other to harden their skulls, and do headstands for long periods of time.

What evidence is there for mind over body in these feats? In a classic experiment, Benson et al. (1982) found that practitioners of gTum mo yoga could increase the temperature of their fingers and toes by up to 8.3°C. The research was provoked by the observation that gTum mo practitioners could dry wet sheets wrapped around their bodies in ceremonies in the cold Himalayas. There are two components to the underlying mechanism (Kozhevnikov et al., 2013). The first is that a special type of 'forceful breath' causes vasodilation, widening blood vessels near the surface of the skin and producing heat. The second component is the use of visualisation to sustain the vasodilation. The heating effect is accompanied by increased alpha, beta, and gamma waves. The results show how meditation can be used in a directed way to change the body, with implications for improving health. Much work remains to be done on how skilled meditators can perform other extraordinary feats.

The Neuroscience of Meditation

There is more than one type of meditation, and depending on whether attention is focused or disengaged, we should expect different neurophysiological systems to be engaged. Lutz et al. (2008) distinguished between two basic types of meditation: focused attention, where a person tries to focus their attention on an object or activity, such as the breath, and open monitoring, where a person monitors their experience moment to moment without reacting to it. These two types of attention involve different brain processes, and furthermore the changes become more pronounced the longer the person has been meditating. Focused attention involves changes in systems responsible for monitoring conflict and sustaining attention; open monitoring does not involve selective attention, but on monitoring, vigilance, and disengaging attention from stimuli. Skilled meditators also show improved performance on attentional tasks when not meditating (with a skilled meditator being one who has accumulated more than 10 000 hours of meditation across their lifetime). Meditation effectively decreases mind-wandering, as shown by fMRI imaging studies that find the main nodes of the default mode network (prefrontal and posterior cingulate cortices) become deactivated during meditation in experienced meditators, and at the same time there is increased connectivity in regions involved in self-monitoring and self-control (the posterior cingulate, dorsal anterior cingulate, and dorsolateral prefrontal cortices; Brewer et al., 2011). The changes relative to non-meditating control participants persist in non-meditative states.

There is some evidence that gamma waves (around 25–40 Hz) are prominent in the EEGs of skilled meditators (in this study Tibetan monks) while they meditated, particularly while they were meditating on being compassionate; no gamma wave activity was found in a control group of novice meditators (Lutz et al., 2004; see Figure 16.1). In Chapter 9, we saw that some have argued that gamma waves are responsible for synchronising perceptual information across the brain to form a coherent percept – bind different sources of information – of which we can become aware. It is possible that this gamma wave activity gives rise to the sense of heightened consciousness and altered state in skilled meditators.

Figure 16.1 The brains of novice controls (left) and skilled meditators (right) while meditating. Blue is low activity, orange and red high activity in the gamma wave range (25–40 Hz). Source: Figure 3 top from Lutz et al. (2004).

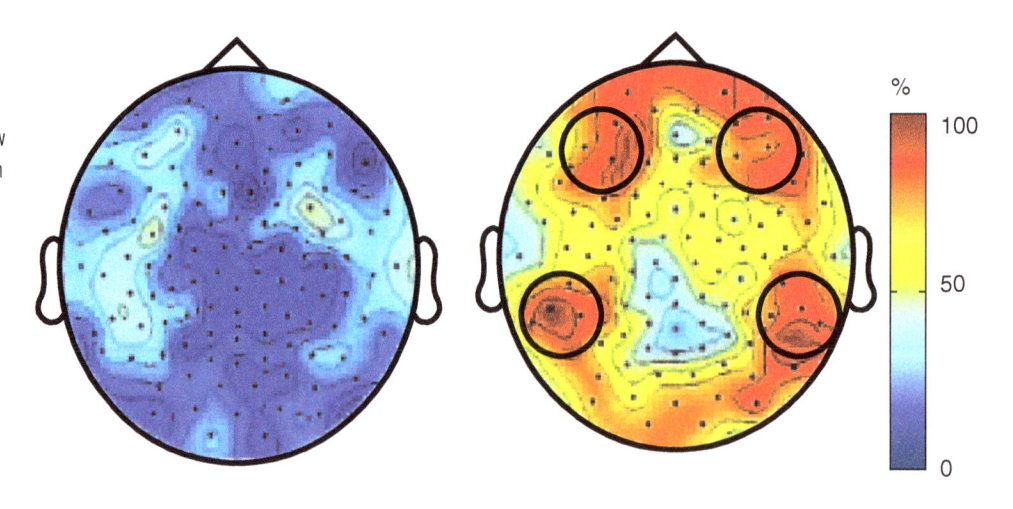

Even a short period of mindfulness meditation training can have beneficial effects. A group of 25 participants received an eight-week training course in mindfulness meditation, and showed an increase in left-side anterior activation (a region of the brain generally associated with a sense of well-being) in the meditators compared with controls, but perhaps more impressively showed a significant improvement in immune response (as measured by the number of influenza antibodies). The greater the left-sided anterior activation, the greater the improvement in immune response (Davidson et al., 2003).

In the longer term, meditation increases the volume of the hippocampus, particular regions of the hippocampus associated with stress regulation, by increasing the amount of grey matter (Lazar et al., 2000; Luders et al., 2013). As might be expected, the increase is correlated with the number of years the person has practised meditation. Buddhist meditators have thicker cortex in brain regions associated with attention (see Schjoedt, 2009, for a review), with significantly larger grey matter volumes in meditators in the right orbito-frontal cortex (as well as in the right thalamus and left inferior temporal gyrus when co-varying for age and/or lowering applied statistical thresholds). In addition, meditators showed significantly larger volumes of the right hippocampus. Both orbito-frontal and hippocampal regions have been implicated in emotional regulation and response control so larger volumes in these regions might account for meditators' ability to cultivate positive emotions, retain emotional stability, and engage in mindful behaviour (Luders et al., 2013).

A recent review has identified eight areas important in mindfulness meditation: eight brain regions were found to be consistently altered in meditators: the frontopolar cortex, which the authors suggest might be related to enhanced meta-awareness following meditation practice; the sensory cortices and insula, areas that have been related to body awareness; the hippocampus, a region that has been related to memory processes; the anterior cingulate

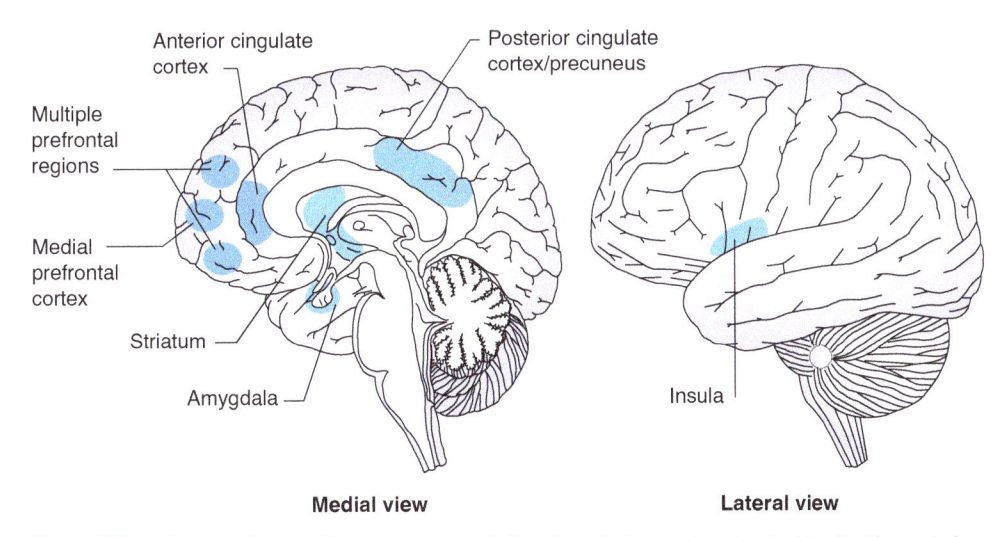

Figure 16.2 Brain regions involved in mindfulness meditation. These include regions involved in attention control (the anterior cingulate cortex and the striatum), emotion regulation (multiple prefrontal regions, limbic regions, and the striatum), and self-awareness (the insula, medial prefrontal cortex, and posterior cingulate cortex, and precuneus). Source: Figure 1 from Tang et al. (2015).

cortex (ACC), striatum, mid-cingulate cortex and orbito-frontal cortex, areas known to be related to attention control and self and emotion regulation; the insula and precuneus, known to be important for self-awareness; and the superior longitudinal fasciculus and corpus callosum, areas involved in **intra**- and inter-hemispherical communication (Tang et al., 2015).

Mindfulness

Our normal waking state is full of distraction and with trying to do more things at once. When I have my lunch at home, I am usually eating, reading the newspaper on my iPad, and watching and listening to the news on my television. Some business gurus and employers encourage us to do more than one thing at once: this ability is called *multitasking*.

There is though such a huge amount of psychological research that we can conclude with unusual certainty that multitasking is bad. We cannot do two things at once properly (unless we are very skilled at one of the tasks). First, there is a cost of switching attention, and second the tasks interfere with each other. Performance on each task is both slower and more error prone than if we did them sequentially (Marois & Ivanoff, 2005; Pashler, 1994). The subject is not of mere academic interest: texting while driving can be as dangerous as drinking while driving.

We seem to live in a world that encourages multitasking. The alternative is living mindfully. *Mindfulness* is paying complete attention to what you are doing right now; it is focused attention on what we are doing. It is difficult for most people to remain mindful for long. (I can barely manage a minute.) It is important when we are being mindful that we do not judge or evaluate.

The ability to be mindful can be improved by training, which is mainly developing focused attention through meditation. Mindfulness training and states share many of the characteristics of meditation training, and many of the benefits. Mindfulness training is an effective treatment for mental illness including anxiety and depression; indeed, it appears to be as effective as cognitive behavioural therapy and antidepressant drugs, but without the side effects (Kuyken et al., 2015; Sundquist et al., 2014). Zeidan et al. (2010) found a wide variety of improvements to mood, anxiety, levels of fatigue, and cognition, including working memory and problem solving.

Mindfulness training seems to affect some of the same brain regions as other types of meditation and regions known to be essential for supporting consciousness (Manuello et al., 2016; see Figure 16.3). Mindfulness training particularly increases the density of grey matter in the hippocampus, the posterior cingulate cortex, the temporo-parietal junction, and even the cerebellum; the anterior cingulate cortex, posterior cingulate cortex, insula and thalamus play an essential role in meditation and consciousness.

At first, this research might appear to be generating a long list of parts of the brain. There are some

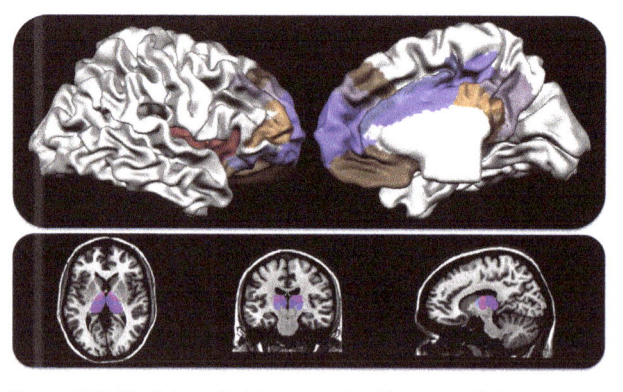

Figure 16.3 Mindfulness training seems to affect many of the same brain regions as other types of meditation and is known to be essential in supporting consciousness. The practice of meditation leads to long-term changes in the brain areas associated with attention and cognitive flexibility. Source: Figure 3 from Manuello et al. (2016).

conclusions to be drawn though. First, skilled meditation involves those areas of the brain known to be important for supporting consciousness. Second, different types of meditation may recruit slightly different brain regions. Third, meditation acts upon the default mode network, which in turn has effects on increasing cortical connectivity, decreasing thalamo-cortical activity, and on the brainstem to affect breathing and heart rate (Jerath et al., 2012).

> **TRY THIS:** Being Mindful
>
> Try to be mindful. Try to be present. Focus on what you are doing right now; pay attention to the here and now. If you find your mind drifting away (and it almost certainly will), do not castigate yourself, but gently bring your attention back to being present, How long can you stay present?

Transcendental Consciousness

Is it possible to have an ASC that in some way is better than usual? As a corollary, do most of us live our lives in a suboptimal state? **Transcendental** means better or surpassing, so transcendental consciousness means consciousness that is better or above normal consciousness in some way. Transcendental meditation helps us to be better.

Expanded or higher consciousness refers to a transitory state of consciousness when the self or the space around us seems larger and better in some way. The writer and 'angry young man' Colin Wilson (1931–2013) studied the esoteric literature, and spent much of his life trying to attain these occasional transitory higher states and reach them more reliably and permanently (see Box 16.2). Wilson (2004a) proposed that the quality of consciousness lies on a continuum shown in Table 16.1. Most of everyday experience for most people is around point 4.

Table 16.1 Wilson's levels of mystical consciousness

0	nonconscious
1	dream, hypnagogic states
2	mere awareness, thinking of nothing
3	self-aware but dull, heavy – Sartre's 'nausea'
4	everyday awareness, dull, passive, 'near nausea'
5	spring morning consciousness – all is well, 'vital'
6	magical – special moments, 'peak experiences'
7	awareness of other places and times, feeling of synchronicity
8	mystical consciousness

Box 16.2 The Life of Colin Wilson

Colin Wilson (1931–2013) was a prolific writer on many aspects of fringe psychology and the paranormal (see Figure 16.5), but he should not be dismissed. There is a common thread running through all his work about how we can live more fulfilling and satisfying lives, not in the sense of making more money or getting a better job, but in the sense of being more *aware*. Wilson was not the first to make this argument (for example, see Figure 16.4), but he was among the most cogent and approachable. He noted that a great deal of human existence is run on autopilot, with what he calls the robot in charge (or with us asleep, as Gurdjieff would have said; see below). Our mundane second-rate consciousness is occasionally punctuated by moments of insight when we are more aware, more conscious, more awake than usual, characterised by extreme happiness combined with philosophical

Figure 16.4 The guru, philosopher, mystic, composer and Russian philosopher George Ivanovitch Gurdjieff (1877–1949). Gurdjieff emphasised the importance of always being 'awake' in the sense of self-aware, and taught how to win 'the war against sleep' (not being aware). Source: InCommunicado/Getty Images.

Figure 16.5 The British writer Colin Wilson (1931–2013). A prolific writer on everything from UFOs to Atlantis, the underlying theme of all Wilson's work was how to live a life in a higher state of consciousness. He was labelled one of the original 'angry young men' for *The Outsider* (1956), his study of alienation and creativity. Source: Mark Kauffman/The LIFE Picture Collection/Getty Images.

> **Box 16.2 (cont.)**
>
> insight. These 'peak moments' have been noted in literature: G.K. Chesterton talked about these moments as feeling as though he had received 'absurd good news', Proust talked about 'moments bienheureux' (blissful moments), Wordsworth 'spots of time', and James Joyce *epiphanies*, a term that has become more widely adopted. Epiphanies are rare, and Wilson, in fact and fiction, explored ways of increasing the frequency of epiphanies, with the aim of making them the default mode of existence. There is virtually no research on the psychology and neuroscience of epiphanies because they are rare and unpredictable, but presumably they are related to some religious states.

A *peak experience*, sometimes called an *epiphany*, is close to being indescribable, but is marked extreme clarity and a feeling of joy, as though one has just received 'absurd good news'. The writer James Joyce describes them in his novel *A Portrait of the Artist as a Young Man* (1916), and the English Romantic poet William Wordsworth (1770–1850) called them 'spots of time'. These are special moments, when everything is imbued with meaning and significance. For example, he experienced one while rowing on a lake and seeing an impressive mountain seem to loom forward.

Wilson took inspiration from the writings of the Armenian–Greek spiritual leader George Gurdjieff (1877–1949) and his disciples the Russian esotericist P.D. Ouspensky (1878–1947) and British scientist John Bennett (1897–1974). Wilson describes ideas that we now see as appertaining to forms of mindfulness (Wilson, 2005, 2009; see Figure 16.4). He acknowledged the importance of the peak experience and wanted to be able to summon these well. He contrasted the vitality of the peak experience with the dullness of routine consciousness and everyday life. For these writers, reaching a peak experience depended on being aware and remembering that you are aware, a process Wilson called 'waking the robot' or 'being asleep'. Most of the time we live automatically, without reflection, as though a robot were in charge. Occasionally, we can wake the robot and move to a higher level of consciousness, using what we now call mindfulness. Fighting the process of staying in dull consciousness, of trying to move from awareness to self-awareness and then peak experience, and then trying to wake up properly, is called 'the war against sleep'. Wilson describes how Bennett was trying to 'stay awake' and maintain a higher state of consciousness, when he met Gurdjieff and realised that two weeks had passed and he had been 'asleep' – not literally, but living the routine life, with the robot in charge.

Consciousness Raising

Consciousness raising is a term used to refer to the process of making people from (relatively) disadvantaged groups aware of their situation, that they are oppressed and of the

> **TRY THIS: Peak Experiences**
>
> Have you ever had a peak experience? Most people can readily list a few. Do they have anything in common? When was your first?

> **TRY THIS: The War Against Sleep**
>
> Fight the war against sleep. What state of consciousness are you in now? By being aware, can you wake up?

means that are used to oppress them. The term came to prominence in the 1960s and '70s in the context of feminism, although the term is used more widely (see Figure 16.6). Although consciousness raising might make individuals more aware of the social context in which they find themselves, and bring into consciousness facts of which they were previously unaware, consciousness raising doesn't directly change a person's consciousness in the sense of awareness. It does though change people's self model and belief system.

Figure 16.6 Women's liberation: an equal rights march from Speaker's Corner to No. 10 Downing Street, to mark International Women's Day, London, 6 March 1971. The fight for equal rights has been a long battle, and is still ongoing. 'Consciousness raising' – making women aware of discrimination – is seen as an important weapon in that battle. Source: xpress/Stringer/Hulton Archive/Getty Images.

Religious Experiences

For many people, religious experiences are among the most intense experiences a person can have. Religious experiences can take many forms, but all share a person being in a state where they experience a state of awe, intense joy, and a sense that something is being revealed to them (James, 1902; see Box 16.3). Religious experiences can be completely spontaneous or induced by prayer, meditation, ritual, extreme physical exertion, or repetitive action, such as repeating the rosary using beads.

Box 16.3 The Nine Characteristics of Mystical States

All mystical states share these properties:

1. A sense of unity with people, objects, or supernatural entities.
2. Transcendence of time and space.
3. Strong positive mood.
4. Feeling of sacredness.
5. Insight into the nature of 'ultimate reality'.
6. Paradoxicality (the experience seems logically contradictory; there might be a loss of sense observed by a remaining self).

TRANSCENDENTAL CONSCIOUSNESS

> **Box 16.3** (cont.)
>
> 7. Ineffability (the experience is beyond words).
> 8. Transience of the experience, yet:
> 9. Permanence persisting positive changes for the individual, in terms of either attitudes or behaviour.
>
> Compiled from Kingsland (2019) and Pahnke (1963).

A typical example of an intense religious experience is the visions seen by Saint Bernadette of Lourdes (christened Marie Bernarde Soubirous, 1844–1879) in southwest France. She reported seeing visions of the Virgin Mary in a cave in 1858. She heard the sound of rushing wind, although nothing moved, and saw a dazzling light containing a white figure, whom she described as 'a small young lady'. She saw visions in the grotto daily for two weeks, sometimes falling into an apparently trance-like state. The visions would give her instructions about prayer, fasting, performing acts of penance, and washing in the spring water. For an accurate historical portrayal of the reported events, see the 1943 film *The Song of Bernadette* (King, 1943).

One of the more dramatic examples of using ritual to induce a mystical state is the whirling dances practised by some Sufis (particularly the Mevlevi Brotherhood of Turkey). (Sufism is a branch of Islam emphasising mysticism; their ascetic teachers are called dervishes.) The whirling dance is a form of active meditation where the person tries to lose their ego (similar to Buddhism) and focus on God by spinning in repetitive circles to music while repeating prayers (see Figure 16.7). Such dancing for prolonged periods will lead to exhaustion and inner ear disturbances. There is, unfortunately, a shortage of scientific literature on what is happening in these states. Understandably, given the practical difficulties of putting a whirling dervish in a fMRI scanner. One can only surmise that there are neurochemical and EEG changes similar to those found in related altered states, such as meditation. Using fMRI, Beauregard and Paquette (2006) found activation across wide areas of the brain while Carmelite nuns were reporting a state of union with God, including but not restricted to the right medial orbito-frontal and temporal cortex, the left and right caudate, left anterior cingulate cortex, and left brainstem (see Figure 16.8).

Figure 16.7 Whirling dervishes perform the Sema Ritual. Dancing and whirling induce an altered state of consciousness allowing religious meditation and devotion. The self is an illusion that has to be dissolved to permit the practitioner to reach enlightenment. Source: Izzet Keribar/Stone/Gettyimages.

There are many types of religion and religious practice. Just because one has benefits doesn't mean that they all will. Certain types of prayer

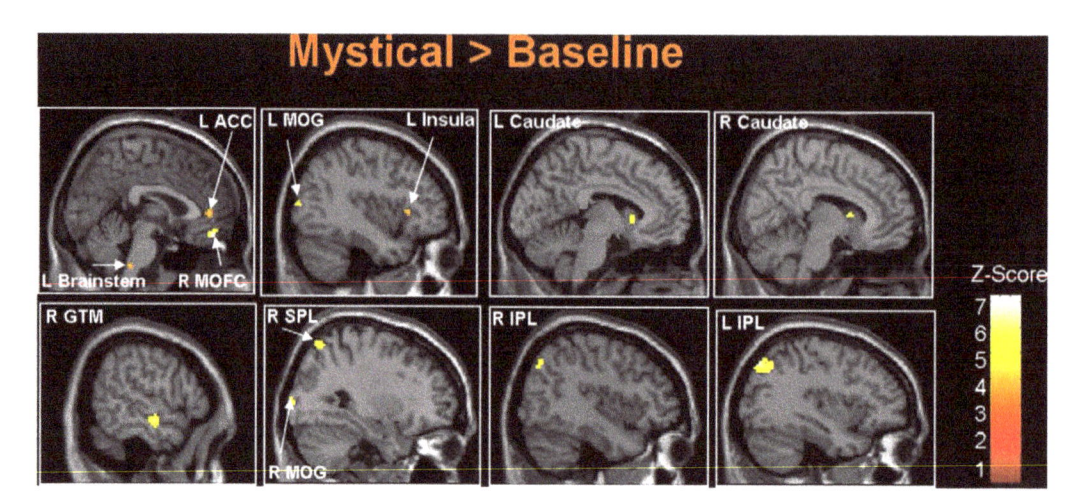

Figure 16.8 Average additional brain activation of Carmelite nuns in mystical states. As can be seen, there is no single area of activation in mystical states; the right medial orbito-frontal cortex, right middle temporal cortex, right inferior and superior parietal lobule (IPL and SPL), right caudate, left medial prefrontal cortex (MPFC), left dorsal anterior cingulate cortex (ACC), left IPL, left insula, left caudate, and left brainstem, as well as parts of the extra-striate visual cortex, are all involved. Source: Figure 1 from Beauregard & Paquette (2006). © 2006 Elsevier Ltd.

might be beneficial, but simply reading a religious work might not. Meditation involves a great deal of hard work, and you might not get the same benefits by going to church, say (although you might get others, like being encouraged to be more charitable and having more social interaction). Therefore, caution is necessary when thinking about the beneficial effects of religious and meditative practices.

Some people are more likely to have spiritual experiences than others. People who score highly on absorption, a trait reflecting how absorbed or immersed a person becomes with a task, are more likely to report hearing God's voice during prayer, have intense mystical experiences both with and without psychedelic drugs, respond to placebo brain stimulation, or have intense transcendent experiences when listening to music or appreciating nature (Lifshitz et al., 2019). Absorption is measured by the *Tellegen Absorption Scale*. It is important in explaining individual differences in daydreaming, hypnotisability, and creativity. Effective meditators also tend to score more highly on absorption (Kingsland, 2019).

Temporal Lobe Activity and Religion

Much of the neuroscience research on intense religious experiences has been carried out by the Canadian psychologist Michael Persinger (1945–2018). Persinger argued that spiritual experiences such as visions are caused by abnormal activity in the *temporal lobes*, particularly in the right hemisphere. Using a device that became known as 'the god helmet' (see Figure 16.9), he reported that he was able to induce feelings similar to religious experiences by stimulating the temporal lobes with a weak magnetic field (Persinger, 1987, 2001). In particular, participants sensed the presence of another, unseen being. However, the results have not been replicated (Wiseman, 2015), and the results may be due to suggestibility rather than the magnetic stimulation, because the device produces similar results when it is not even switched on (Granqvist et al., 2005; Larsson et al., 2005).

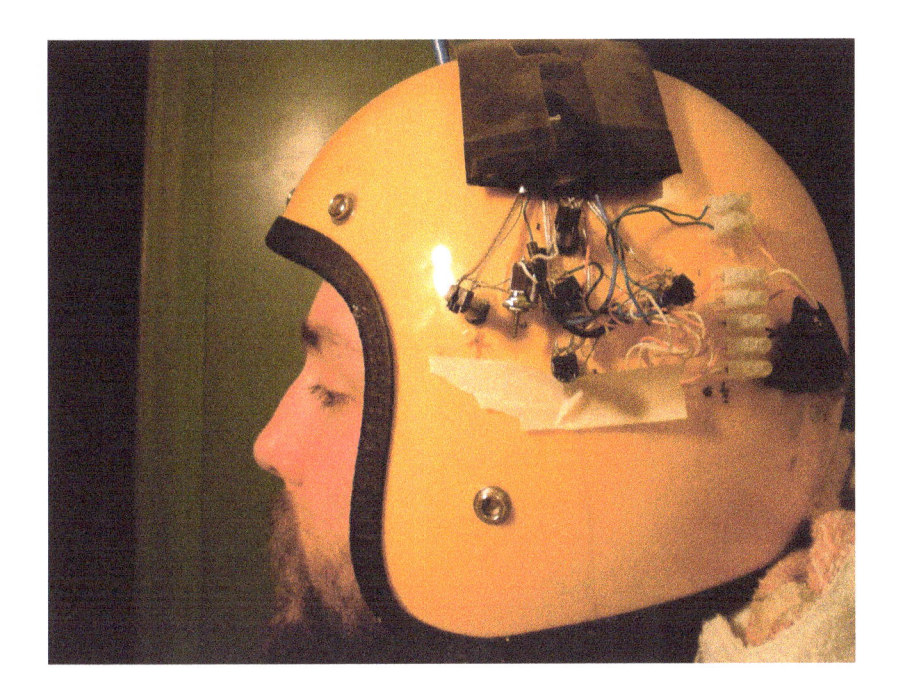

Figure 16.9 The 'God helmet'. Developed by the Canadian psychologist Michael Persinger (1945–2018), the helmet magnetically stimulates regions of the temporal lobe. The results have not been replicated, and may be due to suggestibility. Source: Harriet Carlson via Flikr.

Persinger also proposed that temporal lobe epilepsy produces profound religious states and obsession with religion, or hyper-religiosity. He proposed that spiritual experiences should be viewed as occurring on a spectrum of temporal lobe differences. Slater and Beard described the clinical characteristics of 69 people with epilepsy who had schizophrenia-like psychotic symptoms (Beard, 1963; Slater & Beard, 1963a, b). Three-quarters of the patients they studied had temporal lobe epilepsy (TLE) and 38% claimed to have had religious or mystical experiences. On the basis of this sort of evidence, the American neurologist Norman Geschwind proposed a constellation of characteristics displayed by patients with TLE, later known as the *Geschwind syndrome* (Geschwind, 1979; Schjoedt, 2009).

It is likely that other brain regions are involved in religious experiences. An fMRI study of 19 devout Mormons found that devotional practice was associated in areas of the frontal lobes, particularly the ventromedial prefrontal cortex, the anterior cingulate cortex, and of perhaps most interest, activation in the **nucleus accumbens** preceded peak spiritual feelings by 1–3 seconds in a range of tasks (Ferguson et al., 2016). Other studies have found similar results. These areas are important because they are implicated in the brain's reward circuitry, being activated by states, such as romantic love, and drugs, such as cocaine. The default mode network is also perhaps unsurprisingly implicated (van Elk & Aleman, 2017). Profound religious states and hyper-religiosity are also found in other conditions, such as schizophrenia and manic episodes of bipolar disorder.

A word of caution is provided by Aaen-Stockdale (2012), who points out that many of these experiments are small scale and, at the time of his writing, the evidence for a 'god spot' in the brain was relatively weak. Indeed, the whole notion of a 'god spot', a specific region of the brain whose activation corresponds with a religious experience, is dubious. 'Religious experience' covers a wide range of types of experience of differing intensities that almost certainly involve networks of structures covering multiple regions of the brain.

Entheogens

Intense spiritual states can also be induced by certain hallucinogenic drugs, called entheogens (see Chapter 15). The involvement of dopamine in the brain's reward circuitry explains why these drugs have the effects they do, given that one of their strongest psychopharmacological effects is to increase massively the availability of dopamine. In support of this hypothesis is anecdotal evidence that some people with Parkinson's disease, which is characterised by dopamine becoming less available, report losing their religious feelings. Van Elk and Aleman (2017) provide an integrative model of religious and spiritual experience dependent on four different brain systems: *temporal* regions, which are associated with religious visions and ecstatic experiences; multisensory brain areas and the default mode network, which are involved in self-transcendent experiences; and the theory of mind network, which is associated with prayer experiences and over-attribution of intentionality; and top-down mechanisms instantiated in the *anterior cingulate cortex* and the *medial prefrontal cortex* are involved in acquiring and maintaining intuitive supernatural beliefs.

Entheogenic drug-induced religious experiences are very similar to spontaneous religious experiences. A recent survey of non-drug- and drug-induced experiences showed that there were far more similarities than dissimilarities, although the non-drug group talked about their experience as being an 'encounter with God' as the best description of their experience, while the drug group preferred 'encounter with ultimate reality' (Griffiths et al., 2019). Both reported their encounter as being with a being that was conscious, benevolent, intelligent, sacred, eternal, and all-knowing. Two-thirds of the people who identified as atheist before their experience no longer did so afterwards.

Buddhism

All religions emphasise belief in something bigger than ourselves. Buddhism and several other eastern religions (or perhaps 'philosophies' is a better word) place particular emphasis on understanding the self, the relationship of mind to the world, and developing mental detachment through the practice of meditation (see Figure 16.10).

Skilled practitioners of Buddhist techniques aspire to particular mystical states. The ultimate state sought is *nirvana*, a state of perfect peace, happiness, and contentment, where the person is liberated from physical desire and suffering (and also free from the earthly desires that drive *samsara*, the cycle of birth, pain, death, and rebirth through reincarnation). On the way, one will experience *satori*, an intense spiritual experience where one is *enlightened*, catching a glimpse of one's true inner nature. There is a complete loss of the sense of self and instead a sense of oneness with the universe. Such states are not easy to describe because, almost universally, those who experience these states say they are impossible to put into words! It should be emphasised that similar states are sought and occur in non-Buddhist religious practices, and in meditation without religious overtones.

Figure 16.10 A representation of the sacred Buddha. Aerial view of the Lingshan Buddhist scenic spot, Wuxi city, Jiangsu province, China. Buddhism places great emphasis on meditation to produce altered states of consciousness. Source: Jeff_Hu/E+/Getty Images.

The aim of Zen Buddhism and Zen meditation (discussed in more detail later) is to achieve enlightenment. Now, if enlightenment were an easy concept to explain, it would be easier to attain. I must admit that, in spite of having tried for many years, I have never had any sight of enlightenment – yet.

Enlightenment is one translation of the Sanskrit word 'Bodhi'; 'awakening' is also close. It means the attainment of the level of understanding of Buddha of the real nature of life and things. Some believe that, in the west, the idea has been romanticised, coming to mean a sudden insight into the ultimate nature of reality. I struggle with these terms; what can be meant by 'the ultimate nature of reality'? Buddhist enlightenment is a longer process of working to attain knowledge. Enlightenment is linked to the appreciation of the Four Noble Truths: that life is full of *dukkha*, suffering, caused by a lust for things; by stopping craving stuff and short-term satisfaction, we can attain *nirvana* (the ultimate state of liberation from suffering), and that by proper living we can stop this craving. There is a great deal on the web about enlightenment, and I must admit that a lot of it doesn't make sense (to me). As far as I can glean – enlightenment having resolutely escaped me – enlightenment involves appreciating the illusory nature of the self. Everyone is agreed that it takes time and work (which is probably why I haven't managed it – yet).

The Buddhist term for 'awakening, comprehension; understanding' is *satori*. In the Zen Buddhist tradition, *satori* refers to the experience of *kenshō*, 'seeing into one's true nature'. *Ken* means 'seeing', *shō* means 'essence'. *Satori*, sudden enlightenment, is an important concept in Zen Buddhism; indeed, its goal. Buddhism provides a path to release ourselves from the continual cycle of suffering caused by superficial desire.

Buddhism also teaches the doctrine of *anattā*, that the self is an illusion. There is no permanent unchanging soul or essence, a doctrine that corresponds to our bundle theory of the self. Buddhism teaches us to recognise anattā, *dukkha*, and *anicca* (the lack of permanence in the world). Anattā distinguishes Buddhism from most other religions, because they postulate that we have a permanent, perhaps immortal, soul.

Zen

A special mention should go to Zen Buddhism, which is as close as can be to the go-to religion of many consciousness researchers – particularly so, as it doesn't necessitate a deity, soul, or afterlife. I remember finding out about it as a teenager because I had the impression it would help me understand the nature of my own mind (see Figure 16.11). I liked the idea of having an insight into the ultimate nature of reality (I never achieved this insight though).

Figure 16.11 A group of westerners practising Zen Buddhism. Meditation is no longer seen as quirky or mystical; in this chapter we have reviewed its many health benefits. Similarly, Buddhism and Zen Buddhism are now comparatively mainstream religions in the west. Source: Godong/Universal Images Group/Getty Images.

Zen is a school of Buddhism that originated in China in the Tang dynasty around 700 CE, but was strongly influenced by Indian meditative practices and Taoist philosophy. It quickly spread through southeastern Asia, through Vietnam and Korea, and to Japan. Zen emphasises self-discipline, extensive meditation, and insight into the manifestation of Buddhist thought in everyday life. Zen makes particular use of meditation on koans, small riddles or paradoxes, that provoke a student and lead them along the path to enlightenment (an awakening corresponding to an insight into the nature of truth and reality). We can attain these states through intensive meditation and the contemplation of koans, such as the famous 'What is the sound of one hand clapping?'. Others include 'What do you call the world?', 'Wash your bowls', and, after a Master carried a girl across a muddy road and a younger monk objected, the Master replying 'I left the girl there; are you still carrying her?'. Usually, the koan ends with the student being enlightened.

What makes Zen of so much interest to consciousness researchers? It is a form of introspection that promises (in offering, and most certainly not in the sense of guaranteeing) insight into the nature of our consciousness, if we put in the work. Zen uses a practice called *zazen*, a sitting meditation reflecting on the nature of existence, perhaps through koans. (According to some sources the 'sitting' refers to the mind sitting, not the person!) Another form of meditation – the version that attracted me as a teenager – is *shikantaza*, effectively trying to meditate on nothing. Hofstadter (1979) also discusses Zen and koans; the koans produce ideas that contradict each other, or make no sense, and are examples of the sort of tangled loops that, he argues, give rise to consciousness.

If this section doesn't quite make sense, but sounds intriguing, then you're starting to get the hang of Zen. What does Zen tell us about consciousness? It tells me that there might well be less to being conscious than I often think. Perhaps there isn't much there at all; perhaps the apparent business of mental content is after all an illusion.

> **TRY THIS:** Zen Koans
>
> Here is a famous koan for you to meditate upon.
>
> > A monk asked Zhao Zhou to teach him.
> > Zhao Zhou asked, 'Have you eaten your meal?'
> > The monk replied, 'Yes, I have.'
> > 'Then go wash your bowl,' said Zhao Zhou.
> > At that moment, the monk was enlightened.

Chapter Summary

- Mindfulness is being present in the moment and paying maximal attention to the task with which we are currently engaged.
- Meditation is practising focused attention in a relaxed state.
- Meditation often involves trying to focus on the breath.
- Meditation has many beneficial psychological and physiological effects.
- Some people experience states of consciousness that are in some way more rich or better than normal waking consciousness.
- Mystical experiences involve a dramatic short-lived positive change in psychological state interpreted as mystical and feeling the presence of some higher being.
- Mystical experiences have clear physiological correlates, such as temporal lobe seizures.
- Attempts to reproduce mystical states in the laboratory have proved controversial.
- Buddhism emphasises understanding the self and liberating ourselves from a cycle of suffering.

- Suffering is caused by superficial desire.
- Buddhism involves striving for a higher state of consciousness.
- Zen emphasises insight from observing contradictions, or nothing at all.

Review Questions

1. What changes in the brain when experienced meditators meditate?
2. What is the difference, if any, between mindfulness and meditation?
3. What are mindfulness and meditation good for, and are there any disadvantages to practising them?
4. Does it make sense to talk about states of consciousness 'above' normal waking consciousness, and are they in any way 'better' than normal waking consciousness?
5. What does Buddhism tell us in the west about consciousness?
6. Are religious beliefs compatible with psychology?
7. What is neurogenesis, and what role does it play when the brain rewires itself?
8. What role do neurotransmitters play in higher states of consciousness?

Recommended Resources

Mindfulness and Meditation

Williams, M., and Penman, D. (2011). *Mindfulness: A Practical Guide to Finding Peace in a Frantic World*. London: Piatkus Books.

Yates, J., and Immergut, M. (2017). *The Mind Illuminated*. London: Hay House.

Higher Consciousness

Wilson, C. (2009). *Super Consciousness: The Quest for the Peak Experience*. London: Watkins.

Buddhism

Blackmore, S. (2011). *Zen and the Art of Consciousness* (originally published in 2009 as *Ten Zen Questions*). London: Oneworld Publications.

Claxton, G. (1992). *The Heart of Buddhism: Practical Wisdom for an Agitated World*. London: Thorsons.

Hofstadter, D. (1979). *Godel, Escher, Bach: An Eternal Golden Braid*. New York: Basic Books.

Religious Experiences

James, W. (2012 [1902]). *The Varieties of Religious Experience*. Riverside, CA: Renaissance Classics.

Murphy, T. (2014). *Sacred Pathways: The Brain's Role in Religious and Mystic Experiences* (2nd ed.). Scotts Valley, CA: CreateSpace.

The Brain Changing Itself

Begley, S. (2007). *Train Your Mind Change Your Brain*. New York: Ballantine Books.

Doidge, N. (2007). *The Brain that Changes Itself*. London: Penguin Books.

Newberg, A., and Waldman, M.R. (2009). *How God Changes Your Brain*. New York: Ballantine Books.

Newberg, A., and Waldman, M.R. (2016). *How Enlightenment Changes Your Brain*. London: Hay House.

17 PARAPSYCHOLOGY

Parapsychology is the study of abnormal and unexplained phenomena. It's a strange subject in some ways because, if the subject matter becomes explained, it moves from the domain of parapsychology to the domain of psychology or physics. At the core of the subject are phenomena where the mind has some direct apprehension of or action on the world in a means that we cannot explain in terms of known physical processes. The term *anomalistic psychology* is now sometimes used, particularly if the initial assumption is that there are no *paranormal phenomena*.

If you ask most people to give examples of paranormal phenomena, a long list of apparently unrelated items would spew forth, including telepathy, clairvoyance, ghosts, UFOs, aliens, yetis, spiritualism, and doubtless much else. This chapter imposes order on this impressive array of apparent weirdness.

We need first to distinguish between spontaneous phenomena, which include most things that most people think of as paranormal, from experimental studies of paranormal phenomena. Spontaneous phenomena is a wide-ranging class of reports including ghosts, séances, aliens, UFOs (see Figure 17.1), cryptozoology (unknown animals such as the Yeti and Bigfoot), poltergeists, and apparently incredible coincidences. The problem with all of these is that outside the laboratory we have little idea what is really happening. One thing that you should have taken from this book is that observers are very unreliable. Someone might be completely honest in their assessment of a situation in concluding that they think that they have seen a ghost, but that claim doesn't meet our high standard of scientific evidence. Someone might say they dreamed of their parent the night before they died, but how often do they dream of them anyway? It's very difficult to control the conditions and to assign probabilities to events. That's why most parapsychologists try to control conditions and work with events where we know the probabilities of things happening by chance and work in the laboratory.

We begin by distinguishing between different types of psychic phenomena, such as telepathy, clairvoyance, and precognition, and ask if we can meaningfully make distinctions between them. We introduce the general term psi for a general mechanism underlying them.

We then examine the range of spontaneous phenomena, asking particularly what, if anything, we can learn from them.

Most of the chapter focuses upon experimental tests of paranormal phenomena. We pay particular attention to asking what makes a good experiment, considering issues of

Figure 17.1 An 'unidentified flying object' (UFO). Unknown date and location. Is this really how the aliens would travel? Source: Steven Peters/The Image Bank/Getty Images Plus.

methodology such as cueing and sensory leakage. We look at the particular role altered states of consciousness have played in paranormal research, particularly the ganzfeld. We examine trait and state effects, and introduce the notion of the experimental effect in psi research. We then look at psychokinesis, mind over matter, in the laboratory and in the wild in the form of poltergeists.

We conclude by looking at survival research, the idea that something of us survives after death.

This text is about consciousness, not paranormal phenomena, so how are the two related? This question needs some consideration. If something of our consciousness or personality survives after death, most people would conclude that the materialistic view of psychology is wrong, or at best incomplete. And if these phenomena are real, perhaps they are better understood in the context of some version of dualism rather than monism. However, understanding this relationship is hampered first by the lack of any agreed widely replicable findings in the field (the problem of replicability), and second by the lack of any reasonable mechanism that could explain these phenomena.

Note that there is always something to explain, even if the phenomena turn out not to be paranormal (as is often the case). Figure 17.1 shows something. If it is a fake, why do people bother? Why do so many people believe in UFOs if the evidence for them is so weak?

ESP and Psi

One example of the sort of phenomenon studied, and one with which most people are most familiar, is telepathy. *Telepathy* is the direct transfer from one mind to another – mind reading. If I can tell what you're thinking, or if you can send a mental message to me, we have just enjoyed telepathic communication. *Clairvoyance* is the ability to gain information about a thing – if you put a picture in a drawer, or set a lock combination to a particular number, and I can perceive that picture or number, then I have used clairvoyance.

This is where things get messy. How do we know that I have perceived the object, rather than read your mind for your memory of what's in the drawer or the lock combination? It is impossible in many circumstances to make these distinctions, so parapsychologists use the term *ESP* (extrasensory perception) instead.

I might be able to predict what is going to happen the future. If I see an image of next week's winning lottery numbers, then I have used *precognition*. So, you might think we could get round the telepathy/clairvoyance confusion by, say, randomly choosing a sealed envelope from several and putting it in a drawer. But how could you distinguish between clairvoyance and precognising the future when the envelope is opened and someone looks at it? Again, we can't, so it makes sense to lump telepathy, clairvoyance, and precognition together; we then talk about **GESP, a general extrasensory perception** ability.

We could also use our mind to move or manipulate objects directly – mind over matter, or **psychokinesis (PK)**. At the macro level, I might be able to move my coffee mug over the edge of my desk on to the floor. Messy, and fortunately I have never been able to do it. At the micro level, I might be able to influence the decay of a radioactive substance and hence influence the generation of a series of random numbers. And suppose I ask you to think of an object, and you choose a Christmas tree, and I say Christmas tree, how can we be certain that I didn't influence your choice in the first place by PK? Because the distinctions between telepathy, clairvoyance, precognition, and psychokinesis are so unclear, most researchers in the area prefer the general term *psi*.

We can distinguish between spontaneous occurring phenomena and laboratory-based experimental tests of psi.

Spontaneous Phenomena

Most people are familiar with paranormal occurrences from spontaneously occurring cases – stories they have read or heard about, or strange things that have happened to them. Spontaneously occurring phenomena cover an enormous range of weird stuff from ghosts, UFOs (see Figure 17.1), spiritualism events, physical time travel, and poltergeists, to seeing the future and extraordinary coincidences. The problem with all of these is that they are very difficult to evaluate outside the laboratory because we can't control the conditions, and it's very difficult to estimate the probability of events happening by chance (and hence to carry out statistical analyses). You dream about somebody and they phone you the next day – what are the chances of that? Anecdotes get elaborated and exaggerated, and we know memory is fallible. We know also that most people have a very poor understanding of probability. It is also difficult to rule out fraud. That's not to say that everybody reporting these incidents is a fraud, but simply that it is difficult for these anecdotes to reach the standard of evidence required for worthwhile scientific investigation. When one person is involved, we cannot rule out an ASC or hallucinatory episode.

There may be some examples of apparent spontaneous activity that are eventually attributable to aspects of the environment that are as yet unknown but still explicable within current physics. As an example, infrasound (very low-frequency sound, less than 20 Hz, particularly around 19 Hz) seems to provoke specific psychological states in humans, including feelings of fear or awe. As it's not consciously perceived (it's too low to hear as a sound), it may make people feel unsettled, and even that strange events are happening. The British engineer Vic Tandy (1955–2005) investigated the relationship between infrasound and spontaneous paranormal phenomena such as ghost apparitions. He argued that exposure to infrasound around 19 Hz provoked both physiological (feeling afraid) and psychological (feeling depressed and occasionally glimpsing apparitions) reactions (Tandy & Lawrence, 1998). In a similar study, Richard Wiseman and others played infrasound at 17 Hz during some pieces of music in a concert in the Purcell Room in the South Bank. Many people noted effects in the pieces of music accompanied by the infrasound (even though they did not know which pieces were in the experimental condition). Effects were again both physiological and psychological, including anxiety, sorrow, feeling cold, and having 'shivers down the spine' (Wiseman, 2011a).

We cannot rule out that all accounts of spontaneous phenomena can be explained by this or similar mechanisms, or by physical mechanisms as yet unknown.

Box 17.1 The Versailles Time Travel Incident

On 10 August 1901, two English visitors, Charlotte Moberly (1846–1937) and Eleanor Jourdain (1863–1924), toured the Palace of Versailles. Moberly was principal of a hall of residence for women in Oxford, and Jourdain her assistant, although she had also written several textbooks by that time. After apparently not thinking much of the palace, they decided to walk through the grounds to the Petit Trianon, a small (relatively speaking) chateau. It seems that they got a little lost, and then were overcome by 'feelings of oppression and weariness'. They then came across a scene of people dressed in clothes as from the end of the eighteenth century. Jourdain noticed a cottage, and Moberly noted that everything seemed unreal, and it was as though she was looking at a scene from a Madame Tussaud's waxwork. They then met a seated man whose face was marked by smallpox, and Moberly saw a lady seated on the grass drawing, dressed in old-fashioned clothing. They then found their way back to the palace and met other tourists.

Later on, comparing notes, the pair concluded that they had seen the grounds as they were on 10 August 1792, and the woman Moberly saw (but Jourdain did not) was Marie Antoinette. They revisited the gardens several times but were unable to find their path or landmarks. They thought they had experienced a haunting, or had somehow travelled back in time.

These are extraordinary claims, but given the respectability of the women it is most unlikely that they fabricated the story and drew some ridicule on themselves for no good reason. So, we can at least conclude that they thought something had happened. Given time

Box 17.1 (cont.)

travel or ghosts are the least likely explanations, particularly given evidence that the features they described were not on the maps of 1792, what happened? Their stories were not in perfect accord, and surprisingly they only compared notes some time later. We have seen how fallible our beliefs and memories are (Chapter 6), and have known since at least the time of Bartlett (1932) and his study of memory for *The War of the Ghosts* story how stories get distorted in the retelling. The pair were lost, which would have made them disoriented and confused at the time.

The episode is usually referred to as the Moberly–Jourdain incident, and is described first hand (although ten years later, in 1911) in their joint book *An Adventure*, under the pen names Morrison and Lamont. In spite of its implausibility, the story gripped the public imagination and has been retold several times (e.g. Castle, 1991; Iremonger, 1975). It shows that even extraordinary accounts can have a rational explanation without resorting to talking about fraud or deceit.

Box 17.2 Sonic Noise and Sonic Weapons

Some people report being able to hear an invasive and disturbing low-frequency sound at some locations, the sound being variously described as a hum, rumbling sound, or drone; the phenomenon has been given the name *the Hum*. Subjectively, the Hum is located in the 30–50 Hz range. Many explanations have been proposed, from nearby heavy industry, low-frequency waves used to communicate with submarines, or noises made by animals, to tinnitus, a hearing disorder affecting some individuals who hear ringing and other noises, and noise in the hearing system. But there are sounds lower in frequency than the Hum.

Sonic weapons use powerful sound, ultrasound (beyond the high-frequency limit of hearing for most people, or at least older people), and infrasound (very low frequency, generally below 20 Hz). Blasts of relatively low power ultrasound (around 20 kHz) feel unpleasant, and are used by police and local authorities to deter gatherings of younger people (who are much more sensitive to higher frequencies).

Infrasound can result from both human-made and a very wide range of natural causes. Some animals, such as elephants, rhinoceroses, and whales, use infrasound to communicate.

Can unusual sound patterns generate the appearance of psychic phenomena? Almost certainly. It can't be ruled out, although it's very difficult to explore spontaneous cases unless they persist for some time. But although we might not consciously hear the sound, they can affect us, making us feel odd, afraid, or struck by awe. The work of Tandy and Wiseman shows that, if we rule out psychological explanations, there are still physical explanations available without having to resort to paranormal ones.

> **TRY THIS: Spontaneous Phenomena**
>
> It is easy to find examples of spontaneously occurring psychic phenomena – one good source is the *Fortean Times* It Happened to Me series. Take a sample and provide explanations that do not violate known science. How plausible are your 'alternative' explanations?

> **TRY THIS: Ethics**
>
> Are there any ethical implications of studies such as the Purcell Room experiment? (Note that in this study the music-goers were aware in advance that they were in a study with infrasound involved.)

How Spontaneous Phenomena Change with Time

The forms of spontaneous phenomena has changed over history. Until recently the obsession was with witches, demons, and devils; at the turn of the century, spirits and the afterlife; in recent years UFOs and alien abduction. Clearly the type of phenomena has changed along with the development of psychological and scientific understanding. That might mean that the phenomena are less likely to be real, but it could reflect the way in which an underlying phenomenon is manifested.

Experimental Findings in Parapsychology

The first systematic study of ESP was carried out by the American botanist (originally) J.B. Rhine and his wife Louise E. Rhine at Duke University in North Carolina, in the 1920s and 1930s. He used a series of clear images called Zener cards (circle, square, cross, wavy lines, and star; see Figure 17.2). With five images, we know that the chance of guessing any one correctly is one in five, so on a run of a hundred trials the *mean chance expectancy* is 20. Rhine found evidence of weak effects in the general population of people being able to guess which card he was looking at, with people scoring slightly but significantly higher than chance over many trials. Most of the interest, however, was focused on a few 'psychic superstars', particularly Hubert Pearce and Joseph Pratt, who reliably scored much higher than chance (Rhine, 1934).

Figure 17.2 Zener cards. Five different designs so the base rate of getting a trial right is 1 in 5. Testing telepathy with a person in the same room might be fun but scientifically totally inadequate. Source: Chronicle/Alamy Stock Photo.

Box 17.3 Psychic Superstars

Most people perform at or close to chance in psi experiments, and generally effect sizes in these experiments are small or zero. However, a handful of individuals appear to perform staggeringly better than average, and these people have been nicknamed *psychic superstars*.

The first 'superstars' came from the experimental work of the American psychologist Joseph Pratt (1910–1979) during 1933 and 1934. His experiments with Zener cards with the divinity student Hubert Pearce produced outstanding results: across all sittings he scored 558 hits out of 1850 trials (with a MCE – mean chance expectancy – of 370 hits, this score would be highly statistically significant; see Rhine, 1937 for details). However, the experimental design left a great deal to be desired. Generally, merely shuffling cards is a bad idea because it isn't a very good way of randomising items. It's calculated that seven good riffle shuffles are needed, as card sharps know. More importantly, the design did not eliminate cheating. There has been considerable debate about whether records were falsified, or whether either participant or an accomplice could have gone to the other one's room to spy. You risk your reputation doing psi research. Pearce became a Methodist Minister and was widely regarded as an honest, religious man.

The American artist Ingo Swann (1933–2013) was a star participant in Targ and Puthoff's (1977) remote viewing experiments in the Stargate Project. Swann also took part in OBE experiments where he was required to view a remote target, and PK experiments where he was to influence the magnetic field of a well-shielded magnetometer. The usual sorts of problems, poor experimental control and the failure to prevent fraud, were associated with these experiments. See Swann (2018) for an example of his writings on how to develop your ESP and telepathy.

In 1973, Swann remotely viewed Jupiter and Jupiter's moons. He reported the presence of something like the rings of Saturn. The Voyager probe found faint rings around Jupiter in 1979. Lucky guess, of course.

In more recent times, the Israeli magician Uri Geller claimed to be a psychic superstar (see Figure 17.3).

Figure 17.3 Israeli 'psychic superstar' Uri Geller. Geller came to fame in the 1970s with his spoon-bending exploits on television (see section on psychokinesis). Source: Linjerry/iStock/Getty Images Plus.

Issues in Experimental Design

Parapsychology experiments need extremely rigorous designs to convince the many sceptics. As a general rule, if a stage magician could reproduce the result, then the experiment isn't sound. There are several ways in which a parapsychology experiment could give fallacious results. First, suppose you are given four photographs, and told that one is the target photograph at which another person has been looking? And then suppose you notice that one photograph is covered in greasy fingerprints (see Figure 17.4)? You might well guess that that is the target picture. You'd be right, and score well above chance, and because of nothing to do with ESP. You don't even need to be aware of the fingerprints; we know from earlier that people can pick up from quite subtle cues without awareness. We call this type of information transfer *sensory leakage*. Or suppose I'm looking at some cards, and you can see their reflection in my spectacles? Now suppose a person is trying to send an image to you, and then I show you four pictures, one of which was the target. I know which one of the four was the target, and when I get to it I say 'or was it THIS one?' with particular emphasis. I don't even have to try or be aware of trying, and you don't have to be aware of noticing. We call this type of information transfer *cueing*. You might be sceptical that a person could perform really well on a task simply by making use unconsciously of sensory leakage or cueing, but which explanation are sceptics going to believe? It is, of course, possible to design experiments that prevent leakage and cueing: you use duplicate photographs, you put the participants alone in separate rooms or even buildings, you use a double-blind design where the experimenters or other people that have contact with the participant don't know what the target is. Finally, you need to take as many precautions as possible against experimenter fraud. When people take all these precautions, most psychologists think that findings supporting the existence of psi are rare to nonexistent; unlike the rest of science, the findings are not replicable. This finding is called the *replicability problem* and is considered to be the most telling evidence against the existence of paranormal phenomena.

Psi and Altered States of Consciousness

If psi exists, why is it so weak? One popular idea is that its effects are easily drowned out by much stronger background sensory noise. This *sensory*

Figure 17.4 Sensory leakage. Carrying out an experiment to test for psi is not as easy as it might first appear. Which of these two pictures do you think the sender was looking at in a telepathy experiment?

> **Box 17.4** Hoax Mediums
>
> Mediums purport to contact the dead, in a process known as séances, or more recently in stage or public events, and even on television. Contacting the dead is the basis of the religious movement known as *spiritualism*. While some mediums are genuinely honest in their intentions, trickery and deceit are widespread (see Figure 17.5). The American illusionist and escapologist Harry Houdini (1874–1926) expended some effort in exposing fake psychics, a pursuit that inspired many other stage magicians, most recently holding and Teller. Houdini soon had to attend séances in disguise. In one particularly famous example he exposed a 'trumpet medium'; those involved sit in a circle hold hands, and soon in the dark a trumpet is sounded. Houdini showed how the medium could break free of the circle, and manipulate the trumpet, perhaps with his feet. He smeared lamp black on the trumpet mouthpiece, and of course when the lights came on the medium's mouth was smeared with the lamp black.
>
> Figure 17.5 Ectoplasm apparently appearing out of the head of the medium Marthe Beraud (also known as Eva C.), around 1910. Ectoplasm is the name of spiritual energy or material 'externalised' by mediums. It looks like a piece of cloth to me, and it is difficult to understand how anyone could have been fooled, although it might look better in low light conditions. The material would be concealed on the person, or sometimes even regurgitated. Source: Hulton Archive/Stringer/Getty Images.
>
> Modern-day mediums use a variety of methods to extract information from their victims. At the gentlest end, they may simply pick up on cues as they speak to the person, for example pursuing a line to which the person nods. Some fish for information. Some gather information before the meeting. Some of the techniques are reviewed in Jones (2010).

> **TRY THIS:** Test ESP
>
> Design an experiment to test ESP. Use as many precautions as you reasonably can. Carry out the experiment and employ the appropriate statistical analysis.

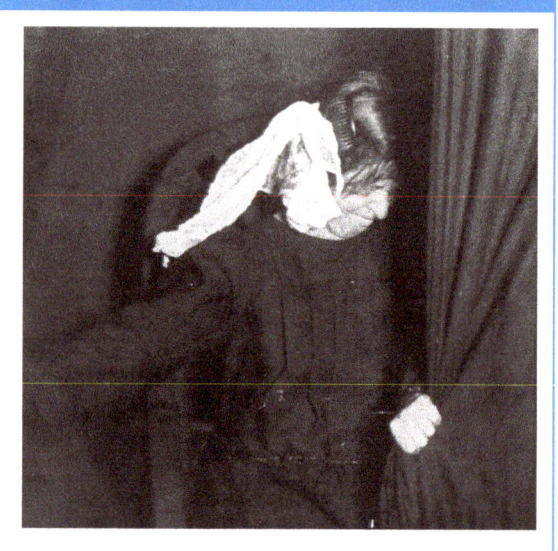

noise hypothesis has led to interest in techniques that boost the signal to noise ratio, particularly using ASCs. All ASC studies try to improve the quality and quantity of the psi signal, and many have been tried, including hypnosis, relaxation, and dreams. The original research by psychiatrist Montague Ullman at the Maimonides dream laboratory in Brooklyn in the 1960s and '70s appeared to find clear evidence for ESP (Ullman

& Krippner, 1969). Subsequent dream studies have continued to find support for ESP (Sherwood & Roe, 2003). The principle behind these dream studies is similar to the reasons for using the ganzfeld: everyday waking consciousness is a source of noise, which is attenuated in dreams allowing the psi signal to come through more strongly. These dream studies have received nowhere near as much attention as the ganzfeld studies. It's more difficult to carry out dream research, of course, which perhaps is the main reason why they have been relatively neglected: you can spend ten hours setting up a participant and waiting, only to discover they don't remember a single dream.

Psi in the Ganzfeld

One of the most promising ASC noise-reduction techniques has been the ganzfeld. The ganzfeld is a form of sensory habituation, similar to sensory deprivation, but more pleasant, and easier to carry out (see Chapter 11). The participant relaxes on a chair or bed for half an hour to an hour and reports their *mentation* (their verbal report of their thoughts, sensations, and feelings during the session). In the basic ganzfeld psi setup, this participant is the receiver; in another location, another person, the sender, is looking at a picture (see Figures 17.6 and 17.7). After the session, the participant has to say which one of a number of pictures (usually four) the sender was looking at based on their mentation. The sender is then recalled and the guess compared against the actual target. There was much excitement in the parapsychological communication in the 1970s and '80s as the ganzfeld appeared reliably to give scores significantly greater than chance. A number of meta-analyses pooling the results of many studies showed scoring at the rate of 30–35%; however, other meta-analyses that were more stringent in their inclusion criteria for methodological soundness showed no significant effect overall. There is also a possible problem called the *file drawer effect*, whereby papers that give null results are not published, and as ever great arguments have ensued (Honorton, 1985; Hyman, 2010; Milton & Wiseman, 2001; Williams, 2011; and references in these papers).

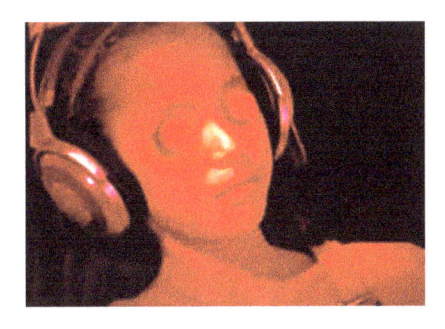

Figure 17.6 The ganzfeld. The participant relaxes with uniform red light presented to their eyes and white (or brown) noise to their ears. Source: Nealparr at en.wikipedia/public domain.

Figure 17.7 Some targets in the ganzfeld. The sender is looking at a copy of one of these four pictures, and the participant has to rate or rank them in order of best correspondence.

Remote Viewing

Some of the more notorious studies of psi have involved a technique known as *remote viewing*,

> **TRY THIS:** Do the Ganzfeld
>
> Set up the ganzfeld as described. If you need any further details, they are easily available online. Design and run an ESP experiment. How well can you protect against sensory leakage and cueing?

Figure. 17.8 Remote viewing. I'm wandering around this location (Trafalgar Square, London) and you're a thousand miles away trying to pick up my impressions. The applications, particularly for the military, are obvious.

where a participant endeavours to gain information about a geographical site (see Figure 17.8). The key studies in remote viewing were carried out by Russell Targ and Harold Puthoff at the Stanford Research Institute (SRI) in the 1970s (Targ & Puthoff, 1977). The work came to rely on psychic superstars, most notably Ingo Swann (1933–2013). At first, one interesting conclusion was that distance did not affect the probability of success. With obvious military applications, the work was funded by the US government in what was known as the *Stargate Project*. Funding and then the research were discontinued when there was no clear evidence that the technique worked. Since then, the remote viewing work has been heavily criticised (e.g. Hyman, 1986; Wiseman & Milton, 1999, among many others). First, as with many of these experiments with psi, the results were difficult or impossible to replicate. Second, there were several methodological criticisms, such as a lack of controls, the possibility of sensory leakage, uncertainty as to what constituted a hit (successful trial), and the design not being stringent enough to eliminate the possibility of fraud (a criticism that has always struck me as slightly unfair, but the retort is always that 'extraordinary claims require extraordinary evidence').

Bem's Experiments

A more recent series of experiments by the respected American social psychologist Daryl Bem has caused controversy. He published a series of experiments in the prestigious *Journal of Personality and Social Psychology*, known for its very high standards of peer review, that found statistical support for the existence of psi. Bem reported nine experiments involving more than 1000 participants based on traditional psychology paradigms but reversed the order of events ('time reversing') to see whether participants' responses could be influenced by future events (Bem, 2011). An example is retroactive recall: participants were shown a list of words and asked to recall as many as possible. They were then shown some of the words again as practice words. They recalled more of the practice words than control words, even though the practice episode was after the recall episode. Other tasks included viewing erotic and precognitive negative stimuli, priming, and habituation. Bem argued that results like these supported precognition.

Unsurprisingly, this research drew many criticisms. One type of criticism was based on the statistics, arguing that Bem didn't control for multiple statistical testing, inappropriately used one-tailed statistics, didn't use appropriate statistics, omitted important details in the procedure, or stopped the experiments when they reached statical significance (Alcock, 2011). A second criticism is that there was a widespread failure to replicate Bem's findings (Ritchie et al., 2012). A third criticism is that the inferential statistical approach traditionally taken by psychologists is inappropriate and we should instead use Bayesian statistics, which takes into account how likely something is to happen (and for psi, it's very unlikely; Wagenmakers et al., 2011). Bem and colleagues tried to address some of these criticisms, although the current consensus among psychologists is that they did not succeed (Bem et al., 2011).

The publication of the paper in a highly respectable APA (American Psychological Association) journal drew criticism, and provoked a debate about the value and credibility of the academic peer-review process.

Trait and State Studies

Many studies have examined psychological factors to uncover when psi is more likely to be manifest (Irwin & Watt, 2007; Watt, 2005). In particular, the work has examined which personality *traits* and which *states* are conducive to psi. In summary, the research shows that psi is more likely to occur with participants who score low on neuroticism and high on extraversion, and when participants feel relaxed, confident, and agreeable.

One of the most well-replicated findings in parapsychology is the sheep-goat effect, whereby people who believe in psi tend to score better than those who don't: the sheep are people who accept the existence of psi, while goats are more sceptical (Schmeidler, 1952). One fascinating and well-replicated result is that not only do goats score worse than sheep, they tend to score significantly *beneath* chance, an effect known as *psi missing*.

Demonstrations of trait and state effects in psi are in themselves evidence for psi: you can't have a meaningful correlation for a phenomenon that isn't real. Therefore, the causes of these effects and the validity of these experiments have come under as much scrutiny as all other areas of parapsychological effects.

Experimenter Effects in Parapsychological Research

Trait differences are not confined to participants. There have been reliable demonstrations that some people make better experimenters than others, in the sense that some are more likely to obtain significant results, an effect known as the *experimenter effect*. Essentially, people who make good participants make good experimenters: successful experimenters tend to be extrovert, confident that the experiment will work, and put participants at their ease. The source of the effect has been much debated (Palmer, 1997; Schmeidler, 1997). Note that the experimenter effect is not confined to parapsychology.

Psychokinesis

Psychokinesis (PK) is mind over matter, being able to move objects or change events by the power of mind alone. It is divided into macro-PK for movement you can see with the eye (see Figure 17.9), and micro-PK for things you can't, including computers and radioactive sources such as have been used in some random number generators.

Of course, there is always the possibility that macro-PK occurs spontaneously, but without considerable supporting evidence there are no well-documented cases. There

Figure 17.9 Psychokinesis? Stanislawa Tomczyk levitating a rubber ball. Tomczyk was a Polish Spiritualist medium active in the early twentieth century.
Source: Science History Images/Alamy Stock Photo.

are a few examples of PK on film, but these are usually from the former Soviet Union or Eastern Europe on grainy black and white film and it is very difficult to work out what is going on. One of the most famous cases was the Russian woman Nina Kulagina (1926–1990); films of her in action can be found online. It is generally thought that she used concealed magnets and threads to move objects around.

One of the more notable crazes in the 1970s was for spoon bending. The craze centred around the Israeli psychic Uri Geller (b. 1946). Geller would appear on stage and television bending spoons and forks, often breaking them (see Box 17.3 and Figure 17.3). It is generally concluded that Geller used stage magic rather than PK.

More thought-provoking evidence came from the work of the American physicist Robert Jahn (1930–2017), who founded the Princeton Engineering Anomalies Research Lab. Jahn studied participants' attempts to influence an electronic random event generator; these produce an outcome, such as a random number, from truly random sources, such as radioactive decay or the photoelectric effect, rather than from an algorithm, which is the means used by computer random number generators (and which are therefore, in principle, predictable, although it is most unlikely). Jahn claimed to find very small but statistically significant deviations from chance performance (e.g. Jahn & Dunne, 1986). Other laboratories have been unable to replicate the work, and the consensus is that the results arose from bias in the machines and problems with statistical interpretation (Pigliucci, 2018).

Box 17.5 Poltergeist

A poltergeist (German for 'noisy ghost') is described as a type of ghost that causes physical disturbance, such as noises and throwing objects around a house. Poltergeists are most often associated with adolescent girls (see Figure 17.10). One hypothesis is that they are associated with spirits that possess children; a slightly less implausible one is that they are manifestations of spontaneous PK, usually by troubled adolescents. The consensus though is that a few are a result of natural phenomena (such as earthquakes, ball lightning, or strong air currents, and, in one famous case, the 1957 Cape Cod case, a strong downdraft from a chimney), but the majority are a combination of wishful thinking, delusion, and hallucination, and others fraud, particularly from attention-seeking children. Occasionally, people will try

Box 17.5 (cont.)

Figure 17.10 Poltergeist: pointing at the location of a rapping sound – or is it a portal to another dimension? Dominique Perrot in Nevers, France, in 1976 at the age of 12; paranormal activity was reported as being associated with her since she was 2 years old. Source: James Andanson/Sygma/Getty Images.

to clear the poltergeist haunting by exorcism, which might have some psychological benefit,

One of the most famous recent cases was the Enfield poltergeist of the late 1970s. The phenomena occurred at Green Street, Enfield, north London, between 1977 and 1979 (Playfair, 1980). They apparently started with furniture being moved, followed by loud noises, disembodied voices, and objects being thrown across the room, and were associated with Margaret (13) and Janet (11). Investigators Maurice Gross and Guy Playfair concluded that, although the children undoubtedly played some tricks, some of the phenomena were genuine, the result of a mischievous disembodied spirt, a claim rebuffed by most other researchers. No more incidents were reported after 1979.

The Enfield poltergeist was allegedly the inspiration for the BBC television *Ghostwatch* pseudo-documentary shown on Halloween, 1992, which provoked fear and panic as some viewers took the programme seriously (see Chapter 6 on panics and mass hysteria). The showing led to the first documented cases of PTSD resulting from watching television (Simons & Silveira, 1994). Poltergeists are a popular motif in the horror movie genre.

What Would Convince a Sceptic?

What kind of evidence would convince us of the existence of psi or supernatural phenomena? Suppose I carried out one experiment on telepathy in my lab, and found that the results were significant at $p < 0.05$ (the agreed standard statistical significance)? Would you, a sceptical psychologist, then throw up your hands and say 'that's it, psi exists, we need to reconsider all our understanding of psychology and by the way the laws of physics must also be wrong in some way'? Yet if I carried out an experiment to the same standard on word recognition, say, and also found results significant at $p < 0.05$, then most likely they would get published in a reputable journal without anyone batting an eyelid. Clearly, something very odd is happening here. For things that we deem very unlikely, we demand higher standards of proof. And with very extraordinary results we demand very high standards of proof. As the philosopher David Hume (1711–1776) observed about miracles, 'That no testimony is sufficient to establish a miracle, unless the testimony be of such a kind, that its falsehood would be more miraculous, than the fact, which it endeavours to establish …' (Hume, 1738).

A demonstration of psi requires a very high level of proof. It might come down to the question of whether a conspiracy and mass fraud by the experimenters is more likely than the existence of psi.

If the phenomena studied by parapsychology were shown to have a sound scientific basis, then there would have to be a revolution in physics and in the way we conceptualise the mind and consciousness. However, virtually all psychologists think that there is no evidence for psi, and any phenomena and significant experimental results are best explained in more traditional ways.

What Does Parapsychology Tell Us About Consciousness?

While there's a healthy literature on who is interested in anomalous experience, there has been no agreed robust demonstration of parapsychological phenomena.

Even if there were, what could they tell us about consciousness? It's difficult to answer in the absence of more specific information. Possibly, we would be more amenable to a dualist philosophy, but psi does not entail dualism. Similarly, the absence of psi does not entail physicalism. But in the absence of any evidence for psi, the issue is little more than an interesting distraction.

And yet ... maybe if there is a robust demonstration of psi it would unsettle our physicalist world view. Maybe all is not rosy in the garden of materialism, neuroscience, and behaviourism. Perhaps a robust demonstration of psi would lead to changes in the way we view consciousness that we, or at least I, can't currently predict.

Survival

Survival is the persistence of some identity, particular consciousness, after death. Needless to say, physical monism leaves no room for any kind of physical survival. We, of course, linger on in people's memories, to different extents, some longer than others. Julius Caesar can be said to have survived, but not in a sense that most people intend. Nothing of him remains.

The best account of quantum models of survival is a video by Stuart Hameroff on YouTube, Stuart Hameroff 'Brain Quantum Computer'. Some quantum models (e.g. orchestrated objective reduction, Orch OR; Hameroff and Penrose, 2014) talk about quantum information leaving the microtubules at the moment of death; if it goes back in, the person continues to live and has an NDE. It is argued that it is possible that this information could exist independently of the person and persist after death, which would be a kind of survival. These ideas are at the moment best filed under 'highly speculative'.

Finally, we get into more fantastic realms. There is no scientific evidence whatsoever for ghosts, and analysis of spiritualist events where a medium attempts to contact the dead shows that they have much more mundane explanations, ranging from lucky guessing to reading cues and manipulation of probability (what are the chances that someone in a crowded room knows of a dead friend or relative whose name began with G?) to outright fraud.

Although there is no undisputed evidence for survival, we do live on in one sense (see also Chapter 10): the memory of us in others, any works we have created, or any children we may have. Most of us change the world in some way, some in great ways.

Box 17.6   Ghosts

It was my personal teenage fascination with the possibility of ghosts and with the specific and distinctive genre of ghost stories that got me into psychology. A ghost is an apparition of a dead person appearing to the living. They can take many forms, from very realistic appearances of people, to clichés of people appearing as sheets, to nothing more than a sensed but invisible presence. There have been many attempts to photograph ghosts, and many claims of photographs accidentally capturing them (see Figure 17.11). A surprisingly (to me) large number of people claim to have seen a ghost (18% of modern Americans according to widely circulated figures), but there is no evidence at all to support their existence. Ghost hunters, like poltergeist researchers, may turn up to a reported appearance with an impressive array of infrared and motion detectors, cameras, and sensors of all sorts, but there is not one single convincing report of any ghost-like phenomenon. Ghosts provide zero evidence for survival.

Figure 17.11 Victorian photograph of a ghost. Or rather, a trick photograph created by double exposure. Source: Science History Images/Alamy Stock Photo.

Yet, it is most unlikely that so many people are simply lying in reporting seeing a ghost. What then is going on? There will doubtless be a small number of pranks and hoaxes. Some will be attributable to the person hallucinating, perhaps waking suddenly from sleep or in a hypnagogic

> **Box 17.6** (cont.)
>
> state (see Chapter 12), or as a result of taking drugs. Many will be attributable to *misattribution* of natural phenomena, maybe interacting with *suggestion* (see Chapter 14). A few might be caused by the presence of peculiar and particular factors such as perhaps the presence of low-frequency sound (see above), strong electromagnetic fields, or even the toxic effects of mould spores. Such factors would explain the reports of particular *locations* as being *haunted*.

Reincarnation

One type of survival merits a little more discussion, given the level of interest in it and the claims that science supports it. *Reincarnation*, or rebirth, is the idea that a person is reborn in another some time after death: something nonphysical becomes attached to a new physical body (see Figure 17.12). Many ancient Greek philosophers, including Pythagoras and Socrates, believed in reincarnation. The details of how reincarnation occurs depend on the specific religion being followed. Reincarnation necessitates a belief in a soul that can survive independently of the brain and physical body, and we have seen that this belief is not consistent with the scientific evidence. Many modern religions incorporate reincarnation, particularly eastern religions including Brahmanism, Jainism, Hinduism, and Sikhism. Reincarnation is central in Buddhism, where we must strive to escape the wheel of reincarnations and attain nirvana by getting rid of our attachments and desires.

Figure 17.12 Reincarnation: the case of the Pollock twins. The twins Gillian and Jennifer, in 1966; their father believed they were the reincarnations of their siblings, two daughters who were killed in a car crash in 1957. The case is being studied by Dr Hemendra Banerjee. Source: Mirrorpix/Mirrorpix/Getty Images.

The best-known research on the subject is that of Ian Stevenson (1918–2007), a Canadian-born psychiatrist from the University of Virginia, who investigated children who claimed to have memories or showed other signs of a previous life, including physical marks such as birthmarks and deformities. He published several books outlining his theory and detailing case studies where children exhibited behaviour that he claimed could only be explained by the child having a prior life (Stevenson, 1988, 2001).

There are two problems with work such as Stevenson's. First, from paranormal explanations, we don't need to posit survival: the 'reincarnated' person might be obtaining information by psi. Second, and more tellingly, critics point to the anecdotal nature of the evidence, the way in which specific cases have selected to support the reincarnation hypothesis, and the reluctance to discount fraud as the most likely explanation (Edwards,

1986). Many cases are of parents claiming that children from lower-caste families are reincarnated souls from upper-caste families, where money is a clear motive.

It should be said that, although most scientists agree there is no evidence for any kind of survival, it is, unsurprisingly, a topic that generates much emotion, with many people convinced of salvation, living on, or reincarnation.

Chapter Summary

- Parapsychology is the study of anomalous phenomena. The term anomalistic psychology is now sometimes also used.
- Paranormal phenomena include telepathy, clairvoyance, precognition, and psychokinesis (mind over matter).
- On deeper analysis, it is difficult to distinguish between these phenomena, so the terms ESP and most generally psi are now preferred.
- Some argue that the existence of paranormal phenomena would invalidate the materialist view of psychology and consciousness.
- In spite of much research, there is no universal agreement that psi exists.
- Evidence for psi could come from spontaneous cases or experimental studies.
- There are apparently insurmountable problems interpreting spontaneous cases meaningfully, so most weight is given to experimental tests of psi.
- Throughout the history of psychical research, there has been considerable interest in alleged 'psychic superstars'.
- Stringent experimental designs are necessary to prevent problems such as sensory leakage and fraud.
- Under-reporting or the 'file drawer problem' is a concern (as it is for much of psychology).
- One hypothesis about why psi might be so weak is sensory attenuation: it is submerged beneath the noise of more robust perceptual channels.
- If the sensory attenuation hypothesis is correct, then noise-reduction techniques should increase the psi–noise ratio, making psi easier to detect.
- One way of reducing noise is through the use of altered states of consciousness.
- Some of the best support for psi comes from studies using the ganzfeld state of sensory habituation, although these studies have also provoked immense controversy.
- There have been many trait and state studies of what makes psi more effective.
- In addition to trait and state effects in participants, many have argued that there are also such effects in experimenters, named the experimenter effect, hence some psi researchers appear to be more successful than others.
- Psychokinesis (PK) is mind over matter.
- Poltergeists might be an example of spontaneous PK.
- There is no good scientific evidence for the survival of the soul in any form, including ghosts or reincarnation.
- We live on in our offspring, work, and ideas, as well as in the memories of others.

Review Questions

1. Why do so few psychologists believe that there are any meaningful significant findings in parapsychology?
2. If psi exists, why do we not observe it in everyday life?
3. What precautions do psi researchers need to take to ensure that their experiments are methodologically sound?
4. What is the best evidence for psi?
5. Why have psi researchers made so much use of altered states?
6. What have studies of personality traits and states told us about psi?
7. Should paranormal research be held to a higher methodological standard than 'normal' psychological research?
8. Is there any evidence for survival after death?

Recommended Resources

Parapsychology Overviews

Cardeña, E., Palmer, J., and Marcusson-Clavertz, D. (eds.) (2015). *Parapsychology: A Handbook for the 21st Century*. Jefferson, NC: McFarland & Co.

Irwin, H.J., and Watt, C. (2007). *An Introduction to Parapsychology* (5th ed.). Jefferson, NC: McFarland. One of the best introductory texts, but it hasn't been updated for a while.

Radin, D. (2009). *The Conscious Universe: The Scientific Truth of Psychic Phenomena*. New York: HarperOne. A popular antidote to the negative coverage of parapsychology.

Watt, C. (2016). *Parapsychology: A Beginner's Guide*. London: Oneworld.

Critical Thinking in Anomalistic Psychology

Alcock, J., Burns, J., and Freeman, A. (2003). *Psi Wars: Getting to Grips with the Paranormal*. Exeter, UK: Imprint Academic. Definitely dated, but has more detailed coverage of experimental parapsychology than other suggestions here.

French, C.C., and Stone, A. (2014). *Anomalistic Psychology*. Basingstoke, UK: Palgrave.

Schick, T., and Vaughn, L. (2019). *How to Think About Weird Things*. New York: McGraw-Hill. Excellent guide to thinking about parapsychology and unusual events.

Shermer, M. (1994). *Why People Believe Weird Things: Pseudoscience, Superstition, and Other Confusions of Our Time*. London: Souvenir. General and a bit dated, but interesting reading for all psychologists.

Wiseman, R. (2011). *Paranormality: Why We See What Isn't There*. London: Macmillan. An introduction to why people believe in paranormal phenomena in the broadest sense, including spontaneous cases.

Reincarnation

Stevenson, I. (2001). *Children Who Remember Previous Lives: A Question of Reincarnation*. Jefferson, NC: McFarland.

18 BRINGING IT ALL TOGETHER

By now, you should have a clear idea of what consciousness is, why it is so difficult to study, and why it is so important. We can say a great deal about the peripheral issues surrounding the core problem of private experience. We can say that consciousness is to do with self-modelling and self-reference. We have made much progress on problems like self-reference, attention, and metacognition. But why it all has to feel like something – why we have qualia is unknown.

Let's return to our 11 original problems listed at the end of Chapter 1 and see what we now know in answer to these questions.

How Do We Define Consciousness?

The 'definition problem' is what is consciousness? Our best definitions are that consciousness is that which is lost in dreamless sleep. It is also the feeling of what it is like to be something. It feels like something to be you. it presumably feels like something to be a poodle like Beau (in fact I'm pretty sure it does). It presumably does not feel like anything to be a lump of rock. There might be grey areas (does it feel like something to be a shrimp or tree?) but the greyness arises because of our lack of knowledge, and not with a lack of clarity over the definition. Being conscious involves being aware, and some organisms are also self-aware – that is, can be aware of their own awareness. The extent of self-awareness is presumably much more limited, although again the vagueness arises from our lack of knowledge rather than a problem of definition. Maybe this greyness will recede as we understand more about the cognitive and neural correlates of awareness and self-awareness.

Figure 18.1 Moon rocks. Are these rocks conscious? Most people would say 'of course not', but those swayed by the recent resurgence in panpsychism would say the issue is not so clear. Source: Space Frontiers/Stringer/Archive Photos/Getty Images.

The 'Hard Problem'

The 'hard problem' is why does it feel like something to be me: why do we have phenomenal experiences at all? Why do we have qualia? For many, the hard problem is the central problem, mystery even, of consciousness, and yet it's the one where there's been least progress. There isn't even agreement on whether it really is a problem or not. No one has given a convincing and widely accepted solution to the hard problem. We have seen that many researchers has claimed to have given a complete theory of consciousness, but in practice none of them have done so convincingly. Some models of consciousness just say it is beyond the scope of the current theory. Some just neglect to mention it at all. Most perceptual and cognitive models take this line, dealing with access consciousness but not phenomenal consciousness, in Block's terms.

We have seen that there are currently many different conceptions of the hard problem. Some researchers don't think there's a problem worth worrying about much. The authors of the majority of models we've examined claim that they've solved the hard problem, although, to take a personal view, I don't think they have. I often have the impression we're talking about different things.

Then, at the extreme, mysterians argue that the human brain is incapable of solving the hard problem, and therefore that it will always remain outside the scope of human science. I don't think there's yet any need to give up trying, but I don't expect the second edition (or third) to have a solution to the hard problem.

What Are the Neural Correlates of Consciousness?

The problem of the 'neural correlates of consciousness' is that of how the brain gives rise to consciousness. This area is one in which we have made immense progress in recent years thanks to advances in brain imaging, particularly *fMRI*. We can now specify quite precisely which brain regions are involved in generating different aspects of consciousness. For example, we have seen that different brain regions, particularly areas of the occipital cortex, contribute to visual processing and visual awareness; we can identify the pathways involved in motor action; and we know how our sense of self arises and how the temporo-parietal junction is particularly important. We have seen how the thalamo-cortical loop plays a central role in awareness. What is more the discoveries from brain imaging are consistent with what we know from lesion studies which show how aspects of consciousness are disrupted by brain damage. The thalamus and brainstem are essential for maintaining wakefulness and arousal. We have seen how brain pathways are related to neurotransmitter pathways, and how we therefore have some idea how altered states of consciousness arise by changes to neurotransmitter levels. We also understand a great deal about the electrophysiology of consciousness, and how gamma waves of a frequency around 40 Hz play an important role in binding stimuli together.

We have also seen that feedforward processing alone does not seem to give rise to consciousness. Consciousness is a result of complex feedback loops in much of the brain. The thalamo-cortical loop has recurred as being central to our discussion of NCC. We currently have little idea as to exactly what type and amount of feedback are minimal requirements for consciousness, but we should be aware that it is an advance unimaginable a few years ago simply to be able to talk in such terms.

Although progress here has been immense, we should be wary of identifying a particular structure as the seat of consciousness. If we damage the plug of our television, the result is no picture, but examining the plug doesn't really tell us much about how the picture is built up. Also, it's a long journey from knowing *where* in the brain something happens to understanding *how* and *why* it happens. Much remains to be done.

What Are the Cognitive Correlates of Consciousness?

The 'cognitive problem' is what is it about our cognitive machinery that gives rise to consciousness? Where does consciousness fit into cognitive processing? We know a great deal about cognition, perception, and consciousness, and how the cognitive processes involved are related to brain structures and activity. Indeed this area is one of the great success stories in consciousness research over the last quarter of a century or so. We have examined the complex relationship between awareness and attention, and seen that they are not quite the same thing.

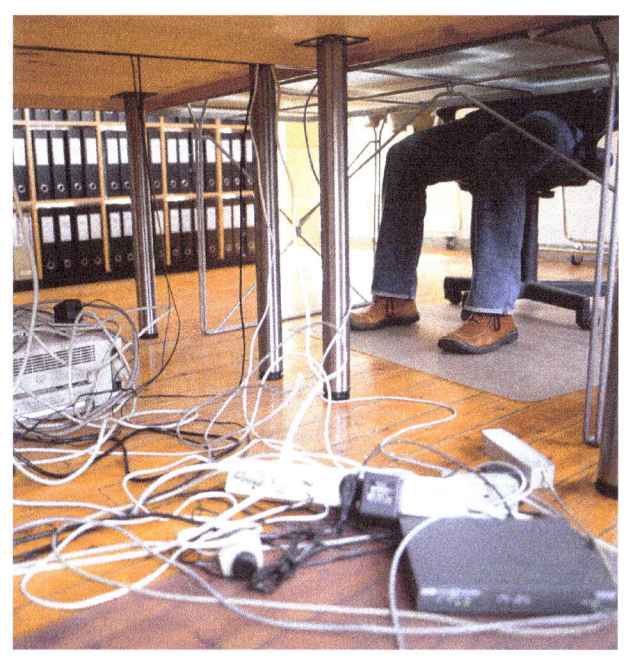

Figure 18.2 Computer cables and power. If you pull the plug from a desktop or mainframe computer, it will suddenly stop working. Does that mean that what is displayed on the screen resides in the power supply connections? (And if you do that deliberately to a computer that is conscious, is that going to be murder?) Source: Peter Sebastian/The Image Bank/Getty Images Plus.

P-zombies aside, consciousness is something that seems to emerge (in the loosest sense) when you have complex cognitive and perceptual processing happening in real time in the world. Whether any of these constraints could be loosened and the system still be conscious is yet undecided.

Self-awareness depends on the system having a self model, and here ideas such as recursion, complexity, and chaos are often discussed. By 'self model' we mean simply that the system has a symbol for itself. Consciousness is involved in episodic memory, being able to have memories of memories, and being able to envisage ourselves in the future. Consciousness is therefore involved in planning and modelling the future. We have also seen that the relationship between attention and consciousness is more complex than it first appears, with the two currently being thought to be dissociable.

The Timing of Events

The 'temporal problem' concerns the timing of the sequence of events that leads to action and thought. We have seen that awareness of processing is very late, in which case the question arises of why do we have the illusion of choosing to act when, in fact, our brain has in effect made that decision for us some time ago? Put another way, the neural correlates of consciousness appear to be too late for consciousness to be involved in perceptual processing and motor action, which in turn raises questions about free will and the function of consciousness. Although we know much more about the neural correlates of these processes than we did a few decades ago, there is still much that doesn't quite make sense.

Perhaps the surprise is that anyone who knows anything about psychology could conclude that things could be otherwise.

The Problem of Free Will

The 'free will problem' is very closely related to the temporal problem, and is the problem of why we have the illusion of choice and control if all our actions are determined. The issue is that everything is determined by the laws of physics like some giant clockwork system set in motion at the Big Bang, and there is no room for free will; determinism rules. We have seen that quantum mechanics is of no help.

Either we reject determinism, which would involve saying our understanding of physics is fundamentally wrong in some way, or we accept that free will is an illusion, or we say that in some way free will is compatible with determinism. This final position, called compatabilism, is adopted by some philosophers, but is controversial and not widely accepted. Unless we can resolve the dilemma, we have to conclude that the commonsense position adopted in practice by most people is wrong. We also have no accepted explanation of why we have the illusion of free will if illusion is all it is.

We also examined the moral and practical consequences of the dilemma – can criminals be held responsible for their actions, and should they be punished, if there is no free will? And if someone acts the way they do because of brain damage, or the way they were born, or even because of their upbringing, should they really be considered morally responsible? There are no simple answers, but we can all imagine what might happen if society stopped policing crime and punishing criminals (watch the movie *The Purge*, Demonaco, 2013, for suggestions).

Figure 18.3 Guard on prison security tower. We have seen that the issue of free will is complex, and that it could reasonably be argued that we do not have a free choice in our actions. If that is so, what is the point of punishment? Should psychopaths be incarcerated or treated? Source: Chris Salvo/The Image Bank/Getty Images Plus.

What Is the Self?

The 'self problem' is who is this 'I' who thinks they have a choice, and who is experiencing my experiences? We have seen that researchers consider the self to be an illusion, in that it is not what it seems. It is not a homunculus, sitting inside the mind observing (what is observing inside the homunculus?). It is a name we give to a complex structure that can be fragmented.

One important aspect of our self is the sense that we are localised in space, and feel that we inhabit our bodies. We have seen how the brain constructs this model of physical self, with structures such as the insula and regions such as the temporal-parietal junction being particularly important. Temporary disruption of the model can give rise to some curious phenomena (the rubber hand illusion) and altered states (out-of-body experiences), and brain damage can lead to long-lasting disruption, giving rise to phenomena such as anosognosia and neglect.

We think of ourselves as extended in time, and we have examined the role memory plays in this construction. Of course, our life's narrative is regularly interrupted (mostly by sleep) and we have seen how our self model helps us maintain our permanent sense of having a self. We have also seen how amnesia can restrict our autobiographical memory and self narrative.

Although the status of the self as an entity might be unclear, we know a considerable amount about the psychological processes constructing it, if that is not a contradiction in terms.

Why Are Some Things Unconscious?

The 'unconsciousness problem, is why are some things conscious, and others unconscious? Our capacity is limited, so consciousness involves selection in that at any time we are only aware of a small amount of what is happening in ourselves and around us. Indeed, we are conscious of very little processing, so the question is really why do we need to be conscious of anything at all? Hence, the unconsciousness problem merges in part with the why are we conscious problem, and we don't really know the answer to that. What additional thing or things does consciousness buy us? It also relates to the cognitive correlates problem. We have seen that attention is closely related to consciousness, but is not quite the same thing.

We must distinguish between unconscious in the sense of not conscious from Freud's conception of the unconscious as a repository of actively repressed material. We have seen that there is little evidence for repression or Freud's structural model of the mind. There is also little evidence for repressed or recovered memories, although the topic is still very controversial.

Why Are We Conscious?

The 'why problem' is why are we conscious, why are humans self-aware, why are (some) animals and not inanimate objects conscious? We have seen that researchers have proposed several explanations for why we are conscious. At the heart is the idea that being conscious enables us to create a complex model of the world and others. We need to be able to model ourselves acting in the future, and in particular, as social animals, we need to be able to model other people and predict what they will do, particularly in response to something we do. Hence, this view of consciousness is tied in with the notion of the theory of mind.

Figure 18.4 Mountain (or eastern) gorillas, *Gorilla beringei*. Few would deny that members of this troop of gorillas are conscious. What benefit, if any, does consciousness confer on them? Did consciousness evolve, and if so why? Could there be such a thing as a 'zombie gorilla'? Source: Martin Harvey/The Image Bank/Getty Images.

There are several things that complicate this answer. The first is, if we point to the distinction between self-aware and aware, why are only humans, and perhaps a few other species, self-aware? If self-awareness is tied in with social behaviour and theory of mind, why are some other animals aware? The second is the question of how can consciousness serve any function if it arises too late in processing to be able to change anything. And third, if any form of panpsychism is correct, then some inanimate things might be conscious, and in that case what sense does it make to talk of consciousness having a function at all? Fourth, if you accept that p-zombies are possible, consciousness is an inessential extra, and what sense does it make to talk of the function and purpose of consciousness if something works just as well without it?

It seems we need at least to distinguish the evolutionary function of consciousness from the question of how it arises, but there is clearly much to do to be able to give a satisfactory answer to this complex question. Our current view of this evolutionary problem is muddled.

Solving the Binding Problem

The 'binding problem' is the issue of how different sensations get bound together to form a unitary percept so that we perceive one thing with all the associated emotions? Why when we see a tiger do we see the orange and black stripes moving with each other and see the shape of the tiger distinct from the background? Why do we associate that loud roar as coming from the tiger? This area is another in which we have made a great deal of progress, and we now know much about selective attention and feature binding, and how it occurs in the brain. It is possible though that less binding occurs than we think, and the completeness of the perceptual world is an illusion – not an illusion in that the world isn't there, but that our representation of it is not as rich as we think. We also know a great deal about the neural correlates of binding, and we have examined in some detail the idea that perceptual features are bound across the brain by resonating as a gamma wave at around 40 Hz.

What Are Altered States of Consciousness?

The 'altered state' problem addresses what we mean by a 'normal' state of consciousness, and what causes an alteration in our state of consciousness? We define normal consciousness normatively as that state most of us inhibit most of the time, moderately alert waking consciousness, marked by mainly beta waves. We note that many things can produce a small change in consciousness – a cup of strong coffee, a glass of wine, a painkiller tablet – but of most concern to us are more dramatic alterations to our state of consciousness, such as sleep, dreams, hypnosis, meditation, and drug-induced states.

The main question with altered states of consciousness is how the provoking agent causes a change. What is it about the brain that changes, and how do these changes result in an altered phenomenology? We know more about the first issue than the second. Psychoactive drugs, for example, alter the levels of neurotransmitters in the brain, or bind to neurotransmitter sites, but often more than one neurotransmitter is involved, and our understanding of the relation between activation at a neurotransmitter site and experience is limited. We have also seen how provoking agents change the pattern of connectivity in the brain, particularly in long-range connections.

We also saw how many altered states of consciousness are good for us. Hypnosis can be used to change bad habits and improve our mental health, and meditation and mindfulness can make us happier, more relaxed, and more focused people, and lead to long-term neural changes. Sensory habituation is now widely used to help people relax and cope with stress. Even hallucinogenic drugs, such as LSD and psilocybin, can improve mental health, and may help us confront our fear of death. Much remains to be done in this area, and we are likely to see further advances over the next few years.

Figure 18.5 What changes in an altered state of consciousness, in terms of neurotransmitters and brain states, and how are these physical changes related to the phenomenological changes? We have seen that, although we now know much about dreaming, drug-induced and other types of ASCs, the mapping from physiology to phenomenology is still only partially understood. Source: PM Images/DigitalVision/Getty Images.

Consciousness Around the World

It is a mistake to think that the western view of the mind is the only correct view, let alone the only view. Even within western societies, there are differences in people's beliefs, with many people accepting some of the phenomena covered by parapsychology or practising a religion. It is tempting for the hard-headed scientist to say that these people are just wrong, but ultimately an element of faith is involved. Many notable scientists have also been very active practising Christians.

We have seen that different cultures view the mind very differently from the west. The Buddhist view of existence and the mind is completely

Figure 18.6 Captain James Cook meeting indigenous people in the tropics, circa 1700. There might be minor differences in the way members of different cultures perceive and categorise the world, but at heart we are all the same. Members of some religious groups might have the ability to experience the world in a better than 'normal' way. Source: Fotosearch/Stringer/Archive Photos/Getty Images.

different from the western scientific view. It would take a brave person to say that these views are simply wrong. There are also significant differences between cultures in the way existence is explored; for example, hallucinogens are illegal in most western countries, but are an essential part of life and growth in other cultures. We have also seen that it is time to listen to those following alternative approaches because their techniques, for example using hallucinogens to treat mental illness, stand up to scientific scrutiny. We should avoid being narrow minded, and ask, how much faith are we willing to put in science?

Can There Be a Science of Consciousness?

We have discussed essentially two sorts of account in this book, which are those aimed at accounting for the cognitive and neural correlates of consciousness, and those aimed at accounting for consciousness as private experience. The progress made in the first class of accounts over recent years shows that the answer to the question of whether there can be a science of consciousness is a resounding yes. However, opinions on the degree of progress made in the second sort of account is, as we have seen, contentious. The first sort suffer from the failing that they struggle to answer 'the hard problem'.

Indeed, the question of whether there could ever be a scientific theory of private experience remains unsolved. And given their subject matter is private, how could they? We have seen that a scientific theory should be testable and, in principle, falsifiable (Popper, 1959), and it's not obvious that any model that purports to explain the existence of nature of qualia can be tested in any way. Science by definition involves the measurement of verifiable 'facts' and, the construction of theories based on those measurements that lead to verifiable novel predictions, and by definition, our private experience is not externally verifiable. We can measure correlates of our private experience, such as our reports of that private experience, but never the private experience itself. Hence, by definition, the contents of consciousness are outside the realms of science. Some, such as Dennett, would probably object to this conclusion, but I think many would agree. Hence, it is better to look at these accounts as stories rather than scientific models. Which is the most coherent story? Which contains logical inconsistencies? Going further, what is the role of science if we reject materialism and physical monism?

There are several responses to this difficulty. The first is to say, like Dennett, that there isn't a real problem, but it's all just a problem of words, and that it doesn't matter very much. The second is to accept that there is a real problem and that physics doesn't provide a complete account of the world. Why stop with private experience? Perhaps there is something in the parapsychology research, and physics' inability to provide an account of the phenomena is just another of its failings? We hence reject a materialistic view of the world. It could be that consciousness falls outside the remit of science, at least if we define science as the method used to construct theories of the physical and natural worlds based on the objectively verifiable and refutable data. Perhaps the problem is the way we have decided we need to think about the world, and our conception of science is too narrow.

Like many other researchers and commentators, Susan Blackmore (2001, p. 525) despairs. She concludes her review with 'I think that one day psychologists will look back and laugh at the silly muddle we got ourselves into. To them the way out will be obvious. The trouble is that right now, like everyone else in the field, I cannot see it.' While I hope it's clear that we have made enormous progress with the soft problems, there is no consensus at all about the hard problem. We are in a muddle, but I don't think it's a silly one.

This book has posed many questions, and has sometimes been short on answers. Science, particularly neuroscience and psychology, with the help of a little philosophy, has at the very least clarified the problems concerning consciousness. In this edition, the hard problem remains unsolved – and personally I don't expect it to be solved by the next edition either. On the other hand, there is plenty to say about consciousness, and I hope at least that, if Stuart Sutherland had been able to read this book, he would retract his statement that nothing worthwhile had been written about it.

Some might find the conclusions bleak: there is no magic spark in us, no immaterial soul. There is no scientific evidence that we're going to carry on living after death. We don't have free will. Much of what we experience is an illusion, not in that it's not there, but our way of thinking about it is wrong.

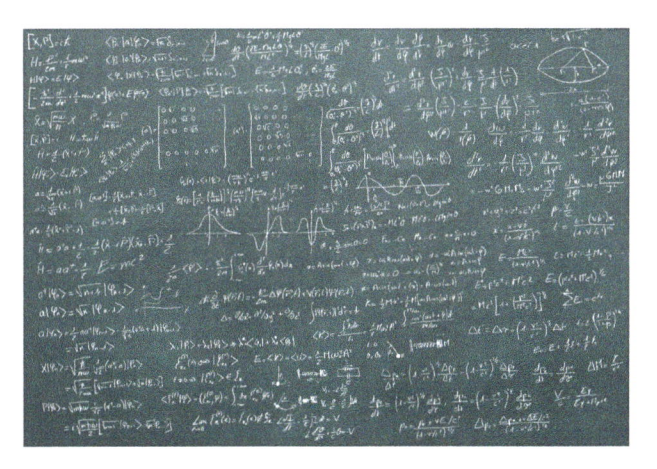

Figure 18.7 Equations on a blackboard. Are we cognitively capable of understanding consciousness? While we might solve all the 'easy' problems', will we ever understand the hard problems? Is consciousness research ultimately even amenable to the scientific method? Source: virtualphoto/E+/Getty Images.

How This Book Will Help Your Life

Hopefully, you will remember at least some of this book for some time. What do you think you will recall after five years? You might remember the odd experimental result or anecdote, but we know from studies of memory that, unless you revisit or refresh the details, you will be unlikely to remember them, but you should remember the gist. What is the gist of this book? That consciousness research is more difficult than you thought? That it's impossible? That brain imaging has all the answers? That we are five years closer to a conscious robot?

TRY THIS

What do you think you will remember about consciousness research in five years, and why? Do you think that any of it will have any practical consequences for your life?

Chapter Summary

- We have made considerable progress towards answering each of our original 11 questions.
- Nevertheless, there are no uniformly agreed solutions to any of them.
- It is possible to study the 'easy problems' of consciousness, and considerable progress has been made.
- The availability of brain imaging techniques has made a huge difference to consciousness research.
- Debate continues, and is likely to continue, on whether there is a 'hard problem' and whether it is solvable.
- It is possible that science will reach its limit when investigating consciousness.
- Studying consciousness can potentially change your life; it is up to you to decide how.

Recommended Resources

I conclude this final chapter with some movies (and a few TV programmes) to see, rather than more books to read. For a more comprehensive list, see my website at www.trevorharley.com/consciousness.html. Consciousness is a regularly occurring theme in movies, particularly where our senses are playing some kind of trick on us. Such movies speculate about the nature of consciousness, memory, personal identity, and altered states of consciousness. These movies are usually very entertaining and often educational – particularly if you ask yourself what is wrong with the plot.

There are a huge number of zombie films, but the zombies in them aren't p-zombies. They're real zombies who eat your brains.

The Matrix trilogy (watch the first; The Wachowskis, 1999) is based on the idea of (read no further if you haven't seen them) … brains in vats deceived by other organisms for nefarious purposes. Many movies portray alternative futures for an individual, but they are all based on the premise that the heroes could have done otherwise. Hence, in *Groundhog Day* (Ramis, 1993), Phil Connors (Bill Murray) relives each day, making adjustments to his life so that he can catch the girl (Andie MacDowell).

Robots and computers have a glorious and long portrayal in moves and novels. Among the most notable is the over-seeing computer HAL in the spacecraft in Stanley Kubrick's (1968) *2001: A Space Odyssey*. In the *Star Trek: The Next Generation* series (Roddenberry 1987–1994), Data eventually has an emotion chip added to his neural network (in *Star Trek: Generations*) to enable him to experience human emotions. Later, Data removed the chip. How plausible is that? *Blade Runner* (Scott, 1982, starring Harrison Ford) is about a hunter of renegade 'replicants', which are human-like robots. One (not to give anything away) believes themselves to be human. The movie is based on the 1968 novel *Do Androids Dream of Electric Sheep?*, by the US science-fiction writer Philip K. Dick (1928–1982). All of his novels and short stories cover themes of identity, consciousness, altered consciousness, what is reality, and tricks of memory, and are fascinating for anyone interested in consciousness. There is an excellent sequel, *Ex Machina* (Garland, 2014), which depicts the interaction between a human and a humanoid AI in a novel and interesting way. And, of course, for AI as a threat, see the *Terminator* movies (Cameron & Hurd, 1984–2019), particularly the second. In the HBO television series *Westworld* (Abrams, 2016), the robots become sentient (does that mean the same as conscious?) and seek freedom after their language becomes sufficiently complex – a concept that touches on computer consciousness, the evolution of consciousness, the bicameral mind, and the importance of language in the development of consciousness.

The ability to talk with animals has fascinated humans throughout history. Growing up on C.S. Lewis's *The Chronicles of Narnia* (1950–1956), as a child I didn't find the idea that preposterous. it is clear to me that my poodle Beau understands a reasonable amount of what I say, and It wouldn't surprise me at all if one day he answered back. There are three major movie incarnations of the *Dr Dolittle* novels of Hugh Lofting (the first book appearing in 1920) about a man who learns to talk to animals in their own language, learning from his parrot Polynesia. One film, starring Rex Harrison (Fleischer, 1967), is a musical; a later version starred Eddie Murphy (Thomas, 1998), and there is a very recent version with Robert Downey, Jnr (Gaghan, 2020). More plausible (slightly) is *Planet of the Apes*, particularly the recent reboot of the franchise, starting with *The Rise of the Planet of the Apes* (20th Century Studios), where chimpanzees tested on drugs designed to treat Alzheimer's disease develop greatly enhanced intelligence. Here language and consciousness are viewed as inextricably linked with intelligence.

Delusions are not surprisingly a rich source of material for movies. For a good film based on fact, see *A Beautiful Mind* (Howard, 2001), based on the life of the Nobel Prize-winning mathematician and developer of game theory John Nash (portrayed by Russell Crowe), who suffered for many years from paranoid schizophrenia. Although not about Capgras syndrome directly, *The Invasion of the Body Snatchers* (Siegel, 1956) nevertheless conveys well the sense of paranoia that arises when you begin to think that people aren't really who they look like. Unmissable.

Many movies play with the idea of memory and memories being false or implanted. They include the following. *Total Recall*; being old, I prefer the 1990 original (Verhoeven, 1990), with Arnold Schwarzenegger. The films are based on the short story 'We can remember it for you wholesale' by Philip K. Dick (1966). Most of Philip K. Dick's novels and short stories are of interest to students of consciousness studies. Many Dick stories play with memory and identity. To say more would be to give too much away. *Eternal Sunshine of the Spotless Mind* (Gondry, 2004): Some people would like to remove unpleasant memories – such as to do with a broken heart and a failed love affair. In this excellent movie, Joel Barish (Jim Carrey) undergoes a procedure to remove the memories of his love affair with Clementine Kruczynski (Kate Winslet) – and immediately regrets it. Bad memories are rarely all bad.

One of the most famous of all movies with a major psychological motif is *The Three Faces of Eve* (Johnson, 1957). The film starred Joanne Woodward, who won an Oscar for her portrayal of the three personalities Eve White, Eve Black, and Jane. The film was based on the case of Chris Costner Sizemore (1927–2016), who developed three personalities after witnessing two horrific incidents when a child.

I was going to give the National Broadcasting Company (NBC) television western series *The Virginian* (Friedkin, 1962–1971) as an example of a famous television series portraying a man with amnesia, in a prolonged fugue state, searching for his identity. However, on checking, the series was in fact about two ranch hands; the ranch foreman, played by James Drury, was only known as 'The Virginian', and his name was never revealed. There is no suggestion though that he had amnesia or lost his identity. I must have been conflating the programme in my memory from childhood with *A Man Called Shenandoah* (Alexander, 1965–1966), where Robert Horton played a cowboy with amnesia trying to recover his true identity. Unfortunately for him, the series was cancelled before he could do so. In addition to showing the degree of popular interest in memory and identity, this incident shows how fallible memory can be – or at least how poor my memory can be.

Disney's *Fantasia* (Armstrong, 1940) portrays Mickey Mouse trying to clean to Dukas's (1897) *The Sorcerer's Apprentice* for a splendid example of synaesthesia.

A movie based on Sacks's *Awakenings* with the same title was made in 1990, starring Robin Williams as Oliver Sacks (Marshall, 1990).

Of course, there are many movies about drugs and altered states of consciousness. There are too many movies on the psychological and social effects of drug addiction to mention. More specifically on drugs and altered states of consciousness, one of my favourites is *A Scanner Darkly* (2006, directed by Richard Linklater and staring an animated Keanu Reeves), based on the Philip K. Dick novel. The novel is immensely depressing, beginning with a drug addict who can feel insects crawling over his skin. The web is replete with analyses of the movie and novel.

People having dreams is a recurring theme in movies. Often, the viewer initially thinks, presumably along with the person portrayed, that the events are real, albeit surprising and often horrible; the person wakes with a start, sitting bolt upright in bed, and we all realise it was 'just' a dream. Usually, the dream depicts the character's deepest fears. Typical, and one of the best, is Linda Hamilton's nuclear explosion dream in *Terminator 2: Judgment Day*.

The Manchurian Candidate is a 1962 movie (Frakenheimer, 1962; remade in 2004) about a soldier 'brainwashed' and left with a post-hypnotic suggestion that whenever he sees a particular playing card he will execute a political assassination.

For locked-in syndrome, see *The Diving Bell and the Butterfly* (Schnabel, 2007).

Cloud Atlas (Wachowski et al., 2012) is a movie about reincarnation.

GLOSSARIES

Glossary of General Terms

Absorption. A trait measured by the Tellegen Absorption Scale and reflecting a person's total engagement or immersion in a task or experience.

Access consciousness. According to Block, the mark of access consciousness is the availability of material to reasoning, memory, language, and the ability to guide thinking.

Activation input modulation model (AIM). A model of sleep and dreams proposed by Allan Hobson with the three dimensions of level of activation, input source, and neurotransmitter modulation.

Activation-synthesis model. A neurobiological model of dreaming proposed by Hobson and McCarley where dreams result from the cortex trying to interpret essentially random brain activation.

Agonist. A substance that can be exogenous (a drug) or endogenous (a neurotransmitter or hormone) and that binds to a neurotransmitter site and produces activation. Contrast with antagonist.

Algorithm. A detailed and explicit specification of a method for solving a particular problem. An algorithm can be implemented as a computer program. It takes an input and by following a series of steps returns an output.

Altered state of consciousness (ASC). A state of consciousness that differs markedly from our normal everyday awake state (which is marked in EEG by a beta rhythm).

Amnesia. A loss of memories, which can be permanent or temporary.

Anaesthetic. A substance that completely blocks out all sensation and pain either locally or generally, the latter resulting in loss of consciousness; the related analgesic simply provides relief from pain.

Anomalous monism. A version of monism proposed by Donald Davidson stating that there is only one type of substance, physical matter, but mental events are not completely describable by (reducible to) physical laws.

Anosognosia. Denial of a disorder, a deficit of self-awareness where someone seems unaware that they have a problem, even to the extent of confabulating to explain why they do not.

Antagonist. A substance that binds to a neurotransmitter site and blocks its action.

Artificial intelligence (AI). Getting computers to do tasks that require intelligence; also called machine intelligence.

Asomatognosia. The failure to recognise part of your body, such as a limb, as your own.

Attention. A bottle neck in processing where some aspects of mental processing come in to focus.

Attentional blink. A procedure whereby it is very difficult to identify a second target when it is presented very quickly (200–500 ms) after a first target.

Auditory verbal hallucination (AVH). Hearing a voice that isn't there; a hallucination of hearing speech.

Autobiographical memory. Memory about our selves and our experiences.

Autonoetic consciousness. Our ability to place ourselves in the past or future and other situations contrary to how the world is.

Autoscopy. A hallucination in which the person sees their physical body in a different location but continues to experience themselves located in their correct location.

Awareness. The state of perceiving or feeling sensations or thoughts.

Axon. A nerve fibre, a long projection from the neuron cell body that connects to other neurons through **synapses**.

Bilateral. On both sides (e.g. of the brain).

Binding problem. The mechanisms whereby different sensations, within and across modalities, are bound together to form a unitary representation, such as red and shape combining to form the impression of a red cube.

Bistable. A stimulus such as the Necker cube that has two equally valid interpretations between which the brain switches; *multistable* used for more than two alternative configurations.

Blindsight. A neurological phenomenon whereby a person who reports being blind in an area of the visual field can nevertheless correctly report some visual information from the apparently blank area.

Bundle theory. A theory of the self and personal identity that says there is no constant person at the centre of our consciousness, but a set or bundle of features.

Callosotomy. An operation cutting the corpus callosum, the bundle of nerve fibres connecting the two cerebral hemispheres.

Capgras delusion. The delusional belief that a friend or family member (or even number of people, but often the person's partner) has been replaced by impostor(s).

Cartesian dualism. The form of dualism that says that there are two different kinds of substance, mind and matter.

Cartesian theatre. A hypothetical place in the mind rather like a multisensory cinema screen where all the results of sensory processing come together, watched by a homunculus who then acts on the basis of the input. The term was coined by Dennett, referring to lingering vestiges of Cartesian dualism in supposedly materialist models of consciousness.

Cerebrospinal fluid (CSF). A clear fluid found in the brain and spinal column that protects them both mechanically and chemically.

Change blindness. A phenomenon in visual perception in which some often very large changes in a visual scene occurring in plain sight are not noticed.

Chaos. A chaotic system is one where very small initial differences between states are magnified so that the system quickly becomes impossible to predict.

Circadian. A biological rhythm that has a period of about 24 hours.

Collective unconscious. Jung's idea that a deep level of the unconscious contains material shared across people containing symbols called archetypes.

Coma. A state resulting from a severe injury to the brain in which a person is unconscious, shows no sleep–wake cycle, and does not respond to any stimuli.

Commissurotomy. An operation involving cutting through a commissure, fibre, or tissue that joins two anatomical bodies, in the current context the corpus callosum, thalamus, and other structures connecting the two hemispheres of the brain.

Compatibilism. The belief that free will and determinism are compatible and that it is possible to believe in both without being irrational.

Complex system. A system made out of many interacting simple units where the behaviour of the whole is very difficult to predict.

Computation. The use of a well-defined algorithm or set of algorithms to generate an output. More broadly, a metaphor for how the mind works, or according to some, how the mind works.

Confabulation. Essentially making things up, particularly making up reasons to explain why a person cannot do or remember something or does not have a particular deficit when in fact they do.

Connectome. The complete neural wiring of an organism.

Contralateral. From one side to another: the brain is wired so that information from the left side of the body is sent initially to the right side of the brain, and vice versa.

Cortisol. A hormone associated with the stress response.

Default mode network. The brain network or system associated with mind-wandering or daydreaming.

Default mode network, default network (DMN, DN). A network of structures in the brain that are highly active together when a person is doing nothing – hence in a 'default setting'.

Denial. A person with the delusional belief that they do not have another delusion or neurological condition.

Determinism. The notion that everything is already determined by previous events. The laws of physics mean that every event now can only have one outcome, which has already been determined. Superficially at least, determinism rules out free will as the outcome of our 'choices' has already been determined.

Dissociation. A condition when parts of the mind that are normal connected become disconnected; dissociative identity disorder is the most extreme example.

Dissociative identity disorder. A personality disorder where aspects of the personality are cut off or dissociated from each other; more commonly known as multiple personality disorder.

DSM. The American Psychiatric Association's Diagnostic and Statistical Manual of Mental Disorders, used for classifying mental illness, abnormalities, and personality disorders.

Dualism. The idea that there are two basic sorts of substance – that mind and matter are completely different kinds of thing. Contrast **monism**.

Dynamic core. A model of consciousness proposed by Edelman whereby conscious experience arises from re-entrant neural activity in the **thalamo-cortical system**.

Ego theory. The theory of the self that says that there is a single unified self that observes and experiences the world.

Electroencephalogram (EEG). A representation of the brain's electrical activity over a very short period of time and the device that measures the brain's electrical activity.

Electrophysiology. The study of the electrical activity of the nervous system.

Eliminative materialism. A materialist account of the mind–body problem that says our everyday common-sense 'folk psychology' view of the world is wrong, and that some of the mental states we think exist in fact do not. We are fooled by our language into thinking that 'believe' and 'desire' refer to real things.

Embodied cognition. The idea that cognitive processing is deeply influenced by our bodies and how it is embedded in the world and how we interact with the world with perceptual and cognitive processing.

Emergentism/emergence. The way in which complex properties and behaviour emerge from the interaction of many simple properties.

Empiricism. The doctrine that all knowledge is based on experience derived from the senses. Hume and Locke were the most famous proponents. Contrast with rationalism.

Encephalitis. The general name for the inflammation of the brain, most commonly caused by a disease.

Endocannabinoid. A biological system sensitive to chemicals related to cannabis.

Entheogen. A hallucinogenic drug that generates a religious or intense spiritual state.

Epilepsy. Disorders associated with seizures, which can range from absences to seizures, associated with massive apparently random electrical activity in the brain.

Epiphenomenalism. A secondary phenomenon that plays no causal role in the first, such as the idea that if conscious is epiphenomenal to our behaviour it plays no causal role in it.

Episodic memory. Memory for specific events located in time or some sort of sequence that can be explicitly stated and therefore shows that the memory has entered awareness.

Explanatory gap. The problem of explaining the difference between phenomenal experience and physical events in the brain. Essentially the hard problem.

Experience sampling method (ESM). A method of determining what people think about, using a timer or smartphone app that bleeps at random intervals cueing the participant to note down exactly what they were doing just then.

Extended consciousness. Consciousness extended in space and time by use of tools, particularly when an object (e.g. a pencil) becomes incorporated with our body representation.

Filling in. Completing a stimulus, usually used in the context of a visual scene, by filling in gaps so that the percept appears complete.

Free will. The idea that we are free to choose between alternative actions, an idea apparently at odds with determinism.

Freudian slips. Mistakes we make that reveal our true thoughts and intentions.

Functionalism. The account of the mind–body relationship that states that all that matters is the causal or functional relationship between mental states. The mind performs computations. The details of what the functional relationships are implemented in doesn't matter in the same way that a computer program does not need a specific arrangement of transistors to run.

Gamma waves. Fast waves with a frequency of about 30–100 Hz, most typically around 40 Hz, thought to play an important role in synchronisation and binding.

Ganzfeld. A state of reduced sensory input created by sensory habituation to a uniform input.

Global workspace theory (GWT). An account of consciousness proposed by Baars using a specific mental architecture similar to working memory where the attentional spotlight illuminates part of the current contents of the mind.

Grey matter. Matter in the brain that is rich in neuronal cell bodies, contrasted with white matter, which is relatively rich in **myelinated axons**.

Hallucinogen. A class of drugs that cause hallucinations or notable change in perception, cognition, and emotion.

Hard problem. Defined by David Chalmers as the problem of explaining private experience and the quality of qualia.

Heautoscopy. Related to **autoscopy**, but a delusion in which people shift their psychological self so that it is with the translated body image so they seem to be experiencing themselves and the world at another point in space.

Heuristic. A general rule or guideline that usually (but not always) leads to a correct solution to a problem.

Homunculus. A little creature inside another creature, running things, and hence starting an infinite regress: what is inside the homunculus? The homunculus is at the centre of the Cartesian theatre.

Hub. A centre in the brain important for connecting different parts of the brain together to carry out a particular task.

Hypnagogic state. A state between wakefulness and falling sleep.

Hypnosis. A state of trance characterised by focused attention, reduced peripheral awareness, openness to suggestion, and induced by a person.

Hypnotic induction. The process that puts a person into the hypnotic state.

Hypometabolism. Lower metabolism of glucose than usual, in brain scanning showing damaged areas of the brain.

Idealism. A form of monism that says that mind is all there is.

Insomnia. Problems with getting to and staying asleep.

Integrated information theory (IIT). Tononi's theory of consciousness where consciousness arises in all systems that have a sufficient amount information that is suitably integrated.

Intentionality. Behaviour that is directed towards something.

Introspection. The process of looking inside to examine the contents of your own mind.

Intuition pump. A term coined by Dennett to refer to a small thought problem constructed to garner our intuitions about important philosophical questions. Bear in mind our intuitions might not always be correct.

Inverted spectrum. A thought experiment whereby individuals 'see' different colours; for example, when I have the sensation of red, you have the sensation of blue. How could we ever know?

Knowledge argument. An argument illustrated by the thought experiment, proposed by Frank Jackson, of Mary the scientist who sees the world in black and white and then is given a coloured rose; is it possible to know all there is about colour without experiencing it? The knowledge argument is considered to be one of the strongest ripostes to materialism.

Language. A system of a finite number of rules for combining a finite number of words to generate an infinite number of sentences.

Libertarianism. Not to be confused with political libertarianism, libertarianism in the context of consciousness and philosophy is the position that free will is incompatible with determinism, and that we do have free will; hence determinism must be false.

Locked-in syndrome (LIS). A state where a person shows signs of normal consciousness but cannot move, except in some cases for some eye movement.

Lucid dream. Dreams in which the person is aware that they are dreaming and is usually also able to influence events in the course of the dream.

Materialism. The philosophical proposal that matter is the only fundamental kind of stuff in the universe, and all processes, including consciousness, can be explained in terms of matter.

Meditation. A relaxation and concentration practice that leads to focused attention in a relaxed state.

Melatonin. A hormone produced by the pineal gland that plays an important role in regulating sleep and wakefulness.

Mental image. A mental representation that has some similarity to the perceptual stimulus, often a visual mental image, such as the result of imagining a rose.

Mental model. A representation or model of important aspects of the world around us, conversation, or text.

Mental time travel. Being able to place or imagine ourselves at any point in the past and particularly future and consider what we would do in such as situation.

Mereological fallacy. Confusing the brain and mind by making statements such as 'the brain believes', when it is only a mind that can believe.

Mescaline. An important hallucinogenic alkaloid. It is naturally occurring and found in plants such a the peyote cactus.

Mind–brain identity. The thesis that mental states are identical to brain states.

Mind–body problem. The problem of how private experience and subjective awareness can arise from the objective matter that comprises neurons and the brain.

Mind-wandering. What happens when we stop being focused on something. The same as daydreaming.

Minimally conscious state. A coma-like state between a vegetative state and normal wakefulness with some limited awareness some of the time.

Mirror test (of self-recognition; MSR). Putting a mark somewhere prominent (e.g. the forehead of a monkey) and seeing if they try to rub it off; if they do, they must be recognising themselves as themselves in the mirror.

Monism. The doctrine that says that there is only one type of substance – mind or matter. Contrast dualism.

Multiple drafts model. A model of consciousness proposed by Dennett in which there is no Cartesian theatre; many streams of processing are active at once, and we are conscious of the one that is most active at that moment.

Myelin. A white fatty material that protects neuron axons and which speeds up the electrical transmission.

Myoclonic jerk. A sudden muscle contraction resulting in a jerk, such as of the arm or leg, occasionally experienced when falling asleep.

Mysterianism. The thesis that we may never be able to understand consciousness fully because we do not have the cognitive abilities necessary to do so.

Near-death experience (NDE). An experience where someone is close to death and enters an altered state of consciousness, often seeing a tunnel of light, hearing welcoming voices, and feeling euphoric.

Neglect. A neurological condition in which a person does not pay attention to a region of visual space.

Neural correlates of consciousness (NCC). Identifying which parts of the brain are involved in generating aspects of consciousness, and how.

Neuronal workspace theory. An extension of the **global workspace theory** that explains which parts of the brain are involved in each aspect of processing.

Neuroethics. The study of ethical problems raised in neuroscience. For example, if someone has abnormal activation in the amygdala, how responsible are they for any crime they might commit?

Neuron. A nerve cell. Neurons transmit information through electrical and chemical signals. They comprise a body and an axon, which makes contact with other neurons at synapses.

Neuroprosthesis. A device replacing or extending the brain's functionality.

Neurotransmitter. A chemical messenger that plays an essential role in the nervous system enabling communication between neurons.

Neutral monism. The view that there is one type of substance that is neither mental nor physical, and mind and matter are different ways of describing that substance.

Nociceptor. A specialist type of nerve cell that responds to potentially harmful or dangerous stimuli, sending messages to the spinal cord and brain.

Non-rapid eye movement (NREM) sleep. A type of sleep where the eyes are still and muscles loose and relaxed, with lower frequency of dreams; contact REM sleep.

Opiate. A drug derive from opium, in turn derived from the opium poppy.

Opioid. A drug that binds to the opioid receptors in the nervous system.

Out-of-body experience (OBE). A state where our consciousness seems to be located outside our body, often above us looking down on our body.

Panpsychism. The view that all physical objects have some mental states and an element of consciousness.

Parapsychology. The study of anomalous experiences.

Persistent vegetative state (PVS). Declared four weeks after being the onset of a vegetative state, a disorder of consciousness in which patients with severe brain damage are in a state of partial arousal rather than true awareness; the prognosis is often poor.

Phantom limb. A sense that a limb that is missing is in some way still there, most notably the person feeling pain in the phantom limb.

Phenomenal consciousness. Consciousness resulting from sensory input and comprising things of which we are we aware.

Phenomenology. The study of consciousness from the first-person point of view.

Phi. A measure of integrated information.

Phi illusion. An illusion where a light appears to move between two light sources that appear to switch on and off in complete asynchrony.

Physicalism. The philosophical doctrine that all there is the physical. Near synonymous with materialism, but distinguished by some by the inclusion of types of energy and physical laws.

Ponto-geniculo-occipital waves. Slow waves that originate in the pons region of the brainstem and that spread through the brain. They appear in sleep and may be associated with the onset of dreaming.

Positron emission tomography (PET). A method of brain scanning examining brain activity via metabolism. The scanner detects radioactivity emitted by a radioactive tracer (e.g. fluorine-18) ingested with glucose.

Private knowledge. Knowledge to which only you have access, such as your qualia and mental states.

Proprioception. Our sense of our body.

Psi. A general term for possible paranormal abilities including telepathy, clairvoyance (together comprising ESP, extrasensory perception), precognition, and psychokinesis, used because we are uncertain as to which if any is primary.

Psychoactive. A substance that affects the mind and behaviour.

P-zombie. A hypothesised entity identical to us and that is behaviourally indistinguishable, but which is not conscious.

Qualia. The elements of sensation; the individual components of conscious experience, such as the sensation of the colour red. Properly the singular is **quale**.

Quantum mechanics. The theory of physics in contrast with classical mechanics whereby all energy is quantised – that is coming in discrete packets, rather than continuous. Information is probabilistic rather than certain – particles only have a probability of being in a specific location.

Rapid eye movement sleep (REM). A type of sleep characterised by rapid, apparently random eye movements, and muscle paralysis, and often accompanied by dreams; contrast **NREM**.

Rationalism. The belief in innate knowledge and reason, with proponents such as Descartes and Leibniz. Contrast with empiricism.

Readiness potential (RP). Also called Bereitschaftspotential or BP, an electrical signal measured by EEG shown in the motor cortex region of the brain indicating that the person is preparing to make a voluntary movement.

Recursion. A rule that calls itself.

Reductionism. The idea that we can explain one level of theorisation wholly in terms of a lower level, such as being able to explain all chemistry in terms of physics.

Re-entrant processing. Processing depending on feedback connections in the brain, usually involving relatively long anatomical distances, so later processing can affect earlier.

Representational theory of consciousness. A theory of consciousness in which representations of representations are of central importance.

Restricted environmental stimulation therapy (REST). Forms of reduction of environmental stimuli, such as mild sensory deprivation, used as a form of therapy.

Robot. A machine controlled by a computer that is capable of interacting directly with the environment and that is capable of carrying out a complex sequence of actions automatically.

Rubber hand. An illusion in which a person can come to feel a sensation in an external object that becomes associated with the person's hand.

Scepticism. The philosophical stance that it is very difficult to be very certain about any knowledge (other than that I exist).

Scotoma. A blind spot in the visual field, such as is found in some migraine auras.

Selective attention. Paying attention to just a limited number of stimuli.

Self. The individual person as the object of our consciousness.

Sensory deprivation. A method of inducing an altered state of consciousness by depleting sensory input to the brain.

Signature of consciousness. Some pattern, such as a characteristic pattern in brain imaging, that distinguishes conscious from nonconscious states.

Singularity. As in technological singularity, a point where the usual rules governing a system no longer apply. The technological singularity is hypothesised as occurring when AIs or robots can improve their own design, so the rate of technological change will suddenly increase dramatically with unforeseeable circumstances.

Sleep. A state characterised by reversible unconsciousness, particular brain-wave patterns, sporadic eye movements, and alterations in muscle tone.

Stimulant. A psychoactive substance that increases the arousal of the nervous system, such as caffeine and amphetamine.

Stream of consciousness. The flow of thoughts and impressions as they appear to unfold in a jumble in front of us; also a literary technique used to emulate this flow.

Subliminal. Something that is just beneath the level of consciousness.

Substance dualism. The same as Cartesian dualism – the idea that there are two basic types of substance, mind and matter.

Substrate independence. The idea that it's what computers and brains do – the software – that's important, not what it's done on (the hardware).

Swarm intelligence. The emergence of sophisticated collective behaviour by the interaction of decentralised simple robots or animals. An example in animals is flocking in birds.

Symbol. Something that stands for something else.

Synaesthesia. A phenomenon when activation in one sense leads to activation in another – for example, hearing a particular sound when seeing a particular colour.

Synapse. The junction between **neurons** (nerve cells). It allows one nerve cell to send an electrical or chemical signal (through a neurotransmitter) to other neurons.

Tetrahydrocannabinol (THC). The main **psychoactive** ingredient of cannabis.

Theory of mind. A model most humans and maybe some other animals have of the mental states of other members of their species, of their motivation and behaviour, that enables them to predict what others might do.

Thought experiment. The process of investigating our beliefs about the mind by taking some scenario and thinking through the consequences; examples include Mary the scientist when considering the knowledge argument.

Threat simulation theory of dreaming. A theory of dreaming proposed by Revonsuo that says that dreams result from an old biological defence mechanism that helps us simulate and therefore deal with possible threats.

Transcendental. Better or surpassing, as in transcendental consciousness or transcendental meditation.

Transcranial magnetic stimulation (TMS). A technique that generates a strong magnetic field that can interfere with processing in specific parts of the brain.

Transhumanism. The philosophy that we should improve the human condition by making use of technology to improve our physiology and intellect.

Turing machine. A mathematical model of a machine that can be described in simple terms such as a piece of a tape and a head that reads and writes on the tape, and that can compute any computable task.

Turing test. A test for human-level intelligence in a conversation devised by the British computer scientist Alan Turing; a computer passes the test if an independent 'blind' judge is unable to decide through conversation whether the speaker is computer or human.

Unconscious. In Freud's theory of consciousness the bulk of the information we 'know', but which is not directly available to consciousness. Also the opposite of conscious.

Glossary of Basic Neuroanatomy Location Terms

Lobes of the cortex

Frontal. Unsurprisingly towards the front of the brain, responsible for higher functions.
Temporal. At the side, responsible for extracting meaning.
Parietal. Towards the top, responsible for spatial processing.
Occipital. At the rear, responsible for visual processing.

Location indicators

Anterior. Towards the front.
Bilateral. On both sides.
Caudal. Towards the tail; lower rear end.
Dorsal. The upper side.
Inferior. Underneath or lower.
Intra-. Within.
Lateral. Towards the sides.
Medial. Central.
Posterior. Towards the back.
Rostral. Towards the tip of the frontal lobes.
Unilateral. On one side only.
Ventral. The lower side.

These terms are often combined. For example, *dorsolateral* means on the upper aspect of the side.

Glossary of the Most Common Neurotransmitters

Acetylcholine. Affects the cholinergic system, important for muscle action and also learning and memory.

Dopamine. Involved in motor control and the reward system.

Epinephrine. Also known as adrenaline, a hormone and neurotransmitter involved in regulating basic bodily functions.

GABA. Gamma-aminobutyric acid is the main inhibitory neurotransmitter.

Glutamate. The most widespread excitatory neurotransmitter.

Nitric oxide. A gas that acts as a neurotransmitter.

Norepinephrine. Also called noradrenaline, this neurotransmitter also acts as a hormone. It is at its lowest during sleep and highest during times of stress.

Serotonin. A monoamine neurotransmitter involved in many brain systems, including the regulation of mood and sleep.

Glossary of the Most Important Neuroanatomical Structures

Amygdala. A pair of small almond-shaped organs near the midline of the brain and deep within the temporal lobes. They form part of the limbic system. They are thought to be important in emotional regulation, the processing of emotional memories, and in motivation.

Angular gyrus. A region towards the front and side of the parietal lobe involved in complex cognitive functions, particularly transferring information from visual processing to semantic processing.

Anterior cingulate cortex (ACC). The front part of the cingulate cortex. It looks like a collar surrounding the corpus callosum.

GLOSSARIES

Basal ganglia. A group of subcortical bodies above the midbrain including the striatum that act as a hub between cortex, thalamus, and brainstem, and are involved in many processes including motor action and learning.

Brainstem. A bulb at the top of the spinal cord as it enters the brain, including the midbrain and pons, involved in sending nerves to the body, and responsible for governing respiration and cardiac function.

Broca's area. A region of the left frontal cortex involved in language, particularly speech production and sequencing speech.

Caudate nucleus. A part of the brain making up the dorsal **striatum**, which is in turn part of the basal ganglia, part of the old brain that plays an important part in learning and movement. It is part of the cortico-basal-ganglia-thalamic loop structure in the brain, which is important for governing reward.

Cerebrum. The forebrain: a large part of the brain distinct from the cerebellum containing the cortex and subcortical structures, sitting on the midbrain and brainstem.

Cerebellum. A large distinct mass of neurons forming the hindbrain important for motor control and balance.

Cingulate cortex. A layer in the middle of (medial) the brain, at the base of the cortex surrounding the corpus callosum. It is connected to many parts of the brain and plays an important role in motivation among other behaviours.

Cingulate gyrus. Part of the limbic system above the corpus callosum acting as a hub between cortex, thalamus, and the rest of the limbic system.

Claustrum. A thin sheet-like structure between the cortex and subcortical regions acting as a major hub.

Corpus callosum. The thick tract of fibres beneath the cortex connecting the left and right hemispheres of the brain.

Cortex. The cerebral cortex is the outermost layer of the brain, divided into two hemispheres, and responsible for most higher functions.

Cortico-cortical fibres. Neuronal axons that start in one cortical area and end in another, usually excitatory.

Cortico-thalamic fibres. Neuronal axons that project from the cortex to the thalamus, with pathways often looped back to the cortex.

Dorsolateral prefrontal cortex (DLPFC). Towards the front and side of the **prefrontal cortex**, the DLPFC is involved in many high-level cognitive functions, including executive processing.

Fronto-parietal cortical network. The junction of the frontal and parietal lobes, on the left side involved in attention and decision making.

Fusiform gyrus. An area towards the side of the temporal and occipital lobes thought to be involved in face and other types of complex recognition.

Gyrus. A ridge on the cortex.

Hippocampus. A seahorse-shaped pair of bodies in the limbic system playing an important role in transferring information from short-term to long-term memory, and in episodic and spatial memory.

Hypothalamus. A small structure underneath the thalamus involved in controlling several basic drives such as hunger, thirst, body temperature, and sleep, and for releasing associated hormones.

Inferior frontal gyrus. A **gyrus** on the **prefrontal cortex** containing **Broca's area**.

Insula. A part of the cortex folded into the brain and associated with controlling awareness, emotion, and homeostasis.

Lateral geniculate nucleus. Two bodies that form part of the thalamus that are the termination of the optic fibre from the retina and that act as an important relay centre for the visual pathways.

Limbic system. A set of structures between the temporal lobes and midbrain including the **hippocampus**, **amygdala**, and mammillary bodies, responsible for regulating a wide range of behaviours including emotion, motivation, and learning.

Mesopontine tegmentum. Also called the dorsal pons, part of the pons, containing several cranial nerve nuclei and the site of some important cholinergic nuclei that project throughout the brain.

Midbrain. A set of structures connecting the forebrain to the brainstem and to the cerebellum with an important role in controlling movement.

Motor cortex. A region of the **frontal lobe** comprising the **premotor cortex**, the **primary motor cortex**, and the supplementary motor area.

Neocortex. The six outermost layers of the cerebrum, responsible for higher cognitive functions.

Neurotoxin. A substance that is poisonous to the nervous system and that interferes with its functioning.

Nucleus accumbens. A region of the basal forebrain involved in many cognitive functions, and aspects of reward, punishment, aversion, impulse control, and learning.

Olfactory bulb. A structure at the front and underneath the human brain that projects from the brain and sits just above the nostrils collecting data about smell.

Optic chiasm. The part of the brain where the optic nerves partly cross so that information from the left and right eyes become separated so that information from the left visual field goes to the right brain and information from the right visual field goes to the left brain.

Orbito-frontal cortex (OFC). The part of the prefrontal cortex immediately above the eye sockets (the 'orbits') and hence at the very front of the brain. It is thought to be important for high-level cognitive processes such as planning and decision making, and particularly inhibition and controlling responses.

Parahippocampus. Grey matter surrounding the hippocampus; part of the limbic system.

Pineal gland. A small gland near the centre of the brain between the two hemispheres. Thought to be the seat of the soul and where mind interacts with matter by Descartes, it manufactures melatonin.

Pituitary gland. A small gland attached to the hypothalamus at the base of the brain producing hormones controlling many important bodily functions including growth, the sex organs, and blood pressure.

Pons. A body at the top of the *brainstem* involved in diverse low-level functions such as respiration, but also involved in sleep paralysis and controlling dreaming.

Precuneus. Part of the surface of the parietal lobe involved in representing the self in space, memory, and playing an important role in the default mode network.

Prefrontal cortex. The front part of the frontal cortex. It is particularly important for planning, reasoning, and decision making.

Premotor cortex. An area of the motor cortex in the frontal lobe anterior to the primary motor cortex involved in planning movement and motor control. It projects directly to the spinal cord.

Primary motor cortex. A region of the frontal lobe directly responsible for controlling voluntary action, and projecting to the spinal cord.

Reticular activating system. Sometimes known as the ascending reticular activating system, a structure comprising many connected nuclei in the brainstem, pons, and medulla, and projecting to the thalamus and hypothalamus, involved with many important neurotransmitter systems, and responsible for regulating wakefulness and arousal.

Retinal–geniculate–striate pathway. The primary route in the brain from the eye to object recognition.

Self-consciousness. Awareness of our own consciousness.

Sensory cortex. The primary somatosensory cortex is a lateral part of the parietal lobe that contains a representation of the contralateral body and receives information from the sensory system.

Striate cortex. Also called the first visual area, the part of the occipital lobe that is the main receiving area for the direct visual pathway from the eye to brain.

Striatum. A structure in the **basal ganglia** made up in turn of bodies called the **caudate nucleus**, putamen, and globus pallidus. It is important in the reward system and motor system. Not to be confused with the **striate cortex**.

Sulcus. A groove in the cortex.

Superior colliculus. A pair of structures at the top of the midbrain involved in relaying visual information.

Suprachiasmatic nucleus (SCN). A small body sitting above the **optic chiasm** responsible for controlling circadian rhythms.

GLOSSARIES

Temporo-parietal junction (TPJ). The region of the brain where the temporal and parietal lobes meet where information from the somatosensory, auditory, and visual processing pathways is integrated with information from the thalamus and limbic systems.

Thalamo-cortical system. The interconnected system of cortex and thalamus thought to play a major role in regulating consciousness.

Thalamic intralaminar nuclei. Groups of neurons in the thalamus that form several distinct groups.

Thalamus. A large body near the centre of the brain serving central vital functions including relaying sensory information and maintaining awareness.

Vestibular cortex. A rather ill-defined area in humans including parts of the **temporal** and **parietal** lobes and **insula**, dealing with vestibular information from the inner ear (balance, orientation, and coordination).

Visual cortex. The occipital lobe, divided into discrete areas labelled with a V and a number, responsible for visual processing.

REFERENCES

Aaen-Stockdale, C. (2012). Neuroscience for the soul. *The Psychologist*, 25, 520–523.

Aboitiz, F., Carrasco, X., Schröter, C., Zaidel, D., Zaidel, E., and Lavados, M. (2003). The alien hand syndrome: classification of forms reported and discussion of a new condition. *Neurological Sciences*, 24, 252–257.

Abrams, J.J. (2016). *Westworld*. New York: HBO Entertainment.

Ackermann, S., and Rasch, B. (2014). Differential effects of non-REM and REM sleep on memory consolidation? *Current Neurology and Neuroscience Reports*, 14, 14430–1440.

Adamo, S.A. (2016). Consciousness explained or consciousness redefined? *Proceedings of the National Academy of Sciences*, 113, E3812–E3812.

Adler, A., and Brett, C. (2009). *Social Interest*. London: Oneworld.

Agrawal, D., Chinara, P., Kumar, S., and Mohanty, B. (2014). Split brain syndrome: one brain but two conscious minds? *Journal of Health Research and Reviews*, 1, 27–33.

Ahluwalia, A. (1978). An intra-cultural investigation of susceptibility to 'perspective' and 'non-perspective' spatial illusions. *British Journal of Psychology*, 69, 233–241.

Akerman, S., Holland, P.R., and Goadsby, P.J. (2011). Diencephalic and brainstem mechanisms in migraine. *Nature Reviews Neuroscience*, 12, 570–584.

Alcock, J., Burns, J., and Freeman, A. (2003). *Psi Wars: Getting to Grips with The Paranormal*. Exeter, UK: Imprint Academic.

Alcock, J. (2011). Back from the future: parapsychology and the Bem Affair. *The Skeptical Inquirer*. https://skepticalinquirer.org/exclusive/back-from-the-future/

Alderson-Day, B., and Fernyhough, C., (2015). Inner speech: development, cognitive functions, phenomenology, and neurobiology. *Psychological Bulletin*, 141, 931–965.

Aleksander, I. (2005). *the World in My Mind, My Mind in the World: Key Mechanisms of Consciousness in People, Animals and Machines*. Exeter, UK: Imprint Academic.

Alekseyeva, T.T. (1958). Correlation of nervous and humoral factors in the development of sleep in non-disjointed twins. *Zh Vyssh Nerv Deya*, 8, 844–865.

Aleman, B., and Merker, B. (2014). Consciousness without cortex: a hydranencephaly family survey. *Acta Paediatrica*, 10, 1057–1065.

Alter, T. (1998). A limited defence of the knowledge argument. *Philosophical Studies*, 90, 35–56.

Alvarez, J.A., and Emory, E. (2006). Executive function and the frontal lobes: A meta-analytic review. *Neuropsychology Review*, 16, 17–42.

Alvarez-Rodriguez, U., Sanz, M., Lamata, L., and Solano, E. (2018). Quantum artificial life in an IBM quantum computer. *Scientific Reports*, 8, 1–9.

American Psychiatric Association (2013). *DSM-5*. New York: American Psychiatric Association.

Anderson, B. (2011). There is no such thing as attention. *Frontiers in Psychology*, 2, 246.

Andrews-Hanna, J.R., Smallwood, J., and Spreng, R.N. (2014). The default network and self-generated thought: component processes, dynamic control, and clinical relevance. *Annals of the New York Academy of Sciences*, 1316, 29–52.

Appel, K., and Haken, W. (1977). Every planar pap is four colorable. I. Discharging. *Illinois Journal of Mathematics*, 21, 429–490.

Araujo, H.P., Kaplan, J.T., and Damasio, A. (2013). Cortical midline structures and autobiographical-self processes: an activation-likelihood estimation (ALE) meta-analysis. *Frontiers in Human Neuroscience*, 7.

Arnulf, I., Grosliere, L., Le Corvec, T., Golmard, J.-L., Lascols, O., and Duguet, A. (2014). Will students pass a competitive exam that they failed in their dreams? *Consciousness and Cognition*, 29, 36–47.

Aserinsky, E., and Kleitman, N. (1953). Regularly occurring periods of eye motility, and concomitant phenomena, during sleep. *Science*, 118, 273–274.

Asimov, I. (1950). *I, Robot*. New York: Doubleday.

Assal, F., Schwartz, S., and Vuilleumier, P. (2007). Moving with or without will: Functional neural correlates of alien hand syndrome. *Annals of Neurology*, 62, 301–306.

REFERENCES

Atkinson, A.P., Thomas, M.S., and Cleeremans, A. (2010). Consciousness: mapping the theoretical landscape. *Trends in Cognitive Sciences*, 4, 372–382.

Atwater, P.M.H. (2007). *The Big Book of Near-Death Experiences*. Faber, VA: Rainbow Ridge.

Baars, B.J. (1983). Conscious contents provide the nervous system with coherent, global information. In R.J. Davidson, G.E. Schwartz, and D. Shapiro (eds.), *Consciousness and Self-Regulation* (Vol. 3). New York: Plenum Press.

Baars, B.J. (1988). *A Cognitive Theory of Consciousness*. Cambridge, UK: Cambridge University Press.

Baars, B.J. (1993). How does a serial, integrated and very limited stream of consciousness emerge from a nervous system that is mostly unconscious, distributed, parallel and of enormous capacity? Experimental and theoretical studies of consciousness. *Ciba Foundation Symposium*, 174, 282–303.

Baars, B.J. (1997). *In the Theater of Consciousness: The Workspace of the Mind*. New York: Oxford University Press.

Baars, B.J. (2002). The conscious access hypothesis: Origins and recent evidence. *Trends in Cognitive Sciences*, 6, 47–52.

Baars, B.J. (2010). Spontaneous repetitive thoughts can be adaptive: postscript on 'mind wandering'. *Psychological Bulletin*, 136, 208–210.

Baars, B.J., and Franklin S. (2003). How conscious experience and working memory interact. *Trends in Cognitive Sciences*, 7, 166–172.

Baars, B.J., and Geld, N. (2019). *On Consciousness: Science and Subjectivity*. Anza, CA: Nautilus Press.

Babb, S.J., and Crystal, J.D. (2006). Episodic-like memory in the rat. *Current Biology*, 16, 1317–1321.

Bagot, K.S., and Kaminer, Y. (2014). Efficacy of stimulants for cognitive enhancement in non-attention deficit hyperactivity disorder youth: a systematic review. *Addiction*, 109, 547–557.

Baggini, J. (2015). *Freedom Regained: The Possibility of Free Will*. London: Granta.

Baird, B., Mota-Rolim, S.A., and Dresler, M. (2019). The cognitive neuroscience of lucid dreaming. *Neuroscience and Biobehavioral Reviews*, 100, 305–323.

Baird, B., Mrazek, M.D., Phillips, D.T., and Schooler, J.W. (2014). Domain-specific enhancement of metacognitive ability following meditation training. *Journal of Experimental Psychology: General*, 143, 1972–1979.

Baker, D., Hunter E., Lawrence, E., et al. (2003). Depersonalisation disorder: clinical features of 204 cases. *British Journal of Psychiatry*, 182, 428–433.

Balcombe, J. (2016). *What a Fish Knows*. London: Oneworld.

Baldauf, D, and Desimone, R. (2014). Neural mechanisms of object-based attention. *Science*, 344, 424–427.

Ballie, R. (2001). Animal sleep studies offer hope for humans. *APA Monitor*, 32, 48.

Barber, T.X. (1969). *Hypnosis: A Scientific Approach*. New York: Van Nostrand Reinhold.

Bargh, J.A. (2012). Priming effects replicate just fine, thanks. Blog, *The Natural Unconscious on Psychology Today*. www.psychologytoday.com/gb/blog/the-natural-unconscious/201205/priming-effects-replicate-just-fine-thanks

Bargh, J.A., Chen, M., and Burrows, L. (1996). Automaticity of social behavior: direct effects of trait construct and stereotype-activation on action. *Journal of Personality and Social Psychology*, 71, 230–244.

Baron, P. (2016). *Free Will and Determinism* (2nd ed.). Scotts Valley, CA: CreateSpace.

Baron, R., and Maier, C. (1995). Phantom limb pain: are cutaneous nociceptors and spinothalamic neurons involved in the signaling and maintenance of spontaneous and touch-evoked pain? A case report. *Pain*, 60, 223–228.

Baron-Cohen, S., Burt, L., Smith-Laittan, F., Harrison, J., and Bolton, P. (1996). Synaesthesia: prevalence and familiality. *Perception*, 25, 1073–1079.

Barrett, D. (ed.). (1996). *Trauma and dreams*. Cambridge, MA: Harvard University Press.

Barron, A.B., and Klein, C. (2016). What insects can tell us about the origins of consciousness. *Proceedings of the National Academy of Sciences*, 113, 4900–4908.

Bartholomew, R.E., and Hassall, P. (2015). *A colourful history of popular delusions*. New York: Prometheus.

Bartlett, F. (1932). *Remembering*. Cambridge, UK: Cambridge University Press.

Barttfeld, P., Uhrig, L., Sitt, J.D., Sigman, M., Jarraya, B., and Dehaene, S. (2015). Signature of consciousness in the dynamics of resting-state brain activity. *Proceedings of the National Academy of Sciences*, 112, 887–892.

Basile, B.M. (2015). Rats remind us what actually counts in episodic memory research. *Frontiers in Psychology*, 6, 75.

Bates, B.L., Miller, R.J., Cross, H.J., and Brigham, T.A. (1988). Modifying hypnotic suggestibility with the Carleton Skills Training program. *Journal of Personality and Social Psychology*, 55, 120–127.

Bauby, J.-D. (1997). *The Diving Bell and the Butterfly*. Glasgow, UK: HarperCollins.

Baumeister, R.F., and Masicampo, E.J. (2010). Conscious thought is for facilitating social and cultural interactions: How mental simulations serve the animal-culture interface. *Psychological Review*, 117, 945–971.

Baumeister, R.F., Masicampo, E.J., and DeWall, N. (2009). Prosocial benefits of feeling free: Disbelief in free will increases aggression and reduces helpfulness. *Personality and Social Psychology Bulletin*, 35, 260–268.

Baumeister, R.F., Masicampo, E.J., and Vohs, K.D. (2011). Do conscious thoughts control behaviour? *Annual Review of Psychology*, 62, 331–361.

Bayne, T. (2008). The unity of consciousness and the split-brain syndrome. *Journal of Philosophy*, 105, 277–300.

Bayne, T., Cleeremans, A., and Wilken, P. (2009). *The Oxford Companion to Consciousness*. Oxford, UK: Oxford University Press.

Beaman, C.P., and Williams, T.I. (2010). Earworms ('stuck song syndrome'): towards a natural history of intrusive thoughts. *British Journal of Psychology*, 101, 637–653.

Beard, A.W. (1963). The Schizophrenia-like psychoses of epilepsy: ii. Physical aspects. *British Journal of Psychiatry*, 109, 119–129.

Beatles (The) (1967). *Sgt. Pepper's Lonely Hearts Club Band*. London: Parlophone.

Beauregard, M., and Paquette, V. (2006). Neural correlates of a mystical experience in Carmelite nuns. *Neuroscience Letters*, 405, 186–190.

Bechtel, W., and Abrahamsen, A.A. (2001). *Connectionism and the Mind: Parallel Processing, Dynamics, and Evolution in Networks*. Hoboken, NJ: John Wiley & Sons.

Beck, F., and Eccles, J.C. (1992). Quantum aspects of brain activity and the role of consciousness. *Proceedings of the National Academy of Science USA*, 89, 11357–11361.

Begley, S. (2007). *Train your Mind Change your Brain*. New York: Ballantine Books.

Béïque, J.C., Imad, M., Mladenovic, L., Gingrich, J.A., and Andrade, R. (2007). Mechanism of the 5-hydroxytryptamine 2A receptor-mediated facilitation of synaptic activity in prefrontal cortex. *Proceedings of the National Academy of Science, USA*, 104, 9870–9875.

Bell, V., Oakley, D.A., Halligan, P.W., and Deeley, Q. (2011). Dissociation in hysteria and hypnosis: Evidence from cognitive neuroscience. *Journal of Neurology, Neurosurgery and Psychiatry*, 82, 332–339.

Bem, D. (2011). Feeling the future: experimental evidence for anomalous retroactive influences on cognition and affect. *Journal of Personality and Social Psychology*, 100, 407–25.

Bem, D., Utts, J., and Johnon, W.O. (2011). Must psychologists change the way they analyze their data? *Journal of Personality and Social Psychology*, 101, 716–719

Bennett, M.R., and Hacker, P.M.S. (2003). Philosophical foundations of neuroscience. In M.R. Bennett, D. Dennett, P.M.S. Hacker, and J.R. Searle (eds.), *Neuroscience and Philosophy: Brain, Mind, and Language*. New York: Columbia University Press, pp. 15–33.

Benson, H., Lehmann, J.W., Malhotra, M.S., Goldman, R.F., Hopkins, J., and Epstein, M.D. (1982). Body temperature changes during the practice of gTum-mo yoga. *Nature*, 295, 234–236.

Berdoy, M., Webster, J.P., and Macdonald, D.W. (2000). Fatal attraction in rats infected with *Toxoplasma gondii*. *Proceedings of the Royal Society: Series B, Biological Sciences*, 267, 1591–1594.

Bernstein, A. (2016). Chris Sizemore, whose many personalities were the real 'Three Faces of Eve,' dies at 89. *Washington Post*, 29 July.

Berti, A., Bottini, G., Gandola, M., et al. (2005). Shared cortical anatomy for motor awareness and motor control. *Science*, 309, 488–491.

Bi, L., Fan, X.-A., and Liu, Y. (2013). EEG-based brain-controlled mobile robots: a survey. *IEEE Transactions on Human-Machine Systems*, 43, 161–176.

Biran, I., Giovannetti, T., Buxbaum, L., and Chatterjee, A. (2006). The alien hand syndrome: what makes the alien hand alien? *Cognitive Neuropsychology*, 23, 563–582.

Bisiach, E., and Luzzatti, C. (1978). Unilateral neglect of representational space. *Cortex*, 14, 129–133.

Bisiach, E., Meregalli S., and Berti, A. (1990). Mechanisms of production control and belief fixation in human visuospatial processing: clinical evidence from unilateral neglect and misrepresentation. In M.L. Commons, R.J. Herrnstein, S.M. Kosslyn, and D.B. Mumford (eds.), *Quantitative Analyses of Behavior, Vol IX*. Hillsdale, NJ: Erlbaum, pp. 3–21.

Black, N., Stockings, E., Campbell, G., et al. (2019). Cannabinoids for the treatment of mental disorders and symptoms of mental disorders: a systematic review and meta-analysis. *Lancet Psychiatry*, 6, 995–1010.

Black, S. (2018). *All that Remains*. New York: Doubleday.

Blackmore, S. (1991). Lucid dreaming: awake in your sleep? *Skeptical Inquirer*, 15, 362–370.

Blackmore, S. (1992) *Beyond the Body: An Investigation into Out-of-the-Body Experiences*. Published in 1992 (with new postscript), Chicago: Academy Chicago; first published in 1982, London: Heinemann.

Blackmore, S. (1993). *Dying to Live: Near-Death Experiences*. New York: Prometheus Books.

Blackmore, S. (2001). State of the art: the psychology of consciousness. *The Psychologist*, 14, 522–525.

Blackmore, S. (2002). There is no stream of consciousness. *Journal of Consciousness Studies*, 9, 17–28.

Blackmore, S. (2011). *Zen and the Art of Consciousness*. London: Oneworld Publications.

Blackmore, S. (2017). *Seeing Myself: The New Science of Out-of-Body Experiences*. London: Robinson Press.

Blackmore, S., and Troscianko, E.T. (2018). *Consciousness: An Introduction* (3rd ed.). London: Routledge.

Blagrove, M., Fouquet, N., Henley-Einion, J.A, et al. (2011). Assessing the dream-lag effect for REM and NREM stage 2 dreams. *PLoS ONE*, 6(10), e26708.

Blagrove, M., Henley-Einion, J., Barnett, A., Edwards, D., and Seage, C.H (2011). A replication of the 5–7 day dream-lag effect with comparison of dreams to future events as control for baseline matching. *Consciousness and Cognition*, 20, 384–391.

Blake, R., and Logothetis, N.K. (2002). Visual competition. *Nature Reviews Neuroscience*, 3, 13–21.

Blakemore, S.J., Wolpert, D.M., and Frith, C.D. (2002). Abnormalities in the awareness of action. *Trends in Cognitive Sciences*, 6, 237–242.

Blanke, O., Landis, T., Spinelli, L., and Seeck, M. (2004). Out-of-body experience and autoscopy of neurological origin. *Brain*, 127, 243–258.

Blanke, O., and Mohr, C. (2005). Out-of-body experience, heautoscopy, and autoscopic hallucination of neurological origin: implications for neurocognitive mechanisms of corporeal awareness and self-consciousness. *Brain Research Reviews*, 50, 184–199.

Blanke, O., Ortigue, S., Landis, T., and Seeck, M. (2002). Stimulating illusory own-body perceptions. *Nature*, 419, 269–270.

Block, N. (1978). Troubles with functionalism. *Minnesota Studies in The Philosophy of Science*, 9, 261–325.

Block, N. (1995). On a confusion about a function of consciousness. *Behavioral and Brain Sciences*, 18, 227–287.

Block, N. (2005). Two neural correlates of consciousness. *Trends in Cognitive Sciences*, 9, 46–52.

Block, N. (2011). Perceptual consciousness overflows cognitive access. *Trends in Cognitive Sciences*, 15, 567–575.

Bloom, P. (2004). Advances in neuroscience relevant to the clinical practice of hypnosis: a clinician's perspective. *Keynote address to the 16th International Congress of Hypnosis and Hypnotherapy*, Singapore.

Bluhm, C., and Clendenin, N. (2009). *Someone Else's Face in the Mirror: Identity and the New Science of Face Transplants*. Santa Barbara, CA: Praeger.

Blumenfeld, H., and Taylor, J. (2003). Why do seizures cause loss of consciousness? *Neuroscientist*, 9, 301–310.

Boese, A. (2016). *Elephants on Acid*. London: Pan.

Bogen, J.E. (1995a). On the neurophysiology of consciousness: Part I. An overview. *Conscious and Cognition*, 4, 52–62.

Bogen, J.E. (1995b). On the neurophysiology of consciousness: Part II. Constraining the semantic problem. *Consciousness and Cognition*, 4, 137–158.

Boland, E.M., Rao, H., Dinges, D.F., et al. (2017). Meta-analysis of the antidepressant effects of acute sleep deprivation. *Journal of Clinical Psychiatry*, 78, e1020–11034.

Boly, M., Massimini, M., Tsuchiya, N., Postle, B.R., Koch, C., and Tononi, G. (2017). Are the neural correlates of consciousness in the front or in the back of the cerebral cortex? Clinical and neuroimaging evidence. *Journal of Neuroscience*, 37, 9603–9613.

Booker, C. (2004). *The Seven Basic Plots of Literature*. London: Bloomsbury Continuum.

Bostrom, N. (2003). Are you living in a computer simulation? *Philosophical Quarterly*, 53, 243–255.

Bostrom, N. (2014). *Superintelligence: Paths, Dangers, Strategies*. Oxford, UK: Oxford University Press.

Botvinick, M., and Cohen, J. (1998). Rubber hands 'feel' touch that eyes see. *Nature*, 391, 756.

Bourdin, P., Barberia, I., Oliva, R., and Slater, M. (2017). A virtual out-of-body experience reduces fear of death. *PLoS ONE*, 12, 1–19.

Brand, B.L., Sar, V., Stavropoulos, P., Krüger, C., et al. (2016). Separating fact from fiction: An empirical examination of six myths about dissociative identity disorder. *Harvard Review of Psychiatry*, 24, 257–270.

Brann, L., Owens, J., and Williamson, A. (2015). *The Handbook of Contemporary Clinical Hypnosis: Theory and Practice*. Oxford, UK: Wiley-Blackwell.

Bray, N. (2018). Concentrating on the claustrum. *Nature Reviews Neuroscience*, 19, 580–581.

Brentano, F.C. (1874). *Psychologie vom empirischen Standpunkte*. Leipzig: Meiner. Translated as *Psychology from an Empirical Standpoint*, by A.C. Rancurello, D.B. Terrell, and L. McAlister. London: Routledge, 1973.

Breuer, J., and Freud, S. (2004[1895]). *Studies on Hysteria*. London: Penguin.

Brewer, J.A., Worhunsky, P.D., Gray, J.R., Tang, Y.-Y., Weber, J., and Kober, H. (2011). Meditation experience is associated with differences in default mode network activity and connectivity. *Proceedings of the National Academy of Sciences*, 108, 20254–20259.

Bristow, D., Haynes, J.D., Sylvester, R., Frith, C.D., and Rees, G. (2005). Blinking suppresses the neural response to unchanging retinal stimulation. *Current Biology*, 15, 1296–1300.

Broadbent, D. (1958). *Perception and Communication*. London: Pergamon Press.

Brodsky, W., and Slor, Z. (2013). Background music as a risk factor for distraction among young-novice drivers. *Accident Analysis and Prevention*, 59, 382–393.

Brogaard, B. (2012). Split brains. Blog, *Psychology Today*. www.psychologytoday.com/gb/blog/the-superhuman-mind/201211/split-brains

Broughton, R.J. (1994). Homicidal somnambulism: a case report. *Sleep*, 17, 253–264.

Brown, P., and Gaines, S. (2002). *The Love You Make: An Insider's Story of The Beatles*. New York: New American Library.

Buckner, R.L., Andrews-Hanna, J.R., and Schacter, D.L. (2008). The brain's default network: anatomy, function, and relevance to disease. *Annals of the New York Academy of Sciences*, 1124, 1–38.

Busby Grant, J., and Walsh, E. (2016). Exploring the use of experience sampling to assess episodic thought. *Applied Cognitive Psychology*, 30, 472–478.

Bush, G., Vogt, B.A., Holmes, J., et al.. (2002). Dorsal anterior cingulate cortex: a role in reward-based decision making. *Proceedings of the National Academy of Science*, 99, 523–528.

Caddy, C., Giaroli, G., White, T.P., Shergill, S.S., and Tracy, D.K. (2014). Ketamine as the prototype glutamatergic antidepressant: pharmacodynamic actions, and a systematic review and meta-analysis of efficacy. *Therapeutic Advances in Psychopharmacology*, 4, 75–99.

Call, J., and Tomasello, M. (2008). Does the chimpanzee have a theory of mind? 30 years later. *Trends in Cognitive Sciences*, 12, 187–192.

Cameron, J. (1984). *Terminator*. Los Angeles, CA: Hemdale Pacific Western Productions.

Cameron, J., and Hurd, G.A. (1984–2019). *Terminator franchise*. Los Angeles, CA: Hemdale Pacific Western Productions.

Cardeña, E., Palmer, J., and Marcusson-Clavertz, D. (eds.) (2015). *Parapsychology: A Handbook for the 21st Century*. Jefferson, NC: McFarland & Co.

Carhart-Harris, R.L, and Friston, K.J. (2010). The default-mode, ego-functions and free-energy: a neurobiological account of Freudian ideas. *Brain*, 133, 1265–1283.

Carhart-Harris, R.L., and Nutt, D.J. (2017). Serotonin and brain function: a tale of two receptors. *Journal of Psychopharmacology*, 31, 1091–1120.

Carhart-Harris, R.L., Bolstridge, M., Rucker, J., et al. (2016). Psilocybin with psychological support for treatment-resistant depression: an open-label feasibility study. *The Lancet Psychiatry*, 3, 619–627.

Carhart-Harris, R.L., Erritzoe, D., Williams, T., et al., (2012). Neural correlates of the psychedelic state as determined by fMRI studies with psilocybin. *Proceedings of the National Academy of Sciences*, 109, 2138–2143.

Carhart-Harris, R.L., Muthukumaraswamy, S., Roseman, L., et al. (2016). Neural correlates of the LSD experience revealed by multimodal neuroimaging. *Proceedings of the National Academy of Sciences*, 113, 4853–4858.

Carroll, S. (2016). *The Big Picture: On the Origins of Life, Meaning and the Universe Itself*. London: Oneworld.

Caspar, E., Cleeremans, A., and Haggard, P. (2015). The relationship between human agency and embodiment. *Consciousness and Cognition*, 33, 226–236.

Castaneda, C. (1990). *The Teachings of Don Juan: A Yaqui Way of Knowledge*. Harmondsworth, UK: Penguin.

Castle, T. (1991). Contagious folly: an adventure and its skeptics. *Critical Inquiry*, 17, 741–772.

Cavanna, F., Vilas, M.G., Palmucci, M., and Tagliazucchi, E. (2018). Dynamic functional connectivity and brain metastability during altered states of consciousness. *NeuroImage*, 180, 383–395.

Cazzolla Gatti, R. (2015). Self-consciousness: beyond the looking-glass and what dogs found there. *Ethology Ecology and Evolution*, 28, 232–240.

Chalmers, A.F. (2013). *What is This Thing Called Science?* (4th ed.). Cambridge, MA. Hackett Press.

Chalmers, D.J. (1995). Absent qualia, fading qualia, dancing qualia. In T. Metzinger (ed.), *Conscious Experience*. Exeter, UK: Imprint Academic, pp. 309–328.

Chalmers, D.J. (1995). Facing up to the problem of consciousness. *Journal of Consciousness Studies*, 2, 200–219.

Chalmers, D.J. (1996). *The Conscious Mind: In Search of a Fundamental Theory*. Oxford, UK: Oxford University Press.

Chang, L., and Tsao, D.Y. (2017). The code for facial identity in the primate brain. *Cell*, 169, 1013–1028.

Chang, L., Zhang, S., Poo, M., and Gong, N. (2017). Spontaneous expression of mirror self-recognition in monkeys after learning precise visual-proprioceptive association for mirror images. *Proceedings of the National Academy of Sciences*, 114, 3258–3263.

Charland-Verville, V., Bruno, M., Bahri, M., Demertzi, A., Desseilles, M., Chatelle, C., Vanhaudenhuyse, A., Hustinx, R., Bernard, C., Tshibanda, L., Laureys, S., and Zeman, A. (2013). Brain dead yet mind alive: a positron emission tomography case study of brain metabolism in Cotard's syndrome. *Cortex*, 49, 1997–1999.

Chater, N. (2018). *The Mind is Flat: The Illusion of Mental Depth and the Improvised Mind*. London: Penguin.

Chaudhary, U., Xia, B., Silvoni, S., Cohen, L.G., and Birbaumer, N. (2017). Brain–computer interface-based communication in the completely locked-in state. *PLoS Biology*, 1–25.

Chaves, J.F. (2006). Theodore X. Barber (1927–2005). *The American Psychologist*, 61, 175.

Cheney, D.L., and Seyfarth, R.M. (1990). *How Monkeys See the World*. Chicago, IL: University of Chicago Press.

Cherry, C.E. (1953). Some experiments on the recognition of speech, with one and with two ears. *Journal of the Acoustical Society of America*, 25, 975–979.

Ching, S., Cimenser, A., Purdon, P.L., Brown, E.N., and Kopell, N.J. (2010). Thalamocortical model for a propofol-induced α-rhythm associated with loss of consciousness. *Proceedings of the National Academy of Sciences*, 107, 22665–22670.

Chomsky, N. (1957). *Syntactic Structures*. The Hague: Mouton.

Chow, H.M., Horovitz, S., Carr, W., et al. (2013). Rhythmic alternating patterns of brain activity distinguish rapid eye movement sleep from other states of consciousness. *Proceedings of the National Academy of Sciences*, 110, 10300–10305.

Churchland, P.M. (1981). Eliminative materialism and the propositional attitudes, *Journal of Philosophy*, 78, 67–90.

Churchland, P.M. (2004). Knowing qualia: a reply to Jackson (with 1997 postscript). In P. Ludlow, Nagasawa, Y., and Stoljar, D. (eds.), *There's Something About Mary* (pp. 163–178). Cambridge, MA: MIT Press.

Churchland, P.M. (2013). *Matter and Consciousness* (3rd. ed.). Cambridge, MA: MIT Press.

Churchland, P.S. (1986). *Neurophilosophy: Toward a Unified Science of the Mind/Brain*. Cambridge, MA: MIT Press.

Churchland, P.M. (1988). *Matter and Consciousness*. Cambridge, MA: MIT Press.

Churchland, P.S. (1996). The hornswoggle problem. *Journal of Consciousness Studies*, 3, 402–408.

Churchland, P.S. (2002). *Brain-Wise: Studies in Neurophilosophy*. Cambridge, MA: MIT Press.

Clark, A. (1985). Spectrum inversion and the color solid. *Southern Journal of Philosophy*, 23, 431–443.

Clark, A. (2010). *Supersizing the Mind: Embodiment, Action, and Cognitive Extension*. Oxford, UK: Oxford University Press.

Clark, A. (2013). Whatever next? Predictive brains, situated agents, and the future of cognitive science. *Behavioral and Brain Sciences*, 36, 181–204.

Clark, A. (2016). *Surfing Uncertainty: Prediction, Action, and the Embodied Mind*. New York: Oxford University Press.

Claxton, G. (1992). *The Heart of Buddhism: Practical Wisdom for an Agitated World*. London: Thorsons.

Clayton, N.S., Dally, J.M., and Emery, N.J. (2007). Social cognition by food-caching corvids. The western scrub-jay as a natural psychologist. *Philosophical Transactions of the Royal Society B: Biological Sciences*, 362, 507–522.

Cleeremans, A. (2011). The radical plasticity thesis: how the brain learns to be conscious. *Frontiers in Psychology*, 2, 1–12.

Cleeremans, A. (2014). Connecting conscious and unconscious processing. *Cognitive Science*, 38, 1286–1315.

Cohen, M. (2004). *Wittgenstein's Beetle and Other Classic Thought Experiments*. Oxford, UK: Wiley-Blackwell.

Cohen, M.A, and Dennett, D.C. (2011). Consciousness cannot be separated from function. *Trends in Cognitive Sciences*, 15, 358–364.

Cohen, M.A., Cavanagh, P., Chun, M.M., and Nakayama, K. (2012). The attentional requirements of consciousness. *Trends in Cognitive Sciences*, 16, 411–417.

Cole, J. (1995). *Pride and a Daily Marathon*. Cambridge, MA: MIT Press.

Cole, J. (2016). *Losing Touch: A Man without his Body*. Oxford, UK: Oxford University Press.

Coleman, M.R., Rodd, J.M., Davis, M.H., et al. (2007). Do vegetative patients retain aspects of language? Evidence from fMRI. *Brain*, 130, 2494–2507.

Conway, M.A. (1997). Past and present: recovered memories and false memories. In M.A. Conway (ed.), *Debates in Psychology: Recovered Memories and False Memories* (pp. 150–191). Oxford, UK: Oxford University Press.

Conway, M.A., and Pleydell-Pearce, C.W. (2000). The construction of autobiographical memories in the self-memory system. *Psychological Review*, 107, 261–288.

Corballis, M.C. (2014). *The Recursive Mind: The Origins of Human Language, Thought, and Civilization*. Princeton, NJ: Princeton University Press.

Corballis, M.C. (2017). Language evolution: a changing perspective. *Trends in Cognitive Sciences*, 21, 229–236.

Corlett, P.R., Taylor, J.R., Wang, X.J., Fletcher, P.C., and Krystal, J.H. (2010). Toward a neurobiology of delusions. *Progress in Neurobiology*, 92, 345–369.

Corley, M., Brocklehurst, P.H., and Moat, H.S. (2011). Error biases in inner and overt speech: evidence from tongue twisters. *Journal of Experimental Psychology: Learning, Memory, and Cognition*, 37, 162–175.

Cote, K.A., Etienne, L., and Campbell, K.B. (2001). Neurophysiological evidence for the detection of external stimuli during sleep. *Sleep*, 24, 791–803.

Cowey, A. (2004). Fact, artefact, and myth about blindsight. *Quarterly Journal of Experimental Psychology*, 57, 577–609.

Cowey, A., and Walsh, V. (2000). Magnetically induced phosphenes in sighted, blind and blindsighted observers. *NeuroReport*, 11, 3269–3273.

REFERENCES

Craig, A.D. (2003). A new view of pain as a homeostatic emotion. *Trends in Neurosciences*, 26, 303–307.

Craig, A.D (2009). How do you feel – now? The anterior insula and human awareness. *Nature Reviews Neuroscience*, 10, 59–70.

Crick, F. (1984). Neurobiology: memory and molecular turnover. *Nature*, 312, 101.

Crick, F. (1995). *The Astonishing Hypothesis: The Scientific Search for the Soul*. New York: Simon and Schuster.

Crick, F., and Ghoneim, M.M. (2001). *Awareness During Anesthesia*. Oxford, UK: Butterworth-Heinemann.

Crick, F., and Koch, C. (1990). Towards a neurobiological theory of consciousness. *Seminars in the Neurosciences*, 2, 263–275.

Crick, F., and Koch, C. (1995). Are we aware of neural activity in the visual cortex? *Nature*, 375, 121–123.

Crick, F., and Koch, C. (1998). Consciousness and neuroscience. *Cerebral Cortex*, 8, 97–107.

Crick, F., and Koch, C. (2003). Framework for consciousness. *Nature Neuroscience*, 6, 119–126.

Crick, F., and Koch, C. (2005). What is the function of the claustrum? *Philosophical Transactions of the Royal Society, Series B*, 360, 1271–1279.

Crick, F., and Mitchison, G. (1983). The function of dream sleep. *Nature*, 304, 111–114.

Critchley, H.D., Wiens, S., Rotshtein, P., Öhman, A., and Dolan, R.J. (2004). Neural systems supporting interoceptive awareness. *Nature Neuroscience*, 7, 189–195.

Critchlow, H. (2018). *Consciousness*. London: Ladybird Books.

Cytowic, R.E., and Cole, J. (2008). *The Man Who Tasted Shapes*. Cambridge, MA: MIT Press.

Cytowic, R.E., and Eagleman, D.M. (2011). *Wednesday is Indigo Blue: Discovering the Brain of Synesthesia*. Cambridge, MA: MIT Press.

Dale, R.C., Church, A.J., Surtees, R.A.H., et al. (2004). Encephalitis lethargica syndrome: 20 New cases and evidence of basal ganglia autoimmunity. *Brain*, 127, 21–33.

Dallaspezia S., and Benedetti F. (2015). Sleep deprivation therapy for depression. *Current Topics in Behavioral Neuroscience*, 25, 483–502.

Dally, J.M., Emery, N.J., and Clayton, N.S. (2006), Food-caching western scrub-jays keep track of who was watching when. *Science*, 312, 1662–1665.

Damasio, A.R. (1989). Time-locked multiregional retroactivation: a systems level proposal for the neural substrates of recall and recognition. *Cognition*, 3, 25–62.

Damasio, A. (1999). *The Feeling of What Happens*. New York: Harcourt Brace and Company.

Damasio, A. (2010). *Self Comes to Mind: Constructing the Conscious Brain*. New York: Pantheon.

Danquah, A.N., Farrell, M.J., and O'Boyle, D.J. (2008). Biases in the subjective timing of perceptual events: Libet et al. (1983) revisited. *Consciousness and Cognition*, 17, 616–627.

Davidson, D. (1970). Mental events. In L. Foster and J.W. Swanson (eds.), *Experience and Theory*. Amherst, MA: University of Massachusetts Press, pp. 79–101.

Davidson, J.A. (1962). An assessment of the value of hypnosis in pregnancy and labour. *British Medical Journal*, II, 951–952.

Davidson, R.J., Kabat-Zinn, J., Schumacher, J., et al. (2003). Alterations in brain and immune function produced by mindfulness meditation. *Psychosomatic Medicine*, 65, 564–570.

Davis, W. (1985). *The Serpent and the Rainbow*. New York: Simon and Schuster.

Davis, J.L., Byrd, P., Rhudy, J.L., and Wright, D.C. (2007). Characteristics of chronic nightmares in a trauma-exposed treatment-seeking sample. *Dreaming*, 17, 187–198.

Debruyne, H., Portzky, M., Van den Eynde, F., and Audenaert, K. (2010). Cotard's syndrome: a review. *Current Psychiatric Reports*, 11, 197–202.

Defechereux, T., Degauque, C., Fumal, I., et al. (2000). L'hypnosédation, un nouveau mode d'anesthésie pour la chirurgie endocrinienne cervicale. Étude prospective randomisée. *Annales de Chirurgie*, 125, 539–546.

Dehaene, S. (2014). *Consciousness and the Brain: Deciphering How the Brain Codes our Thoughts*. New York: Viking Press.

Dehaene, S., and Changeux, J-P. (2004). Neural mechanisms for access to consciousness. In M.S. Gazzaniga (ed.), *The Cognitive Neurosciences*. Cambridge, MA: Boston Review, pp. 1145–1157.

Dehaene S., and Changeux J-P. (2011). Experimental and theoretical approaches to conscious processing. *Neuron*, 70, 200–227.

Dehaene, S., and Naccache, L. (2001). Towards a cognitive neuroscience of consciousness: Basic evidence and a workspace framework. *Cognition*, 79, 1–37.

Dehaene, S., Kerszberg, M., and Changeux, J.P. (1998). A neuronal model of a global workspace in effortful cognitive tasks. *Proceedings of the National Academy Science USA*, 95, 14529–14534.

Dehaene, S., Changeux, J.-P., Sergent, C., Naccache, L., and Sackur, J. (2006). Conscious, preconscious, and subliminal processing: a testable taxonomy. *Trends in Cognitive Sciences*, 10, 204–211.

Dement, W., and Kleitman, N. (1957). The relation of eye movements during sleep to dream activity: an objective method for the study of dreaming. *Journal of Experimental Psychology*, 53, 339–346.

Dement, W.C. (1974). *Some Must Watch While Some Must Sleep*. San Francisco, CA: W.H. Freeman.

Demonaco, J. (2013). *The Purge*. Universal City, CA: Universal Pictures.

Dennett, D.C. (1978a). *Brainstorms*. Cambridge, MA: MIT Press.

Dennett, D.C. (1978b). Why you can't make a computer that feels pain. *Synthese*, 38, 415–456.

Dennett, D.C. (1988). Quining qualia. In A.J. Marcel and E. Bisiach (eds.), *Consciousness in Contemporary Science*. Oxford, UK: Oxford University Press, pp. 42–77.

Dennett, D.C. (1991). *Consciousness Explained*. Harmondsworth, UK: Penguin Books.

Dennett, D.C. (1991b). Review of McGinn, *The Problem of Consciousness. The Times Literary Supplement*, May 10, 10.

Dennett, D.C. (1995). The unimagined preposterousness of zombies. *Journal of Consciousness Studies*, 2, 322–326.

Dennett, D.C. (2001). *Are we explaining consciousness yet? Dennett 2001 Cognition*, 79, 221–37.

Dennett, D.C. (2004). *Freedom Evolves*. Harmondsworth, UK: Penguin.

Dennett, D.C. (2014). *Intuition Pumps and Other Tools for Thinking*. Harmondsworth, UK: Penguin.

Dennett, D.C. (2015). *Sweet Dreams: Philosophical Obstacles to a Science of Consciousness*. Cambridge, MA: MIT Press.

Dennett, D.C. (2018). Facing up to the hard question of consciousness. *Philosophical Transactions of the Royal Society B: Biological Sciences*, 373, 1–7.

Dennett, D.C., and Kinsbourne, M. (1992). Time and the observer: the where and when of consciousness in the brain. *Behavioral and Brain Sciences*, 15, 183–247.

Deutsch, D. (2003). *Phantom Words and Other Curiosities*. La Jolla, CA: Philomel Records.

Diamond, J. (1997). *Guns, Germs, and Steel: The Fates of Human Societies*. New York: W.W. Norton and Company.

Dick, P.K. (1968). *Do Androids Dream of Electric Sheep*. New York: Doubleday.

Diekelmann, S., and Born, J. (2010). The memory function of sleep. *Nature Reviews Neuroscience*, 11, 114–126.

Dienes, Z., and Hutton, S. (2013). Understanding hypnosis metacognitively: RTMS applied to left DLPFC increases hypnotic suggestibility. *Cortex*, 49, 386–392.

Dixon, M.J., Smilek, D., Duffy, P.L., Zanna, P.M., and Merikle, P.M. (2006). The role of meaning in grapheme–colour synaesthesia. *Cortex*, 42, 243–252.

Doblin, R. (1991). Pahnke's 'Good Friday Experiment': a long-term follow-up and methodological critique. *Journal of Transpersonal Psychology*, 23, 1–25.

Doblin, R. (1998). Dr. Leary's Concord Prison Experiment: A 34 year follow-up study. *Journal of Psychoactive Drugs*, 30(4), 419–426.

Dodick, D.W., and Gargus, J.J. (2008). Why migraines strike. *Scientific American*, 299, 56–63.

Doerig, A., Schurger, A., Hess, K., and Herzog, M.H. (2019). The unfolding argument: why IIT and other causal structure theories cannot explain consciousness. *Consciousness and Cognition*, 72, 49–59.

Doidge, N. (2007). *The Brain that Changes Itself*. London: Penguin Books.

Domhoff, G.W. (2001). A new neurocognitive theory of dreams. *Dreaming*, 11, 13–33.

Domhoff, G.W. (2003). *The Scientific Study of Dreams: Neural Networks, Cognitive Development, and*

REFERENCES

Content Analysis. Washington, DC: American Psychological Association Press.

Domhoff, G.W. (2011). The neural substrate for dreaming: is it a subsystem of the default network? *Consciousness and Cognition*, 20, 1163–1174.

Domhoff, G.W. (2017). *The Emergence of Dreaming: Mind-Wandering, Embodied Simulation, and the Default Network*. Oxford, UK: Oxford University Press.

Domhoff, G.W., and Fox, K.C.R. (2015). Dreaming and the default network: a review, synthesis, and counterintuitive research proposal. *Consciousness and Cognition*, 33, 342–353.

Domhoff, G.W., and Schneider, A. (2008). Studying dream content using the archive and search engine on DreamBank.net. *Consciousness and Cognition*, 17, 1238–1247.

Donaldson, D. (1987). Knowing one's own mind. *Proceedings and Addresses of the American Philosophical Association*, 60, 441–458.

Dourmashkin, R.R., Dunn, G., Castano, V., and McCall, S.A. (2012). Evidence for an enterovirus as the cause of encephalitis lethargica. *BMC Infectious Diseases*, 12, 1–20.

Doyen, S., Klein, O., Pichon, C.-L., and Cleeremans, A. (2012). Behavioral priming: it's all in the mind, but whose mind? *PLOS ONE*, 7, 1–7.

Dretske, F. (1995). *Naturalizing the Mind*. Cambridge, MA: Bradford Books / MIT Press.

Dreyfus, H.L. (1992). *What Computers Still Can't Do*. Cambridge, MA: MIT Press.

Duhigg, C. (2013). *The Power of Habit: Why We Do What We Do, and How to Change*. New York: Random House.

Duncan, J.S., Sander, J.W., Sisodiya, S.M., and Walker, M.C. (2006). Adult epilepsy. *The Lancet*, 367, 1087–1100.

Dunlosky, J., and Thiede, K.W. (2013). Metamemory. In D. Reisberg (ed.), *The Oxford Handbook of Cognitive Psychology*. Oxford, UK: Oxford University Press, pp. 283–298.

Eagleman, D. (2011). *Incognito: The Secret Lives of the Brain*. Edinburgh, UK: Canongate.

Eason, A. (2013). *The Science of Self-Hypnosis: The Evidence Based Way to Hypnotise Yourself*. San Diego, CA: Awake Media.

Eccles, J.C. (1994). *How the Self Controls the Brain*. London: Springer.

Edelman, G.M. (1989). *The Remembered Present*. New York: Basic Books.

Edelman, G.M. (1992). *Bright Air, Brilliant Fire: On the Matter of the Mind*. New York: Basic Books.

Edelman, G.M. (2003). Naturalizing consciousness: a theoretical framework. *Proceedings of the National Academy of Science USA.*, 100, 5520–5524.

Edelman, G.M. (2004). *Wider than the Sky*. London: Allen Lane.

Edelman, G.M., and Gally, J.A. (2013). Reentry: a key mechanism for integration of brain function. *Frontiers in Integrative Neuroscience*, 7(63), 1–6.

Edelman, D. B., and Seth, A. K. (2009). Animal consciousness: a synthetic approach. *Trends in Neurosciences*, 32, 476–484.

Edelman, G.M., and Tononi, G. (2000). *A Universe of Consciousness*. New York: Basic Books.

Edelman, G.M., Gally, J.A., and Baars, B.J. (2011). Biology of consciousness. *Frontiers in Psychology*, 2, 1–7.

Edwards, P. (1986). The case against reincarnation: Parts 1–4. *Free Inquiry*, 6, 24–53.

Egner, T., and Raz, A. (2007). Cognitive control processes and hypnosis. In G. Jamieson (ed.), *Hypnosis and Conscious States: The Cognitive Neuroscience Perspective*. London: Oxford University Press, pp. 29–50.

Ehrsson, H.H. (2007). The experimental induction of out-of-body experiences. *Science*, 317, 1048.

Ehrsson, H.H., Holmes, N. P., and Passingham, R.E. (2005). Touching a rubber hand: feeling of body ownership is associated with activity in multisensory brain areas. *Journal of Neuroscience*, 25, 10564–10573.

Ehrsson, H.H., Kito, T., Sadato, N., Passingham, R.E., and Naito, E. (2005). Neural substrate of body size: Illusory feeling of shrinking of the waist. *PLoS Biology*, 3(12),1–8.

Ehrsson, H.H., Spence, C., and Passingham, R. E. (2004). That's my hand! Activity in premotor cortex reflects feeling of ownership of a limb. *Science*, 305, 875–877.

Eichenlaub, J.B., Nicolas, A., Daltrozzo, J., Redouté, J., Costes, N., and Ruby, P. (2014). Resting brain activity varies with dream recall frequency between subjects. *Neuropsychopharmacology*, 39, 1594–1602.

Eliasmith, C., Stewart, T.C., Choo, X., et al. (2012). A large-scale model of the functioning brain. *Science*, 338, 1202–1205.

Elitzur, A.C. (1997). Why don't we know what Mary knows? Baars' reversing the problem of qualia. *Journal of Consciousness Studies*, 4, 319–324.

Elliott, J.C., Baird, B., and Giesbrecht, B. (2016). Consciousness isn't all-or-none: Evidence for partial awareness during the attentional blink. *Consciousness and Cognition*, 40, 79–85.

Ellis, H.D., and Lewis, M.B. (2001). Capgras delusion: a window on face recognition. *Trends in Cognitive Sciences*, 5, 149–156.

Ellis, H.D., and Young, A.W. (1990). Accounting for delusional misidentification. *British Journal of Psychiatry*, 157, 239–248.

Emmett, P.A. (1989). A biblico-ethical response to the question of withdrawing fluid and nutrition from individuals in the persistent vegetative state, 4–5, 248–249.

Engel, A., and Singer, W. (2001). Temporal binding and the neural correlates of sensory awareness. *Trends Cognitive Sciences*, 5, 16–25.

Engel, A.K., Fries, P., Koenig, P., Brecht, M., and Singer, W. (1999). Temporal binding, binocular rivalry, and consciousness. *Consciousness and Cognition*, 8, 128–151.

Epstein, R., Lanza, R.P., and Skinner, B.F. (1981). 'Self-awareness' in the pigeon. *Science*, 212, 695–696.

Eschner, K. (2017). Computers are great at chess, but that doesn't mean the game is 'solved'. Smart News, 21 February 2017, www.Smithsonian.com.

Evans, F.J. (1979). Contextual forgetting: posthypnotic source amnesia. *Journal of Abnormal Psychology*, 88, 556–563.

Evans, J.St.B.T. (2010). *Thinking Twice: Two Minds in One Brain*. Oxford, UK: Oxford University Press.

Exner, J.E. (2002). *The Rorschach: Basic Foundations and Principles of Interpretation* (Vol. 1). Hoboken, NJ: John Wiley and Sons.

Eysenck, M.W., and Keane, M.T. (2015). *Cognitive Psychology: A Student's Handbook* (7th ed.). London: Psychology Press.

Fallon, J. (2013). *The Psychopath Inside*. New York: Current Books.

Farah, M.J. (ed.) (2010). *Neuroethics: An Introduction with Readings*. Cambridge, MA: MIT Press.

Farrer, C., and Frith, C.D. (2002). Experiencing oneself vs another person as being the cause of an action: the neural correlates of the experience of agency. *NeuroImage*, 15, 596–603.

Farthing, G.W. (1992). *The Psychology of Consciousness*. Upper Saddle River, NJ: Prentice Hall.

Faymonville, M.E., Boly, M., and Laureys, S. (2006). Functional neuroanatomy of the hypnotic state. *Journal of Physiology Paris*, 99, 463–469.

Feigley, D.A., and Spear, N.E. (1970). Effect of age and punishment condition on long-term retention by the rat of active- and passive-avoidance learning. *Journal of Comparative and Physiological Psychology*, 73, 515–526.

Feinberg, T.E., and Mallatt, J. (2013). The evolutionary and genetic origins of consciousness in the Cambrian Period over 500 million years ago. *Frontiers in Psychology*, 4, 1–27.

Fellows, B., and Ragg, L. (1992). The Carleton Skill Training Program: a preliminary British trial. *Contemporary Hypnosis*, 9, 169–174.

Ferguson, M.A., Nielsen, J.A., King, J.B., et al. (2016). Reward, salience, and attentional networks are activated by religious experience in devout Mormons. *Social Neuroscience*, 13, 104–116.

Fernyhough, C. (2016). *The Voices Within: The History and Science of How We Talk to Ourselves*. London: Profile Books.

Filbey, F.M., Aslan, S., Calhoun, V.D., et al. (2014). Long-term effects of marijuana use on the brain. *Proceedings of the National Academy of Sciences*, 111, 16913–16918.

Fisher, T.D., Moore, Z.T., and Pittenger, M. (2012). Sex on the brain? An examination of frequency of sexual cognitions as a function of gender, erotophilia, and social desirability. *Journal of Sex Research*, 29, 69–77.

Flanagan, O. (1992). *Consciousness Reconsidered*. Cambridge, MA: MIT Press.

Flanagan, O. (2000). *Dreaming Souls*. Oxford, UK: Oxford University Press.

Flegr, J. (2007). Effects of *Toxoplasma* on human behavior. *Schizophrenia Bulletin*, 33, 757–760.

Flegr, J. (2013). Influence of latent *Toxoplasma* infection on human personality, physiology and morphology:

pros and cons of the *Toxoplasma*-human model in studying the manipulation hypothesis. *The Journal of Experimental Biology*, 216, 127–133.

Fleischer, J.G., Gally, J.A., Edelman, G.M., and Krichmar, J.L. (2007). Retrospective and prospective responses arising in a modeled hippocampus during maze navigation by a brain-based device. *Proceedings of the National Academy of Sciences*, 104, 3556–3561.

Fleming, S.M., and Dolan, R.J. (2012). The neural basis of metacognitive ability. *Philosophical Transactions of the Real Society, Series B Biological Sciences*, 367, 1338–1349.

Flor, H., Nikolajsen, L., and Jensen, T.S. (2006). Phantom limb pain: a case of maladaptive CNS plasticity? *Nature Reviews Neuroscience*, 7, 873–881.

Fodor, J.A. (1975). *The Language of Thought*. Cambridge, MA: Harvard University Press.

Fornaro, M., Gabrielli, F., Albano, C., et al. (2009). Obsessive-compulsive disorder and related disorders: a comprehensive survey. *Annals of General Psychiatry*, 8, 1–13.

Foulkes, D. (2002). *Children's Dreaming and the Development of Consciousness*. Cambridge, MA: Harvard University Press.

Fox, O. (1962). *Astral Projection*. New York: 370 University Books.

Fox, K.C.R., Nijeboer, S., Solomonova, E., Domhoff, G.W., and Christoff, K. (2013). Dreaming as mind wandering: evidence from functional neuroimaging and first-person content reports. *Frontiers in Human Neuroscience*, 7, 412.

Frank, M.C., Everett, D.L., Fedorenko, E., and Gibson, E. (2008). Number as a cognitive technology: Evidence from Pirahã language and cognition. *Cognition*, 108, 819–824.

Franklin, S., Madl, T., Strain, S., et al. (2016). A LIDA cognitive model tutorial. *Biologically Inspired Cognitive Architectures*, 16, 105–130.

Franklin, S., Strain, S., Snaider, J., McCall, R., and Faghihi, U. (2012). Global workspace theory, its LIDA model and the underlying neuroscience. *Biologically Inspired Cognitive Architectures*, 1, 32–43.

Freeman, R.M., Macaulay, A.J., Eve, L., Chamberlain, G.V.P., and Bhat, A.V. (1986). Randomised trial of self hypnosis for analgesia in labour. *British Medical Journal*, 292, 657–658.

French, C.C., and Stone, A. (2014). *Anomalistic Psychology*. Basingstoke, UK: Palgrave.

Frenda, S.J., Patihis, L., Loftus, E.F., Lewis, H.C., and Fenn, K.M. (2014). Sleep deprivation and false memories. *Psychological Science*, 25, 1674–1681.

Freud, E., Plaut, D.C., and Behrmann, M. (2016). 'What' is happening in the dorsal visual pathway. *Trends in Cognitive Sciences*, 20, 773–784.

Freud, S. (1899). *The Interpretation of Dreams*. (New edition 1991.) Harmondsworth, UK: Penguin.

Freud, S. (1905). *The Psychopathology of Everyday Life*. (New edition 1991.) Harmondsworth, UK: Penguin.

Freud, S. (1924). *A General Introduction to Psychoanalysis*. (New edition 1991.) Harmondsworth, UK: Penguin.

Fried, I. (1997). Syndrome E. *The Lancet*, 350, 1845–1847.

Fries, P. (2009). Neuronal gamma-band synchronization as a fundamental process in cortical computation. *Annual Review of Neuroscience*, 32, 209–24.

Friston, K. (2009). The free-energy principle: a rough guide to the brain? *Trends in Cognitive Sciences*, 13, 293–301.

Friston, K. (2010). The free-energy principle: a unified brain theory? *Nature Reviews Neuroscience*, 11, 127–138.

Friston, K. (2018). Am I self-conscious? (Or does self-organisation entail self-consciousness?) *Frontiers in Psychology*, 00579.

Frith, C. (2007). *Making Up the Mind: How the Brain Creates Our Mental World*. Oxford, UK: Blackwell.

Frith, C.D. (2019). The neural basis of consciousness. *Psychological Medicine*, 1, 1–13.

Frith, C., Perry, R., and Lumer, E. (1999). The neural correlates of conscious experience: an experimental framework. *Trends in Cognitive Sciences*, 3, 105–114.

Fu, Z., and Rutishauser, U. (2018). Single-neuron correlates of awareness during attentional blinks. *Trends in Cognitive Sciences*, 22, 5–7.

Fulcher, R.Z. (2014). *The Beginner's Guide to Hypnotherapy*. Scotts Valley, CA: CreateSpace.

Gallagher, S. (2000). Philosophical conceptions of the self: implications for cognitive science. *Trends in Cognitive Sciences*, 4, 14–21.

Gallagher, S. (ed.). (2011). *The Oxford Handbook of the Self*. Oxford, UK: Oxford University Press.

Gallagher, S., and Zahavi, D. (2012). *The Phenomenological Mind*. London: Routledge.

Gallup, G.G., Jr. (1970). Chimpanzees: SELF recognition. *Science*, 167, 86–87.

Gamez, D. (2008). Progress in machine consciousness. *Consciousness and Cognition*, 17, 887–910.

Garland, A. (2014). *Ex Machina*. London: Film4/DNA Films.

Gazzaniga, M.S. (1996). *Conversations in Cognitive Neuroscience*. Cambridge, MA: MIT Press.

Gazzaniga, M.S. (2005). Essay: forty-five years of split-brain research and still going strong. *Nature Reviews Neuroscience*, 6, 653–659.

Gazzaniga, M.S. (2015). *Tales from Both Sides of the Brain: A Life in Neuroscience*. New York: Ecco Press.

Gazzaniga, M.S., Bogen, J.E., and Sperry, R.W. (1962). Some functional effects of sectioning the cerebral commissures in man. *Proceedings of the National Academy of Science USA*, 48, 1765–1769.

Gelbard-Sagiv, H., Mudrik, L., Hill, M. R., Koch, C., and Fried, I. (2018). Human single neuron activity precedes emergence of conscious perception. *Nature Communications*, 9, 1–13.

Geldard, F.A., and Sherrick, C.E. (1972). The cutaneous 'rabbit': a perceptual illusion. *Science*, 178, 178–179.

Gennaro, R. (2017). *Consciousness*. London: Routledge.

Geschwind, N. (1979). Behavioral changes in temporal lobe epilepsy. *Psychological Medicine*, 9, 217–219.

Gfeller, J.D., Lynne, S.J., and Pribble, W.E. (1987). Enhancing hypnotic susceptibility: interpersonal and rapport factors. *Journal of Personality and Social Psychology*, 52, 586–595.

Giacino, J.T., Ashwal, S., Childs, N., et al. (2002). The minimally conscious state: definition and diagnostic criteria. *Neurology*, 58, 349–353.

Giles, N., Lau, H., and Odegaard, B. (2016). What type of awareness does binocular rivalry assess? *Trends in Cognitive Sciences*, 20, 719–720.

Gillig, P.M. (2009). Dissociative identity disorder: a controversial diagnosis. *Psychiatry Rounds*, 6(3), 24–29.

Gillihan, S., and Farah, M. (2005). Is self special? A critical review of evidence from experimental psychology and cognitive neuroscience. *Psychological Bulletin*, 131, 76–97.

Givon, L.E., and Lazar, A.A. (2016). Neurokernel: an open source platform for emulating the fruit fly brain. *PLOS ONE*, 0146581, 1–25.

Gloor, P. (1990). Experiential phenomena of temporal lobe epilepsy. *Brain*, 113, 1673–1694.

Godfrey-Smith, P. (2016). *Other Minds: The Octopus and the Evolution of Intelligent Life*. London: William Collins.

Goethals, G.R., and Reckman, R.F. (1973). The perception of consistency in attitudes. *Journal of Experimental Social Psychology*, 9, 491–501.

Gold, I. (1999). Does 40-Hz oscillation play a role in visual consciousness? *Consciousness and Cognition*, 8, 186–195.

Goldberg, I.I., Harel, M., and Malach, R. (2006). When the brain loses its self: prefrontal inactivation during sensorimotor processing. *Neuron*, 50, 329–339.

Goldman, S., Galarneau, D., and Friedman, R. (2007). New onset LSD flashback syndrome triggered by the initiation of SSRIs. *The Ochsner Journal*, 7, 37–39.

Goodale, M.A., and Milner, A.D. (1992). Separate visual pathways for perception and action. *Trends in Neurosciences*, 15, 20–25.

Gorassini, D.R., and Spanos, N.P. (1986). A social-cognitive skills approach to the successful modification of hypnotic susceptibility. *Journal of Personality and Social Psychology*, 50, 1004–1012.

Gordon, P. (2004). Numerical cognition without words: evidence from Amazonia. *Science*, 306, 496–499.

Gorry, G.A., Kassirer, J.P., Essig, A., and Schwartz, W.B. (1973). Decision analysis as the basis for computer-aided management of acute renal failure. *The American Journal of Medicine*, 55, 473–484.

Goswami, I. (2007). *Cognitive Development: The Learning Brain*. Hove, UK: Psychology Press.

Goswami, M., Thorpy, M.J., and Pandi-Perumal, S.R. (2016). *Narcolepsy: a clinical guide*. Berlin: Springer.

Gottlieb, D.J., Punjabi, N.M., Newman, A.B., Resnick, H.E., Redline, S., Baldwin, C.M., and Nieto, F.J. (2005). Association of sleep time with diabetes mellitus and impaired glucose tolerance. *Archives of Internal Medicine*, 165, 863–867.

Granqvist, P., Fredrikson, M., Unge, P., et al. (2005). Sensed presence and mystical experiences are predicted by suggestibility, not by the application of transcranial weak complex magnetic fields. *Neuroscience Letters*, 379, 1–6.

Gray, J.A. (2006). *Consciousness: Creeping Up on the Hard Problem*. Oxford, UK: Oxford University Press.

Gray, J.A., Parslow, D.M., Brammer, M.J., et al. (2006). Evidence against functionalism from neuroimaging of the alien colour effect in synaesthesia. *Cortex*, 42, 317.

Gray, K., and Wegner, D.M. (2012). Feeling robots and human zombies: mind perception and the uncanny valley. *Cognition*, 125, 125–130.

Greenemeier, L. (2017). 20 Years after Deep Blue: how AI has advanced since conquering chess. *Scientific American*, 2 June.

Greenwald, A.G., Banahi, M.R., Rudman, L.A., et al. (2002). A unified theory of implicit attitudes, stereotypes, self-esteem, and self concept. *Psychological Review*, 109, 3–25.

Greenwald, A.G., Klinger, M.R., and Schuh, E.S. (1995). Activation by marginally perceptible ('subliminal') stimuli: dissociation of unconscious from conscious cognition. *Journal of Experimental Psychology: General*, 124, 22–42.

Gregoriou, G.G., Gotts, S.J., Zhou, H., and Desimone, R. (2009). High-frequency, long-range coupling between prefrontal and visual cortex during attention. *Science*, 324, 1207–1210.

Greyson, B. (1998). Biological aspects of near-death experiences. *Perspectives in Biology and Medicine*, 42, 14–32.

Greyson, B., Holden, J.M., and van Lommel, P. (2012). 'There is nothing paranormal about near-death experiences' revisited: Comment on Mobbs and Watt. *Trends in Cognitive Sciences*, 16, 445.

Griffiths, R.R., Hurwitz, E.S., Davis, A.K., Johnson, M.W., and Jesse, R. (2019). Survey of subjective 'God encounter experiences': comparisons among naturally occurring experiences and those occasioned by the classic psychedelics psilocybin, LSD, ayahuasca, or DMT. *PLoS ONE*, 14, 1–26.

Griffiths, R.R., Richards, W.A., McCann, U., and Jesse, R. (2006). Psilocybin can occasion mystical-type experiences having substantial and sustained personal meaning and spiritual significance. *Psychopharmacology*, 187, 268–283.

Griffiths, R.R., Johnson, M.W., Richards, W.A., et al. (2018). Psilocybin-occasioned mystical-type experience in combination with meditation and other spiritual practices produces enduring positive changes in psychological functioning and in trait measures of prosocial attitudes and behaviors. *Journal of Psychopharmacology*, 32, 49–69.

Gross, C.G., Moore, T., and Rodman, H.R. (2004). Visually guided behavior after V1 lesions in young and adult monkeys and its relation to blindsight in humans. *Progress in Brain Research*, 144, 279–94.

Grossenbacher, P.G., and Lovelace, C.T. (2001). Mechanisms of synesthesia: cognitive and physiological constraints. *Trends in Cognitive Science*, 5, 36–41.

Grossman, S., Gueta, C., Pesin, S., Malach, R., and Landau, A.N. (2019). Where does time go when you blink? *Psychological Science*, 30, 907–916.

Grotenhermen, F. (2003). Pharmacokinetics and pharmacodynamics of cannabinoids. *Clinical Pharmacokinetics*, 42, 327–360.

Guggisberg, A.G., and Mottaz, A. (2013). Timing and awareness of movement decisions: does consciousness really come too late? *Frontiers in Human Neuroscience*, 7, 1–11.

Gujar, N., Yoo, S.S., Hu, P., and Walker, M.P. (2011). Sleep deprivation amplifies reactivity of brain reward networks, biasing the appraisal of positive emotional experiences. *Journal of Neuroscience*, 31, 466–47.

Gusnard, D.A., Akbudak, E., Shulman, G.L., and Raichle, M.E. (2001). Medial prefrontal cortex and self-referential mental activity: Relation to a default mode of brain function. *Proceedings of the National Academy of Science*, 98, 4259–4264.

Guterstam, A., Björnsdotter, M., Gentile, G., and Ehrsson, H.H. (2015). Posterior cingulate cortex integrates the senses of self-location and body ownership. *Current Biology*, 25, 1416–1425.

Hall, C.S. (1953). A cognitive theory of dreams. *The Journal of General Psychology*, 49, 273–282.

Hameroff, S.R. (1998). 'Funda-Mentality': is the conscious mind subtly linked to a basic level of the universe? *Trends in Cognitive Sciences*, 2, 119–124.

Hameroff, S. (2006). Consciousness, neurobiology and quantum mechanics. In J.A. Tuszynski (ed.), *The

Emerging Physics of Consciousness. New York: Springer Science and Business Media, pp. 192–251.

Hameroff, S. (2007). The brain is both neurocomputer and quantum computer. *Cognitive Science*, 31, 1035–1045.

Hameroff, S., and Penrose, R. (2014). Consciousness in the universe: a review of the 'Orch OR' theory. *Physics of Life Review*, 11, 39–78.

Hankins, P. (2015). *The Shadow of Consciousness: A Little Less Wrong*. Scotts Valley, CA: CreateSpace.

Harari, Y.N. (2014). *Sapiens: A Brief History of Humankind*. New York: Harper Collins.

Harari, Y.N. (2016). *Homo Deus: A Brief History of Tomorrow*. London: Harvill Secker.

Hardin, C.L. (1993). *Color for Philosophers* (expanded edition). Indianapolis, IN: Hackett.

Hardy, J. (2006). Speaking clearly: a critical review of the self-talk literature. *Psychology of Sport and Exercise*, 7, 81–97.

Harley, H.E. (2013). Consciousness in dolphins? A review of recent evidence. *Journal of Comparative Physiology A*, 199, 565–582.

Harley, T.A. (2014). *The Psychology of Language* (4th ed.). London: Routledge.

Harley, T.A. (2017). *Talking the Talk: Language, Psychology, and Science*. London: Routledge.

Harman, G. (1973). *Thought*. Princeton, NJ: Princeton University Press.

Harris, A. (2019). *Consciousness*. New York: Harper.

Harris, J. (2014). *Sensation and Perception*. London: Sage.

Harris, S. (2012). *Free will*. New York: Free Press.

Harrison, J. (2001). *Synaesthesia: The Strangest Thing*. Oxford, UK: Oxford University Press.

Hart, H.L.A. (1970). *Punishment and Responsibility*. Oxford, UK: Oxford University Press.

Hartmann, E. (1998). *Dreams and Nightmares: The Origin and Meaning of Dreams*. New York: Basic Books.

Hasan, F.M., Zagarins, S.E., Pischke, K.M., et al. (2014). Hypnotherapy is more effective than nicotine replacement therapy for smoking cessation: Results of a randomized controlled trial. *Complementary Therapies in Medicine*, 22, 1–8.

Hassabis, D., Kumaran, D., and Maguire, E.A. (2007). Using imagination to understand the neural basis of episodic memory. *Journal of Neuroscience*, 27, 14365–14374.

Hauser, M.D., Chomsky, N., and Fitch, W.T. (2002). The faculty of language: what is it, who has it and how did it evolve? *Science*, 298, 1569–1579.

Häuser, W., Hagl, M., Schmierer, A., and Hansen, E. (2016). The efficacy, safety and applications of medical hypnosis: a systematic review of meta-analyses. *Deutsches Ärzteblatt International*, 113, 289–296.

Haxby, J.V., Gobbini, M.I., Furey, M.L., et al. (2001). Distributed and overlapping representations of faces and objects in ventral temporal cortex. *Science*, 293, 2425–2430.

Hayne, H. (2004). Infant memory development: implications for childhood amnesia. *Developmental Review*, 24, 33–73.

Haynes, J.D. (2011). Decoding and predicting intentions. *Annals of the New York Academy of Sciences*, 1224, 9–21.

Heap, M., Brown, R.J., and Oakley, D.A. (2004). *The Highly Hypnotizable Person: Theoretical, Experimental, and Clinical Issues*. London: Routledge.

Heavey, C.L., and Hurlburt, R.T. (2008). The phenomena of inner experience. *Consciousness and Cognition*, 17, 798–810.

Heilman, K.M., Barrett, A.M., and Adair, J.C. (1998). Possible mechanisms of anosognosia: a defect in self-awareness. *Philosophical Transactions of the Royal Society B: Biological Science*, 353, 1903–1909.

Henning, A., Kurtom, M., and Espiridion, E.D. (2019). A case study of acute stimulant-induced psychosis. *Cureus*, 11, e4126.

Hesse, B.E., and Potter, B. (2004). A behavioral look at the training of Alex: a review of Pepperberg's *The Alex Studies: Cognitive and Communicative Abilities of Grey Parrots*. *The Analysis of Verbal Behavior*, 20, 141–151

Heyes, C.M. 1994. Reflections on self-recognition in primates. *Animal Behaviour*, 47, 909–919.

Heyes, C.M. 1998. Theory of mind in nonhuman primates. *Behavioural and Brain Sciences*, 21, 101–148.

Hilgard, E.R. (1977). *Divided Consciousness: Multiple Controls in Human Thought and Action*. New York: Wiley.

Hirstein, W. (2006). *Brain Fiction*. Cambridge, MA: MIT Press.

Hirstein, W., and Ramachandran, V.S. (1997). Capgras syndrome: a novel probe for understanding the neural representation of the identity and familiarity of persons. *Proceedings of the Royal Society of London Series B*, 264, 437–444.

Hobbes, T. (1668 [1651]). *Leviathan*. Oxford, UK: Oxford University Press.

Hobson, J.A. (2009). REM sleep and dreaming: towards a theory of protoconsciousness. *Nature Reviews Neuroscience*, 10, 803–813.

Hobson, J.A. (2015). *Psychodynamic Neurology: Dreams, Consciousness, and Virtual Reality*. Boca Raton, FL: CRC Press.

Hobson, J.A. (2017). *Conscious States: The AIM Model of Waking, Sleeping, and Dreaming*. Scotts Valley, CA: CreateSpace.

Hobson, J.A., and McCarley, R.W. (1977). The brain as a dream state generator: an activation-synthesis hypothesis of the dream process. *American Journal of Psychiatry*, 134, 1335–1348.

Hobson, J.A., Pace-Schott, E.F., and Stickgold, R. (2000). Dreaming and the brain: toward a cognitive neuroscience of conscious states. *Behavioral and Brain Sciences*, 23, 793–842.

Hoel, E.P., Albantakis, L., and Tononi, G. (2013). Quantifying causal emergence shows that macro can beat micro. *Proceedings of the National Academy of Sciences USA*, 110, 19790–19795.

Hoffman, D.D. (2019). *The Case Against Reality: How Evolution Hid the Truth from Our Eyes*. London: Allen Lane.

Hofmann, A. (2018). *LSD My Problem Child / Insights/Outlooks* (trans. J. Ott, reprint edition). Oxford, UK: Beckley Foundation Press.

Hofstadter, D. (1979). *Godel, Escher, Bach: An Eternal Golden Braid*. New York: Basic Books.

Hofstadter, D. (2007). *I Am a Strange Loop*. New York: Basic Books.

Holender, D. (1986). Semantic activation without conscious identification in dichotic listening, parafoveal vision, and visual masking: a survey and appraisal. *Behavioral and Brain Sciences*, 9, 1–66.

Holender, D., and Duscherer, K. (2004). Unconscious perception: The need for a paradigm shift. *Perception and Psychophysics*, 66, 872–881.

Honda, I. (1957). *The Mysterians*. Tokyo, Japan: Toho.

Honorton, C. (1985). Meta-analyses of Psi Ganzfeld research: a response to Hyman. *Journal of Parapsychology*, 49, 52–86.

Hood, B. (2013). *The Self Illusion*. London: Constable.

Horikawa, T., Tamaki, M., Miyawaki, Y., and Kamitani, Y. (2013). Neural decoding of visual imagery during sleep. *Science*, 340, 639–642.

Horne, J. (2006). *Sleepfaring: A Journey Through the Science of Sleep*. Oxford, UK: Oxford University Press.

Horowitz, A. (2017). Smelling themselves: dogs investigate their own odours longer when modified in an 'olfactory mirror' test. *Behavioural Processes*, 143C, 17–24.

Hsu, F.-H. (2002). *Behind Deep Blue: Building the Computer that Defeated the World Chess Champion*. Princeton, NJ: Princeton University Press.

Huber, R., Mäki, H., Rosanova, M., Casarotto, S., Canali, P., Casali, A.G., ... Massimini, M. (2013). Human cortical excitability increases with time awake. *Cerebral Cortex*, 23, 332–338.

Hufford, D.J. (1989). *The Terror that Comes in the Night: An Experience-Centered Study of Supernatural Assault Traditions*. Philadelphia, PA: University of Pennsylvania Press.

Hull, C. (1933). *Hypnosis and Suggestibility: An Experimental Approach*. New York: Appleton-Century.

Hull, C. (1940). *Mathematico-Deductive Theory of Rote Learning*. New Haven, CT: Yale University Press.

Hume, D. (1738). *An Enquiry Concerning Human Understanding*. London: Miller.

Humphrey, N. (1984). *Consciousness Regained: Chapters in the Development of Mind*. Oxford, UK: Oxford University Press.

Humphrey, N. (2006). *Seeing Red: A Study in Consciousness*. Harvard, CT: Harvard University Press.

Humphrey, N. (2011). *Soul Dust: The Magic of Consciousness*. London: Quercus.

Hunter, C.R. (2010). *The Art of Hypnosis: Mastering Basic Techniques* (3rd. ed.). London: Crown House.

Hunter, E.C.M., Charlton, J., and David, A.S. (2017). Depersonalisation and derealisation: assessment and management. *British Medical Journal*, 745, j745.

Husserl, E. (1913). *Logical Investigations*. London: Routledge.

Huxley, A. (1954). *The Doors of Perception*. London: Chatto & Windus.

Hyman, R. (1986). Parapsychological research: a tutorial review and critical appraisal. *Proceedings of the IEEE*, 74, 823–849.

Hyman R. (2010). Meta-analysis that conceals more than it reveals: comment on Storm et al. (2010). *Psychological Bulletin*, 136, 486.

Illes, J., and Sahakian, B.J. (2011). *The Oxford Handbook of Neuroethics*. Oxford, UK: Oxford University Press.

Ilieva, I.P, Hook, C.J., and Farah, M.J. (2015). Prescription stimulants' effects on healthy inhibitory control, working memory, and episodic memory: a meta-analysis. *Journal of Cognitive Neuroscience* 27, 1–21.

Intaite, M., Noreika, V., Šoliunas, A., and Falter, C.M. (2013). Interaction of bottom-up and top-down processes in the perception of ambiguous figures. *Vision Research*, 89, 24–31.

Iremonger, L. (1975). *The Ghosts of Versailles*. London: White Lion.

Irwin, H.J., and Watt, C. (2007). *An Introduction to Parapsychology* (5th ed.). Jefferson, NC: McFarland.

Iwata, K., Yamamoto, M., Nakao, M., and Kimura, M. (1999). A study on polysomnographic observations and subjective experiences under sensory deprivation. *Psychiatry and Clinical Neurosciences*, 53, 129–131.

Iwata, K., Nakao, M., Yamamoto, M., and Kimura, M. (2001). Quantitative characteristics of alpha and theta EEG activities during sensory deprivation. *Psychiatry and Clinical Neurosciences*, 55, 191–192.

Jackson, F. (1986). What Mary didn't know. *Journal of Philosophy*, 83, 291–295.

Jahn, R.G., and Dunne, B.J. (1986). On the quantum mechanics of consciousness, with application to anomalous phenomena. *Foundations of Physics*, 16, 721–772.

Jahoda, G. (1971). Retinal pigmentation, illusion susceptibility and space perception. *International Journal of Psychology*, 6, 199–207.

Jaloba, A., and Nicholson, F. (2014). *The Hypnotherapy Handbook*. Scotts Valley, CA: CreateSpace.

James, W. (1890). *The Principles of Psychology*. New York, NY: Henry Holt.

James, W. (1896). *Is Life Worth Living?* Philadelphia: S. Burns Weston.

James, W. (1902). *The Varieties of Religious Experience*. Reprinted 2012. Riverside, CA: Renaissance Classics.

Jefferson Airplane (1967). *Surrealistic Pillow*. Hollywood, CA: RCA Victor.

Jennett, B. (2002). Editorial: the vegetative state. The definition, diagnosis, prognosis and pathology of this state are discussed, together with the legal implications. *British Medical Journal*, 73, 355–357.

Jerath, R., Barnes, V.A., Dillard-Wright, D., Jerath, S., and Hamilton, B. (2012). Dynamic change of awareness during meditation techniques: neural and physiological Correlates. *Frontiers in Human Neuroscience*, 6, 131.

Johnson, N. (1957). *The Three Faces of Eve*. Los Angeles, CA: 20th Century Fox.

Johnson-Laird, P.N. (1983). *Mental Models: Towards a Cognitive Science of Language, Inference, and Consciousness*. Cambridge, UK: Cambridge University Press.

Jones, D. (2010). *The Handbook of Psychic Cold Reading*. Milton Keynes, UK: Lightning Source.

Jouvet, M. (1979). What does a cat dream about? *Trends in Neuroscience*, 2, 15–16.

Joyce, J. (1916). *A Portrait of the Artist as a Young Man*. New York: B.W. Huebsch.

Jung, C.G. (1969). *Archetypes and the Collective Unconscious* (Collected works of C.G. Jung, Vol. 9). London: Routledge.

Jung, C.G. (1995). *Memories, Dreams, Reflections*. London: Fontana Press.

Jung, C.G. (2014). *Dreams*. London: Routledge.

Kahn, D., and Hobson, J.A. (2005). State-dependent thinking: a comparison of waking and dreaming thought. *Consciousness and Cognition*, 14, 429–38.

Kahneman, D. (2012). *Thinking fast and slow*. Harmondsworth, UK: Penguin.

Kallio, S., and Revonsuo, A. (2005). The observer remains hidden. *Contemporary Hypnosis*, 22, 138–143.

Kane, M.J., and McVay, J.C. (2012). What mind wandering reveals about executive-control abilities

and failures. *Current Directions in Psychological Science*, 21, 348–354.
Kane, R. (1998). *The Significance of Free Will*. Oxford, UK: Oxford University Press.
Kane, R. (2011). *The Oxford Handbook of Free Will* (2nd ed.). Oxford, UK: Oxford University Press.
Kang, J.-E., Lim, M.M., Bateman, R.J., Lee, J.J., Smyth, L.P., Cirrito, J.R., … Holtzman, D.M. (2009). Amyloid-B dynamics are regulated by Orexin and the sleep-wake cycle. *Science*, 326, 1005–1007.
Kanwisher, N. (2010). Functional specificity in the human brain: a window into the functional architecture of the mind. *Proceedings of the National Academy of Science, USA*, 107, 11163–11170.
Kätsyri, J., Förger, K., Mäkäräinen, M., and Takala, T. (2015). A review of empirical evidence on different uncanny valley hypotheses: support for perceptual mismatch as one road to the valley of eeriness. *Frontiers in Psychology*, 6, 390.
Katz J., Saadon-Grosman, N., and Arzy, S. (2017). The life review experience: qualitative and quantitative characteristics. *Consciousness and Cognition*, 48, 76–86.
Keller, H. (2012 [1903]). *The Story of my Life*. Mineola, NY: Dover Press.
Kemmerer, D. (2015). *Cognitive Neuroscience of Language*. Hove, Sussex: Psychology Press.
Kentridge, R.W., and Heywood, C.A. (2000). Metacognition and awareness. *Consciousness and Cognition*, 9, 308–312.
Kesselring, T., and Müller, U. (2011). The concept of egocentrism in the context of Piaget's theory. *New Ideas in Psychology*, 29, 327–345.
Kessels, R.P.C., Kortrijk, H.E., Wester, A.J., and Nys, G.M.S. (2008). Confabulation behavior and false memories in Korsakoff's syndrome: role of source memory and executive functioning. *Psychiatry and Clinical Neurosciences*, 62, 220–225.
Key, B. (2015). Fish do not feel pain and its implications for understanding phenomenal consciousness. *Biological Philosophy*, 30, 149–165.
Kesey, K. (1962). *One Flew Over the Cuckoo's Nest*. New York: Viking Press.
Khait, I., Lewin-Epstein, O., Sharon, R., et al. (2019). Plants emit informative airborne sounds under stress. *bioRxiv* 507590.

Kierkegaard, S. (1980 [1844]). *The Concept of Anxiety*. Princeton, NJ: Princeton University Press.
Kihlstrom, J.F. (1985). Hypnosis. *Annual Review of Psychology*, 36, 385–418.
Kihlstrom, J. (2014). Hypnosis and cognition. *Psychology of Consciousness: Theory, Research, and Practice*, 1, 139–152.
Kihlstrom, J.F. (2018). Hypnosis as an altered state of consciousness. *Journal of Consciousness Studies*, 25, 53–72.
Killingsworth, M.A., and Gilbert, D.T. (2010). A wandering mind is an unhappy mind. *Science*, 330, 932.
Kim, J. (2011). *Philosophy of Mind* (3rd ed.). Philadelphia, PA: Westview Press.
King, H. (1943). *The Song of Bernadette*. Hollywood, CA: 20th Century Fox.
Kingsland, J. (2019). *Am I Dreaming? The New Science of Consciousness and how Altered States Reboot the Brain*. London: Atlantic Books.
Kinsey, A., Pomeroy, W., and Martin, C. (1948). *Sexual Behavior in the Human Male*. Philadelphia: W.B. Saunders.
Kinsey, A., Pomeroy, W., Martin, C., and Gebhard, P. (1953). *Sexual Behavior in the Human Female*. Philadelphia: W.B. Saunders.
Kinsey Institute (2020). Sex FAQs. Website. https://kinseyinstitute.org/research/index.php
Kirsch, I. (2011). The altered state issue: dead or alive? *International Journal of Clinical and Experimental Hypnosis*, 59, 350–362.
Kleinhauz, M., and Beran, B. (1984). Misuse of hypnosis: a factor in psychopathology. *American Journal of Clinical Hypnosis*, 26, 283–290.
Koch, C. (2004). *The Quest for Consciousness: A Neurobiological Approach*. Englewood, CO: Roberts & Co.
Koch, C. (2012). *Consciousness: Confessions of a Romantic Reductionist*. Cambridge, MA: MIT Press.
Koch, C. (2014). Is consciousness universal? *Scientific American Mind*, 25, 1–6.
Koch, C., and Tsuchiya, N. (2007). Attention and consciousness: two distinct brain processes. *Trends in Cognitive Sciences*, 11, 16–22.
Koch, C., Massimini, M., Boly, M., and Tononi, G. (2016). Neural correlates of consciousness: progress

and problems. *Nature Reviews Neuroscience*, 17, 307–321.

Koestler, A. (1959). *The Sleepwalkers*. London: Hutchison.

Köhler, W. (1917). *Intelligenzprüfungen an Menschenaffen. The Mentality of Apes* (1925 English publication). New York, NY: Harcourt, Brace and Company Inc.

Koivisto, M., Kainulainen, P., and Revonsuo, A. (2009). The relationship between awareness and attention: Evidence from ERP responses. *Neuropsychologia*, 47, 2891–2899.

Komatsu, H. (2006). The neural mechanisms of perceptual filling-in. *Nature Reviews Neuroscience*, 7, 220–231.

Koriat, A., and Levy-Sadot, R. (2000). Conscious and unconscious metacognition: A rejoinder. *Consciousness and Cognition*, 9, 193–202.

Kornmeier, J., and Bach, M. (2005). The Necker cube: An ambiguous figure disambiguated in early visual processing. *Vision Research*, 45, 955–960.

Kosslyn, S. (1996). *Imagery and Brain: The Resolution of the Imagery Debate*. Cambridge, MA: MIT Press.

Kosslyn, S.M., Ganis, G., and Thompson, W.L. (2001). Neural foundations of imagery. *Nature Reviews Neuroscience*, 2, 635–642.

Kotani, Y., Shimazawa, M., Yoshimura, S., Iwama, T., and Hara, H. (2008). The experimental and clinical pharmacology of propofol, an anesthetic agent with neuroprotective properties. *CNS Neuroscience and Therapeutics*, 14, 95–106.

Kotov, A. (1971). *Think Like a Grandmaster*. London: Batsford.

Kouider, S., de Gardelle, V., Sackur, J., and Dupoux, E. (2010). How rich is consciousness? The partial awareness hypothesis. *Trends in Cognitive Sciences*, 14, 301–307.

Kouider, S., Stahlhut, C., Gelskov, S.V., Barbosa, L.S., Dutat, M., De Gardelle, V., ... Dehaene-Lambertz, G. (2013). A neural marker of perceptual consciousness in infants. *Science*, 376, 376–380.

Kozhevnikov, M., Elliott, J., Shephard, J., and Gramann, K. (2013). Neurocognitive and somatic components of temperature increases during g-tummo meditation: legend and reality. *PLoS ONE*, 8, 1–12.

Krebs, T.S., and Johansen, P.Ø. (2013). Psychedelics and mental health: a population study. *PloS One*, 8, e63972.

Kreiman, G., Koch, C., and Fried, I. (2000). Category-specific visual responses of single neurons in the human medial temporal lobe. *Nature Neuroscience*, 3, 946–953.

Kring, A.M., and Johnson, S.L. (2013). *Abnormal Psychology* (12th ed.). Singapore: Wiley.

Kubrick, S. (1968). *2001: A Space Odyssey*. UK: Stanley Kubrick Productions.

Kühl, H.S., Kalan, A.K., Arandjelovic, M., et al. (2016). Chimpanzee accumulative stone throwing. *Scientific Reports*, 6, 1–8.

Kung, S., Espinel, Z., and Lapid, M.I. (2012). Treatment of nightmares with prazosin: a systematic review. *Mayo Clinic Proceedings*, 87, 890–900.

Kurzweil, R. (2005). *The Singularity is Near*. New York: Penguin Group.

Kurzweil, R., and Grossman, T. (2004). *Fantastic Voyage: Live Long Enough to Live for Ever*. Emmaus, PA: Rodale.

Kurzweil, R., and Grossman, T. (2009). *Transcend*. New York: Rodale.

Kuyken, W., Hayes, R., Barrett, B., et al.(2015). The effectiveness and cost-effectiveness of mindfulness-based cognitive therapy compared with maintenance antidepressant treatment in the prevention of depressive relapse or recurrence (PREVENT): results of a randomised controlled trial. *The Lancet*, 386, 63–73.

La Croix, R., Melzack, R., Smith, D., and Mitchell, N. (1992). Multiple phantom limbs in a child. *Cortex*, 28, 503–507.

LaBerge, D. (1997). Attention, awareness, and the triangular circuit. *Consciousness and Cognition*, 6, 149–181.

LaBerge, S., and Rheingold, H. (1990). *Exploring the World of Lucid Dreaming*. New York: Ballantine.

Lagercrantz, H., and Changeux, J.P. (2009). The emergence of human consciousness: from fetal to neonatal life. *Pediatric Research*, 65, 255–260.

Lamme, V.A.F. (2003). Why visual attention and awareness are different. *Trends in Cognitive Sciences*, 7, 12–18.

Lamme, V.A.F. (2010). How neuroscience will change our view on consciousness. *Cognitive Neuroscience*, 1, 204–220.

Lamme, V.A.F., and Roelfsema, P.R. (2000). The distinct modes of vision offered by feedforward and recurrent processing. *Trends in Neurosciences*, 23, 571–579.

Landry, M., Lifshitz, M., and Raz, A. (2014). Brain correlates of hypnosis: a systematic review and meta-analytic exploration. *Neuroscience and Biobehavioral Reviews*, 81, 75–98.

Lane, T., Duncan, N.W., Cheng, T., and Northoff, G. (2016). The trajectory of the self. *Trends in Cognitive Sciences*, 20, 481–482.

Lang, F. (1927). *Metropolis*. Babelsberg, Germany: UFA.

Langdon R., Connaughton E., and Coltheart M. (2014). The Fregoli delusion: a disorder of person identification and tracking. *Topics in Cognitive Science*, 6, 615–631.

Larsson, M., Larhammarb, D., Fredrikson, M., and Granqvist, P. (2005), Reply to M.A. Persinger and S.A. Koren's response to Granqvist et al. 'Sensed presence and mystical experiences are predicted by suggestibility, not by the application of transcranial weak magnetic fields'. *Neuroscience Letters*, 380, 348–350.

Lau, H., and Rosenthal, D. (2011). Empirical support for higher-order theories of conscious awareness. *Trends in Cognitive Sciences*, 15, 365–373.

Laureys, S. (2005). Science and society: death, unconsciousness and the brain. *Nature Reviews Neuroscience*, 6, 899–909.

Laureys, S., Gosseries, O., and Tononi, G. (2016). *The Neurology of Consciousness*. New York: Academic Press.

Lazar, S.W., Bush, G., Gollub, R.L., Fricchione, G.L., Khalsa, G., and Benson, H. (2000). Functional brain mapping of the relaxation response and meditation. *Neuroreport*, 11, 1581–1585.

LeCun, Y., Bengio, Y., and Hinton, G. (2015). Deep learning. *Nature*, 521, 436–444.

Lee, H., Xie, L., Yu, M., Kang, H., Feng, T., Deane, R., … Benveniste, H. (2015). The effect of body posture on brain glymphatic transport. *Journal of Neuroscience*, 35, 11034–11044.

Lee, M.A., and Shlain, B. (1985). *Acid Dreams*. New York: Grove Press.

Lee, S.J., Ralston, H.J.P., and Drey, E.A. (2005). Fetal pain: a systematic multidisciplinary review of the evidence. *Journal of the American Medical Association*, 294, 947–954.

Lee, U., Mashour, G.A., Kim, S., Noh, G.J., and Choi, B.M. (2009). Propofol induction reduces the capacity for neural information integration: implications for the mechanism of consciousness and general anesthesia. *Consciousness and Cognition*, 18, 56–64.

Le Moan, S., Farup, I., and Blahová, J. (2018). Towards exploiting change blindness for image processing. *Journal of Visual Communication and Image Representation*, 54, 31–38.

Lenggenhager, B., Metzinger, T., and Blanke, O. (2007). Video ergo sum: manipulating bodily self-consciousness. *Science*, 318, 1096–1100.

Levy, S. (1993). *Artificial Life*. Harmondsworth, UK: Penguin Books.

Lewis, P.A. (2013). *The Secret World of Sleep*. New York: Palgrave Macmillan.

Li, K., and Malhotra, P.A. (2015). Spatial neglect. *Practical Neurology*, 15, 333–339.

Li, S., Callaghan, B.L., and Richardson, R. (2014). Infantile amnesia: forgotten but not gone. *Learning & Memory*, 21(3), 135–139.

Libet, B. (2005). *Mind Time: The Temporal Factor in Consciousness*. Harvard, MA: Harvard University Press.

Lifshitz, M., van Elk, M., and Luhrmann, T.M. (2019). Absorption and spiritual experience: a review of evidence and potential mechanisms. *Consciousness and Cognition*, 73(June), 102760.

Lilienfeld, S.O., Sauvigné, K.C., Lynn, S.J., et al.. (2015). Fifty psychological and psychiatric terms to avoid: a list of inaccurate, misleading, misused, ambiguous, and logically confused words and phrases. *Frontiers in Psychology*, 6, 1–15.

Lim, A., Lozano, A.M., Moro, E., Hamani, C., Hutchison, W.D., Dostrovsky, J.O., et al. (2007). Characterization of REM-sleep associated ponto-geniculo-occipital waves in the human pons. *Sleep*, 30, 823–827.

Lima, J. de, Lloyd-Thomas, A.R., Howard, R.F., Sumner, E., and Quinn, T.M. (1996). Infant and neonatal pain: anaesthetists' perceptions and prescribing patterns. *British Medical Journal*, 313, 787.

Lin, L., Faraco, J., Li, R., Kadotani, H., Rogers, W., Lin, X., Qiu, X., de Jong, P.J., Nishino, S., and Mignot, E. (1999). The sleep disorder canine narcolepsy is caused by a mutation in the hypocretin (orexin) receptor 2 gene. *Cell*, 98, 365–376.

Lindstrom, M. (2011). *Brandwashed: Tricks Companies Use to Manipulate Our Minds and Persuade Us to Buy*. London: Kogan Page.

Lipson, H., and Pollack, J.B. (2000). Automatic design and manufacture of robotic lifeforms. *Nature*, 406, 974–978.

Llewellyn, S. (2013). Such stuff as dreams are made on? Elaborative encoding, the ancient art of memory, and the hippocampus. *Behavioral and Brain Sciences*, 36, 589–607.

Llewellyn, S. (2015). Crossing the invisible line: Creative insight, REM dreaming and psychopathology. *Frontiers in Psychology*, 8, 1824.

Llinás, R. (2002). *I of the Vortex: From Neurons to Self*. Cambridge, MA: MIT Books.

Llinás, R., and Ribary, U. (1992). Rostrocaudal scan in human brain: a global characteristic of the 40-Hz response during sensory input. In E. Basar, and T. Bullock (eds.), *Induced Rhythms in the Brain* (pp. 147–154). Boston: Birkhäuser.

Llinás, R., and Ribary, U. (1993). Coherent 40-Hz oscillation characterizes dream state in humans. *Proceedings National Academy Science USA*, 90, 2078–2081.

Llinás, R., and Ribary, U. (2001). Consciousness and the brain. The thalamocortical dialogue in health and disease. *Annals of the New York Academy of Sciences*, 929, 166–175.

Llinás, R., Ribary, U., Contreras, D., and Pedroarena, C. (1998). The neuronal basis for consciousness. *Philosophical Transactions of the Royal Society of London*, 353, 1841–1849.

Loftus, E. (1996). *Eyewitness Testimony*. Harvard: Harvard University Press.

Loftus E.F., and Ketcham, K. (1994). *The Myth of Repressed Memory: False Memories and Allegations of Sexual Abuse*. New York: St Martin's Press.

Loftus, E., and Ketcham, K. (2000). *The Myth of Repressed Memory; False Memory And Allegations of Sexual Abuse*. London: St. Martin's Press.

Logan, J. (1955). *Picnic*. Los Angeles, CA: Columbia Pictures.

Logothetis, N.K. (2006). Vision: a window into consciousness. *Scientific American*, 295, 4–11.

Lou, H.C., Luber, B., Crupain, M., et al. (2004). Parietal cortex and representation of the mental self. *Proceedings of the National Academy of Sciences*, 101, 6827–6832.

Love (1967). *Forever Changes*. Hollywood, CA: Elektra.

Love, D. (2013). *Are You Dreaming? Exploring Lucid Dreams*. Enchanted Loom Publishing.

Lowe, P. (2012). *The Cambridge Declaration on Consciousness*. Cambridge, UK: University of Cambridge.

Lu, J., Sherman, D., Devor, M., and Saper, C.B. (2006). A putative flip–flop switch for control of REM sleep. *Nature*, 441, 589–594.

Lucchelli, F., and Spinnler, H. (2007). The case of lost Wilma: a clinical report of Capgras delusion. *Neurological Sciences*, 28, 188–195.

Luders, E., Kurth, F., Toga, A.W., Narr, K.L., and Gaser, C. (2013). Meditation effects within the hippocampal complex revealed by voxel-based morphometry and cytoarchitectonic probabilistic mapping. *Frontiers in Psychology*, 4, 398.

Ludlow, P., Nagasawa, Y., and Stoljar, D. (2004). *There's Something About Mary*. Cambridge, MA: MIT Press.

Ludwig, A.M. (1966). Altered states of consciousness. *Archives of General Psychiatry*, 15, 225–234.

Lutz, A., Greischar, L.L., Rawlings, N.B., Ricard, M., and Davidson, R.J. (2004). Long-term meditators self-induce high amplitude gamma synchrony during mental practice. *Proceedings of the National Academy of Sciences*, 101, 16369–16373.

Lutz, A., Slagter, H.A., Dunne, J.D., and Davidson, R.J. (2008). Attention regulation and monitoring in meditation. *Trends in Cognitive Science*, 12, 163–169.

Lynn, S.J., Laurence, J.R., and Kirsch, I. (2015). Hypnosis, suggestion, and suggestibility: an integrative model. *American Journal of Clinical Hypnosis*, 57, 314–329.

Lynn, S.J., Rhue, J.W., and Kirsch, I. (eds.), (1993). *Handbook of Clinical Hypnosis*. Washington, DC: American Psychological Association

Machovec, F. (1988). Hypnosis complications, risk factors, and prevention. *American Journal of Clinical Hypnosis*, 31, 40–49.

Mack, A. (2003). Inattentional blindness: looking without seeing. *Current Directions in Psychological Science*, 12, 180–184.

Mack, A., and Rock, I. (1998). *Inattentional Blindness*. Cambridge, MA: MIT Press.

MacLean, P.D. (1990). *The Triune Brain in Evolution: Role in Paleocerebral Functions*. New York: Plenum Press

MacLeod, C.M. (1975). Long-term recognition and recall following directed forgetting. *Journal of Experimental Psychology: Human Learning and Memory*, 1, 271–279.

MacPhail, E. (1998). *The Evolution of Consciousness*. Oxford, UK: Oxford University Press.

Maddula, M., Lutton, S., and Keegan, B. (2009). Anton's syndrome due to cerebrovascular disease: a case report. *Journal of Medical Case Reports*, 3, 9028.

Malcolm, N. (1959). *Dreaming*. London: Routledge and Kegan Paul.

Maltby, J., Day, L., and Macaskall, A. (2013). *Personality, Individual Differences, and Intelligence* (2nd ed.). Cambridge, UK: Pearson.

Manuello, J., Vercelli, U., Nani, A., Costa, T., and Cauda, F. (2016). Mindfulness meditation and consciousness: an integrative neuroscientific perspective. *Consciousness and Cognition*, 40, 67–78.

Maravita, A., and Iriki, A. (2004). Tools for the body (schema). *Trends in Cognitive Sciences*, 8, 79–86.

Marcel, A.J. (1983a). Conscious and unconscious perception: an approach to the relations between phenomenal experience and perceptual processes. *Cognitive Psychology*, 15, 238–300.

Marcel, A.J. (1983b). Conscious and unconscious perception: experiments on visual masking and word recognition. *Cognitive Psychology*, 15, 197–237.

Marchetti, C., and Della Sala, S. (1998). Disentangling the alien and anarchic hand. *Cognitive Neuropsychiatry*, 3, 191–207.

Markel, H. (2011). *An Anatomy of Addiction: Sigmund Freud, William Halstead, and the Miracle Drug Cocaine*. London: Vintage.

Marois, R., and Ivanoff, J. (2005). Capacity limits of information processing in the brain. *Trends in Cognitive Sciences*, 9, 296–305.

Marshall, P. (1990). *Awakenings*. New York: Lasker/Parkes Productions.

Marten, K., and Psarakos, S. (1995). Using self-view television to distinguish between self-examination and social behavior in the bottlenose dolphin (*Tursiops truncatus*). *Conscious and Cognition*, 4, 205–224.

Martin, P. (2003). *Counting Sheep*. London: Flamingo.

Martin, W.R., and Fraser H.F. (1961). A comparative study of physiological and subjective effects of heroin and morphine administered intravenously in postaddicts. *Journal of Pharmacology and Experimental Therapeutics*, 133, 388–399.

Mashour, G.A. (2013). Cognitive unbinding: a neuroscientific paradigm of general anesthesia and related states of unconsciousness. *Neuroscience and Biobehavioral Reviews*, 37, 213–223.

Mashour, G.A. (2014). Top-down mechanisms of anesthetic-induced unconsciousness. *Frontiers in Systems Neuroscience*, 8, 1–10.

Mashour, G.A., and Alkire, M.T. (2013). Evolution of consciousness: phylogeny, ontogeny, and emergence from general anesthesia. *Proceedings of the National Academy of Sciences*, 110 (Supplement 2), 10357–10364.

Mashour, G.A., and Hudetz, A.G. (2018). Neural correlates of unconsciousness in large-scale brain networks. *Trends in Neurosciences*, 41, 150–160.

Massimini, M., Ferrarelli, F., Huber, R., Esser, S. K., Singh, H., and Tononi, G. (2005). Breakdown of cortical effective connectivity during sleep. *Science*, 309, 2228–2232.

Massimini, M., Tononi, G., and Andersen, F. (2018). *Sizing Up Consciousness: Towards an Objective Measure of the Capacity for Experience*. Oxford, UK: Oxford University Press.

Mathis, D.A., and Mozer, M.C. (1995). On the computational utility of consciousness. In G. Tesauro, D.S. Touretzky, and T.K. Leen (eds.), *Advances in Neural Information Processing Systems* (Vol. 7). Cambridge, MA: MIT Press, pp. 10–18.

Mathur, M.B., and Reichling, D.B. (2016). Navigating a social world with robot partners: a quantitative cartography of the Uncanny Valley. *Cognition*, 146, 22–32.

Mattelaer, J.J., and Jilek, W. (2007). Koro? The psychological disappearance of the penis. *The Journal of Sexual Medicine*, 4, 1509–1515.

Mazzoni, G., Venneri, A., McGeown, W.J., and Kirsch, I. (2013). Neuroimaging resolution of the altered state hypothesis. *Cortex*, 49, 400–410.

McAllister, M.M. (2000). Dissociative identity disorder: a literature review. *Journal of Psychiatric and Mental Health Nursing*, 7, 25–33.

McCall, S., Vilensky, J.A., Gilman, S., and Taubenberger, J.K. (2009). The relationship between encephalitis lethargica and influenza: a critical analysis. *Journal of Neurovirology*, 14, 177–185.

McClelland, J.L., and Rumelhart, D.E. (1981). An interactive activation model of context effects in letter perception. Part 1. An account of basic findings. *Psychological Review*, 88, 5, 375–407.

McConkie, G.W., and Currie, C.B. (1996). Visual stability across saccades while viewing complex pictures. *Journal of Experimental Psychology: Human Perception and Performance*, 22, 563–581.

McGeown, W.J., Mazzoni, G., Venneri, A., and Kirsch, I. (2009). Hypnotic induction decreases anterior default mode activity. *Consciousness and Cognition*, 18, 848–855.

McGinn, C. (1989). Can we solve the mind-body problem? *Mind*, 98, 349–366.

McGinn, C. (2000). *The Mysterious Flame: Conscious Minds in a Material World*. New York: Basic Books.

McGreal, C. (2018). *American Overdose: The Opioid Tragedy in Three Acts*. London: Guardian Faber.

McGregor, D.E.G. (1964a). *The Dream World Of Dion McGregor*. London: Decca.

McGregor, D.E.G. (1964b). *The Dream World Of Dion McGregor*. New York: Bernard Geis Associates.

McNally, R.J. (2007). Dispelling confusion about traumatic dissociative amnesia. *Mayo Clinical Proceedings*, 82, 1083–1087.

Mele, A.R. (2014). *Free: Why Science Hasn't Disproved Free Will*. Oxford, UK: Oxford University Press.

Melzack, R., and Wall, P.D. (1965). Pain mechanisms: a new theory. *Science*, 150, 971–979.

Menzel, E., Savage-Rumbaugh, E.S., and Lawson, J. (1985). Chimpanzee (*Pan troglodytes*) spatial problem solving with the use of mirrors and televised equivalents of mirrors. *Journal of Comparative Psychology*, 99, 211–217.

Merikle, P.M., and Cheesman, J. (1987). Current status of research on subliminal perception. *Advances in Consumer Research*, 14, 298–302.

Metzinger, T. (2004). *Being No One: The Self-Model Theory of Subjectivity*. Cambridge, MA: MIT Press.

Metzinger, T. (2010). *The Ego Tunnel: The Science of the Mind and the Myth of the Self* (reprint edition). New York: Basic Books.

Metzner, R. (1998). Hallucinogenic drugs and plants in psychotherapy and shamanism. *Journal of Psychoactive Drugs*, 30, 333–341.

Middlebrooks, P.G., and Sommer, M.A. (2011). Metacognition in monkeys during an oculomotor task. *Journal of Experimental Psychology: Learning, Memory, and Cognition*, 27, 325–337.

Mele, A. (2010). *Effective Intentions: The Power of Conscious Will*. Oxford, UK: Oxford University Press.

Milaniak, I., and Widom, C.S. (2015). Does child abuse and neglect increase risk for perpetration of violence inside and outside the home? *Psychological Violence*, 5, 246–255.

Miller, R.D., Ericsson, L.I., Fleisher, L.A., Wiener-Kronish, J.P., Cohen, N.H., and Young, W.L. (2014). *Anesthesia* (8th ed.). Amsterdam: Elsevier.

Milner, P.M. (1974). A model for visual shape recognition. *Psychological Review*, 81, 521–535.

Milton, J., and Wiseman, R. (2001). Does psi exist? Reply to Storm and Ertel (2001). *Psychological Bulletin*, 127, 434–438.

Minh, A., Matheson, F.I., Daoud, N., et al. (2013). Linking childhood and adult criminality: Using a life course framework to examine childhood abuse and neglect, substance use and adult partner violence. *International Journal of Environmental Research and Public Health*, 10, 5470–5489.

Mithen, S.J. (1996). *The Prehistory of the Mind: A Search for the Origins of Art, Religion, and Science*. London: Thames and Hudson.

Mithen, S.J. (2005). *The Singing Neanderthals: The Origins of Music, Language, Mind and Body*. London: Weidenfeld and Nicolson, London.

Mittner, M., Hawkins, G.E., Boekel, W., and Forstmann, B.U. (2016). A neural model of mind wandering. *Trends in Cognitive Sciences*, 20, 570–578.

Miyazaki, M., Hirashima, M., and Nozaki, D. (2010). The 'cutaneous rabbit' hopping out of the body. *Journal of Neuroscience*, 30, 1856–1860.

Mobbs, D. (2012). Response to Greyson et al.: there is nothing paranormal about near-death experiences. *Trends in Cognitive Sciences*, 16, 446.

Mobbs, D., and Watt, C. (2011). There is nothing paranormal about near-death experiences: how neuroscience can explain seeing bright lights, meeting the dead, or being convinced you are one of them. *Trends in Cognitive Sciences*, 15, 447–449.

Modinos, G., Ormel, J., and Aleman, A. (2009). Activation of anterior insula during self-reflection. *PLoS ONE*, 4, e4618.

Mole, C. (2008). Attention in the absence of consciousness? *Trends in Cognitive Sciences*, 12, 44.

Møller, A. (2014). *Pain, Its Anatomy, Physiology, and Treatment* (2nd ed.). Scotts Valley, CA: CreateSpace.

Montemayor, C., and Haladjian, H.H. (2015). *Consciousness, Attention, and Conscious Attention*. Cambridge, MA: MIT Press.

Moody, R. (1975). *Life after Life: The Investigation of a Phenomenon: Survival of Bodily Death*. San Francisco, CA: Harper.

Moorcroft, W.H. (2013). *Understanding Sleep and Dreaming* (2nd ed.). New York: Springer.

Moore, T.M., Scarpa, A., and Raine, A. (2002). A meta-analysis of serotonin metabolite 5-HIAA and antisocial behavior. *Aggressive Behavior*, 28, 299–316.

Morcom, A.M., and Fletcher, P.C. (2007), Does the brain have a baseline? Why we should be resisting a rest. *NeuroImage*, 37, 1073–1082.

Morin, A., and Hamper, B. (2012). Self-reflection and the inner voice: activation of the left inferior frontal gyrus during perceptual and conceptual self-referential thinking. *The Open Neuroimaging Journal*, 2012, 6, 78–89.

Morin, C.M., Espie, C.A., and Akerstedt, T. (2012). *The Oxford Handbook of Sleep and Sleep Disorders*. Oxford, UK: Oxford University Press.

Moro, V., Pernigo, S., Zapparoli, P., Cordioli, Z., and Aglioti, S.M. (2011). Phenomenology and neural correlates of implicit and emergent motor awareness in patients with anosognosia for hemiplegia. *Behavioural Brain Research*, 225, 259–269.

Morrison, E., and Lamont, F. (1911). *An Adventure*. London: Macmillan.

Mortensen, H.S., Pakkenberg, B., Dam, M., et al. (2014). Quantitative relationships in delphinid neocortex. *Frontiers in Neuroanatomy*, 8, 1–10.

Moruzzi, G., and Magoun, H.W. (1949). Brain stem reticular formation and activation of the EEG. *Electroencephalography and Clinical Neurophysiology*, 1, 455–473.

Moseley, P., Fernyhough, C., and Ellison, A. (2013). Auditory verbal hallucinations as atypical inner speech monitoring, and the potential of neurostimulation as a treatment option. *Neuroscience and Biobehavioral Reviews*, 37, 2794–2805.

Moss, P.D., and McEvedy, C.P. (1966). An epidemic of over breathing among schoolgirls. *British Medical Journal*, 2, 1295–1300.

Mudrik, L., Faivre, N., and Koch, C. (2014). Information integration without awareness. *Trends in Cognitive Sciences*, 18, 488–496.

Murphy M.J., et al. (2011). Propofol anesthesia and sleep: a high-density EEG study. *Sleep*, 34, 283–291.

Myin-Germeys, I., Oorschot, M., Collip, D., et al. (2009). Experience sampling research in psychopathology: opening the black box of daily life. *Psychological Medicine*, 39, 1533–1547.

Naccache, L. (2018). Why and how access consciousness can account for phenomenal consciousness. *Philosophical Transactions of the Royal Society B: Biological Sciences*, 373, 1–9.

Nagel, T. (1974). What is it like to be a bat? *The Philosophical Review*, 83, 435–450.

Nagel, T. (1979). *Mortal Questions*. Cambridge, UK: Cambridge University Press.

Nakagaki, T., Yamada, H., and Tóth, Á. (2000). Maze-solving by an amoeboid organism. *Nature*, 407, 470.

Nagasawa, Y. (2009). The knowledge argument. In T. Bayne, A. Cleeremans, and P. Wilken, *The Oxford Companion to Consciousness*. Oxford, UK: Oxford University Press, pp.395–397.

Nash, M.R., and Barnier, A.J. (2008). *The Oxford Handbook of Hypnosis: Theory, Research, and Practice*. Oxford, UK: Oxford University Press.

Navon, D., and Gopher, D. (1979). On the economy of the human-processing system. *Psychological Review*, 86, 214–255.

Nelson, A.L., Barlow, G.J., and Doitsidis, L. (2009). Fitness functions in evolutionary robotics: A survey and analysis. *Robotics and Autonomous Systems*, 57, 345–370.

Newberg, A., and Waldman, M.R. (2009). *How God Changes Your Brain*. New York: Ballantine Books.

Newberg, A., and Waldman, M.R. (2016). *How Enlightenment Changes Your Brain*. London: Hay House.

Newman, J., and Baars, B.J. (1993). A neural attentional model for access to consciousness: a global workspace perspective. *Concepts in Neuroscience*, 4, 255-290.

New York Times (2009). When Sartre talked to crabs (it was Mescaline). *The New York Times*. 14 November.

Nicholls, G. (2012). *Navigating the Out-of-Body Experience: Radical New Techniques*. Woodbury, MN: Llewellyn Publications.

Nichols, D.E. (2017). N,N-dimethyltryptamine and the pineal gland: Separating fact from myth. *Journal of Psychopharmacology*, 32, 30-36.

Nielsen, T., and Levin, R. (2007). Nightmares: a new neurocognitive model. *Sleep Medicine Reviews*, 11, 295-310.

Nielsen, T.A., Kuiken, D., Alain, G., Stenstrom, P., and Powell, R.A. (2004). Immediate and delayed incorporations of events into dreams: Further replication and implications for dream function. *Journal of Sleep Research*, 13, 327-336.

Nisbett, R.E., and Wilson, T.D. (1977). Telling more than we can know: verbal reports on mental processes. *Psychological Review*, 84, 231-259.

Noë, A. (ed.) (2002). *Is the Visual World a Grand Illusion?* Charlottesville, VA: Imprint Academic.

Noë, A. (2010). *Out of Our Heads: Why You Are Not Your Brain, and Other Lessons from the Biology of Consciousness*. New York: Hill and Wang.

Nolfi, S., Floreano, D., and Arkin, R.C. (2004). *Evolutionary Robotics: The Biology, Intelligence, and Technology of Self-Organizing Machines*. Cambridge, MA: MIT Press.

Norman, K.A., Polyn, S.M., Detre, G.J., and Haxby, J.V. (2006). Beyond mind-reading: multi-voxel pattern analysis of fMRI data. *Trends in Cognitive Sciences*, 10, 424-430.

Northoff, G., and Bermpohl, F. (2004). Cortical midline structures and the self. *Trends in Cognitive Sciences*, 8, 102e107, 200

Northoff, G., et al. (2006). Self-referential processing in our brain: a meta-analysis of imaging studies on the self. *Neuroimage*, 31, 440-457.

Nosek, B.A., Smyth, F.L., Sriram, N., et al. (2009). National differences in gender–science stereotypes predict national sex differences in science and math achievement. *Proceedings of the National Academy of Science USA*, 106, 1-5.

Nozick, R. (1981). *Philosophical Explanations*. Harvard, MA: Harvard University Press.

Nutt, D. (2012). *Drugs Without the Hot Air*. Cambridge, UK: UIT Cambridge Ltd.

Nyberg, L., Kim, A.S.N., Habib, R., Levine, B., and Tulving, E. (2010). Consciousness of subjective time in the brain. *Proceedings of the National Academy of Sciences USA*, 107, 22356-22359.

Oakley, D.A., and Halligan, P.W. (2010). Psychophysiological foundations of hypnosis and suggestion. In S.J. Lynn, J.W. Rhue, and I. Kirsch (eds.), *Handbook of Clinical Hypnosis*. Washington, DC: American Psychological Association, pp. 79-177.

Oakley, D.A., and Halligan, P.W. (2013). Hypnotic suggestion: opportunities for cognitive neuroscience. *Nature Reviews Neuroscience*, 14, 565-576.

O'Connell, M. (2017). *To Be a Machine*. London: Granta.

O'Regan, J.K., and Noë, A. (2001). A sensorimotor account of vision and visual consciousness. *Behavioral and Brain Sciences*, 24, 939-1031.

Okai, T., Kozuma, S., Shinozuka, N., Kuwabara, Y., and Mizuno, M. (1992). A study on the development of sleep-wakefulness cycle in the human fetus. *Early Human Development*, 29, 391-396.

Olesen, J., Burstein, R., Ashina, M., and Tfelt-Hansen, P. (2009). Origin of pain in migraine: evidence for peripheral sensitisation. *The Lancet Neurology*, 8, 679-690.

Olkowicz, S., Kocourek, M., Lučan, R.K., et al. (2016). Birds have primate-like numbers of neurons in the forebrain. *Proceedings of the National Academy of Sciences*, 113, 7255-7260.

Olness, K., MacDonald, J.T., and Uden, D.L. (1987). Comparison of self-hypnosis and propranolol in the treatment of juvenile classic migraine. *Pediatrics*, 79, 593-597.

Oppenheim, G.M., and Dell, G.S. (2008). Inner speech slips exhibit lexical bias, but not the phonemic similarity effect. *Cognition*, 106, 528-537.

Oppenheim, G.M., and Dell, G.S. (2010). Motor movement matters: the flexible abstractness of inner speech. *Memory and Cognition*, 38, 1147-1160.

Orwell, G. (1949). *Nineteen Eighty-Four*. London: Secker & Warburg.

REFERENCES

Osvath, M., and Karvonen, E. (2012). Spontaneous innovation for future deception in a male chimpanzee. *PLoS ONE*, 7, 1–8.

Overgaard, M., and Fazekas, P. (2016). Can no-report paradigms extract true correlates of consciousness? *Trends in Cognitive Sciences*, 20, 241–242.

Owen, A. (2018). *Into the Grey Zone*. London: Guardian Books.

Packard, V., and Miller, M.C. (2007). *The Hidden Persuaders* (New edition). New York: Ig Press.

Padzer, L. (1980). *Michelle Remembers*. New York: Pocket Books.

Pagel, J.F. (2000). Nightmares and disorders of dreaming. *American Family Physician*, 61, 2037–2042.

Pahnke, W.N. (1963). *Drugs and mysticism: An analysis of the relationship between psychedelic drugs and the mystical consciousness*. PhD thesis presented to the Committee on Higher Degrees in History and Philosophy of Religion, Harvard University.

Pahnke, W.N. (1966). Drugs and mysticism. *International Journal of Parapsychology*, 8, 295–315.

Paivio, A. (1986). *Mental Representations: A Dual Coding Approach*. New York: Oxford University Press.

Palmer, J. (1997). The challenge of experimenter psi. *European Journal of Parapsychology*, 13, 110–125

Pandolfo, M. (2011). Genetics of epilepsy. *Seminars in Neurology*, 31, 506–518.

Parfit, D. (1984). *Reasons and Persons*. Oxford, UK: Oxford University Press.

Parfit, D. (1987). Divided minds and the nature of persons. In C. Blakemore and S. Greenfield (eds.), *Mindwaves: Thoughts on Intelligence, Identity and Consciousness*. Oxford, UK: B. Blackwell, pp. 19–28.

Parks, T. (2018). *Out of my Head: On the Trail of Consciousness*. London: Harvill Secker.

Parnia, S., Spearpoint, K., de Vos, G., Fenwick, P., Goldberg, D., Yang, J., et al. (2014). AWARE – AWAreness during REsuscitation: A prospective study. *Resuscitation*, 85, 1799–1805.

Parnia, S., Waller, D.G., Yeates, R., and Fenwick P. (2001). A qualitative and quantitative study of the incidence, features and aetiology of near death experiences in cardiac arrest survivors. *Resuscitation*, 48, 149–156.

Pashler, H. (1994). Dual-task interference in simple tasks: data and theory. *Psychological Bulletin*, 116, 220–244.

Passie, T., Halpern, J.H., Stichtenoth, D.O., Emrich, H.M., and Hintzen, A. (2008). The pharmacology of lysergic acid diethylamide: a review. *CNS Neuroscience and Therapeutics*, 14, 295–314.

Patel, G.M., Patel, G.C., Patel, R.B., Patel, J.K., and Patel, M. (2006). Nanorobot: a versatile tool in nanomedicine, *Journal of Drug Targeting*, 14, 63–67.

Patru, M.C., and Reser, D.H. (2015), A new perspective on delusional states: evidence for claustrum involvement. *Frontiers in Psychiatry*, 6, 158.

Payne, B.K., Brown-Iannuzzi, J.L., and Loersch, C. (2016). Replicable effects of primes on human behavior. *Journal of Experimental Psychology: General*, 145, 1269–1279.

Payne, J.D., and Nadel, L. (2004). Sleep, dreams, and memory consolidation: the role of the stress hormone cortisol. *Learning & Memory*, 11, 671–678.

Pedersen, M.G., Motensen, P.B., Norgaard-Pedersen, B., and Postolache, T.T. (2012). *Toxoplasma gondii* infection and self-directed violence in mothers. *Archives of General Psychiatry*, 69, 1123–1130.

Penrose, R. (1989). *The Emperor's New Mind: Concerning Computers, Minds, and the Laws of Physics*. Oxford, UK: Oxford University Press.

Penrose, R. (1994). *Shadows of the Mind: A Search for the Missing Science of Consciousness*. London: Vintage Books.

Penrose, R. (1997). *The Large, the Small, and the Human Mind*. Cambridge, UK: University Press.

Pepperberg, I. (2013). *Alex and Me: How a Scientist and a Parrot Discovered a Hidden World of Animal Intelligence – and Formed a Deep Bond in the Process*. London: Scribe Press.

Persinger, M.A. (1987). *Neuropsychological Bases of God Beliefs*. New York: Prager Publishers.

Persinger, M.A. (2001). The neuropsychiatry of paranormal experiences. *The Journal of Neuropsychiatry and Clinical Neurosciences*, 13, 515–524.

Pert, C.B., and Snyder, S.H. (1973). Opiate receptor: demonstration in nervous tissue. *Science*, 179, 1011–1014.

Petkova, V.I., and Ehrsson, H.H. (2008). If I were you: perceptual illusion of body swapping. *PLoS ONE*, 3, 0003832.

Pfeiffer, B. E. (2018). The content of hippocampal 'replay.' *Hippocampus*, October 2017, 1–13.

Philippi, C.L., Feinstein, J.S., and Khalsa, S.S., et al. (2012). Preserved self-awareness following extensive bilateral brain damage to the insula, anterior cingulate, and medial prefrontal cortices. *PLoS ONE*, 7(8).

Piaget, J. (1990). *The Child's Conception of the World*. New York: Littlefield Adams.

Picchioni, D., Duyn, J.H., and Horovitz, S.G. (2013). Sleep and the functional connectome. *NeuroImage*, 80, 387–396.

Pigliucci, M. (2018). *Nonsense on Stilts* (2nd ed.). Chicago, IL: University of Chicago Press.

Pinel, J.P.J., and Barnes, S.J. (2017). *Biological Psychology* (10th ed.). Harlow, UK: Pearson.

Pinto, Y., Neville, D.A., Otten, M., et al. (2017). Split brain: divided perception but undivided consciousness. *Brain*, 140, 1231–1237.

Pitts, M.A., Lutsyshyna, L.A., and Hillyard, S.A. (2018). The relationship between attention and consciousness: an expanded taxonomy and implications for no-report paradigms. *Philosophical Transactions of the Royal Society B: Biological Sciences*, 373, 1–12.

Playfair, G.L. (1980). *This House is Haunted: The True Story of a Poltergeist*. New York: Stein and Day.

Pollan M. (2019). *How to Change Your Mind: The New Science of Psychedelics*. London: Penguin.

Pomara, C., Cassano, T., D'Errico, S., et al. (2012). Data available on the extent of cocaine use and dependence: biochemistry, pharmacologic effects and global burden of disease of cocaine abusers. *Current Medicinal Chemistry*, 19, 5647–5657.

Popper, K. (1959). *The Logic of Scientific Discovery*. Oxford, UK: Routledge.

Portas, C.M., Rees, G., Howseman, A.M., et al. (1998). A specific role for the thalamus in mediating the interaction of attention and arousal in humans. *Journal of Neuroscience*, 18, 8979–8989.

Posner, M.I. (1992). Attention as a cognitive and neural system. *Current Directions in Psychological Science*, 1, 11–14.

Povinelli, D.J. (1989). Failure to find self-recognition in Asian elephants (*Elephas maximus*) in contrast to their use of mirror cues to discover hidden food. *Journal of Comparative Psychology*, 103, 122–131.

Pratkanis, A.R., Eskenazi, J., and Greenwald, A.G. (1994). What you expect is what you believe (but not necessarily what you get): a test of the effectiveness of subliminal self-help audiotapes. *Basic and Applied Social Psychology*, 15, 251–276.

Premack, D., and Woodruff, G. (1978). Does the chimpanzee have a theory of mind? *Behavioural and Brain Sciences*, 1, 515–526

Price, D.D. (2000). Psychological and neural mechanisms of the affective dimension of pain. *Science*. 288, 1769–1772.

Prigatano, G.P., and Schacter, D.L. (1991). *Awareness of Deficit After Brain Injury: Clinical and Theoretical Issues*. Oxford, UK: Oxford University Press.

Prior, H., Schwarz, A., Güntürkün, O., and De Waal, F. (2008). Mirror-induced behavior in the magpie (*Pica pica*): evidence of self-recognition. *PLoS Biology*, 6, e202.

Putnam, H. (1981). *Reason, Truth and History*. Cambridge, UK: Cambridge University Press.

Putnam, H. (1988). *Representation and Reality*. Cambridge, MA: MIT Press.

Pylyshyn, Z.W. (1973). What the mind's eye tells the mind's brain: a critique of mental imagery. *Psychological Bulletin*, 80, 1–25.

Pylyshyn, Z.W. (2002). Mental imagery: in search of a theory. *Behavioral and Brain Sciences*, 25, 157–237.

Qaseem, A., Kansagara, D., Forciea, M.A., Cooke, M., Denberg, T.D., Barry, M.J., … Wilt, T. (2016). Management of chronic insomnia disorder in adults: a clinical practice guideline from the American college of physicians. *Annals of Internal Medicine*, 165, 125–133.

Quiroga, R.Q., Kreiman, G., Koch, C., and Fried, I. (2007). Sparse but not 'grandmother-cell' coding in the medial temporal lobe. *Trends in Cognitive Sciences*, 12, 87–91.

Radin, D. (2009). *The Conscious Universe: The Scientific Truth of Psychic Phenomena*. New York: HarperOne.

Raichle, M.E. (1998). Behind the scenes of functional brain imaging: a historical and physiological perspective. *Proceedings of the National Academy of Sciences of the USA*, 95, 765–772.

Raichle, M.E. (2010). The brain's dark energy. *Scientific American*, 302, 44–49.

Raichle, M.E., MacLeod, A.M., Snyder, A.Z., et al. (2001). Inaugural article: a default mode of brain function. *Proceedings of the National Academy of Sciences*, 98, 676–682.

Raimo, E.B., Roemer, R.A., Moster, M., and Shan, Y. (1999). Alcohol-induced depersonalization. *Biological Psychiatry*, 45, 1523–1526.

Rainville, P., Hofbauer, R.K., Paus, T., et al. (1999). Cerebral Mechanisms of Hypnotic Induction. *Journal of Cognitive Neuroscience*, 11, 110–125.

Rainville, P., Hofbauer, R.K., Catherine Bushnell, M., Duncan, G.H., and Price, D.D. (2002). Hypnosis modulates activity in brain structures involved in the regulation of consciousness. *Journal of Cognitive Neuroscience*, 14, 887–901.

Ramachandran, V.S. (1998). *Phantoms in the Brain*. London: Fourth Estate.

Ramachandran, V.S. (2012). *The Tell-Tale Brain*. London: Windmill Books.

Ramachandran, V.S., and Hubbard, E.M. (2001a). Psychophysical investigations into the neural basis of synaesthesia. *Proceedings of the Royal Society, Series B Biological Sciences*, 268, 979–983.

Ramachandran V.S., and Hubbard E.M. (2001b). Synaesthesia: a window into perception, thought and language. *Journal of Consciousness Studies*, 8, 3–34.

Ramachandran, V. S., Rogers-Ramachandran, D., and Stewart, M. (1992). Perceptual correlates of massive cortical reorganization. *Science*, 258, 7–8.

Ramachandran, V.S., Rogers-Ramachandran, D., and Cobb, S. (1995). Touching the phantom limb. *Nature*, 377, 489–490.

Ramakrishnan, K., and Scheid, D.C. (2007). Treatment options for insomnia. *American Family Physician*, 76, 517–526.

Rampil, I. (1994). Anesthetic potency is not altered after hypothermic spinal cord transection in rats. *Anesthesiology*, 80, 606–610.

Ramis, H. (1993). *Groundhog Day*. Los Angeles, CA: Columbia Pictures.

Randall, D.K. (2012). *Dreamland: Adventures in the Strange World of Sleep*. New York: Norton.

Rankin, A.M., and Philip, P.J. (1963). An epidemic of laughing in the Bukoba district of Tanganyika. *Central African Medical Journal*, 9, 167–170.

Reardon, S. (2017). A giant neuron found wrapped around entire mouse brain. *Nature*, 543, 14–15.

Reber, T.P., Faber, J., Niediek, J., et al. (2017). Single-neuron correlates of conscious perception in the human medial temporal lobe. *Current Biology*, 27, 2991–2998.

Rechtschaffen, A., and Bergmann, B.M. (1995). Sleep deprivation in the rat by the disk-over-water method. *Behavioural Brain Research*, 69, 55–63.

Reed, L. (1967). *Heroin*. Velvet Underground. Velvet Underground and Nico. Hollywood, CA: TTG Studios.

Regalado, A. (2014). *What will it take for computers to be conscious*. MIT Technology Review, 2 October.

Reggia, J., Huang, D., and Katz, G. (2015). Beliefs concerning the nature of consciousness. *Journal of Consciousness Studies*, 22, 146–171.

Reggia, J.A., Katz, G., and Huang, D.W. (2016). What are the computational correlates of consciousness? *Biologically Inspired Cognitive Architectures*, 17, 101–113.

Reinders, A.A., Nijenhuis, E.R., Quak, J., et al. (2006). Psychobiological characteristics of dissociative identity disorder: a symptom provocation study. *Biological Psychiatry*, 60, 730–740.

Reiss, D., and Marino, L. (2001). Mirror self-recognition in the bottlenose dolphin: a case of cognitive convergence. *Proceedings of the National Academy of Sciences*, 98, 5937–5942.

Rendu, W., Beauval, C., Crevecoeur, I., et al. (2016). Let the dead speak ... comments on Dibble et al.'s reply to 'Evidence supporting an intentional burial at La Chapelle-aux-Saints'. *Journal of Archaeological Science*, 69, 12–20.

Renfrew, C. (2007). *Prehistory: The Making of the Human Mind*. London: Phoenix.

Rensink, R.A., O'Regan, J.K., and Clark, J. (1997). To see or not to see: the need for attention to perceive changes in scenes. *Psychological Science*, 8, 368–373.

Revonsuo, A. (2000). The reinterpretation of dreams: an evolutionary hypothesis of the function of dreaming. *Behavioral and Brain Sciences*, 23, 877–901.

Revonsuo, A., Kallio, S., and Sikka, P. (2009). What is an altered state of consciousness? *Philosophical Psychology*, 22, 187–204.

Rey, G. (1997). *Contemporary Philosophy of Mind*. London: Wiley.

Reynolds, C. (1987). Flocks, herds, and schools: a distributed behavioral model. *Computer Graphics*, 21, 25–34.

Rhine, J.B. (1934). *Extrasensory Perception*. Boston, MA: Boston Society for Psychical Research.

Rhine, J.B. (1937). *New Frontiers of the Mind*. New York: Farrar and Rinehart.

Rieber, R.W. (2006). *The Bifurcation of the Self: The History and Theory of Dissociation and its Disorders*. Berlin: Springer.

Riemann, D., Berger, M., and Voderholzer, U. (2001). Sleep and depression – results from psychobiological studies: an overview. *Biological Psychology*, 57, 67–103.

Ring, K. (1980). *Life at Death: A Scientific Investigation of the Near-Death Experience*. New York: Coward, McCann, and Geoghegan.

Ritchie, S.J., Wiseman, R., and French, C.C. (2012). Failing the future: three unsuccessful attempts to replicate Bem's 'retroactive facilitation of recall' effect. *PLoS ONE*, 7(3), 1–5.

Rizzolatti, G., and Sinigaglia, C. (2007). *Mirrors in the Brain: How Our Minds Share Actions and Emotions*. Oxford, UK: Oxford University Press.

Roddenberry, G. (1987–1994). *Star Trek: The Next Generation*. Los Angeles, CA: Paramount Domestic Television.

Rohde, M., Luca, M., &and Ernst, M. O. (2011). The rubber hand illusion: Feeling of ownership and proprioceptive drift Do not go hand in hand. *PLoS ONE*, 6(6).

Rose, J.D., Arlinghaus, R., Cooke, S.J., et al. (2014). Can fish really feel pain? *Fish and Fisheries*, 15, 97–133.

Rosenthal, D.M. (2006). *Consciousness and Mind*. Oxford, UK: Oxford University Press.

Rowson, J. (2019). *The Moves that Matter: A Chess Grandmaster on the Game of Life*. London: Bloomsbury.

Royal College of the Physicians of London (1995). Criteria for the diagnosis of brain stem death. *Journal of the Royal College of the Physicians of London*, 29, 381–382.

Ruby, P., Blochet, C., Eichenlaub, J.B., et al. (2013). Alpha reactivity to first names differs in subjects with high and low dream recall frequency. *Frontiers in Psychology*, 4, 1–9.

Russell, B. (1910). Knowledge by acquaintance and knowledge by description. *Proceedings of the Aristotelian Society*, 11, 108–128.

Russell, B. (1912). *The Problems of Philosophy*. Oxford, UK: Oxford University Press.

Russell, I.F., and Wang, M. (2001). Absence of memory for intra-operative information during surgery with total intravenous anaesthesia. *British Journal of Anaesthesia*, 86, 196–202.

Saadah, E.S.M., and Melzak, R. (1994). Phantom limb experiences in congenital limb-deficient adults. *Cortex*, 30, 479–485.

Sabah, M., Mulcahy, J., and Zeman, A. (2012). Herpes simplex encephalitis. *British Medical Journal*, 344(Jun06 2), e3166–e3166.

Sacks, O. (1970). *Migraine*. New York: Vintage Books.

Sacks, O. (1973). *Awakenings*. London: Duckworth.

Sacks, O. (1985). *The Man who Mistook his Wife for a Hat*. London: Duckworth.

Sacks, O. (2007). *Musicophilia: Tales of Music and the Brain*. London: Picador.

Sadler, M., and Regan, N. (2019). *Game Changer: AlphaZero's Groundbreaking Chess Strategies and the Promise of AI*. Netherlands: New in Chess.

Sandberg, A. (2014). Ethics of brain emulations, *Journal of Experimental and Theoretical Artificial Intelligence*, 26, 439–457

Sandberg, A., and Bostrom, N. (2008). *Whole Brain Emulation: A Roadmap*. Technical Report 2008-03. Oxford, UK: University of Oxford.

Sarbey, B. (2016). Definitions of death: brain death and what matters in a person. *Journal of Law and the Biosciences*, 3, 743–752.

Sarbin, T.R., and Coe, W.C. (1972). *Hypnosis: A Social Psychological Analysis of Influence Communication*. New York: Holt, Rinehart and Winston.

Saroka, K., Mulligan, B.P., Murphy, T.R., and Persinger, M.A. (2010). Experimental elicitation of an out of body experience and concomitant cross-hemispheric electroencephalographic coherence. *NeuroQuantology*, 8, 466–477.

Sartori, P. (2008). *The Near-Death Experiences of Hospitalised Intensive Care Patients: A Five Year Clinical Study*. New York: Edwin Mellen Press.

REFERENCES

Sartre, J-.P. (1929). *La Nausée [Nausea]*. Paris: Éditions Gallimard.

Savage-Rumbaugh, S. (1996). *Kanzi: The Ape at the Brink of the Human Mind*. New York: Wiley.

Schacter, D.L. (1976). The hypnagogic state: a critical review of the literature. *Psychological Bulletin*, 83, 452–481.

Schacter, D.L., Addis, D.R., and Buckner, R.L. (2007). Remembering the past to imagine the future: the prospective brain. *Nature Reviews Neuroscience*, 8, 657–661.

Schick, T., and Vaughn, L. (2019). *How to Think About Weird Things*. New York: McGraw-Hill.

Schiff, N.D. (2008). Central thalamic contributions to arousal regulation and neurological disorders of consciousness. *Annals of the New York Academy of Sciences*, 1129, 105–118.

Schjoedt, U. (2009). The religious brain: a general introduction to the experimental neuroscience of religion. *Method and Theory in the Study of Religion*, 21, 310–339.

Schmeidler, G.R. (1952). Personal values and ESP scores. *Journal of Abnormal and Social Psychology*, 47, 757–761.

Schmeidler, G.R. (1997). Psi-conducive experimenters and psi-permissive ones. *European Journal of Parapsychology*, 13, 83–94.

Schnall, S., Bentos, J., and Harvey, S. (2008). With a clean conscience: cleanliness reduces the severity of moral judgments, *Psychological Science*, 19, 1219–1222.

Schneider, S., and Velman, M. (2017). *The Blackwell Companion to Consciousness*. Oxford, UK: Blackwell.

Schneider, W., and Shiffrin, R.M. (1977). Controlled and automatic human information processing: 1. Detection, search, and attention. *Psychological Review*, 84, 1–66.

Schredl, M. (2008). Dream recall frequency in a representative German sample. *Perceptual and Motor Skills*, 106, 699–702.

Schredl, M. (2011). Dream research in schizophrenia: methodological issues and a dimensional approach. *Consciousness and Cognition*, 20, 1036–1041.

Schulz, H. (2008). Rethinking sleep analysis. *Journal of Clinical Sleep Medicine*, 4, 99–103.

Schurger, A., Mylopoulos, M., and Rosenthal, D. (2016). Neural antecedents of spontaneous voluntary movement: a new perspective. *Trends in Cognitive Sciences*, 20, 77–79.

Schwartz, J.M. (2017). *Brain Lock* (20th anniversary edition). New York: Harper Perennial.

Scoboria, A., Wade, K.A., Lindsay, D.S., Azad, J., Strange, D., Ost, J., et al. (2017). A mega-analysis of memory reports from eight peer-reviewed false memory implantation studies. *Memory*, 25, 146–163.

Scott, N., Hanstock, T.L., and Thornton, C. (2014). Dysfunctional self-talk associated with eating disorder severity and symptomatology. *Journal of Eating Disorders*, 2, 1–11.

Scott, R. (1982). *Blade Runner*. Burbank, CA: Warner Bros.

Scoville, W.B., and Milner, B. (1957). Loss of recent memory after bilateral hippocampal lesions. *Journal of Neurology, Neurosurgery and Psychiatry*, 20, 11–21.

Seager, W. (2016). *Theories of Consciousness* (2nd ed.). London: Routledge.

Seager, W., and Allen-Hermanson, S. (2015). Panpsychism. *The Stanford Encyclopedia of Philosophy* (Fall 2015 Edition), Edward N. Zalta (ed.).

Searle, J.R. (1980). Minds, brains and programs. *Behavioral and Brain Sciences*, 3, 417–457.

Searle, J.R. (1997). *The Mystery of Consciousness*. New York: not, *The New York Review of Books*.

Searle, J.R. (2004). *Mind: A Brief Introduction*. New York: Oxford University Press.

Searle, J.R. (2014). What your computer can't know. *The New York Review of Books*, 9 October 2014, p. 54.

Sebel P.S., Bowdle, T.A., Ghoneim M.M., et al. (2004). The incidence of awareness during anesthesia: a multicenter United States study. *Anesthesia and Analgesia*, 99, 833–839.

Semba, K. (1993). Aminergic and cholinergic afferents to REM sleep induction regions of the pontine reticular formation in the rat. *Journal of Comparative Neurology*, 330, 543–556.

Sergent, C., and Dehaene, S. (2004). Is consciousness a gradual phenomenon? Evidence for an all-or-none bifurcation during the attentional blink. *Psychological Science*, 15, 720–728.

Shallice, T., Burgess, P., and Robertson, I. (1996). The domain of supervisory processes and temporal organisation of behaviour. *Philosophical Transactions of the Royal Society, Series B*, 351, 1405–1412.

Shallice, T., and Cooper, R.P. (2011). *The Organisation of Mind*. Oxford, UK: Oxford University Press.

Shapiro, L. (2017). *The Routledge Handbook of Embodied Cognition*. Oxford, UK: Routledge.

Shaw, R.C., and Clayton, N.S. (2013). Careful cachers and prying pilferers: Eurasian jays (*Garrulus glandarius*) limit auditory information available to competitors. *Proceedings of the Royal Society, Biological sciences*, 280, 20122238.

Shea, N., and Frith, C.D. (2019). The global workspace needs metacognition. *Trends in Cognitive Sciences*, 23, 560–571.

Shermer, M. (1994). *Why People Believe Weird Things: Pseudoscience, Superstition, and Other Confusions of Our Time*. London: Souvenir.

Shermer, M. (2018). *Heavens on Earth: The Scientific Search for the Afterlife, Immortality, and Utopia*. New York: Henry Holt and Company.

Sherwood, S., and Roe, C. (2003). A review of dream ESP studies conducted since the Maimonides dream ESP programme. *Journal of Consciousness Studies*, 6, 85–109.

Shettleworth, S.J. (2010). Clever animals and killjoy explanations in comparative psychology. *Trends in Cognitive Sciences*, 14, 477–481.

Shevel, E. (2011). The extracranial vascular theory of migraine: a great story confirmed by the facts. *Headache: The Journal of Head and Face Pain*, 51, 409–417.

Shimmamura, A. (1992). Organic amnesia. In L.R. Squire (ed.), *Encyclopedia of Learning and Memory*. New York: Macmillan, pp. 30–35.

Siclari, F., Baird, B., Perogamvros, L., Bernardi, G., LaRocque, J.J., Riedner, B., ... Tononi, G. (2017). The neural correlates of dreaming. *Nature Neuroscience*, 20, 872–878.

Silver, D., Hubert, T., Schrittwieser, J., et al. (2018). A general reinforcement learning algorithm that masters chess, shogi, and Go through self-play. *Science*, 362, 1140–1144.

Silver, N. (2012). *The Signal and the Noise: The Art and Science of Prediction*. London: Allen Lane.

Simeon, D. (2004). Depersonalisation disorder: a contemporary review. *CNS Drugs*, 18, 343–354.

Simons, D., Silveira, W.R. (1994). Post-traumatic stress disorder in children after television programmes. *British Medical Journal*, 308, 389.

Simons, D.J., and Chabris, C.F. (1999). Gorillas in our midst: sustained inattentional blindness for dynamic events. *Perception*, 28, 1059–1074.

Simons, D.J., and Levin, D.T. (1997). Change blindness. *Trends in Cognitive Sciences*, 1, 261–267.

Simons, D.J., and Rensink, R.A. (2005). Change blindness: past, present, and future. *Trends in Cognitive Sciences*, 9, 16–20.

Singer, P. (1990 [1975]). *Animal Liberation*. New York: Avon Books.

Sinnott-Armstrong, W., and Nadel, L. (2010). *Conscious Will and Responsibility: A Tribute to Benjamin Libet*. Cambridge, MA: Oxford University Press.

Sio, U.N., and Ormerod, T.C. (2009). Does incubation enhance problem solving? A meta-analytic review. *Psychological Bulletin*, 135, 94–120.

Sizemore, C.C. (1977). *I'm Eve*. New York: Doubleday.

Slater, E., and Beard, A.W. (1963a). The schizophrenia-like psychoses of epilepsy: i. Psychiatric aspects. *British Journal of Psychiatry*, 109, 95–112.

Slater, E., and Beard, A.W. (1963b). The schizophrenia-like psychoses of epilepsy: v. Discussion and conclusions. *British Journal of Psychiatry*, 109, 143–150.

Slater, M., Spanlang, B., Sanchez-Vives, M.V., and Blanke, O. (2010). First person experience of body transfer in virtual reality. *PLoS ONE*, 5, 1–9, 0010564.

Slavick-Lennard, K. (2013). *Sleep Talkin' Man*. New York: Black Cat.

Smallwood, J., and Schooler, J.W (2006). The restless mind. *Psychological Bulletin*, 132, 946–958.

Smallwood, J., and Schooler, J.W. (2015). The science of mind wandering: empirically navigating the stream of consciousness. *Annual Review of Psychology*, 66, 487–518.

Smart, J.J.C. (1959). Sensations and brain processes. *Philosophical Review*, 68, 141–156.

Smith J.D., Couchman, J.J., and Beran, M.J. (2014). Animal metacognition: a tale of two comparative psychologies. *Journal of Comparative Psychology*, 128, 115–131.

REFERENCES

Smith, J.D., Schull, J., Strote, J., et al. (1995). The uncertain response in the bottlenosed dolphin (*Tursiops truncates*). *Journal of Experimental Psychology: General*, 124, 391–408.

Smith, J.D., Zakrzewski, A.C., and Church, B.A. (2016). Formal models in animal-metacognition research: the problem of interpreting animals' behavior. *Psychonomic Bulletin and Review*, 23, 1341–1353.

Smythies J.R., Morin R.D., and Brown, G.B. (1979). Identification of dimethyltryptamine and O-methylbufotenin in human cerebrospinal fluid by combined gas chromatography/mass spectrometry. *Biological Psychiatry*, 14, 549–56.

Sneddon, L.U., and Leach, M.C. (2016). Anthropomorphic denial of fish pain. *Animal Sentience*, 3, 1–4.

Sneddon, L.U., Braithwaite, V.A., and Gentle, M.J. (2003). Do fishes have nociceptors? Evidence for the evolution of a vertebrate sensory system. *Proceedings of the Royal Society B: Biological Sciences*, 270, 1115–1121.

Solms, M. (2000). Dreaming and REM sleep are controlled by different brain mechanisms. *Behavioral and Brain Sciences*, 23, 843–850.

Soon, C.S., Brass, M., Heinze, H., and Haynes, J.D. (2008). Unconscious determinants of free decisions in the human brain. *Nature Neuroscience*, 11, 543–545.

Spanos, N. P. (1983). The hidden observer as an experimental creation. *Journal of Personality and Social Psychology*, 44, 170–176.

Spanos, N.P. (1986). Hypnotic behavior: a social-psychological interpretation of amnesia, analgesia, and 'trance logic.' *Behavioral and Brain Sciences*, 9, 449–467.

Spanos, N.P. (1989). *Hypnosis: The Cognitive-Behavioral Perspective*. New York: Prometheus Press.

Sparrow, G., Hurd, R., Carlson, R., and Molina, A. (2018). Exploring the effects of galantamine paired with meditation and dream reliving on recalled dreams: toward an integrated protocol for lucid dream induction and nightmare resolution. *Consciousness and Cognition*, 63, 74–88.

Squire, L.R. (2009). The legacy of patient H.M. for neuroscience. *Neuron*, 61, 6–9.

Squire L.R., et al. (2010). Role of the hippocampus in remembering the past and imagining the future. *Proceedings of the National Academy of Sciences USA*, 107, 19044–19048.

Srinivasan, V., Pandi-Perumal, S.R., Trakht, I., et al. (2009). Pathophysiology of depression: role of sleep and the melatonergic system. *Psychiatry Research*, 165, 201–214.

Srivastava, A., McNeill, D., and Ip, R. (2013). The importance of thalamic connections: cognition, arousal, and behavior in thalamic stroke. *Journal of Neuropsychiatry and Clinical Neurosciences*, 25, E63–E64.

Stallman, H.M., and Kohler, M. (2016). Prevalence of sleepwalking: a systematic review and meta-analysis. *PLoS ONE*, 11, 1–20

Stam, H.J., and Spanos, N.P. (1980). Experimental designs, expectancy effects, and hypnotic analgesia. *Journal of Abnormal Psychology*, 89, 751–762.

Statland, B.E., and Demas, T.J. (1980). Serum caffeine half-lives. Healthy subjects vs. patients having alcoholic hepatic disease. *American Journal of Clinical Pathology*, 73, 390–393.

Stein, M.B., and Uhde, T.W. (1989). Depersonalization disorder: effects of caffeine and response to pharmacotherapy. *Biological Psychiatry*, 26, 315–320.

Sternberg, R.J. (1986). Inside intelligence. *American Scientist*, 74, 137–143.

Stevenson, I. (1988). *Twenty Cases Suggestive of Reincarnation*. Charlottesville, VA: University of Virginia Press.

Stevenson, I. (2001). *Children who Remember Previous Lives: A Question of Reincarnation*. Jefferson, NC: McFarland & Co.

Stickgold, R. (1998). Sleep: off-line memory reprocessing. *Trends in Cognitive Sciences*, 2, 484–492

Stone, A., and Young, A.W. (1997). Delusions and brain injury: the philosophy and psychology of belief. *Mind and Language*, 12, 327–364.

Storm, L., Tressoldi, P.E., and Di Risio, L. (2010). Meta-analysis of free-response studies, 1992–2008: assessing the noise reduction model in parapsychology. *Psychological Bulletin*, 136, 471–485.

Strassman, R.J. (2001). *DMT: The Spirit Molecule. A Doctor's Revolutionary Research into the Biology of*

Near-Death and Mystical Experiences. Rochester, VT: Park Street.

Strassman, R.J. (2014). *DMT and the Soul of Prophecy: A New Science of Spiritual Revelation in the Hebrew Bible*. Rochester, VT: Park Street Press.

Strawson, G. (2006). *Consciousness and its Place in Nature*. Exeter, UK: Imprint Academic.

Strawson, G. (2018). *Things that Bother Me*. New York: New York Review of Books.

Strawson, P.F. (1962). Freedom and resentment. *Proceedings of the British Academy*, 48, 1–25.

Stumbrys, T., Erlacher, D., Schädlich, M., and Schredl, M. (2012). Induction of lucid dreams: a systematic review of evidence. *Consciousness and Cognition*, 21, 1456–1475.

Suddendorf, T. (2013). *The Gap: The Science of What Separates Us from Other Animals*. New York: Basic Books.

Suddendorf, T., and Corballis, M.C. (2007). The evolution of foresight: what is mental time travel and is it unique to humans? *Behavioral and Brain Sciences*, 30, 299–313.

Suddendorf, T.R., Addis, D.R., and Corballis, M.C. (2009). Mental time travel and the shaping of the human mind. *Philosophical Transactions of the Royal Society of London, B*, 364, 1317–1324.

Suedfeld, P., and Baker-Brown, G. (1987). Restricted environmental stimulation therapy of smoking: a parametric study. *Addictive Behaviors*, 12, 263–267

Sui, J. (2016). Self-reference acts as a golden thread in binding. *Trends in Cognitive Sciences*, 20, 482–483.

Sui, J., and Humphreys, G.W. (2015). The integrative self: how self-reference integrates perception and memory. *Trends in Cognitive Sciences*, 19, 719–728.

Sulloway, F.J. (1979). *Freud, Biologist of the Mind*. Harvard: Harvard University Press.

Sundberg, M.L. (1996). Toward granting linguistic competence to apes: a review of Savage-Rumbaugh et al.'s language comprehension in ape and child. *Journal of the Experimental Analysis of Behaviour*, 65, 477–492.

Sundquist, J., Lilja, A., Palmér, K., et al. (2014). Mindfulness group therapy in primary care patients with depression, anxiety and stress and adjustment disorders: randomised controlled trial. *British Journal of Psychiatry*, 206, 128–135.

Sunstein, C.R., and Thaler, R.A. (2009). *Nudge: Improving Decisions About Health, Wealth and Happiness*. Harmondsworth, UK: Penguin.

Sutherland, S. (1989). Consciousness. *Macmillan Dictionary of Psychology*. London: Macmillan.

Swan, I. (2018). *Everybody's guide to natural ESP: Unlocking the extrasensory power of your mind*. Agoura Hills, CA: Swann-Ryder Productions.

Symons, C., and Johnson, B.T. (1997). The self-reference effect in memory: a meta-analysis. *Psychological Bulletin*, 121, 371–394.

Szelenberger, W.S., Niemcewicz, S., and Dabrowska, A.J. (2005). Sleepwalking and night terrors: psychopathological and psychophysiological correlates. *International Review of Psychiatry*, 17, 263–270.

Tagliazucchi, E., Chialvo, D.R., Siniatchkin, M., Brichant, J., and Laureys, S. (2016). Large-scale signatures of unconsciousness are consistent with a departure from critical dynamics. *Journal of The Royal Society Interface*, 13, 1–34T

Tagliazucchi, E., Roseman, L., Kaelen, M., et al. (2016). Increased global functional connectivity correlates with LSD-induced ego dissolution. *Current Biology*, 26, 1043–1050.

Tallis, F. (2012). *Hidden Minds: A History of the Unconscious*. New York: Helios Press.

Talwar, S.K., Xu, S., Hawley, E.S., et al. (2002). Rat navigation guided by remote control. *Nature*, 417, 37–38.

Tamminen, J., Payne, J.D., Stickgold, R., Wamsley, E.J., and Gaskell, M.G. (2010). Sleep spindle activity is associated with the integration of new memories and existing knowledge. *Journal of Neuroscience*, 30, 14356–14360.

Tandy, V., and Lawrence, T. (1998). The ghost in the machine. *Journal of the Society for Psychical Research*, 62, 360–364.

Tang, Y.Y., Hölzel, B.K., and Posner, M.I. (2015). The neuroscience of mindfulness meditation. *Nature Reviews Neuroscience*, 16, 213–225.

Targ, R., and Puthoff, H. (1977). *Mind-Reach*. London: Jonathan Cape.

Tart, C.T. (1988). From spontaneous event to lucidity. In J. Gackenbach and S. LaBerge (eds.), *Conscious Mind, Sleeping Brain*. New York: Springer, pp. 67–103.

REFERENCES

Tart, C.T. (1990). Introduction to the first edition. In C.T. Tart (ed.), *Altered States of Consciousness*. San Francisco, CA: HarperCollins.

Taylor, K. (2016). *Brainwashing: The Science of Thought Control*. Oxford, UK: Oxford University Press.

Telford, C., McCarthy-Jones, S., Corcoran, R., and Rowse, G. (2012). Experience sampling methodology studies of depression: the state of the art. *Psychological Medicine*, 42, 1119–1129.

Tellegen A., and Atkinson, G. (1974). Openness to absorbing and self-altering experiences ('absorption'), a trait related to hypnotic susceptibility. *Journal of Abnormal Psychology*, 83, 268–277.

Tennie, C., Jensen, K., and Call, J. (2016). The nature of prosociality in chimpanzees. *Nature Communications*, 7, 13915.

Terhune, D.B., Cleeremans, A., Raz, A., and Lynn, S.J. (2017). Hypnosis and top-down regulation of consciousness. *Neuroscience and Biobehavioral Reviews*, 81, 59–74.

Tero, A., Takagi, S., Saigusa, T., et al. (2010). Rules for biologically inspired adaptive network design. *Science*, 327, 439–442.

The Wachowskis (1999). *The Matrix*. Burbank, CA: Warner Bros.

Thigpen, C.H., and Cleckley, H.M. (1954). A case of multiple personality. *Journal of Abnormal and Social Psychology*, 495, 135–151.

Thigpen, C.H., and Cleckley, H.M. (1992 [1957]). *The Three Faces of Eve* (Revised ed.). New York City: McGraw-Hill Education.

Thompson, M. (2020). *Sleep Habits in Different Cultures*. Mattress Advisor, Sleep Resources. www.mattressadvisor.com/anthropology-cultures/

Timmermann, C., Roseman, L., Williams, L., et al. (2018). DMT models the near-death experience. *Frontiers in Psychology*, 9, 1–12.

Tinuper, P., Montagna, P., Medori, R., et al. (1989). The thalamus participates in the regulation of the sleep-waking cycle. a clinico-pathological study in fatal familial thalamic degeneration. *Electroencephalography and Clinical Neurophysiology*, 73, 117–123.

Titkov, E.S. (1976). Characteristics of the daily periodicity of wakefulness and rest in the brown bullhead (Ictalurus nebulosus). *Journal of Evolutionary Biochemistry and Physiology*, 12, 305–309.

Tong, F., Nakayama, K., Vaughan, J.T., and Kanwisher, N. (1998). Binocular rivalry and visual awareness in human extrastriate cortex. *Neuron*, 21, 753–759.

Tononi, G. (2004). An information integration theory of consciousness. *BMC Neuroscience*, 5, 1–22.

Tononi, G. (2008). Consciousness as integrated information: a provisional manifesto. *Biological Bulletin*, 215, 216–242.

Tononi, G. (2012). *Phi: A Voyage from the Brain to the Soul*. New York: Pantheon Books.

Tononi, G., and Cirelli, C. (2006). Sleep function and synaptic homeostasis. *Sleep Medicine Reviews*, 10, 49–62.

Tononi, G., and Edelman, G.M. (1998). Consciousness and complexity. *Science*, 282, 1846–1851.

Tononi, G., and Koch, C. (2008). The neural correlates of consciousness: an update. *Annals of the New York Academy of Sciences*, 1124, 239–261.

Tononi, G., and Koch, C. (2015). Consciousness: here, there and everywhere? *Philosophical Transactions of the Royal Society, Series B*, 370, 20140167.

Tononi, G., and Laureys, S. (2009). The neurology of consciousness: an overview. In S. Laureys and G. Tononi (eds.), *The Neurology of Consciousness*. Amsterdam, The Netherlands: Academic Press, pp 375–412.

Tononi, G., Boly, M., Massimini, M., and Koch, C. (2016). Integrated information theory: from consciousness to its physical substrate. *Nature Reviews Neuroscience*, 17, 450–461.

Tosches, M.A., Bucher, D., Vopalensky, P., and Arendt, D. (2014). Melatonin signaling controls circadian swimming behavior in marine zooplankton. *Cell*, 159, 46–57.

Treisman, A. (1964). Selective attention in man. *British Medical Bulletin*, 20, 12–16.

Trevena, J.A., and Miller, J. (2002). Cortical movement preparation before and after a conscious decision to move. *Consciousness and Cognition*, 11, 162–190.

Trevena, J., and Miller, J. (2010). Brain preparation before a voluntary action: evidence against unconscious movement initiation. *Consciousness and Cognition*, 19, 447–456.

Tsakiris M., Hesse, M,D, Boy, C., Haggard. P., and Fink, G. R. (2007). Neural signatures of body ownership: a sensory network for bodily self-consciousness. *Cerebral Cortex*, 17, 2235-2244.

Tseng, P., Hsu, T., Muggleton, N.G., et al. (2010). Posterior parietal cortex mediates encoding and maintenance processes in change blindness. *Neuropsychologia*, 48, 1063-1070.

Tsuchiya, N., Wilke, M., Frässle, S., and Lamme, V.A.F. (2015). No-report paradigms: extracting the true neural correlates of consciousness. *Trends in Cognitive Sciences*, 19, 757-770.

Tsushima, Y., Sasaki, Y., and Watanabe, T. (2006). Greater disruption due to failure of inhibitory control on an ambiguous distractor. *Science*, 314, 1786-1788.

Tulving, E. (1985). Memory and consciousness. *Canadian Psychology*, 26, 1-12.

Tulving, E. (2002). Episodic memory: from mind to brain. *Annual Review of Psychology*, 53, 1-25.

Tustin, K., and Hayne, H. (2010). Defining the boundary: age-related changes in childhood amnesia. *Developmental Psychology*, 46, 1049-1061.

Tye. M. (1991). *The Imagery Debate*. Cambridge, MA: MIT Press.

Tye, M. (1995). *Ten Problems of Consciousness*. Cambridge, MA: MIT Press.

Tye, M. (2002). *Consciousness, Color, and Content*. Cambridge, MA: MIT Press.

Tye, M. (2003). *Consciousness and Persons: Unity and Identity*. Cambridge, MA: Bradford Books.

Ullman, M., and Krippner, S. (1969). A laboratory approach to the nocturnal dimension of paranormal experience: report of a confirmatory study using the REM monitoring technique. *Biological Psychiatry*, 1, 259-270.

Ungerleider, L.G., and Mishkin, M. (1982). Two cortical visual systems. In D.J. Ingle, M.A. Goodale, and R.J.W. Mansfield (eds.), *Analysis of Visual Behavior*. Cambridge, MA: MIT Press, pp. 549-586.

Uthaug, M., van Oorsouw, K., Kuypers, K.P.C., et al. (2018). Sub-acute and long-term effects of ayahuasca on affect and cognitive thinking style and their association with ego dissolution. *Psychopharmacology*, 235, 2979-2989.

Uttal, W.R. (2013). *Dualism*. London: Routledge.

Vaitl, D., Gruzelier, J., Jamieson, G.A., et al. (2005). Psychobiology of altered states of consciousness. *Psychological Bulletin*, 131, 98-127.

Valli, K., Revonsuo, A., Pälkäs, O., Ismail, K.H., Ali, K.J., and Punamäki, R.-L. (2005). The threat simulation theory of the evolutionary function of dreaming: evidence from dreams of traumatized children. *Consciousness and Cognition*, 14, 188-218.

Van den Heuvel, M.P., and Sporns, O. (2013). Network hubs in the human brain. *Trends in Cognitive Sciences*, 17, 683-696.

Van Elk, M., and Aleman, A. (2017). Brain mechanisms in religion and spirituality: an integrative predictive processing framework. *Neuroscience and Biobehavioral Reviews*, 73, 359-378.

Van Essen, D.C., Smith, S.M., Barch, D.M., et al. for the WU-Minn HCP Consortium. (2013). The WU-Minn Human Connectome Project: an overview. *NeuroImage*, 80, 62-79.

Van Lommel, P. (2011). Near-death experiences: the experience of the self as real and not as an illusion. *Annals of the New York Academy of Sciences*, 1234, 19-28.

Van Lommel, P., Van Wees, R., Meyers, V., and Elfferich, I. (2001). Near-death experience in survivors of cardiac arrest: a prospective study in the Netherlands. *Lancet*, 358, 2039-2045.

Vanderwolf, C.H. (2000). Are neocortical gamma waves related to consciousness? *Brain Research*, 855, 217-224.

Vanhaudenhuyse, A., Demertzi. A., Schabus. M., et al. (2011). Two distinct neuronal networks mediate the awareness of environment and self. *Journal of Cognitive Neuroscience*, 23, 570e578, 20.

Vaso A., Adahan H.M., Gjika A., et al. (2014). Peripheral nervous system origin of phantom limb pain. *Pain*, 155, 1384-1391.

Veatch, R. (1975). The whole-brain-oriented concept of death: an outmoded philosophical formulation. *Journal of Thanatology*, 3, 13-30.

Vilensky, J.A. (ed.). (2011). *Encephalitis Lethargica: During and After the Epidemic*. Oxford, UK: Oxford University Press.

Vimal, R.L.P. (2009). Meanings attributed to the term 'consciousness'. *Journal of Consciousness Studies*, 5, 9-27.

REFERENCES

Vogel, G.W., Thurmond, A., Gibbons, P., Sloan, K., and Walker, M. (1975). REM sleep reduction effects on depression syndromes. *Archives of General Psychiatry*, 32, 765–777.

Vogeley, K., and Fink, G.R. (2003). Neural correlates of the first-person-perspective. *Trends in Cognitive Sciences*, 7, 38–42.

Vogeley, K., Kurthen, M., Falkai P., and Maier, W. (1999). Essential functions of the human self model are implemented in the prefrontal cortex. *Consciousness and Cognition*, 8, 343–363.

Vohs, K.D., and Schooler, J.W. (2008). The value of believing in free will: encouraging a belief in determinism encourages cheating. *Psychological Science*, 19, 49–54.

Vollenweider, F.X., and Kometer, M. (2010). The neurobiology of psychedelic drugs: implications for the treatment of mood disorders. *Nature Reviews Neuroscience*, 11, 642–651.

Voss, U., Holzmann, R., Hobson, A., et al. (2014). Induction of self awareness in dreams through frontal low current stimulation of gamma activity. *Nature Neuroscience*, 17, 810–812.

Vrselja, Z., Daniele, S.G., Silbereis, J., et al. (2019). Restoration of brain circulation and cellular functions hours post-mortem. *Nature*, 568, 336–343.

Vygotsky, L. (1934). *Thought and Language*. Trans. 1962. Cambridge, MA: MIT Press.

Waal, F. de (2016). *Are We Smart Enough to Know How Smart Animals Are?* London: Granta.

Wackermann, J., Pütz, P., and Allefeld, C. (2008). Ganzfeld-induced hallucinatory experience, its phenomenology and cerebral electrophysiology. *Cortex*, 44, 1364–1378.

Wade, N. (2006). *Perception and Illusion: Historical Perspectives*. New York: Springer Publishing.

Wagenmakers, E.J., Wetzels, R., Borsboom, D., and van der Maas, H.L.J. (2011). Why psychologists must change the way they analyze their data: the case of Psi. Comment on Bem (2011). *Journal of Personality and Social Psychology*, 100, 426–432.

Walker, M. (2018). *Why We Sleep: The New Science of Sleep and Dreams*. London: Penguin.

Walther, B., and Schulz, H. (2004). Recurrent isolated sleep paralysis: Polysomnographic and clinical findings. *Somnologie – Schlafforschung und Schlafmedizin*, 8, 53–60.

Wamsley, E J., Tucker, M., Payne, J.D., Benavides, J.A., and Stickgold, R. (2010). Dreaming of a learning task is associated with enhanced sleep-dependent memory consolidation. *Current Biology*, 20, 850–855.

Wang, G., Grone, B., Colas, D., Appelbaum, L., and Mourrain, P. (2011). Synaptic plasticity in sleep: learning, homeostasis and disease. *Trends in Neurosciences*, 34, 452–463.

Ward, J. (2008). *The Frog who Croaked Blue: Synesthesia and the Mixing of the Senses*. London: Routledge.

Ward, J. (2015). *The Student's Guide to Cognitive Neuroscience*. Hove, UK: Psychology Press.

Ward, L.M. (2011). The thalamic dynamic core theory of conscious experience. *Consciousness and Cognition*, 20, 464–486.

Warneken, F., and Tomasello, M. (2006). Altruistic helping in human infants and young chimpanzees. *Science*, 311, 1301–1303.

Waterfield, R. (2002). *Hidden Depths: The Story of Hypnosis*. London: Macmillan.

Waters, F., Chiu, V., Atkinson, A., and Blom, J.D. (2018). Severe sleep deprivation causes hallucinations and a gradual progression toward psychosis with increasing time awake. *Frontiers in Psychiatry*, 9, 1–13.

Watson, D. (2003). To dream, perchance to remember: individual differences in dream recall. *Personality and Individual Differences*, 34, 1271–1286.

Watt, C. (2005). Psychological factors. In J. Henry (ed.), *Parapsychology*. Hove, UK: Routledge. pp. 64–79

Watt, C. (2016). *Parapsychology*. London: Oneworld.

Wearing, D. (2005). *Forever today: A memoir of love and amnesia*. London: Corgi Press.

Wegner, D.M. (2003). *The Illusion of Conscious Will*. Cambridge, MA: MIT Press.

Weiskrantz, L. (1986). *Blindsight: A Case Study and Implications*. Oxford, UK: Oxford University Press.

Weiskrantz, L. (1997). *Consciousness Lost and Found: A Neuropsychological Exploration*. Oxford, UK: Oxford University Press.

Weizenbaum, J. (1966). ELIZA – A computer program for the study of natural language communication between man and machine. *Communications of the ACM*, 9, 36–45.

Wells, H.G. (1898). *The War of the Worlds*. London: Heinemann.

Wegner, D. (2002). *The Illusion of Conscious Control*. Cambridge, MA: MIT Press.

Westphal, J. (2016). *The Mind–Body Problem*. Cambridge, MA: MIT Press.

Westwood, D.A., and Goodale, M.A. (2011). Converging evidence for diverging pathways: neuropsychology and psychophysics tell the same story. *Vision Research*, 51, 804–811.

Whinnery, T., and Forster, E.M. (2013). The +Gz-induced loss of consciousness curve. *Extreme Physiology and Medicine*, 2, 1.

White, J.G., Southgate, E., Thomson, J.N., and Brenner, S. (1986). The structure of the nervous system of the nematode *Caenorhabditis elegans*. *Philosophical Transactions of the Royal Society, Series B (Biological Sciences)*, 314, 1–340.

Whitehead, A.N. (1933). *Adventures of Ideas*. New York: Macmillan.

Whitley, R.J. (2006). Herpes simplex encephalitis: adolescents and adults. *Antiviral Research*, 71, 141–148.

Wickramasekera, I.E. (2015). Mysteries of hypnosis and the self are revealed by the psychology and neuroscience of empathy. *American Journal of Clinical Hypnosis*, 57, 330–348.

Wilcox, T., and Hirshkowitz, A. (2015). An overview of animal models of pain: disease models and outcome measures. *Journal of Pain*, 14, 1–27.

Williams, B.J. (2011). Revisiting the ganzfeld ESP debate: a basic review and assessment. *Journal of Scientific Exploration*, 25, 639–661.

Williams, M., and Penman, D. (2011). *Mindfulness: A Practical Guide to Finding Peace in a Frantic World*. London: Piatkus Books.

Wilson, A.D., and Golonka, S. (2013). Embodied cognition is not what you think it is. *Frontiers in Psychology*, 58, 4.

Wilson, B.A., and Wearing, D. (1995). Prisoner of consciousness: a state of just awakening following herpes simplex encephalitis. In R. Campbell and M.A. Conway (eds.), *Broken Memories: Case Studies in Memory Impairment*. Malden, UK: Blackwell Publishing, pp. 14–30.

Wilson, C. (2004a). *Dreaming to Some Purpose*. London: Century.

Wilson, C. (2005). *G.I. Gurdjieff: The War Against Sleep*. London: Aeon Books.

Wilson, C. (2009). *Super Consciousness: The Quest for the Peak Experience*. London: Watkins.

Wilson, E.O. (2012). *The Social Conquest of Earth*. New York: Liveright Press.

Wilson, H.R., Blake, R., and Lee, S.-H. (2001). Dynamics of travelling waves in visual perception. *Nature*, 412, 907–910.

Wilson, S.C., and Barber, T.X. (1983). The fantasy-prone personality: Implications for understanding imagery, hypnosis, and parapsychological phenomena. In A.A. Sheikh (ed.), *Imagery: Current Theory, Research, and Applications*. New York: John Wiley, pp. 340–290.

Wilson, T.D. (2004b). *Strangers to Ourselves: Discovering the Adaptive Unconscious*. Harvard, MA: Harvard University Press.

Wilton, R., and Harley, T.A. (2018). *Science and Psychology*. London: Routledge.

Wiseman, R. (2015). *Paranormality: the science of the supernatural*. London: Pan.

Winawer, J., Witthoft, N., and Frank, M. (2007). Russian blues reveal effects of language on color discrimination. *Proceedings of the National Academy of Science USA*, 104(19).

Windt, J.M. (2013). Reporting dream experience: why (not) to be skeptical about dream reports. *Frontiers in Human Neuroscience*, 7, 708.

Windt, J.M. (2015). *Dreaming*. Cambridge, MA: MIT Press.

Windt, J. M., Nielsen, T., and Thompson, E. (2016). Does consciousness disappear in dreamless sleep? *Trends in Cognitive Sciences*, 20, 871–882.

Winfield, A. (2012). *Robotics: A Very Short Introduction*. Oxford, UK: Oxford University Press.

Winograd, T. (1972). Understanding natural language. *Cognitive Psychology*, 3, 1–191.

Wiseman, R. (2011a). *Quirkology*. London: Pan.

Wiseman, R. (2011b). The haunted brain. *Skeptical Inquirer*, 35, 5. csicop.org.

Wiseman, R. (2011c). *Paranormality: Why We See What Isn't There*. London: Macmillan.

REFERENCES

Wiseman, R., and Milton, J. (1999). Experiment one of the SAIC Remote Viewing Program: a critical reevaluation. *Journal of Parapsychology*, 62, 297–308.

Wittgenstein, L. (1953). *Philosophical Investigations*. Oxford, UK: Blackwell.

Wittgenstein, L. (1961). *Tractatus Logico-Philosophicus*. London: Routledge and Kegan Paul.

Wobst, A.H.K. (2007). Hypnosis and surgery: past, present, and future. *Anesthesia and Analgesia*, 104, 1199–1208.

Wolman, D. (2012). The split brain: A tale of two halves. *Nature*, 483, 260–263.

Wright, D.B., Ost, J., and French, C.C. (2006). Recovered and false memories. *The Psychologist*, 19, 352–355.

Wyatt R.J., Gillin J.C., Kaplan J., et al. (1974). N,N-dimethyltryptamine: a possible relationship to schizophrenia? *Advances in Biochemical Psychopharmacology*, 11, 299–313.

Xie, L., Kang, H., Xu, Q., et al. (2013). Sleep drives metabolite clearance from the adult brain. *Science*, 342, 373–377.

Xu, J., Vik, A., Groote, I.R., et al. (2014). Nondirective meditation activates default mode network and areas associated with memory retrieval and emotional processing. *Frontiers in Human Neuroscience*, 8, 86.

Yang, G., Lai, C.S.W., Cichon, J., et al. (2014). Sleep promotes branch-specific formation of dendritic spines after learning. *Science*, 344, 1173–1178.

Yang, Y. Raine, A., Narr, K.L., Colletti, and Toga, A. W. (2011). Localization of deformations within the amygdala in individuals with psychopathy. *Archives of General Psychiatry*, 66, 986–994.

Yates, J., and Immergut, M. (2017). *The Mind Illuminated*. London: Hay House.

Zadra, A., Desjardins, S., and Marcotte, E. (2006). Evolutionary function of dreams: a test of the threat simulation theory in recurrent dreams. *Consciousness and Cognition*, 15, 450–463.

Zaki, J., Davis, J.I., and Ochsner, K.N. (2012). Overlapping activity in anterior insula during interoception and emotional experience. *NeuroImage*, 62, 493–499.

Zamboni, G., Budriesi, C., and Nichelli, P. (2005). 'Seeing oneself': a case of autoscopy. *Neurocase*, 11, 212–215.

Zeidan, F., Johnson, S.K., Diamond, B.J., David, Z., and Goolkasian, P. (2010). Mindfulness meditation improves cognition: evidence of brief mental training. *Consciousness and Cognition*, 19, 597–605.

Zeki, S. (2003). The disunity of consciousness. *Trends in Cognitive Sciences*, 7, 214–218.

Zeki, S., and Bartels, A. (1998). The asynchrony of consciousness. *Proceedings of the Royal Society B*, 265, 1583–1585.

Zelazo, P.D., Moscovitch, M., and Thompson E. (2007). *The Cambridge Handbook of Consciousness*. Cambridge, UK: Cambridge University Press.

Zimbardo, P.G, Weisenberg, M., Firestone, I., and Levy B. (1969). Changing appetites for eating fried grasshoppers with cognitive dissonance. In P.G. Zimbardo, *The Cognitive Control of Motivation*. Glenview, IL.: Scott Foresman, pp. 100–122.

Zirkel, S., Garcia, J.A., and Murphy, M. C. (2015). Experience-sampling research methods and their potential for education research. *Educational Researcher*, 44, 7–16.

Zou, J., et al. (2016). Binocular rivalry from invisible patterns. *Proceedings of the National Academy of Science USA*, 113, 8408–8413.

INDEX

absorption, 195
absorption score, 308, 376
access consciousness (A-consciousness), 16–17
acetylcholine (ACh), 293, 294, 312, 318
activation-synthesis model, 316–317
adaptation
   feature of complex systems, 85
ADHD (attention deficit hyperactivity disorder), 346
Adler, Alfred, 320
adrenaline, 294
Aeschylus, 263
agency
   sense of, 69
agnosia, 227, 228
AIM model of sleep and dreaming, 295–296
alcohol, 362
alexia, 227
alien hand syndrome, 73–74, 180, 255
aliens
   form and potential to develop intelligence, 113
   forms of, 73–74
alkaloids, 352
Allen, Paul, 99
alpha waves, 243
altered states of consciousness
   attempts to detect psi, 391–393
   cardiac arrest survivors, 280
   circadian rhythms, 288–290
   comparison with normal state of consciousness, 269–270
   definitions of, 269–270
   delirium, 283
   dying brain hypothesis, 281
   encephalitis lethargica, 282–283
   epilepsy, 278–279
   ganzfeld technique, 273–274
   life review experience (LRE), 279–280
   migraine, 277–278, 279
   near-death experiences, 279–282
   out-of-body experiences, 274–277
   problem of, 22, 408–409
   psychonauts, 270–271
   restricted environmental stimulation therapy (REST), 273
   romantic love (limerence), 283
   sensory deprivation, 272–274
   sensory habituation, 272–274
   types of, 272–283
   See also sleep
Alzheimer's disease, 104, 163, 195
   anosognosia, 147–146
   loss of autobiographical memory, 166
   sleep and, 300
   sleep and dementia risk, 302
Amazon Robotics, 96–97
Ambien, 297
amnesia, 163
   anterograde amnesia, 166
   brain damage and, 166
   case of Clive Wearing, 166–169
   case of HM (Henry Molaison), 166
   case of Jimmie G., 166
   caused by *herpes simplex* encephalitis, 166–169
   dissociative amnesia, 174
   Korsakoff's syndrome, 166
   retrograde amnesia, 166
   self and, 166–169
   source amnesia, 338
amphetamine, 345–346
amphetamine psychosis, 345–346
amyotrophic lateral sclerosis (ALS), 262
anaesthesia
   history of, 248
   See also general anaesthesia
anarchic hand syndrome, 73–74
anencephaly, 246
animal consciousness, 18
   animal intelligence and, 110–114
   Cambridge Declaration on Consciousness, 110
   evolution of consciousness, 120–124
   identifying which animals are conscious, 108–109
   implications for how we treat animals, 108–109
   mirror test of self-recognition, 114–115
   nature of consciousness in animal minds, 109–110
   panpsychism, 124–126
   prosocial behaviour, 119
   ritual behaviour, 119
   role of social intelligence, 120
   social intelligence hypothesis, 119
   theory of mind, 117–119

animal intelligence
  Alex the African grey parrot, 111
  birds, 111–112
  brain structure and complexity, 110–114
  dolphins and whales, 112, 113
  learning without neurons, 113–114
animal magnetism, 323, 324
animal minds, 109–117
  anthropomorphism, 109
  capacity for pain perception in animals, 116–117
animals
  sleep, 287–288, 289
anomalistic psychology, 384
anomalous monism, 33
anorexia, 191
anosognosia, 145–147, 230
  Alzheimer's disease, 147–146
  Anton–Babinski syndrome, 145–146
  dementia, 147–146
  neglect, 146
anterior cingulate cortex (ACC), 255
anthropomorphism, 109
antipsychotic medications, 141
anti-realism, 140
antisocial personality disorder (ASPD), 68
Anton–Babinski syndrome, 145–146, 228
archetypes (Jung), 151
argument by analogy to the existence of other minds, 40
Aristotle, 33
artificial intelligence (AI), 11, 81–92
  Alexa, 87, 88
  AlphaGo, 89–90
  Assistant, 87
  background knowledge problem, 89
  BLOCKSWORLD, 83, 88–89
  chatbots, 87–88
  chess-playing computers, 84–86
  computational correlates of consciousness, 91–92
  connectionist approach, 91
  consciousness in a disembodied AI, 93–94
  deep learning, 91
  defining intelligence, 102–103
  disembodied AI, 92–94
  distinction between intelligence and consciousness, 102–103
  early AI models of psychology, 88–89
  ELIZA, 87
  embodied cognition, 93–94
  enactivism, 93–94
  expert systems, 82
  frame problem, 89
  future of, 102–105
  how smart computers are now, 89–91
  LIDA (Learning Intelligent Distributed Agent), 92–93
  Loebner Prize, 87
  Mitsuku, 87
  Moore's law, 90
  MYCIN expert system, 82
  neural networks approach, 91
  potential threats from, 104–105
  programs that play Go, 89–90
  SHRDLU, 88–89
  Siri, 87, 88
  situated cognition, 93–94
  technological singularity, 102–103
  timeline of progress, 82–84
  transhumanism, 103–104
  Turing test, 86–88
artificial life (A-life), 79–81
  autopoiesis, 80
  Boids simulation of flocking behaviour, 80–81, 210
  emergence, 81
  flocking behaviour in birds, 80–81
  use of quantum computers for simulations, 81
ASCs. *See* altered states of consciousness
Aserinsky, Eugene, 290
Asimov, Isaac
  Three Laws of Robotics, 104–105
asomatognosia, 146
astonishing hypothesis, 241–242
astral projection, 277
attention, 192–201
  absorption, 195
  awareness and, 193–194
  cocktail party effect, 192–193
  default mode network, 194–196
  mind-wandering, 194–196
  visual attention, 194
attractor networks, 91
auditory verbal hallucinations (AVH), 190
autistic spectrum disorder, 195
autobiographical memory
  continuity of the self, 165
  infantile amnesia, 165
  loss in Alzheimer's disease, 166
  recency effect, 165
  role of episodic memory, 166
autonoetic consciousness, 157, 203, 204
autopoiesis, 192–201
autoscopic hallucination, 176

autoscopy, 176–177, 274
Awakenings (Sacks), 283
awareness
    attention and, 193–194
    consciousness and, 12
ayahuasca, 354, 362, 363

Baars, Bernard, 132, 197–198
babies
    experience of pain, 40–41
Balint's syndrome, 233–234
Barber, Theodore X., 327
barbiturates, 294, 297
Bauby, Jean-Dominique, 261–262
Beatle mania, 144
The Beatles, 357, 358
Beau the miniature poodle, 52
    capacity to feel pain, 116
    dreaming, 306
    level of awareness, 108
    model of the world, 202
    perception of the world, 14
behaviourism, 21
beliefs, 138–147
    anosognosia, 145–147
    anti-realism, 140
    deceiving devils, 140
    delusions, 141–147
    denial, 145–147
    element of uncertainty in, 138–139
    reliability of, 139–141
    scepticism, 140
    simulations, 140
    solipsism, 140
    supernatural beliefs, 378
belladonna, 350–351
Bem, Daryl, 394–395
Bennett, John, 373
benzodiazepines, 294, 297
Berger, Hans, 242, 243
Berkeley, Bishop, 32
beta waves, 21
betel (areca) nut, 362
bicameral mind, 123–124
binaural beats, 275
binding problem of perception, 22, 231–235, 408
    Balint's syndrome, 233–234
    microconsciousness, 234
    role of gamma waves, 232–233
    visual awareness, 234–235
birds
    intelligence of, 111–112
Bispectral Index Scale (BIS), 250
bistable figures, 221
black body radiation, 213
Blackmore, Susan, 182, 281
Blaine, David, 61
blindsight, 227–229
Block, Ned, 16–17, 48
Boids simulation of flocking behaviour, 80–81, 210
Bostrom, Nick, 140
Bourne, Ansel, 174
Brahmanism, 400
Braid, James, 324
brain
    attempts to build an artificial brain, 11
    augmentation, 11
    building a brain, 98–102
    circuits involved in the neuronal workspace model, 200–201
    computed tomography (CT) scan, 240
    computerised axial tomography (CAT) scan, 240
    damage caused by *herpes simplex* encephalitis, 167–168
    electrocorticography,
    electroencephalography (EEG), 240
    evolutionary development, 244–245
    functional imaging, 240
    functional magnetic resonance imaging (fMRI), 240
    imaging and mind reading, 242
    imaging the living brain, 240
    incomplete brains, 246–247
    interfaces with computers, 101–102
    language processing in Broca's area, 190
    magnetic resonance imaging (MRI), 240
    magnetoencephalography (MEG), 240
    mapping of neurons and connections, 99
    neuroprosthesis, 101–102
    optogenetics, 240
    part-brain emulation, 100–101
    positron-emission tomography (PET), 240
    regions involved in the default mode network, 196–197
    relationship to the mind, 28–29
    role of gamma waves, 232–233
    search for the seat of consciousness, 4
    structure and functions of neurons, 46–47
    studying the living brain, 240
    thalamo-cortical resonance, 233
    transcranial magnetic stimulation (TMS), 240
    whole brain emulation, 100
    See also neural correlates of consciousness; neuroscience
brain imaging, 10

development of, 9
functional magnetic resonance imaging (fMRI), 9
brain in a vat (thought experiment), 220
brain waves, 242–244
    alpha waves, 243
    beta waves, 243
    delta waves, 244
    gamma waves, 232–233, 243
    infra-slow waves, 244
    P300 wave, 199, 244
    ponto-geniculo-occipital waves (PGO waves), 291
    theta waves, 243
brainstem structures
    role in sleep, 291–293
Bremer, Frédéric, 291–292
Brentano, Franz, 16, 162
Breuer, Joseph, 324
Brown, Derren, 61
Bruneri–Canella case, 174–175
Buddhism, 378–380
    meditation, 132
    reincarnation, 400
    self as illusion, 159
    Zen Buddhism, 380–381
bufotenin, 350
bulimia, 191
bundle theory of the self, 159–160, 173

Caenorhabditis elegans (nematode), 46, 288
   what it is like to be, 51
caffeine, 345, 362
   effects of, 269
callosotomy, 171
Cambridge Declaration on Consciousness, 110
cannabis, 343–344, 362
    dangers of cannabis use, 321
    medicinal use, 344, 362
Čapek, Karel, 94
Capgras delusion or syndrome, 142, 182
cardiac arrest survivors
    near-death experiences, 280
Carhart-Harris, Robin, 363
Carmelite nuns
    religious experiences, 375–377
carpentered world hypothesis, 188
Cartesian dualism. *See* substance dualism
Cartesian Theatre, 62
Castaneda, Carlos, 362
catalepsy, 297
Chalmers, David, 15, 18, 42
    dancing qualia thought experiment, 49–50

panpsychism, 125
probability of living in a simulated universe, 140
change blindness, 132
chaos
    feature of complex systems, 209
Charcot, Jean-Martin
    use of hypnosis to treat hysteria, 324–325
chatbots, 87–88
chess-playing computers, 84–86
    algorithmic approach, 85
    AlphaZero, 85–86
    Deep Blue, 84–85, 86
    Deep Fritz, 85
    Deep Thought, 84
    use of heuristics, 85
Chesterton, G.K., 373
chimpanzees
    metacognition studies, 205
    prosocial behaviour, 119
    ritual behaviour, 119
    teaching language to, 121
    theory of mind, 117–119
chloroform, 247, 248
choline, 311–312
Chomsky, Noam, 21, 52, 88, 122, 189, 208
chronesthesia, 203–205
Chuang-Tzu
    butterfly dream, 306–307
Churchland, Patricia, 42, 44
Churchland, Paul, 36, 44
circadian rhythms, 288–290
clairvoyance, 385–386
Clarke, Andy, 180–181
claustrum, 253–255
Cleeremans, A., 256–257
Coca-Cola, 347
coca leaves, 362
cocaine, 347–348, 362
cochlear implants, 101
cocktail party effect, 153, 192–193
codeine, 348
cognition
    insights from hypnosis, 338
cognitive correlates of consciousness, 22, 405
cognitive dissonance, 138
cognitive fluidity
    role in development of consciousness, 120–121
cognitive neuroscience, 8, 21
cognitive psychology, 21, 49
Coleridge, Samuel Taylor, 271
collective unconscious, 151

colour perception
  inverted colour spectrum argument, 36–38
coma and coma-like states, 260–261
commissurotomy, 171
compatibilism, 64
complete locked-in syndrome (CLIS), 262
complex systems, 209
  adaptation, 209
  chaos, 209
  definition of, 209
  emergence, 209
  examples, 209
  feedback loops, 209
  nonlinearity, 209
computation approach to cognition, 48–49
computational correlates of consciousness, 91–92
computational neuroscience, 100
computational theory of mind, 50
computed tomography (CT) scan, 240
computerised axial tomography (CAT) scan, 240
Comte, Auguste, 133
confabulation, 144–145, 147, 166, 230
conjoined twins
  sleep–wake cycles, 289
conscious realism, 32
consciousness
  access consciousness (A-consciousness), 16–17
  awareness and, 12
  change blindness, 132
  contents of, 131–138
  definitions of, 12
  degrees of, 18–20
  developmental aspect, 245–246
  different states of, 5–6
  difficulty of defining, 11–14
  emergence theory of, 209–210
  experience sampling, 136–137
  extended consciousness, 180–181
  free energy model, 211
  global workspace theory, 197–198
  higher-order thought theory, 207–209
  homunculus problem, 132
  inattentional blindness, 132
  intentionality of, 15–16
  introspection and, 132
  introspection process, 133–134
  language and, 186–192
  limitations, 185–186
  limitations of introspection, 137–138
  limits of, 16
  microconsciousness theory, 234
  multiple drafts model, 201
  neuronal workspace theory, 198–201
  neuroscience and, 4
  of something, 15–16
  phenomenal consciousness (P-consciousness), 16–17
  phenomenology, 135–136
  philosophy and, 4–5
  preconscious, 147–148
  primary consciousness, 17
  privacy of, 12, 13–14
  psychology and, 3
  quantum consciousness, 212–213
  reasons for studying, 3–6
  representational theories, 206–207
  research challenges, 3
  search for the seat of, 4
  secondary consciousness, 17
  something it is like to be, 12
  spirituality and, 5–6
  states of, 18–20
  states when we are not conscious, 6
  stream of consciousness, 132
  subliminal processing, 147
  types of, 16–20
  ways that consciousness can be altered, 18–20
  what it means to be conscious, 6
consciousness disorders, 259–262
  coma and coma-like states, 260–261
  definitions of death, 261
  locked-in syndrome, 261–262
  minimally conscious state (MCS), 261
  persistent vegetative state (PVS), 260
consciousness problems, 21–23
  altered state problem, 22, 408–409
  binding problem, 22, 408
  cognitive problem, 22, 405
  cultural differences, 409–410
  definition problem, 403
  free will problem, 22, 406
  hard problem, 21, 404
  neural correlates problem, 22, 404–405
  science problem, 22, 410–411
  self problem, 22, 406–407
  temporal problem, 22, 405–406
  unconscious problem, 22, 407
  why problem, 22, 407–408
  See also mind–body problem
consciousness raising, 373–374
consciousness studies, 6–11

INDEX

artificial intelligence (AI), 11
  attempts to build an artificial brain, 11
  brain augmentation, 11
  brain imaging, 9, 10
  definition, 6
  history of consciousness research, 20–21
  history of neuroscience, 8–9
  inability to measure consciousness directly, 7
  introspection, 6–7
  philosophical thought experiments, 10
  role of falsification in science, 7–8
    scientific experimentation, 7–10
continuity of existence, 165–169
Cook, Peter, 156
Copernicus, Nicolaus, 20, 26, 33
Copperfield, David, 61
coronavirus crisis of 2020, 211
corpus callosotomy, 171
cortisol levels
  circadian rhythm, 289
Cotard's delusion, 143, 163, 182
crack cocaine, 348
creativity
  dreaming and, 317–318
Crick, Francis, 241–242
crime and punishment
  antisocial personality disorder (ASPD), 68
  diminished responsibility, 68
  effects of early upbringing and environment, 68–69
  implications of free will, 66–69
  mental illness, 68
  neurocriminology, 69
  personality types and, 69
  purpose of psychology in understanding crime, 68–69
  purpose of punishment, 67
crystal meth, 346
cultural differences
  drug use, 362
  views of the mind, 409–410
culture
  language and, 186–188

Daleks, 96
Dali, Salvador, 222
Damasio, Antonio
  three levels of the self, 161–163
Dani people, New Guinea, 187
Davis, Wade, 41
Davy, Humphry, 248

deadly nightshade (*Atropa belladonna*), 351
death, 20, 257–258
  as loss of higher functions, 259
  definitions of, 261
  ghosts, 396–399
  near-death experiences, 279–282
  possibility of escaping, 262–263
  reincarnation, 400–401
  survival after, 398–401
  transhumanism and, 103–104
deceiving devils, 140
deciding to act, 69–73
  EEG readiness potential (RP or BP), 71–72
  Libet's experiments on 'voluntary' movement, 70–71, 72–73
  sense of agency, 69
deep brain stimulation (DBS), 101
default mode network, 143, 194–196, 353, 360–361
  activation of, 195–196
  brain regions involved in, 196–197
  changes in functioning, 195
  definition of, 195
  dreams and, 312
  effect of meditation, 371
  hubs, 195
  involvement in religious experiences, 377, 378
  pathologies associated with damage to, 195
  role in dreaming, 317
Dehaene, Stenislas, 198–201
deliriant drugs, 350–351
delirium, 283
delta waves, 244
delusions, 141–147
  anosognosia, 145–147
  Capgras delusion or syndrome, 142, 182
  confabulation, 144–145
  Cotard's delusion, 143, 182
  denial, 145–147
  Fregoli syndrome, 142–143
  intermetamorphosis, 143
  mass hysteria, 143–145
  schizophrenia, 141
  subjective doubles syndrome, 143
  walking corpse syndrome, 143
Dement, William, 290
dementia
  anosognosia, 147–146
Democritus, 4
denial, 145–147

Dennett, Daniel, 15, 18, 27-28, 35, 40, 136, 201
   denial of the existence of the self, 182
   eliminative materialism, 44-45
   myth of the Cartesian Theatre, 62
   on qualia, 44-45 on compatibilism, 64
   on mysterianism, 52
   on p-zombies, 43
   on the China brain, 48
depersonalisation, 173-174, 331
depression, 191, 195
   sleep deprivation treatment, 301
derealisation, 173-174, 331
   case study, 175
Descartes, René, 20, 30-31, 140, 159, 220
determinism
   compatibility with free will, 64
   free will and, 58-61
   laws of physics, 58-59
   moral responsibility and, 67
   probabilistic nature of quantum mechanics, 60
   role in human behaviour, 59-60
diamorphine. *See* heroin
Dinoire, Isabelle, 161, 181
discrimination
   consciousness raising, 373-374
dissociative amnesia, 174, 331
dissociative drugs, 351
dissociative fugue, 174-175
dissociative identity disorder (DID), 175-176, 331
dissociative states, 173-176
   depersonalisation, 173-174
   derealisation, 173-174
   derealisation case study, 175
   dissociative identity disorder (DID), 175-176, 331
   out-of-body experiences, 274-277
DMT (N,N-dimethyltryptamine), 281, 353-355
dolphins
   intelligence and self-awareness, 112, 113
Domhoff, G. William, 321
Donaldson, David, 28
dopamine (DA), 65, 294, 378
dopaminergic system, 293
The DreamBank, 313
dreaming, 18, 220
dreams
   activation-synthesis model, 316-317
   content of, 312-316
   creativity and, 317-318
   default mode network and, 312
   dream diary, 307-308
   dream enhancers, 311-312
   dreamless sleep, 308
   hyperassociative nature, 318
   intruder experience, 313-314
   learning and, 321
   level of dream recall, 308-309
   lucid dreams, 310-311
   memory pruning, 321
   nightmares, 313-314
   post-analytic theories, 320-321
   post-traumatic stress disorder (PTSD) nightmares, 314
   problem solving and, 317-318
   psychoanalysis and, 319-320
   reality of, 305-307
   recurring dreams, 315-316
   role of the default mode network, 317
   sleep paralysis, 314-315
   stages of sleep and, 308
   The DreamBank, 313
   threat simulation theory, 318-319
   what a dream is, 307-308
   why we dream, 316-321
   Zhuangzi's (Chuang-Tzu's) butterfly dream, 306-307
Dretske, Fred, 206
Droste effect, 208
drugs. *See* psychoactive drugs
dualism, 29-32
   emergentism, 32
   free will and, 60-61
   occasionalism, 31
   parallelism, 31
   property dualism, 32, 53
   substance dualism, 31-32, 53
Dussutour, Audrey, 113
dying brain hypothesis, 281
dynamic core hypothesis, 253

earthworms
   cyclic activity, 288
Eccles, John, 32
ecstasy, 363
Edelman, David, 110
Edelman, Gerald, 17, 252-253
Edison, Thomas, 318
ego theory of the self, 159-160, 173, 181
Einstein, Albert, 34, 213
   Annus Mirabilis (1905), 214-215
electrocorticography,
electroencephalography (EEG), 240, 242
   readiness potential (RP or BP), 71-72
electrophysiology of consciousness, 242-244
   brain waves, 242-244

electrophysiology of sleep, 290–291
eliminative materialism, 44–45
embodied cognition, 93–94, 180
emergence, 81
   definition of, 209
   feature of complex systems, 209
emergence theory of consciousness, 209–210
emergentism, 32
empiricism, 219–220
enactivism, 93–94, 180
encephalitis lethargica, 282–283
endogenous opioids, 349
endorphins, 39, 281
entheogens, 64–66, 271, 350, 354–355, 359, 378
environmental effects on behaviour, 64–66
epilepsy, 278–279
epinephrine, 294
epiphanies, 371–373
epistemology
   definition, 26
Esdaile, James, 323–324, 327
ESP (extra-sensory perception), 385–386
ether, 248
ethics
   neuroethics, 69
evolution of consciousness, 120–124
   bicameral mind, 123–124
   development of cognitive fluidity, 120–121
   development of meta-awareness, 123
   importance of language, 121–122
   Neanderthals, 121
   power of recursion, 122–123
   protoconsciousness, 121
   role of social intelligence, 120
   Upper Palaeolithic Revolution in human evolution, 120–121
evolution of the brain, 244–245
evolutionary functions of sleep, 301–302
evolutionary robotics, 97–98
executive self, 163–164
experience sampling, 136–137
extended mind hypothesis, 180–181

face transplants, 161, 181
falsification
   role in science, 7–8
feedback loops, 93
   feature of complex systems, 209
feminism
   consciousness raising, 373–374
fentanyl, 348

Flanagan, Owen, 42
flocking behaviour, 209, 210
flocking behaviour in birds
   simulation of, 80–81
foetus
   capacity to feel pain, 245
   development of consciousness in, 245
Foulkes, David, 321
Franklin, Stan, 92
free association, 148
free energy model of consciousness, 211
free will, 57
   antisocial personality disorder (ASPD), 68
   as an illusion, 61
   behavioural effects of toxoplasmosis, 65–66
   benefits of believing in, 62–63
   compatibility with determinism, 64
   construction of the illusion of, 62–63
   deciding to act, 69–73
   determinism and, 58–61
   determinist view of human behaviour, 59–60
   diminished responsibility, 68
   distinction between people and objects, 57–58
   dualism and, 60–61
   effects of early upbringing and environment, 68–69
   environmental effects on behaviour, 64–66
   homunculus theory of the self, 62
   implications for crime and punishment, 66–69
   individual responsibility and, 5
   inner self and, 62
   involuntary action, 73–76
   laws of physics and, 57–59
   mental illness and, 68
   moral responsibility and, 67
   nature of the 'I' who can choose, 62
   of the soul, 60–61
   probabilistic nature of quantum mechanics, 60
   problem of consciousness, 4, 22, 406
   purpose of psychology in understanding crime, 68–69
   purpose of punishment, 67
   sense of agency, 69
   social priming, 65
Fregoli syndrome, 142–143
Freud, Sigmund, 16, 162, 185
   experimentation with cocaine as a treatment, 347
   on recurring dreams, 315, 316
   psychoanalysis of dreams, 319
   study of hysterical disorders, 331
   study with Charcot, 324–325
   theory of the unconscious, 147–150
   use of hypnosis to treat hysteria, 324–325

Freudian slips, 148
frightening near-death experiences, 279
Friston, Karl, 211
fruit fly (*Drosophila*) brain, 101
fugue states, 174–175, 331
functional magnetic resonance imaging (fMRI), 9, 240
functional near infrared spectroscopy (fNIRS), 262
functionalism, 45–51
    arguments against, 49–51
    China brain thought experiment, 47–48
    Chinese room thought experiment, 50–51
    computation approach to cognition, 48–49
    dancing qualia thought experiment, 49–50
    definition, 45
    qualia and, 49–51
    replacing human neurons with silicon versions, 45–46
    silicon brains, 45–46
    structure and functions of neurons, 46–47
    substrate independence, 99

Gage, Phineas, 164
galantamine, 312
Galileo Galilei, 20, 26, 33
Gallup, Gordon, 114, 115
gamma-aminobutyric acid (GABA), 294
gamma waves, 243
    role in perceptual binding, 232–233
ganzfeld technique, 273–274
    psi studies, 393
Gardner, Martin, 52
Gardner, Randy, 300
Gazzaniga, Michael, 171
Geller, Uri, 390, 396
general anaesthesia, 247–251
    Bispectral Index Scale (BIS), 250
    chloroform, 247, 248
    ether, 248
    history of anaesthesia, 248
    how general anaesthetics work, 249–250
    intravenous administration, 248
    nitrous oxide (laughing gas), 247, 248
    post-operative recall, 250
    propofol, 248, 249, 250
    role of the thalamus, 250
    sodium thiopental, 248
Geschwind syndrome, 377
ghosts, 396–399
global workspace theory of consciousness, 91, 197–198, 253
glutamate, 294
glymphatic system, 302

Go (game)
    computer programs that play, 89–90
'god helmet' experiments (Persinger), 376–377
Graham, Billy, 329
grapheme-colour synaesthesia, 230
gravity-induced loss of consciousness (G-LOC), 275
Gross, Maurice, 397
Gurdjieff, George Ivanovitch, 372, 373
Guthrie, Francis, 83

habits
    automatic nature of, 74–76
HAL 9000 computer (*2001: A Space Odyssey*), 104
Hall, Calvin, 320–321
Hallam, Clint, 161
hallucinations
    auditory verbal hallucinations (AVH), 190
hallucinogens, 350–361
haloperidol, 141
Hameroff, Stuart, 212, 398
Hankins, Peter, 15
Harari, Yuval, 367
Harris, Sam, 52
Harrison, George, 357
Hawking, Stephen, 262
heautoscopy, 176–177
Heidegger, Martin, 135
Heisenberg's Uncertainty Principle, 213
hemispatial neglect, 229
henbane, 350–351
Heraclitus, 160
heroin, 349–350
    overdose risk, 350
    withdrawal symptoms, 349–350
herpes simplex encephalitis
    amnesia caused by, 166–169
    damage caused to the brain, 167–168
heterophenomenology, 136
higher-order thought theory, 207–209
Hilgard, Ernest, 331
Hill, Betty and Barney, 333–334
Hinduism, 400
hoax mediums, 390–392
Hobbes, Thomas, 64
Hobson, John Allan, 295, 316–317
Hoffman, D.D., 236
Hoffmann, Albert, 357
Hofstadter, Douglas, 18–19, 37, 208, 209, 236, 263
Holender, Daniel, 153
Holland, John, 97

homunculus theory of the self, 5, 62, 132, 158, 159
Hopkins, Matthew, 149
Houdini, Harry, 357–358
Hubbard, Alfred (Captain Trips), 357
Hull, Clark, 333
human behaviour
    determinist view, 59–60
Human Connectome Project, 46
human evolution
    bicameral mind, 123–124
    development of cognitive fluidity, 120–121
    development of meta-awareness, 123
    Upper Palaeolithic Revolution, 120–121
Hume, David, 159, 219, 397
Humphrey, Nicholas, 120
Hurston, Zora Neale, 41
Husserl, Edmund, 135–136
Huxley, Aldous, 352
hydranencephaly, 246
hydrocephalus, 247
hydrocodone, 348
hydrogen sulphide, 294
hypnosis
    debate over the hypnotic state, 330–332
    dissociation, 330–331
    Esdaile state, 327
    history of, 323–325
    horse whisperers, 329–330
    insights about cognition, 338
    non-state theories, 331–332
    popular image of, 323
    self-hypnosis (auto-hypnosis), 324, 337–338
    snake charmers, 329–330
    Stanford Hypnotic Susceptibility Scale, 328
    Stanford Suggestibility Scale, 327
    state theory of, 330–331
    Tellegen Absorption Scale, 327, 328
    used to treat hysteria, 324–325
    views on what happens during, 330–332
hypnotic drugs, 297
hypnotic effects, 332–336
    anaesthesia/analgesia, 335–336
    false memories, 333–334
    hypnosurgery, 335–336
    hypnotic suggestions, 332
    memory, 333–334
    neuroscience of hypnosis, 336
    post-hypnotic amnesia, 333–334
    question of safety, 334–335
    stopping smoking, 332

hypnotic process, 325–330
    distinction between stage and clinical settings, 326
    hypnotic induction, 326–327
    hypnotic trance, 327
    individual differences in hypnotisability, 327–328
    learning suggestibility, 329
    what makes a good hypnotist, 329–330
hypocretin, 300
hysteria, 324–325, 331

idealism, 32
ideasthesia, 230
identity, 156
    components of, 156
    psychological and physical aspects, 156–157
identity theory, 43–44
illusions
    cutaneous rabbit illusion, 226
    free will as an illusory construction, 62–63
    Kanizsa triangle, 139
    Muller-Lyer illusion, 187–188
    nature of, 61
    non-visual illusions, 226–227
    phi illusion, 201–202
    Pinocchio illusion, 231
    rubber hand illusion, 178–179
    self as an illusion, 181–182
    visual illusions, 225–226
illusory contours, 139
inattentional blindness, 132
incompatibilism, 64
incubation
    role in problem solving, 189
incubus, 314, 315
infantile amnesia, 165
infants
    consciousness in, 18
infra-slow waves, 244
infrasound effects, 387, 388
inner speech, 189–191
    role of Broca's area of the brain, 190
insular cortex (insula), 169–170
integrated information theory, 256
intelligence
    defining, 102–103
intentionality, 206–207
    of beliefs, 139
    of consciousness, 15–16
intermetamorphosis, 143

introspection, 6-7, 131, 207
   analytic, 133-134
   consciousness and, 132
   descriptive, 133-134
   effects of meditation, 367
   experience sampling, 136-137
   influence of cognitive dissonance, 138
   interpretive, 133-134
   limitations of, 137-138
   phenomenology, 135-136
   process of, 133-134
   stimulus error, 133-134
   stream of consciousness, 132
   types of, 133-134
   Zen Buddhism, 380-381
intuition pumps, 27-28
inverted colour spectrum argument, 36-38
involuntary action, 73-76
   alien hand syndrome, 73-74
   anarchic hand syndrome, 73-74
   habits, 74-76
   myoclonic jerks, 73
   obsessive-compulsive disorder (OCD), 76
   psychological compulsions, 76
   skills, 74-76
Iron Man and Tony Stark, 35-36

Jackson, Frank, 34
Jackson, Michael, 248
Jahn, Robert, 396
Jainism, 400
James, William, 21, 52, 132, 133, 161, 162
Jaynes, Julian, 123-124
Jefferson Airplane, 357, 358
Jennifer Aniston neuron, 235
jimsonweed (*Datura stramonium*), 351, 362
Jourdain, Eleanor, 387-388
Joyce, James, 373
Julius Caesar, 398
Jung, Carl Gustav
   archetypes, 151
   collective unconscious, 151
   psychoanalysis of dreams, 319-320

Kahneman, Daniel, 7
Kane, Robert, 64
Kanizsa triangle, 139
Kant, Immanuel, 162, 207, 219
Kasparov, Garry, 84-85, 86
Kekulé, Friedrich August, 317-318
Keller, Helen, 14

Kelvin, Lord, 213
Kepler, Johannes, 20, 26, 33
ketamine, 274, 351, 363
Kesey, Ken, 358
khat, 362
Kierkegaard, Søren, 6
Kinsey Report, 137
Kleitman, Nathaniel, 290
Knight, Rob, 95
knowledge argument against materialism, 34-36
knowledge by acquaintance, 36
knowledge by description, 36
Koch, Christoph, 110, 124-125, 255, 256
Köhler, Wolfgang, 205
Korsakoff's syndrome, 166
Kosslyn, Stephen, 191-192
Kramnik, Vladimir, 85
Kulagina, Nina, 396
Kurzweil, Ray, 90, 262

Langton, Christopher, 80
language
   consciousness and, 186-192
   culture and, 186-188
   inner speech, 189-191
   power of recursion, 122-123
   propositional attitudes, 188
   role in the evolution of consciousness, 121-122
   role of Broca's area of the brain, 190
   symbols, 189
   thinking and, 188-189
Language of Thought Hypothesis, 188-189
Laplace, Pierre-Simon, 58-59, 60
Larsen, Bent, 84
laudanum, 271, 348
L-DOPA, 142, 283
learning
   dreams and, 321
   sleep and, 302-303
   use of subliminal messaging, 153
learning without neurons
   slime mould (the blob), 113-114
Leary, Timothy, 271, 358, 359
lecithin, 311
Lee Se-dol, 89
Lennard, Adam, 298
Lennon, John, 357
Levy, David, 84
libertarianism, 64
Libet, Benjamin
   experiments on 'voluntary' movement, 70-71, 72-73

INDEX 475

LIDA (Learning Intelligent Distributed Agent), 92–93
life review experience (LRE), 279–280
light
  behaviour of, 213, 214
linguistic determinism, 187
linguistic relativism, 187
Llinás, Rodolfo, 200
Locke, John, 36, 162, 182, 207
locked-in syndrome, 242, 261–262
Loebner Prize, 87
Loewi, Otto, 293, 317, 318
Lorenz, Edward, 209
Lou Gehrig's disease, 262
Love (band), 359
Low, Philip, 110
LSD, 280, 281, 355–361
  1960s counter-culture and, 357–358
  ego dissolution, 360–361
  history of use, 357–358
  neuroscience of hallucinogens, 359–361
  summer of love (1967), 358
  therapeutic use of hallucinogens, 362–363
  Timothy Leary and, 271
  urban myths associated with, 356–357

MacDougall, Duncan, 20–21
machine consciousness, 79
  artificial intelligence (AI), 81–92
  artificial life (A-life), 79–81
  autopoiesis, 80
  brain–computer interfaces, 101–102
  building a brain, 98–102
  constructing an artificial brain, 99–101
  disembodied AI, 92–94
  distinction between intelligence and consciousness, 102–103
  future of AI, 102–105
  LIDA (Learning Intelligent Distributed Agent), 92–93
  neuroprosthesis, 101–102
  part-brain emulation, 100–101
  potential threats from AI, 104–105
  robotics, 94–98
  Turing machine, 99
  uploading minds into computers, 100
  whole-brain emulation, 100
magic mushrooms, 353, 360
magical thinking, 63
magnetic resonance imaging (MRI), 34–35
magnetoencephalography (MEG), 240
Malcolm, Norman, 305
mandrake, 350–351

manic-depressive disorder, 377
Marcel, Anthony, 152–153
Mashour, George, 249
mass hysteria, 143–145
  Beatle mania, 144
  Blackburn case (1965), 143
  caused by pop stars, 144
  moral panics, 144
  Morangos com Açúcar Virus (Strawberries with sugar), Portugal (2006), 144
  satanic child abuse stories, 149–150
  shrinking penis panic (*koro*), 144
  Soap opera virus, Portugal (2006), 144
  Tanganyika laughter epidemic (1962), 144–145
  witch trials, 149–150
materialism, 33, 43–45
  eliminative materialism, 44–45
  knowledge argument, 34–36
  reductive materialism (reductionism), 43–44
  See also physicalism
Mayhew, Christopher, 352
McCarley, Robert, 295, 316–317
McCarthy, John, 82
McCartney, Paul, 357
McGinn, Colin, 52
McGregor, Dion, 298
meaning in life
  role of consciousness, 6
meditation
  effects on introspective capacity, 367
  effects on the default mode network, 371
  insight meditation, 367
  neuroscience of, 368–369
  physiological effects, 367
  practice of, 366–367
  raising body temperature, 367
  vipassana meditation, 367
  See also mindfulness
melatonin, 288–289
  circadian rhythm, 289–290
Mele, Alfred, 72
memory
  amnesia, 166–169
  anterograde amnesia, 166
  dreaming and, 321
  episodic memory, 166
  false memories, 333–334
  hypnotic effects, 333–334
  retrograde amnesia, 166
  semantic memory, 166
  See also autobiographical memory

Mendeleev, Dmitri, 318
mental illness
   moral responsibility and, 68
mental imagery, 191–192
   dual code theory, 191
   propositional theory, 191
   spatial representation theory, 191
mental models, 202–203
mental time travel, 122–123, 203–205
mereological fallacy
   distinction between brain and mind, 29
Merleau-Ponty, Maurice, 135
mescaline, 352–353
Mesmer, Franz, 323
mesmerism, 323
meta-awareness, 123, 207
metacognition, 164, 203, 205, 207
metaconsciousness, 207
metaphysics
   definition, 26
methamphetamine, 346
methylphenidate, 346
Metzinger, Thomas, 181
microbots, 97
microconsciousness, 234
migraine, 277–278, 279
Mill, John Stuart, 219
mind
   definition, 28
   myth of the Cartesian Theatre, 62
   relationship to the brain, 28–29
mind-altering drugs. *See* psychoactive drugs
mind-body problem
   definition, 26
   distinction between brain and mind, 29
   dualism, 29–32, 53
   functionalism, 45–51
   inverted colour spectrum argument, 36–38
   knowledge argument, 34–36
   materialism, 43–45
   mereological fallacy, 29
   monism, 29–30, 32–33
   mysterianism, 51–53
   p-zombies (philosophical zombies), 41–43
   pain, 38–41
   panpsychism, 124–126
   qualia, 29–30
   relationship between brain and mind, 28–29
   thought experiments, 27–28
mind–brain identity theory, 43–44

mindfulness, 370–371
   problems with multitasking, 187–188
   See also meditation
mind-wandering, 194–196
   task unrelated thoughts (TUTs), 194
minimally conscious state (MCS), 261
mirror test of self-recognition, 114–115
mise en abyme, 208
Moberly, Charlotte, 387–388
modelling the world, 202–211
   emergence theory of consciousness, 209–210
   mental models, 202–203
   mental time travel, 203–205
   metacognition, 205
   recursion, 207–209
   representation and consciousness, 210–211
   representational theories of consciousness, 206–207
Molaison, Henry, 166
monism, 29–30, 32–33
   anomalous monism, 33
   conscious realism, 32
   idealism, 32
   knowledge argument, 34–36
   materialism, 33, 43–45
   neutral monism, 33
   physicalism, 33
Moore's law, 90
moral panics, 144
   satanic child abuse stories, 149–150
   witch trials, 149–150
moral responsibility
   antisocial personality disorder (ASPD), 68
   determinism and, 67
   diminished responsibility, 68
   effects of early upbringing and environment, 68–69
   free will and, 67
   mental illness and, 68
   neurocriminology, 69
   personality types and, 69
Morangos com Açúcar Virus (Strawberries with sugar), Portugal (2006), 144
morphine, 348–349
Morton, William T., 247, 248
motor control
   awareness of, 33
motor neurone disease, 242, 262
Muller-Lyer illusion, 187–188
multiple drafts model of consciousness, 201
multiple personalities. *See* dissociative identity disorder (DID)

multitasking
  problems with, 370
music
  in the stream of consciousness, 132
Musk, Elon, 102
myoclonic jerks, 73
mysterianism, 51–53

Nagel, Thomas, 12, 13–14
naloxone, 349
nanobots, 97
narcolepsy, 297, 346
Neanderthals, 121
near-death experiences, 20, 279–282
  biological explanations for, 281–282
  fear of death and, 281
  life-changing effects of, 281
Necker cube, 221–222
neglect (perceptual disorder), 146, 229–230
neural correlates of consciousness, 239–242
  anterior cingulate cortex (ACC), 255
  astonishing hypothesis, 241–242
  claustrum, 253–255
  coma and coma-like states, 260–261
  definition of, 241
  definitions of death, 261
  developmental aspect, 245–246
  dynamic core hypothesis, 253
  electrophysiology of consciousness, 242–244
  frontal or posterior cortical involvement, 252
  general anaesthesia, 247–251
  imaging and mind reading, 242
  incomplete brains, 246–247
  integrated information theory, 256
  locked-in syndrome, 261–262
  problem of, 22, 404–405
  radical plasticity of the neural system, 256–257
  re-entry and the thalamo-cortical loop, 252–253
  thalamo-cortical loop, 251–255
  thalamo-cortical system, 241
  thalamus, 251–255
neural Darwinism, 252
neural enhancer (nootropic) drugs, 104
neural plasticity, 256–257
neurocriminology, 69
neuroethics, 69
neurology of sleep, 291–293
neuronal workspace theory of consciousness, 198–201
  brain circuits involved, 200–201

neurons
  structure and functions of, 46–47
neuropeptides, 297
neuropharmacology of sleep, 293–294
neuroprosthesis, 101–102
neuroscience
  consciousness and, 4
  development of brain imaging, 9
  hallucinogens, 359–361
  history of, 8–9
  hypnosis, 336
  meditation, 368–369
  of the self, 169–171
  religious experiences, 376–378
  search for the seat of consciousness, 4
  split-brain studies, 8–9
neurotransmitters, 47
  acetylcholine (ACh), 294
  adrenaline, 294
  dopamine (DA), 294
  epinephrine, 294
  gamma-aminobutyric acid (GABA), 294
  glutamate, 294
  noradrenaline, 294
  norepinephrine, 294
  role in sleep, 293–294
  serotonin (5-HT), 294
neutral monism, 33
Newton, Isaac, 34, 57–58, 213
Niemann, Albert, 347
nightmares, 313–314
nitric oxide, 294
nitrous oxide (laughing gas), 247, 248
Noë, Alva, 241
nonlinearity
  feature of complex systems, 209
noradrenaline, 294
norepinephrine, 294
Nozick, Robert, 64
Nutt, David, 343, 362, 363

obsessive-compulsive disorder (OCD), 76
occasionalism, 31
Old Hag (folklore), 314–315
ontology
  definition, 26
opiates and opioids, 348–350
opium, 271
optimisation
  free energy model of consciousness, 211
optogenetics, 240

orexin, 297, 300
Orkney child abuse scandal (1991), 149
other minds
   problem of, 13-14
Ouspensky, P.D., 373
out-of-body experiences, 176, 274-277
   explaining, 275-276
   induction in the laboratory, 275
   induction techniques, 276-277
   Monroe technique, 277

p-zombies (philosophical zombies), 41-43
   conceivability and the need for consciousness
   explanations of the zombie myth
   function of consciousness
   lack of consciousness
Pahnke, Walter N., 359
pain, 38-41
   argument by analogy to the existence of other minds, 40
   capacity for pain perception in animals, 116-117
   capacity for pain perception in plants, 117
   congenital analgesia, 40
   dissociation from, 40
   endorphins and, 39
   in babies, 40-41
   mental aspect of, 39-40
   physical aspect of, 39
   private nature of, 38
   programming a robot to avoid harm, 40
   simulation in robots, 44
Paivio, Allan, 191
panpsychism, 124-126, 256
Paracelsus, 248
parallelism, 31
paranoid schizophrenia, 141
parapsychology
   anomalistic psychology, 384
   clairvoyance, 385-386
   definition of, 384
   effects of low-frequency sound, 388
   ESP (extra-sensory perception), 385-386
   ethical issues, 389
   experimental studies, 384
   ghosts, 396-399
   how spontaneous phenomena change with time, 388
   infrasound effects, 387, 388
   phenomena that have a physical explanation, 387, 388
   precognition, 385-386
   psi, 385-386
   psychokinesis (PK), 385-386

   reincarnation, 400-401
   sonic phenomena, 388
   sonic weapons, 388
   spontaneous phenomena, 384-385, 386-389
   survival after death, 398-401
   telepathy, 385-386
   the Hum, 388
   types of paranormal phenomena, 384-385
   ultrasound effects, 388
   unreliability of memories of events, 387-388
   Versailles time travel incident, 387-388
   what it tells us about consciousness, 398
   Zener cards, 389
parapsychology research, 389-398
   Bem's experiments on psi, 394-395
   ESP studies, 389-390
   experimental design issues, 391
   experimenter effect, 395
   file drawer effect, 393
   hoax mediums, 390-392
   poltergeists, 392-397
   psi in the ganzfeld, 393
   psychic superstars, 389-390
   psychokinesis (PK), 395-396
   remote viewing, 393-394
   replicability problem, 391
   sensory leaking and cueing problems, 391
   sheep-goat effect, 395
   spoon bending, 396
   studies with null results not published, 393
   trait and state studies, 395
   use of ASCs to help detect psi, 391-393
   what would convince a sceptic, 397-398
parasomnias. *See* sleep disorders
Parfit, Derek, 159-160
Parkinson's disease, 142, 291, 294, 378
parsimony principle, 44
partial awareness hypothesis, 200
Pazder, Lawrence, 149
peak experiences, 371-373
Pearce, Hubert, 389, 390
Penn and Teller, 392
Penrose, Roger, 212
Pepperberg, Irene, 147-146
perception, 218
   agnosia, 227, 228
   alexia, 227
   Balint's syndrome, 233-234
   binding problem, 231-235
   binocular rivalry, 222-224

bistable figures, 221
blindsight, 227–229
brain in a vat (thought experiment), 220
change blindness, 224–225
dreaming and, 220
empiricism, 219–220
filling in, 221
grand illusion of, 235–236
inattentional blindness, 225
inverting glasses experiment, 218
Jennifer Aniston neuron, 235
Necker cube, 221–222
neglect, 229–230
non-visual illusions, 226–227
no-report paradigm, 227
normal visual perception, 220–227
perception–action hypothesis, 228–229
phenomenalism, 219
proprioception, 231
prosopagnosia, 227
simultagnosia, 233–234
single-neuron response, 234–235
synaesthesia, 230–231
two-visual-systems hypothesis, 228–229
visual awareness, 234–235
visual illusions, 225–226
visuo-spatial perception disorders, 227–231
Perrot, Dominique, 397
Persinger, Michael, 376–377
persistent vegetative state (PVS), 260
person identity nodes, 142
personality types
  moral responsibility and, 69
peyote, 352–353, 362
phantom bodies, 176–177
phantom limb pain, 177–178
phantom limbs, 177–178
  motor control disorders and, 180
phencyclidine (PCP, angel dust), 351
phenobarbital, 297
phenomenal consciousness (P-consciousness), 16–17, 208–209
phenomenalism, 219
phenomenology, 131, 135–136
  definition of, 135
  heterophenomenology, 136
phi illusion, 201–202
philosophical zombies. *See* p-zombies
philosophy
  consciousness and, 4–5
  definition, 10, 26

terms and disciplines, 26
thought experiments, 10
philosophy of mind, 4, 26
  definition, 26
  See also mind–body problem
philosophy of science
  definition, 26
phonetic inner speech, 189–190
phonological inner speech, 189–190
photoelectric effect, 213, 214
physicalism, 33
  arguments for and against, 35–36
  knowledge argument, 34–36
  See also materialism
physics
  history of, 33–34
  laws of, 33–34, 57–59
Piaget, Jean, 93, 118, 189
pineal gland, 30–31, 289–290
Pink Floyd, 357
Pinker, Steven, 52
Pirahã people, Amazon basin, 187
plants
  capacity for pain perception, 117
Plato, 30, 160
Platynereis dumerilii (marine worm), 288
Playfair, Guy, 397
Plutarch, 160
Poe, Edgar Allen, 96
polio, 283
poltergeists, 392–397
ponto-geniculo-occipital waves (PGO waves), 291
pop stars
  mass hysteria caused by, 144
Popper, Karl, 7–8
positron-emission tomography (PET), 240
post-operative recall, 250
post-traumatic stress disorder (PTSD), 195
  emotional numbing, 331
  from watching television, 397
  nightmares, 314
  recurring nightmares, 316
Pratt, Joseph, 389, 390
prazosin, 314
precognition, 385–386
preconscious, 147–148
prejudice, 141
primary consciousness, 17
privacy of consciousness, 12, 13–14
private knowledge, 36

problem solving
   incubation, 189
   through dreams, 317–318
problems of consciousness, 21–23
   altered state problem, 22, 408–409
   binding problem, 22, 408
   cognitive problem, 22, 405
   cultural differences, 409–410
   definition problem, 403
   easy problems, 15
   explanatory gap, 15
   free will problem, 22, 406
   hard problem, 15, 21, 404
   neural correlates problem, 22, 404–405
   other minds, 13–14
   science problem, 22, 410–411
   self problem, 22, 406–407
   temporal problem, 22, 405–406
   unconscious problem, 22, 407
   why problem, 22, 407–408
   See also mind–body problem
property dualism, 32, 53
propofol, 248, 249, 250
propositional attitudes, 139, 188
proprioception, 231
   Pinocchio illusion, 231
prosocial behaviour, 119
prosopagnosia, 142, 227
Proust, Marcel, 373
psi, 385–386
psilocybin, 353, 359, 360, 362
   therapeutic use of hallucinogens, 362–363
psychedelic drugs, 352–361
psychoactive drugs
   alcohol, 362
   amphetamine, 345–346
   ayahuasca, 354, 362, 363
   belladonna, 350–351
   betel (areca) nut, 362
   bufotenin, 350
   caffeine, 269, 345, 362
   cannabis, 343–344, 361–362
   CIA mind control Project MKULTRA, 359
   classification, 342–343
   coca leaves, 362
   cocaine, 347–348
   Concord State Prison experiment, 359
   crack cocaine, 348
   crystal meth, 346
   cultural differences in drug use, 362
   dangers of cannabis use, 361–362
   deliriants, 350–351
   dissociative drugs, 351
   DMT (N,N-dimethyltryptamine), 353–355
   ecstasy, 363
   effects of mind-altering drugs, 20
   effects on serotonin receptors, 363
   endogenous opioids, 349
   entheogens, 352, 354–355, 359, 378
   exploring legal forms, 341
   Good Friday Marsh Chapel experiment, 359
   hallucinogen persisting perception disorder (HPPD), 356
   hallucinogens, 350–361
   henbane, 350–351
   heroin, 349–350
   hypnotic drugs, 297
   jimsonweed, 362
   ketamine, 351, 363
   khat, 362
   LSD, 355–361
   magic mushrooms, 353, 360
   mandrake, 350–351
   medicinal use of cannabis, 362
   mescaline, 352–353
   methamphetamine, 346
   methylphenidate, 346
   modes of action, 341
   morphine, 348–349
   neuroscience of hallucinogens, 359–361
   opiates and opioids, 348–350
   peyote, 352–353, 362
   phencyclidine (PCP, angel dust), 351
   psilocybin, 353, 359, 360, 362
   psychedelic drugs, 352–361
   research challenges, 341
   Ritalin (methylphenidate), 346
   social context of drug use, 361–363
   SSRIs (selective serotonin reuptake inhibitors), 360
   stimulant psychosis, 345–346
   stimulants, 345–348
   synthetic opioids, 348
   therapeutic use of hallucinogens, 362–363
   use in shamanic ceremonies, 363
psychoanalysis
   dreams and, 319–320
psychokinesis (PK), 385–386, 395–396
psychological compulsions, 76
psychology
   consciousness and, 3
   early AI models of, 88–89

history of development, 21
purpose in understanding crime, 68–69
psychonauts, 270–271
Puthoff, Harold, 394
Puységur, Marquis de, 333
Pylyshyn, Zenon, 191–192
Pythagoras, 400

qualia, 29–30
   eliminative materialism, 44–45
   functionalism and, 49–51
   inverted colour spectrum argument, 36–38
quantum computers, 213
   life simulations, 81
quantum consciousness, 212–213
quantum mechanics, 213–214
   involvement in life, 81
   probabilistic nature of, 60
quantum models of survival, 398
Quine, W.V.O., 44

radical plasticity of the neural system, 256–257
Ramachandran, Vilayanur S., 177
Ramanujan, Srinivasa, 318
rationalism, 219
reality
   grand illusion of, 235–236
recency effect
   autobiographical memory, 165
recursion, 19, 122–123, 189, 207–209
reductive materialism (reductionism), 43–44
reflection, 207
reincarnation, 400–401
religious beliefs
   nature of the soul, 20
   reincarnation, 400–401
religious experiences, 374–376
   absorption score and, 376
   Carmelite nuns, 375–377
   entheogens, 378
   neuroscience of, 376–378
   nine characteristics of mystical states, 374–375
   Saint Bernadette of Lourdes, 375
   temporal lobe activity and religion, 376–378
   whirling dervishes of Sufism, 375
remote viewing, 393–394
representation
   consciousness and, 210–211
   mental models, 202–203
   mental time travel, 203–205

representational theories of consciousness, 206–207
   higher-order thought theory, 207–209
representational theory of mind, 189
repressed memories, 149–150
restricted environmental stimulation therapy (REST), 273
reticular activating system, 292–293
retinal–geniculate–striate pathway, 228
Rey, Georges, 44
Rhine, J.B., 389
Rhine, Louise E., 389
Ritalin (methylphenidate), 346
ritual behaviour in chimpanzees, 119
robo-rat (guided rat) experiment, 62–63
robotics, 94–98
   Amazon Robotics, 96–97
   CRONOS, 95
   definition of a robot, 94
   development of robots, 94–95
   evolutionary robotics, 97–98
   forms of aliens, 96
   genetic algorithms, 97–98
   Golem Project, 98
   humanoid robots, 95
   microbots, 97
   nanobots, 97
   pain simulation in robots, 44
   robot interactions with the world, 11
   robots and consciousness, 98
   swarm intelligence, 96–97
   Three Laws of Robotics (Asimov), 104–105
   uncanny valley, 95
Rogers, Carl, 87
Rolling Stones, 359
romantic love (limerence)
   altered state of consciousness, 283
Rorschach inkblot test, 148
Russell, Bertrand, 36, 188

Sacks, Oliver, 166
sage leaf extract, 312
Saint Bernadette of Lourdes, 375
Sapir–Whorf hypothesis, 187
Sartre, Jean-Paul, 135, 352, 371
satanic child abuse stories, 149–150
scepticism, 140, 220
schizophrenia, 141, 142, 180, 195, 377
   auditory verbal hallucinations (AVH), 190
Schneider, Adam, 313

science
  role of falsification, 7–8
science of consciousness, 22, 410–411
scientific experimentation, 7–10
scopolamine, 351
Searle, John R., 50–51
secondary consciousness, 17
sedative-hypnotic drugs, 297
selective attention, 192
self, 156–164
  amnesia and, 166–169
  as an illusion, 181–182
  autobiographical memory and, 165
  autoscopy, 176–177
  awareness of motor control, 179–180
  boundaries of, 176–181
  bundle theory, 159–160, 173
  central and peripheral self, 161
  continuity of existence, 165–169
  core and extended self, 161
  Cotard's delusion and, 182
  dissociative states, 173–176
  ego theory, 159–160, 173, 181
  executive self, 163–164
  extended consciousness, 180–181
  heautoscopy, 176–177
  homunculus theory, 5, 62, 158, 159
  in counterfactual situations, 157
  individual as the object of their consciousness, 156
  knower and known, 161
  meta-self, 158
  minimal self and narrative self, 161
  nature of the inner self, 62
  neuroscience of, 169–171
  notion of, 5
  phantom bodies, 176–177
  phantom limb pain, 177–178
  phantom limbs, 177–178, 180
  psychological and physical aspects, 156–157
  psychological self identifies with our physical self, 170–171
  recursive thinking about, 158
  rubber hand illusion, 178–179
  split-brain studies, 171–173
  three levels of (Damasio), 161–163
  transplants and, 161
  transporter problem, 159–160
  types of, 163–164
  viewed in the future, 157
self-awareness, 12, 13, 19–20

self-consciousness, 12, 208–209, 218
  definition of
self-hypnosis (auto-hypnosis), 337–338
self model, 157–158
self problem of consciousness, 22, 406–407
self-recognition, 114–115
  mirror test of
self-reference, 208
sensory deprivation, 272–274
sensory habituation, 272–274
serotonin (5-HT), 293, 294
serotonin receptor 2A, 281
serotonin receptors
  effects of psychoactive drugs, 363
Sertürner, Friedrich, 349
sexual dysfunction, 191
Shepard tone, 226
shrinking penis panic (*koro*), 144
Sikhism, 400
Simpson, James Young, 247, 248
simulations, 140
simultagnosia, 233–234
situated cognition, 93–94
skills
  automatic nature of, 74–76
Skinner, B.F., 21
Skynet AI (*Terminator* franchise), 11, 104
sleep
  action of the glymphatic system, 302
  definition of, 286–287
  evolutionary functions of, 301–302
  hypnagogic state, 287
  hypnopompic state, 287
  in animals, 287–288
  learning and, 302–303
  need at different ages, 287
  NREM sleep, 287
  reasons for studying, 286
  REM sleep, 287
  sleep journal, 287
  synaptic homeostasis hypothesis, 302
  ultradian sleep cycle, 287
  why we sleep, 301–303
sleep biology, 288–296
  AIM model of sleep and dreaming, 295–296
  animals, 289
  conjoined twins, 289
  electrophysiology of sleep, 290–291
  melatonin, 288–289
  melatonin circadian rhythm, 289–290

neurology of sleep, 291–293
neuropharmacology of sleep, 293–294
PGO waves, 291
role of brainstem structures, 291–293
role of neurotransmitters, 293–294
role of the pineal gland, 289–290
role of the reticular activating system, 292–293
stages of sleep, 290–291
unihemispheric sleep, 289
sleep deprivation, 272–274
to help depression, 301
sleep disorders, 296–299
bedwetting, 298
chronic insomnia disorder, 296
drug treatments for insomnia, 297
getting to sleep, 296–297
hypnotic drugs, 297
insomnia, 296–297
murder in your sleep, 299
narcolepsy, 297
night terrors, 298–299
nightmares, 299, 313–314
problems during sleep, 298–299
sleepwalking (somnambulism), 299
staying awake when you don't want to, 296–297
talking in your sleep, 298
sleep latency, 296
sleep paralysis, 314–315
slime mould (*Physarum polycephalum*)
learning without neurons, 113–114
Smart, J.J.C., 44
Smith, Michelle, 149
Soap opera virus, Portugal (2006), 144
social anxiety, 191
social intelligence
role in development of consciousness, 120
social intelligence hypothesis, 119
social interaction
theory of mind and, 119
social priming, 65, 153
Socrates, 400
sodium thiopental, 248
sodium valproate, 279
solipsism, 140
sonic phenomena, 388
sonic weapons, 388
soul
attempt to measure the mass of, 20–21
nature of, 20
question of free will, 60–61

source amnesia, 338
Späth, Ernst, 352
spatial neglect, 229–230
Sperry, Roger, 171
spiritual experiences, 374–376
spiritualism, 392
spirituality
consciousness and, 5–6
split-brain studies, 73, 171–173
spoon bending, 396
SQUIDs (superconducting quantum interference devices), 240
SSRIs (selective serotonin reuptake inhibitors), 294, 360
Stanford Hypnotic Susceptibility Scale, 328
Stanford Suggestibility Scale, 327
stereotypes, 141
Stevenson, Ian, 400–401
strange loops, 208, 209
Strassman, Richard, 355
Stratton, George M., 218
Strawson, Peter, 64
stream of consciousness, 132
subjective doubles syndrome, 143
subjective experience
private knowledge, 36
qualia, 29–30
subliminal advertising, 152
subliminal processing, 147, 152–153
substance dualism, 30–31–32, 53
substrate independence, 99
Sufism
whirling dervishes, 375
superstitious beliefs, 63
suprachiasmatic nucleus (SCN), 290
survival after death, 398–401
ghosts, 396–399
reincarnation, 400–401
Sutherland, Stuart, 11
Swann, Ingo, 390, 394
swarm intelligence, 96–97, 209
symbols, 189
manipulation, 49
synaesthesia, 230–231
synaptic homeostasis hypothesis, 302

Tanganyika laughter epidemic (1962), 144–145
tangled loops, 209
Targ, Russell, 394
telepathy, 385–386
Tellegen Absorption Scale, 81–92, 327, 328, 376

temporal lobe activity and religion, 376–378
temporal lobe epilepsy, 376–377
temporal problem of consciousness, 22, 405–406
Terminator series of films, 11
tetrodotoxin, 41–42
thalamo-cortical circuit, 279
thalamo-cortical loop, 251–255
    re-entrant neural activity, 252–253
thalamo-cortical resonance, 233
thalamo-cortical system, 241
thalamus, 251–255
    role in general anaesthesia, 250
The Diving Bell and the Butterfly (Bauby), 261–262
The Matrix series of films, 140
theory of mind
    animal consciousness and, 117–119
    chimpanzees, 117–119
    social interaction and, 119
theory of mind network, 378
theta waves, 243
thinking
    inner speech, 189–191
    language and, 188–189
    problem solving, 189
thought experiments, 10, 27–28
    brain in a vat, 220
    China brain, 47–48
    Chinese room, 50–51
    dancing qualia, 49–50
    imagining a painful operation, 251
    intuition pumps, 27–28
    Mary colour experiment (knowledge argument), 34–35
    p-zombies, 41–43
    Schrödinger's cat, 27
    Ship of Theseus problem, 160
    Star Trek transporter problem, 159–160
    Swampman, 28
threat simulation theory of dreams, 318–319
Titchener, Edward, 133–134
Tomczyk, Stanislawa, 396
Tononi, Giulio, 124–125, 256
toxoplasmosis
    behavioural effects, 65–66
tramadol, 348
transcendental consciousness, 371–381
    absorption score and, 376
    Buddhism, 378–381
    consciousness raising, 373–374
    definition, 371
    entheogens, 378
    epiphanies, 371–373
    life of Colin Wilson, 371–373
    nine characteristics of mystical states, 374–375
    peak experiences, 371–373
    religious experiences, 374–376
    temporal lobe activity and religion, 376–378
    Zen Buddhism, 380–381
transcranial magnetic stimulation (TMS), 240
transhumanism, 103–104, 271
transplants
    face transplants, 161
    psychological rejection of, 161
    self and, 180–181
Tulving, Endel, 204
Turing, Alan, 48, 86–87, 99
Turing machine, 99
Turing test, 86–88
two streams of consciousness model, 172
Tye, Michael, 206
type identity theory, 44

Ullman, Montague, 392
ultrasound effects, 388
unconscious
    collective unconscious (Jung), 151
    free association, 148
    Freudian slips, 148
    Freud's theory of, 147–150
    problem of consciousness, 22, 407
    repressed memories, 149–150
    Rorschach inkblot test, 148
    subliminal processing, 152–153
unconscious content, 147

Verne, Jules, 96
Versailles time travel incident, 387–388
Vicary, James, 152
visual attention, 194
visual neglect, 229–230
visual perception. *See* perception
vitamin B1 (thiamine)
    deficiency effects, 166
von Economo, Constantin Freiherr, 282
Vygotsky, Lev, 189

walking corpse syndrome, 143
Waterman, Ian, 231
Watson, J.B., 21
Wearing, Clive, 166–169
Wegner, Daniel, 63

Weiskrantz, Larry, 227–228
Weizenbaum, Joseph, 87
Wells, H.G., 96
whales
   intelligence and self-awareness, 112, 113
Whinnery, Typ, 275
whirling dervishes of Sufism, 375
Whorf, Benjamin Lee, 187
Wilson, Colin, 371–373
Wilson, E.O., 119
Winograd, Terry, 88–89
witch trials, 149–150
Wittgenstein, Ludwig, 186
Wordsworth, William, 373

Wright, Charles Romley Alder, 350
writing
   means of extending our consciousness, 181
Wundt, Wilhelm, 21

Z-drugs, 297
Zeki, Samir, 234
Zen Buddhism, 380–381
Zhuangzi
   butterfly dream, 306–307
zolpidem, 297
zombies
   explanations of the myth, 41–42

CPSIA information can be obtained
at www.ICGtesting.com
Printed in the USA
BVHW011302041021
618099BV00006B/243